BLACKSTONE'S GUIDE TO
The Mental Capacity Act 2005

SECOND EDITION

BLACKSTONE'S GUIDE TO

The Mental Capacity Act 2005

SECOND EDITION

Peter Bartlett

OXFORD
UNIVERSITY PRESS

OXFORD

UNIVERSITY PRESS

Great Clarendon Street, Oxford OX2 6DP

Oxford University Press is a department of the University of Oxford.
It furthers the University's objective of excellence in research, scholarship,
and education by publishing worldwide in

Oxford New York

Auckland Cape Town Dar es Salaam Hong Kong Karachi
Kuala Lumpur Madrid Melbourne Mexico City Nairobi
New Delhi Shanghai Taipei Toronto

With offices in

Argentina Austria Brazil Chile Czech Republic France Greece
Guatemala Hungary Italy Japan Poland Portugal Singapore
South Korea Switzerland Thailand Turkey Ukraine Vietnam

Oxford is a registered trade mark of Oxford University Press
in the UK and in certain other countries

Published in the United States
by Oxford University Press Inc., New York

First published 2005
Second edition 2008

British Library Cataloguing in Publication Data

Data available

Library of Congress Cataloging in Publication Data

Data available

Typeset by Cepha Imaging Private Ltd, Bangalore, India
Printed in Great Britain
on acid-free paper by
Ashford Colour Press Limited., Gosport, Hampshire

ISBN 978-0-19-923904-7

1 3 5 7 9 10 8 6 4 2

Preface

The Mental Capacity Act 2005 took full effect on 1 October 2007. It revolutionizes the way in which the law deals with people who, because of an impairment or disturbance of functioning of mind or brain, lack capacity to make decisions. New rules are created for how the best interests of these people are to be determined, and how, in anticipation of incapacity, individuals may make decisions to refuse medical treatment. For the first time, individuals can while competent appoint an individual to make decisions during later incapacity regarding their personal care and treatment. And all of this is supervised by a newly created Court of Protection.

The first edition of this guide was published shortly after the Mental Capacity Act 2005 received Royal Assent. The preface to that edition noted the considerable amount of new material that was to come: regulations, a Code of Practice, legislative reforms to mental health law, and a variety of guidance were all expected in the period between Royal Assent to the 2005 statute and its implementation. These are now largely complete, with the exception of some regulations concerning research on people lacking capacity. The result is a veritable deluge of information. Where the problem in writing the first edition was how to guide the reader into largely uncharted territory, the problem of this edition is to make this vast array of law and guidance comprehensible to non-professional readers, while ensuring that sufficient detail is provided to alert those charged with administration of the Act with meaningful assistance, and indications of where pitfalls may lie. With that in mind, the first chapter provides an overview of the Act, specifically designed for people without legal knowledge. That should provide the grounding needed to make sense of the more detailed discussion in the remainder of the book.

As noted, the Act as passed in 2005 is now in full effect. In the period leading up to implementation, however, the legislature was not idle. Major reforms to the Mental Health Act 1983 were passed in the summer of 2007. Most significantly for current purposes, these deal with when people lacking capacity may be deprived of their liberty, for example in care homes where they might not be permitted to leave at will. These provisions, and other amendments introduced in 2007, are currently expected to take effect in April 2009, and a Code of Practice concerning those amendments is under development. These new provisions are discussed in this volume, mainly in Chapter 4.

In closing, I would like to thank a number of people who have made this volume possible. As usual, I have received sterling support from the staff of Oxford University Press, and in particular Kathryn Grant, Jane Kavanagh, Jodi Towler, Marjorie Francois, and Ruth Freestone King. Once again, I would also like to express my particular thanks to my partner, Rick Savage, who not merely provided emotional support, but once again read considerable parts of the manuscript to ensure its comprehensibility to non-lawyers.

Peter Bartlett
December 2007

Contents—Summary

Contents—Detailed

4. DEPRIVATION OF LIBERTY OF PEOPLE LACKING CAPACITY: THE 2007 AMENDMENTS

5. ROUGH EDGES?

Table of Cases

Canada

European Union

United States of America

Table of Legislation

Table of Statutory Instruments
and Codes of Conduct

Table of Abbreviations

CTO   Community Treatment Order under ss 17A–17G and 64A–64K of the Mental Health Act 1983, as amended by the Mental Health Act 2007

D   Person making a decision on behalf of a person lacking capacity

ECHR   European Convention for the Protection of Human Rights and Fundamental Freedoms

ECtHR   European Court of Human Rights

EPA   Enduring Power of Attorney

EPAA   Enduring Powers of Attorney Act 1985

IMCA   Independent Mental Capacity Advocate

LPA   Lasting Power of Attorney (see Mental Capacity Act 2005 ss 9–14)

MCA   Mental Capacity Act 2005

MHA   Mental Health Act. Unless otherwise stated, the reference is to the MHA 1983, as amended. Where relevant amendments are introduced by the MHA 2007 (not yet in effect), these changes are noted.

P   Person who lacks capacity, or (in some contexts) is thought to lack capacity

PG   Public Guardian

REC   Research Ethics Committee, as established under the by the Department of Health *Research Governance Framework* (2nd edn, 2005)

1

THE MENTAL CAPACITY ACT 2005:
THE BASIC STRUCTURE

A. INTRODUCING THE MENTAL CAPACITY ACT 2005

This Guide has been written with a variety of readers in mind. Some—for example, 1.01 lawyers experienced in representing clients with mental disabilities, will already be well-versed in many of the issues discussed. Others, such as medical practitioners specializing in disorders of old age, or high street lawyers wishing to offer advice on planning for incapacity to a general client base, will have important pockets of knowledge, but will need an introduction to the specifics relevant to the Mental Capacity Act 2005 itself (hereinafter referred to as MCA). Still others may have no background knowledge at all. They may be people who find themselves called upon to make decisions about an incapacitated loved one, or people wishing to make arrangements anticipating their own incapacity later in life.

Since many readers of this book will need some grounding in fundamentals, this 1.02 chapter is intended to provide the broad picture. It will be clear from a quick perusal of the appendices to this book that there is now a wealth of information available to direct and to guide. The MCA Code of Practice alone runs to just under 300 pages in the version published by the Department of Constitutional Affairs. The risk is that the uninitiated reader will be lost in the detail. With that in mind, this chapter commences with an overview of how decisions are made under the Act (paras 1.04 to 1.47 below). This explanation is deliberately light on detail; for that, readers will be cross-referenced to the relevant sections of this book, the MCA, and other supporting documents. As some readers may have purchased this book with a view to planning for incapacity, there is a basic discussion of what options are available to do so (paras 1.48 to 1.69 below). The book then goes on to introduce the relevant legal instruments by listing the appendices to this book, and clarifying their respective status (paras 1.70 to 1.85 below). Finally, there is a brief look ahead to what the future holds. The MCA as passed in 2005 was only fully implemented on 1 October 2007, so matters of interpretation are still open to speculation. This chapter section provides an initial sense of what may be at issue in such interpretation. Amendments introduced by the Mental Health Act 2007 (hereinafter referred to as the 2007 amendments), which are not yet in force, will also be foreshadowed.

1.03   Chapter 1 thus provides a basic framework to understand the Act. The rest of this book builds on that framework. The statutory and common law that was previously in effect provides a context for interpretation of the new statute, and this legal back-drop is discussed in Chapter 2. The remainder of the book examines the MCA in detail. Chapter 3 provides a commentary to the provisions of the statute. Chapter 4 examines the 2007 amendments. Chapter 5 looks at a number of specific issues where tensions and problems may arise in the implementation of the new Act.

B. MAKING DECISIONS ON BEHALF OF PEOPLE WHO LACK CAPACITY

1.04   This section introduces the fundamental legal mechanisms and processes of the MCA. There is no discussion here of research on persons lacking capacity, nor on the new criminal offence of ill-treatment or neglect of a person lacking capacity, both of which are dealt with elsewhere in the book.[1]

1.05   To start, let us be clear on what the MCA does, and does not do. It does provide a mechanism by which decisions may be made and legal relations entered into on behalf of a person who lacks capacity (hereinafter referred to as P), thereby creating a legal framework where, for example, care and treatment may be provided to P, contracts may be entered on behalf of P, a will may be drafted on behalf of P, and financial, property, and some legal decisions may be made on behalf of P. The MCA goes no further than this. P remains subject to the same law as if P had capacity. Where consent is not required for care or treatment to be provided to P (as is the case for compulsory treatment under the Mental Health Act 1983, for example), that care or treatment may still be provided, even though the relevant decision-maker under the MCA objects. Furthermore, the MCA does not allow services to be demanded on behalf of P that P could not demand had he or she been competent. For example, the MCA will facilitate P's admission to a particular care home where accommodation is offered by that care home, but it does not oblige the care home to offer a place any more than P could have forced the care home to offer a place when he or she had capacity. Entitlements to services, insofar as they exist, are to be

---

[1] For research, see paras 3.137–3.149 below; for the new criminal offence, see paras 3.150–3.157 below.

found in other areas of law (including social services law and medical law). Neither does the MCA overrule other law, even if that law deals with people with mental disabilities. If P were to commit an illegal act, for example, whether he or she would be convicted of a crime would depend on the relevant criminal law, including the law of insanity and the law relating to fitness to stand trial. A substitute decision-maker under the MCA (hereinafter D) may be involved in the issues, by arranging for such things as legal bills to be paid, but whether or not P is found guilty is not a matter for the MCA.

The easiest way to introduce the basic structure and terminology of the MCA is to consider the position of a person about to provide care or medical treatment to a mentally vulnerable person. Such a carer ought to make the determinations in the following text box, in the order they appear. This chapter will then discuss those determinations briefly. They are all discussed in more detail in Chapter 3.   1.06

While some parts of the Act do apply to minors, for purposes of this example, it is assumed that the vulnerable person is over the age of eighteen.   1.07

The principles at the beginning of the MCA[2] will guide all the decisions in the matters above.   1.08

Before elaborating on the items in the text box, it will be helpful to identify a few of the key players in the administration of the MCA.   1.09

The MCA creates a new Court of Protection, staffed by judges of the High Court Family Division. The Court has a broad jurisdiction under the MCA, and can provide decisions regarding contested law or facts. It may make orders, for example, to determine whether an individual has capacity to make a specific decision; to determine the validity of any document or decision made regarding P; and to determine the best interests of P—so pretty much anything that may be doubted or disputed under the Act. In practice, this means that the Court of Protection can always provide a definitive legal judgment as to what is to happen to a person lacking capacity or thought to be lacking capacity.   1.10

The Office of the Public Guardian provides many of the administrative services related to the MCA. In particular, it is responsible for registering any Lasting Power of Attorney (hereinafter referred to as LPA), supervising court-appointed deputies, and administrative functions such as receiving any security or reports required of donees of LPAs or deputies appointed by the Court of Protection. The Public Guardian also supervises the Court of Protection Visitors, who can visit and report on people lacking capacity and their decision-makers.   1.11

In addition to the provisions just set out, the MCA also provides particular safeguards when especially serious decisions are at issue. In cases of care home or hospital admissions for extended periods and in cases of 'serious treatment', Independent Mental Capacity Advocates (IMCAs) provide an assessment of best interests when P is without any non-professional carers. In the event that care home or hospital admissions would deprive P of his or her liberty, the 2007 amendments will introduce   1.12

---

[2] See paras 3.15–3.21 below; MCA s 1; Code Ch 2.

Does the person have capacity?

1. Does the person have capacity to make the decision in question? If so, the person is legally entitled to make the decision, and the MCA has no further application.

Is the decision outside the MCA, or is there a valid and applicable advance refusal of medical treatment?

2. Does the decision involve voting, consent to sexual relations, or other precluded decision? If so, the MCA has no further application, and no person can consent on behalf of the person lacking capacity (hereinafter called P).
3. Does the decision involve treatment for mental disorder of a person confined under the Mental Health Act 1983 (hereinafter MHA 1983) or other form of compulsion authorized by that Act, or treatments otherwise regulated by that Act? If so, the terms of the MHA 1983 take precedence and the MCA in practice will cease to be relevant for that decision.
4. If the decision concerns provision of a medical treatment other than that discussed in point 3, is there a valid and applicable advance decision to refuse that treatment? If so, the treatment cannot be given.
5. [Once the 2007 amendments take effect:] Does the decision involve admission to a hospital or care home in conditions that deprive P of his or her liberty, and if so, is there a valid and applicable advance decision by P refusing treatment to be offered in that admission? If so, the admission may not take place under the MCA. The MCA does not preclude admissions in these circumstances under the MHA 1983, however, when the requirements of that Act are met.

If not, who should make the decision, and on what grounds?

6. Is there a Lasting Power of Attorney (LPA), registered with the Official Guardian, which covers the decision? If so, the decision should be made by the donee of the LPA, according to the statutory definition of best interests.
7. Is there a deputy appointed by the Court of Protection with jurisdiction to make the relevant decision? If so, the deputy should make the decision, according to the statutory definition of best interests.
8. Does the decision concern the care or treatment of P, and is the action proposed in the best interests of P as defined by the statute? If so, and assuming there is no contrary decision flowing from the points above, the MCA deems that P consents to the proposed action.

a system of formalized and independent assessments to ensure the appropriateness of the admission.[3]

Given this framework of actors, let us return to consider the items in the text box   1.13
with some additional introductory comments.

1. Does the person have capacity to make the decision in question? If so, the person is legally entitled to make the decision, and the MCA has no further application

This is the fundamental gateway provision to the Act: where a person has the capacity   1.14
to make the particular decision in question, the Act does not apply, and the apparently mentally vulnerable person can make the decision in the same way as any other person can. The capacity decision attaches to the specific decision in question: it is expected that many people will have capacity for some decisions, and not for others. The capacity determination should be read in the context of the principles of the Act.[4] These principles provide that there is a legal presumption in favour of capacity: people have capacity unless the evidence demonstrates the contrary. In addition, all reasonable steps must be taken to assist the person to make a capable decision before any finding of incapacity may be made. Incapacity may not be inferred merely because an individual has made or would make an unwise decision. Nor may incapacity be inferred from unjustified assumptions based on criteria such as age or appearance: just because someone is old or frail it does not follow that they lack capacity.

In substance, the individual has capacity if he or she can understand the informa-   1.15
tion relevant to the decision in question, retain it (at least briefly) and weigh it as part of a decision-making process, then communicate the decision.[5] The information must be provided in a form appropriate to the individual's needs.

The definition of capacity is contained in ss 2 and 3 of the MCA. It is discussed   1.16
in detail below at paras 3.22 to 3.32 and in Chapter 4 of the Code of Practice.

2. Does the decision involve voting, consent to sexual relations, or other precluded decision? If so, the MCA has no further application, and no person can consent on behalf of the person lacking capacity (hereinafter P)

The MCA takes the view that there are some decisions for which no one ought to be   1.17
able to consent on behalf of P. Voting in parliamentary, municipal and similar elections and referenda is an obvious example,[6] as are consenting to marriage/civil partnership and sexual relations.[7] Also precluded are consents made under the Human

---

[3] See further Ch 4 below; MCA Sch A1 and 1A.
[4] See paras 3.15–3.21 below; MCA s 1; Code Ch 2.
[5] MCA s 3(1).
[6] MCA s 29.
[7] MCA s 27(1)(a) and (b).

Fertilisation and Embryology Act 1990—effectively, decisions regarding P becoming a parent through artificial insemination or any other new reproductive technologies. The MCA would seem to be clear: if P cannot exercise a competent choice in these cases, the event should not occur.

1.18   Section 27 also precludes from the MCA consents related to adoptions and to divorces based on two years of separation. On these decisions, it should be noted that what is precluded is proceeding based on an imputed consent of P. The relevant legislation provides other ways of placing children for adoption and of getting divorced, and these other ways are not precluded by the MCA.

1.19   These exceptions to the MCA are discussed further at para 3.14 below.

3. Does the decision involve treatment for mental disorder of a person confined under the Mental Health Act 1983 (hereinafter MHA 1983) or other form of compulsion authorized by that Act, or treatments otherwise regulated by that Act? If so, the terms of the MHA 1983 take precedence and the MCA will, in practice, cease to be relevant for that decision

1.20   The interrelations between the MCA and the Mental Health Act 1983 (hereinafter referred to as MHA 1983), specifically as amended by the 2007 amendments, are not straightforward, and are discussed at length in paras 5.38 to 5.70 below. The present comments give a brief introduction to that discussion.

1.21   The MHA 1983 restricts some treatments—most importantly psychosurgery— to situations where not merely a second and independent medical opinion is provided in favour of the treatment but also the patient offers competent consent. The MCA cannot be used to avoid this provision of the MHA 1983: psychosurgery cannot be performed if a patient lacks capacity to consent to it. In the same way, the 2007 amendments will preclude electro-convulsive therapy (ECT) being performed on people without capacity when a valid and applicable advance decision to refuse that treatment is in effect. Unlike psychosurgery, ECT will be allowed to be performed on persons lacking capacity when no such advance decision is in place, subject to safeguards introduced to the MHA 1983 by the 2007 amendments.

1.22   The MHA 1983 also permits a variety of interventions even where a person— whether capable or not—refuses to consent to them. The provisions contained in Parts II and III of the MHA 1983 allow an individual to be detained against his or her will in a psychiatric facility, and the provisions of Part IV of the Act allow these detained patients to be treated without their consent under specified conditions. As these provisions do not require the consent of the individual, they can proceed outside the scope of the MCA regarding persons who lack capacity.

1.23   The significant majority of people receiving treatment for mental disabilities, including the bulk of psychiatric inpatients, are not detained under the MHA 1983. In law, their rights to leave hospital and their rights to consent to or refuse treatment are identical to those enjoyed by people receiving non-psychiatric treatment. The MCA does apply to these people if they lack capacity to make a decision. The particular safeguards relating to institutional admissions and decisions regarding serious medical treatment may be of particular relevance to such people.[8]

4. If the decision concerns provision of a medical treatment other than that discussed in point 3, is there a valid and applicable advance decision to refuse that treatment? If so, the treatment cannot be given

The MCA allows people, while competent, to refuse treatments in anticipation of incapacity. Obvious examples would include a Jehovah's Witness who wishes to refuse treatment with blood products, or a person wishing to control treatment provided in a period of severe and permanent incapacity at the end of his or her life. If the treatment in question is proposed during a subsequent period of incapacity, it is regarded in law as though the individual had a momentary return to capacity and gave a competent refusal of the treatment.   1.24

For the refusal to be upheld, it must be 'valid' and 'applicable'. The refusal would be inapplicable if the refusal actually did not refer to the treatment proposed, or in circumstances where preconditions in the refusal are not present. The refusal would also be inapplicable if new circumstances had arisen, unanticipated by P, that would have affected P's decision to refuse the treatment. The advance decision to refuse would be invalid if: 1.25

- it had been withdrawn by P while he or she had capacity to do so; or
- P had, since the refusal, created an LPA with the authority to consent to or refuse the treatment in question; or
- P had done anything inconsistent with the advance refusal.

For most decisions, there are no requirements that the advance decision to refuse treatment be in writing or witnessed. At least in theory, an oral refusal is sufficient. The exception is where the refusal may involve life-sustaining treatment, in which case the decision has to be in writing and witnessed, and must expressly state that it applies even if life is at risk.   1.26

Advance decisions to refuse treatment are codified by ss 24 and 26 of the MCA. They are discussed further in paras 3.112 to 3.136 below, and in Chapter 9 of the Code of Practice.   1.27

5. [Once the 2007 amendments take effect:] Does the decision involve admission to a hospital or care home in conditions that deprive P of his or her liberty, and if so, is there a valid and applicable advance decision by P refusing treatment to be offered in that an admission? If so, the admission may not take place under the MCA.

---

[8] See paras 5.46–5.50 and 3.57–3.59 below.

The MCA does not preclude admissions in these circumstances under the MHA 1983, however, when the requirements of that Act are met

1.28 As regards the MCA, the 2007 amendments deal primarily with the situation of persons admitted to care homes or hospitals in situations where they are deprived of their liberty within the meaning of Article 5 of the European Convention on Human Rights (hereinafter referred to as ECHR). These are often referred to as 'Bournewood' patients, after the defendant in the litigation that brought the situation of these patients to a head.[9] The amendments are drafted with astonishing complexity, and will be discussed in detail in Chapter 4 below.

1.29 Fortunately for non-professional carers, the complexity rests on those in charge of care homes and hospitals ('managing authorities'). If a carer is responsible for accommodation of P outside those environments (in a private home, for example) in conditions that deprive P of liberty, the carer is required to obtain approval of this arrangement from the Court of Protection: this is one of the unusual cases where, as a matter of law, court authorization is required for personal care and treatment. The meaning of 'deprivation of liberty' will be discussed in detail below.[10] Rather unhelpfully, a full definition is impossible, but in brief, the issue will be whether the carer exercises 'complete and effective control over [P's] care and movements.'[11]

1.30 If the admission is to a care home or hospital in circumstances that would deprive P of liberty, the 2007 amendments will require the managing authority to trigger a number of assessments. Many of these (capacity and best interests, for example) flow directly from the MCA itself. The assessments do, however, have a few factors that remove the applicability of the MCA. Some of these relate to overlaps with the MHA 1983, as amended.[12] Another is where P has, while competent, made an advance refusal of some or all of the treatment that will be offered in the facility.[13] In that case, the person may not be admitted to the facility under the MCA, although he or she may be so admitted under the MHA 1983 as amended, if the provisions of that Act are met.

1.31 If admission is to a care home or hospital, people other than the managing authorities continue to make decisions as normal. The donee of an LPA or court-appointed deputy with authority to make accommodation decisions, for example, would apply the best interest test in the same way he or she would for any other decision, and if the admission is not in the best interests of P, the donee should refuse to allow the admission. In that event, the admission is likewise taken out of the realm of the MCA, although it can potentially be effected under the MHA 1983.

---

[9] See *R v Bournewood Community and Mental Health NHS Trust, ex p L* [1999] AC 458.
[10] Paras 4.26–4.34.
[11] *HL v United Kingdom* (2005) 40 EHRR 32, para 91.
[12] See paras 4.61–4.73 below.
[13] MCA Sch A1 para 19.

As originally passed in 2005, most of the MCA specifically fails to provide author- 1.32
ity to deprive persons lacking capacity of their liberty.[14] Until those amendments
take effect, therefore, the only way deprivation of liberty may be authorized under
the MCA is by order of the Court of Protection.

The 2007 amendments relating to 'Bournewood' patients are contained primar- 1.33
ily in schedules A1 and 1A of the MCA. At the time of writing, a Draft Code of
Practice was available on the Department of Health website, and was subject to
consultation.[15]

6. Is there a Lasting Power of Attorney (LPA), registered with the Official Guardian, which covers the decision? If so, the decision should be made by the donee of the LPA, according to the statutory definition of best interests

If we get as far as point 6, the only question is who is to take responsibility for the 1.34
decision. Whoever takes that responsibility, the criteria for reaching the decision will
have been settled: the decision must be taken in the best interests of the person lacking capacity, as defined by MCA s 4. It is therefore appropriate to introduce the test
of best interests here.

The best interests criteria will be discussed at various stages in this book.[16] They 1.35
are also discussed in Chapter 5 of the Code of Practice. The test contains both substantive and procedural requirements. In determining best interests, the decision-
maker (D) is required:

- to consider the likelihood that P will regain capacity, and if so when that will be;
- to involve P in the decision as much as is practicable;
- to consider P's wishes, feelings, beliefs, and values both prior to the decision being
  made and at the time it is made; and in particular any relevant document written by P;
- to consult, insofar as it is practical and appropriate, with anyone named by P as
  someone to be consulted; anyone engaged in caring for P or interested in P's
  welfare; and any donee of an LPA or deputy. These consultations are to ascertain
  the consultees' views of what would be in P's best interest, and in particular his or
  her relevant wishes, feelings, beliefs, and values as above.

This list is not exhaustive. D is expressly required to consider *all* relevant information.[17] The test is to be read in the context of the principles in s 1. Of particular
relevance will be the requirement in that section that actions must involve the least
restriction possible of P's rights and freedom of action.

The best interests test thus contains both substantial elements (the first and third 1.36
bullet points) and process (the second and fourth bullet points). While the general

---

[14] See MCA ss 6(5), 11(6), 20(13), all of which will be repealed by the 2007 amendments.
[15] <http://www.dh.gov.uk> gateway reference 8319. Accessed 5 October 2007.
[16] See, most significantly, paras 3.33–3.52 below.
[17] MCA s 4.

requirement to consider all relevant information leaves the field of determination open—D is not bound by P's previous competent views, for example—the material in the bullet points above should not be considered mere window dressing. All aspects of the test are mandatory, although the reference to practicality in the second and fourth bullet points does provide some flexibility in the application. How the various factors should be balanced in reaching a decision will depend on the circumstances of each case.

1.37 Additional requirements apply if the decision in question would involve the 'restraint' of P, defined as a situation where D either uses or threatens to use force to secure the doing of an act that P resists, or restricts P's liberty of movement, whether or not P resists.[18] For such restraint to be in P's best interests, it must be necessary to prevent harm to P, and the restraint must be proportionate to the seriousness and likelihood of the harm occurring.

1.38 In determining who should make the decision on this basis, the first thing to ascertain is whether there is a valid and applicable LPA that covers the decision. An LPA allows forward planning by an individual in anticipation of incapacity; by creating it, a person with capacity (the donor) appoints someone (the donee) to make decisions for him or her during a period of subsequent incapacity. The donor has considerable flexibility in deciding what decisions are to be covered by an LPA. Prior to the implementation of the MCA, a broadly similar mechanism was available for decisions relating to property and financial affairs (the Enduring Power of Attorney—EPA). Existing EPAs may still be registered and relied upon after the introduction of the MCA, although no new EPAs can be signed. The MCA changes some of the technicalities of the EPA, such as making them less complicated to register, and it expands their remit so that they can now cover decisions relating to personal care and treatment as well as property and financial affairs.

1.39 The LPA must be in the relevant official form,[19] and must be registered with the Official Guardian before the donee can use it.

1.40 The legislative provisions concerning LPAs are contained in MCA ss 9–14, and further provisions regarding their creation are contained in Part 2 of the Regulation in Appendix 3 below. They are discussed further in paras 3.70 to 3.93 below, and by the Code of Practice at Chapter 7.

7. Is there a deputy appointed by the Court of Protection with jurisdiction to make the relevant decision? If so, the deputy should make the decision, according to the statutory definition of best interests

1.41 In the event that there is no relevant LPA, the next possibility is that the Court of Protection may have appointed a deputy with authority to make the decision. The Court has broad discretion in making these appointments, although the authority

---

[18] MCA s 11(5).
[19] See App 3 below which contains SI 2007/1253, Sch 1.

of the deputy may not conflict with the authority of a donee of an LPA. The appointments may be limited in such terms as the Court sees fit.

The deputy is required to decide according to the statutory definition of best   1.42
interests (see point 6 above). Unlike the donee of an LPA, however, the deputy may
not be given authority to refuse life-sustaining treatment.[20] If the deputy thinks that
such treatment is not in the best interests of P, the matter will need to be referred to
the Court of Protection.

The appointment and role of deputies is determined by the MCA at ss 16–21. It   1.43
is discussed further in paras 3.94 to 3.111 below, and by the Code of Practice at
Chapter 8.

**8. Does the decision concern the care or treatment of P, and is the action proposed
   in the best interests of P as defined by the statute? If so, and assuming there is no
   contrary decision flowing from the points above, the MCA deems that P consents
   to the proposed action**

In the event that there is no other decision-maker, the MCA deems P to consent to   1.44
decisions regarding care and treatment, if the care or treatment proposed is in the
best interests of P as defined by the statute (see point 6 above).

The result of this is that a wide variety of carers are afforded a defence in civil and   1.45
criminal law to acts that would otherwise be illegal. This defence will be broad
enough to cover most care and treatment decisions, except those decisions resulting
in a loss of P's liberty (see point 5 above). For care and treatment decisions, therefore, applications to the Court of Protection are intended to be uncommon, although
the Court remains available to determine cases of dispute or for guidance when a
particularly serious decision is at issue.

Some care or treatment decisions may have financial ramifications. The MCA   1.46
requires that P must pay expenses that are reasonably necessary and incurred on his
or her behalf: s 7. The Act is somewhat less flexible here than in the area of care
and treatment decisions, however. While moneys in the actual possession of the
decision-maker (D) may be applied to reimburse expenses, the authority does not
extend to accessing P's bank accounts or sale of P's property to meet the debt. Such
steps would require a decision of the donee of an LPA or deputy with authority in
such financial matters, or an order of the Court of Protection.

The general defence is created by MCA s 5, and provisions regarding payment of   1.47
expenses are governed by MCA ss 7–8. These matters are discussed in paras 3.53 to
3.69 below, and in the Code of Practice at Chapter 6.

---

[20] MCA s 20(5).

C. PLANNING FOR INCAPACITY

1.48 The previous section described the overall decision-making structure that comes into effect when an individual lacks capacity. This section engages the decision-making structures of the MCA from a slightly different angle: what options does a person with capacity have to plan for incapacity in the future?

1.49 The MCA offers a considerable range of options here, resulting in remarkable flexibility for advance planning. People may designate who is to be involved in decision-making and have different options as to the degree of their involvement. The clearest ways to do this are by creating one or more LPAs, and/or by designating someone to be consulted in ascertaining the individual's best interests. People planning for incapacity may also, to varying degrees depending on the decision, influence the substantive matters considered in reaching the decision. This might involve making an advance decision to refuse treatment, or making an expression of wishes to be taken into account in the determination of best interests.

1.50 Mixing and matching these mechanisms is certainly permitted and will often be desirable. It may well be appropriate, for example, to give one person the authority to make a decision by creating an LPA, but requiring that person to consult someone else in deciding best interests.

1.51 A few words of warning are nonetheless appropriate. First, in the event of perceived conflict between different documents, undesired results may occur. As an obvious example, an advance decision to refuse treatment is rendered invalid by a subsequent LPA, if the LPA includes authority to make the decision covered by the refusal.[21] How the courts and other decision-makers will construe other documents they see as potentially divergent may be unpredictable. Consolidating views in a small number of documents may offer some assistance here.

1.52 Second, people planning for incapacity should ensure that any resulting arrangements are practical. It may well make sense, for example, to sign two LPAs for property and affairs—one covering management of investments and the other covering day-to-day expenditures for care and the household finances. It would generally be unwise to sign a wide variety of LPAs, however, if the result would be the donees tripping over each other's jurisdiction. Registration of LPAs—a precondition of their being relied upon—will also cost £150 each,[22] making multiple LPAs potentially expensive.

1.53 In all this, it is important to recall that the MCA does not provide options that the individual would not have if competent. Such entitlements, insofar as they exist at all, are found in other areas of law such as social services law.

1.54 Once again, this section is introductory, and is thus kept light on detail. People considering planning for incapacity should therefore follow the references to the

---

[21] MCA s 25(2)(b).
[22] SI 2007/2051, Sch 1.

remainder of this text for further detail. With that introduction, the possibilities afforded by the MCA to plan for incapacity may be summarized as follows.

1. Advance Decisions to Refuse Treatment

The obvious way to influence decisions relating to medical treatment is to make an advance decision refusing specified treatment. The result of such a decision, so long as it is valid and applicable, is that the treatment is deemed to be competently refused.   1.55

There are, in general, no formalities requirements for such refusals: the MCA envisages that an oral decision is effective. The exception is when life-sustaining treatment is at issue, in which case the refusal must be in writing, signed, witnessed, and make clear expressly that it is intended to apply when life is at risk. Particularly when the results would be serious, however, it is appropriate to note that the courts have been extremely reluctant to enforce these advance refusals. One must have some sympathy with this reluctance, in the event of ambiguities in evidence. It is therefore likely to be advisable for evidential purposes that the decision be in writing in any event, and made in a context that its consequences are clearly intended. It will often be advisable to discuss the advance decision with one's general practitioner or another medical carer, who would then be in a position to attest that the maker of the decision was aware of the consequences of what he or she was doing.   1.56

If valid and applicable, the advance decision absolutely precludes the provision of the treatment in question. It cannot be undone once the person loses capacity. It should therefore be made only when the individual is absolutely sure that he or she would never want the treatment in question, given the circumstances articulated in the advance decision. If the individual wishes merely to provide non-binding guidance to future decision-makers, an expression of wishes should be used instead.   1.57

While a valid and applicable advance decision to refuse treatment has the effect of refusing consent to the treatment, there is no clear requirement anywhere in the MCA that the doctor performing the treatment be informed of the advance decision. Further, and more troubling, there have in the past been persistent anecdotes about advance refusals going missing from clinical files. While destruction of a written advance decision may well violate criminal law,[23] that is a different question from ensuring the treating physician is aware of the decision at the time it is to be acted upon. For these reasons, it is likely to be advisable to sign several copies of the decision, and lodge some with people who can be relied upon to bring the decision to light when it is needed.   1.58

Advance decisions to refuse treatment are codified by MCA ss 24 and 26. They are discussed further in paras 3.112 to 3.136 below, and in the Code of Practice at Chapter 9.   1.59

---

[23] See paras 3.131–3.136 below.

2. The Content of the Best Interest Test

1.60   The advance refusal of treatment is the only time when decisions relating to care, treatment, property, or affairs will be made without reference to the best interests test contained in MCA s 4. As noted above at para 1.36, the best interest test includes both substantive and procedural requirements. Some of these requirements will be relevant to advance planning for incapacity. Engaging with these requirements does not determine the outcome of the best interests test; it merely ensures that the wishes of the person are taken into account on either substance of what is in best interests, or who should be consulted to determine best interests.

1.61   The best interests test requires the decision-maker to take into account the present and past wishes, feelings, beliefs, and values of the person then lacking capacity, and in particular any written statement made by the individual concerning wishes or feelings.[24] Provision of such a statement will be the appropriate course of action for an individual who wishes to provide guidance to decision-makers regarding future medical treatment, but who does not wish to preclude that treatment outright. Unlike the advance refusals mechanism, statements as to wishes, feelings, beliefs, and values are not restricted to cases of medical treatment—guidance may be given to D on any potential decision.

1.62   As noted above, the MCA does not create a context where an individual can demand specific forms of care, treatment, or services. That said, the individual recording his or her competent wishes, feelings, beliefs, or values may certainly express preferences between alternative treatments or courses of action. This would be likely to be very helpful in the event that a service provider offers D a choice of services or courses of action for P.

1.63   This allows an individual with capacity to make their views known on substantive questions of best interests. The best interest test also requires D to consult with a variety of people in determining P's best interest. This list includes 'anyone named by [P] as someone to be consulted on the matter in question or on matters of that kind'.[25] The individual can thus identify someone who is to be consulted regarding his or her best interests. The list also includes the donee of an LPA, so it is not necessary to name that individual separately.

1.64   The statute requires that consultation regarding best interests is made not only with the person named by P and the holder of an LPA, but also with anyone engaged in P's care or interested in P's welfare, and a court-appointed deputy. Consultation is to be to the extent 'practicable and appropriate'. The scope of this phrase will be discussed elsewhere,[26] but if the individual planning for incapacity does not wish consultation with someone on this list to occur, it is appropriate that he or she make those views known in advance. It is not clear whether such a view would be binding,

---

[24] MCA s 4(6).
[25] MCA s 4(7)(a).
[26] See para 3.44.

but it would certainly be highly relevant in determining whether consultation was appropriate.

Once again, these mechanisms will only work if D is aware of them at the time   1.65
the decision is to be made. The person planning for incapacity would therefore be well-advised to notify potential decision-makers (such as the individual's general practitioner, the donees of any LPA, or the managers of the care home in which the individual resides) of their wishes in this regard, and to provide them with copies of any written documentation. Here, as with the advance decision, there is no requirement that the wishes be expressed in writing, but it is likely to be evidentially useful if they are. And once again, it would be wise to provide a trusted friend with copies of the documents, to ensure that they are drawn to the attention of relevant people in the event of administrative oversight.

The best interests criteria will be discussed at various stages in this book, but   1.66
primarily at paras 3.33 to 3.52 below. They are also discussed in the Code of Practice at Chapter 5.

3. Lasting Powers of Attorney

As noted above, the best interests test allows a person planning for incapacity to   1.67
involve specified people in advising D as to what is in P's best interest. That is a different question from determining who will decide what is in P's best interest—that is, who will be D? The MCA allows P when competent to make that decision, through the creation of one or more LPAs. As noted above, until the introduction of the MCA, such an appointment could only be made regarding financial affairs broadly conceived. That is no longer the case, and LPAs can be designed to cover personal care and treatment decisions as well.

In some ways, LPAs are inflexible: they must be made on the required form, and   1.68
they must be registered with the Official Guardian before they can be relied upon. In other ways, however, they are very flexible. Different people may be appointed to make different kinds of decisions, and authority can be tailored to the individual's needs. There is no requirement for there to be only one donee for a given set of decisions; multiple individuals may be appointed if that is the donor's wish. That said, in the end what the LPA does is to select one or more individuals to serve as decision-makers. While they may well be selected because they have particularly good insights into the donor's best interests, they are obliged to make their decisions based on the statutory best interest test.

LPAs are governed by MCA ss 9–14 and are discussed in detail elsewhere in this   1.69
book[27] and by the Code of Practice at Chapter 7. Further guidance concerning LPAs is contained in Part 2 of Appendix 3 below.

---

[27] See paras 3.70–3.93 below.

D. THE BUILDING BLOCKS: THE ACT,
THE CODE OF PRACTICE, RULES, AND GUIDANCE

1.70   The first edition of this book was written shortly after the MCA received Royal Assent. It was clear at that time that the Act itself was just the starting point. The introduction to that edition lists a further seven types of regulation, guidance, and similar material to be published pursuant to the Act in the roughly two years between Royal Assent and implementation.

1.71   That process has now largely been completed. Table 1.1 at the end of this chapter provides an annotated list of all statutory instruments related to the Act. The most significant of these, along with the Act itself and the Code of Practice, are contained as appendices to this book. It can no longer be said that there is a lack of information—rather the reverse. The problem for uninitiated readers is not likely to be a lack of information, but rather too much. With that in mind, it is appropriate to provide a brief introduction to the appendices to this book.

1. Mental Capacity Act 2005, as amended by the Mental Health Act 2007 (see Appendix 1)

1.72   The MCA provides the basic legal framework for decision-making on behalf of people lacking capacity: all the other items discussed below flow back to this, since it creates the authority for those other documents. At the risk of stating the obvious, it is a statute passed by Parliament, and as such, it is binding: people making decisions must follow the Act. Should they not do so (and assuming their actions are not justified by common law or other statute, such as the MHA 1983), they run the risk of being held liable under the civil or criminal law for their actions and, if professionals, being censured by their professional bodies as well.

1.73   Because the Act is legally binding, and because it is so central to the administration of the affairs of people lacking capacity, all readers are strongly encouraged to read the parts of it that are relevant to them, as identified in the references above and elsewhere in this book. At a bare minimum, anyone involved with making decisions on behalf of persons thought to be lacking capacity should read s 1 (principles), ss 2 and 3 (definition and determination of incapacity), s 4 (best interests), and either s 6(1)–(5), 11(1)–(6), or 20(7)–(13) (restraint). Fortunately for readers, these provisions, like most of the MCA as passed in 2005, are remarkably clearly drafted.

1.74   The implementation of the MCA as passed in 2005 took place in stages, but has been in full force from 1 October 2007. As noted above, however, amendments were introduced to the MCA by the MHA 2007 (the '2007 amendments') in the summer of 2007. At the time of writing this book (autumn 2007), the 2007 amendments have not yet been brought into effect, and it is expected that implementation will occur in April 2009. The 2007 amendments both add and delete text from the 2005 version. In Appendix 1, text to be added by the 2007 amendments and thus not yet in force is in square brackets [so added material looks like this]; text to be deleted by the 2007 amendments and thus still in force until those amendments take effect is in italics *and thus appears like this*.[28] The most up-to-date information regarding implementation may be found at the Department of Health website, <http://www.dh.gov.uk>.

2. Code of Practice (see Appendix 2)

In addition to the statutory instruments and the MCA itself, the Department   1.75
of Justice has provided a Code of Practice for the MCA ('the Code'). This is an extensive document, running to almost 300 pages in the version published by the government. The MCA provides that professional carers, paid carers, IMCAs, donees of LPAs, deputies, and researchers all have a duty to 'have regard' to the Code (MCA s 42(4)).

Even for those not obliged to consult it, the Code has much to recommend it. It   1.76
provides a wealth of information on a wide variety of subjects associated with the MCA. It is peppered with examples and is in user-friendly language throughout. Helpful tips are provided on everything from assisting a vulnerable person to make a capable decision to making complaints about poor service. It is strongly recommended that anyone engaging with the MCA take account of what it has to offer.

And yet some hesitation is required. First, unlike the other appendices to this   1.77
book, a Code of Practice is guidance, not hard law. Unlike the terms of the MCA and the statutory instruments above, views or procedures contained only in the Code may be departed from when there is appropriate reason to do so. Indeed, in a case concerning a similar Code of Practice under the MHA 1983, the courts have held that a hospital may depart from a provision of a Code of Practice not merely on a case-by-case basis when individual circumstances warrant it, but as a matter of general policy.[29] The MCA requires courts to 'take into account' relevant provisions of the Code;[30] it does not require the courts to abide by the Code, and courts do find Codes of Practice to be in error in appropriate circumstances.[31] It is thus not 'law' in the sense that the other appendices are.

The MCA Code makes this point expressly on the first page of its introduction,   1.78
and goes on to note that people outside those mentioned in MCA s 42(2) are not required by the MCA to have regard to the Code. Both these comments must in turn must be read with some care, however. Insofar as the Code's provisions are surplus to legal provisions, the Code is quite right. As one might expect, though,

---

[28] The 2007 amendments also corrected a typographical error, changing the last word of s 20(11)(a) from 'or' to 'and'. This change took effect on 1 October 2007, and the change is thus neither italicized nor in square brackets. Readers referring to older copies of the statute may nonetheless wish to be aware of this change.

[29] *R (Munjaz) v Mersey Care NHS Trust and Others* [2005] UKHL 58.

[30] MCA s 42(5).

[31] See, eg, *R (E) v Bristol City Council* [2005] EWHC 74 (Admin) para 28, regarding the Code of Practice under the MHA 1983.

much of the Code closely reflects the statutory and other legal requirements and, where it does so, those statutory requirements are *not* mere guidance: they are the law and they must be followed.

1.79   Here, there is room for some concern about the Code: it is not always as clear as it might be when advice offered is mere guidance, and when it reflects hard law. For this reason, readers are strongly encouraged not to rely solely on the Code, but to be aware of the core provisions of the MCA itself and the relevant statutory instruments.

3. Lasting Powers of Attorney, Enduring Powers of Attorney and Public Guardian Regulations, SI 2007/1253 (see Appendix 3)

1.80   This fleshes out the requirements of the MCA regarding LPAs, EPAs, and the role and function of the Public Guardian. It provides the form that must be followed for the creation of a valid LPA, for example, as well as detailing the forms and processes that must be followed to register the LPA—a precondition before the donee can rely on it.

1.81   It further details the legal framework in which the Public Guardian is required to act. Thus the MCA makes it the duty of the Public Guardian to keep registers of LPAs, EPAs, and court orders that appoint deputies. This statutory instrument defines how this is to be done, and who will have access to the registers. The MCA provides that the Public Guardian is responsible for overseeing court-appointed deputies; this statutory instrument explains some of the mechanics as to how this will be done.

1.82   As they are contained in a statutory instrument, these provisions have the power of law, and are directly enforceable. They are not mere guidance or statements of good practice. For example, for the creation of a valid LPA, a person from the list must attest that the donor understands the effect of the LPA, and that the LPA is signed without fraud or undue influence on the donor.[32] As is envisaged by the MCA, this statutory instrument provides the list of people eligible to provide that statement, and requires in some cases that two such statements be provided. These rules must be complied with, and whatever the donor's intent, a document that does not comply with them does not create an LPA.

4. Court of Protection Rules, SI 2007/1744 (L12) (see Appendix 4)

1.83   As noted in para 1.10 above, the MCA creates a new Court of Protection. While the jurisdiction of the Court is defined by the MCA itself, the MCA provides authority for the Court Rules to be set by statutory instrument. It is these Rules that are contained as Appendix 4.

---

[32] See MCA Sch 1 para 2(1)(e).

Many of the Rules are purely procedural: how documents must be organized and   1.84
how other parties to litigation must be informed of them, for example, or how P is
to be notified of litigation concerning him or her. Some of the Rules deal with more
than mere mechanics, however. Thus Part 8 of the Rules defines who must ask for
permission of the Court before commencing litigation. Part 17 requires that P, if a
party to the proceedings, must have a litigation friend, that is, a person to act on
behalf of P and advise P's lawyers (if any) on P's behalf.

As with the LPA Regulations, the Court Rules are a statutory instrument, and are   1.85
thus binding.

E. THE WAY AHEAD

As noted above, the MCA as passed in 2005 came into full effect only on 1 October   1.86
2007, shortly before publication of this book. There are as yet no judicial decisions
under the MCA, and matters of interpretation are therefore a matter of speculation
to a considerable degree. That said, the MCA had a long gestation period. In the
long wait for legislative reform, the courts themselves began to fashion remedies in
the cases confronting them.

Chapter 2 charts this legislative history, providing a context for the MCA. In   1.87
many ways, the courts' judgments in recent years mirror the provisions of the MCA,
and will no doubt serve to some degree as a guide to interpretation of the new statute. Nonetheless, the courts now have a statute to interpret, and they are meant to
be governed by that, not their own case law, at least to the extent of any divergences.
The discussion in Chapter 2 further shows that the courts' approach had its problems, both doctrinally and practically. While it is no doubt desirable that the courts
have an eye to their previous jurisprudence, the MCA does represent a new start,
and it would be unfortunate if the courts were to sleepwalk into applying their previous jurisprudence uncritically.

As noted at the beginning of the previous section, most of the statutory instru-   1.88
ments, guidance, and official publications envisaged by the original Act are now in
place. The most significant exceptions concern the conduct of research involving
people lacking capacity.

It has already been noted that the MCA has been amended by the Mental Health   1.89
Act 2007 (the '2007 amendments', not yet in force). Those amendments allow and
provide safeguards for the deprivation of liberty of people lacking capacity, and clarify some of the interrelations between the MCA and the MHA 1983 (also as
amended by the 2007 amendments). While a Draft Code of Practice for these
amendments as they affect the MCA has been published for consultation,[33] final
versions of this Code and any statutory instruments are not available at the time
of writing. The substance of the 2007 amendments as they affect the MCA are
discussed at length in Chapter 4 and paras 5.62 to 5.70 below.

---

[33] <http://www.dh.gov.uk> gateway reference 8319. Accessed 5 October 2007.

Table 1.1: Statutory instruments issued pursuant to Mental Capacity Act 2005, as of 1 October 2007

SI number	Title
2006/1832	The Mental Capacity Act 2005 (Independent Mental Capacity Advocates) (General) Regulations 2006 • Defines NHS Body • Defines 'serious medical treatment' • Defines role of IMCA
2006/2810	The Mental Capacity Act 2005 (Appropriate Body) (England) Regulations 2006 • Defines 'appropriate body' for purposes of research. Amended by SI 2006/3474
2006/2814 (C95)	The Mental Capacity Act 2005 (Commencement No 1) Order 2006 • Re research provisions of MCA
2006/2883	The Mental Capacity Act 2005 (Independent Mental Capacity Advocates) (Expansion of Role) Regulations 2006 • Permits appointment of IMCA when care home or hospital placements under review, or during adult protection proceedings
2006/3473	The Mental Capacity Act 2005 (Commencement No 1) (Amendment) Order 2006
2006/3474	The Mental Capacity Act 2005 (Appropriate Body) (England) (Amendment) Regulations 2006 • Re appropriate body to approve research projects
2007/563 (C24)	The Mental Capacity Act 2005 (Commencement No 1)(England and Wales) Order 2007
2007/679	The Mental Capacity Act 2005 (Loss of Capacity during Research Project) (England) Regulations 2007
2007/833 (W71)	The Mental Capacity Act 2005 (Appropriate Body) (Wales) Regulations 2007 • Defines body to approve research in Wales involving people lacking capacity
2007/837 (W72)	The Mental Capacity Act 2005 (Loss of Capacity during Research Project) (Wales) Regulations 2007
2007/852 (W77)	The Mental Capacity Act 2005 (Independent Mental Capacity Advocates) (Wales) Regulations 2007 • Defines 'NHS Body' and 'serious medical treatment' in Wales
2007/856 (W79)	The Mental Capacity Act 2005 (Commencement) (Wales) Order 2007 • Commencement of ss 35–41 in Wales
2007/1253	The Lasting Powers of Attorney, Enduring Powers of Attorney and Public Guardian Regulations • Detail on LPAs, EPAs, and Public Guardian role and procedures
2007/1744 (L12)	The Court of Protection Rules 2007 • Rules of Practice for the Court of Protection
2007/1770	The Public Guardian Board Regulations 2007 • Establishes appointment and regulations re PG Board
2007/1897 (C72)	The Mental Capacity Act 2005 (Commencement No 2) Order 2007 • Final commencement order for MCA as passed in 2005
2007/1898	The Mental Capacity Act 2005 (Transitional and Consequential Provisions) Order 2007 • Transitional matters re litigation commenced prior to 1 October 2007, advance decisions to refuse treatment made prior to 1 October 2007 • Minor statutory amendments to bring conformity with MCA

SI number	Title
2007/1899	The Mental Capacity Act 2005 (Transfer of Proceedings) Order 2007 • Transfer of proceedings from Court of Protection to court with jurisdiction under Children Act
2007/2051	The Public Guardian (Fees, etc) Regulations 2007
2007/2635	The Mental Health Act 2007 (Commencement No 2) Order 2007 • Amendment to MCA s 20(11) to take effect on 1 October 2007

2

THE LEGISLATIVE HISTORY AND
THE ROLE OF THE COMMON LAW

A. THE DEMISE OF *PARENS PATRIAE* AND
THE LEGAL LACUNA

For much of English history, the care of persons lacking capacity was governed by   2.01
the *parens patriae* jurisdiction of the Crown, one of the Royal Prerogative powers.
That was certainly the case by the fourteenth century, when the power was codified.[1]
In modern times, this *parens patriae* power was generally delegated to Chancery
judges. By the end of the mid-twentieth century, it had become subject to an array
of statutes. In 1957, the Percy Commission[2] recommended placing the entire jurisdiction on a statutory footing, and its recommendations were implemented by the
Mental Health Act 1959 (hereinafter referred to as MHA 1959). Since then, the
parens patriae power as such has ceased to exist for adults lacking capacity.

1. Estate-Related Matters

For matters relating to property and affairs, the MHA 1959 created the 'Court of   2.02
Protection', less a formal court than an office within the Supreme Court under the
jurisdiction of a Master. In substantive terms, the MHA 1959 changed little for
estate-related matters. The threshold standards remained flexible, requiring only

---

[1] *De Prerogativa Regis* (1324) 17 Edw. II, stat. I, esp c ix, x.
[2] *Report of the Royal Commission on the Law Relating to Mental Illness and Mental Deficiency 1954–1957*
(the Percy Report), Cmnd 169.

that the individual, based on medical evidence, be incapable by reason of mental disorder of managing and administering his or her property and affairs. If that standard was met, the Court took control of the property, depriving the individual of the legal authority to contract.[3] Normally the Court appointed a receiver, often a family member, to handle the day-to-day administration of the estate. In law, the Court was in control of the estate, and the receiver was required to account to the Court.

2.03   These provisions of the 1959 Act were carried over into Part VII of the Mental Health Act 1983 (hereinafter referred to as MHA 1983).

2.04   While this process was considerably less formal than most court applications, it was regarded as unduly intrusive in what was otherwise thought to be a family matter. Furthermore, it had no flexibility: in law, the appointment of the Court of Protection deprived the individual of all powers over his or her estate, even if he or she may still have had some limited areas of capacity. Partly to rectify these difficulties, the Enduring Powers of Attorney Act 1985 (the EPAA) was passed. Prior to the EPAA, powers of attorney lapsed with the incapacity of the donor.[4] The EPAA allowed powers to continue in effect after the donor became incapable, if the power of attorney so provided. Further, it allowed powers to take effect only upon the individual losing capacity. The holder of an Enduring Power of Attorney (EPA) was required to register it with the Court of Protection when the individual was losing capacity. This required serving the donor and prescribed family members with notice prior to registration, but provided there was no objection from any of these people, formalities of registration were minimal.

2.05   For the first time the EPA allowed people themselves, rather than the Court, to designate who would control their affairs. Involvement of the Court in overseeing the powers following registration was minimal.[5] Nonetheless, they remained powers of attorney; they did not remove any legal power from the donor, even when that individual lacked capacity. This had the advantage that donors with partial capacity could still exercise their autonomy in the areas of their capacity. EPAs affected estate matters only, however; they could not extend to personal decisions.

2. Personal Decisions

2.06   The provisions of the MHA 1959 relating to estates were in many ways similar to the provisions of the old *parens patriae* powers. The same cannot be said of personal decision-making, which was given an entirely new approach. The MHA 1959 superseded not only the statutes relating to the Royal Prerogative, but also the Mental Deficiency Acts 1913, 1926, and 1939, the Lunacy Act 1890, the Mental Treatment Act 1930, and related mental health legislation. No general authority defined in

---

[3] *Re Walker* [1905] 1 Ch 160; *Re Beaney (deceased)* [1978] 2 All ER 595, 600.

[4] *Drew v Nunn* (1879) 4 QB 661.

[5] *Re R (Enduring Power of Attorney)* [1990] 1 Ch 647.

terms similar to incapacity was created relating to personal decisions. The most closely analogous mechanism was guardianship, but that was not phrased in terms of incapacity. Rather, it required the individual to be suffering from one of four specific types of mental disorder: mental illness, 'subnormality', 'severe subnormality', or psychopathy. The last three of these were in turn subject to further definition, with the mental impairments requiring 'arrested or incomplete development of mind'. Subnormality further had to be treatable through medicine or 'training', and severe subnormality had to render the individual incapable of independent living or open to exploitation.[6] These definitions would already have been difficult to apply, for example, to adults with intellectual difficulties following a stroke, as their impairment did not stem from arrested or incomplete development. The other substantive criteria were minimal: the individual's disorder had to be of a nature or degree warranting reception into guardianship; and such reception had to be in the interests of the welfare of the individual or the protection of others. The legal status of personal decisions for incapable people not fitting the guardianship criteria under the MHA 1959 must have been dubious, although it does not appear to have attracted litigation.

The MHA 1983 altered guardianship in several ways. First, cosmetically, it altered   2.07
the language from 'subnormality' and 'severe subnormality' to 'mental impairment', and 'severe mental impairment'. Second, while maintaining the 1959 'arrested or incomplete development of mind' criteria, it altered the definition of these conditions by requiring 'abnormally aggressive or seriously irresponsible conduct'.[7] Recent case law took these new restrictions remarkably seriously, holding for example that the desire of an incapable adult to return to the family home did not meet this threshold, even if allegations were true that the standards of hygiene in the home were manifestly inadequate and the incapable adult had suffered sexual exploitation there.[8]

Third, and perhaps most significantly, the MHA 1983 limited the powers of a   2.08
guardian. Under the MHA 1959, the guardian had the powers of a parent over a fourteen-year-old child. Under the MHA 1983, these powers were reduced to the power to require the patient to reside at a specific place (but not a power to have them returned there, or to confine them there); the power to require the patient to attend at a place for treatment (but not to consent to treatment on the patient's behalf); and the power to require access to the patient to be given to various persons such as doctors or social workers. Outside these decisions, it was at best unclear who, if anyone, could make personal decisions on behalf of adults lacking

---

[6] MHA 1959 s 4.

[7] MHA 1983 s 1(2). The Mental Health Act 2007 (MHA 2007) in general removes the different categories of mental disorder, but nonetheless keeps the 'abnormal and aggressive or seriously irresponsible conduct' criterion for 'learning disability' (as the new Act labels it) in various contexts, including guardianship: see MHA 2007 s 2A and 2B.

[8] *Re F (Mental Health Act: Guardianship)* [2000] 1 FLR 192.

capacity. Such decisions were clearly being made, but in a legal vacuum, and so the common law was called in to fill the lacuna.

B. THE DEVELOPMENT OF THE COMMON LAW

2.09 The creative use of common law in response to the gap in statutory provision since 1989 has been astonishing. While it is difficult to criticize the motives of those concerned and their desire to craft a pragmatic solution to the statutory difficulties discussed above, the development was doctrinally unsatisfactory. At issue have been the questions of how incapacity was to be defined, what legal jurisdiction existed to make decisions on behalf of persons lacking capacity and who could exercise it; and how the best interests of the person lacking capacity were to be determined.

2.10 An understanding of these issues is relevant to the statute for two reasons. First, nothing in the Mental Capacity Act 2005 (hereinafter referred to as the MCA) expressly overrules the common law. While some must be taken to have been overruled by implication, the remainder will continue in effect. Most of the recent developments in the common law occurred after the Law Commission had published its recommendations. At the time, however, legislative reform remained uncertain. It seemed likely that common law remedies would be the only way forward for some time to come. Although that may have appeared necessary at the time, it is now fair to ask whether it is appropriate to continue with these measures. Second, the courts will almost certainly look to the common law as they seek for interpretative aids to the new statute. While this is no doubt desirable to some degree and in some contexts, it should approached with care. The new statute is different in some important respects to the common law responses developed by the courts. The determination of best interests, as an obvious example, is markedly different from the common law approach. To use the common law overly prescriptively to interpret the MCA may therefore undermine the statute. The statute also provides a new opportunity to re-assess the old case law, and where appropriate, a chance to right previous false starts and doubtful decisions. Consequently, the question becomes where and to what extent the common law can or should serve to guide development of the new statute.

1. A New Jurisdiction?

2.11 The problem of the legislative gap first attracted the courts' attention in *Re F (Mental Patient: Sterilisation)*, in 1989.[9] At issue was a sterilization operation for an adult woman lacking capacity. The immediate practical problems were who, if anyone, could consent to the operation and whether a sterilization for contraceptive purposes would be in the best interests of the woman in question. The legal question

---

[9] [1990] 2 AC 1.

was thus whether doctors performing the surgery would be guilty of a crime or liable in tort for battery.

The House of Lords addressed the issue by expanding the doctrine of necessity. 2.12 The Court held that treatment of a person unable to consent owing to incapacity would not incur liability provided the treatment were in the best interests of the incapacitated person. No further consent was required. The procedural mechanism used to reach this result was the Court's declaratory jurisdiction, that is, the general authority of the Court to make determinations of the rights of parties. Since the case of *F*, there has been an expansion in the wording of the scope of the relevant Civil Procedure Rule taking it beyond 'rights' narrowly construed,[10] but the jurisdictional approach is generally the same. The declaratory procedure creates no new substantive jurisdiction in the Court; it only allows declarations of law found elsewhere. The declaration in the case of *F*, for example, related to the law of tort and crime.

This approach is not without its limitations. In a purely legal sense, the Court's 2.13 decision means nothing. The proposed surgery in the case of *F* was not made legal by the decision; legality was dependent upon the surgery being in F's best interests. While the House of Lords has since stated that an application ought to be made in cases of non-therapeutic sterilization and for the termination of treatment for persons in a permanent vegetative state,[11] it would seem that the court has no mechanism to enforce this, and the judgment itself does nothing per se to affect the legality of even these treatments.[12] The judicial decision was in that sense little more than a security blanket.

Even as a security blanket, it had its problems, as it did not bind the patient unless 2.14 the patient was a party.[13] It became standard practice to make the patient a party,[14] but from the perspective of a patient's rights, this approach is odd. The patient's participation after all would in some cases be merely symbolic. If the patient's incapacity is caused by unconsciousness, to pick a clear example, it would be fair to ask what meaningful role the patient would have in a hearing as to how that decision would be taken. Adults lacking capacity are often represented by the Official Solicitor. Such representation is of course desirable, but in cases of urgency, the ability of the Official Solicitor to assess the situation will be severely limited, circumscribing the meaningfulness of the representation provided. In any event, the logic of the rule that parties will be bound by decisions lies in the notion that they will have had a chance to contest the merits. When the patient's incapacity is such that he or she is unable to engage with the hearing, even if represented by the Official Solicitor, it is difficult to see that this premise is met. This is a problem that hovers over incapacity law.

---

[10] See CPR r 40.20.

[11] See *Re F (Sterilisation)*, n 9 above, for sterilizations; *Airedale NHS Trust v Bland* [1993] AC 789 for permanent vegetative states. See also *Practice Note (Family Div: Incapacitated Adults)* [2002] 1 WLR 325.

[12] *Re F (Sterilisation)*, see n 9 above, at 63–65 and 80–83.

[13] ibid at 64 and 81–82; *St George's Healthcare NHS Trust v S* [1998] 3 All ER 673, 698.

[14] *St George's Healthcare NHS Trust v S*, see n 13 above, 703; *Practice Note (Family Div: Incapacitated Adults)* [2002] 1 WLR 325.

What happens if an individual who regains capacity can point to factors not made known to the court that might well have affected the court's decision? Particularly if those factors were or ought to have been known to the individual applying to the court, is the individual precluded from legal action?

2.15   Subsequent cases drew the courts' jurisdiction into new territory in two ways. As has already been noted, the declaratory jurisdiction proper is parasitic on existing law: for example, it allows a declaration as to whether a proposed action would be tortious. Recent cases appeared to expand this into a new substantive jurisdiction of the court to make declarations in the best interests of an individual lacking capacity without reference to such law: at least insofar as applications concerned people lacking capacity, the jurisdiction apparently ceased to be parasitic, and acquired its own substantive realm. Second, courts began to involve third parties, typically family members, in the decision-making process in a formal way.

2.16   The first of these flowed from a dubious interpretation of *In re S (Hospital Patient: Court's Jurisdiction)*.[15] That case involved a dispute between the estranged wife and the current common law partner of a man who had suffered a stroke. The overarching question was where the man would live, and the specific issue in the hearing was whether the common law partner had sufficient interest in the matter to be permitted to bring the case. The Court of Appeal held that she did, on the basis that 'in cases of controversy and cases involving momentous and irrevocable decisions, the courts have treated as justiciable any genuine question as to what the best interests of a patient require or justify'.[16]

2.17   This was taken in *Re TF (An Adult: Residence)*[17] as authority for the proposition that the courts had a near-unfettered authority to make declarations in the best interests of persons lacking capacity.[18] While Butler-Sloss P acknowledged in that case that the *S* case was on its face about standing, she held that 'the underlying issue, recognised by counsel and by this court, was the best interests of S'.[19] She further stated that the substantive question of S's future residence was the focus of the decision when S's case was remitted to the trial court for determination on the merits. This is not clear. In fact, the published version of the trial court's decision when S was remitted appears to be concerned with conflict of laws questions.[20]

2.18   The broad reading of the court in the *TF* case goes a long way toward re-introducing a system akin to *parens patriae*. Butler-Sloss P addressed this by asking whether the statutory scheme under the MHA 1959 was intended to oust the common law

---

[15] [1996] Fam 1 (CA).

[16] At 18.

[17] [2000] 1 MHLR 120.

[18] See also *Re S (Adult Patient)(Inherent Jurisdiction: Family Life)* [2002] EWHC 2278; [2003] 1 FLR 292, where Munby LJ states: 'The court has jurisdiction to grant whatever relief in declaratory form is necessary to safeguard and promote the incapable adult's welfare and interests' [para 50].

[19] Para 29.

[20] [1996] Fam 23.

of necessity. She held that it was not.[21] The MHA 1959 was held not to have been intended to cover all eventualities, and the MHA 1983, its successor legislation, was thus held similarly not to be a complete code. Certainly, there is jurisprudential support for the notion that the Mental Health Act is not a complete code,[22] but the suggestion that it intended to leave common law remedies for situations such as that of TF is problematic. TF had a developmental disorder, and prior to 1959, she would almost certainly have been under the jurisdiction of the Mental Deficiency Acts. The Percy Commission reported that on 31 December 1954, 76,987 people, of whom 59,221 were over the age of sixteen, were receiving care in the community under these Acts.[23] In 1955, 79,300 people were under voluntary or statutory supervision or guardianship.[24] Whether or not the Percy Commission would have understood the Mental Health Act as a complete code, it beggars belief to suggest that its intent was to remove these people from statutory provision to the common law, without troubling to mention it.

In any event, the difficulty with expanding the declaratory jurisdiction into broad questions of best interests is that it is unclear what power the court is purporting to exercise. If the question is whether specified conduct will be tortious, it is clear what the court is declaring; but what, at common law, is the legal effect of a decision merely that a course of conduct is in the best interests of a person lacking capacity? If an individual does not abide by the court's decision, where is the illegality? It cannot be that a general decision-making authority has been violated; that authority was provided only under *parens patriae*, and that authority is gone. Is a cause of action created between the incapacitated person and the person not following the court's order? If so, we have a new tort, and there is no suggestion that the court wished to proceed in that direction. If not, is the individual in contempt of court? If so, a criminal sanction would be being used to enforce a court order enforcing a non-legal norm. If not, then the court order becomes unenforceable.   2.19

In *Re S (Adult Patient) (Inherent Jurisdiction: Family Life)*,[25] the Court went yet another step back towards the *parens patriae* framework by holding that it could appoint a surrogate decision-maker for a person lacking capacity. The case flowed from the more specific decision in *Re R (Adult: Medical Treatment)*,[26] where the Court held that a decision by a physician to withhold treatment could be made if, and only if, one of the patient's parents consented. It is difficult to see that this is a coherent position. Under the case of *F*, a defence in crime and tort existed if   2.20

---

[21] Paras 26–27. The concurring judgments of Thorpe JA and Sedley JA have similar conceptual problems.

[22] *R v Kirklees MBC, ex p C* [1993] 2 FLR 187.

[23] United Kingdom. *Report of the Royal Commission on the Law Relating to Mental Illness and Mental Deficiency 1954–1957* (the Percy Report), Cmnd 169, table 10a. An additional 58,119 people were receiving institutional care under these Acts.

[24] Percy Report, table 15.

[25] [2002] EWHC 2278 (Fam); [2003] 1 FLR 292.

[26] [1996] 2 FLR 99; cf criticism by Ian Kennedy in his note on the case at [1997] *Medical Law Review* 104, 108.

treatment was in the best interests of the patient. Best interests is a question of fact: either the cessation of treatment is in the best interests of the patient, in which case a defence must lie; or it is not, in which case a defence cannot lie. Either way, while the views of the parents may provide relevant information, their formal consent is not relevant. Indeed, in the case of *F* itself, Lord Goff made it clear that it was merely good practice to consult close family of the patient; it was not a legal necessity.[27] Following the 1996 case of *S*, the family could be parties to any subsequent declaration proceedings. There would therefore be nothing objectionable in requiring the family to be given notice prior to the cessation of treatment, allowing them to return to court if they thought it appropriate; but that is quite different from requiring their consent. The generalization of this approach allowing a global surrogate decision-maker in the case of *Re S* does not escape this problem: necessity attaches as a defence to the person who would otherwise be civilly or criminally liable.

2.21   In the view of the common law courts, the declaratory jurisdiction could make considerable intrusions into the liberty of the individual. In *Norfolk v Norwich Healthcare (NHS) Trust*,[28] it was held that where medical treatment was in the best interests of the adult lacking capacity, reasonable force could be used to effect the treatment. A more expansive view was taken by Sedley LJ in *TF (Adult: Residence)*:

> If returning to her mother is in truth a source of danger to her, I agree that, absent any statutory inhibition, the court may, by declaring what is in T's best interests, sanction not only the provision of local authority accommodation (which in any case needs no special permission) but the use of such moral or physical restriction as may be needed to keep T there and out of harm's way.[29]

This expansiveness must now be read in the context of the decision of the European Court of Human Rights in *HL v UK*.[30] That case involved the admission of a person lacking capacity to a psychiatric hospital. Had he attempted to leave the facility, he would have been prevented from doing so, but he never attempted to do so. Nonetheless, the intrusiveness of his admission was sufficient that the ECtHR held that he was deprived of his liberty under Article 5 of the ECHR, and that this deprivation was not justified by the common law necessity provisions, in effect at that time. Specifically, it held that the law in 1997 provided neither sufficient procedural safeguards nor sufficiently well-defined substantive criteria, to pass scrutiny under Article 5.[31]

2.22   If a declaratory judgment by the court were viewed as a prerequisite to intrusive interventions, it would presumably solve the first of these difficulties. Under the traditional understanding of the declaratory jurisdiction, however, it is not a prerequisite

---

[27] At p 78.
[28] [1996] 2 FLR 613.
[29] *TF*, see n 17 above, para 47.
[30] Application No 45508/99, judgment of 5 October 2004. Prior to the ECHR application, this case was reported in the English courts as *R v Bournewood Community and Mental Health NHS Trust, ex p L* [1998] 3 WLR 107 (HL).
[31] Paras 118–124.

that makes actions legal, it is a security blanket confirming the legality of actions that are legal in themselves through being in the best interests of the incapable person. Furthermore, the approach of the court to defining best interests became broader rather than narrower in the decade following the facts in the case of *HL*.[32] This suggests that the substantive criteria for Article 5 compliance have not been met by the common law.

While the government amended aspects of the Mental Capacity Act during the 2.23 legislative process to take account of some aspects of the case of *HL*, it is only with the passage of the amendments to the MCA in 2007 (contained in MHA 2007) that a response to the *HL* case has been made. These amendments, not yet in force, are discussed in detail in Chapter 4 below.

In a sense, it is difficult to criticize the courts for the jurisdictional developments 2.24 they have undertaken. The legal exclusion of family members from decisions regarding the loved ones for whom they, at least as much as the doctor, may be caring appears on its face to be callous. A hard line insistence that decisions regarding best interests be delayed until the law of tort or crime engages would be unlikely to foster considered decision-making with reasonable standards of evidence. If the issue were intervention into allegedly inadequate social care of an individual, for example, a hearing might well not be held until a *quia timet* injunction would lie.[33] This would result in hearings occurring at times of urgency, and it is difficult to see that this would work to the benefit of anyone in the process. At the same time, the common law's endeavours to move outside the narrow reading of the declaratory jurisdiction was doctrinally problematic.

Much less legally problematic are the jurisprudential developments relating to 2.25 advance directives. It was recognized in the case of *Re T*[34] that the wishes of a competent adult regarding future treatment were binding in a subsequent period of incapacity. In terms of practical enforceability, this was something of a false start in that Butler-Sloss and Staunton LLJ further held that a failure to honour such wishes would give rise to only nominal damages,[35] but the principle was established. In *Re C (Adult: Refusal of Medical Treatment)*,[36] Thorpe J went so far as to issue an injunction precluding future treatment that would conflict with the patient's competent wishes, so providing a remedy in contempt in the event that the wishes were contravened. More than a decade after the *Re T* case, such advance directives are sufficiently part of the legal consciousness that it is no longer obvious that failure to comply with them would attract only nominal damages.[37] That said, the standards imposed by the courts do suggest considerable hesitancy at enforcement of such

---

[32] See paras 2.35–2.42 below.
[33] See the judgment of Hale J (as she then was) in *Cambridgeshire County Council v R (An Adult)* [1995] 1 FLR 50.
[34] [1992] 4 All ER 649.
[35] 665, 669; cf *Malette v Schulman* (1990) 67 DLR (4th) 321, 72 OR (2d) 417 (CA) contra.
[36] [1994] 1 All ER 819.
[37] *Re T*, see n 34 above, 665 and 669.

advance directives. They may always be revoked by the competent patient, and such revocation may be either express or implied. They do not apply if they appear to be based on a premise or belief which proves unfounded: they must represent the real wish of the competent patient, applicable to the circumstances. The burden of proof is on the individual seeking to establish the continuing validity and applicability of the directive. Where life is at stake, clear and convincing evidence must be presented as to the continuing validity and applicability of the directive, and any doubt falls to the preservation of life.[38]

2.26   There remain practical difficulties with the law as it relates to advance directives. There are no formalities requirements for them, raising difficulties as to what statements meet the threshold of validity. It is also unclear whether a patient now lacking capacity but outwardly consenting to treatment is bound by his or her previous advance directive precluding it.[39]

2. Defining Incapacity

2.27   The legal need to define incapacity has as long a history as the legal jurisdiction relating to incapable people, so at least as far back as the fourteenth century. Capacity determination has occurred not only in the *parens patriae* context, however, but also in the context of individual disputes: validity of wills, fitness to plead at trial, enforceability of contracts, fitness to serve as trustee, and ability to consent to treatment are obvious examples. The tradition in English law has been that capacity is a functional concept: it is assessed according to whether the individual can make the specific decision at issue. There is no necessary inconsistency, for example, in an individual being competent to execute a will, but incompetent to consent to treatment, or even in being competent to consent to one treatment and not to others. The only recent exception to this concerned Part 7 of the MHA 1983: once the court took control of individuals' property and affairs under that legislation, they lost the right to conduct all their affairs as defined by that Part, even if they retained capacity over some parts of their affairs.

2.28   The result has been a multiplicity of legal approaches to incapacity, with some common law tests of incapacity being more similar than others. Space does not permit a systematic canvassing of these tests,[40] but it is fair to note that if diverse strands survive the introduction of the MCA, there may be misalignments. Some of these will be identified in the sections that follow, as context requires.

2.29   Certainly, there is a presumption across the common law that an individual has capacity, and the onus to demonstrate incapacity falls to the party alleging incapacity. The presumption of capacity is not displaced simply because an individual has a

---

[38] See *Re T*, n 34 above and *HE v A Hospital NHS Trust, AE* [2003] EWHC 1017.

[39] This question is raised, but not decided, by Munby J in *HE*, see n 38 above.

[40] Regarding determination of capacity generally, see P Bartlett and R Sandland, *Mental Health Law: Policy and Practice* (Oxford University Press, 2007, 3rd edn) Ch 10.

mental disorder.[41] Some cases and academic works are phrased as if capacity must be shown. While this may make grammatical sense and has the advantage of deleting double negatives, it should not be allowed to mislead on the presumption of capacity.

Much of the recent academic literature has focused on the capacity to consent to medical treatment. The criteria for capacity in this regard were established in *Re C (Adult: Refusal of Treatment)*, where it was held that capacity implied that the patient could comprehend and retain treatment information, believe it, and weigh it in the balance to arrive at a choice as to whether or not to consent.[42] This standard, with its insistence that the individual have the ability to weigh matters in the balance, may appear to set a high threshold for capacity. Such an approach was not evident on the decision in the case of *C* itself. C had a gangrenous leg. Against medical advice, he refused amputation, but accepted less invasive treatment. He was apparently aware of the risk of death, but was content to run the risk. He had long suffered from schizophrenia and had delusions that he had once been an outstanding surgeon who had never lost a patient. He further identified himself as religious, and believed that he would survive his malady through the aid of God. Nonetheless, it was held that he had capacity to refuse treatment, apparently on the somewhat surprising basis that the delusions did not affect his judgement regarding the treatment. This case supports the proposition that though the threshold of capacity may be relatively high, the presumption of capacity is strong and requires a considerable weight of evidence to rebut.

2.30

Other cases have been more ready to find the patient lacking capacity. This may flow in part from the fact that the reported cases appear to derive from a small number of situations: an inordinate number deal with women in the late stages of pregnancy, and refusals of blood transfusions on religious grounds. Whatever the reason, patients have seldom been held to have capacity when the matter is disputed in court. The tendency is to find that even if the individual is able to understand the information, he or she is unable to 'weigh it in the balance' to arrive at a choice. Thus courts have held that a woman in labour described as having a needle phobia was not competent to decide on whether she should receive an injection: her refusal did not represent a 'real choice'.[43] In theory, if individuals are not incapable, the reasons for their decisions are not relevant; such treatment decisions are to be respected even if 'the reasons for the refusal were rational or irrational, unknown or non-existent'.[44] While that is certainly true in law, it is equally true that in the rare

2.31

---

[41] *Re C (Adult: Refusal of Medical Treatment)* [1994] 1 All ER 819, 824; *Masterman-Lister v Brutton and Co, Jewell and Home Counties Dairies* [2002] EWCA Civ 1889.

[42] [1994] 1 All ER 819, 824.

[43] In *Re MB (Medical Treatment)* [1997] 2 FLR 426, 437.

[44] *Re T (Adult: Refusal of Medical Treatment)* [1992] 3 WLR 782, 799.

cases where courts have upheld refusals of treatment, they have also tended to explain that apparently irrational decisions may not be so irrational after all.[45]

2.32   None of this addresses the question of what the patient must understand to have capacity. The complication is that a defence to battery exists if the patient has given valid consent based on an understanding 'in broad terms of the nature of the procedure which is intended'.[46] That may be considerably less information than the reasonable doctor is required to give under the law of negligence.[47] Which level of understanding is required for the individual to have capacity? There does not appear to be a satisfactory theoretical answer here. If the battery approach is adopted, a refusal may be honoured of a patient who cannot understand the information that a reasonable doctor is required to provide (the negligence standard). If the negligence approach is adopted, a refusal may not be honoured of a patient who understands the nature of the procedure in broad terms and refuses for cogent reasons, but is unable to understand some of the finer points required by negligence law.

2.33   At its core, the law of consent is a defence to battery, and if that approach is adopted for determination of capacity, understanding the lower standard of information would be required. That does not appear to be the standard of the *C* case discussed above, however, which is stated in terms of understanding risks and benefits, and weighing information in the balance. Nothing in the law of battery would appear to require that.

2.34   These difficulties invited a practical problem of how the law was to approach the situation where the doctor incorrectly considered an individual to be lacking capacity, and treated an individual without consent in purported reliance on the defence of necessity. The legally correct answer was that a battery was committed in this situation. The defence of necessity could apply only if the individual in fact lacked capacity; there was no obvious way to introduce wiggle room to this. In theory, the answer was for the practitioner to apply to the court, but that was likely to be expensive and time-consuming, and could be impractical if a treatment had to be given in haste. While the matter was not been litigated in these terms, the logic of the common law required a doctor's assessment of capacity to be correct, not merely not negligent in these circumstances.

3. Defining Best Interests

2.35   The recent pre-MCA jurisprudence regarding the definition of best interests, like the jurisprudence relating to the declaratory jurisdiction, flowed from *F (Mental Patient: Sterilisation)*. As noted in para 2.12 above, that case held that further

---

[45] See, eg, *Re B (Consent to Treatment: Capacity)* [2002] EWHC 429; [2002] 2 All ER 449; [2002] 1 FLR 1090.

[46] *Chatterton v Gerson* [1981] QB 432, 443.

[47] *Sidaway v Board of Governors of the Bethlem Royal Hospital* [1985] AC 871; *Pearce v United Bristol Healthcare NHS Trust* [1999] PIQR 53. Regarding conflicting capacities, see M Gunn, 'The Meaning of Incapacity' (1994) 2 Medical Law Review 8, 10–12.

consent was not required for medical treatment carried out in the 'best interests' of a person lacking capacity. The articulation of best interests in that case was embryonic. Treatment would be in the best interests of patients if it would save their lives or ensure improvement or prevent deterioration of their physical or mental health.[48] Consistent with this medical vision of best interests, the House of Lords adopted the then standard approach to liability:[49] if the view of the treating physician as to best interests was consistent with that of a responsible body of his or her professional colleagues, liability would not attach. This was a decision for the doctor alone. Consultation with close relatives or carers was a matter of good practice, not a legal requirement.[50]

Even in a medical context, subsequent cases have moved outside the strictly medical definition of best interests. In the case of *MB*, it was specifically held that the concept of best interests was not limited to medical criteria, and that the wishes of the patient prior to losing capacity—in this case wishes mitigating in favour of the treatment—were major factors in determining best interests.[51] The following articulation by Thorpe LJ would suggest that the factors for consideration were exceptionally broad:

2.36

> There can be no doubt in my mind that the evaluation of best interests is akin to a welfare appraisal. . . . [T]he first instance judge with the responsibility to make an evaluation of the best interests of a claimant lacking capacity should draw up a balance sheet. The first entry should be of any factor or factors of actual benefit. . . . Then on the other sheet the judge should write any counterbalancing dis-benefits to the applicant. . . . Then the judge should enter on each sheet the potential gains and losses in each instance making some estimate of the extent of the possibility that the gain or loss might accrue. At the end of that exercise the judge should be better placed to strike a balance between the sum of the certain and possible gains against the sum of the certain and possible losses. Obviously, only if the account is in relatively significant credit will the judge conclude that the application is likely to advance the best interests of the claimant.[52]

While these comments were written in the context of medical treatment, the approach was later applied in the context of other personal decisions, in particular with regard to the removal of incapacitated persons from family care by social service agencies.[53]

There was no objective threshold to intervention beyond the best interests test. *Newham LBC v S (Adult: Court's Jurisdiction)*[54] involved an adult without capacity in the care of her father. Social services sought to remove her from the father's care,

2.37

---

[48] *Re F (Sterilisation)*, see n 9 above, at 66–68, per Lord Brandon.

[49] Flowing from *Bolam v Friern Hospital Management Committee* [1957] 2 All ER 118.

[50] *Re F (Sterilisation)*, see n 9 above, at 78, per Lord Goff.

[51] *MB*, see n 43 above, at 439. See also *Re A (Male Sterilisation)* [2000] 1 FLR 549 at 555; *Re S (Adult Patient: Sterilisation)* [2001] Fam 15 at 30.

[52] *Re A (Male Sterilisation)*, see n 51 above, at 560.

[53] *Re S (Adult Patient) (Inherent Jurisdiction: Family Life)*, see n 25 above, and *Newham London Borough Council v S and Another (Adult: Court's Jurisdiction)* [2003] EWHC 1909 (Fam); [2003] All ER (D) 550.

[54] See n 53 above.

based on the father's alleged problems relating to alcohol and violence. The Court found that these problems did not exist, but at the same held that the balance sheet approach to best interests justified the removal of the adult from family care by social services. Similarly, in *S (Adult Patient) (Inherent Jurisdiction: Family Life)*,[55] the uncontested expert evidence was that an adult lacking capacity was given generally satisfactory care by his family; the intervention of social services was nonetheless approved by the court. The Court specifically rejected a requirement for a threshold of significant harm, which must be demonstrated in similar cases regarding children, before the local authority could intervene.

2.38　　This raises potential difficulties regarding the right to family life under Article 8 of the ECHR. If the incapable adult is still understood to be part of the family unit, he or she may have a right to be cared for within the family, and that the family may have a right to care for him or her under Article 8. Certainly that cannot be an absolute right—an individual lacking capacity should not be left in an abusive family— but it does suggest the appropriateness of a more substantive threshold than is provided by the existing case law. *S (Adult Patient)(Inherent Jurisdiction: Family Life)*[56] acknowledged this difficulty, but held that the best interests of the incapacitated person remained the sole test for intervention. Since the family of a capacitated adult could not enforce family care and contact, so the family of an incapacitated adult's Article 8 rights were similarly limited. The court, placing itself in the position of the incapacitated adult, could thus terminate contact or care.[57] This begs too many questions. Understanding how the incapable adult would have exercised their Article 8 rights if competent may be highly speculative. In the absence of evidence of harm within the family, the threshold denied by the court, the options may be finely balanced. In such a circumstance, is it really convincing that the Article 8 rights of the family count for nought? Further, the approach of the court assumes that it has jurisdiction to act as substitute decision-maker for the adult lacking capacity. As discussed regarding the jurisprudence on common law jurisdiction above, this is a tenuous argument.[58]

2.39　　The move to the broad 'balance sheet' approach carried with it a move away from a determination of best interests based on the view of the relevant professional. Where under the case of *F*, best interests were a matter of professional judgment, to which liability would not attach if the view were consistent with a reasonable body of medical opinion, subsequent cases required something more similar to a correctness test. Such an approach is theoretically unproblematic in the context of a court hearing, but cases such as *Re A (Male Sterilisation)* required such a standard of doctors as well:

Doctors charged with the decisions about the future treatment of patients and whether such treatment would, in the cases of those lacking capacity to make their own decisions, be in their best

---

[55] See n 25 above.
[56] ibid.
[57] Paras 38–39 and 42.
[58] See paras 2.16–2.20 above.

interests, have to act at all times in accordance with a responsible and competent body of relevant professional opinion. That is the professional standard set for those who make such decisions. The doctor, acting to that required standard, has, in my view, a second duty, that is to say, he must act in the best interests of a mentally incapacitated patient. I do not consider that the two duties have been conflated into one requirement.[59]

This significantly reduced the permitted margin of error in the determination of best interests by those charged with the care of adults lacking capacity. The necessity defence would appear to be available only if the caregiver is correct in his or her assessment of best interests. The only legally sound advice at common law to a caregiver in cases of doubt would be to commence court proceedings, with all the inconvenience and expense that would be entailed.

It was in this set of contexts that the MCA was passed in 2005. As will be clear   2.40 from the preceding discussion, the overwhelming direction of the case law was to expand the definition of best interests to include factors that were not strictly medical, and to apply the approach developed in the context of treatment to other issues of personal care. If this represents the overall consensus of the jurisprudence, the case of *R (Burke) v GMC*[60] strikes a somewhat discordant note. This case involved a challenge to the guidance of the General Medical Council (GMC) on the provision of artificial nutrition and hydration. The applicant, Mr Burke, suffered from a degenerative condition, and would in the future become incapacitated. He was concerned that following the GMC guidance, his doctors would withdraw artificial nutrition and hydration before he would wish it to be withdrawn. He therefore applied to court for an order that his best interests would be in the provision of this treatment, even in circumstances beyond the GMC guidance.

Mr Burke lost before the Court of Appeal, primarily on the basis that his case was   2.41 premature. Nonetheless, the Court adopted a much more circumspect tone to its discussion of best interests and the judicial role than was evident in previous cases. The Court firmly criticized the use of the balance sheet approach to best interests by the trial judge. It held that the balance sheet approach flowed primarily from sterilization cases, and was of little assistance in cases such as Mr Burke's. It adopted a much more circumspect approach to best interests determination:

It seems to us that it is best to confine the use of the phrase 'best interests' to an objective test, which is of most use when considering the duty owed to a patient who is not competent and is easiest to apply when confined to a situation where the relevant interests are purely medical.[61]

The overall tone of the *Burke* case appears much more conservative in its view of the judicial role, and of the determination of best interests. In particular, it seems to suggest that best interests are to be determined in a medical context by consideration of medical factors.

---

[59] See n 51 above, at 555, per Butler-Sloss P.
[60] [2005] EWCA 1003.
[61] [2005] EWCA 1003, para 29.

2.42   The sense from the *Burke* case is that at least this panel of the Court of Appeal wished to rein in the mushrooming jurisprudence of the declaratory jurisdiction in this area. That said, a number of other cases noted above are also from the Court of Appeal, so it is not obvious how far the less expansive approach in the *Burke* case reflects the overall view of the Court. Of perhaps more significance, as will be discussed below, is the fact that much of the expansive view of best interests and of court jurisdiction is reflected in the MCA. Whatever its merits, the *Burke* case's circumspection may thus be of little effect.

C. THE LAW COMMISSION PROPOSALS
AND THE ROAD TO LEGISLATIVE REFORM

2.43   The origins of the MCA lie in an investigation, discussion documents, and a final report including a draft bill by the Law Commission. The impetus for the Commission project flowed from a discussion document by the Law Society in 1989.[62] The Commission published an initial general consultative document in 1991,[63] followed by more specific papers in 1993 on formalizing, amending, and clarifying the rights of carers;[64] medical treatment and research;[65] and public law protection for people lacking capacity.[66] These met with broad academic approval,[67] and a final report was published in 1995.[68] Green and White Papers followed in 1997 and 1999.[69] A draft bill in 2003 received pre-legislative scrutiny,[70] and

---

[62] *Decision Making and Mental Incapacity: A Discussion Document* (1989).

[63] *Mentally Incapacitated Adults and Decision-Making: An Overview* (Consultation Paper 119) (1991).

[64] *Mentally Incapacitated Adults and Decision-Making: A New Jurisdiction* (Consultation Paper 128) (1993),

[65] *Mentally Incapacitated Adults and Decision-Making: Medical Treatment and Research* (Consultation Paper 129) (1993).

[66] *Mentally Incapacitated and Other Vulnerable Adults: Public Law Protection* (Consultation Paper 130) (1993).

[67] P Fennell, 'Statutory Authority to Treat, Relatives and Treatment Proxies' (1994) 2 Medical Law Review 30; P Fennell 'The Law Commission Proposals on Mental Incapacity' (1995) Family Law 420; M Freeman, 'Deciding for the Intellectually Impaired' (1994) 2 Medical Law Review 77; M Gunn, 'The Meaning of Incapacity' (1994) 2 Medical Law Review 8; A Parkin, 'Where now on Mental Incapacity?' (1996) 2 Web Journal of Current Legal Issues; P Wilson, 'The Law Commission's Report on Mental Incapacity: Medically Vulnerable Adults or Politically Vulnerable Law?' (1996) 4 Medical Law Review 227. For more critical views, see P Bartlett, 'The Consequences of Incapacity' (1997) 4 Web Journal of Current Legal Issues; D Carson, 'Disabling Progress: The Law Commission's Proposals on Mentally Incapacitated Adults' Decision-Making' (1993) Journal of Social Welfare and Family Law 304.

[68] *Mental Incapacity* (Law Com 231) (1995).

[69] Lord Chancellor's Department, *Who Decides? Making Decisions on Behalf of Mentally Incapacitated Adults* Cm 3803 (1997); Lord Chancellor's Department, *Making Decisions: The Government's Proposals for Making Decisions on Behalf of Mentally Incapacitated Adults* Cm 4465 (1999).

[70] See *House of Commons and House of Lords Joint Committee Report on the Draft Mental Incapacity Bill* (HL Paper (2002–3) no 189; HC Paper (2002–3) no 1083). See also government response, February 2004. Both these documents are available at <http://www.parliament.uk/bills/draftbills/draftbills0203.cfm>, accessed 15 November 2007. This bill also received the attention of the Joint Committee of the House of Commons

a further draft bill with explanatory notes was published in 2004. It was this bill, in a somewhat amended form, that eventually made its way to the statute books in the dying hours of Parliamentary time before the 2005 election.

The MCA as passed in 2005 remains in structure and content remarkably similar 2.44
to the Commission's draft bill. The most significant exception is that the public law protections proposed by the Law Commission were not included in the bills before Parliament, and so have not been implemented. These would have placed a threshold on intervention by local authorities into the lives of vulnerable people in the community. The provisions would have allowed such intervention only in cases of significant harm or serious exploitation. Temporary orders for the protection of such vulnerable persons would have been allowed for up to eight days to allow for the consideration of long-term options.[71] At the end of the eight-day period, it would have been necessary to resort to other law, such as the MHA 1983, for which the Commission proposed slightly expanded powers of guardianship. These proposals were directed to 'vulnerable' adults, a group considered to be wider than adults lacking capacity.

Instead of these public law protections, the MCA has provision for the establish- 2.45
ment of a system of independent advocates who must be consulted at key moments in the intervention of social services and similar organizations. These advocates will have authority to challenge decisions made for adults lacking capacity, but will operate within the substantive framework of the remainder of the MCA.

Notwithstanding the similarity between the Commission's proposals and the 2.46
eventual statute, the ten-year delay in its passage onto the statute book cannot solely be attributed to a shortage of parliamentary time. There were several stumbling blocks. First and most significant was the Commission's view that advanced decisions in matters of medical treatment should be enforceable, a view that was taken to be a move to allow euthanasia.[72] Whatever the political relevance of such concerns, it is difficult to see them as having legal merit. By the time of the Commission's proposals, the common law had already accepted the efficacy of advanced directives for medical treatment. Indeed, in the case of *Re C* an injunction precluding apparently life-saving treatment had been granted on the basis of such a competent advanced wish.[73] It is not obvious that the Commission's proposals would have extended this in any way. Advance directives were nonetheless excluded from the Green Paper, apparently to continue to be governed by common law. Their codification was re-introduced into the bill, but concerns about euthanasia continued throughout its parliamentary life. Prime Minister Tony Blair was eventually required

---

and House of Lords on Human Rights in their 23rd Report, Appendix I (2003–4, HL 210, HC 1282); see also government response <http://www.dca.gov.uk/menincap/response.pdf>, accessed 15 November 2007.

[71] Law Com 231, part IX. These provisions would have replaced the National Assistance Act 1948 s 47 and MHA 1983 s 135(1) and (3).

[72] See Wilson, see n 67 above, 228.

[73] See para 2.25 above.

to provide assurances that the Act would not alter the law relating to murder, manslaughter, and assisted suicide, and at the last moment s 62 was added to that effect.

2.47   The Commission's proposals on medical research involving adults lacking capacity were similarly viewed with some trepidation. Once again the reasons are unconvincing. Prior to the Commission's work, there were no formal legal restrictions relating to research involving people lacking capacity. Such research was taking place on patients unable to consent owing to incapacity, but with no other formal safeguards as to the appropriateness of the research. It is difficult to see how an outright ban of such research could be desirable. Research into conditions such as Alzheimer's disease requires the involvement of people affected by the condition; a ban on their involvement would effectively prohibit research into the condition. The Commission's approach took account of the desirability of appropriate research, but sought to impose certain procedural structures and substantive limitations. The research was already happening in an uncontrolled environment. The Commission's proposals were about providing a structure of appropriate controls, not a research free-for-all. Given this, those who were hesitant about research on adults lacking capacity ought to have favoured them. The proposals were re-introduced prior to the passage of the bill by Parliament.[74]

2.48   The Commission's proposals and draft bill were published in the beginning of 1995. The structure and content of most of the MCA dates from that period. The remainder of law however did not stand still in this ensuing decade. The Hague Convention on the International Protection of Adults[75] was signed in 2000, and is implemented by the MCA Sch 3. Of more pervasive relevance is the Human Rights Act 1998, passed and brought into effect in 2000. The Strasbourg jurisprudence involving people lacking capacity has been limited, but it is clear (if it could ever have been in doubt) that such people are within the purview of the Convention.[76] The *HL* case, discussed above (para 2.21), was decided by the ECtHR too late in the legislative timetable fully to be taken into account in the MCA in 2005. The Act did take some cognizance of the case by precluding people other than courts from restricting an incapacitated person's right to liberty under Article 5, but it is only with the passage of the 2007 amendments that a developed response to the *HL* case has been introduced.[77]

2.49   Finally, the growth in the common law described in the first sections of this chapter took effect largely after the Commission's report. In that time, we have seen the creation of a new jurisdiction to determine (and presumably enforce) actions done in the best interests of an individual lacking capacity, a jurisdiction that apparently allows the appointment of a substitute decision-maker. 'Best interests' has been

---

[74] The provisions regarding research are discussed at paras 3.137–3.149 below.
[75] Cm 5881 (2000).
[76] See, eg, the *HL* case, n 30 above.
[77] These provisions are discussed in Ch 4 below.

re-defined in a broad and flexible way. Advance directives, recognized prior to the Commission's report but still in their infancy, have begun to attract a jurisprudential canon. Even the definition of incapacity itself has become applied much more comfortably by the courts. None of this could have been in the minds of the Commission. The Commission expressly intended its proposals to sit beside the common law, and there is nothing in the MCA to alter this approach. If the new jurisprudential developments continue to exist unaltered, however, many of the approaches of the MCA will be able to be circumvented by appeal to the common law. At the same time, it is difficult to believe that the courts, now increasingly used to dealing with matters of incapacity, will fail to view the new statute in the light of their existing jurisprudence. As the MCA creates a totally new statutory space, how these divergences will be played off against one other is currently a matter of speculation.

3

AN OVERVIEW OF THE STATUTE

A. THE LEGISLATIVE STRUCTURE
AND THE CODE OF PRACTICE

The MCA received Royal Assent on 17 April 2005. It was introduced into force   3.01
in stages in 2007, with the result that it took full effect in England and Wales on
1 October 2007.[1] As noted above, the MCA as passed in 2005 did not fully deal
with the issues surrounding deprivation of liberty of people lacking capacity that
were raised by *HL v UK*.[2] Amendments to the MCA to address those issues were
introduced by the MHA 2007, and are not yet in force. For purposes of the present
chapter, the 2007 amendments are not taken into account, and the law is taken to
be as it is in force on 1 October 2007. The 2007 amendments are considered separately, in Chapter 4.

The statute as passed in 2005 is buttressed by seven schedules. Four of these   3.02
involve the usual collection of repeals, amendments, and transitional provisions.

---

[1] See SI 2007/1897 (C72).
[2] (2005) 40 EHRR 32; see paras 1.28, 1.32, 2.23, and 2.48 above.

Schedule 5 of the MCA repeals all of the Enduring Powers of Attorney Act 1985 and Part 7 of the Mental Health Act 1983 (which concerns property and affairs of 'patients'), and Schedule 4 contains transitional provisions for those persons under the jurisdiction of those provisions at the time of their repeal. Schedule 6, among other things, amends references to incapacity in other statutes to reflect the MCA definition. Schedules 1, 3, and 4, the three substantive schedules, concern formalities of lasting powers of attorney (LPAs), transitional provisions regarding enduring powers of attorney (EPAs), supplemental provisions relating to the property and affairs of those lacking capacity, and the international protection of adults lacking capacity.

3.03   A number of statutory instruments have also been issued pursuant to the MCA. The most significant of these are contained as appendices to this book: the LPAs, EPAs and Public Guardian Regulations, SI 2007/1253 (App 3), and the Court of Protection Rules, SI 2007/1744 (L12) (App 4). A full list of statutory instruments relating to the MCA (as of 1 October 2007) is to be found in Table 1.1, at the end of Chapter 1.

3.04   In addition, a Code of Practice has been issued pursuant to s 42 of the MCA, and is contained in this book as Appendix 2. The MCA imposes a duty to have regard to the Code on donees of LPAs, court-appointed deputies, researchers using mentally incapable subjects, mental health advocates under the Act, those acting in a professional capacity, and those acting for remuneration.[3] Courts are also to take departures from the Code of Practice into account, when relevant to a matter arising before them (s 42(5)). That said, as discussed above,[4] the Code is guidance. It is not binding in the same sense as the statute or statutory instruments, and people implementing the MCA may depart from the Code when they have cogent reason to do so,[5] so long as that departure is not inconsistent with the MCA itself or its statutory instruments.

B. THE OVERALL PICTURE

3.05   The MCA is an attempt to introduce flexible and supportive measures to ensure that appropriate decisions are taken in the best interests of adults lacking capacity, with no more procedural difficulty than is required. As the detail can be complex, an overview may be of assistance.

3.06   In the MCA, and in the discussion that follows here, persons lacking capacity or reasonably thought to be lacking capacity are labelled P, and persons caring for them or making decisions for them are labelled D. A set of principles is initially

---

[3] MCA s 42(4).
[4] See para 1.77 above.
[5] *R (Munjaz) v Mersey Care NHS Trust and Others* [2005] UKHL 58.

established to colour the overall interpretation of the Act.[6] Statutory definitions are established for 'people who lack capacity',[7] 'inability to make decisions' (MCA s 3), and 'best interests'.[8]

The Act codifies the right to make advance decisions to refuse medical treatment. When such a valid decision exists for a treatment, it is in law as if the individual were competent and making the decision at the time the decision is relied on. In this sole case, issues of best interests or substituted decision-making cease to be relevant: the decision stands.[9] Unless there is a valid advance directive for health care, the Act is primarily concerned with substitute decision-making, based on the best interests definition.

3.07

Alternatively, an individual can execute an LPA, a power that can withstand or indeed commence upon the incapacity of the donor. This allows the holder of the power to make personal or property decisions, as delineated by the power, in those areas where the donor lacks cpacity. Unlike the older version, however, LPAs can be granted for personal decisions as well as for financial decisions.[10]

3.08

At the most formal level, and generally intended to be used as a last resort, a new Court of Protection can make decisions on behalf of P, or can, subject to some restrictions, appoint a deputy to make those decisions.[11] A deputy cannot be appointed to make decisions inconsistent with the holder of a valid LPA,[12] although the Court can declare an LPA void in the event that it was obtained by fraud or undue influence, or that the donee is behaving in contravention of the authority or other than in the best interests of P.[13] The structure and administration of the new Court of Protection forms Part II of the MCA.

3.09

At the least formal level, D can act to provide care or treatment in the best interests of P, and the act will be treated as though P had consented to it. No liability will therefore attach, as long as there is no negligence in the performance of the care or treatment. There are provisions relating to expenses to ensure that D has access to funds to pay for the care or treatment, and any suppliers of necessaries will be paid.[14] This 'general defence' does not apply to decisions being taken by a donee of an LPA, a court, or a court-appointed deputy, or within the scope of a valid and applicable advance decision to refuse medical treatment. While it is expected that this general defence will be the mechanism most frequently relied on in care provision, it is in this sense a default mechanism, taking effect when no more formal authority exists under the MCA.

3.10

---

[6] MCA s 1.
[7] MCA s 2.
[8] MCA s 4.
[9] MCA ss 24–26.
[10] MCA ss 9–14.
[11] MCA ss 15–21.
[12] MCA s 20(4).
[13] MCA s 22(3)–(4).
[14] MCA ss 5–8.

3.11   The MCA provides some additional procedural safeguards against interventions by public authorities. If there is no person other than a professional carer who would be appropriate to consult regarding P's best interests, an independent mental capacity advocate must be consulted prior to the NHS engaging in serious medical treatment of P, or the NHS or a local authority providing accommodation to P beyond the short term. The advocate's role is to support P as far as possible to be involved in the decision, to obtain further information including additional medical reports if appropriate, to determine P's best interests, and to ascertain alternative courses of action if appropriate.

3.12   The Act further lays down a regulatory structure for the approval of 'intrusive' research involving adults lacking capacity. 'Intrusive' research is defined as research that would otherwise require the consent of the participants. To obtain approval, the MCA requires that such research be into the impairing condition affecting P or the treatment of such a condition, that the proposed protocols are the most effective for gaining the knowledge, and that the risks or inconvenience of participation to research subjects be limited. As part of the recruitment of research subjects, a non-professional carer must be consulted for each subject to determine the appropriateness of the subject's participation in the research, including what his or her views about participation in the research would have been if capable.[15]

3.13   An offence is created for carers, including donees of LPAs and court-appointed deputies, who ill-treat or wilfully neglect persons without capacity.[16]

3.14   The Act specifically excludes some decisions from its ambit. The MCA does not extend to a variety of decisions related to family relations, including consent to marriage or civil partnership, consent to sexual relations, consent to divorce based on two years' separation, consent to a child's placement for adoption or making of an adoption order, discharging parental responsibilities over a child's property, or giving consent under the Human Fertilisation and Embryology Act.[17] Further, the MCA does not extend to decisions on behalf of a person lacking capacity regarding voting for any public office or in a referendum.[18] For all these decisions, if a person lacks capacity to make the decision himself or herself, the decision cannot be made at all. Decisions regarding treatment regulated by the Mental Health Act are also outside the MCA. This will be discussed in more detail below in the overall context of the interface between the Mental Health Act and the MCA.[19]

---

[15] MCA ss 30–34.

[16] MCA s 44.

[17] MCA s 27.

[18] MCA s 29.

[19] MCA s 28, see further paras 5.38–5.70 below, and regarding the 2007 amendments, paras 4.61–4.73 below.

C. THE PRINCIPLES

The following five principles are set out in s 1 to guide interpretation of the   3.15
legislation:

. . .

(2) A person must be assumed to have capacity unless it is established that he lacks capacity.

(3) A person is not to be treated as unable to make a decision unless all practicable steps to help him to do so have been taken without success.

(4) A person is not to be treated as unable to make a decision merely because he makes an unwise decision.

(5) An act done, or decision made, under this Act for or on behalf of a person who lacks capacity must be done, or made, in his best interests.

(6) Before the act is done, or the decision is made, regard must be had to whether the purpose for which it is needed can be as effectively achieved in a way that is less restrictive of the person's rights and freedom of action.

Guidance regarding the principles is given in the Code of Practice at Chapter 2.

What is striking about the principles is not how much, but how little new law   3.16
they contain. The principles in s 1(2) and (4) flow directly from the common law. The principle in s 1(3) grows out of the presumption of capacity. All of these reflect a desire to protect the autonomy of the capable individual. The requirement to provide assistance is not mere window-dressing. People who have difficulty communicating their decisions risk being considered unable to make decisions under s 3(1)(d). The requirement to provide assistance should ensure that such persons fall under the MCA only if they really are unable to communicate their wishes, not merely because they may require specialist assistance in being understood. Similarly, this principle would suggest that individuals who may have difficulty assimilating information should not be found to lack capacity because it is inconvenient to spend the required time working through the information with them. Moreover, the degree of support an individual receives in his or her overall environment may affect the decisions he or she can make. The presence of carers, professional or lay, may make it possible to organize the individual's life so that decisions are simplified to a degree where an individual of marginal capacity can make the decision. While it would seem that such support as is 'practicable' must be taken into account, there is no duty in the Act to provide such services. While rights to care may exist under other statutes, they are normally subject to fiscal restraints, a restriction that may well be read by the courts into the word 'practicable'.[20]

The principle in s 1(5) is similar in spirit to the fiduciary duties traditionally gov-   3.17
erning those charged with the administration of estates of persons lacking capacity,

---

[20] Courts have traditionally been notoriously reluctant to enforce the provision of care services when confronted by public authorities crying impecuniousness: see, eg, *R v Gloucestershire CC, ex p Barry* [1997] 2 All ER 1 (HL).

although as will become clear, the definition of best interests is something of a departure from that developed by the law. The principle of least restrictive alternative in s 1(6) is common in legal ethics relating to coercion and mental disorder. The precise phrasing of such principles varies. The phrasing in the MCA directs attention to both the individual's rights and freedom of action. At issue therefore is both protecting the individual's legal autonomy and maximizing his or her practical experience of living.

3.18   Implicit in the Act is also the old common law notion that capacity is a functional concept. Throughout the MCA and the Code of Practice, reference is made to lacking capacity to make particular decisions. The individual retains legal authority to make those decisions for which he or she continues to have capacity. Previously, the exception had been for people found to lack capacity to administer their property and affairs: at least after 1905, a *parens patriae* determination regarding property resulted in a complete inability to deal with one's own property and affairs, even in areas where the individual continued to have capacity.[21] That is no longer the case for court appointments. Section 20(1) states specifically that court-appointed deputies do not have any power where the deputy knows or has reasonable cause to believe that P has capacity to make the decision in question. Once again, this is part of the overall approach of the MCA to ensure that those people with capacity can exercise their autonomy.

3.19   The bounds of the presumption of capacity contained in s 1(2) warrant comment. Certainly, any real doubt as to whether an individual has capacity must be resolved in favour of capacity. In this regard, the courts are likely to be influenced by the common law here, that significant evidence is required to displace the presumption.[22] That said, the MCA does not allow wilful blindness to incapacity. If the evidence of incapacity is there to be seen, the MCA applies: it cannot be ignored. This will be more relevant under the MCA than at common law, since incapacity triggers procedures that must be followed. The person making a decision for P might be a donee of an LPA or court-appointed deputy, who must be approached to make the decision in question if P lacks capacity. Further, the best interests test has procedural requirements that must be followed, regarding involvement of P and consultation with others. These provisions cannot be avoided by a reliance on the presumption in s 1(2) in the face of clear evidence of incapacity.

3.20   The principle in s 1(3) that all practicable steps must be made to help an individual to make a decision reflects an overall requirement of the MCA, that vulnerable people will be as involved as possible in decisions made about them (see also ss 3(2), (3), 4(4)). Consistent with this, Chapter 3 of the Code of Practice contains helpful

---

[21] See *Re Walker* [1905] 1 Ch 160. This continued under the codified controls over property and estates of incapable persons under the MHA 1959 and MHA 1983: see *Re Beaney (deceased)* [1978] 2 All ER 595, 600.

[22] See para 2.30 above, and Code of Practice para 4.10.

information as to how to assist vulnerable people to be involved in decision-making.

The Act applies to people over the age of sixteen.[23] There are several exceptions.　3.21

- An LPA may be signed only by an individual over the age of eighteen (MCA s 9(2)(c)).
- An advance decision to refuse treatment may be made only by a person over the age of eighteen (MCA s 24(1)).
- The court can deal with the property of an incapable minor below the age of sixteen if the court considers it likely that the minor will continue to lack capacity at the age of eighteen (MCA s 18(3)).
- The offence of ill-treatment or wilful neglect of a person lacking capacity has no age limit (MCA s 44).

The situation regarding minors will be discussed at paras 5.09 to 5.11 below.

D. THE MEANING OF INCAPACITY

The meaning of incapacity flows from ss 2 and 3 of the MCA. Further guidance as　3.22
to its interpretation is provided in the Code of Practice at Chapter 4.

The MCA states that a person lacks capacity in relation to a matter if at the mate-　3.23
rial time he is 'unable to make a decision for himself in relation to the matter because of an impairment of, or a disturbance in the functioning of, the mind or brain'.[24] Such impairment or disturbance may be permanent or temporary[25] and is decided on the balance of probabilities.[26] This is intended to introduce a diagnostic threshold to the determination of capacity under the MCA.[27] The presence of such a threshold, originally proposed by the Law Commission, was criticized as being stigmatizing.[28] The Law Commission did not agree that a stigma would follow from this requirement, and viewed it as an important substantive protection against the overuse of the statute.[29]

The result is not without its problems, however. How are we to cope with inca-　3.24
pacity that is outside the diagnostic criterion? The Code of Practice anticipates that incapacity caused by drunkenness is within the scope of the MCA, for example.[30]

---

[23] MCA s 2(5)–(6).

[24] MCA s 2(1).

[25] MCA s 2(2).

[26] MCA s 2(4).

[27] Department of Health, 'Explanatory Notes to the Mental Capacity Act' (London: Queen's Printer, 2005) para 22.

[28] Carson 'Disabling Progress: The Law Commission's Proposals on Mentally Incapacitated Adults' Decision-making' (1993) Journal of Social Welfare and Family Law 304. .

[29] Law Com 231, para 3.8.

[30] Code of Practice paras 4.9 and 4.12.

However, it is not obvious that this is within the scope of a diagnostic criterion: having had too much to drink is not in itself a medical condition. If that is the case, notwithstanding the Code of Practice, drunkenness would be outside the terms of the MCA. That seems to have been Parliament's intention. Section 3 of the Sale of Goods Act 1979 governed the sale of 'necessaries' to minors, people lacking capacity, and people who are drunk. That is now dealt with for people lacking capacity by s 7 of the MCA, and people with mental incapacity are duly removed from the scope of the 1979 Act. People unable to contract because of drunkenness are not removed from the 1979 Act, suggesting that Parliament did not consider them to be within the scope of the MCA. The requirement of an impairment to the mind or brain further ignores the possibility of an individual whose purely physical impairment results in incapacity. An individual without brain damage who falls unconscious following an accident, or is immobilized by a severe muscular disease, or is so distracted by physical pain as to be unable meaningfully to consent, could be examples where inclusion within the ambit of disorder to the 'mind or brain' might tax language to breaking point. If such individuals were held to be outside the provisions of the Act decisions about them would still need to be made. In the event that they are outside the MCA, recourse to the common law might still be necessary.

3.25   The lack of capacity cannot be established 'merely' by reference to age or appearance, or a 'condition' or 'aspect of his behaviour' which would lead to 'unjustified' assumptions about incapacity.[31] This is presumably intended to ensure that incapacity is not decided by stereotype: extreme age, an unkempt appearance, or an ingrained mistrust of service providers do not of themselves bespeak incapacity. The wording of the provision is nonetheless unfortunate, in that 'merely' suggests that these factors can be included in an assessment of capacity, even if they would lead to 'unjustified' assumptions, so long as there is additional evidence corroborating incapacity. This is illogical. If assumptions based on the criteria would be unjustified, the criteria should not be considered at all in an assessment of capacity. In that circumstance, the criterion would be irrelevant, and use of the criterion at all would perpetuate the unfair bias the subsection is intended to challenge.

3.26   The inability to make a decision for oneself is defined in s 3 of the Act. Such inability occurs when the individual is unable:

(a) to understand the information relevant to the decision, even if the information is presented in a culturally appropriate way such as through the use of simple language or visual aids;
(b) to retain that information, even if only for a short period;
(c) to use or weigh that information as part of the process of making the decision; or
(d) to communicate his decision (whether by talking, using sign language or any other means).

---

[31] MCA s 2(3).

The similarity with the common law definition of capacity to consent to medical treatment discussed at paras 2.27 to 2.34 above will be obvious to the reader, and there can be little doubt that the courts will use the existing common law jurisprudence as a guide to the interpretation of this section. The section contains a flexibility similar to the common law approach, particularly in the requirement that the individual be able to 'use or weigh that information as part of the process of making the decision'. When the courts have made controversial findings of incapacity in the past, it has often been as a result of applying this rather amorphous standard.

The MCA requires that the incapable individual must be unable to understand   3.27
the reasonably foreseeable consequences of deciding one way or another, and of failing to decide.[32] This would seem to include reasonably foreseeable risks and benefits flowing from the various decisions possible, or of failing to make a decision. There had been a strand of scholarship in the past that has claimed that capacity to choose is contingent on the severity of the choice made. Thus an individual might have capacity to consent to a specific treatment, but not to refuse it, because the consequences of having the treatment might be less severe than the consequences of not having the treatment.[33] This is no longer a sustainable argument in England and Wales. This subsection of the MCA requires an understanding of all possible choices, including failure to make a choice; it follows that the standard of capacity is the same, no matter what choice P is to make.

Through all this, it should be emphasized that the MCA is phrased in terms of   3.28
ability. Certain academic literature has drawn a distinction between ability to understand and actual understanding.[34] In the legal context of the MCA, where capacity determination is so closely related to specific decisions, the distinction may seem somewhat precious, but insofar as it is an issue, the MCA speaks in terms of ability. It follows from this that people of marginal capacity have the same rights as those of robust capacity to waive information provision. The fact that an individual chooses to hush the warnings of his or her stockbroker regarding equity transactions or doctor regarding adverse effects of treatment may be manifestly unwise, but it does not of itself bespeak incapacity.

Conspicuous by its absence from the definition is any express requirement that   3.29
an individual believe the information provided.[35] What is required is an ability to understand and weigh the information. If the information is not believed, enquiries should be made as to the circumstances. If it were the result of a psychotic delusion, the effect of the delusion on the belief of the information would unquestionably be relevant to the assessment of incapacity. If the lack of belief flowed for example from a view that the person providing the information was not adequately qualified,

---

[32] MCA s 3(4).

[33] See, eg, B Dickens, 'Medical Consent Legislation in Ontario' (1994) 2 Medical Law Review 283, 287.

[34] See, eg, the classic paper on capacity, L Roth, A Meisel and C Lidz, 'Tests of Competency to Consent to Treatment' (1977) 134 American Journal of Psychiatry 279, 282. The distinction is made regarding capacity under the MHA 1983 in *R v MHAC, ex p X* (1988) 9 BMLR 77, 85.

[35] Such a requirement is contained in the common law: see *Re C* [1994] 1 WLR 290, 295.

however—a house officer rather than a consultant, for example—it would not necessarily bespeak incapacity. In other cases, the failure to believe may flow from a refusal to accept that the facts are as presented—a manifestly unrealistic view that P can return to his or her own home and a consequent refusal to move to a nursing home, for example. Once again, a failure to be realistic about one's prospects does not necessarily bespeak incapacity. The robustly capable may behave in this fashion without any challenge to their right to do so; it does not follow from the fact that an individual has marginal capacity or is in a position of relative vulnerability that this should change.

3.30   There is similarly no requirement in the legislation that an individual should respect, trust, or even be civil to doctors, local authorities, police officers, carers, family, or other service providers. There may be a wide variety of reasons for such behaviour and responses; they do not all bespeak incapacity by any means. Being difficult, obstreperous, ornery, or rude is not the same as being incapable.

3.31   Consequently, ascertaining whether an individual lacks capacity may in some circumstances be a difficult question. The individual who must satisfy himself or herself as to the capacity of P is D, the individual who will in the end be liable if the relevant decision is taken wrongly. The incapacity definitions themselves, discussed above, provide guidance on how the decision ought to be addressed, and the Code of Practice provides further useful pointers.[36] In the event that the decision will interfere with P's rights under Article 5 of the Human Rights Act,[37] medical evidence of such incapacity will be necessary, to comply with the requirements of *Winterwerp v the Netherlands*.[38] Otherwise such formal evidence is not required, so long as D is satisfied that there is an impairment or disturbance of functioning of the mind or brain leading to the required inability to make decisions. That said, if D is in doubt as to P's ability, medical views should be appropriately obtained.

3.32   While the responsibility to determine whether P lacks capacity falls on D, the Act is in general sufficiently satisfied if D reasonably believes that P lacks capacity. The Code of Practice discusses this at paras 4.44 to 4.45, noting that D will be required to have reasonable grounds and objective reasons for this view, as well as being able to describe the process he or she has taken to reach this conclusion.[39] This is no doubt sound advice. Different sections of the MCA deal with this reasonable belief slightly differently. For that reason, they will be dealt with separately below.

---

[36] Code of Practice Ch 3 and paras 4.35–4.36.
[37] Until the 2007 amendments to the MCA come into force, such decisions may be taken only by the court: see ss 6(5), 11(6), and 20(13).
[38] *Winterwerp v the Netherlands* (A/33) (1979–80) 2 EHRR 387, para 39.
[39] Code of Practice para 4.44.

E. BEST INTERESTS

Decisions made under the MCA must be made in the 'best interests' of P. The major **3.33**
exception to this is that a valid and applicable advance treatment directive must be
followed whether or not it is in the best interests of P: otherwise, best interests
rules.[40] It is of course to be remembered that decision-making under the MCA only
occurs when P lacks capacity relative to the decision in question: people who do not
lack capacity make their own decisions, in their best interests or otherwise as they
see fit. The best interests test is contained as s 4 of the MCA, and is discussed in the
Code of Practice at Chapter 5.

As discussed at paras 2.35 to 2.42 above, best interests at common law are deter- **3.34**
mined in a somewhat amorphous fashion, based on a balance sheet of the pros and
cons for a proposed course of action. What is to be taken into consideration and
how it is to be discovered are largely undefined. The page-long definition of best
interests in s 4 of the MCA is therefore an important departure from the common
law approach. This section does not purport to be a complete code of what must
be considered in determining P's best interests. Indeed, it expressly instructs the
decision-maker to take into account all relevant circumstances in assessing best
interests.[41] Instead, it provides a list of factors that must always be considered and a
set of consultations and enquiries that must be pursued in each case.

The enumerated substantive criteria combine three different broad sets of factors **3.35**
into the best interests determination, which may be summarized as follows:

• protecting P's position, in the event that P is likely to regain capacity;
• considering the wishes, feelings, values, and beliefs P had when competent, or
  would have now if P were competent;
• considering P's current, incompetent, wishes and feelings, and notwithstanding
  the incapacity, involving P in the decision-making.

These approaches may be in conflict, and the section establishes no priority between
them. Best interests will in this sense be a balancing act based on the facts of the
individual situation. The above general themes are embodied in the following way
in the statute.

Section 4(3) requires that D consider whether P is likely to regain capacity, and **3.36**
if so, when. This is in part a practical set of questions, allowing D to organize his
or her decision-making in the context of the period D will be making decisions.
If P is unlikely ever to regain capacity, long-term care strategies are appropriate. If
P is expected to regain capacity, the object should be to ensure that decisions are not
taken during P's incapacity that will continue to bind P long into his or her capacity.

---

[40] Decisions as to whether P will be included in research are also not decided on the basis of best interests:
see further paras 3.137–3.149 below.

[41] MCA s 4(2).

Failure to protect P's position in this way would result in P being effectively pre-cluded from decision-making after capacity is regained, a clear violation of the spirit of the MCA.

3.37   The substantive criteria that must be considered in determining best interests are contained in s 4(6):

(6) He must consider, so far as is reasonably ascertainable—
    (a) the person's past and present wishes and feelings (and, in particular, any relevant written statement made by him when he had capacity),
    (b) the beliefs and values that would be likely to influence his decision if he had capacity, and
    (c) the other factors that he would be likely to consider if he were able to do so.

The explanatory notes to the 2005 bill states that 'best interests is not a test of "substituted judgement" (what the person would have wanted), but rather it requires a determination made by applying an objective test as to what would be in the person's best interests'.[42] At least in this unqualified form, this statement is not in conformity with s 4(6). The focus on P's wishes, feelings, beliefs, and values makes it clear that the test has an important and express subjective component. These are the classic features of a substituted judgement approach. In this it is to be distin-guished from the common law best interests assessment, which is markedly more objective. Certainly, other factors are also relevant to the test, and P's wishes will not always carry the day; but they are not irrelevant, as the explanatory notes may suggest.

3.38   The provision makes it clear that account is to be taken not merely of past com-petent views, but also of P's current wishes and feelings. On one level, this just reflects common humanity. People without capacity experience fear and joy as much as the rest of us do, and it would be inhuman to ignore those factors in determining best interests. It is also one of the ways the statute takes into account the fact that while in law responsibility for decisions must be clearly defined with capacity as a dividing line, in practice abilities vary in an infinite number of ways. The fact that P loses the right to make a decision through incapacity does not therefore mean that P is excluded from the decision, as he or she may have much to contribute notwith-standing legal incapacity. This approach is also reflected in s 4(4), which requires D, as far as reasonably practicable, to 'permit and encourage' P to 'participate, or to improve his ability to participate, as fully as possible in any act done for him and any decision affecting him'. In the approach of the Act, the loss of capacity is not meant necessarily to entail a complete loss of autonomy.

3.39   The criteria require particular regard to be had to statements written by P when he or she had capacity. It does not follow from this that non-written views expressed by P when competent are irrelevant. Such views, depending on the context in which they were expressed, may retain considerable force. Similarly, the context of written statements will be significant. There is a world of difference between a casual view expressed in an informal letter to a friend and a formal statement in express

---

[42] Department of Health, Explanatory Notes, para 28.

anticipation of incapacity made following professional advice. The relevance and weight of any view expressed while competent, be it in writing or oral, will depend on the circumstances.

Unless the view constitutes a valid and applicable advance decision to refuse treatment, it will not be the sole controlling factor in the determination of best interests. The other factors in the section remain relevant. That said, the philosophy of the MCA places considerable weight on advance planning by P and the autonomy of P. It is therefore to be hoped that competent statements providing clear indications of P's wishes will be accorded considerable weight in the determination of best interests.
3.40

Special considerations apply to best interests determinations relating to the provision or withholding of life-sustaining treatment. The issues surrounding this situation under the Act will be discussed at paras 5.12 to 5.29 below. Suffice it to say here that s 4(6) requires that this decision cannot be motivated by a desire to bring about the death of P. It does not follow from this that medically appropriate treatment which is otherwise in the best interests of P cannot be given because it may shorten P's life. Similarly, if treatment has ceased to be effective, there is nothing in the section that requires its continuation, assuming its termination would otherwise be in the best interests of P.
3.41

Section 4(7) requires D, insofar as it is practicable and appropriate, to consult the following people as to what would be in P's best interests:
3.42

(a) anyone named by the person as someone to be consulted on the matter in question or on matters of that kind,

(b) anyone engaged in caring for the person or interested in his welfare,

(c) any donee of an LPA granted by the person, and

(d) any deputy appointed for the person by the court.

A donee of an LPA or a deputy is to be consulted even if he or she does not have jurisdiction to make the decision in question. As the person assessing best interests will be the person with decision-making authority—the donee of an LPA or deputy who has the relevant authority if such exists—any other reading of the session would be nonsensical. The Code of Practice suggests that consultation with donees of LPAs is merely 'good practice'.[43] In this, the Code is misleading. It is not merely good practice, it is a requirement of s 4, unless such consultation is impracticable.

The purpose of this consultation is specific. It is not to ask what the consultee thinks ought to happen; it is to ask the consultee for information about P's best interests as defined by the statute, and in particular the views, feelings, beliefs, and values of P as defined in s 4(6). In the common law, it is unclear whether the best interests of third parties such as carers are relevant to the determination of best interests.[44]
3.43

---

[43] Code of Practice para 7.57.

[44] In support of the relevance of such factors, see *Airedale NHS Trust v Bland* [1993] AC 789 at 869 (per Lord Goff), *Re S (Medical Treatment: Adult Sterilisation)* [1998] 1 FLR 944, 946–947. In support of the

Such third party interests are not mentioned in the substantive criteria in s 4, and this subsection does nothing to include them. Once again, of course, many people in P's position would have the interests of those around them in their consideration if making the relevant decision at a time when they were competent. These views will therefore often be relevant under s 4(6)(c). If the evidence is to the contrary, however, there is nothing in the section to make relevant the views of carers as to their own best interests.

3.44   The requirements to consult apply when such consultation is 'practicable and appropriate'. There are two obvious questions flowing from this provision: how hard must D try to have a consultation with a relevant person; and when is a consultation inappropriate? Regarding the former, reasonable and bona fide efforts ought to be made to consult with the individuals named in the provision. These might include:

- ringing the most recent telephone numbers of which D is aware;
- if necessary, checking the telephone directory in the jurisdiction in which the individuals were last known to reside to see if there is a more recent telephone number;
- if time permits, writing to the individuals at their last known address;
- asking P's other friends and family for more recent contact details for the individuals.

Real attempts should be made to contact at least the enumerated people, along with others close to P, but if, for example, some appear to have disappeared, to be unreachable, to have lost capacity themselves, or refuse to speak with D, D should satisfy himself or herself that adequate consultation has occurred to get a good and rounded sense of the views, feelings, beliefs, and values of P as defined in s 4(6).

3.45   The requirement of consultation should not be read as destroying P's right to privacy. Just as P may have nominated a person to be consulted in these matters, there may be cogent reasons why he or she would not want some individuals consulted. The requirement in the Mental Health Act to consult with a specific 'nearest relative' was found to be in violation of Article 8 of the ECHR on this basis, when the nearest relative was alleged to have a history of sexually abusing the person who was the subject of the consultation.[45] This is a particularly extreme example; more generally, particularly outside the range of enumerated people, D should consider whether P would wish the potential consultee to be made privy to his or her private affairs.[46]

3.46   Laudable though the criteria in s 4 may be, they do become problematic in cases where the individual has never had capacity, and has minimal abilities to engage with the decision. This latter point should not be overstated: even people with very minimal abilities are likely to have emotional responses that the criteria require to be taken into account. Nonetheless, determination of the beliefs, values, and other

---

irrelevance of such factors, see *Bland* at 896 (per Lord Mustill); *Re A (Male Sterilisation)* [2000] 1 FLR 549, 556.

[45] See *JT v UK* [2000] 1 FLR 909; *R (M) v Secretary of State for Health* [2003] EWHC 1094.

[46] On matters of confidentiality generally, see Code of Practice Ch 16.

factors that would have influenced P had he had capacity is bound to be highly speculative when P has never had capacity, and where there is consequently little upon which to base the analysis. Such an approach has been used by the common law in the drafting of wills for people without capacity, with results that are not entirely convincing.[47] The Law Commission seems to anticipate that the test will become more objective for such persons,[48] but there is little in the statutory criteria to support such a re-interpretation. The alternative is equally problematic, however. Does it follow, for example, that the adult child of Jehovah's Witnesses ought to be deemed to be a member of that faith and subject to its restrictions on use of blood products, or that the adult child of socialists would never invest her money in large corporations? Resort to 'objective' criteria does not escape these problems, since an 'objective' decision that a blood transfusion is in the best interests of P would by implication be a finding that P would not have been a Jehovah's Witness. It is difficult to escape the view that this would be making a religious decision about P as much as the reverse finding would be. In the event that individuals providing some aspects of P's care have strong views about the values in question, failure to take those views into account may put those exercising the legal framework on a collision course with the individuals providing aspects of P's care. In this situation, there is a risk that the carers' views as decision-makers on behalf of P as to his or her best interests merge with their own personal views and value systems. There is nothing in the statute to suggest that this is the intent of the legislation.

The best interests criteria limit the use of age, appearance, conditions and aspects   3.47
of behaviour in the same way as the criteria regarding incapacity, and are subject to the same criticisms as those in para 3.25 above. The restrictions are nonetheless important, and perhaps never more so than for the individual who has always lacked capacity. In the absence of a basis of information regarding competent wishes in the past, decision-makers will be forced to use more speculative information. The risk is that such speculative factors may cross the line into stereotype or unwarranted paternalism. The use of such unjustified assumptions is exactly what this subsection is there to protect against.

As noted at the beginning of this section, the statute does not purport to create a   3.48
complete code for the determination of best interests. Other factors may be taken into account in appropriate circumstances.[49] While the flexibility of this approach can work to the considerable advantage of persons lacking capacity, there are difficulties with such an open-ended approach. First, how is D to determine what other factors ought to be taken into consideration? Often it will seem obvious, but some of these apparently obvious factors may serve to undercut the statutory approach. The enumerated statutory criteria are already quite broad. The section already allows

---

[47] See, eg, *Re C* [1991] 3 All ER 866, and comment in P Bartlett and R Sandland, *Mental Health Law: Policy and Practice* (Oxford University Press, 2007, 3rd edn) 532–533.

[48] Law Com 231, para 3.25.

[49] See Code of Practice paras 5.18–5.20.

consideration of any factor P would consider if competent; by definition, therefore, expansion into new territory means considering things which P would not have considered if competent. Unfettered inclusion of such factors risks undercutting the overarching ethos of the best interests test as discussed above. The carefully defined approach of the statute would risk being reduced to the crude balance sheet of the common law. At the same time, the statute is designed to establish practical regimes of care for adults lacking capacity. The criteria must function in the real world, and that may, in practice, require the inclusion of factors not articulated in the section. The difficulty to be faced by decision-makers, and ultimately by the courts, is how to ensure respect for the statutory structure while ensuring the system can actually function. Inevitably, that will be decided on a case-by-case basis, but decision-makers moving outside the statutory criteria ought to be prepared to explain the appropriateness of their decision.

3.49   The criteria and their open-endedness raise particular problems when rights under the Human Rights Act are at issue. Under the MCA as passed in 2005, only the court will be permitted to infringe the rights to liberty under the ECHR, limiting the difficulties of the best interests approach here,[50] but nonetheless the problem remains for the judicial level of decision-makers. When the Article 5 right to liberty is infringed, the infringement will only be permitted if, inter alia, the deprivation is 'prescribed by law'. The decision of the European Court of Human Rights in *Kudlow v Poland* establishes a standard:

> It is therefore essential that the conditions for deprivation of liberty under domestic law should be clearly defined, and that the law itself be foreseeable in its application, so that it meets the standard of 'lawfulness' set by the Convention, a standard which requires that all law should be sufficiently precise to allow the person – if needed, to obtain the appropriate advice – to foresee, to a degree that is reasonable in the circumstances, the consequences which a given action may entail.[51]

Of concern is whether the best interests criteria are sufficiently defined to satisfy this requirement. The statutory criteria may themselves give rise to problems in this regard. The statutory criteria provide a framework for the determination of best interests, but it is a deliberately open-ended framework based on flexible concepts such as values and presumed wishes, not a clear set of criteria such as is usual for Article 5 detentions. It is fair to ask whether this set of flexible and subjective criteria will be such that an individual could foresee the consequences of his or her actions. The open-endedness of the criteria extends this problem. The court in *HL v UK* was concerned that there were no substantive criteria for the deprivation of liberty.[52] It is not clear that an open-ended set of criteria will convince the ECtHR of the clarity of English law any more than the absence of criteria. How, after all, can the individual foresee the consequences of his or her actions, when the criteria on which those actions will be judged are limited only by relevance?

---

[50] For the situation once the 2007 amendments take effect, see Ch 4.
[51] Application No 25874/94, judgment 9 January 2001, para 49.
[52] Application No 45508/99, judgment of 5 October 2004, paras 119–124.

It is for the decision-maker, D, to satisfy himself or herself that the proposed 3.50 course of action is in the best interests of P. As discussed above in paragraph 2.34, at common law such a determination apparently needed to be correct in order for the decision to be protected from liability. The MCA is much less harsh. The best interests test will be taken to be satisfied by decision-makers (other than courts) if the requirements of s 4 discussed above have been met, and if D 'reasonably believes' the course of action is in the best interests of P. D may sometimes be faced with conflicting views among those with whom he or she is required to consult. The Code of Practice encourages D to seek consensus in this situation, but rightly notes that agreement is not necessarily the same as deciding in P's best interests under the statute.[53] Decision-makers must remain alive to the provisions of the Act, and in particular that the issue is what is in the best interests of P, not the broader realm of family politics and interests except insofar as P would have considered that relevant.

In the event that D is unable to make a clear determination of best interests, it 3.51 may be desirable to seek the advice of the independent advocacy service. While this is not defined as one of their core functions under the Act, the Code of Practice does suggest this as a possible way forward.[54] The Code of Practice also suggests mediation.[55] While this may indeed be helpful, it must be approached with some care. The usual approach of mediation is to reach a jointly acceptable solution and to build on consensus. This may sometimes involve a flexible approach to legal and statutory rights, in the attainment of an optimal solution as perceived by the parties. Mediation under the MCA will need to be markedly different. The best interests criteria set an agenda for what will be relevant to the mediation, and as a matter of law must form the framework for the decision reached. Further, mediation works best when all parties are of roughly equal bargaining power. This will almost certainly not be the case if P lacks capacity. Mediation must therefore be approached with some care in the context of a dispute over best interests.

In the event of real doubt in the context of a significant decision, it may well be 3.52 appropriate to seek the advice of the court.

F. A GENERAL DEFENCE IN CIVIL AND CRIMINAL LAW, AND CONTRACTS FOR NECESSARY GOODS AND SERVICES

The 'general defence' is the least formalistic and most innovative of the legal devices 3.53 in the MCA. The essential thrust of the provision is that people who care for people without capacity should be protected from liability for so doing, provided that such care is in the best interests of P and is performed without negligence. The phrasing of this provision has changed between the Law Commission draft and the final

---

[53] Code of Practice paras 5.63–5.64.
[54] Code of Practice paras 5.68–5.69.
[55] Code of Practice paras 5.68 and 15.7–15.13.

statute, although the overall intent has remained the same. The Law Commission provision stated that 'it shall be lawful to do anything for the personal welfare or health care . . . [of P] if it is in all the circumstances reasonable for it to be done by the person who does it.'[56] This would have created a legal power or positive authority for persons engaging in welfare or health care of P. The MCA provision is instead structured as a defence:

5(1) If a person ('D') does an act in connection with the care or treatment of another person ('P'), the act is one to which this section applies if—

(a) before doing the act, D takes reasonable steps to establish whether P lacks capacity in relation to the matter in question, and

(b) when doing the act, D reasonably believes—

(i) that P lacks capacity in relation to the matter, and

(ii) that it will be in P's best interests for the act to be done.

(2) D does not incur any liability in relation to the act that he would not have incurred if P—

(a) had had capacity to consent in relation to the matter, and

(b) had consented to D's doing the act.

The difference between the Law Commission power and the statutory defence is not obviously material. Certainly, both will provide a defence to reasonable care provided directly to P, so long as the care is in P's best interests. Appropriate surgery provided to P is an obvious example: the surgeon can rely on s 5, as it would similarly have been possible to rely on the Law Commission's positive authority. The Law Commission also had third party relationships in mind, however. Their general authority was to be available for carers acting effectively as agents to arrange contractual care provided by third parties, from the delivery of milk to the replacement of P's roof.[57] These agency arrangements would also appear to be within the scope of s 5: as competent consent of P to such arrangements would be sufficient to establish them, so they would be established under the terms of s 5(2). This applies only to arrangements that require minimal legal formality. The word 'consent' could not be stretched for example to include transactions that need to be in writing such as the sale of land.

3.54   The statutory provision therefore places care on a legal, albeit informal, footing. 'Care' is not defined by the Act, and 'treatment' is defined merely as including 'a diagnostic or other procedure',[58] but it is reasonable to surmise that the courts will accord both a wide ambit. The Code of Practice provides an illustrative list of routine physical care, routine shopping or purchase of services, health care procedures and similar duties.[59] The range of activities does not appear to be restricted to such

---

[56] Law Com 231, cl 4(1).

[57] Law Com 231, para 4.7.

[58] MCA s 64(1).

[59] Code of Practice para 6.5.

routine duties, however. The Law Commission includes roof repairs as an example,[60] and the Code of Practice includes arranging admission to a care home.[61]

Section 6 provides particular constraints in reliance on the general defence regarding the 'restraint' of P. Restraint occurs when D 'uses, or threatens to use, force to secure the doing of an act which P resists' or 'restricts P's liberty of movement, whether or not P resists'.[62] Restraint does not include the deprivation of P's liberty under Article 5 of the ECHR, however.[63] Until the 2007 amendments take effect, such deprivations of liberty under the MCA can be sanctioned only by the court.[64] Otherwise, restraint is permitted only if two conditions are met: 3.55

6(2) The first condition is that D reasonably believes that it is necessary to do the act in order to prevent harm to P.
(3) The second is that the act is a proportionate response to
   (a) the likelihood of P's suffering harm, and
   (b) the seriousness of the harm . . .

The first condition speaks to the necessity of the intervention to prevent harm, the second acknowledges that, in some instances, the proposed response may be more invasive than the harm that is set out to be prevented, especially if the harm is relatively unlikely to occur. Harm is not defined in the Act, although the Code of Practice provides a few examples.[65] The statutory provisions can be invoked of course only if the person is also incapable of making the specific decision in question. Vulnerability without incapacity does not justify the use of the MCA.

The focus of the definition of restraint is on the response of P to D's actions, or   3.56
the restriction of P. Restrictions placed on a third party in the best interests of P are not within the definition, unless P objects or unless restriction of P's movement is required. For example, if P lives in D's house and D takes the view that association with a third party is not in P's best interests, the exclusion of the third party from D's property would not be restraint within the meaning of the section unless P objects.

Special provisions are provided when 'serious treatment' is to be provided by an   3.57
NHS body, or where defined accommodation is to be provided by an NHS body or local authority. If no appropriate individual is available to be consulted about P's best interests except a professional who provides care of P for remuneration, the accommodation or serious treatment can only be provided after an Independent Mental Capacity Advocate (IMCA) has been appointed to represent P.[66] The specific role of the IMCA may vary depending on the circumstances of appointment.

---

[60] Law Com 231, para 4.7.
[61] Code of Practice para 6.1.
[62] MCA s 6(5).
[63] ibid.
[64] This is by implication, since all other decision-makers are expressly precluded from depriving P of Article 5 rights: see ss 6(5), 11(6), and 20(13). Regarding the 2007 amendments, see Ch 4 below.
[65] Code of Practice para 6.45.
[66] See MCA ss 35–41; Code of Practice Ch 10.

Nonetheless, the IMCA is expected to consult documents and people providing professional care to P and those with knowledge of P's wishes, feelings, beliefs, and values. The IMCA is then to support P's involvement as far as possible in the decision in question, call for further medical opinions if appropriate; ascertain alternative courses of action if any; and ascertain what P's wishes, feelings, beliefs, and values would be. The advocate may also act on P's behalf to challenge the decision, including before the Court of Protection.[67]

3.58   These provisions are mandatory only for 'serious medical treatment' and defined accommodation of persons lacking capacity. 'Serious medical treatment' includes not merely treatment where the consequences to P are serious, but also treatment where the risks and benefits of treatment are finely balanced or where the choice between treatment options is finely balanced.[68] In these latter cases, there is no requirement that consequences of the treatment be serious. Accommodation, when provided by the NHS, means admission to hospital that is expected to exceed 28 days or to a care home for a period expected to be longer than eight weeks.[69] These provisions are meant to include aftercare provided under s 117 of the Mental Health Act.[70] Accommodation when provided by a local authority means residential accommodation for a period expected to exceed eight weeks.[71] In any of these circumstances, the prior involvement of the advocate may be waived in cases of urgency (undefined), but in cases concerning accommodation, the advocate must nonetheless be involved following the reception of P into the accommodation. The local authority or NHS body may also appoint an IMCA, if it wishes, when accommodation in the care home or hospital is under review, if P has resided there for at least twelve weeks.[72] These provisions do not apply when another person is appropriate to be consulted regarding P's best interests, and in particular, s 40 of the MCA precludes the application of these provisions if there is a person nominated by P to be consulted in matters affecting his or her interests, a donee of an LPA created by P, a deputy appointed by the court for P, or a donee of an EPA created by P.

3.59   An NHS body or local authority is also permitted, but not required, to appoint an IMCA when it intends to take adult protection proceedings, when it is alleged that P is being abused or neglected.[73] Such appointments may be made even if there is an available donee of an LPA or EPA, deputy, or nominated person.

3.60   Section 5 takes effect if, prior to taking the action in question, D has taken reasonable steps to determine P's capacity, and if while doing the act D reasonably believes that P lacks capacity and that the act is in P's best interests. While the section provides protection for D in cases of reasonable belief, the section does provide

---

[67] SI 2006/1832, paras 6, 7.
[68] ibid, para 4.
[69] MCA s 38.
[70] Explanatory notes to MCA para 121.
[71] MCA s 39(4)(a).
[72] SI 2006/2883, para 3.
[73] ibid, para 4.

an express requirement for D to have taken 'reasonable steps' to determine P's capacity. Belief alone is therefore insufficient for the section; it must be a belief founded on a reasonable investigation. The belief in P's incapacity must also itself be reasonable. D's determination that the action is in the best interests of P is not expressly subject to the requirement that reasonable steps be taken, but need only be a reasonable belief. That said, the statutory definition of best interests itself contains a variety of procedural requirements and substantive criteria, including the likelihood that P will regain capacity, maximizing the involvement of P in the decision, the view P would have taken if competent, and consulting with other carers and similar figures.[74] It is difficult to see that D could arrive at a 'reasonable belief' that an act would be in P's best interests as defined without taking the appropriate procedural steps.

The MCA anticipates that a variety of individuals may be involved in making   3.61 decisions about P's care. This raises the possibility of dispute among decision-makers or carers as to the appropriate course of action. Obviously, attempts should be made to reach consensus in these situations, within the framework of the statutory best interests criteria. In the end, it is the person who will be relying on the general defence who must be satisfied that P lacks capacity and the P's best interests are met by the actions he or she is taking. The defence will apply so long as that belief is reasonable. Nonetheless, where contradictory views are entrenched concerning significant decisions and litigation appears likely at some point, it will usually be preferable to seek a court opinion before embarking on the controversial course of action.

The Code of Practice suggests that in determinations of capacity and best inter-   3.62 ests, professionals will be held to a higher standard than lay persons.[75] This makes some sense if the determination is viewed according to standards analogous to the law of negligence, where professionals are expected to exercise a higher standard of care than non-professionals in their field of expertise.[76] Such a differential standard is not obvious, however, on the face of the statute. Indeed, the common law tendency has been to view the capacity determination as a multi-disciplinary matter. The statutory test is consistent with that change, requiring consultation with non-professionals in the determination of best interests. As the law becomes less focused on these determinations as within the competence of specific professionals, the argument for a higher standard of care for those professionals becomes less convincing. If these determinations are not just a medical matter, why should the courts expect doctors to be better at them than other people?

Professionals can of course be expected to know about the statutory provisions,   3.63 and their failure to comply with them should meet with little judicial sympathy. The same applies to court-appointed deputies, and to donees of LPAs, who receive information about the MCA when the LPA is registered. Should the same apply to other

---

[74] See paras 3.33–3.52 above.
[75] Code of Practice para 6.33.
[76] See, eg, *Wilsher v Essex Area Health Authority* [1986] 3 All ER 801.

lay persons? Should the protection of the general defence be afforded to a D who honestly thinks he or she is doing right by P even if his or her actions are outside the statutory definition of best interests? There would seem to be three possibilities here: stretch the statutory definition of best interests to include D's actions; deny the statutory protection but allow a defence under the common law jurisdiction; or fail to provide a defence at all. None of these possibilities is attractive. The first would go a considerable way to gutting the statutory definition that has been so carefully developed by the Law Commission and is one of the real strengths of the statute. The second would have a similar effect, because it would allow the substantive and procedural statutory safeguards to be circumvented by an appeal to the common law. The third could result in well-intentioned carers, who may think they are acting in the benefit of P, being subjected to legal sanction. How this will play out in court remains to be seen. One would suspect that case-specific facts such as the manner and personality of individual protagonists, may figure significantly in the making of precedent-setting decisions.

3.64   The general defence does not affect the operation of an advance decision to refuse medical treatment.[77] Treatments refused by P in advance cannot then be given by reliance on the general defence. It also does not authorize any individual acting in conflict with decisions made by a donee of an LPA or a court-appointed deputy acting within the scope of their respective authorities.[78] The general defence is still available for decisions outside the respective authorities of these individuals. This raises the potentially difficult question as to how an informal carer, the sort that is intended to be assisted by the general defence, is meant to know of these individuals and the scope of their authorities. He or she could apply to the Public Guardian to search the registers of deputies and LPAs if he or she knows to do so and is prepared to pay the fee of £25 for each of the two searches—fees from which medical practitioners and local authorities are exempt.[79] If D does not search the registers, there is the possibility that persons acting in good faith in reliance on the general defence may find that it does not apply in their case. If the act in question is otherwise tortious, or if significant financial commitments are made that cannot be avoided, the result could be unfortunate for D.

3.65   In the event of legal uncertainty flowing from apparent conflicting authorities, however, the MCA is clear that life-sustaining treatment may be given and any act done to prevent the deterioration of P's condition, pending a decision of the court.[80]

3.66   The MCA acknowledges that payment may be required for the provision of care to P. This is primarily covered in s 7, under which P must pay a 'reasonable price' for 'necessary goods and services' supplied to him or her. While this will most frequently be applicable to care provided under the general defence, nothing in s 7 restricts it

---

[77] MCA s 5(4).
[78] MCA s 6(6).
[79] SI 2007/2052, para 6.
[80] MCA s 6(7).

to such care. If an individual with a valid LPA for personal decisions did not have a valid LPA for financial decisions, for example, s 7 would apply to ensure payment for the financial ramifications of the personal decisions, as long as the goods and services provided were 'necessary'. In practice, reliance on s 7 may sometimes be unwieldy, so it should not be viewed as a substitute for a well-drawn LPA with included financial powers.

The provision contained in the MCA is a development of the common law regarding services and s 3 of the Sale of Goods Act 1979 regarding goods. While the MCA formally supersedes the 1979 Act as regards people lacking capacity, it does so in language identical to that statute. As a result, the relevant jurisprudence relating to this other law will continue to be relevant to the MCA provision.[81] 'Necessary' is in a sense a misleading term, insofar as it implies a restrictive ambit of what must be paid for. In fact, the MCA reflects the existing jurisprudence that takes a broader approach. 'Necessary' under the MCA means 'suitable to a person's condition in life and to his actual requirements at the time when the goods or services are supplied'.[82] The term therefore extends not merely to minimal food and shelter, but assuming they are appropriate to P's financial resources, requirements and condition in life, also for example to home repairs, a new television, holidays, and restaurant meals. A particularly expansive example can be found in *Re Bevan* where the person lacking capacity made a living letting property. Necessaries in that case were taken to include all expenses related to rent audit of the properties and the expenses for renovation of one of the rental properties.[83]
3.67

While s 7 creates a liability on P to pay for necessaries, it does not create a new process to ensure actual payment for expenditures. Section 8 goes part of the way to doing this for acts permitted under the general defence in s 5, by allowing D to pledge P's credit or to apply money in P's possession towards the expenditure. These mechanisms may be used whether the payment is actually owed to D or to a third party: there are no express provisions regarding conflicts of interests, and no requirement that such expenditure be reported to any public body. The Code of Practice makes it clear that it does nothing to give D signing authority over P's bank accounts or investments, however,[84] so D's actual access to funds to disburse may be limited. If P's incapacity is likely to be of some duration, creditors may lack patience and press for more formal steps to be made to the court in order to effect payment.
3.68

Other mechanisms may be of more assistance. The Social Security Regulations allow a carer to act as an 'appointee' of a person lacking capacity, and so to claim benefits on his or her behalf. This may be of practical importance, as it provides a steady (albeit modest) stream of income into a carer's hands, with which payment for necessaries may be made.
3.69

---

[81] For an overview, see P Matthews, 'Contracts for Necessaries and Mental Incapacity' (1982) 33 Northern Ireland Legal Quarterly 149.

[82] MCA s 7(2).

[83] [1912] 1 Ch 196.

[84] Code of Practice para 6.64.

G. LASTING POWERS OF ATTORNEY (LPAs)

3.70   At common law, powers of attorney were deemed to be terminated upon the incapacity of the donor.[85] The statutory provisions of the Enduring Powers of Attorney
Act 1985 (EPAA) allowed the power to continue in these circumstances if it was
clear on its face that this was intended by the donor and provided that the statutory
criteria were met, most significantly that the enduring power of attorney (EPA) was
registered with the Court of Protection consistent with the procedures in the EPAA
as P, the person signing the LPA, was losing capacity. These powers of attorney could
extend only to matters of property and affairs, however—the traditional realm of
powers of attorney. They could not extend to purely personal decisions regarding
social care or medical treatment.

3.71   The MCA provides a new statutory framework for powers of attorney intended
to survive the incapacity of the donor (now called 'lasting' powers of attorney, hereinafter LPAs). This framework is broadly similar to the one provided under the
EPAA, except that the MCA allows them to extend beyond decisions relating to P's
property and affairs to personal decisions.[86] The general provisions regarding LPAs
are contained in ss 9–14 of the MCA. Specifics related to completion and registration of LPAs are contained as Schedule 1 to the MCA, supplemented by SI 2007/1253
(contained in App 3 below). Although the new provisions allow the creation of LPAs
to cover personal care decisions as well as property decisions, this cannot be done on
the same form. An individual P who wishes to give authority to one individual to
manage all P's affairs will have to execute two LPAs: one for property and affairs and
another for personal welfare decisions.[87]

3.72   The MCA revokes the EPAA.[88] While all new powers of attorney must be executed pursuant to the MCA if they are to survive the incapacity of the donor, the
salient provisions of the EPAA regarding registration and legal effect of EPAs are
contained in Schedule 4 of the MCA.[89] EPAs that were validly executed under the
statutory framework at the time of their execution need not therefore be re-executed
under the new legislation. Some clients may nonetheless wish to execute a new LPA,
for example to take advantage of somewhat different registration procedures. Clients
may in any event wish to execute an LPA for personal care decisions, as these will
not be covered by the EPA.

---

[85] *Drew v Nunn* (1879) 4 QB 661.
[86] MCA s 9(1).
[87] See SI 2007/1253, Sch 1.
[88] MCA s 66.
[89] There are a few minor variations between the EPAA and Sch 4 in the procedures applicable. Eg, where
the EPAA accorded a variety of duties to the Court of Protection, most of these are now given to the Office of
the Public Guardian.

The case of Re K, Re F[90] held that a donor could have the capacity to execute an   3.73
EPA even if he or she did not have capacity to manage his or her property and
affairs. This may appear to be a somewhat surprising result, as it allows the donor to
appoint an agent to do things that the donor as principal is incapable of doing,[91] but
it seems entrenched in the current law. It seems likely that a similar approach will be
adopted under the MCA.

In *Re K, Re F* the following standard of capacity was adopted: 3.74

What degree of understanding is involved? Plainly one cannot expect that the donor should have
been able to pass an examination on the provisions of the 1985 Act. At the other extreme, I do not
think that it would be sufficient if he realised only that it gave cousin William power to look after
his property. Counsel as amicus curiae [for the Official Solicitor] helpfully summarised the matters
which the donor should have understood in order that he can be said to have understood the
nature and effect of the power: first, if such be the terms of the power, that the attorney will be able
to assume complete control over the donor's affairs; second, if such be the terms of the power, that
the attorney will in general be able to do anything with the donor's property which the donor
could have done; third, that the authority will continue if the donor should be or become mentally
incapable; fourth, that if he should be or become mentally incapable, the power will be irrevocable
without the confirmation of the court.[92]

While the capacity to execute an LPA is governed by the general definitions of persons lacking capacity in ss 2 and 3 of the MCA, the language in *Re K* may serve as a
guide, in particular to the breadth of the 'information relevant to the decision' in
s 3(1)(a). References to 'property' and 'affairs' will of course have to be varied to
reflect the terms of the LPA in question.

While the Act makes it clear that LPAs may give authority to make decisions   3.75
related to either or both of P's 'personal welfare' and 'property and affairs',[93] the statute does little further to define these terms. 'Property' is defined in s 63(1) as including any thing in action and any interest in real or personal property. Insofar as the
provisions relate to property and affairs, it seems reasonable to conclude that the
range of powers granted can be as broad as is otherwise permitted by the general law
relating to powers of attorney.[94] The scope as it relates to personal welfare lacks
this established precedent, but is likely to be read broadly by the courts. A non-
exhaustive and illustrative list is contained in the Code of Practice and includes,
among other things, decisions as to where P should live, decisions regarding day-to-
day care and dress, determining with whom P will have contact, decisions regarding

---

[90] [1988] 1 All ER 358.

[91] For a critical analysis of this decision, see P Bartlett and R Sandland, *Mental Health Law: Policy and Practice* (Oxford University Press, 2007, 3rd edn) 565–566.

[92] [1988] 1 All ER 358, 363.

[93] MCA s 9.

[94] The EPAA was express on this point: see s 3(2). While the language has disappeared from the MCA, it is difficult to see how else the potential breadth of the LPA relating to property and affairs would be construed.

medical consent and accessing medical treatment, and applying for access to confidential documents and personal information relating to P.[95]

3.76   LPAs are subject to the same restrictions regarding restraint, and the same definition of restraint, as persons who act in reliance on the general defence.[96] LPAs are subject to advance decisions to refuse.[97] Some caution is appropriate here, however, as s 25(2)(b) holds that an advance decision to refuse treatment is invalid if a subsequent LPA appears to include authority to give or refuse consent to the treatment. As a matter of caution, a well-drafted LPA should state clearly that the advance treatment refusal remains in effect, if that is P's wish. Finally, while the LPA may extend to making treatment decisions for P, it does not authorize the giving or refusing of consent to life-sustaining treatment unless the instrument contains express provisions to that effect.[98] As treatment decisions in an end-of-life context will be one of the situations where many clients will want the LPA to be effective, this presumption should be drawn to clients' attention and specific instructions obtained as to whether the LPA should have effect in these circumstances.

3.77   The MCA provides further express restrictions on the use of LPAs in the context of personal welfare decision-making. First, even when the LPA has been registered, it extends only to making decisions in areas where P actually lacks capacity or where D reasonably believes that P lacks capacity.[99] This is not the case in matters of property and affairs: upon registration, D receives the full range of authorities relating to property and affairs contained in the LPA even if P has capacity to make the decision in question.[100] That does not, of course, remove any authority from P. An LPA is in the end a power of attorney, and although it gives authority to the attorney, it does not remove any from the donor. Contracts signed by P would therefore remain enforceable if P had capacity to sign them, and in the event that he or she did not have capacity, would be dealt with by the contractual law relating to contracts by people lacking capacity.

3.78   Section 9(4) of the MCA provides that the authority conferred by the LPA is subject to:

. . .

(a) the provisions of this Act and, in particular, sections 1 (the principles) and 4 (best interests), and

(b) any conditions or restrictions specified in the instrument . . .

Section 9(4)(a) engages decisions under the LPA with the overall philosophy of the MCA. As a consequence, it will be necessary for D, when making decisions about P,

---

[95] Code of Practice para 7.21. Cf s 17, which defines 'personal welfare' for purposes of court-appointed deputies.

[96] See paras 3.55–3.56 above.

[97] MCA ss 11(7)(b) and 25(7).

[98] MCA s 11(7)(c) and (8).

[99] MCA s 11(7)(a).

[100] This reflects previous practice regarding EPAs: see Re F, Re K, n 92 above; D Lush, *Cretney and Lush on Enduring Powers of Attorney* (Blackwell, 2001, 5th edn) para 4.2.2.

to consider P's current (incapable) views and feelings on the matter and the likelihood that P will regain capacity, the requirement that P be involved as far as possible in the decision-making process, and the other substantive conditions and processes in the best interests definition.

Section 9(4)(b) is more problematic. Certainly, it allows P to restrict the type of decision D can make. If for example, P wishes to restrict D to making health care decisions, s 9(4)(b) would allow P to do so. What is the effect of substantive conditions or restrictions as to how D is to make decisions, however? What if P wishes to restrict D to making specific ethical investments with her money (or, indeed, investing only in company XYZ), or wishes to express a preference for or against a specific nursing home (or requiring D to ensure that P resides in her current residence until she dies)? It may well be the case that compliance by D with restrictions under s 9(4)(b) would be in contravention of P's best interests under s 9(4)(a), since while P's views are relevant to determination of best interests under s 4, they are not determinative of best interests. Section 9(4)(a) and (b) have equal status in the statute; it is not obvious which one should prevail.

3.79

The MCA is in general very restrictive about allowing P when competent to make binding substantive decisions in anticipation of incapacity. The specific codification of advance decisions to refuse treatment is notable as an exception, and, as discussed below, they do not extend beyond refusals of medical treatment.[101] If the substantive direction under s 9(4)(b) held sway, it would effectively allow other advance decisions, through the back door of LPA appointments. Whether or not this is desirable, it does not appear to be the intent of the Act.

3.80

It may, perhaps, be possible to re-cast the apparent substantive directions as speaking to the scope of D's authority, rather than directing how that authority is to be exercised. If the donor had capacity, the fact that she gave a regular power of attorney to D to make investments in company XYZ for her would restrict the shares D could buy for her; it would not preclude her from making other investments herself. Using that as a parallel, D's decision under the LPA would not be 'I choose not to buy investments other in than company XYZ' but rather 'I have no jurisdiction to consider whether to buy investments in company XYZ'. In that event, a different substitute decision-maker acting on proper authority presumably could make non-ethical investments, if that were in P's best interests. For investment decisions, this would almost certainly have to be arranged by the court. As these other investment decisions would be considered to be outside D's remit under the LPA, however, the role could be passed on to a deputy, notwithstanding the general rule that a deputy cannot make decisions inconsistent with the donee of an LPA acting within the authority of the LPA.[102]

3.81

Such an approach would significantly limit the role of s 9(4)(b) in personal care decisions. In the example above, the requirement that D make decisions that would

3.82

---

[101] See para 3.113 below.
[102] MCA s 20(4).

keep P in her own home would be re-cast as any decisions that reach another result are outside the scope of D's authority under the LPA. The procedural barriers associated with a court application would provide some protection to P's wishes in the context of a decision related to property and affairs. For personal care decisions, it is not merely the court or a deputy, but anyone relying on the general defence under s 5, who would have authority to make a countervailing decision. The procedural barrier of the court application would not need to exist, and the restriction in the LPA could be overridden much more easily. The restriction might indeed become little more than a statement of wishes, required to be considered under the best interests determination under s 4, notwithstanding that P intended it to be much more robust. Further, P's attempt to have decisions made about her by the person of her choosing would be undermined. It is difficult to see that this is the intent of the Act.

3.83   Special provisions are made regarding the attorney's power to make gifts. Subject to any conditions or restrictions in the instrument, the attorney with authority over P's property and affairs may make gifts on customary occasions as defined in the Act to those related to or connected with P, and may donate to any charity to which P might be expected to make donations. In any event, such gifts and donations must always be reasonable, having regard to all the circumstances and in particular the size of P's estate.[103]

3.84   The mechanics of making, registering and revoking LPAs are contained in MCA ss 10 and 13 and Sch 1, and in SI 2007/1253, Part 2 and Sch 1. Both donor and attorney must be over the age of eighteen. The instrument must be in writing, on the prescribed form in Schedule 1 of SI 2007/1253, with the duly witnessed signatures of the donor and the donee. In addition, an 'LPA certificate' must be provided attesting to the fact that the donor understands the nature of the LPA, that the LPA does not flow from undue pressure or fraud, and that there is no other reason the instrument would not create an LPA.[104] This certificate may be signed by a person who has known the donor for at least two years, or a suitable professional such as a health care professional, lawyer, social worker, or IMCA. A number of people are specifically precluded from signing such certificates, however, including:

- the donor's family members;
- the donee of the LPA, or any other LPA or EPA signed by the donor, even if revoked, or a family member of such a person;
- if the donee is a trust company, an employee of the trust company;
- a business partner or associate of the donor or donee;
- an owner, director, manager, or employee of a care home in which the donor resides, or a family member of such a person (SI 2007/1253, paras 7–8).

---

[103] MCA s 12.
[104] MCA Sch 1 para 2(1)(2).

For personal decisions, the attorney must be an individual, although for property **3.85** and affairs, it may also be a trust corporation.[105] In general, the mechanics are similar to those previously in effect for EPAs, with a few exceptions. Where there is more than one attorney, it is now assumed that the attorneys will act jointly, unless the instrument specifies otherwise.[106] Where attorneys are to act jointly, the failure of either one of them to meet the criteria of the MCA prevents an LPA from being created.[107] While the instrument cannot give the donee the power to appoint a substitute or successor attorney, the instrument itself may appoint such a substitute.[108]

The rather complex provisions regarding notification prior to registration which **3.86** applied to EPAs have been removed. In their stead, the instrument itself is now required to indicate such person or persons as must be notified prior to registration.[109] Up to five people may be so identified.[110] If no one is so identified, two LPA certificates as described in para 3.84 above must be provided.

The LPA is registered at first instance with the Public Guardian.[111] The Public **3.87** Guardian cannot register an LPA with powers trespassing on those of a court-appointed deputy.[112] The court has increased jurisdiction to sever provisions in conflict with the MCA.[113] Registration remains a largely administrative affair. No formal evidence of P's incapacity is routinely required, although P or any of the people identified in the LPA to be notified may of course object to the registration. In that event, the LPA cannot be registered without an order of the court.[114]

Section 13 of the Act concerns revocation of LPAs. While packaged somewhat **3.88** differently from the EPA, its effects are similar. P may revoke the power, at any time he or she has capacity.[115] The power is revoked if P becomes bankrupt, and is suspended if P is subject to an interim bankruptcy order. The power is also revoked if D disclaims the appointment, dies, loses capacity, or, except insofar as the LPA gives authority over P's personal welfare, D becomes bankrupt. Unlike the previous legislation, it does provide that dissolution or annulment of a marriage or civil partnership between donor and donee will terminate the power, unless the power specifically provides to the contrary.[116]

The LPA creates a fiduciary relationship between P and D. The Code of Practice **3.89** provides a good overview of how a donee ought to approach his or her duties.[117]

---

[105] MCA s 10(1).
[106] MCA s 10(5).
[107] MCA s 10(6).
[108] MCA s 10(8).
[109] MCA Sch 1 s 2(c).
[110] SI 2007/1253, reg 6.
[111] MCA Sch 1 para 11.
[112] MCA Sch 1 para 12.
[113] MCA Sch 1 para 11.
[114] MCA Sch 1 paras 13–14.
[115] MCA s 13(2).
[116] MCA s 13(6)(c), (10).
[117] Code of Practice paras 7.58–7.68.

3.90   The powers of the court over LPAs are set out primarily in ss 22–23 of the MCA. The court has a general power to determine points of law relating to an LPA. It can revoke or refuse to register the power if there has been undue influence or fraud, or if the donee is not acting in the best interests of P or in contravention of authority. Pending a court determination on these matters, the general defence allows life-sustaining treatment to be given to P, and for caregivers to do such acts as are reasonably believed to be necessary to prevent a serious deterioration in P's condition.[118] The court can also give directions to D as to how to exercise the powers contained in the LPA and provide consents the donee would need to get from P. It can insist on rendering of accounts or production of information, and allow remuneration or payment of expenses of donee. The court may also relieve the donee from liability.

3.91   The Code of Practice states that the donee of an LPA may have their powers extended by the court, if the donor has lost capacity.[119] The statutory basis for this claim is not obvious. While the court certainly has the authority to provide consents or authorizations that would otherwise need to be provided by P,[120] it is not obvious that this should be read so broadly as to allow the court to alter the terms of the LPA.

3.92   In the past, the courts have been reluctant to intervene to any considerable extent in the implementation of EPAs, holding that their role extended to administrative matters only and not to the core of the power.[121] The wording of the sections relating to the court's powers in the MCA is not particularly more expansive than that of the previous legislation, but the overall context of the MCA itself does point towards a more interventionist role for the courts. It remains to be seen how the courts will approach their role in overseeing these instruments.

3.93   LPAs are no doubt a welcome development. They are flexible—a donor P may give different people different powers of decision relating to all or part of P's personal welfare, estate, or property. They have the tremendous advantage of allowing P to decide whom he or she trusts to make the decisions P would want made. That said, a slight note of caution is appropriate. While the Office of the Public Guardian has authority to investigate allegations of abuse,[122] it is not obvious how abuses will come to the attention of that Office. Particularly if the courts continue their laissez-faire approach, P may be left vulnerable. There is in any event unlikely to be routine scrutiny to ensure that the system is operating as it ought. It is therefore essential that donors of these powers give serious consideration into whose hands they wish to commit their lives.

---

[118] MCA s 6(7).

[119] Code of Practice para 7.48.

[120] MCA s 23(2)(b).

[121] See *In Re R (Enduring Power of Attorney)* [1990] 1 Ch 647. For a critical view of this approach, see P Bartlett and R Sandland, *Mental Health Law: Policy and Practice* (Oxford University Press, 2007, 3rd edn) 563–565.

[122] MCA s 58; SI 2007/1253, regs 46–47.

H. THE POWERS OF THE COURT AND APPOINTMENT OF DEPUTIES

Under the MCA, the Court of Protection is re-constituted and receives a significantly 3.94 expanded statutory jurisdiction over the personal and financial affairs of persons lacking capacity. The court is constituted under ss 45–49 of the MCA. Additional guidance on the administration of property and affairs is contained in Schedule 2 of the MCA. The Court of Protection Rules, which define its operating practices, have been published and are contained in Appendix 4 to this book. Part 7 of the Mental Health Act is repealed by the MCA, and transitional arrangements for those currently under its jurisdiction are contained in Schedule 5, Part 1 of the MCA.

The court is assisted in its functions by the Public Guardian and the Court of 3.95 Protection Visitors. The former has a variety of functions enumerated in s 58 of the MCA, related to administrative oversight of LPAs and court-appointed deputies. Specific duties include maintaining registers of LPAs and deputies, supervising deputies, receiving reports from donees of LPAs and deputies. The Public Guardian also has to investigate complaints regarding the exercise of powers by LPAs and deputies, and can direct a Court of Protection Visitor to visit and report on donees of LPAs, deputies, and those for whom donees and deputies are making decisions. The Court of Protection Visitors include 'special' visitors who have medical qualifications and are knowledgeable about mental disorder, and 'general' visitors. As their name suggests, their role is to visit donees of LPAs, deputies, and those for whom they make decisions, in response to requests from the Public Guardian or Court of Protection. In carrying out these duties, the Visitors and the Public Guardian may examine and copy health records, social services records held by local authorities, and records held by persons registered under Part 2 of the Care Standards Act 2000, as far as they relate to the person lacking capacity who is the subject of their enquiries.

The Court of Protection has three sorts of function. It has a general supervisory 3.96 jurisdiction to make declarations regarding the care provided under the provisions of the MCA. It is given its own jurisdiction to make orders over the personal welfare and property and affairs of persons lacking capacity allowing it, for example, to make specific decisions concerning the sale of a major asset or the drafting of a will. Finally, it can appoint receivers for ongoing decision-making.

The general supervisory jurisdiction includes the authority to determine whether 3.97 P lacks capacity regarding a specific decision or class of decisions, and whether acts either done or proposed to be done in relation to P are lawful.[123] The court therefore has jurisdiction to consider any issue which may arise under the general defence, as well as the applicability and effect of any advanced refusal of treatment. The court also has jurisdiction to determine whether a document creates an effective LPA and

---

[123] MCA s 15.

whether an LPA ought to be registered.[124] It may further provide directions on matters within the scope of an LPA, require the donee to submit accounts or records, and set remuneration of the donee.[125] The court therefore has jurisdiction to adjudicate on all relevant matters that may arise under the care provisions of the Act.

3.98　　The court's power to make orders over personal welfare and property and affairs of P are defined by the MCA. For personal welfare decisions, the definition is non-exhaustive, but includes:

(a) deciding where P is to live;
(b) deciding what contact, if any, P is to have with any specified persons;
(c) making an order prohibiting a named person from having contact with P;
(d) giving or refusing consent to the carrying out or continuation of a treatment by a person providing health care for P;
(e) giving a direction that a person responsible for P's health care allow a different person to take over that responsibility.[126]

The powers of the court as regards property and affairs are coextensive with the court's previous powers in this area, which were contained in s 96 of the Mental Health Act. They include a wide array of powers, including disposition or acquisition of property, carrying on of a trade or profession, discharge of debts, the execution of a will, and the conduct of legal proceedings.[127] Where normally the provisions of the MCA do not apply to persons under the age of sixteen, for matters relating to property and affairs the court may make decisions on behalf of, and appoint deputies for, persons under that age if it appears that they will continue to lack capacity at the age of eighteen years.[128]

3.99　　The court's powers are, of course, subject to the remainder of the MCA, and in particular the principles in s 1 and best interests criteria.[129] The court is not necessarily bound by the terms of the application before it, and can make whatever order it views as best promoting the best interests of P.[130]

3.100　　While it must be ensured that the statutory criteria are followed for decision-making, care should be given to avoiding unnecessary court applications. Costs of litigation have in the past often been paid for from the estate of P, and as litigation can be expensive, this is not necessarily going to be in the best interests of P. The Law Commission intended the court to be the decision-maker of last resort.[131] Similarly, the Code of Practice encourages informal resolution of disputes, but acknowledges there will be times when court applications are appropriate. By way of example it

---

[124] MCA s 22.
[125] MCA s 23.
[126] MCA s 17.
[127] MCA s 18(1).
[128] MCA s 18(3).
[129] MCA s 16(3).
[130] MCA s 16(6).
[131] Law Com 231, para 8.2.

mentions situations where P wishes to challenge a finding that he or she lacks capacity, disagreements between professionals or family members as to the capacity of P.[132] Within the terms of the MCA itself, if violation of an individual's liberty under Article 5 of the ECHR is to be imposed, it may only be done by the court.[133] In the absence of express provision in an LPA, many legal decisions will require court applications, including the sale of property and access to bank accounts to make funds available for care.

The Code of Practice, relying on jurisprudence before the passage of the MCA, states that court applications ought to be made when the following are at issue: 3.101

- proposed withholding or withdrawal of artificial nutrition or hydration from people in a permanent vegetative state;
- organ or bone marrow donations by P;
- non-therapeutic (ie, contraceptive) sterilization of P;
- cases where there is doubt or dispute as to whether a treatment is in P's best interests.[134]

Most of these are serious decisions, and court applications may well be appropriate when they are proposed. It is not obvious that such applications are legally required, however. At common law, the authority of the court to insist on such applications was at best dubious.[135] Further, the MCA contains no formal requirement for such applications, and it does seem to envisage that decisions to refuse life-sustaining treatment by the donee of an LPA may be relied upon without court intervention in some circumstances.[136] That said, anyone carrying out these procedures would wish to be particularly sure that the P lacked capacity and that the procedure was, indeed, in P's best interests.

Only the court can make or amend a will on behalf of P. A will can only be made   3.102 if P has reached the age of eighteen years. The mechanics of the court's jurisdiction to make wills are contained in Schedule 2 to the MCA. The relevant portions of that schedule are coextensive to s 97 of the MHA 1983. The body of law that has developed under the Mental Health Act in this regard is therefore likely to continue to apply to wills made under the MCA.[137] While the will must conform to the whole of the best interests test in s 4, it is reasonable to surmise that the past and present wishes of P, as well as the beliefs, values, and other factors which would have been likely to influence P if he or she had capacity, should be pivotal in the drafting of the will.

The court further has jurisdiction to appoint deputies to make decisions on   3.103 behalf of P. In coming to its decision, the court must in addition to the best interests

---

[132] Code of Practice para 8.16.
[133] This will change when the 2007 amendments to the MCA come into effect: see Ch 4 below.
[134] Code of Practice para 8.18.
[135] See paras 2.11–2.26, and esp 2.13 above.
[136] See MCA s 11(8)(a).
[137] See, eg, *Re B (Court of Protection)* [1987] 2 FLR 155 and *Re D (J)* [1982] 1 Ch 237 re drafting generally and *Re C (A Patient)* [1991] 3 All ER 866 regarding bequests to charities.

criteria in s 4, have regard to the principles that a decision by a court is preferable to the appointment of a deputy, and that the powers conferred on a deputy should be as limited in scope and duration as reasonably possible.[138] The objective here is to minimize the scope and duration of control: specific decisions of the court are to be preferred to the ongoing appointment of a deputy; and when a deputy must be appointed, it is to be for the narrowest scope and shortest time reasonably practicable. Deputies for personal welfare decisions must be individuals aged eighteen or over. For decisions relating to property and affairs, they may also be public trust corporations. Holders of offices for the time being may be appointed,[139] so a director of a social services agency could be appointed to make personal decisions regarding a person lacking capacity.[140] Deputies must consent to their appointment, but once appointed have a duty to act.[141]

3.104   Section 20 of the MCA creates restrictions on the powers of deputies. Notwithstanding the terms of his or her appointment, a deputy does not have power to make a decision if he or she has reasonable reason to believe that P has capacity in relation to the matter. Deputies cannot require a change in the individual responsible for P's health care. They may not settle P's property, or exercise powers vested in P. They may not make decisions that are within the scope of a valid LPA, and they may not refuse life-sustaining treatment on behalf of P. Their powers regarding restraint are similar to those imposed on donees of LPAs and persons acting under the general defence.[142]

3.105   The overall duties of deputies are described in the Code of Practice.[143] They will normally be expected to post security, and are subject to the supervision of the court. That will normally include periodic reports to the Public Guardian, who also has an authority to investigate complaints regarding the exercise of the authority of a deputy.

3.106   Whether the application is for a declaration, an order, or for the appointment of a deputy, the application process is governed by s 50. The following persons may apply to the court as of right:

(a) a person who lacks, or is alleged to lack, capacity,
(b) if such a person has not reached the age of eighteen, by anyone with parental responsibility for that person,
(c) the donor or donee of an LPA relating to the application,
(d) a deputy for the person to whom the application relates,
(e) a person named in an order of the court, if the application relates to that order.[144]

---

138 MCA s 16(4).
139 MCA s 19(2).
140 See Code of Practice para 8.41.
141 ibid para 8.47.
142 See paras 3.55–3.56 above.
143 Code of Practice paras 8.50–8.68.
144 MCA s 50(1).

Other persons must receive the leave of the court to apply. In deciding whether to grant leave, the following factors are to be considered by the court:

(a) the applicant's connection with the person to whom the application relates,
(b) the reasons for the application,
(c) the benefit to the person to whom the application relates of a proposed order or directions; and
(d) whether the benefit can be achieved in any other way.[145]

The provisions regarding leave are more systematic than the common law approach to standing in declaration applications. While they do not represent an entirely new direction in this regard, they should serve to clarify the jurisprudence in this area.

In the hearing of the application, the court has all the powers of a superior court, as well as the power to call for reports enumerated in s 49. This provides the court with investigative resources not generally available to courts in an adversarial system. The court can require investigations and reports to be made by the Public Guardian, a Court of Protection Visitor, or a local authority or NHS body or one of its officers or employees. In complying with such a requirement, the Public Guardian or Court of Protection Visitor may examine and copy any health record, local authority social services record, or record held by a person registered under Part 2 of the Care Standards Act 2000 relating to P. 　3.107

The introduction of a statutory court jurisdiction in personal welfare matters is to be greeted with enthusiasm. In general, here as in the remainder of the statute, standards of drafting are refreshingly good. There are however a few places of potential uncertainty. 　3.108

The MCA makes it clear that acts done by an individual acting on the general defence or pursuant to an LPA sufficiently meet the standards of best interests if D reasonably believes them to be in P's best interests.[146] Certainly, the court on application has the authority to overrule such decisions taken in good faith; the more difficult question is whether it will choose to exercise some deference to ground-level decision-makers, particularly those selected by P through an LPA. These individuals have after all been entrusted by the donor to make the relevant decisions; if they are making the decisions to the standard anticipated in s 4(9), should the court intervene if its view of best interests is different? 　3.109

The view since 1905 of the *parens patriae* power over property and affairs, carried over into the jurisprudence under Part 7 of the Mental Health Act, was that it extinguished any authority of P to deal with his or her property. Once P became subject to these powers, any purported contracts with him or her were void, as P was not legally able to contract.[147] This was not the previously traditional view. Earlier nineteenth-century authority held that a contract signed in a so-called 'lucid interval' 　3.110

---

[145] MCA s 50(3).
[146] MCA s 4(9).
[147] See *Re Walker* [1905] 1 Ch 160; *Re Beaney (deceased)* [1978], 2 All ER 595, 600.

was valid.[148] This appears to have been restored by the MCA: it is clear that P has authority to make decisions if competent to do so, as notwithstanding the content of an order of appointment, the deputy ceases to have jurisdiction in areas where he knows or reasonably believes P to have capacity.[149]

3.111 While this works to the advantage of the competent individual, the twentieth-century rule worked to the protection of the individual lacking capacity. When such individuals were subject to the *parens patriae* or statutory scheme, contracts signed by them were void. This saved them from the common law of contract, where the contract was enforceable if the other party contracted without knowledge of the incapacity of P.[150] What is the situation now that the court order may not preclude P's exercising his or her rights in a period of capacity? Contracts signed by P during the period of the court order presumably cannot now be assumed to be void. They would be enforceable in any event if P has capacity; but if he or she does not, it is at least arguable that they will still be enforceable, unless the other party was aware or ought reasonably to have been aware of P's incapacity.

I. ADVANCE DECISIONS TO REFUSE TREATMENT

3.112 The MCA places the common law authority to make advance decisions refusing treatment on a statutory footing. Such advance decisions may be made by any person with capacity, age eighteen or over. The MCA states that if:

(a) at a later time and in such circumstances as he may specify, a specified treatment is proposed to be carried out or continued by a person providing health care for him, and
(b) at that time he lacks capacity to consent to the carrying out or continuation of the treatment,

the specified treatment is not to be carried out or continued.[151]

This provision contains considerable flexibility, and carries considerable power. The person making the statement, P, may specify the disorder or the treatments at issue, and specify any conditions for its application. It applies not merely to the commencement of treatment, but to the continuation of treatment. P could, for example, decide that treatment should not be continued beyond a specified period, if a particular level of result were not obtained. It is, however, an advance *refusal* of treatment. Under an LPA, P may state treatment preferences, but such views are not within the scope of an advance decision to refuse treatment. Neither the LPA nor the advance decision can require a treatment provider to offer a specific treatment.[152] Nor does an advance decision permit the active intervention of a treatment provider

---

[148] See, eg, *M'Adam v Walker* (1813) 1 Dow 148, 177–178.
[149] MCA s 20(1).
[150] *Imperial Loan Company v Stone* [1892] 1 QB 599.
[151] MCA s 24(1).
[152] See *R (Burke) v General Medical Council* [2005] EWCA 1003.

to hasten the death of P: the criminal laws relating to homicide, euthanasia and assisted suicide are unchanged by the MCA.[153] It acts instead as equivalent to a competent refusal of consent to treatment. Consistent with that, it will not operate to prevent treatment where consent is not necessary, such as where enforced treatment is provided under Part 4 of the Mental Health Act to patients who are civilly or criminally detained.[154]

The provision allows P to refuse 'treatment . . . by a person providing health care to him'.[155] The definition of 'treatment' in the MCA includes 'a diagnostic or other procedure',[156] but offers no further clarification. Unlike the wording of s 5 regarding the general defence, the term 'care' is not contained within s 24, and the advance refusal must therefore cover a narrower range of decisions, typically those related to consent in a medical context. P could not, for example, refuse care home admission.[157] The proposals of the Law Commission would further expressly have precluded advance refusals of 'basic care', defined as 'care to maintain bodily cleanliness and to alleviate severe pain and the provision of direct oral nutrition and hydration.'[158] This is in part reflected in the wording of para 9.28 of the Code of Practice:

> An advance decision cannot refuse actions that are needed to keep a person comfortable (sometimes called basic or essential care). Examples include warmth, shelter, actions to keep a person clean and the offer of food and water by mouth.

The examples in the Code of Practice are unobjectionable, as they concern care, not treatment. Some actions that keep a person comfortable and arguably falling within the realm of basic care are however medical in nature, such as the provision of drugs to alleviate pain. The MCA does not include the Law Commission's restrictions on refusing such treatment, and an individual could therefore refuse it if he or she wished. Similarly, the Code of Practice elsewhere takes the view that artificial nutrition and hydration (ie, provision of nutrients or fluids by tube) are medical treatments;[159] they can therefore be refused using an advance decision, if an individual wishes to do so.

As the Code of Practice acknowledges,[160] the MCA allows P to refuse all treatment, if that is his or her wish. Elsewhere, the Code of Practice states that the advance decision 'must state precisely what treatment is to be refused—a statement giving a general desire not to be treated is not enough'.[161] This should be read as insisting that P be clear in what he or she is refusing, and in particular clear that he or she is making a refusal of the treatment(s) rather than offering a statement of wishes.

3.113

3.114

---

[153] MCA s 62.
[154] See Code of Practice para 9.37, and paras 5.51–5.56 below.
[155] MCA s 24(1)(a).
[156] MCA s 64(1).
[157] Regarding the effect of advance refusals of treatment on deprivations of liberty under the 2007 amendments, see paras 4.74–4.76 below.
[158] Law Com 231, draft bill, cl 9(7) and (8).
[159] Code of Practice para 9.26.
[160] ibid para 9.13.
[161] ibid para 9.11.

The reference to stating 'precisely' the treatment in question should not be read as restricting P's right to refuse all treatment, if that is his or her wish; there would be no support for that restriction under the statute.

3.115   The advance decision will take effect only if P lacks capacity at the time treatment is to be provided or continued; should P have capacity at that time, he or she will be able to consent to or refuse the treatment as any other competent person would. Where P lacks capacity to consent and the advance decision is valid and applicable to the treatment proposed, the advance decision has the same effect as if P had competently refused the treatment.[162] It thus takes precedence over any consent provided by donees of LPAs, court-appointed deputies, or pursuant to the general defence in s 5. While the Court of Protection has jurisdiction to determine whether the advance decision is valid and applicable to the proposed treatment, it does not have jurisdiction in any other way to alter or override the decision.

3.116   For most treatments, there are no formalities requirements for the advance decision: oral refusals will suffice. This apparent flexibility is somewhat illusory. To be realistic, whatever the Act may say, a practitioner or court will be hesitant to rely on a refusal without clear evidence that it was meant to be taken seriously. A written, signed, and witnessed statement is not the only way to do this—discussing it with a medical practitioner and having it noted in the clinical record would no doubt also suffice—but for evidential purposes, something concrete will significantly increase the likelihood that the refusal will be effective.

3.117   Further, advance decisions to refuse life-sustaining treatment, probably the most frequent use of such advance decisions, do have formalities requirements. While there is no statutory form for such advance decisions, the MCA does require them to state specifically that they are to apply when life is at risk, and they must be in writing, either signed by P or by another person under P's direction, and witnessed.[163] These are new requirements: the common law had no such requirements in these circumstances. Very limited transitional provisions have been put in place. Advance decisions to refuse life-sustaining treatment that were made prior to 1 October 2007 will continue to be in effect if they are otherwise valid and applicable, if they are in writing, and if P has lacked capacity since 1 October 2007. In this limited circumstance, they need not contain the specific statement that they are to apply even if life is at risk, nor need they be signed and witnessed.[164] The effect of this is that people with capacity on or after 1 October 2007 must make new advance decisions that comply with s 25.

3.118   The Law Commission draft would have also included a presumption that advance refusals of treatment would not apply if the viability of a foetus were at risk.[165] This presumption is not contained expressly in the MCA, but given the court's reluctance

---

[162] MCA s 26(1).
[163] MCA s 25(6).
[164] SI 2007/1898, para 5.
[165] Law Com 231, para 5.26.

to uphold treatment refusals in this situation,[166] it would be prudent for women of child-bearing age to address this contingency expressly in the advance decision.

An advance decision will only preclude treatment if it is valid and applicable. It   3.119
will not be valid if P has withdrawn the decision at a time when he or she had capacity; has since the decision executed an LPA that gives the donee authority to give or refuse consent to the treatment in question; or done anything else 'clearly inconsistent' with the advance decision remaining his or her fixed decision.[167] While an LPA which does not overlap with the advance decision does not affect its validity,[168] it may be prudent in drafting an LPA that touches on treatment to state expressly that it is subject to the advance decision, if that is P's wish.

The scope of the final provision, doing something 'clearly inconsistent' with the   3.120
advance decision, is potentially remarkably expansive. An obvious example would be if P has, while competent and since the advance decision, consented to similar treatment in circumstances similar to those contained in the advance decision. The ambit is however considerably wider than this. In *HE v A Hospital NHS Trust, AE*[169] an advance refusal was held to be invalid because of subsequent inconsistent conduct. The key inconsistency in this advance refusal of a blood transfusion lay in P's religious conversion from Jehovah's Witness to Muslim, coupled with her failure to mention the advance treatment refusal for two days during a previous hospital admission. While one may have sympathy with this result, the inconsistency is not immediately apparent. Certainly, Jehovah's Witnesses do not accept blood transfusions; but is it obvious that a conversion to Islam is inconsistent with a decision to refuse such treatment? The court in that case suggests that advance refusals of life-sustaining treatment will be honoured only in cases of manifest and unambiguous validity. If this approach is followed in the implementation of the MCA provisions, persons making advance treatment refusals will have to be vigilant for their views to be respected.

The conditions for an advance decision to be held inapplicable are as follows: 3.121

(a) that treatment is not the treatment specified in the advance decision,
(b) any circumstances specified in the advance decision are absent, or

---

[166] See, eg, *Norfolk and Norwich Healthcare (NHS) Trust v W* [1996] 2 FLR 613; *Re MB (An Adult: Medical Treatment)* [1997] 2 FLR 426 ; *Re T (Adult: Refusal of Medical Treatment)* [1992] 3 WLR 782; *Tameside and Glossop Acute Services Trust v CH* [1996] 1 FLR 762; *A Metropolitan Borough Council v DB* [1997] 1 FLR 767; *Re S (Adult: Refusal of Medical Treatment)* [1994] 2 FLR 671. In *St George's Healthcare NHS Trust v S* [1998] 2 FLR 728; [1998] 3 All ER 673, the patient was permitted to sue following a court application granting the treating professionals the authority to enforce treatment on her, although the situation in this case was highly unusual in that the facts as presented to the court granting the authority to treat her had been materially incorrect.

[167] MCA s 25(2).
[168] MCA s 25(7).
[169] [2003] EWHC 1017.

(c) there are reasonable grounds for believing that circumstances exist which P did not anticipate at the time of the advance decision and which would have affected his decision had he anticipated them.[170]

Once again, considerable elasticity is provided in these provisions. If P wishes his or her wishes to be honoured, clarity of articulation will be significant. The third condition is intended to allow changes of circumstance, most obviously progress in medical science, that would have affected P's decision. The aim is to ensure that P does not become a prisoner of prior conditions, unable to take advantage of new developments. While there is merit in such a condition, there are risks that a court reluctant to allow a refusal of treatment to stand could exploit its relatively broad language. The Code of Practice takes the view that the length of time since the expression of the decision, and 'changes in the patient's personal life' will be relevant.[171] There is no reference to these criteria in the MCA itself, and while it is inappropriate to rule these factors out, they should be approached with considerable caution. The fact that an advance refusal was made a considerable length of time ago does not mean it is forgotten. Especially if the decision has been made with some formality, it may be the case that P has not reiterated the decision specifically because he or she believes the previous decision still to be in effect. This might be the case, for example, if the decision is made as part of a package at a lawyer's office, along with a will and an LPA, as is frequently the case in countries where there is experience of these mechanisms. The insistence that such documents be re-executed periodically to ensure their ongoing validity would create an unjustifiable gravy train for lawyers. Changes in personal circumstances should similarly be approached carefully. It does not follow for example that marriage or an increase in religious fervour affects an individual's view regarding consent to life-sustaining treatment. The risk is that the views holding sway become those of the treatment provider, family, or individual judge, rather than those of P himself or herself. That is not the intent of the provision. That said, because of the approach in the Code of Practice, it would be prudent for persons with advance decisions to reiterate or re-execute them upon significant changes in their life.

3.122   In the first instance, it is for the person who would be providing the treatment to determine whether an advance decision to refuse treatment is valid and applicable. An individual will not incur liability for providing treatment unless 'satisfied' that a valid and applicable advance decision to refuse the treatment exists; an individual will not incur liability for withholding treatment if he or she 'reasonably believes' that a valid and applicable advance decision to refuse the treatment exists.[172] These standards of certainty differ: satisfaction implies a higher level of certainty than reasonable belief. A margin is thus created within the system, serving to protect treatment providers from liability in cases of honest doubt. A valid and applicable advance

---

[170] MCA s 25(4).
[171] Code of Practice para 9.43; see also Code paras 9.29–930.
[172] MCA s 26(2)–(3).

decision is effective as if P were competent and refusing the treatment at the time the treatment is offered, however, so treatment of P if the provider is satisfied that such a valid and applicable advance decision exists would be a battery and, potentially, a criminal offence. Similarly, failure to treat when there is no reasonable belief that such an advance decision exists is likely to constitute negligence.

That offers little by way of understanding how the standards are to be under- 3.123
stood. The Code of Practice notes that if a practitioner has 'genuine doubts'[173] as to the existence, validity or applicability, they would not be satisfied of its existence, but it is not clear how much this paraphrase adds to understanding. Treatment providers should consider the overall circumstances of the alleged advance decision. Certainly, the formality of the setting in which the decision is made will be relevant: wishes expressed after sober reflection in doctors' or lawyers' offices will have more credence than those expressed informally and with less forethought. The provider should also consult with those well-known to P, to determine whether the decision is consistent with P's values and wishes as understood by those people. If a consistent view comes back that the wishes are reliably the wishes of P, and that the decision is in other respects valid and applicable, it is to be hoped that the courts would hold that the provider should be satisfied that the advance decision is in effect.

The Code of Practice places particular responsibility on 'the relevant health care 3.124
professional who is in charge of the patient's care'[174] to determine the validity and applicability of an advance decision. While it may well be appropriate for this individual to have primary responsibility for ensuring appropriate investigation into the matter, it does not follow that others in the treatment team are absolved of their responsibilities. Anyone whose role would require the consent of the patient if competent, and who would therefore be relying on the effectiveness or not of an advance directive as a defence under s 26, must bring himself or herself within the terms of the section. Thus anyone treating must not be 'satisfied' that a valid and applicable advance decision exists; and anyone under a duty of care to P who does not treat must 'reasonably believe' that a valid and applicable advance decision does exist. There is no reason why reliance on superior officers will apply here any more than anywhere else in the law of consent.

In the event of doubt, the matter of validity and applicability can be referred to 3.125
the Court of Protection. The Court can rule on whether an advance decision exists, is valid, and is applicable to the treatment proposed.[175] If the Court holds that it is, the decision must be honoured. There is no mechanism for the Court to overrule a valid and applicable decision to refuse treatment. Pending such court determination, and notwithstanding any apparent advance decision to the contrary, life-sustaining

---

[173] Code of Practice para 9.58.
[174] ibid para 9.64.
[175] MCA s 26(4).

treatment may be provided to P, and care provided if it is reasonably believed to be necessary to prevent a serious deterioration in P's condition.[176]

3.126　　Courts in the past have indicated that court determinations *ought* to be made prior to the cessation of or failure to provide life-sustaining treatment.[177] Such a requirement is not contained in the MCA itself, and the Code of Practice mentions it only in the specific context of withholding artificial hydration and nutrition from people in a permanent vegetative state.[178] It remains to be seen whether it will be introduced by judicial interpretation. In any event, because of the seriousness of the situation, treatment providers with honest and reasonable doubts regarding validity or applicability of an advance decision may wish to consider a court application in these circumstances when time allows. If such court applications are not formally required, however, and if the provider is satisfied that the advance decision is valid and applicable, it would be binding.

3.127　　An advance decision may be distinguished from an LPA that covers matters relating to medical consent. The LPA appoints someone to make treatment decisions, subject to the best interests criteria and such restrictions as are contained in the instrument itself. The advance decision makes the decision: there is at least in theory no routine assessment of the wisdom or desirability of the decision. The inclusion of medical decision-making in an LPA will be appropriate to deal with unforeseen maladies occurring after the onset of incapacity. The advance decision will be appropriate when P has firm and fixed views about refusal of a definable treatment, set of treatments, or course of treatment in definable future situations.

3.128　　The MCA is clear that a person may withdraw or alter their advance decision while they have capacity to do so.[179] Withdrawals need not be in writing.[180] This would appear to apply even when the advance decision was in writing, and even when the advance decision was required to be in writing.[181] Except for a withdrawal or partial withdrawal, an alteration of the decision does need to be in writing if it concerns life-sustaining treatment.[182]

3.129　　This raises the question as to whether the decision may be varied by the individual after losing capacity: is an individual who appears compliant with and perhaps enthusiastic about treatment following a loss of capacity bound by the advance decision refusing the treatment? The answer is not entirely obvious. On the one hand, the point of the advance refusal is that an individual may make decisions to apply during their subsequent incapacity. These are not matters to be entered lightly, and persons making these decisions must be taken to have adopted a considered view of

---

[176] MCA s 26(5).

[177] See *Airedale NHS Trust v Bland* [1993] AC 789. See also *Practice Note (Family Div: Incapacitated Adults)* [2002] 1 WLR 325.

[178] Code of Practice para 8.18.

[179] MCA s 24(3).

[180] MCA s 24(4).

[181] See Code of Practice para 9.31, and *HE*, see n 169 above, para 39.

[182] MCA s 24(5).

their wishes. The sections of the statute referring to withdrawal or amendment refer specifically to P having capacity when that occurs. Passive compliance with treatment on its own can surely be insufficient to circumvent this. Otherwise people who were unconscious might not have their decisions respected, and that cannot be the intent of the legislation. On the other hand, the statute provides that the advance decision will be invalid if the individual 'has done anything . . . clearly inconsistent with the advance decision remaining his fixed decision'.[183] That provision is not expressly limited to matters arising during the individual's capacity. It may thus at least arguably be broad enough to include decisions made when P has lost capacity.

Different issues arise if the treatment is life-sustaining, as the termination of such   3.130
treatment raises questions regarding the right to life in Article 2 of the ECHR. Article 2 rights are enjoyed by everyone, including those lacking capacity. In at least some circumstances, most obviously when P indicates an incompetent but clear wish to receive the treatment, failure to provide such treatment could raise questions of Article 2 compliance. Alternatively, the right to make advance decisions could be considered an aspect of the right to privacy under Article 8. There is no ECHR jurisprudence that assists in ascertaining how the presence of a competent, advance refusal of a treatment should be considered to affect the current and incompetent views of an individual apparently now wishing that treatment.

The Law Commission proposed that concealing or destroying an advance deci-   3.131
sion ought to be an offence, punishable by imprisonment up to two years.[184] While the Commission took the view that any forgery of such documents was covered under existing law relating to fraud, it considered the existing law to be uncertain as to whether destroying or concealing such a document was a crime. Curiously, this provision was dropped from the final legislation. This is a matter of some concern, as anecdotal evidence suggests that such decisions do sometimes disappear from medical records.

Notwithstanding the failure to include the specific offence in the MCA, legal   3.132
consequences may nonetheless flow from the concealment or destruction of an advance decision. Certainly, when the concealment or destruction is by a member of a medical, legal or similar profession, it would constitute grounds for professional discipline. Whether destruction of such a document is a property crime depends on the ownership of the document. If the document is owned by the NHS trust, which would be the case for example for hospital records, a doctor, nurse, or other person destroying the document might well be guilty of criminal damage. Further, if the advance decision were signed and witnessed in circumstances where P would own it and then given to someone else, be it doctor or anyone else, P may retain some rights over it. Section 5(3) of the Theft Act 1968 holds that where a person receives property from another, and is under an obligation to the other to retain and deal with that property in a particular way, the property is to be considered as regards the

---

[183] MCA s 25(2)(c).
[184] Law Com 231, para 5.38.

recipient as belonging to the giver. A credible argument could be made that this provision applies to an advance decision given to a medical professional for placement in a clinical record, and the destruction of the record therefore constitutes theft from P. The legal duty to retain and deal with the property is less clear if the advance decision is instead given to a non-professional such as a friend; the argument for criminal liability here is still coherent, but less convincing.

3.133   The above analysis applies whether or not the precluded treatment has actually been performed. If that absence were discovered prior to the provision of the treatment, P could of course execute a new decision if he or she continues to have the capacity to do so. If P lacks capacity to execute a new decision, it may be worth considering an application to the Court of Protection for an order precluding the treatment in question. In some circumstances, it may be appropriate to consider whether the person destroying the original decision should be required to pay the costs of such an application.

3.134   If the precluded treatment has occurred, other criminal law may also become relevant. It is not obvious that the destruction of the written evidence of the decision destroys the decision. A decision that was valid when it was signed and witnessed may remain a valid decision, even if the evidence of the decision is 'misplaced'. A doctor who is satisfied of the existence of such a decision but performs the precluded treatment anyway may thus still be guilty of a criminal assault. The case would be particularly strong if the treating physician had destroyed the decision himself or herself; it would be more problematic if the decision had been destroyed by another, but the doctor had strong grounds for believing it had existed and had never been withdrawn by P.

3.135   It is a more difficult question whether criminal consequences flow if a doctor performs the treatment innocently, unaware that the decision has been destroyed or concealed by someone else (C). Clearly, the innocent doctor is protected by s 26(2). The situation regarding C is less straightforward. The initial question concerns the scope of s 26(2). If that provision renders the treatment not a criminal act at all, then it is difficult to see that C is guilty of anything related to the treatment. That seems unlikely, however. Medical treatments are assaults, to which consent provides a defence. The scope of s 26(2) would seem to be analogous to the provision of a defence of consent to the treating physician. In that case, the treatment could still constitute a criminal act as regards C, if the precluded treatment is a sufficiently foreseeable result of C's actions. If C actively conceals the existence of the advance decision in the face of an express enquiry from the treating physician, for example, C may well be inciting an assault. Even absent such a direct request, if the provision of the precluded treatment is sufficiently foreseeable from the destruction of the advance decision, C may also be guilty of assault.[185]

---

[185] The arguments here are by analogy from cases such as *R v Bourne* (1952) 36 Cr App R 125 and *R v Cogan and Leak* [1976] QB 217.

The application of criminal law to the situation where an advance decision is   3.136
concealed or destroyed is a matter of speculation. It is not a set of facts that the court
has been called on to deal with, and the approach of judge and jury may well be
dependent on the specific facts before it. Cases of this sort may prove evidentially
problematic. All this makes a word of warning appropriate. The person making an
advance decision may find it prudent to make several copies, lodging one with his
or her medical adviser, and one or more others with friends who can draw the decision to the attention of any successor medical advisers if necessary.

J. RESEARCH RELATING TO PEOPLE LACKING CAPACITY

The research provisions in the MCA supplement the legal and ethical regulations,   3.137
governance and guidance relating to research generally. Of particular relevance in
this regard is the Research Governance Framework for Health and Social Care,[186]
which establishes Research Ethics Committees (RECs) to approve any clinical or non-
clinical research to be carried out within the NHS. The Research Governance Framework emphasizes the importance of each research subject providing informed consent.[187]
It does not contain specific provisions relating to research subjects who lack capacity.
That is provided by the MCA. Where the Research Governance Framework is government guidance, the MCA is primary legislation. In the event of conflict, the MCA
therefore takes priority. The MCA provisions are also in some ways broader than the
Research Governance Framework. The Framework covers research occurring in the
Department of Health and NHS broadly conceived, including social care services.[188]
The MCA applies whenever people lacking capacity are involved as subjects of research,
whether or not the research occurs in the DOH/NHS environment.

The MCA provisions do not affect research governed by the Medicines for Human   3.138
Use (Clinical Trials) Regulations 2004,[189] introduced consequent on the EU Clinical
Trials Directive.[190] These regulations apply to 'clinical trials', defined as follows:

'clinical trial' means any investigation in human subjects, other than a non-interventional trial,
intended—

(a) to discover or verify the clinical, pharmacological or other pharmacodynamic effects of one or
     more medicinal products,

(b) to identify any adverse reactions to one or more such products, or

(c) to study absorption, distribution, metabolism and excretion of one or more such products
with the object of ascertaining the safety or efficacy of those products.[191]

---

[186] Department of Health (2nd edn, 2005).
[187] *Research Governance Framework*, para 2.2.3.
[188] *Research Governance Framework*, para 1.2.
[189] SI 2004/1031.
[190] See J McHale ' Clinical Research' in A Grubb (ed), *Principles of Medical Law* (Oxford University Press,
2004, 2nd edn).
[191] SI 2004/1031, reg. 2(1).

Schedule 1 Part 5 of these regulations contain provisions relating to incapacitated adults. Consent to participation in clinical trials is provided by the subject's 'legal representative', defined as an individual who 'by virtue of their relationship with that adult . . . is suitable to act as their legal representative for the purposes of that trial' and is available and willing to do so. If there is no such person, the legal representative is the doctor primarily responsible for adult's treatment, or his or her nominee.[192] A donee of an LPA covering health care decisions or a court-appointed deputy with a similar remit would be obvious people to function as legal representatives in this context. While the views of P against participating in such a clinical trial are to be considered, they do not appear to be binding.[193] Instead, informed consent provided by the legal representative 'shall represent that adult's presumed will.'[194]

3.139　　The MCA provisions apply to 'intrusive' research, defined as research which would be unlawful if it were performed on a person with capacity without his or her consent (s 30(2)). Under traditional English law, this would have applied to any research involving the touching of an individual, as without consent this would have constituted a battery. Purely observational research however would probably have been outside the scope of the provision. That was the intent of the Law Commission,[195] but the situation has become more complicated with the introduction of the right to privacy under Article 8 of the ECHR. Research on people lacking capacity is likely to occur on a hospital ward, in a doctor's office, in a care home, or in the subject's own home. In all of these situations, the individual would have a reasonable expectation of privacy to some degree or other. In the doctor's office, when the subject is undergoing a medical examination, the expectation of privacy is particularly strong. On an open hospital ward where routine visits by other members of the public are permitted, it is more questionable whether mere observation by a researcher on the ward would be a sufficient intrusion to trigger Article 8. In either case, it may be relevant if the researcher is already a member of the medical team who already has access to the otherwise privileged environment. If the research protects the anonymity of the research subject, it is less obvious that Article 8 will be triggered. If the research infringes the right to privacy under Article 8, such research will be within the definition of 'intrusive'.

3.140　　Similar concerns might well be raised about researchers using clinical records, if the researcher would not otherwise have been made privy to the information. It does seem that notwithstanding government guidance, data anonymized by a person who has already had access to the information such as the individual's treating physician may be made available to researchers with no breach of the law of confidentiality occurring.[196] Such use of information would probably not reach the threshold of an Article 8 violation, and would therefore be outside the scope of the MCA.

---

[192] SI 2004/1031, Sch 1, pt 1, reg 2.
[193] ibid, Sch 1, pt 5, reg 7.
[194] ibid, Sch 1, pt 5, reg 12.
[195] See Law Com 231, draft bill, cl 11(4)(d).
[196] *R v Department of Health, ex p Source Informatics* [2001] QB 424 (CA).

Intensive research where all or some of the subjects are unable to consent to the   3.141
research are within the scope of the MCA. That means that such research projects
must be approved by the 'appropriate body'[197] and comply with the conditions of
the Act. The appropriate body is specified by regulation as the existing RECs.[198]
The MCA provisions can be seen to buttress rather than to cut across current systems of research governance.

The MCA provides substantive limitations on the research that may be carried   3.142
out on people lacking capacity,[199] and process requirements regarding the attainment of substitute consent.[200] The substantive provisions require that the research
project in question must be connected with an impairing condition affecting P, or
the treatment of that condition. 'Impairing condition' is further defined as a condition which is or may be attributable to, or which does or may cause or contribute to,
disturbance in the functioning of the mind or brain. The researcher must further
demonstrate that research of comparable effectiveness cannot be carried out using
only people who have capacity to consent.[201] Historically, people in psychiatric and
long-stay institutions, many or most of whom lacked capacity to consent, were
sometimes used as captive subjects in research unrelated to the disorder thought to
cause their mental impairment. The view expressed through the MCA is that this is
unethical: research on people lacking capacity must be related to the causes or effects
of their incapacity. People lacking capacity may not simply be used for research as a
matter of convenience.

Very unusually for the MCA, the sections concerning research do not refer to the   3.143
best interests test, but rather introduce their own substantive thresholds. The research
must either have the potential to benefit P without imposing a disproportionate
burden on him or her, or be intended to provide knowledge of the causes or treatments of, or care of people affected by, the same or a similar condition. In the latter
case, where the treatment is to provide knowledge and will not potentially benefit P
directly, there must also be reasonable grounds for believing the following:

(a) that the risk to P from taking part in the project is likely to be negligible, and
(b) that anything done to, or in relation to, P will not—
    (i) interfere with P's freedom of action or privacy in a significant way, or
    (ii) be unduly invasive or restrictive.[202]

Projects that are for the increase in knowledge of P's condition but which offer no
obvious benefit to him or her must therefore carry virtually no burden of participation. The interests of P are expressly stated to outweigh those of science and society.[203]

---

[197] MCA s 30(1).
[198] SI 2006/2810. For Wales, see SI 2007/833 (W71).
[199] MCA s 31.
[200] MCA s 32.
[201] MCA s 31(2)–(4).
[202] MCA s 31(6).
[203] MCA s 33(3).

Projects that may benefit P must not bear disproportionate burdens. Clinical trials are not subject to these rules, so these restrictions will not serve to limit drug testing. There may be complications, however, in that some of the factors relating to intrusiveness might vary between individual participants. The rules would seem to require that the appropriate level of intrusiveness not be exceeded for each given research subject prior to approval of the project, but in standard research application procedures, it is unethical to recruit for a study prior to receipt of REC approval. The effect of factors applying differently to different individual research subjects could not be known at the time of project approval.

3.144   For each participant lacking capacity, the researcher is required to identify an individual who is engaged in the participant's care or welfare in a non-professional capacity, and is prepared to advise on whether P should participate in the project.[204] Donees of LPAs and court-appointed deputies relating to P are specifically not precluded from fulfilling this role,[205] and may indeed be the appropriate choice. If no such non-professional carer is available, guidance not yet issued will allow appointment of an individual unconnected to the research project to fulfil this role.[206] The structure of the Act provides that this person advises the researcher. While the researcher is to consult with this person, it remains the researcher's responsibility to ensure that the prerequisites for P's participation in the research are met. The MCA also provides the consultee with concrete controls, however. If at any time before or during the research the consultee informs the researcher that P if competent would be likely to decline participation, then P must be withdrawn from the research.[207]

3.145   Consistent with this, the MCA specifically requires the consultee to advise on what the wishes and feelings of P would have been if P had had capacity.[208] In any event, nothing may be done to P in the name of research that is contrary to an advance decision to refuse treatment or 'any other form of statement made by him and not subsequently withdrawn'.[209]

3.146   Guidance regarding appointment of consultees and their role in research is to be issued by the Department of Health.[210]

3.147   Nothing may be done to P to which he appears to object except where it is to protect P from harm or to reduce or prevent pain or discomfort.[211] There is no capacity requirement here: an incapable objection will require P's removal from

---

[204] MCA s 32(2).
[205] MCA s 32(7).
[206] MCA s 32(3).
[207] MCA s 32(5).
[208] MCA s 32(4).
[209] MCA s 33(2).
[210] Draft guidance has already been made available: Department of Health, 'Guidance on nominating a consultee for research involving adults who lack capacity to consent', available electronically at <http://www.dh.gov.uk/consultations>, gateway reference 8371. Accessed 20 September 2007. This draft guidance is part of a consultation exercise, for which submissions were due by 14 September 2007.
[211] MCA s 33(2).

the research. Such objection need not be verbal, but may for example be by showing signs of resistance. Specifically, if P indicates in any way that he or she wishes to be withdrawn from the project, he or she must be withdrawn without delay.[212] In addition, the balance of benefit outweighing risk, which must be shown for approval of the project, continues to apply to each participant lacking capacity. If burdens at any time outweigh benefits, and if there is any burden inherent in a project from which P will not directly benefit, the researcher must withdraw P from the project forthwith.[213] The sole exception is that treatment may continue if a significant risk to P's health would result from its discontinuance.[214]

In general, P may be involved in the research only if the above criteria are satisfied.   3.148 The exception is when P is about to receive urgent treatment, and where 'having regard to the nature of the research and of the particular circumstances of the case . . . it is also necessary to take action for the purposes of the research as a matter of urgency' and when it is not practicable to engage in the consultation process outlined above.[215] Nonetheless, such treatment may only be given with the agreement of an independent medical practitioner or, if that is not practicable, the researcher acts 'in accordance with a procedure approved by the appropriate body [the REC] at the time when the research project was approved'.[216] This 'urgency' exception is presumably intended to allow research into incapacitating injuries, at the time the injury occurs. One does not know in advance who will be injured, so planning is not necessarily possible. The usual criteria are therefore unable to be met.

If the research protocol approved by the REC under the MCA includes the stor-   3.149 ing or use of human tissue, P is deemed to consent to such storage or use for purposes of the Human Tissue Act 2004.[217]

K. ILL-TREATMENT OR NEGLECT OF PERSONS LACKING CAPACITY

The MCA makes it an offence to ill-treat or neglect people lacking capacity. The   3.150 offence applies to an individual D who either:

(a) has the care of a person (P) who lacks, or whom D reasonably believes to lack, capacity, or
(b) is the donee of a lasting power of attorney or an enduring power of attorney created by P, or
(c) is a deputy appointed by the court for P.[218]

---

[212] MCA s 33(4).
[213] MCA s 33(5).
[214] MCA s 33(6).
[215] MCA s 32(8).
[216] MCA s 32(9).
[217] See SI 2006/1659, reg 3(2)(c).
[218] MCA s 44(1).

3.151   If the relevant relationship is contained under s 44(1)(a), P's incapacity or D's reasonable belief in P's incapacity must be demonstrated. The subsection is disjunctive: either will suffice. The section can therefore be triggered if P lacks capacity unbeknown to D, or alternatively when D has a reasonable belief that P lacks capacity that turns out to be incorrect. There is no minimum age for P, although the statutory definition of incapacity applies, requiring an impairment or disturbance in functioning of the mind or brain.

3.152   The meaning of incapacity is problematic in this subsection. As discussed in para 3.18 above, the MCA is structured around capacity as a functional concept: it relates to a specific decision or set of decisions. In this context, the scope of the offence is unclear: what is it P is meant to lack capacity to do or decide, to trigger the section? It would seem odd if any incapacity could trigger the section. That would mean, for example, that a prosecution for neglect might lie if D does not address P's malnourishment, even when P's only lack of capacity concerns his or her ability to care for his property. It is surely not the case that D is guilty of an offence for failing to provide care in a situation where D rightly believes that P retains capacity to make decisions. D would not, after all, have the legal right to intervene in these circumstances. At the same time, requiring too close an association between the abuse and the specific decisions relating to which P lacks capacity will unduly restrict the offence. As an obvious example, consider a case where D is hitting P, a case that might be expected to fall at the centre of the offence. That abuse does not relate clearly to a type of decision or specific functional incapacity in P. If the abuse must be related to a set of decisions where P lacks capacity, it is not obvious that D would be guilty of the offence here. D would, of course, be guilty of the crime of assault in such circumstances, and P's vulnerability would be an aggravating factor in sentencing. The specific offence in the MCA in no way precludes the application of other criminal law. Nonetheless, it would seem extremely odd for those facts not to constitute a violation of the MCA offence as well.

3.153   Under s 44(1)(a), there must be a relationship of care between D and P. 'Care' is not defined in the Act, but it is reasonable to suspect that the courts will accord it a broad meaning. The first part of the definition would certainly include people providing care in reliance on the general defence, but it is not restricted to them. It presumably extends to situations where P is in a relationship of reliance on D, and D is either legally required to provide goods, services or support in response to that need, or voluntarily agrees to do so. Where P lives with D in D's premises, for example, a care relationship is likely to exist whatever the legal structure of the arrangements between P and D. If D goes to P's home to assist with cleaning, a care relationship is also likely to be found to be established. That may be the case even if the assistance is voluntary. If P is heavily reliant on such care, there is perhaps a question as to how D may cease the arrangement, lest simply terminating the arrangement be viewed as neglect. There can be little doubt that D cannot be forced to continue to provide voluntary care indefinitely; but it might nonetheless be prudent to notify another person involved with P's care, the Public Guardian, or social services in cases where withdrawal of the care will have major adverse consequences to P.

Section 44(1)(b) and (c) lacks some of these ambiguities. These subsections are 3.154 based on legal relationships between D and P. Presumably the definition of P in (a) applies in addition to the other two parts, so that P must lack capacity or reasonably be believed to lack capacity by D. For (b) to apply, D must be the donee of an LPA, but there is no requirement that the LPA be registered. The point is important, ill-treatment or neglect of P, possibly including an extreme case of failing to register an LPA when P was losing capacity, might meet the conditions of the offence. There is no express requirement that the abuse be within the legal authority granted to the donee of the LPA or deputy. As discussed in para 3.152 above, alleged neglect of P relating to acts where D lacks the legal authority to intervene because of P's continuing capacity should not be caught by the provision. If P's capacity in the area is lacking or ambiguous, however, it is perhaps arguable that the donee or deputy cannot turn a blind eye to severe deprivation, but must alert some relevant authority such as social services or the Public Guardian, even if the neglect is outside the scope of D's authority.

The offence occurs when D 'ill-treats' or 'wilfully neglects' P.[219] A similarly worded 3.155 prohibition relating to psychiatric patients is contained in s 127 of the MHA 1983. This may provide a guide to interpretation of the MCA section. The jurisprudence under the Mental Health Act offence holds that 'ill-treatment' and 'wilfully to neglect' were conceptually different, and warranted separate counts in an indictment.[220] The elements of ill-treatment were articulated by the Court of Appeal in *R v Newington*:

In our judgment the judge should have told the jury that for there to be a conviction of ill-treatment contrary to the Act of 1983 the Crown would have to prove (1) deliberate conduct by the appellant which could properly be described as ill-treatment irrespective of whether this ill-treatment damaged or threatened to damage the health of the victim and (2) a guilty mind involving either an appreciation by the appellant at the time that she was inexcusably ill-treating a patient or that she was reckless as to whether she was inexcusably acting in that way.[221]

The Court further held that the actual occurrence of injury or unnecessary suffering was not pivotal to the offence. It has been suggested that the judgment is broad enough to include inadequate feeding or heating, the use of harsh words, or bullying.[222] A course of conduct is not necessarily required; a single slapping incident is sufficient to trigger the offence.[223] Under *Newington*, violence was not necessarily evidence of ill-treatment if it were used for example 'for the reasonable control of a patient'.[224] For purposes of the MCA provisions, that must now be read in light of

---

[219] MCA s 44(2).
[220] *R v Newington* (1990) 91 Cr App R 247.
[221] (1990) 91 Cr App R 247, 254.
[222] M Gunn, 'Casenote on *R v Newington*' (1990) 1 Journal of Forensic Psychiatry 360, 361.
[223] *R v Holmes* [1979] Crim LR 52.
[224] (1990) 91 Cr App R 247, 253.

the provisions on restraining individuals, discussed in paras 3.55 to 3.56, 3.76, 3.104 above and paras 4.26 to 4.34 below.

3.156   There is little jurisprudential guidance on the meaning of 'neglect'. In *Newington*, the court suggested that unlike 'ill-treatment', it would be related to a particular state of mind,[225] but it did little to elaborate. Richard Jones suggests instead that it is an objective state, which would 'probably' include the failure to provide medical care to a patient.[226] Such an objective standard may perhaps define the scope of 'neglect', but the actions of D must also be 'wilful', suggesting a level of knowledge of the relevant circumstances and a choosing not to intervene. Certainly, failures to take due care of P in situations where D has, and is aware that he or she has, a legal obligation to do so might be obvious examples of neglect. A failure to make decisions by the donee of an LPA or court-appointed deputy might be obvious examples. The failure of these individuals or other carers to act on knowledge coming to their attention, or that ought to have come to their attention, is a less clear case, but may perhaps be within the scope of the section. Acting on such knowledge cannot mean enforcing on D an expanded caring role, because the legal recognition of such roles requires the consent of D, but it might mean notifying relevant social services agencies, other carers, or the Public Guardian.

3.157   Persons convicted of offences under s 44 are subject on summary conviction to a maximum of 12 months' imprisonment or a fine not exceeding the statutory maximum; and on indictment to a term of imprisonment not exceeding 5 years or a fine.

---

[225] (1990) 91 Cr App R 247, 252.
[226] R Jones, *Mental Health Act Manual* (Sweet and Maxwell, 2006, 10th edn) para 1-1160.

4

DEPRIVATION OF LIBERTY OF
PEOPLE LACKING CAPACITY:
THE 2007 AMENDMENTS

A. INTRODUCTION

As noted elsewhere in this book, the MCA was amended as part of the government's 4.01
reforms to mental health legislation in 2007.[1] These amendments are not in force at
the time this book is written. The current best guess is that they will be take effect
in April 2009. The 2007 amendments themselves provide for much elaboration in
the form of regulations and statutory instruments. These have not yet been published, so much of the detail remains open to speculation. A Draft Code of Practice
was put out for public consultation in September 2007.[2]

The reforms address the situation of persons without capacity who are deprived 4.02
of their liberty within the meaning of Article 5 of the ECHR. The issue came to a
head in the case of *HL v the United Kingdom*,[3] generally known as the *Bournewood*
case, after the health care trust in which it arose. HL was an adult lacking capacity
who was admitted informally to a psychiatric facility. Had he tried to leave the facility, he would have been civilly confined ('sectioned') under the Mental Health Act.
Such recourse was not taken as he never attempted to do so, although it would seem
that the carers with whom he had lived in the community were discouraged from

---

[1] See Mental Health Act 2007 ss 49–51 and Schs 7, 8, and 9.
[2] <http://www.dh.gov.uk> gateway reference 8319. Accessed 5 October 2007.
[3] (2005) 40 EHRR 32.

visiting him out of a concern that he would have wished to leave with them. At issue was whether in these circumstances his Article 5 right to liberty had been infringed. The ECtHR held that it had, and further that such infringement was not justified by law. It is this infringement that the 2007 amendments are meant to address.

4.03 In the litigation prior to the hearing before the ECtHR, the government had estimated that this issue affected approximately 48,000 people in psychiatric hospitals—more than three times the number otherwise civilly confined there.[4] In the wake of the ECtHR decision, it was further held that people lacking capacity admitted to care homes in similar circumstances were similarly held in violation of Article 5.[5] The issue is thus not small in scale.

4.04 The ECtHR decision was published shortly before the passage of the MCA, too late for a response to be included in that statute. As a result, the MCA as passed in 2005 largely avoided the issue. Persons relying on the general defence, holders of LPAs, and court-appointed deputies were specifically precluded from taking decisions that would deprive P of his or her liberty.[6] These three subsections will be revoked when the 2007 amendments come into effect. In their stead, the 2007 amendments introduce s 4A, which allows P to be deprived of liberty only if that deprivation is consistent with a judgment of the Court of Protection, or is in compliance with the provisions of the new Schedule A1. The new s 4B will allow life-sustaining treatment to be provided while a court decision is sought under s 4A to resolve any doubts as to whether the deprivation of liberty is justified.

4.05 The basic direction of Schedule A1 is simple enough.

- The provisions apply to persons lacking capacity and deprived of their liberty in hospitals or care homes.
- Subject to some fairly minor tweaking, the overall approach and most of the substantive requirements of the MCA will apply to 'Bournewood' residents.
- A 'supervisory body'—generally the relevant primary care trust (for hospitals in England), the National Assembly for Wales (for hospitals in Wales), or local authority (for care homes)—will have to be informed of anyone deprived of their liberty. Those authorities will ensure that the relevant provisions of the MCA are followed.
- When there is no other appropriate person to consult regarding P's[7] best interests, an IMCA will be appointed to assist in this determination.
- A representative will be appointed to maintain contact with P and represent P in matters regarding the detention. While not clear from the 2007 amendments themselves, it would seem that this is expected often to be one of P's friends, family, or an informal carer where such a person is available.

---

[4] *R (L) v Bournewood Community and Mental Health NHS Trust* [1998] 3 WLR 107 (HL) at 112.

[5] *JE v DE and Surrey County Council* [2006] EWHC 3459 (Fam).

[6] MCA ss 6(5), 11(6), and 20(13).

[7] For reasons not entirely clear, the 2007 amendments introduce a new term—the 'relevant person'—for a person lacking capacity. For sake of consistency with the remainder of this book and with the remainder of the statute, the 'relevant person' will continue to be identified as P.

- Particular rules are introduced regarding the intersection of the 'Bournewood' situation and mental health legislation.

As this encapsulates the overall direction of the 2007 amendments, it is astonishing and distressing these amendments take approximately the same space in the statute book as the whole previous MCA, excluding its schedules. The drafting is at times hideously and needlessly complicated. This is highly unfortunate. The MCA as passed in 2005 is the sort of legislation that a reasonable lay person charged with making decisions can reasonably understand; not so the amendments.

The good news for non-professional carers is that the amendments will not affect them directly in any event. If called upon to advise upon or decide whether P should be admitted to a care home or hospital, such non-professional carers and family members should decide with reference to the MCA as described in the earlier chapters of this book. If P is deprived of liberty in that setting (regarding 'deprivation of liberty' see paras 4.26 to 4.34 below), then the duty will be on the care home or hospital to notify the relevant authorities, who will in turn be required to ensure that the new law is complied with. If the carer is of the view that the relevant law is not being followed—that the accommodation is not in the best interests of P, for example—the matter should normally be raised initially with those in charge of P's care. If the matter is not resolved, the carer can raise the matter with the relevant authority—the primary care trust or social services authority. If that is not successful, it may be appropriate to raise the matter with the Public Guardian or the Court of Protection.   4.06

If P is deprived of liberty but not accommodated in a hospital or care home an application to the Court of Protection will be required for the accommodation to be legal. This would be the case, for example, if P were deprived of liberty in his or her own home, or in the home of a private carer. The court application will be based on the MCA as passed in 2005, and as discussed in the remainder of this book; apart from the new rules dividing the MCA from the MHA, the 2007 amendments will not apply to it. It is expected that such private confinements will be uncommon, and thus that few such applications will be required.   4.07

An order of the Court of Protection can also permit P's deprivation of liberty in a hospital or care home. In that event, no recourse to the process in the 2007 amendments will be necessary while the court order remains in effect.   4.08

B. OVERVIEW OF THE 2007 AMENDMENTS

The bulk of the 2007 amendments are contained in new schedules, A1 and 1A, to the MCA. These introduce a new language to speak about people lacking capacity. Rather than using the language of capacity and the abbreviation 'P', as is used in much of the rest of the MCA, the amendments refer to a 'relevant person'. As the prior convention has been used to this point in this book, it will be continued in this chapter, but readers consulting the legislation itself will need to be aware of the   4.09

new vocabulary. A person admitted to a care home or hospital in circumstances depriving him or her of liberty is called a 'detained resident' by the 2007 amendments. An index to key terms in Schedule A1 is helpfully contained in para 187 of that schedule.

4.10   The 2007 amendments are in addition to the provisions already contained in the MCA. If there is a donee of an LPA with the relevant authority, for example, he or she still has the obligation to decide whether a care home or hospital admission is appropriate. Schedule A1 is instead directed to those detaining P in a hospital or care home, a situation which will normally arise after the LPA or other decision-maker has reached a view of best interests under the other terms of the MCA.

4.11   The terms and ethos of the MCA as a whole apply to the 2007 amendments unless contradicted by the specific terms of those amendments. The principles contained in s 1 of the MCA,[8] the definition of incapacity,[9] and the test of best interests,[10] for example, all apply except insofar as they are expressly modified by the 2007 amendments. While their location mainly in schedules A1 and 1A of the MCA makes them appear self-contained and separate to the body of the MCA, this division is illusory.

1. 'Managing Authorities', 'Supervisory Bodies', and 'Standard Authorisations'

4.12   As noted above, the 2007 amendments will require the 'managing authority' of the hospital or care home where P will be accommodated to seek authorization from the relevant 'supervisory body' whenever a deprivation of liberty may occur, unless a court order already permits the deprivation of liberty.

4.13   The managing authority for a hospital will be the primary care trust, NHS trust, foundation trust, strategic health authority or local health board with authority over the hospital. For care homes or private hospitals, the managing authority will be the individual responsible for the home, being registered under Part 2 of the Care Standards Act 2000.

4.14   For care home admissions, the supervisory body will be the local authority where P is ordinarily resident or, if P has no ordinary residence, the local authority where the care home is located. For hospital admissions, the 'supervisory body' will be:

- the primary care trust that commissions the care or treatment that deprives P of liberty; or if none
- the National Assembly for Wales if the hospital is in Wales, or if the care or treatment was commissioned by a Welsh local health board or the National Assembly for Wales; or
- the primary care trust for the area where the hospital is located.[11]

---

[8] See paras 3.15–3.21 above.
[9] MCA ss 2–3, discussed at paras 3.22–3.32 above.
[10] MCA s 4, discussed at paras 3.33–3.52 above.
[11] MCA Sch A1 paras 180–184.

In some cases, this will mean that the managing authority and the supervisory body will be the same for a given institution. This is permitted by the Act, subject to regulations not yet published.[12]

The 2007 amendments anticipate that the initial application for a 'standard' authorization must be made either up to 28 days prior to the admission of P, or if P has already been admitted, if P will meet the 'qualifying requirements' (see paras 4.35 to 4.77 below) within the 28 days.[13] The latter provision would cover the situation, for example, where P is losing capacity over time: the request for authorization would be made as P is approaching the loss of capacity. An application for a standard authorization must also be made if P already meets the qualifying requirements. This would be the case, for example, if P were suddenly rendered incapable, such as by a stroke. New applications for standard authorizations must be when the place of detention changes.[14] 4.15

This application triggers the supervisory body to enquiring whether the qualifying requirements are met.[15] If the qualifying conditions are met, the supervisory body is obliged to issue a standard authorization.[16] This allows P to be detained in the place named by the authorization, for the period stated, and subject to any conditions contained in the authorization. The maximum period will be one year, or such shorter time as is indicated by the person assessing best interests,[17] but new standard authorizations may be sought as previous ones approach expiry. The authorization will also have to provide reasons as to why the qualifying conditions are met, and explain the purpose of the authorization. 4.16

If a standard authorization is granted, a 'representative' will be appointed by the supervising body.[18] Paragraph 140(1) of Schedule A1 states that this person will: 4.17

- maintain contact with P;
- represent P in matters relating to or connected with his or her deprivation of liberty; and
- support P in matters relating to or connected with his or her deprivation of liberty.

The role of the representative is specifically stated not to affect the appointment or authority of the donee of an LPA, a deputy, or the Court of Protection.[19] While there will no doubt be some overlap between the roles, they are not the same. The representative can be understood as akin to an advocate, where as these other roles are decision-makers.

---

[12] MCA Sch A1 para 184.
[13] MCA Sch A1 para 24.
[14] MCA Sch A1 paras 24–26.
[15] See further paras 4.35–4.77 below.
[16] MCA Sch A1 para 50.
[17] MCA Sch A1 paras 42(2) and 51(2).
[18] MCA Sch A1 para 139.
[19] MCA Sch A1 para 141.

4.18   Most of the defining features of the representative are to be determined by regulations not yet published. The Draft Code of Practice envisages that the representative will be recommended as part of the assessment of P's best interests, and may (but will not necessarily) be appointed from among P's friends or carers. It expects that P will be able to choose who the best interests assessor should recommend for this role if he or she has capacity to do so, and otherwise the recommendation of any donee of an LPA or court-appointed deputy should be taken. The supervisory body would be obliged to invite the person recommended through this process to assume the role.[20]

4.19   If a standard authorization is refused, a notice of that refusal must be given to:

- the managing authority of the care home or hospital,
- P,
- any IMCA who has been consulted regarding best interests,
- every interested person consulted in the determination of best interests.[21]

In this case, a new standard authorization need not be sought by the managing authority unless there is a relevant change of circumstances in P's situation.[22]

4.20   If the standard authorization is granted, a copy must be given to each of these people, and also to P's representative.[23] Reviews of such authorizations may be requested by P, the representative, or the managing authority. The managing authority is obliged to request such a review if it appears to it that one or more of the qualifying requirements cease to be met.[24] The review process also provides the only significant way in which a standard authorization may be amended, short of application to the Court of Protection.[25]

2. Urgent Authorizations

4.21   How frequently these authorizations will be sought in advance of P being admitted or losing capacity in situations that deprive him or her of liberty remains to be seen. The 2007 amendments do also allow for an urgent authorization, providing a mechanism to make the deprivation liberty legal pending the determination of whether the qualifying requirements are met. An urgent authorization is made by the managing authority itself, when it is either required to make a request for a standard authorization, or to have already requested one. In addition, the managing authority

---

[20] Draft Code of Practice para 4.21.
[21] MCA Sch A1 para 58(2).
[22] MCA Sch A1 para 28.
[23] MCA Sch A1 para 57(2).
[24] MCA Sch A1 para 103; see further paras 4.35–4.77 below.
[25] MCA Sch A1 para 61. Amendment also occurs when the managing authority changes, so long as the place of detention does not change: see MCA Sch A1 paras 98–100. Thus if an NHS hospital becomes a foundation trust hospital, the foundation trust automatically becomes the managing authority for the purpose of the standard authorizations in force.

must believe that the need for P to be detained 'is so urgent that it is appropriate for the detention to begin before' the request is made or determined.[26] In this event, the managing authority issues the urgent authorization, essentially authorizing itself to detain P for a period of up to seven days. There is no administrative review of the urgent authorization, and any challenge to it must be made to the Court of Protection.

If a standard authorization is given while an urgent authorization is in force, the urgent authorization ceases to have effect when the standard authorization takes effect. If a standard authorization is refused while an urgent authorization is in force, the urgent authorization ceases to have effect when the managing authority receives notice of that refusal.[27] In this case, P and an IMCA, if one exists, must be given notice that the authorization is without further effect.   4.22

The managing authority must take all reasonable steps promptly to explain the effect of the urgent authorization to P, and to notify P of his or her right to challenge the authorization in the Court of Protection, and that explanation must be given orally and in writing.[28] An IMCA, if one exists, must also promptly receive a copy of the urgent authorization,[29] presumably with the expectation that he or she will challenge it in appropriate circumstances. The IMCA will exist, however, only if there is no non-professional carer to offer advice on P's best interests.[30] If there is such a non-professional carer, there will be no IMCA, but there is no requirement to provide that carer with a copy of the urgent authorization. It is not obvious why people with IMCAs receive at least some scrutiny of these detentions, where those without IMCAs receive none.   4.23

There may be only one urgent authorization for each admission, but the managing authority may request the supervisory body to extend that urgent authorization once, for a period of up to seven days.[31] Reasons for requesting this extension must be given, and P must be notified of the request. The extension may be granted only if: 4.24

- the managing authority has made a request for a standard authorization;
- there are 'exceptional reasons' why that request has not been decided; and
- it is 'essential for the existing detention to continue until the request is disposed of'.[32]

If the extension is granted, both P and the IMCA, if there is one, must be notified.   4.25

The reference to 'exceptional reasons' suggests that these extensions should not be granted as a matter of course. The risk is of course that the request has not been decided for systemic reasons, such as the relevant assessments being incomplete

---

[26] MCA Sch A1 paras 76(2) and (3).
[27] MCA Sch A1 para 89.
[28] MCA Sch A1 para 83.
[29] MCA Sch A1 para 82.
[30] MCA s 39A(1)(b).
[31] MCA Sch A1 paras 77 and 84.
[32] MCA Sch A1 para 84(4)

because of inadequate assessors, or an insufficient number of IMCAs. It is appropriate to have some concerns regarding conflicts of interest here: the body deciding on the extension will be the same body as is failing to provide the sufficient personnel. Judicial review of the extension would lie to the Court of Protection, and it remains to be seen how stringently the Court will view this provision.

C. DEPRIVATION OF LIBERTY

4.26 The 2007 amendments only take effect when an individual who lacks capacity is 'deprived of his liberty' within the meaning Article 5 of the ECHR. If instead the individual has capacity to do so, he or she can make his or her own decision regarding accommodation: in this case, as throughout this book, the MCA will have no application. Capacity in this context will be discussed further at paras 4.46 to 4.53 below. If P lacks capacity but is not deprived of liberty, the 2007 amendments will not apply, but the MCA as passed in 2005 and as described elsewhere in this book will apply. That legislation itself contains safeguards for hospital and care home admissions. If the admission is to a care home for more than eight weeks or hospital for more than 28 days, an IMCA must be provided for P if there is no prescribed consultee with whom to consult regarding P's best interests.[33]

4.27   Deprivation of liberty is thus a key threshold to the application of the 2007 amendments. The Draft Code of Practice provides an introduction to the concept.[34] Inevitably, whether the threshold is crossed will depend on the individual circumstances of P's situation. The following passage from the *HL* judgment itself provides a useful starting point:

[T]he Court considers the key factor in the present case to be that the health care professionals treating and managing the applicant exercised complete and effective control over his care and movements from the moment he presented acute behavioural problems on 22 July 1997 to the date he was compulsorily detained on 29 October 1997.[35]

There had been conflicting evidence as to whether Mr L had been kept on a locked ward. The view of the court was that this was not pivotal to the case. It was instead the intensity of the control over him that was relevant: 'the concrete situation was that the applicant was under continuous supervision and control and was not free to leave'.[36]

4.28   While clearly freedom to leave the accommodation will be relevant to determining whether there has been a deprivation of liberty, the issues of control identified by the ECtHR extended further, to whether others were allowed to visit him, and whether

---

[33] See MCA ss 38, 39, and 40.
[34] Draft Code of Practice Ch 2.
[35] *HL v UK*, see n 3 above, para 91.
[36] ibid.

such visits were controlled or supervised.[37] The conditions of accommodation will also, therefore, be relevant.

Throughout, it is clear that Mr L did not need to understand that he was being deprived of his liberty. The question was instead the intensity of the surveillance and control.   4.29

While it is not possible to provide a definitive list, it is possible to provide strong indicators as to when deprivations of liberty will be found to occur. Certainly, if P is precluded from leaving the accommodation on a systematic basis, a deprivation of liberty is likely to exist. That may be by way of distraction, dissuasion, locked doors, doors fitted with 'fumble locks' (doors requiring physical and mental agility to open), physical restraint, or other means. Similarly, if P would be returned to the accommodation by force or by what might be perceived as force (eg, sending the police after him or her), a deprivation of liberty is a serious possibility. The Draft Code of Practice notes that restricted permission to leave the institution would not necessarily constitute a deprivation of liberty.[38] It provides by way of example refusal to allow the individual to leave in the middle of the night, or requiring the individual to be escorted when leaving the accommodation. Certainly, these would be more marginal cases, but even these must be approached with care. If the insistence on an escort would have the effect of dissuading the individual from visiting particular friends, or if the escort was a staff member expected to 'keep an eye on things', a deprivation of liberty would be more likely than if the escort is primarily to provide assistance to a person with a mobility difficulty.   4.30

The Draft Code notes that deprivation of liberty does not flow simply from an individual's condition.[39] The deprivation occurs as a result of acts or decisions of others about that individual. That said, a wicked intention is not required on the part of the person depriving P of liberty. There was no suggestion of bad faith on the part of the hospital carers in the *HL* case, for example, nor any allegation even that their primary purpose was to restrain (rather than to treat) Mr L. Indeed, the conditions of the treatment may make a deprivation of liberty more likely. When sedating medication has the effect of removing an individual's ability to choose, for example, it may deprive the individual of liberty even if there are irreproachable medical arguments for the provision of the medication. This would of course be significantly more telling if one of the purposes of the medication was to restrict P's movements or ability or desire to choose.   4.31

It seems that the ability to maintain contact with the outside world is of particular significance in determining whether there is a deprivation of liberty. This was a significant factor in the *HL* case. The Draft Code refers to precluding or significantly restricting visits of family or friends, or not allowing P to use a telephone to   4.32

---

[37] *HL v UK*, see n 3 above, para 91.
[38] Draft Code of Practice para 2.6.
[39] ibid para 2.10.

maintain contact with family or friends.[40] This example raises the question of how the right to liberty under Article 5 interacts with other ECHR rights, in this case the right to family life provided by Article 8. The concern with access to family and friends suggests that the encroachment onto other ECHR rights by the carer reverberates into whether liberty has been deprived under Article 5. In that event, restrictions on privacy, another Article 8 right, might well be relevant to determining whether a deprivation of liberty has occurred. That view is consistent with the ECtHR's comments regarding the intensity of surveillance by the medical staff in the *HL* case.

4.33   Whether a deprivation of liberty exists must be decided on the basis of the totality of circumstances surrounding P's accommodation. While some factors, such as the ongoing refusal of staff to allow P to leave a locked room or ward, for example, would be sufficient alone to constitute a deprivation of liberty, in more marginal cases it might be a combination of factors that would constitute the deprivation.

4.34   In the event that P is deprived of liberty, formal authorization must be obtained either through a court order, or through Schedule A1. If the deprivation of liberty occurs in a hospital or care home, then it will normally be appropriate to use the latter route and apply for a standard authorization. The process for doing so was described at paras 4.12 to 4.20 above. The substantive matters that will be taken into account in that process—the 'qualifying requirements'—are discussed below. If necessary, and as discussed at paras 4.21 to 4.25 above, an urgent authorization may be required pending the completion of assessments required for the standard authorization. If the deprivation of liberty does not occur in a hospital or care home, an application to the Court of Protection will be required.

D. QUALIFYING REQUIREMENTS

1. General Comments and Introduction

4.35   As discussed at para 4.12 above, it is the duty of the managing authority to notify the supervisory body that P is (or is about to be) accommodated in its facility in conditions constituting a deprivation of liberty, when it is of the view that P meets the qualifying requirements. The managing authority must therefore do its own routine assessments as to whether individuals lack capacity, whether deprivations of liberty occur, and whether the qualifying requirements are met. For persons lacking capacity and deprived of liberty, if it is of the view that the qualifying requirements are not met, a request for a standard authorization is inappropriate, and Schedule A1 does not apply. How it should proceed in such cases will depend on the reason the qualifying requirements are not met. If, for example, P is detained under the MHA, continued detention will be justified by that Act, even though Schedule A1

---

[40] Draft Code of Practice para 2.15.

will not apply.[41] By comparison, if the conditions of accommodation were considered unsuitable, some other form or conditions of accommodation would need to be found such as would satisfy the best interests test.

Once the managing authority notifies the supervisory body, the primary responsibility to determine whether the qualifying requirements are met rests with the supervisory body. It is the supervisory body that will appoint the required assessors to determine whether the qualifying requirements are indeed met, and thus whether a standard authorization should be given. The managing authority is obliged to co-operate with these assessors, by providing copies of relevant documentation for example, but it is not required to administer the process of assessment.

4.36

There are six qualifying requirements for the purposes of Schedule A1. They will be discussed in some detail below, but a brief overview of them is provided in text box 4.1. If all qualifying requirements are met, the managing body is obliged to grant the standard authorization. Once any of the qualifying requirements is found not to be met, the remainder of the assessment process ceases and the standard authorization is refused.

4.37

Text Box 4.1: The Six Qualifying Requirements for Schedule A1

- **Age**: P must be over the age of eighteen.
- **Mental Health**: P must be affected by a disorder or disability of the mind.
- **Mental Capacity**: P must lack the capacity to decide whether he or she should be accommodated in the hospital or care home for the purpose of being given the relevant care or treatment.
- **Best Interests**: Admission to the care home or hospital on the terms proposed must be in the best interests of P, and must be necessary to prevent harm to him. The admission must be a proportionate response to the likelihood and severity of the harm P would suffer if not so admitted.
- **Eligibility**: This requirement determines the dividing line between Schedule A1 and the MHA 1983. In general terms—
  - If P is already covered by compulsory powers under the MHA 1983, the eligibility requirement will not be met if the proposed standard authorization overlaps or conflicts with those compulsory powers.
  - If P is to be admitted to hospital to be treated for mental disorder and objects either to the admission or to that treatment, the eligibility requirement is not met unless P's objection has been overruled by the valid decision of a deputy or donee of an LPA.
- **No Refusals**: This requirement will be met unless (1) P has made an advance decision refusing some or all of the medical treatment to be provided in the care home or hospital; or (2) if the admission is in conflict with a decision of a donee of an LPA or deputy acting within their authority.

---

[41] See 'eligibility requirement', paras 4.61–4.73 below.

4.38   It is required that the person assessing the mental health requirement cannot be the same person as assesses best interests.[42] The managing authority will be permitted to appoint the same assessor for other assessments. Beyond this, the training, selection, and eligibility of assessors is all subject to regulations as yet published only in draft form. These would require the mental health assessor to be a doctor with expertise in matters of mental disorder, satisfying the ECHR requirement that deprivation of liberty of a person of unsound mind must be based on an opinion by a qualified medical practitioner.[43] Best interests would be assessed by an 'approved mental health professional',[44] or appropriately qualified social worker, nurse, occupational therapist, or psychologist. Mental capacity could be assessed by anyone qualified to make either a mental health or a best interests assessment.

4.39   An assessment is not required if the matter in question has been assessed in the previous year, whether for purposes of a standard authorization or not, and if there is no reason for the managing authority to think that this existing assessment is no longer accurate. If it is a previously existing best interests assessment that is to be relied upon, the managing authority must take into account information from and views of any relevant IMCA, and P's representative.[45]

2. The Age Requirement

4.40   The age requirement will be met if P is over the age of eighteen years. Here, as elsewhere, the MCA does not preclude the use of other legislation such as the Children Act 1989 for persons under the age of eighteen.

4.41   The effect of para 24(2) is that a managing authority is obliged to request a standard authorization for P within 28 days of P's eighteenth birthday, if P will then fulfil the other qualifying requirements.

3. The Mental Health Requirement

4.42   The mental health requirement in Schedule A1 para 14 is to be decided by reference to the definition of mental disability in the MHA (as amended by the 2007 amendments), but specifically excluding from that definition the restrictions it contains relating to learning disability. The result requires that P's be affected by 'any disorder or disability of the mind'.[46] Notwithstanding different language, it is not obvious that this will vary much in practice from the diagnostic threshold in the MCA,

---

[42] MCA Sch 1 para 129(5).

[43] *Winterwerp v the Netherlands* (A/33) (1979–80) 2 EHRR 387, para 39.

[44] As defined by s 114(1) of the MHA 1983, as amended in 2007. This category includes appropriately trained social workers, community mental health nurses and similar professions, but does not include psychiatrists or other physicians.

[45] MCA Sch A1 para 49.

[46] MHA s 1(2), as amended in 2007.

which refers to an 'impairment of, or disturbance in functioning of, the mind or brain'.[47]

The MHA definition is however qualified by a requirement that 'dependence on alcohol or drugs is not considered to be a disorder or disability of the mind'.[48] While it is not clear whether incapacity caused by drunkenness or drug intake would be within the scope of the MCA,[49] incapacity caused by alcoholism or addiction would be. This would appear to be the main difference between the MCA and MHA definitions. It is therefore not permitted to use Schedule A1 to deprive P of liberty when P's condition is dependence on alcohol or drugs. That said, it should be noted that such dependence does not preclude the requirement being met if P also suffers from a different disorder or disability of mind. A person with Alzheimer's disease, for example, would meet the requirement even if he or she also had a drink problem. 4.43

There is no requirement concerning the severity of mental disorder that will satisfy the mental health requirement. Theoretically, for purposes of this criterion, it does not need to cause the mental incapacity (although that will be necessary for the mental capacity requirement, albeit based in the MCA diagnostic criterion). At this stage, any mental disorder will suffice. 4.44

The mental health assessor is further required to consider how (if at all) P's mental health will be affected by being deprived of liberty, and must notify the best interests assessor of his or her conclusions on this point.[50] The role of the assessor is thus not merely to decide whether P has a mental disorder, but also to look to any effects of the proposed admission on P's mental disorder. Given the overlap noted above between the mental health requirement and the diagnostic aspect of the mental capacity requirement, it may be that this question of effect of confinement becomes the important aspect of the mental health requirement. Here, the effect—presumably both positive and negative—of the admission on P's mental health must be considered directly. 4.45

4. The Mental Capacity Requirement

This requirement will be met if P lacks the capacity to decide 'whether or not he should be accommodated in the relevant hospital or care home for the purposes of being given the relevant care or treatment.'[51] 4.46

This is to be read in conjunction with the terms of the main Act regarding determination of mental capacity.[52] Thus the incapacity must be causally related to an impairment or disturbance of mind or brain, and undue reliance should not be 4.47

---

[47] MCA s 2(1).
[48] MHA s 1(3), as amended in 2007.
[49] See para 3.24 above.
[50] MCA Sch A1 para 36.
[51] MCA Sch A1 para 15.
[52] MCA ss 2, 3; see further paras 3.22–3.32 above.

made on unwarranted assumptions based on age, appearance, condition, or behaviour. An incapable individual must be unable to required to understand, retain, and weigh information to reach a decision, or be unable to communicate the decision.

4.48   Similarly, the principles in the MCA continue to apply to this assessment. In particular, the presumption of capacity continues to apply; all practicable steps must be taken to assist the person to reach a capable decision; and the fact that an individual makes an unwise choice does not necessarily bespeak incapacity.[53]

4.49   With that prelude, what must the individual be unable to understand in order to lack capacity? There is some academic literature, mainly from the United States, concerning capacity to consent to informal admissions to psychiatric hospitals that may be relevant.[54] Appelbaum and Bateman, writing in 1979, propose a threshold of understanding, based on the following criteria:

(1) Does the patient appreciate the nature of his condition?
   (a) Does he recognize that he has a mental illness?
   (b) Does he think that he requires treatment?
   (c) Does he know of a reasonable alternative to hospitalization?
(2) Does the patient understand the nature of hospitalization?
   (a) Does he understand the role of his doctor?
   (b) Does he understand the role of medication, if indicated?
   (c) Does he understand the nature of an inpatient setting, such as an understanding that there will be closed and open wards, and activities and programmes available?
(3) Is the patient able to comprehend the basis for the doctor's recommendations concerning admission?
(4) Is the patient able to make a decision to co-operate with his doctor's recommendations?
(5) Can the patient act affirmatively to protect himself in the hospital environment? For example, if the patient were experiencing adverse effects, would he know to approach a member of staff?
(6) Is the patient aware of rights as voluntary patient, including
   (a) right to file request for discharge;
   (b) right to refuse medication;
   (c) right to legal representation;
   (d) aware of existence of civil rights adviser in hospital.

---

[53] MCA s 1; see also paras 3.15–3.21 above.

[54] See, eg, American Psychiatric Association, 'Consent to voluntary hospitalization', task force report 34 (APA, 1992); P Appelbaum and A Bateman, 'Competency to Consent to Voluntary Psychiatric Hospitalisation: A Theoretical Approach' (1979) 7 Bulletin of the American Academy of Psychiatry and the Law 390; S Hoge, 'On Being "Too Crazy" to Sign into a Mental Hospital: The Issue of Consent to Psychiatric Hospitalization' (1994) 22 Bulletin of the American Academy of Psychiatry and the Law 431; and B Winick, 'Competency to Consent to Voluntary Hospitalization: A Therapeutic Jurisprudence Analysis of Zinermon v. Burch' (1991) 14 International Journal of Law and Psychiatry 169, esp at 182–191. For a discussion of this literature in an English context, see P Bartlett, 'The Test of Compulsion in Mental Health Law' (2003) 11 Medical Law Review 326.

(7) Is the patient aware of adverse consequences that might result from admission? This would include an awareness of potential of involuntary detention if he requests discharge.

This approach is based on an acknowledgement that even informal psychiatric admissions can have significant consequences, and therefore sets a relatively high threshold for capacity.

The tide of American academic opinion appears to have changed following the 4.50 case of *Zinermon v Burch*,[55] where one of the judges of the American Supreme Court held that informal admission of incapable people to psychiatric facilities might be contrary to the American Constitution.[56] Following this judgment, academic opinion shifted markedly to advocating a significantly lower threshold for capacity. By 1992, the American Psychiatric Association advocated that the patient need only understand that he or she is being admitted to a psychiatric hospital or ward for treatment; that release from the hospital may not be automatic; and that he or she can get help from the staff to initiate procedures for release.[57]

The nature of the understanding that will be required in the context of the MCA 4.51 is not straightforward. The requirement in MCA Sch 1 refers to understanding 'whether or not he should be accommodated in the relevant hospital or care home for the purposes of being given the relevant care or treatment.'[58] The assumption would seem to be that the admission itself (which is key to the question of deprivation of liberty) is so intimately bound up with the care or treatment to be given in the admission that they are one decision. It would seem from the wording of the schedule that an individual must be capable in all aspects of this decision in order to be capable overall. This would seem to suggest a relatively high standard of capacity. That would seem however to countermand the overall approach of the MCA, which is to keep the threshold of capacity low.

This tension will be magnified in a case where there is an array of options, each 4.52 with advantages and disadvantages. The individual may understand parts of what is proposed, and not understand other parts. It would seem counterintuitive that lack of capacity would flow from having a variety of options, but that is arguably the result, since the competent individual is required to understand the consequences of choosing one way rather than another.[59]

It remains to be seen how assessors and the English and Welsh courts will deal 4.53 with these issues.

---

[55] 494 US 113, 110 S Ct 975, 108 L Ed 2d 100 (1990).

[56] Blackmun J at 494 US 133–134.

[57] American Psychiatric Association, 'Consent to voluntary hospitalization', task force report 34 (APA, 1992). For authors in broad support, see eg B Appelbaum, P Appelbaum and T Grisso, 'Competence to Consent to Voluntary Psychiatric Hospitalization: A Test of a Standard Proposed by the APA' (1998) 49 Psychiatric Services 1193; S Hoge, n 54 above and B Winick, n 54 above.

[58] MCA Sch A1 para 15.

[59] MCA s 3(4).

5. The Best Interests Requirement

4.54　The substantive content of the best interests requirement is contained in MCA Sch A1 para 16:

> 16 (1)　The relevant person meets the best interests requirement if all of the following conditions are met.
>
> (2)　The first condition is that the relevant person is, or is to be, a detained resident.
>
> (3)　The second condition is that it is in the best interests of the relevant person for him to be a detained resident.
>
> (4)　The third condition is that, in order to prevent harm to the relevant person, it is necessary for him to be a detained resident.
>
> (5)　The fourth condition is that it is a proportionate response to—
> > (a)　the likelihood of the relevant person suffering harm, and
> > (b)　the seriousness of that harm,
> >
> > for him to be a detained resident.

4.55　　The first condition requires the best interests assessor to determine whether the circumstances of P's admission are such as to amount to a deprivation of liberty.[60] If they do not, then the best interests requirement is not met. As the objective of the 2007 amendments is to take account of the *Bournewood* decision, it makes sense at some point in the process to determine whether P is actually going to be deprived of liberty, and that is what this condition does. Nonetheless, the inclusion of this criterion in the best interests assessment is counterintuitive and very unfortunate. It suggests that if P is not deprived of liberty, it is not in his or her best interests to be accommodated in this way, as the best interest requirement in the schedule is not met. That may be extremely misleading. For purposes of the remainder of the MCA, it may well be in P's best interests to be so accommodated. What the result instead means is that *no authority under schedule A1 is required* to accommodate P in this way.

4.56　　If the best interests condition fails on this ground, the best interests assessment under Schedule A1 will cease and the standard authorization will be refused. Nonetheless, the person responsible under the general terms of the MCA for deciding where P should live should assess the situation using the best interests test in s 4. If under that test the accommodation proposed in the request for a standard authorization is in P's best interests, he or she should be so accommodated even though the standard authorization itself will have been be refused as unnecessary.

4.57　　The remainder of the requirement is more straightforward, reflecting the standards of the remainder of the MCA. 'Best interests' in para 16(3) refers directly to the best interests test in s 4, and para 16(4) and (5) closely resemble the restrictions on restraint contained in MCA ss 6(5), 11(6), and 20(13).[61] The discussion of best

---

[60]　See definition of 'detained resident': MCA Sch A1 para 6.
[61]　See paras 3.55–3.56 above.

interests elsewhere in this book will thus be of relevance to the interpretation of the best interests requirement.[62]

Schedule A1 does enhance the s 4 best interests test somewhat. To assure diversity of opinion, the best interests assessor cannot be the same person as the mental health assessor,[63] but the best interests assessor is required to have regard to conclusions reached by the mental health assessor as to the effects of the proposed arrangements on P's mental health.[64] The managing authority must give the best interests assessor access to any care plan or needs assessment relating to P, and the assessor consider those documents and consult with the managing authority.[65]   4.58

These provisions are additions to the requirements contained in s 4. It will thus be necessary for the best interests assessor to involve P as much as possible, to consider the likelihood of P's regaining capacity, to consider P's current and past wishes, feelings, beliefs and values, and consult carers, donees of LPAs, deputies, and anyone named by P.[66] The assessor will also be subject to the principles of the Act, and most significantly have regard to whether the desired purposes could be achieved in a manner less restrictive of P's rights and freedom of choice.[67]   4.59

If the best interests assessor concludes that the best interests requirement is satisfied, he or she must state the maximum period for which the standard authorization may apply. This can be up to one year, but is to be shorter if the assessor considers it appropriate.[68] The assessor may also recommend conditions that should attach to the authorization.[69] The supervisory body must 'have regard' to this recommendation in deciding whether to impose conditions in the standard authorization.[70] The supervisory body is thus not bound to incorporate the recommendation of the assessor.   4.60

6. The Eligibility Requirement

The substantial provisions of the eligibility requirement are contained in Schedule 1A of the MCA. The objective of the requirement is to delineate between the detention power of the MCA and the powers of compulsion under the MHA 1983 (including, as they come into effect, the amendments to that Act introduced by the MCA 2007).   4.61

The eligibility requirement is unique among the six requirements in that it binds the court in its making of declarations under the MCA, as well as supervisory bodies   4.62

---

62 See paras 3.33–3.52 above.
63 MCA Sch A1 para 129(5).
64 MCA Sch A1 para 39(3)(a).
65 MCA Sch A1 para 39.
66 MCA s 4; see further paras 3.33–3.52 above.
67 MCA s 1(6); see further paras 3.15–3.21 above.
68 MCA Sch A1 para 42.
69 MCA Sch A1 para 43.
70 MCA Sch A1 para 53(2).

in the granting of standard authorizations.[71] If P is 'ineligible' under Schedule 1A, therefore, he or she cannot be deprived of liberty by the MCA at all, and resort will have to be had to the MHA.

4.63   The approach of the eligibility requirement is twofold, and can be summarized in general terms as follows.

- If the matter at issue in the standard authorization is already covered by the MHA compulsory powers regarding P, the eligibility requirement will not be met and the standard authorization will be refused.
- For matters outside the realm of compulsion already applied to P under the MHA, the requirement will not be met if (i) P is to be admitted to hospital to be treated for mental disorder and (ii) P objects either to the admission or to that treatment, unless (iii) P's objection has been overruled by the valid decision of a deputy or donee of an LPA.

How this general approach is applied depends on the MHA legal regime applying to P.

4.64   If P is detained in hospital under a civil or criminal section of the MHA, the eligibility requirement is not met.[72] This applies to virtually all compulsory hospital admissions under the MHA, including admissions for assessment or for treatment,[73] remands to hospital during the criminal process,[74] hospital orders following criminal conviction,[75] and transfers of prisoners to psychiatric facilities.[76] The only obvious exceptions are the short-term removals to places of safety provided by MHA ss 135 and 136. 'Hospital' for the purposes of the section includes independent hospitals registered under Part II of the Care Standards Act 2000 as providing treatment for persons detained under the MHA.[77]

4.65   Under some circumstances, people subject to such orders may be liable to detention, but not actually detained in a hospital. People subject to such orders may be granted leave of absence from the hospital, for example, subject to such conditions as are deemed necessary.[78] In the case of criminal sections, people may be released from hospital in stages that include periods in hostels, half-way houses, or other facilities in the community. In these cases, the MHA section remains in effect, but the individual is not detained in a hospital. In these cases, the eligibility requirement will not be met if *either*:

- the standard authorization or court order would not be in accord with the conditions imposed under the MHA *or*

---

[71] MCA s 16A.
[72] MCA Sch 1A para 2.
[73] MHA ss 2, 3, and 4.
[74] MHA ss 35 and 36.
[75] MHA ss 37, 38, 44, and 45A.
[76] MHA ss 47, 48, and 51.
[77] MCA Sch 1A para 17(1); MHA s 34.
[78] MHA s 17.

- if the standard authorization or court order would involve the treatment for P for mental disorder in hospital.

The logic of the first point would be that it is undesirable to have conflicting legal authorizations. The logic of the latter is presumably that compulsion under the MHA is already involved in these cases, and the MHA should therefore continue to control hospital psychiatric treatment in these cases. This provision appears to refer to where the treatment occurs, not where P is to reside. Thus it would seem that outpatient treatment for mental disorder would result in the eligibility requirement not being met when that treatment was given to P at a hospital.

The 2007 amendments as they apply to the MHA provide that persons detained under that Act may upon their release be subject to community treatment orders.[79] When these amendments take effect, they will allow the imposition of a variety of conditions, including where the individual will live, what medical treatment they will be required to accept, and what conduct they may be precluded from engaging in. The eligibility requirement treats these the same way as it does people liable to detention but not in hospital, that is, any authorization or court order must be in accord with the community treatment order, and the authorization or court order must not involve treatment for mental disorder in hospital. | 4.66

If P is subject to guardianship under MHA s 7 or 37, different rules apply regarding eligibility requirement. Guardianship provides quite specific powers of the guardian over the person subject to guardianship: | 4.67

- the power to require the individual to reside at a specific place (but no power to detain or to force him or her to return there);
- the power to require the individual to attend at a particular place for the purposes of medical treatment, occupation, education, or training (but no power to consent to treatment on his or her behalf); and
- the power to require access to the individual to be given to medical practitioners, social workers, or other specified people.[80]

As with the other community-based regimes, any standard authorization or court order made under the MCA must not conflict with any requirement imposed through the guardianship. Thus if the guardian requires P to live at a specific place, a standard authorization proposing a different place of accommodation would not meet the eligibility requirement.

Unlike those other regimes, when P is subject to guardianship there is no blanket restriction on authorizations or court orders that involve hospital treatment for mental disorder. When admission to a hospital for purpose of such treatment is proposed, however, the eligibility requirement will not be met if: | 4.68

- P objects to the admission or objects to some or all of the treatment to be offered, unless

---

[79] MHA s 17A–17G.
[80] MHA s 8; see further paras 2.6–2.8, above.

- a donee of an LPA or a court-appointed deputy agrees to the admission or treatment to which P objects.[81]

In determining whether P objects, regard must be had to all circumstances that are readily ascertainable, and in particular P's behaviour, P's wishes and feeling, and P's views, beliefs, and values. Circumstances from the past are to be considered, but only so far as it is still appropriate to have regard to them.[82] There is no requirement that P be competent to object. Indeed, if P were so competent, he or she might well also be competent to make the decision as to admission, and the MCA and its schedules would not apply at all. No guidance is provided by the statute as to how strenuous P's objection must be to contravene eligibility. At least arguably, a relatively minor objection would suffice.

4.69   While P's objection can be overridden by the decision of the donee or deputy, it should be recalled that these individuals must decide with reference to the best interests test in s 4.[83] This test specifically requires the decision-maker to take into account P's past and present wishes, feelings, values, and beliefs. While these do not bind the decision-maker, they must be considered seriously.

4.70   The eligibility requirement also addresses the situation of people who are 'within the scope' of the MHA, but subject to no compulsory powers under that Act. For these people, the eligibility requirement will not be met if P objects to the admission or the treatment offered, unless that objection is overridden by the donee of an LPA or a deputy, as described in para 4.69 above.

4.71   P is within the scope of the MHA if he or she could be detained in hospital under s 2 or 3 of the MHA (admission for assessment and admission for treatment), if the relevant officials were minded to do so.[84] This creates a broad category[85] into which an individual will fall if:

- he or she suffers from a mental disorder as defined by the MHA;
- the disorder is such that it warrants his or her detention in hospital for assessment or treatment, as the case may be;
- it is necessary that he or she be so admitted in the interests of his or her own health or safety or for the protection of others;
- if the admission is for treatment (MHA s 3) rather than for assessment (MHA s 2), that appropriate treatment is available.

The effect of this rather flexible language is that most people with serious mental illness and similar conditions, including personality disorder, can be compulsorily

---

[81] MCA Sch 1A para 5(3)–(5).

[82] MCA Sch 1A para 5(6)–(7).

[83] See further paras 3.33–3.52 above.

[84] MCA Sch 1A para 12.

[85] For a detailed discussion of the admission criteria under the MHA, see P Bartlett and R Sandland, *Mental Health Law: Policy and Practice* (Oxford University Press, 2007, 3rd edn) esp Ch 4.

admitted under s 2 or 3, and will thus come within the scope of the MHA for purposes of Sch 1A.

The situation of people with learning disabilities is more complicated. They may   4.72
be admitted for assessment under MHA s 2 according to the criteria just noted, but such compulsion expires at the end of 28 days and is unrenewable. Where people with other forms of mental disorder may then be detained under s 3 if the conditions are met, section 3 does not apply to people with learning disabilities unless their disability 'is associated with abnormally aggressive or seriously irresponsible conduct on his part'.[86]

This leads to a potentially peculiar situation. Assume that P has a learning dis-   4.73
ability, and objects to a proposed admission to a psychiatric hospital. For the first 28 days, he or she can be detained under MHA s 2, and will therefore be ineligible under the MCA schedules. At the end of 28 days, s 2 is not available and, if P's disability is not associated with abnormally aggressive or seriously irresponsible conduct, s 3 is not available either. It would seem therefore that, at this point, the eligibility requirement is met, and P can be detained under the MCA provisions (assuming the other five requirements are met). If at some subsequent time further assessment is appropriate, P will again become ineligible and resort will have to be had once again to s 2, with this cycle potentially repeating itself.

7. The No Refusals Requirement

The no refusals requirement will be met except in two circumstances: 4.74

- when P has made a valid and applicable advance decision to refuse some or all of the treatment for which P is being admitted;
- when the admission would conflict with the decision of a donee of an LPA or a court-appointed deputy acting within their authority.[87]

The first of these does not say that P can make an advance refusal of care home or   4.75
hospital admission per se. The schedule instead refers back to the provisions of the body of the MCA relating to advance refusals, and those sections refer to refusals of treatment alone, not treatment and care.[88] As an example, assume P has made a valid and applicable decision to refuse chemotherapy for cancer. If it is proposed that he be admitted to a hospital ward for that treatment, the advance decision would become relevant, and the admission could not take place. Assuming the advance decision did not extend to palliative treatment, however, the individual could be admitted to a hospital or care home for that purpose.

There is no exception relating to treatments for mental disorder. The no refusals   4.76
requirement will ensure that an individual making a valid and applicable advance

---

[86] MHA s 1(2A).
[87] MCA Sch A1 paras 19–20.
[88] MCA, ss 24–26; see para 3.113 above.

decision to refuse such treatments cannot be admitted on the authority of Schedule A1 to a hospital or care home where they will be administered. In this, the no refusals requirement mirrors the effect of the eligibility requirement, discussed above. Like the eligibility requirement, however, this will often prove of minimal import, as P will often be able to be admitted using the compulsory powers of the MHA, where most treatments will be able to be given.

4.77   The second of these reinforces the fact that the terms of Schedule A1 do not oust the role of other decision-makers. If the donee of an LPA or deputy who has authority to determine where P will live objects to the proposed accommodation, the no refusals requirement is not met and the standard authorization must be refused.

E. SAFEGUARDS

4.78   As noted at the beginning of this chapter, the motivation for the 2007 amendments as they affect the MCA was to provide the safeguards required to prevent deprivation of liberty in violation of the ECHR. The qualifying requirements discussed above provide the government's substantive response to the breach of Article 5 found in *HL v UK*. We turn our attention now to some of the procedural mechanisms that the government has introduced to ensure compliance with the substantive provisions.

1. Right of Any Person to Request Assessments

4.79   As noted above,[89] it is the duty of all managing authorities to request a standard authorization from the relevant supervisory body whenever P is or is about to be accommodated in conditions that would constitute a deprivation of liberty. That request triggers the appointment of assessors to ensure that the qualifying requirements are met.

4.80   It is not merely managing authorities that can trigger the process, however. *Any* person can request the supervisory authority to determine whether there is an unauthorized deprivation of liberty. Prior to approaching the managing authority, the person must notify the managing authority that in his or her view there is an unauthorized deprivation of liberty in the facility, and ask the managing authority to request a standard authorization.[90]

4.81   If the managing authority does not request the standard authorization within a reasonable time, the individual may request the supervisory body to decide whether there is an unauthorized deprivation of liberty. To this end, the supervisory body must appoint an assessor, unless either (i) the supervisory body considers the request frivolous or vexatious; or (ii) the question of whether the deprivation of liberty exists

---

[89] See paras 4.05 and 4.12.
[90] MCA Sch A1 para 68.

has been determined in the past and there is no change of circumstances that would merit the question being reconsidered.[91]

The individual's request does not immediately trigger a full assessment of all six 4.82 qualifying requirements. Instead, the assessor's role at this stage is to determine whether there is an unauthorized deprivation of liberty. It is only if or when that assessor advises the supervisory body that there is such a deprivation, that the supervisory body must appoint the full range of assessors and the full assessment process is undertaken.[92]

The ability of anyone to trigger the process in Schedule A1 may prove to be 4.83 highly important. It means that there is some check to ensure that standard authorizations are requested in appropriate circumstances. The Draft Code of Practice anticipates that checking for unauthorized deprivations of liberty will become a routine part of care home and hospital inspections.[93] This is to be welcomed, as it would mean that an ongoing and systematic overview would be occurring as to whether there was compliance with the 2007 amendments.

2. IMCAs

An IMCA will be appointed for P when the managing authority requests a standard 4.84 authorization or when an urgent authorization is given regarding P, and where the managing authority is satisfied that there is no person appropriate to consult about P's best interests other than a professional carer.[94] Further, if P is without a representative, the supervisory body is required to appoint an IMCA to fulfil this role.[95] Finally, an IMCA will be appointed if P has only an unpaid representative, and where:

- either P or the representative request to instruct an advocate, or
- the supervisory body has reason to believe that where, without assistance, P and the representative (i) would be unable to exercise rights to apply to court or to request a review of the standard authorisation, or (ii) have failed to exercise or are unlikely to exercise those rights in circumstances when it would be reasonable to do so.[96]

All of these duties to appoint are subject to s 40(1), that no IMCA need be appointed where there is a donee of an LPA or court-appointed deputy authorized to make decisions regarding the admission, and no person nominated by P to be consulted on the matters relevant to the authorization. 4.85

---

[91] MCA Sch A1 para 69(3)–(5).
[92] MCA Sch A1 s 71(2).
[93] Draft Code of Practice Ch 8.
[94] MCA ss 39A and 39B.
[95] MCA s 39C.
[96] MCA s 39D.

The IMCAs have a variety of express rights to be kept informed about P, the specifics of which depend on which section of the MCA served as the base of the IMCA's appointment. An IMCA must be informed of the grant or refusal of a standard authorization,[97] and the grant of an urgent authorization.[98] He or she must be informed when a managing body fails to extend an urgent authorization, or when that authorization otherwise ceases to be in force.[99] Any comments provided by an IMCA must be taken into account by all assessors of the qualifying requirements, and an IMCA is to receive copies of all assessments related to the qualifying requirements from the supervisory body.[100] An IMCA will be informed if an enquiry is commenced as to whether a deprivation of liberty exists, when a best interests assessor considers that there has been a deprivation of liberty.[101] The IMCA will also be notified of the outcome of any review of a standard authorization, and of the suspension of a standard authorization during a period of ineligibility.[102]

4.86   The specific role of the IMCA will flow to a considerable degree from the circumstances of his or her appointment. The IMCA appointed under s 39A, whose role is to assist in the determination of best interests in the absence of any non-professional carer, will have quite a different role from an IMCA appointed under s 39D, who is appointed with the expectation that P and his or her representative R are unable adequately to protect P's rights. No doubt all IMCAs will endeavour to assist P to understand the issues surrounding his situation, but the s 39D IMCA's role is expressly more interventionist. That section requires the IMCA to assist P or R to apply to court or for a review of a standard authorization, if P or R wishes to exercise those rights, and has the right to make representations to the supervisory body and assessors in any resulting review process.[103]

4.87   If employed effectively, IMCAs may be of considerable assistance to P and his or her representative. At the same time, some scepticism is appropriate. It is at best doubtful that there has been sufficient funding to provide an appropriate IMCA service. There are further limits to how far this will serve as a safeguard. No doubt it will be of assistance to those for whom an IMCA is appointed, but to a considerable degree the expectation seems to be that those with friends do not need advocacy. But however well-intentioned friends may be, it is not obvious that they will have the specialist knowledge of the variety of options available to P that a competent IMCA should have. If a supervisory body comes to the view that P and his or her representative are unable to safeguard P's rights, an IMCA may be appointed; but it is not obvious how such situations will come to the attention of the supervisory body. Those without IMCAs may have considerably less protection.

---

[97] MCA Sch A1 paras 57(2) and 58(2).
[98] MCA Sch A1 para 82.
[99] MCA Sch A1 paras 86(1) and 90(3).
[100] MCA Sch A1 paras 132 and 135(2).
[101] MCA Sch A1 paras 69(8) and 136(3).
[102] MCA Sch A1 paras 120(1) and 95(3).
[103] MCA s 39D(8)–(9).

3. P's Representative

As discussed above,[104] a representative for P is appointed when a standard authoriza- 4.88
tion is made. Paragraph 140(1) of Schedule A1 states that this person will:

- maintain contact with P;
- represent P in matters relating to or connected with his or her deprivation of liberty; and
- support P in matters relating to or connected with his or her deprivation of liberty.

To that end, the representative receives a copy of the standard authorization, and
must be informed by the managing authority of its effect.[105] The representative may
request a review of a standard authorization, make submissions to assessors during
that review, must receive copies of any assessments made, and must be informed of
the outcome of the review.[106] The representative must be informed when a standard
authorization is placed in abeyance during a period of ineligibility, and when it
ceases to be so suspended.[107]

It is anticipated that in some cases the representative may be paid for his or her 4.89
services. In others it will be a lay person. If a lay person, he or she can request the
assistance of an IMCA.[108] In order for the representative to develop real options for
P, it may well be necessary to engage with and negotiate the social services system.
This is a remarkably complex and technical system, and a lay representative would
often be well-advised to seek the assistance of an IMCA in this regard.

4. Review of Standard Authorization

A review of a standard authorization may be requested by P, by P's representative, or 4.90
by the managing authority.[109] The review may be requested on the basis that P does
not meet one or more of the qualifying requirements, or that P does not meet a
qualifying requirement for the reason stated in the existing authorization, or that a
change in conditions of the authorization is appropriate.[110]

In response to such a request, the supervisory body is not automatically obliged 4.91
to re-assess all qualifying requirements. Instead, it must determine which, if any,
qualifying requirements 'appear to be reviewable',[111] and appoint assessors to review
those requirements. Such assessments are conducted much as they are for the initial

---

[104] Para 4.17.
[105] MCA Sch A1 para 57(1) and 59(5).
[106] MCA Sch A1 paras 102(5), 132, 135(2) and 120(1).
[107] MCA Sch A1 paras 93(5) and 95(3).
[108] MCA s 39D.
[109] MCA Sch A1 para 102.
[110] MCA Sch A1 paras 105–107.
[111] MCA Sch A1 para 109.

standard authorization. Minor alterations in the conditions of a standard authorization may be made without a full best interests re-assessment.[112]

5. Court of Protection

4.92 In the event of dispute, on this as on all matters relating to the MCA, recourse may be had to the Court of Protection as decision-maker of last resort. The Court has jurisdiction to rule on matters related to the 2007 amendments, and can therefore rule on matters of law and process in the application of the 'Bournewood' amendments.

4.93 The Court can alternatively make its own best interests determination regarding a person lacking capacity. In exercising this role, the court is bound by the eligibility requirement in Schedule 1A, but not by the other requirements of Schedule A1. In an unusual circumstance, where the application of the process in Schedule A1 leads to an apparently inappropriate result, an application to the Court may be appropriate, to make use of its greater flexibility in decision-making.

---

[112] MCA Sch A1 para 111(4).

5

ROUGH EDGES?

A. ENFORCEMENT

The overall approach of the Law Commission report and the MCA is facilitative. In   5.01
a legal world of perceived confusion, where decisions taken on behalf of people lacking capacity were of dubious legal validity, the intent was to introduce clarity and to
place decisions on a firm legal foundation. The reform process commenced in the
late 1980s, during a period of particular financial stringency. This may explain why
the Law Commission proposed little by way of specific enforcement mechanisms to
ensure compliance with its substantive proposals. Its proposals would have given the
re-formulated Court of Protection jurisdiction to oversee the administration of
the Act, but it was unclear what machinery would buttress the court in its role. The
objective of the new scheme was specifically to avoid legal formality, and the
Commission proposed no routine hearings to determine whether decisions were
being taken properly. Similarly, while deviation from the new law would be within
the jurisdiction of professional complaints procedures, there was no suggestion that
it would be at the core of the functioning of the relevant professional standards
bodies.

There was some increase in the administrative infrastructure between the Law   5.02
Commission proposals and the MCA as enacted. The Office of the Public Guardian
is included in the MCA. A considerable part of its role will be administrative: it is to
maintain registers of LPAs and court deputies, and receive any security required
by the courts of carers.[1] It also has a substantive role, however: it is to supervise

---

[1] MCA s 58(1)(a),(b),(e); SI 2007/1253, regs 33–37.

deputies; it can direct the Court of Protection Visitors to visit donees of LPAs, court-appointed deputies, and the individuals for whom they make decisions; it receives reports of donees of LPAs and deputies as required by the Court; it deals with representations, including complaints about the exercise of powers by donees of LPAs and deputies; and provides reports to court as the court requires.[2] If the Public Guardian is given sufficient staff and resources, the office may be important in ensuring legal compliance among deputies and donees of LPAs. That said, while they will have jurisdiction to make investigation at their own instigation, it is not obvious how they will know of apparent infringements of the MCA without being told: the protections they offer will depend on whistleblowers.

5.03   The Lord Chancellor's Visitors, under review at the time the Law Commission reported, are retained and re-named the Court of Protection Visitors.[3] They will serve as the investigative arm of the Office of the Public Guardian.[4] The so-called 'special' visitors will have professional expertise in cases of mental impairment, and will in the main be medically qualified. 'General' visitors need not have medical qualifications. Both the visitors and the Public Guardian may, as part of their investigations, consult and take copies of health records, social services records held by local authorities, and records held by those registered under Part 2 of the Care Standards Act. The visitors may also interview the subject of their investigations in private.

5.04   Independent advocacy is also to be provided under the MCA, through the Department of Health in England and National Assembly in Wales.[5] The role expressly envisaged by the Act for these advocates—IMCAs—involves safeguarding P in the event that serious medical treatment is to be provided to P, or long-term accommodation is to be provided by either the NHS or a local authority to P in a hospital, care home, or other local authority facility.[6] A local authority is further permitted, but not required, to appoint an IMCA when such accommodation is under review, or when it plans to institute adult protection proceedings.[7] Either way, the appointment would occur only if there is no non-professional person to advise on P's best interests. The role of the advocates is essentially to advise on best interests and to ensure the fullest possible involvement of P in the decision-making process.

5.05   IMCAs are unusual in the MCA, in that they provide, albeit in a limited range of cases, a routine procedural intervention in specific decisions that will be regulated by the general defence. That is significant because otherwise decisions taken under the general defence are invisible to the system: there is no obligation or process to report the decisions that are being taken under these mechanisms, rendering routine scrutiny impossible. Similarly, while the Court of Protection has jurisdiction to require

---

[2] MCA s 58(c),(d),(f),(g),(h); SI 2007/1253, regs 41, 44–48; Code of Practice paras 14.8–14.22.
[3] MCA s 61.
[4] See SI 2007/1253, reg 44.
[5] MCA s 35; SI 2006/2883, regs 3–4.
[6] See further paras 3.57–3.60 above.
[7] See para 3.59 above.

the holders of LPAs to provide reports or accounts,[8] it would seem that such a requirement will be the exception rather than the rule. Reports and accounts may be more routinely required of deputies, who may also be required to post security during their authority; these conditions will depend on the terms of their appointment by the Court of Protection.

Thus while the Public Guardian has the authority to investigate the exercise of   5.06
powers under the MCA, there is no suggestion that close monitoring of decisions taken under the general authority, under LPAs, or perhaps even by deputies will be closely scrutinized. This is likely to be an issue particularly for personal welfare decisions. Standard and relatively easy accounting practices make financial decision-making relatively easy to monitor. The same cannot be said for personal decision-making, where there is no reporting mechanism that corresponds to the 'balanced books' of financial accounting. Inevitably, personal decisions cannot be subject to the same level of systematic scrutiny. The enforcement of the standards of the MCA are likely therefore be somewhat haphazard in this area, relying on reports of people who see P. This is of particular concern for care decisions taken under the general defence, which need not be reported to any official. While professional caregivers are likely to receive at least rudimentary training on the terms of the MCA, non-professional caregivers under these sections will not necessarily receive any information about the scope of their authority, or the requirements of the MCA. No one will routinely receive any routine information about the scope, provision, or quality of care provided under this mechanism of the MCA. It is difficult to see in these circumstances how a system of enforcement of the MCA's requirements can operate effectively. Similar concerns apply to a somewhat lesser degree for care provided by donees of LPAs and court-appointed deputies, who will at least be identifiable by the Public Guardian and will receive some information as to the terms of the MCA.

Some of these decisions are serious. The MCA for example regulates the restraint   5.07
of people lacking capacity.[9] The resulting acts can be highly intrusive, allowing the use or threat of use of physical force against P and restricting P's movements. As another example, it is difficult to see that carers will not be tempted to allow their own convenience to weigh unduly heavily in the best interests determination, significantly undermining the intent of the MCA. With the best will in the world, it would be naïve to pretend that the administrative capacity in the MCA is sufficient to ensure anything approaching universal compliance with it.

In cases where a deprivation of liberty occurs within the meaning of Article 5 of   5.08
the ECHR, additional safeguards will be introduced once the 2007 amendments are implemented: see Chapter 4 above. As noted in that chapter, these provisions are triggered by the 'managing authority'—the person depriving P of liberty—notifying the supervisory body of P's situation. How effective the provisions will be, therefore,

---

[8] MCA s 23(3)(a).
[9] See further paras 3.55–3.56, 3.72, and 3.104 above.

depends on how careful and astute the managing authorities are in identifying when P is deprived of liberty, and whether systems are in place for inspectors routinely to identify persons lacking capacity deprived of liberty who have not been afforded the legal safeguards. Implementation of the 2007 amendments will in this sense be crucial.

B. MINORS

5.09   The MCA applies in general to people aged of sixteen or over.[10] There are several exceptions. Eighteen is the minimum age to execute an LPA,[11] to make a binding advance decision to refuse treatment,[12] and for the court to draft a will on P's behalf.[13] The courts may also deal with the property of minors lacking capacity if the court considers it likely that the minor will continue to lack capacity at the age of eighteen.[14] When the 2007 amendments regarding deprivation of liberty come into effect, they will apply only to people over the age of eighteen.[15] Finally, there is no lower age limit for the offence of ill-treatment or wilful neglect of a person lacking capacity,[16] although the statutory definition of capacity in s 2(1) applied to that offence means that the victim must be suffering from an impairment or disturbance of functioning of the mind or brain. Incapacity flowing solely from youth will not trigger the offence.

5.10   The result further complicates an already complex situation regarding children. For property, children are in general restricted from conveying until the age of eighteen. Their affairs are generally dealt with by the Official Guardian. For children who lack capacity as defined by the MCA, however, a new possibility has been introduced, not available to non-disabled children. If the child will remain incapable upon attainment of his or her majority, the court may deal with their property under the MCA. The law relating to contracts for necessaries applies to children in any event, so the fact that it applies for mentally incapable minors aged sixteen or older appears to add little.

5.11   In personal matters, including consent to medical treatment, there is already a range of overlapping jurisdictions and legal authorities. The presumption of capacity takes effect at age sixteen. Below that age, while not presumed competent, a child who is in fact competent can make a variety of personal decisions, including consent to treatment.[17] The attainment of age sixteen, however, does not extinguish the

---

[10] MCA s 2(5).
[11] MCA s 9(2)(c).
[12] MCA s 24(1).
[13] MCA s 18(2).
[14] MCA s 2(5)–(6) and 18(3).
[15] MCA Sch A1 para 13.
[16] MCA s 44.
[17] *Gillick v West Norfolk and Wisbech AHA* [1986] AC 112.

parental authority over the child, which remains until the age of eighteen. The parent can therefore consent to treatment on the child's behalf up to the age of eighteen. One might reasonably expect that this would be the usual course of events for minors lacking capacity. Similarly, the court's jurisdiction over the minors does not cease until the age of eighteen.[18] The criteria for the court making decisions on behalf of minors are much more flexible than those under the MCA. Under the court's jurisdiction over minors, the 'balance sheet' approach discussed at para 2.36 above is adopted. It is difficult to see that the MCA will be resorted to with any frequency in the context of personal care decisions. If the care providers and the parents of the child lacking capacity agree, the care can proceed on the basis of the parental consent. If they do not agree, an application to a court for directions is likely to prove necessary. Applications under the court's power over minors will generally prove more flexible, although in cases of urgency, the express power contained in the MCA to provide treatment necessary to sustain life or prevent a serious deterioration of P's condition pending the court's decision may make an MCA application appropriate. In any event, the flexibility of the system is increased by a power awarded by the MCA to the Lord Chancellor to transfer proceedings to courts with jurisdiction under the Children Act 1989 from the Court of Protection, and vice versa.[19] This might allow the more flexible provisions of the MCA relating to property and affairs to be dealt with by the Court of Protection, and personal matters by a court with jurisdiction under the Children Act 1989.

C. END OF LIFE DECISIONS

Experience from other jurisdictions would suggest that resort may frequently be had to the MCA regarding decisions at the end of life. The MCA contains a variety of provisions regarding such decisions, styled in the Act as relating to 'life-sustaining treatment'. While they are discussed elsewhere in this book, they form a particular enough category of decision to warrant consideration as a unit.   5.12

The provisions relating to life-sustaining treatment, as is the case for the remainder of the MCA, apply only if P lacks capacity to make the required decisions himself or herself. If that is not the case, then the individual may consent to or refuse treatment at his or her pleasure. The principles in s 1 of the MCA further provide that all practicable steps must be taken to help the individual to make the decision, and he or she is not to be considered incapable merely because he or she makes an unwise decision. In end of life decisions, as in other decisions, the policy of the   5.13

---

[18] Regarding the continuing rights of parents and courts over *Gillick*-competent minors, see *Re R (A Minor) (Wardship: Medical Treatment)* [1991] 4 All ER 177, 185; *Re W (A Minor) (Medical Treatment)* [1992] 3 WLR 758.

[19] MCA s 21; see also SI 2007/1899.

MCA is that individuals should be supported to make their own, competent, decisions.

5.14 The MCA expressly does not alter the law relating to homicide or assisted suicide.[20] The administration of medication with the object of bringing about the death of an individual, even if it is at that individual's instigation, remains a very serious crime.

5.15 'Life-sustaining treatment' is defined in s 4(10) of the MCA as 'treatment which in a view of a person providing health care for the person concerned is necessary to sustain life'. Notwithstanding its inclusion in s 4, the section defining best interests, this definition applies for purposes of the entire MCA.[21] The definition provides that the decision as to whether the special provisions of the MCA related to life-sustaining treatment apply will fall within the expertise of the health care provider. It does not say that for purposes of determination of best interests in cases of life-sustaining treatment there is any departure from the overall test contained in the section. The full range of procedural and substantive criteria contained in the statutory best interests test must be applied to reach the best interests determination. The views of the doctor as to what is in the best medical interests of P will be relevant; they will not be determinative. Certainly, the decision comes within the realm of 'serious medical treatment' in s 37, and therefore an IMCA will be required when nobody other than a professional carer is otherwise available to be consulted about P's best interests.

5.16 As discussed at paras 3.112 to 3.136 above, the MCA codifies the right of a competent individual to refuse medical treatment in advance, such refusal to take effect during subsequent incapacity. This situation is unique in the care provisions of the MCA in that if an advance decision is valid and applicable, there is no place for the statutory best interests test. That said, the mechanism only allows treatment to be refused. It does not allow a person to insist on the provision of treatment that medical advisers view not to be in the individual's best interests.[22]

5.17 If an individual is determined that they want their wishes regarding refusal of treatment respected in specific circumstances, he or she should execute an advance decision. This is the only way the decision will be binding in the future. Views can also be expressed, with views expressed in writing being particularly relevant, but such views will merely go into the mix of factors that will be relevant in a best interests determination; they will not be binding. Equally, persons making advance decisions to refuse life-sustaining treatment should exercise due care. Often, the decision will be taken when the individual is unaware of when and in what specific circumstances the incapacity may occur and the advance decision may be relied on. Advance decisions should only be made if P is sure that he or she wants to refuse the treatment in the situation defined in the advance decision, whatever other circumstances may be.

---

[20] MCA s 62.
[21] MCA s 64(1).
[22] *R (Burke) v General Medical Council* [2005] EWCA 1003.

When an advance decision concerns refusal of life-sustaining treatment, it must   5.18
be in writing and witnessed. The written advance decision must state expressly that
it is to apply to life-sustaining treatment in the event that P's life is at risk.[23] Any
alterations to such decisions also need to meet these requirements, although withdrawals of the decision can be oral.[24] An advance decision will further be enforced
only if it is 'valid' and 'applicable'.

These requirements concerning formalities are introduced by the MCA. Previously,   5.19
advance decisions to refuse life-sustaining treatment had no such formalities requirements. People who have made their wishes known in the past would be well-advised
to check and ensure that their decisions meet these requirements. Very limited transitional provisions have been put in place. Advance decisions to refuse life-sustaining
treatment that were made prior to 1 October 2007 will continue to be effective if
they are otherwise valid and applicable, if they are in writing, and if P has lacked
capacity since 1 October 2007. In this limited circumstance, they need not contain
the specific statement that they are to apply even if life is at risk, nor need they be
signed and witnessed.[25] The effect of this is that people with capacity on or after
1 October 2007 must make new advance decisions that comply with s 25.

Considerable care must be exercised in drafting these advance decisions. While   5.20
the courts have been clear for a number of years that, in the abstract, they are enforceable,[26] they have shown a marked reluctance actually to enforce them. Indeed, while
there are cases of capable people present in court having orders made either to protect their decisions to refuse life-sustaining treatment during subsequent incapacity[27] or to terminate life-sustaining treatment immediately,[28] there are no reported
cases of the courts in England actually upholding a written advance decision to
refuse life-sustaining treatment when the person lacked capacity at the time of the
court hearing. Instead, the courts in cases such as *HE v A Hospital NHS Trust, AE*[29]
have held that the onus of proof lies on an individual seeking to enforce an advance
decision to refuse treatment, and the proof of validity and applicability must be clear
and convincing.[30] Any doubt as to the validity and applicability of an advance decision to refuse life-sustaining treatment is, according to this case, to be resolved in
favour of life.[31]

Notwithstanding the recommendation of the Law Commission, the destruction   5.21
or concealment of an advance decision to refuse treatment is not made a specific

---

[23] MCA s 25(5).
[24] MCA s 24(4)–(5).
[25] SI 2007/1898, reg 5.
[26] This is the case since at least 1992. See *Re T (Adult: Refusal of Medical Treatment)* [1992] 3 WLR 782.
[27] *Re C (Adult: Refusal of Medical Treatment)* [1994] 1 All ER 819; *Re AK (Medical Treatment: Consent)* [2001] 1 FLR 129.
[28] *Re B (Consent to Treatment: Capacity)* [2002] EWHC 429.
[29] [2003] EWHC 1017.
[30] *HE*, ibid, paras 23–24.
[31] *HE*, ibid, para 46.

offence under the MCA. As discussed at paras 3.131 to 3.136 above, such destruction or concealment may nonetheless have legal consequences.

5.22 Unless there is a valid and applicable advance decision to refuse treatment, the decision whether to provide life-sustaining treatment is to be made in the 'best interests' of P. Section 4(5) of the MCA makes it clear that conduct is never in the best interests of an individual if it is 'motivated by a desire to bring about his death'. This is consistent with the Act's upholding of the prohibition of homicide and assisted suicide. Treatment that is otherwise medically justified will not necessarily be illegal, however, if an adverse effect of the treatment happens to shorten the individual's life. Moreover, while it may be the case that the failure to treat an individual may result in his or her death, it does not follow at common law that the treatment is necessarily in the best interests of the patient. In *Airedale NHS Trust v Bland*,[32] the leading case on the termination of life-sustaining treatment, the withdrawal of artificial feeding was permitted on the basis that the medical consensus was that its continuation would have no therapeutic benefit. *Bland* must now be read in the light of the statutory test of best interests, and some of its peripheral discussion is now open to question, but its basic principles do not appear to be disturbed by the MCA.

5.23 There are a variety of other safeguards that affect life-sustaining treatment. If the donee of an LPA is to have the power to refuse such treatment on P's behalf, the LPA must say so expressly.[33] There is no requirement in the MCA that a court application is required prior to the donee making such a decision. Certainly, if the donee is in any doubt as to P's best interests, the Court of Protection has jurisdiction to determine the matter on the donee's application. Consistent with jurisprudence before the MCA, the Code of Practice also suggests that such applications ought to be made when termination of life-sustaining treatment is proposed for a person in a permanent vegetative state.[34] While that may well be appropriate, it does not appear to be a formal legal requirement.

5.24 Court-appointed deputies are required to consent to life-sustaining treatment.[35] If life-sustaining treatment within the authority of a deputy is to be refused, it must be done by the court. It does not follow that the deputy has a right to demand life-sustaining treatment. If a doctor takes the view that further treatment is not in the best interests of P, the doctor cannot be required to provide it. The deputy is not permitted to change medical professionals to obtain this result, as the change of personnel responsible for P's health care is reserved to the court.[36]

5.25 The MCA envisages a number of situations where the court may be called on to make determinations regarding treatment, including life-sustaining treatment. Where there are disputes as to whether treatment may be given under the general defence, where there is doubt whether the donee of an LPA who refuses such

---

[32] (1993) 1 All ER 821.
[33] MCA s 11(8).
[34] Code of Practice para 8.18.
[35] MCA s 20(5).
[36] MCA s 20(2)(b).

treatment is acting in the best interests of P, or where there are questions as to the validity and applicability of an advance decision, the MCA provides that life-sustaining treatment may be given to P and any other act may be done to prevent a serious deterioration of P's condition, pending a court hearing into the merits of the matter.[37]

When a court application will clearly be required, as for example when the validity or applicability of an advance decision is contested and is likely to become relevant, the application should if at all possible be launched in sufficient time for a considered hearing to occur. The *HE* case provides an example of the difficulties when this does not occur. In that case, the patient was unconscious at all relevant times. She was or had been a Jehovah's Witness, and had signed an advance decision to refuse blood products. Since that time, she had become engaged to a Muslim man, and a condition of the marriage was that she re-converted to her original Muslim faith. She had been absent from Jehovah's Witness services for three months at the time of her hospital admission. During her hospital admission, there were differing views between her family members as to the veracity of her religious conversion, and the applicability of the advance decision. It did not arrive in court until eleven days later, on an urgent application with only the Muslim side of the family present. The treating physician's evidence was in writing only, faxed to the court. Given the urgency of the application, it is difficult to criticize the court's handling of the matter. At the same time, it is fair to wonder whether the Jehovah's Witness side of the family might have presented a different and relevant perspective on the facts. A more timely application would have permitted a more meaningful assessment of the evidence.

5.26

At common law, it was expected that a court application would be made prior to the termination of life-sustaining treatment of persons in a permanent vegetative state.[38] Under the MCA, there is no formal requirement for such applications. It is contained in the Code of Practice,[39] although this is of course guidance, without the force of formal law. Such a requirement has advantages and disadvantages in policy terms. It has the advantage of providing a procedural safeguard to protect against the cessation of life-sustaining treatment in error. In a society that values the sanctity of human life, that is important. At the same time, it makes it effectively impossible to refuse treatment in some circumstances. There will be cases when the judicial system simply cannot act quickly enough. The insistence that a court order is necessary if life-sustaining treatment is to be withheld would mean, for example, that Jehovah's Witnesses may well get blood transfusions immediately following automobile accidents when their lives are in imminent danger, even in situations where there is little, if any, doubt that they would refuse such transfusions. As cases such as the *HE* case show, the courts have in the past made every effort to deal expeditiously with

5.27

---

[37] MCA ss 6(7) and 26(5).
[38] See *Bland* [1993] AC 789. See also *Practice Note (Family Div: Incapacitated Adults)* [2002] 1 WLR 325.
[39] Code of Practice para 8.18.

cases in urgent situations; but the processes cannot be instantaneous. It is also fair to wonder how far these urgent decisions by the court lead to considered decision-making, and correspondingly how much benefit they actually bring to the calibre of decision-making.

5.28   Although court decisions are not formally required in these circumstances, the question arises as to when they ought to be sought. Certainly, if a health care provider or other decision-maker is in honest and legitimate doubt as to the proper legal course to follow, then the courts' views should be sought. If there is no reasonable doubt, the situation is less clear cut. May a treatment provider seek a court declaration not because of a sincere doubt over the validity and applicability of an advance directive, but instead in order to access the provisions of s 26(5) allowing life-sustaining treatment pending the court decision? How expeditiously is the provider required to press for a speedy decision by the court? The use of s 26(5) (or s 6(7), for treatment provided under the general defence) might well be considered ethically dubious in these circumstances. It may also be of dubious legality. Section 26(2) states that a treatment provider does not incur liability unless 'satisfied' that a valid and applicable advance decision exists. If the provider is satisfied that such an advance decision exists without the court order, liability might theoretically attach if the treatment were given.

5.29   Some doctors may have personal ethical beliefs that oppose the withdrawal or failure to provide life-sustaining treatment to patients, even in situations where patients refuse such treatment. The approach of the Code of Practice is that patients should be transferred to the care of other treatment providers if the requirements of the MCA would otherwise draw a practitioner into a practice that he or she views as morally objectionable.[40] This is no doubt appropriate whenever possible, and all reasonable efforts should be made to ensure such transfers occur in a timely fashion. There may be circumstances however (for example when only one doctor is on call) when it is not possible. When this occurs, the provisions of the MCA must nonetheless be followed. A valid and applicable advance decision to refuse life-sustaining treatment has the same legal status as if a competent patient were refusing the treatment in question. It must be honoured, even if that is morally repugnant to the practitioner. While every effort should be made to avoid that situation, the statement in the Code of Practice that health care professionals 'do not have to do something that goes against their beliefs'[41] must be qualified in this situation.

D. THE HUMAN RIGHTS ACT

5.30 The Law Commission report was completed in early 1995, before the passage of the Human Rights Act 1998 and indeed before it became Labour Party policy to

---

[40] Code of Practice paras 9.61–9.63.
[41] ibid para 9.61.

incorporate the ECHR directly into English jurisprudence. While the Law Commission was of course well aware of the ECHR, its direct applicability in domestic law has introduced a new level of immediacy to its substantive and procedural guarantees unforeseen by the Law Commission. This is complicated by the fact that ECHR jurisprudence has not remained static. The first case calling on the ECtHR to interpret the scope of Article 5 relating to persons of unsound mind was not determined until late 1979,[42] almost forty years after the ratification of the ECHR itself. A trickle of cases in the early years has grown considerably in volume more recently, and the sophistication of the ECtHR's jurisprudence has similarly increased markedly. Many of the relevant cases have been framed in a mental health context rather than one of mental incapacity, and implicitly assume a level of comprehension and will on the part of complainants. The ECtHR is still coming to terms with the nuances of the situation when such conditions may not be present. The jurisprudence is thus very much in a process of development.

The ECHR jurisprudence has a different ethos from the MCA. The MCA is   5.31
designed to create a supportive framework in which decisions are taken for the benefit of people lacking capacity. Procedure is to be kept to a minimum, and criteria are intended to be flexible enough to meet a wide variety of needs. The statutory best interests test at the core of the MCA is a particularly clear example of this. It is not restrictive, but rather requires an inclusive approach to decision-making. Matters that must be considered are drawn broadly—the 'beliefs and values' P would have had if competent, for example. Indeed, under s 4(2), anything considered by the decision-maker to be relevant is incorporated into the best interests test. The ECHR by comparison is designed to protect the individual against human rights violations. It therefore tends to favour procedural safeguards and clear criteria. Obvious examples of this approach include Article 5, where the deprivation of liberty must be subject to challenge in a court or court-like process, and Article 6, which requires tribunal or similar hearings to be available when civil rights are violated. In the event of conflict, it is difficult to see how these divergent approaches can be integrated.

A number of ECHR rights may be relevant to the subject matter already dis-   5.32
cussed in this book, including the right to life (Article 2), the right to be free of inhuman or degrading treatment (Article 3), the right to liberty (Article 5), the rights to legal process established by Article 6, the right to respect for private and family life (Article 8), the right to freedom of conscience or religion (Article 9), the right to peaceful enjoyment of possessions (protocol 1, Article 1), and the prohibition of discrimination (Article 14) are obvious examples. The ECtHR has made it clear that particular vigilance is to be exercised to ensure that the rights of vulnerable people, such as those lacking capacity or in institutions, are not violated. [43]

Not all decisions made on behalf of a person lacking capacity will trigger the   5.33
Human Rights Act. The articles of the ECHR have severity thresholds, and unless

---

[42] *Winterwerp v The Netherlands* (A/33) (1979–80) 2 EHRR 387.
[43] *Herczegfalvy v Austria* (1992) 50 EHRR 437 at para 82.

those thresholds are met there is no violation. Questions surrounding the threshold for the deprivation of liberty were discussed at paras 4.26 to 4.34 above, for example. There is further ECHR jurisprudence to the effect that medically approved treatment of an individual lacking capacity will not reach the threshold of severity to trigger Article 3,[44] although there was no advance decision at issue in that case. Further, the terms of some articles of the ECHR restrict the application of rights when such restrictions are in accordance with law and necessary in a democratic society for, among other things, the protection of health or morals, public safety, or protection of rights and freedoms of others.[45] This is not the place for a detailed discussion of the ECHR and incapacity—that is covered in other works[46]—but some indication of the potential problems is appropriate.

5.34   Potential human rights issues arise from a variety of situations discussed elsewhere in this book. The 2007 amendments (discussed in Chapter 4), designed to address issues relating to deprivation of liberty of persons lacking capacity, are one example of many. As discussed at paras 3.32, 3.60, 3.77, 3.104 above, it is possible for an individual to lose his or her rights even though it later transpires that he or she did not actually lack capacity, if the decision-maker has a reasonable belief in his or her incapacity. Particularly if the individual actually has capacity, civil rights issues may arise. Obvious examples include the right to control one's own money, as the MCA allows for P's money to be pledged or otherwise used in payment for services P did not request; and the loss of one's bodily integrity, through the loss of the right to consent to medical treatment. The provision of life-sustaining treatment may raise issues under Article 2 or 8 or, if a factor in the decision is a religious belief, Article 9. The balance between state care and family care may generate issues under Article 8. The court's approach to advance decisions to refuse treatment, where cases often concern religious objections to treatment, may raise issues under Article 9. This is only a taster. No doubt experience of the MCA and its administration will raise a wide variety of unforeseen issues.

5.35   If the substantive and procedural provisions of the MCA are routinely followed, some of these difficulties will be minimized. Those provisions require P to be involved as much as possible in decisions concerning him or her, for example, suggesting broad congruence with the values implicit in human rights law. The use of IMCAs may also prove significant here. Nonetheless, the question of compliance returns us to the question of whether the enforcement provisions of the MCA are adequate: see paras 5.01 to 5.08 above. This may itself raise a question under the Human Rights Act, with reference to Article 1, which requires the state to ensure that individual rights are respected within the state.

---

[44] *Herczegfalvy v Austria* (1992) 50 EHRR 437 at para 82.

[45] See ECHR Art 8; similar but not identical provisions are contained in Arts 9, 10, and 11.

[46] See, eg, P Bartlett, O Lewis and O Thorold, *Mental Disability and the European Convention on Human Rights* (Brill/Martinus Nijhoff, 2006).

It is easy to spot potential tensions; more difficult is to determine how they should 5.36
be resolved. The process-based jurisprudence of the ECtHR works most convinc-
ingly when the rights subject is a competent individual, able to defend his or her
rights. This is precisely what cannot be assumed in matters related to the MCA. It is
not obvious how it helps L in the *Bournewood* case to provide the right to a hearing.
According to the facts of that case, he was unable to express a view as to whether or
not he consented to the admission; it is difficult to see how he would have been able
to take advantage of his new right to a hearing. Allowing that right instead to be
exercised by a family member or other carer does little to solve the problem convinc-
ingly. A perusal of a number of the common law cases regarding the right to make
personal decisions for P suggests that this right is relevant when there is a row
between family carers and social services or medical practitioners.[47] It may well be
appropriate to provide a forum for those disputes, but at times in these cases, the
rights of P seem to be lost in the cross-fire. Further, it is not obvious that P's rights
are protected unless the other parties are prepared to litigate. It is difficult to see that
P's rights are reliably protected through this mechanism. The Court of Appeal in
R(MH) v Secretary of State for Health,[48] held that for one of the civil confinement
provisions of the Mental Health Act, tribunal hearings should routinely be provided
to those lacking the capacity to apply for one. The decision was overruled by the
House of Lords,[49] but it is unclear how successful the approach would have been in
any event. The tribunal and the doctor will be present, but who would represent the
patient, and on what terms? It cannot be assumed that these patients will be able to
instruct counsel, and while a lawyer might be appointed as *amicus*, it is not obvious
how such individuals would understand their role in the proceedings.

Neither the English courts nor the ECtHR have as yet proceeded very far in 5.37
coming to terms with the complexity of these situations. The overarching question
is what these rights mean when an individual lacks capacity to make a decision, and
perhaps when they lack capacity or ability to press for their rights. Unlike most other
European countries, the United Kingdom has a significant number of barristers and
solicitors who devote a considerable part of their practice to work relating to mental
disorder. There are academic journals devoted to law and mental disorder based in
this country,[50] and a good collection of academics working in the field. The MCA
is also an intelligent and reasonably sophisticated statute. There is the potential for
this country to play an important part in articulating how, at the beginning of the
twenty-first century, the rights contained in the ECHR can be made real for individuals lacking capacity.

---

[47] See, eg, *Bournewood* 1 AC 479F, per Lord Goff; *Re S (Adult Patient) (Inherent Jurisdiction: Family Life)*
[2002] EWHC 2278 (Fam); [2003] 1 FLR 292, paras 66, 74, 77(7); *Newham London Borough Council v S and
another (Adult: court's jurisdiction)* [2003] EWHC 1909 (Fam); [2003] All ER (D) 550 para 26(iii), 53.

[48] [2004] EWCA Civ 1609.

[49] [2005] UKHL 60.

[50] In addition to generalist journals devoted to medical law, see Journal of Forensic Psychiatry and
Psychology and Journal of Mental Health Law.

E. INTERFACE WITH THE MENTAL HEALTH ACT

1. Introduction and Treatment under Part 4

5.38 Mental disorder and mental incapacity are different concepts, and the presumption of capacity continues to apply for individuals with mental health problems.[51] Nonetheless, a significant number of individuals with mental health difficulties will also lack capacity for personal welfare and health care decisions, raising questions as to the interface with between the MCA and the MHA 1983.

5.39 The 2007 amendments, due to be proclaimed in force in April 2009, are relevant to the interrelations between the MCA and MHA on three matters:

- the use of electro-convulsive therapy (ECT);
- people subject to community treatment orders under the MHA;
- the respective roles of the MHA and MCA when deprivation of liberty is proposed (the 'eligibility' requirements).

These will be discussed in the final section of this chapter. Until that point, the law is taken to be as contained in the MCA as passed in 2005. While the 2007 amendments are certainly relevant, they also apply to fairly specific situations. The more general discussion of the inter-relations between the MHA and MCA, discussed below, will thus largely continue to be applicable.

5.40 The starting point for the analysis is s 28(1) of the MCA:

Nothing in this Act authorises anyone—

(a) to give a patient medical treatment for mental disorder, or
(b) to consent to a patient's being given medical treatment for mental disorder,

if, at the time when it is proposed to treat the patient, his treatment is regulated by Part 4 of the Mental Health Act.

Part 4 of the Mental Health Act regulates treatment in several ways. First, and most straightforwardly, s 57 prohibits some treatments without the competent and informed consent of the patient as well as a second opinion from an independent doctor registered for the purpose by the Secretary of State for Health. This applies to all patients, whether or not they are sectioned.[52] Currently, the treatments in question are psychosurgery and the surgical implantation of hormones to reduce male sex drive.[53] Of these, only the former is of practical relevance, as male sex drive is now controlled through the use of a hormone analogue rather than an actual hormone, ingested orally rather

---

[51] *Re C (Adult: Refusal of Medical Treatment), Re* [1994] 1 All ER 819 at 824; *Masterman-Lister v Brutton and Co, Jewell and Home Counties Dairies* [2002] EWCA Civ 1889.

[52] MHA s 56. In theory, patients need not be hospitalized either, although it is difficult to see that psychosurgery would occur outside a hospital setting in any event.

[53] MHA s 57(1) and Mental Health (Hospital, Guardianship and Consent to Treatment) Regulations 1983, SI 1983/893, reg 16.

than surgically.[54] Certainly, s 28(1) of the MCA ensures that these safeguards may not be circumvented for persons lacking capacity. Such treatments cannot be given to an individuals lacking capacity to consent to them.

The definition of capacity used for the Mental Health Act is contained in its 5.41 Code of Practice.[55] It is based on the common law of capacity, which lacks some of the nuances of ss 2 and 3 of the MCA. The Mental Health Act Code includes an inability to believe information related to treatment as an indicator of incapacity, a provision not express in the MCA. The MCA by comparison includes a number of factors absent from the Mental Health Act Code:

- incapacity cannot be established merely by age, appearance, or unjustified assumption regarding personal behaviour;[56]
- while P will lack capacity if he or she is unable to retain the information necessary to make a decision, such retention need only be for a short period for an individual to have capacity;[57]
- in determining capacity the information that must be understood relevant to a decision includes the reasonably foreseeable consequences of deciding one way or another, or of failing to make a decision.[58]

While these are not express in the criteria in the Mental Health Act Code, nor are they in opposition to those criteria. It may well be that practitioners read the Mental Health Act Code in light of the MCA criteria, as a categorical clash could prove problematic and unduly confusing with no obvious advantage. The MCA does limit its application to those aged sixteen or over, however. There is no age restriction in the Mental Health Act.

Part 4 also restricts treatment that can be given to involuntarily detained ('sec- 5.42 tioned') patients. For electro-convulsive therapy and when any treatment for mental disorder continues beyond three months from the first day the patient was given treatment for mental disorder during this detention, either informed consent must be obtained or an opinion received from an approved independent doctor.[59] Once again, s 28(1) of the MCA makes it clear that this safeguard cannot be circumvented for patients lacking capacity, if those patients are sectioned.

Under the MHA, a sectioned patient may be given other treatments for mental 5.43 disorder for up to three months without consent or the need for a second opinion.[60] As this treatment is authorized within Part 4, it comes within the purview of s 28 of the MCA. Certainly, treatment under the Mental Health Act must be in the best

---

[54] Such analogues ingested orally are outside the scope of the section: see *R v MHAC, ex p X* (1988) 9 BMLR 77.
[55] MHA Code of Practice (1999) para 15.10.
[56] MCA s 2(3).
[57] MCA s 3(3).
[58] MCA s 3(4).
[59] MHA s 58(1) and SI 1983/893, reg 16.
[60] This is the combined effect of MHA ss 58(1) and 63.

interests of the patient,[61] but the Code reflects the common law approach rather than the statutory framework of the MCA. It is thus considerably more objective than the MCA definition, lacking express reference to the views and values of P and the consultation requirements of the MCA. It does require information about the treatment to be given to the patient,[62] though this information could not be withheld from a patient able to engage with it under the MCA. The Code's guidance on treatment of people lacking capacity offers few formal safeguards, apart from the reminder that sterilization procedures require court approval.[63] Section 28 therefore removes the protections of the MCA for this group of patients, where the Mental Health Act provides few safeguards by way of compensation.

5.44   Once the three months have passed, however, the MHA processes for confined patients do have some advantages over the MCA. The treatment of these patients has to be formally reviewed at this point, with an independent second opinion offered. The doctor offering that opinion must consult with two other professionals who have been involved with the patient's care, one of whom must be a nurse, and the other not a medical practitioner (generally a social worker).[64] This may offer an objective, professional review of treatment considerably more robust than anything routinely on offer under the MCA.

5.45   Section 28 of the MCA applies only to medical treatments for mental disorder regulated by Part 4 of the Mental Health Act. It therefore does not apply to civil confinement or Mental Health Act guardianship, which are governed by Part 2 of that Act, or to informal admissions, which are governed by s 131 in Part 10. It further extends neither to treatment other than for mental disorder[65] for anyone under the jurisdiction of the Mental Health Act, nor to any medical treatment of informal patients, be it for mental disorder or not. In these contexts, the MCA provisions will apply.

2. Informal Patients

5.46   'Informal' patients are those inpatients not civilly confined. At common law, the guardian of a child could admit the child as an informal patient to the psychiatric facility.[66] Similar powers over persons aged sixteen or over are within the remit of those with decision-making authority over where P would live under the MCA, subject to the usual rules regarding best interests and the following restrictions.

---

[61] MHA Code of Practice para 15.21. The Code was last revised in 1999, and therefore does not reflect developments in the common law since that time: see paras 2.35–2.42 above.

[62] ibid para 14.5(a).

[63] ibid paras 15.22–15.24.

[64] MHA s 58(4).

[65] As defined, rather broadly, in MHA s 145. For a summary of relevant jurisprudence regarding this section, see Bartlett and Sandland, *Mental Health Law: Policy and Practice* (Oxford University Press, 2007, 3rd edn) 297–309.

[66] *R v Hallstrom (No 2)* [1986] 2 All ER 306, 312.

Informal admissions to hospitals and care homes under the jurisdiction of the NHS are subject to special provisions contained in s 38 of the MCA. When such hospital admission is expected to be for a period exceeding 28 days, or care home admission for a period exceeding eight weeks, the provider is required to seek the advice of an independent advocate unless there is a donee of an LPA or EPA, an individual named by P to be consulted in matters affecting his interests, or a court-appointed deputy: see para 3.58 above. Insofar as informal admission was resisted by P, required force or the threat of force to effect, or restricted P's liberty of movement, it would constitute restraint and would therefore be subject to the specific provisions discussed at paras 3.55 to 3.56, 3.76, and 3.104 above. Indeed, if the admission constituted a violation of P's right to liberty under Article 5 of the ECHR (see paras 4.26 to 4.34 above) it could only be effected under the MCA by court order, pending the passage of the 2007 amendments: see Chapter 4. In practice, and until the 2007 amendments come into effect, where the sole problematic issue is hospital admission, it will normally be more expeditious and less expensive to invoke the civil confinement sections of the Mental Health Act rather than to resort to the courts under the MCA.

Once admitted to hospital, informal patients are subject to the common law as regards treatment for their mental and other disorders. Informal patients lacking capacity are therefore to be treated under the MCA in much the same way as if they were outside the psychiatric facility. Advance decisions to refuse treatment apply, and donees of LPAs and court-appointed deputies whose authority includes the making treatment decisions have authority to make decisions related to treatment either for mental disorder or other disorder. Otherwise, treatment for mental or other disorder can be provided under the general defence unless it is governed by Part 4, as discussed above. If the treatment proposed is 'serious', the provisions regarding IMCAs will be relevant.[67] In the event that a decision-maker is apparently not exercising his or her authority in the best interests of P, the usual remedies of contacting the Public Guardian or, if the decision-maker is acting in a professional capacity, raising the matter with his or her employer or professional organization remain available here. 5.47

If P remains on informal status, the procedural protections related to electro-convulsive therapy and treatment beyond three months will not apply, as the relevant section of that Act refers only to confined patients. These treatments will therefore not to be regulated by Part 4 of the Mental Health Act, and in law, it would appear that ECT can therefore be given to an informal patient lacking capacity in his or her best interests, provided that the procedures in the MCA are followed. Some people will view this with concern, particularly if the decision is made by a doctor relying on the general defence, rather than a donee of an LPA or deputy specifically appointed to make medical decisions on behalf of P based on his or her knowledge of P. If a doctor has reservations about proceeding in these circumstances, it may well be appropriate to seek the advice of an independent colleague, or to call 5.48

---

[67] See paras 3.57–3.58 above.

in the services of a Court of Protection Special Visitor or an independent advocate. Indeed, this sort of treatment may well be included in the regulation defining 'serious' treatment in s 37. This would trigger the involvement of an advocate as a matter of routine, where there is no LPA, EPA, or court-appointed deputy. Unless that occurs, while the doctor has the option of seeking the advice of others, it will not be possible for others concerned about P to require it. They could instead notify the Public Guardian of concerns that P's best interests were not being met or apply to the Court of Protection. Either of these would however require factual circumstances calling into question whether P's best interests were being served; the mere provision of an unpopular treatment would not suffice.

5.49   As noted above, patients who are civilly confined may be treated without their consent and, as this treatment is governed by Part IV of the MHA, the MCA has no application. Such confinement is sometimes resorted to as a way of circumventing a refusal by individuals with capacity to consent to treatment for their mental disorder. Nothing in the MCA precludes the use of the MHA in this way, to circumvent the refusal of a substitute decision-maker or an advance decision to refuse a proposed treatment. That presupposes, of course, that the legal conditions for civil confinement have been met: see further paras 5.52 to 5.53 below. The approach will also only be effective for treatments for mental disorder, as these are the only treatments for which the requirement of consent is waived under the Mental Health Act. While the definition of medical treatment is broad in this context, including 'nursing, . . . care, habilitation, and rehabilitation under medical supervision',[68] it is not universal. Advance decisions regarding treatments for non-mental disorders cannot be overruled.

5.50   How far the confinement and resulting treatment powers can overrule the views of the patient when competent is something of an open question in any event. It does seem now that the refusal of proposed treatment by a competent patient must be taken into consideration as one of the factors in deciding whether compulsory treatment will be given under the Mental Health Act, but it is only one factor. It does not determine whether treatment will be enforced.[69] An advance decision to refuse medical treatment, if valid and applicable, has the same status as if the decision had been made by P when competent at the time consent was called for.[70] It should therefore have the same impact on the decision to treat involuntarily as the refusal of a competent patient. Broader views would similarly appear to feed into the mix, although none would be able definitively to determine the outcome of the decision to treat involuntarily under the MHA.

---

[68] MHA s 145.
[69] R (PS) v G (RMO) and W (SOAD) [2003] EWHC 2335, para 119.
[70] MCA s 26(1).

3. Civil Confinement

There is nothing in the MCA to preclude the application of the confinement provi-   5.51
sions contained in Part 2 of the Mental Health Act. The Mental Health Act is subject to substantive thresholds and procedural requirements of its own,[71] suggesting
different advantages and disadvantages of people lacking capacity, their doctors and
their other carers relying upon it.

The substantive legal criteria are contained in s 2 (admission for assessment,   5.52
allowing confinement for 28 days, non-renewable) and s 3 (admission for treatment,
allowing admission for six months, renewable) of the Mental Health Act. This is not
the place to examine them in detail. In essence, each requires the individual to be
suffering from mental disorder of a 'nature or degree' that makes it appropriate for
him or her to be admitted for assessment or treatment, as the case may be. Such
admission must also be necessary for the health or safety of the person, or the protection of others. For s 3 admissions, if the individual is suffering from 'psychopathy'
or 'mental impairment', both defined terms, a treatment must exist to alleviate or
prevent a deterioration of the individual's condition; once the 2007 amendments
take effect, 'appropriate' treatment will instead need to be available under s 3, whatever the patient's diagnosis. These 'nature or degree' criteria are not particularly
strong—admission in the interests of the patient's health is sufficient. Meeting this
threshold does not require a doctor to civilly confine the individual, however, and
most doctors, aware perhaps both of the significance of the decision to confine an
individual and the shortage of resources in this area of medical practice, avoid sec-
tioning if reasonably possible.

Where the Mental Health Act does create a significant substantive barrier is in its   5.53
definitions of 'mental impairment' and 'severe mental impairment'. Section 3, unlike
s 2, requires that the mental disorder of the individual be specified as mental illness,
mental impairment, severe mental impairment, or psychopathy. As discussed at para
2.06 above, the definition of the mental impairments requires not merely impairment of intelligence and social functioning, but 'abnormally aggressive or seriously
irresponsible conduct' on the part of the person as a result.[72] The courts have taken
this restriction seriously. As a result, individuals with mental impairments may fall
outside the scope of the longer-term confinement available in s 3. While the specific
categories of mental disorder are abolished for most purposes by the 2007 amendments, this conduct-based requirement remains for people with learning disabilities.[73] For these people, the MCA procedures may be the only long-term option.

---

[71] The substantive and procedural rules regarding civil confinement are complex. For an explanation and
discussion of their operation, see Bartlett and Sandland, *Mental Health Law: Policy and Practice* (Oxford
University Press, 2007, 3rd edn) Chs 4 and 5. Details of the admission criteria will be affected by the 2007
amendments: see P Bowen, *Blackstone's Guide to the Mental Health Act 2007* (Oxford University Press, 2008),
and Bartlett and Sandland (above).

[72] MHA s 1(2).

[73] MHA s 1(2A), (2B), and (4).

5.54   The Mental Health Act provisions are procedurally stronger than the restraint provisions of the MCA, requiring certification by two doctors and a social worker. This may be important for P. The people who make decisions for P under the MCA will not necessarily be professionals, and may lack the knowledge of practical alternatives to hospital admission possessed by a competent social worker. If professional knowledge is at the core of the decision, whether it is the knowledge of social workers or medical professionals, the combination of individuals in the confinement process suggests stronger decision-making than that of a single doctor with or without a lay decision-maker under the MCA. In the Mental Health Act process, of course, the views of the individual while competent and the nuanced views of best interests contained in the MCA do not form a formal part of the consideration. That may work to the advantage or disadvantage of the patient according to the individual case. The substantive threshold criteria under the Mental Health Act are also relatively weak, as discussed above. The individual is therefore subject to some choice of criteria by the professional decision-makers. The principle of least restrictive alternative, for example, will be adopted by most of these professionals, but there is no formal requirement to that effect in the Mental Health Act.

5.55   The nearest relative of the patient normally has the right to block any compulsory admission under the Mental Health Act, unless the patient would be dangerous if not subject to confinement. If the nearest relative as defined by the Mental Health Act is the same person as an MCA deputy or donee of an LPA with authority over the admission, the confinement process may offer a broader range of information and advice relevant to the merits of the decision, while still leaving the decision with the individual chosen by P or the court. Processes do however exist for substitution of the nearest relative when the individual prescribed by statute 'unreasonably objects' to the civil committal. The courts have in the past been primarily interested in the patient's best medical interests in assessing such unreasonable objection. If this trend continues, a deputy or donee of an LPA who refused the admission based on MCA best interests criteria might find himself or herself being removed as nearest relative.

5.56   As part of the Mental Health Act's procedural strength, persons admitted under either s 2 or 3 or their nearest relatives have the right to a review tribunal hearing to challenge the confinement, complete with legal representation for which legal aid is available. There is no corresponding right under the MCA short of an application to the Court of Protection. Probably, success before the review tribunal does not preclude continuing the admission of the individual under the MCA processes. In practice, P might well be perturbed by this approach, and his or her continued admission might therefore be sufficiently intrusive to violate the right to liberty under Article 5 of the ECHR. In that event, pending implementation of the 2007 amendments, his or her continued detention would have to be by court order.

4. Mental Health Act Guardianship

5.57   Particularly for people lacking capacity to make personal decisions who are expected to be resident outside hospitals, the guardianship provisions of the Mental Health

Act warrant at least passing consideration.[74] The criteria require the individual to be suffering from mental illness, mental impairment, severe mental impairment, or psychopathy. The limitations on the definitions of the mental impairments (requiring 'abnormally aggressive or seriously irresponsible conduct') discussed in paras 2.06 and 5.53 above apply here, and will continue to apply after the 2007 amendments take effect.[75] This may have the effect of rendering Mental Health Act guardianship unavailable to many individuals who lack capacity to make personal decisions. The norm in recent years has been that the guardian appointed is the social services authority, although that is not a requirement.

The powers that the Mental Health Act provisions convey to the guardian are   5.58
limited. The guardian can require the patient to reside at a specific place (but does not have power to detain him or her there); the power to require the patient to attend for medical treatment, occupation, education, or training (but no power to consent to treatment); and the power to require access to the patient to be given to specified professionals such as doctors.[76] These are not as extensive as those that may be conveyed under an LPA allowing the donee to make personal welfare decisions, nor as those available to the court to award to deputies. Guardianship is unlikely to be much practical use when these broader mechanisms are already in place. Guardians may be appointed only when it is 'necessary in the interests of the welfare of the patient or for the protection of others'.[77] It is difficult to see that this requirement will be met if the powers of guardianship are already being exercised responsibly by the donee of an LPA or a deputy. For that reason, guardians generally ought not to be appointed in these situations.

The reverse is not necessarily true. As the role of a deputy can be considerably   5.59
broader than that of a Mental Health Act guardian, it may still be appropriate for the court to appoint a deputy even if a guardian under the Mental Health Act exists. In this situation, the existence of the other decision-maker should be disclosed in the application for the appointment of a deputy.

In the event that both a guardian and a donee of an LPA or deputy exist, the   5.60
MCA as passed in 2005[78] is not clear whose views should prevail on matters within both authorities. The procedural rules do not assist here. Guardianship may be challenged first at the review board and then at the High Court, but not in the Court of Protection, which has jurisdiction relating to LPAs and deputies. The litigants might be in the Court of Appeal before both issues could be determined at the same time.

It is less obvious that the appointment of a Mental Health Act guardian will be   5.61
inappropriate when decisions are otherwise being made under the general defence.

---

[74] MHA s 7.

[75] See MHA s 1(2A).

[76] MHA s 8(1).

[77] MHA s 7(2)(b).

[78] For persons deprived of liberty, this situation is clarified by the 2007 amendments: see para 5.70 below and paras 4.61–4.73 above ('eligibility').

If the person lacking capacity meets the criteria, and where the issues of concern are within the guardian's powers listed above, a guardianship application may provide an expeditious way to introduce a specific decision-maker. Certainly, the process for appointment of an MHA guardian would be less cumbersome than an application to the Court of Protection for the appointment of a deputy. The MCA as drafted in 2005 does not address whether the person relying on the general defence may make decisions in contravention of those of a Mental Health Act guardian. [79] The MCA does not revoke Mental Health Act guardianship, however, and therefore must be taken to coexist with it. In that context, the general defence must be subject to the decisions of a guardian, acting within his or her scope of authority.

5. The Effect of the 2007 Amendments

(a) *Electro-Convulsive Therapy (ECT)*

5.62   The 2007 amendments introduce a new regime into the MHA for the provision of electro-convulsive therapy.[80] These are contained within Part 4 of the MHA, and therefore take precedence over the MCA.[81] As required previously, ECT may only be given either (a) when the patient is competent and consents to the treatment, or (b) when a doctor other than the treating physician provides a second opinion to the effect that the patient lacks capacity and the treatment is appropriate for the patient.[82] Unlike the previous regime, however, the doctor providing the second opinion must also certify that providing the treatment would not be in conflict with:

- an advance decision which the doctor is satisfied is valid and applicable;
- a decision made by the donee of an LPA
- a decision of a court-appointed deputy
- an order of the Court of Protection.[83]

These mechanisms operate as they would in any other MCA decision. Thus the donee of the LPA, the deputy, or the court must decide according to P's best interests as defined in the MCA, and the regular MCA rules regarding advance decisions apply. The effect of this is that P will be able, while competent, to make a decision to refuse ECT during his or her incapacity, and substitute decision-makers can prevent ECT being given to P when they reasonably consider such treatment not to be in P's best interests.

5.63   A different approach is adopted by the MHA for ECT when the patient is under the age of eighteen. If that individual has capacity, he or she can consent to the treatment, and it may be given if a doctor other than the treating physician certifies that

---

[79] For persons deprived of liberty, this situation is clarified by the 2007 amendments: see para 5.70 below and paras 4.61–4.73 above ('eligibility').

[80] MHA s 58A.

[81] See paras 5.38–5.45 above.

[82] MHA s 58A.

[83] MHA s 58A(5)(c).

the patient has capacity and that the treatment is appropriate.[84] If P lacks capacity, the doctor providing the independent opinion must certify this and also that the treatment is appropriate, but this alone is not sufficient to allow the treatment.[85] Further legal authority is required. Normally, this will presumably be parental consent, or an order under the Children Act. Section 28(1A) of the MCA however makes the provisions of the MCA applicable to this situation. Consistent with the remainder of the MCA, persons under eighteen cannot make advance decisions to refuse treatment or sign LPAs, but the remainder of the Act will have effect if P is aged sixteen or over. The Court of Protection will therefore have jurisdiction to make treatment decisions for them, and if appropriate to appoint a deputy. Perhaps more troubling, there is nothing in s 28(1A) to preclude the reliance by the treating physician on the general defence in s 5. Absent a conflicting decision from the Court of Protection or a court-appointed deputy, ECT can be given to persons under eighteen lacking capacity because of mental disorder if the relevant second opinion is provided and if the treating physician considers it in the best interests of P. This makes the apparent protection provided by MHA s 58A(7) appear remarkably hollow in these situations.

(b) Community Treatment Orders under the Mental Health Act

In their amendments to the MHA, the 2007 amendments introduce community treatment orders (CTOs) for the first time. The details of these orders are beyond the scope of this book.[86] Essentially, they allow people civilly confined under s 3 of the MHA (admission for treatment) to be released on condition that they follow a prescribed regime of treatment for their mental disorder in the community. If they fail to do so, their re-confinement is pursuant to a simplified administrative procedure, which has the effect of reviving their earlier s 3 confinement.[87] While in the community under such an order, the individual is known as a 'community patient'. The treatment provisions of the CTO regime concern only treatment for mental disorder.[88] Treatments for physical disorders remain outside the scope of the MHA, and the MCA continues to apply to them even when P is subject to a CTO.   5.64

  5.65

Apart from psychosurgery, which remains governed by s 57 in Part 4 of the MHA, the treatment of community patients for mental disorder or for physical disorder is governed by Part 4A of the MHA, being ss 64A to 64K of that Act, not Part 4. As a result, the general provision regarding psychiatric treatment, that the MCA is subject to the MHA,[89] does not apply. The MCA is therefore applicable regarding the treatment of community patients for mental disorder. Section 28(1B) of the MCA   5.66

---

84 MHA s 58A(4).
85 MHA s 58A(7).
86 See P Bowen, *Blackstone's Guide to the Mental Health Act 2007* (Oxford University Press, 2008).
87 MHA ss 17A–17G.
88 MHA s 64A.
89 MCA s 28(1); see para 5.40 above.

makes it clear, however, that the general defence[90] does not apply to treatment of community patients for mental disorder, although as we shall see, s 64D provides a mechanism that is in some ways similar.

5.67   While failure to comply with a CTO may result in an individual being re-confined in hospital, the CTO does not of itself allow treatment to be enforced on a patient. (For adults, the exception to this is when the emergency treatment is required for a patient who lacks capacity.)[91] Otherwise, consent of the patient if capable, or a substitute decision if the patient is not capable, must be provided.[92] The MHA provides additional safeguards for treatment for mental disorder of community patients, primarily in its requirement that certificates of the appropriateness of the treatment be provided by a doctor other than the treating physician. Subject to some exceptions, such certificates are required for ECT and when treatment for mental disorder has continued for three months since the admission to hospital.

5.68   If the patient has capacity, he or she decides whether or not to consent to the relevant treatment. If instead the patient P is over the age of sixteen and lacks capacity, the treatment may proceed only if:

- a donee of an LPA or court-appointed deputy or the Court of Protection consents to the treatment on P's behalf, or
- the provisions of s 64D of the MHA are complied with.[93]

In the former case, the decision will be decided in the same fashion as any other decision under the MCA. In particular, the principles[94] and the substantive and procedural requirements of the best interests test[95] will apply, and advance decisions to refuse the treatment[96] will be binding. That said, what is at issue is whether or not consent should be given to the treatment contained in the CTO; the desirability of the CTO itself is not at issue at this stage. The donee, deputy, or Court of Protection has no obvious role in determining whether the CTO ought to have been given, merely whether the treatment at issue is in P's best interests.

5.69   Section 64D of the MHA allows the treatment to proceed if the approved clinician responsible for the treatment:

- takes reasonable steps to establish whether P has capacity;
- reasonably believes when the treatment is given that P lacks capacity;

---

[90] MCA s 5; see general discussion regarding this defence at paras 3.53–3.69 above.

[91] See MHA s 64G. MHA s 64B(3)(b) further allows emergency treatment where the patient if competent, or otherwise the donee of an LPA, a court-appointed deputy or the Court of Protection consent. This provision removes the need for certification by an independent medical practitioner that the treatment is appropriate; see further below.

[92] MHA s 64B.

[93] MHA s 64C(2).

[94] See paras 3.15–3.21 above.

[95] See paras 3.33–3.52 above.

[96] See paras 3.112–3.136 above.

- has no reason to believe that P objects to the treatment being given, or, if P does object, that it is unnecessary to impose force upon P in order to give the treatment;
- the decision does not conflict with a valid and applicable advance decision, nor with a decision of the donee of an LPA, court-appointed deputy, or the Court of Protection.

While this is broadly similar to the approach of s 5 of the MCA, in that it allows the treating physician to perform the treatment without the consent or authorization of a third party, it conspicuously does not refer to the best interests test of the MCA. That test would become relevant if an individual challenging the provision of the treatment were to raise the matter with the Court of Protection, but the clinician under s 64D instead is required only to consider P's possible objection and whether the treatment can be given without imposing force upon P. The approach to determining whether P objects is contained in s 64J(1) of the MHA:

(1) In assessing for the purposes of this Part whether he has reason to believe that a patient objects to treatment, a person shall consider all the circumstances so far as they are reasonably ascertainable, including the patient's behaviour, wishes, feelings, views, beliefs and values.

Circumstances from the past are, however, to be considered only so far as it is still appropriate to do so.[97] Appropriateness will depend on the facts of the case.

(c) 'Eligibility' and Deprivation of Liberty

When P is to be deprived of his or her liberty, be it in a care home, hospital, or else-   5.70
where, the 2007 amendments introduce rules as to whether this is to occur under the MCA or the MHA. These 'eligibility criteria' are discussed elsewhere in this book,[98] and that discussion will not be repeated here. In essence, they provide that:

- if P is subject to compulsion under the MHA, the MCA should not be applied so as to conflict with that compulsion;
- P should not be admitted to hospital for psychiatric treatment using the MCA if he or she objects to the admission or the treatment, unless that objection is overruled by a deputy or donee of an LPA.

It should be emphasized here that the formal eligibility criteria of the 2007 amendments will apply only if P is to be deprived of liberty. For other interventions involving P, the discussion of interface between MHA and MCA elsewhere in this chapter will continue to apply.

---

[97] MHA s 64J(2).
[98] See paras 4.61–4.73 above.

F. CONTINUATION OF THE COMMON LAW?

5.71　The second chapter of this book described the recent developments of the common law in the field of incapacity. There is therefore a pleasing symmetry in concluding the book by returning to those developments. The question to address here is how much of the common law is superseded by the MCA, and how much of it will be taken to coexist with the new legislation.

5.72　In its original conception by the Law Commission, the legislative developments would have supplanted little of the common law. Various tests of capacity that had been long-established in laws of contract, crime, wills, equity, and other contexts would continue to exist.[99] The new legislation would instead provide new mechanisms creating new authorities to make decisions on behalf of those lacking capacity. The MCA as eventually passed has not departed from that original format. Nothing in the MCA expressly supersedes anything in common law; instead the Act is phrased as a collection of newly created legal responses.

5.73　The common law context of the Law Commission approach did not remain static, however. Indeed, since 1989, there has been a veritable explosion in judicial decision-making related to the law of incapacity. The two cases that serve as the cornerstones of recent thinking, *Re F (Mental Patient: Sterilisation)*[100] regarding the doctrine of necessity and *Re C (Adult: Refusal of Medical Treatment)*[101] regarding the legal definition of incapacity, occurred during the Law Commission's deliberations, the latter very late in those deliberations. The other significant common law developments have occurred since the Law Commission report, and could not reasonably have been anticipated by it. These developments do overlap significantly with the MCA as it has arrived on the statute books. As discussed in Chapter 2 of this book, they refined the common law best interests test, gave the court a new and broader jurisdiction in matters relating to incapacity, and introduced the appointment of substitute decision-makers. As discussed in that chapter, these developments are problematic in practice and on shaky doctrinal foundations, but they cannot be ignored. They are not expressly overruled by the MCA; the question is how far they are overruled by implication, and how far they continue to stand.

5.74　Even in its original conception, prior to the recent developments in the common law, there was potential for discord. The law of testamentary capacity will serve as an example. The test of such capacity at common law is contained in *Banks v Goodfellow*:

> It is essential to the exercise of such a power that a testator shall understand the nature of the act and its effects; shall understand the extent of the property of which he is disposing; shall be able to comprehend and appreciate the claims to which he ought to give effect.[102]

---

[99] Law Com 231, para 3.23.
[100] [1990] 2 AC 1.
[101] [1994] 1 All ER 819.
[102] (1870) 5 QB 549, 565.

This is quite a different wording from the definition of inability to make a decision 5.75
in the MCA. Judicial interpretations of the *Banks* test show a further divergence
from the approach of the MCA. In *Evans v Knight and Moore*, for example, it was
held:

[W]here a mental aberration is proved to have shown itself in the alleged testator, the degree of
evidence necessary to substantiate any testamentary act depends greatly on the character of the act
itself. If it purports to give effect only to probable intentions, its validity may be established by
comparatively slight evidence. But evidence, very different in kind and much weightier in degree,
is required to the support of an act which purports to contain dispositions contrary to the testator's
probable intentions, or savouring, in any degree, of folly or frenzy.[103]

This suggests that the wisdom or appropriateness of the decision is a factor in
whether the testator will be deemed to have capacity. In that case, the fact that the
will was 'precisely such a disposition as natural affection would dictate'[104] was apparently a significant factor in upholding the will. Such an approach is not consistent
with the principle in the MCA that a person will not be treated as lacking capacity
merely because he makes an unwise decision.[105]

Such incomplete alignments, at least in theory, have the potential to be problem- 5.76
atic. The test of incapacity that would allow a court to write a will on behalf of P is
the statutory test under the MCA, not the common law test. Incomplete alignments
between the tests in statute and common law mean that potentially, either both the
court and P might have the authority to write a will, or neither might. The former
situation might result in a posthumous battle between two apparently valid wills;
the latter would result in no one being able to draft a will, defeating the object of the
statutory provision. While the courts may endeavour to interpret cases in ways that
would minimize these anomalous results, and while the difficulties may be inevita-
ble, the result is not ideal.

The issues surrounding the new powers of the court raise different issues. Where 5.77
it is clear that the common law definitions of capacity will coexist with the MCA
provisions, it is not clear how far the common law powers related to the doctrine of
necessity will remain. They certainly will to some degree. The doctrine of necessity
existed long before the case of *F*.[106] It is this doctrine that allows fire-fighters to enter
burning buildings to fight fires, without liability for trespass. The passage of the
MCA clearly does not remove this doctrine in that context. There can similarly be
no doubt that the court retains a jurisdiction to make declarations on the law. As
noted in the second chapter, that power extends well beyond mental capacity; it is
not revoked by the Act. The question is instead whether in areas closely related to
the Act, the other jurisdictions should be taken to have been amended into closer
conformity with the Act.

---

[103] (1822) 1 Add 229 and 237–238.
[104] ibid, 238.
[105] MCA s 1(4).
[106] See n 100 above.

5.78 The advance decision to refuse treatment is a case where some elements of the common law are clearly superseded. The common law provided no formalities requirements for any advance decisions to refuse medical treatment. The MCA instead requires advance decisions of life-sustaining treatment to state expressly that they apply even though life may be put at risk, and requires them to be in writing, signed, and witnessed.[107]

5.79 The continuing extent of broader powers of the court regarding necessity and declarations is less clear. On the one hand, the continuation of these legal mechanisms may provide a safety valve allowing relief to be given in hard cases without unduly stretching the language of the MCA. On the other hand, overuse of the common law powers in these situations may gut the MCA of the very benefits it was designed to promote. Some examples may clarify this tension.

5.80 Consider an individual suffering from a severe physical injury following a car accident. When the ambulance arrives, they may be distracted by pain, and therefore unable to give meaningful consent. It would seem an unduly harsh result to fail to provide pain relief in that situation; yet can it really be said that they are suffering from an 'impairment of, or a disturbance in the functioning of, the mind or brain'?[108] The Law Commission viewed the provision of this diagnostic threshold as a safeguard.[109] Expanding the meaning to suit the facts would risk destroying its value as a safeguard. It might in this example be better to keep a firm grip on the scope of the diagnostic threshold, and refuse to apply the MCA. That would still leave necessity as an available defence,[110] and one that might better fit the facts of the situation. This would be an example of the continued use of necessity used to strengthen the safeguards in the MCA.

5.81 At the same time, overuse of the alternative processes risks undermining the MCA. Decisions that are covered by the statutory general defence in s 5 will often be the same as the decisions previously made under the common law defence of necessity. The definition of best interests will vary, however, depending on which legal mechanism is applied. The MCA has a carefully considered and nuanced definition, much more precise than the simple balance sheet approach of the common law. Allowing reliance on the common law in this context would circumvent the MCA, and effectively undermine one of its key provisions.

5.82 This is not a merely abstract possibility. To be realistic, many (if not most) non-professional people who are in caring relationships of people lacking capacity will be unaware of the MCA or the common law provisions. Indeed, the clarification of the rules surrounding such informal care was one of the objectives of the Law Commission

---

[107] MCA s 25(5)–(6).

[108] MCA s 2(1). As a further example, see the ambiguities relating to drunkenness, noted at para 3.24 above.

[109] Law Com 231, para 3.8.

[110] This approach suits the understanding of necessity prior to the *F* case in 1989: see R Dias, *Clerk and Lindsell on Torts* (Sweet and Maxwell, 1982, 15th edn) para 1-154; J Fleming, *Law of Torts* (Law Book Co., 1977, 5th edn) 92–94, (1998, 9th edn) 106.

proposals in this area.[111] They will not be the donees of LPAs or in receipt of deputy powers from the court. They will, without their express knowledge, be relying on the general defence in s 5 or the doctrine of necessity. They will have no knowledge of the best interests test in s 4, so it will be unsurprising if they do not follow its specific provisions. Such carers may have been acting in good faith and with considerable personal sacrifice. How is the court to react in this situation in the event of difficulties? It would seem insulting to find that such carers acted illegally, let alone to hold them liable in damages or subject to a criminal punishment, particularly if their actions met the common law test of best interests.

One possibility for the court in this situation is to soft-pedal the legislative require-   5.83
ments. It might do this, for example, by suggesting that the statutory best interests test is 'directive' rather than 'mandatory'. It might alternatively give particular weight to s 4(2), which allows 'all relevant circumstances' to be taken into account, at the expense of side-lining the specific determinations under the rest of the section. Best interests is a key concept, however, and such an approach would effectively render the statute ineffective. This approach cannot be the intent of the statute. Certainly, s 4(9) provides that a reasonable belief that a decision is taken in the best interests of P will suffice, but only if the processes are in compliance with s 4(2) to (7). These provisions are not meant to be side-lined.

Another possibility is for the court to hold that the statutory scheme is not satis-   5.84
fied, but that the common law defence of necessity remains open. As discussed above, this would be likely to have the same effect of allowing the MCA to be circumvented, rendering key provisions of the statute meaningless.

The third possibility is to hold that the statute supersedes the law in this area, and   5.85
that the carer has acted illegally. That seems to be the best result if the objective is to protect the integrity of the statutory regime, with the protections it provides to people lacking capacity in general. If the carer is an unattractive witness or of dubious character, this may be the result the court adopts. If however the carer has acted in good faith and with considerable personal sacrifice, there may well be considerable pressures to adopt one of the other results hard cases make bad law. That said, it is difficult to see the justice in the result, when the carer did not even know of the law they should have followed. While ignorance may be no excuse in law, it does tug at the heartstrings.

The new-found common law jurisdiction of the Court to appoint substitute   5.86
decision-makers is easier to deal with. It is discretionary. The arguments in favour of the jurisdiction are eradicated by the new jurisdiction of the Court of Protection to appoint deputies. It may be a nice legal question as to whether the common law jurisdiction continues to exist—it was always on rather shaky legal foundations— but it is difficult to see a circumstance where it would be appropriate for the Court to exercise it.

---

[111] Law Com 231, para 4.2.

APPENDIX 1

Mental Capacity Act 2005

[Please Note: the purpose of this document is solely to help people in understanding the effect of the changes to be made by the Mental Health Act 2007. It should not be relied on for any other purpose.]

PURPOSE

This document is intended to show how the Mental Capacity Act 2005 will look as amended by the Mental Health Act 2007, which received Royal Assent on 19 July 2007.

KEY

Material to be deleted by the 2007 Act is in italics, eg *omitted material looks like this*.

Material to be added by the 2007 Act is in square brackets, eg [added material looks like this].

Existing sections and schedules to be amended by the Act are marked '##'.

ANNOTATIONS

At the end of each section (or paragraph of a Schedule) the relevant provision of the 2007 Act is in italics, square brackets, and also in smaller type.

The 2007 Act itself is available from the Office for Public Sector Information at http://www.opsi.gov.uk/acts/acts2007a.htm

---

MENTAL CAPACITY ACT 2005

CONTENTS

PART 1
PERSONS WHO LACK CAPACITY

The principles

Preliminary

Lasting powers of attorney

General powers of the court and appointment of deputies

[Powers of the court in relation to Schedule A1

SCHEDULE 2
PROPERTY AND AFFAIRS: SUPPLEMENTARY PROVISION

SCHEDULE 3
INTERNATIONAL PROTECTION OF ADULTS

SCHEDULE 4
PROVISIONS APPLYING TO EXISTING ENDURING
POWERS OF ATTORNEY

SCHEDULE 5
TRANSITIONAL PROVISIONS AND SAVINGS

SCHEDULE 6
MINOR AND CONSEQUENTIAL AMENDMENTS

SCHEDULE 7
REPEALS

MENTAL CAPACITY ACT 2005
2005 CHAPTER 9

An Act to make new provision relating to persons who lack capacity; to establish a superior court of record called the Court of Protection in place of the office of the Supreme Court called by that name; to make provision in connection with the Convention on the International Protection of Adults signed at the Hague on 13th January 2000; and for connected purposes. [7th April 2005]

BE IT ENACTED by the Queen's most Excellent Majesty, by and with the advice and consent of the Lords Spiritual and Temporal, and Commons, in this present Parliament assembled, and by the authority of the same, as follows:—

PART 1
PERSONS WHO LACK CAPACITY

The principles

1 The principles

(1) The following principles apply for the purposes of this Act.
(2) A person must be assumed to have capacity unless it is established that he lacks capacity.
(3) A person is not to be treated as unable to make a decision unless all practicable steps to help him to do so have been taken without success.
(4) A person is not to be treated as unable to make a decision merely because he makes an unwise decision.
(5) An act done, or decision made, under this Act for or on behalf of a person who lacks capacity must be done, or made, in his best interests.
(6) Before the act is done, or the decision is made, regard must be had to whether the purpose for which it is needed can be as effectively achieved in a way that is less restrictive of the person's rights and freedom of action.

Preliminary

2 People who lack capacity

(1) For the purposes of this Act, a person lacks capacity in relation to a matter if at the material time he is unable to make a decision for himself in relation to the matter because of an impairment of, or a disturbance in the functioning of, the mind or brain.
(2) It does not matter whether the impairment or disturbance is permanent or temporary.
(3) A lack of capacity cannot be established merely by reference to—
    (a) a person's age or appearance, or
    (b) a condition of his, or an aspect of his behaviour, which might lead others to make unjustified assumptions about his capacity.

(4) In proceedings under this Act or any other enactment, any question whether a person lacks capacity within the meaning of this Act must be decided on the balance of probabilities.

(5) No power which a person ('D') may exercise under this Act—

    (a) in relation to a person who lacks capacity, or

    (b) where D reasonably thinks that a person lacks capacity, is exercisable in relation to a person under 16.

(6) Subsection (5) is subject to section 18(3).

3 Inability to make decisions

(1) For the purposes of section 2, a person is unable to make a decision for himself if he is unable—

    (a) to understand the information relevant to the decision,

    (b) to retain that information,

    (c) to use or weigh that information as part of the process of making the decision, or

    (d) to communicate his decision (whether by talking, using sign language or any other means).

(2) A person is not to be regarded as unable to understand the information relevant to a decision if he is able to understand an explanation of it given to him in a way that is appropriate to his circumstances (using simple language, visual aids or any other means).

(3) The fact that a person is able to retain the information relevant to a decision for a short period only does not prevent him from being regarded as able to make the decision.

(4) The information relevant to a decision includes information about the reasonably foreseeable consequences of—

    (a) deciding one way or another, or

    (b) failing to make the decision.

4 Best interests

(1) In determining for the purposes of this Act what is in a person's best interests, the person making the determination must not make it merely on the basis of—

    (a) the person's age or appearance, or

    (b) a condition of his, or an aspect of his behaviour, which might lead others to make unjustified assumptions about what might be in his best interests.

(2) The person making the determination must consider all the relevant circumstances and, in particular, take the following steps.

(3) He must consider—

    (a) whether it is likely that the person will at some time have capacity in relation to the matter in question, and

    (b) if it appears likely that he will, when that is likely to be.

(4) He must, so far as reasonably practicable, permit and encourage the person to participate, or to improve his ability to participate, as fully as possible in any act done for him and any decision affecting him.

(5) Where the determination relates to life-sustaining treatment he must not, in considering whether the treatment is in the best interests of the person concerned, be motivated by a desire to bring about his death.

(6) He must consider, so far as is reasonably ascertainable—

    (a) the person's past and present wishes and feelings (and, in particular, any relevant written statement made by him when he had capacity),

    (b) the beliefs and values that would be likely to influence his decision if he had capacity, and

    (c) the other factors that he would be likely to consider if he were able to do so.

(7) He must take into account, if it is practicable and appropriate to consult them, the views of—

(a) anyone named by the person as someone to be consulted on the matter in question or on matters of that kind,

(b) anyone engaged in caring for the person or interested in his welfare,

(c) any donee of a lasting power of attorney granted by the person, and

(d) any deputy appointed for the person by the court,as to what would be in the person's best interests and, in particular, as to the matters mentioned in subsection (6).

(8) The duties imposed by subsections (1) to (7) also apply in relation to the exercise of any powers which—

(a) are exercisable under a lasting power of attorney, or

(b) are exercisable by a person under this Act where he reasonably believes that another person lacks capacity.

(9) In the case of an act done, or a decision made, by a person other than the court, there is sufficient compliance with this section if (having complied with the requirements of subsections (1) to (7)) he reasonably believes that what he does or decides is in the best interests of the person concerned.

(10) 'Life-sustaining treatment' means treatment which in the view of a person providing health care for the person concerned is necessary to sustain life.

(11) 'Relevant circumstances' are those—

(a) of which the person making the determination is aware, and

(b) which it would be reasonable to regard as relevant.

[4A Restriction on deprivation of liberty

(1) This Act does not authorise any person ('D') to deprive any other person ('P') of his liberty.

(2) But that is subject to—

(a) the following provisions of this section, and

(b) section 4B.

(3) D may deprive P of his liberty if, by doing so, D is giving effect to a relevant decision of the court.

(4) A relevant decision of the court is a decision made by an order under section 16(2)(a) in relation to a matter concerning P's personal welfare.

(5) D may deprive P of his liberty if the deprivation is authorised by Schedule A1 (hospital and care home residents: deprivation of liberty).]

[Section 4A inserted by section 50(2) of the 2007 Act.]

[4B Deprivation of liberty necessary for life-sustaining treatment etc.

(1) If the following conditions are met, D is authorised to deprive P of his liberty while a decision as respects any relevant issue is sought from the court.

(2) The first condition is that there is a question about whether D is authorised to deprive P of his liberty under section 4A.

(3) The second condition is that the deprivation of liberty—

(a) is wholly or partly for the purpose of—

(i) giving P life-sustaining treatment, or

(ii) doing any vital act, or

(b) consists wholly or partly of—

(i) giving P life-sustaining treatment, or

(ii) doing any vital act.

(4) The third condition is that the deprivation of liberty is necessary in order to—
   (a) give the life-sustaining treatment, or
   (b) do the vital act.
(5) A vital act is any act which the person doing it reasonably believes to be necessary to prevent a serious deterioration in P's condition.]

[Section 4B inserted by section 50(2) of the 2007 Act.]

5 Acts in connection with care or treatment

(1) If a person ('D') does an act in connection with the care or treatment of another person ('P'), the act is one to which this section applies if—
   (a) before doing the act, D takes reasonable steps to establish whether P lacks capacity in relation to the matter in question, and
   (b) when doing the act, D reasonably believes—
       (i) that P lacks capacity in relation to the matter, and
       (ii) that it will be in P's best interests for the act to be done.
(2) D does not incur any liability in relation to the act that he would not have incurred if P—
   (a) had had capacity to consent in relation to the matter, and
   (b) had consented to D's doing the act.
(3) Nothing in this section excludes a person's civil liability for loss or damage, or his criminal liability, resulting from his negligence in doing the act.
(4) Nothing in this section affects the operation of sections 24 to 26 (advance decisions to refuse treatment).

6 Section 5 acts: limitations

(1) If D does an act that is intended to restrain P, it is not an act to which section 5 applies unless two further conditions are satisfied.
(2) The first condition is that D reasonably believes that it is necessary to do the act in order to prevent harm to P.
(3) The second is that the act is a proportionate response to—
   (a) the likelihood of P's suffering harm, and
   (b) the seriousness of that harm.
(4) For the purposes of this section D restrains P if he—
   (a) uses, or threatens to use, force to secure the doing of an act which P resists, or
   (b) restricts P's liberty of movement, whether or not P resists.
(5) *But D does more than merely restrain P if he deprives P of his liberty within the meaning of Article 5(1) of the Human Rights Convention (whether or not D is a public authority).*
(6) Section 5 does not authorise a person to do an act which conflicts with a decision made, within the scope of his authority and in accordance with this Part, by—
   (a) a donee of a lasting power of attorney granted by P, or
   (b) a deputy appointed for P by the court.
(7) But nothing in subsection (6) stops a person—
   (a) providing life-sustaining treatment, or
   (b) doing any act which he reasonably believes to be necessary to prevent a serious deterioration in P's condition, while a decision as respects any relevant issue is sought from the court.

[Subsection (5) omitted by section 50(4)(a) of the 2007 Act.]

7 Payment for necessary goods and services

(1) If necessary goods or services are supplied to a person who lacks capacity to contract for the supply, he must pay a reasonable price for them.

(2) 'Necessary' means suitable to a person's condition in life and to his actual requirements at the time when the goods or services are supplied.

8 Expenditure

(1) If an act to which section 5 applies involves expenditure, it is lawful for D—
   (a) to pledge P's credit for the purpose of the expenditure, and
   (b) to apply money in P's possession for meeting the expenditure.

(2) If the expenditure is borne for P by D, it is lawful for D—
   (a) to reimburse himself out of money in P's possession, or
   (b) to be otherwise indemnified by P.

(3) Subsections (1) and (2) do not affect any power under which (apart from those subsections) a person—
   (a) has lawful control of P's money or other property, and
   (b) has power to spend money for P's benefit.

Lasting powers of attorney

9 Lasting powers of attorney

(1) A lasting power of attorney is a power of attorney under which the donor ('P') confers on the donee (or donees) authority to make decisions about all or any of the following—
   (a) P's personal welfare or specified matters concerning P's personal welfare, and
   (b) P's property and affairs or specified matters concerning P's property and affairs, and which includes authority to make such decisions in circumstances where P no longer has capacity.

(2) A lasting power of attorney is not created unless—
   (a) section 10 is complied with,
   (b) an instrument conferring authority of the kind mentioned in subsection (1) is made and registered in accordance with Schedule 1, and
   (c) at the time when P executes the instrument, P has reached 18 and has capacity to execute it.

(3) An instrument which—
   (a) purports to create a lasting power of attorney, but
   (b) does not comply with this section, section 10 or Schedule 1, confers no authority.

(4) The authority conferred by a lasting power of attorney is subject to—
   (a) the provisions of this Act and, in particular, sections 1 (the principles) and 4 (best interests), and
   (b) any conditions or restrictions specified in the instrument.

10 Appointment of donees

(1) A donee of a lasting power of attorney must be—
   (a) an individual who has reached 18, or
   (b) if the power relates only to P's property and affairs, either such an individual or a trust corporation.

(2) An individual who is bankrupt may not be appointed as donee of a lasting power of attorney in relation to P's property and affairs.

(3) Subsections (4) to (7) apply in relation to an instrument under which two or more persons are to act as donees of a lasting power of attorney.

(4) The instrument may appoint them to act—

(a) jointly,

(b) jointly and severally, or

(c) jointly in respect of some matters and jointly and severally in respect of others.

(5) To the extent to which it does not specify whether they are to act jointly or jointly and severally, the instrument is to be assumed to appoint them to act jointly.

(6) If they are to act jointly, a failure, as respects one of them, to comply with the requirements of subsection (1) or (2) or Part 1 or 2 of Schedule 1 prevents a lasting power of attorney from being created.

(7) If they are to act jointly and severally, a failure, as respects one of them, to comply with the requirements of subsection (1) or (2) or Part 1 or 2 of Schedule 1—

(a) prevents the appointment taking effect in his case, but

(b) does not prevent a lasting power of attorney from being created in the case of the other or others.

(8) An instrument used to create a lasting power of attorney—

(a) cannot give the donee (or, if more than one, any of them) power to appoint a substitute or successor, but

(b) may itself appoint a person to replace the donee (or, if more than one, any of them) on the occurrence of an event mentioned in section 13(6)(a) to (d) which has the effect of terminating the donee's appointment.

11 Lasting powers of attorney: restrictions

(1) A lasting power of attorney does not authorise the donee (or, if more than one, any of them) to do an act that is intended to restrain P, unless three conditions are satisfied.

(2) The first condition is that P lacks, or the donee reasonably believes that P lacks capacity in relation to the matter in question.

(3) The second is that the donee reasonably believes that it is necessary to do the act in order to prevent harm to P.

(4) The third is that the act is a proportionate response to—

(a) the likelihood of P's suffering harm, and

(b) the seriousness of that harm.

(5) For the purposes of this section, the donee restrains P if he—

(a) uses, or threatens to use, force to secure the doing of an act which P resists, or

(b) restricts P's liberty of movement, whether or not P resists, or if he authorises another person to do any of those things.

(6) *But the donee does more than merely restrain P if he deprives P of his liberty within the meaning of Article 5(1) of the Human Rights Convention.*

(7) Where a lasting power of attorney authorises the donee (or, if more than one, any of them) to make decisions about P's personal welfare, the authority—

(a) does not extend to making such decisions in circumstances other than those where P lacks, or the donee reasonably believes that P lacks, capacity,

(b) is subject to sections 24 to 26 (advance decisions to refuse treatment), and

    (c) extends to giving or refusing consent to the carrying out or continuation of a treatment by a person providing health care for P.

(8) But subsection (7)(c)—

    (a) does not authorise the giving or refusing of consent to the carrying out or continuation of life-sustaining treatment, unless the instrument contains express provision to that effect, and

    (b) is subject to any conditions or restrictions in the instrument.

[Subsection (6) omitted by section 50(4)(b) of the 2007 Act.]

12 Scope of lasting powers of attorney: gifts

(1) Where a lasting power of attorney confers authority to make decisions about P's property and affairs, it does not authorise a donee (or, if more than one, any of them) to dispose of the donor's property by making gifts except to the extent permitted by subsection (2).

(2) The donee may make gifts—

    (a) on customary occasions to persons (including himself) who are related to or connected with the donor, or

    (b) to any charity to whom the donor made or might have been expected to make gifts, if the value of each such gift is not unreasonable having regard to all the circumstances and, in particular, the size of the donor's estate.

(3) 'Customary occasion' means—

    (a) the occasion or anniversary of a birth, a marriage or the formation of a civil partnership, or

    (b) any other occasion on which presents are customarily given within families or among friends or associates.

(4) Subsection (2) is subject to any conditions or restrictions in the instrument.

13 Revocation of lasting powers of attorney etc.

(1) This section applies if—

    (a) P has executed an instrument with a view to creating a lasting power of attorney, or

    (b) a lasting power of attorney is registered as having been conferred by P, and in this section references to revoking the power include revoking the instrument.

(2) P may, at any time when he has capacity to do so, revoke the power.

(3) P's bankruptcy revokes the power so far as it relates to P's property and affairs.

(4) But where P is bankrupt merely because an interim bankruptcy restrictions order has effect in respect of him, the power is suspended, so far as it relates to P's property and affairs, for so long as the order has effect.

(5) The occurrence in relation to a donee of an event mentioned in subsection (6)—

    (a) terminates his appointment, and

    (b) except in the cases given in subsection (7), revokes the power.

(6) The events are—

    (a) the disclaimer of the appointment by the donee in accordance with such requirements as may be prescribed for the purposes of this section in regulations made by the Lord Chancellor,

    (b) subject to subsections (8) and (9), the death or bankruptcy of the donee or, if the donee is a trust corporation, its winding-up or dissolution,

    (c) subject to subsection (11), the dissolution or annulment of a marriage or civil partnership between the donor and the donee,

    (d) the lack of capacity of the donee.

(7) The cases are—

    (a) the donee is replaced under the terms of the instrument,

    (b) he is one of two or more persons appointed to act as donees jointly and severally in respect of any matter and, after the event, there is at least one remaining donee.

(8) The bankruptcy of a donee does not terminate his appointment, or revoke the power, in so far as his authority relates to P's personal welfare.

(9) Where the donee is bankrupt merely because an interim bankruptcy restrictions order has effect in respect of him, his appointment and the power are suspended, so far as they relate to P's property and affairs, for so long as the order has effect.

(10) Where the donee is one of two or more appointed to act jointly and severally under the power in respect of any matter, the reference in subsection (9) to the suspension of the power is to its suspension in so far as it relates to that donee.

(11) The dissolution or annulment of a marriage or civil partnership does not terminate the appointment of a donee, or revoke the power, if the instrument provided that it was not to do so.

14 Protection of donee and others if no power created or power revoked

(1) Subsections (2) and (3) apply if—

    (a) an instrument has been registered under Schedule 1 as a lasting power of attorney, but

    (b) a lasting power of attorney was not created, whether or not the registration has been cancelled at the time of the act or transaction in question.

(2) A donee who acts in purported exercise of the power does not incur any liability (to P or any other person) because of the non-existence of the power unless at the time of acting he—

    (a) knows that a lasting power of attorney was not created, or

    (b) is aware of circumstances which, if a lasting power of attorney had been created, would have terminated his authority to act as a donee.

(3) Any transaction between the donee and another person is, in favour of that person, as valid as if the power had been in existence, unless at the time of the transaction that person has knowledge of a matter referred to in subsection (2).

(4) If the interest of a purchaser depends on whether a transaction between the donee and the other person was valid by virtue of subsection (3), it is conclusively presumed in favour of the purchaser that the transaction was valid if—

    (a) the transaction was completed within 12 months of the date on which the instrument was registered, or

    (b) the other person makes a statutory declaration, before or within 3 months after the completion of the purchase, that he had no reason at the time of the transaction to doubt that the donee had authority to dispose of the property which was the subject of the transaction.

(5) In its application to a lasting power of attorney which relates to matters in addition to P's property and affairs, section 5 of the Powers of Attorney Act 1971 (c. 27) (protection where power is revoked) has effect as if references to revocation included the cessation of the power in relation to P's property and affairs.

(6) Where two or more donees are appointed under a lasting power of attorney, this section applies as if references to the donee were to all or any of them.

General powers of the court and appointment of deputies

15 Power to make declarations

(1) The court may make declarations as to—
  (a) whether a person has or lacks capacity to make a decision specified in the declaration;
  (b) whether a person has or lacks capacity to make decisions on such matters as are described in the declaration;
  (c) the lawfulness or otherwise of any act done, or yet to be done, in relation to that person.
(2) 'Act' includes an omission and a course of conduct.

16 Powers to make decisions and appoint deputies: general

(1) This section applies if a person ('P') lacks capacity in relation to a matter or matters concerning—
  (a) P's personal welfare, or
  (b) P's property and affairs.
(2) The court may—
  (a) by making an order, make the decision or decisions on P's behalf in relation to the matter or matters, or
  (b) appoint a person (a 'deputy') to make decisions on P's behalf in relation to the matter or matters.
(3) The powers of the court under this section are subject to the provisions of this Act and, in particular, to sections 1 (the principles) and 4 (best interests).
(4) When deciding whether it is in P's best interests to appoint a deputy, the court must have regard (in addition to the matters mentioned in section 4) to the principles that—
  (a) a decision by the court is to be preferred to the appointment of a deputy to make a decision, and
  (b) the powers conferred on a deputy should be as limited in scope and duration as is reasonably practicable in the circumstances.
(5) The court may make such further orders or give such directions, and confer on a deputy such powers or impose on him such duties, as it thinks necessary or expedient for giving effect to, or otherwise in connection with, an order or appointment made by it under subsection (2).
(6) Without prejudice to section 4, the court may make the order, give the directions or make the appointment on such terms as it considers are in P's best interests, even though no application is before the court for an order, directions or an appointment on those terms.
(7) An order of the court may be varied or discharged by a subsequent order.
(8) The court may, in particular, revoke the appointment of a deputy or vary the powers conferred on him if it is satisfied that the deputy—
  (a) has behaved, or is behaving, in a way that contravenes the authority conferred on him by the court or is not in P's best interests, or
  (b) proposes to behave in a way that would contravene that authority or would not be in P's best interests.

[16A Section 16 powers: Mental Health Act patients etc.

(1) If a person is ineligible to be deprived of liberty by this Act, the court may not include in a welfare order provision which authorises the person to be deprived of his liberty.
(2) If—
  (a) a welfare order includes provision which authorises a person to be deprived of his liberty, and

(b) that person becomes ineligible to be deprived of liberty by this Act, the provision ceases to have effect for as long as the person remains ineligible.

(3) Nothing in subsection (2) affects the power of the court under section 16(7) to vary or discharge the welfare order.

(4) For the purposes of this section—
   (a) Schedule 1A applies for determining whether or not P is ineligible to be deprived of liberty by this Act;
   (b) 'welfare order' means an order under section 16(2)(a).]

[Section 16A inserted by section 50(3) of the 2007 Act.]

17 Section 16 powers: personal welfare

(1) The powers under section 16 as respects P's personal welfare extend in particular to—
   (a) deciding where P is to live;
   (b) deciding what contact, if any, P is to have with any specified persons;
   (c) making an order prohibiting a named person from having contact with P;
   (d) giving or refusing consent to the carrying out or continuation of a treatment by a person providing health care for P;
   (e) giving a direction that a person responsible for P's health care allow a different person to take over that responsibility.

(2) Subsection (1) is subject to section 20 (restrictions on deputies).

18 Section 16 powers: property and affairs

(1) The powers under section 16 as respects P's property and affairs extend in particular to—
   (a) the control and management of P's property;
   (b) the sale, exchange, charging, gift or other disposition of P's property;
   (c) the acquisition of property in P's name or on P's behalf;
   (d) the carrying on, on P's behalf, of any profession, trade or business;
   (e) the taking of a decision which will have the effect of dissolving a partnership of which P is a member;
   (f) the carrying out of any contract entered into by P;
   (g) the discharge of P's debts and of any of P's obligations, whether legally enforceable or not;
   (h) the settlement of any of P's property, whether for P's benefit or for the benefit of others;
   (i) the execution for P of a will;
   (j) the exercise of any power (including a power to consent) vested in P whether beneficially or as trustee or otherwise;
   (k) the conduct of legal proceedings in P's name or on P's behalf.

(2) No will may be made under subsection (1)(i) at a time when P has not reached 18.

(3) The powers under section 16 as respects any other matter relating to P's property and affairs may be exercised even though P has not reached 16, if the court considers it likely that P will still lack capacity to make decisions in respect of that matter when he reaches 18.

(4) Schedule 2 supplements the provisions of this section.

(5) Section 16(7) (variation and discharge of court orders) is subject to paragraph 6 of Schedule 2.

(6) Subsection (1) is subject to section 20 (restrictions on deputies).

19 Appointment of deputies

(1) A deputy appointed by the court must be—
- (a) an individual who has reached 18, or
- (b) as respects powers in relation to property and affairs, an individual who has reached 18 or a trust corporation.

(2) The court may appoint an individual by appointing the holder for the time being of a specified office or position.

(3) A person may not be appointed as a deputy without his consent.

(4) The court may appoint two or more deputies to act—
- (a) jointly,
- (b) jointly and severally, or
- (c) jointly in respect of some matters and jointly and severally in respect of others.

(5) When appointing a deputy or deputies, the court may at the same time appoint one or more other persons to succeed the existing deputy or those deputies—
- (a) in such circumstances, or on the happening of such events, as may be specified by the court;
- (b) for such period as may be so specified.

(6) A deputy is to be treated as P's agent in relation to anything done or decided by him within the scope of his appointment and in accordance with this Part.

(7) The deputy is entitled—
- (a) to be reimbursed out of P's property for his reasonable expenses in discharging his functions, and
- (b) if the court so directs when appointing him, to remuneration out of P's property for discharging them.

(8) The court may confer on a deputy powers to—
- (a) take possession or control of all or any specified part of P's property;
- (b) exercise all or any specified powers in respect of it, including such powers of investment as the court may determine.

(9) The court may require a deputy—
- (a) to give to the Public Guardian such security as the court thinks fit for the due discharge of his functions, and
- (b) to submit to the Public Guardian such reports at such times or at such intervals as the court may direct.

20 Restrictions on deputies

(1) A deputy does not have power to make a decision on behalf of P in relation to a matter if he knows or has reasonable grounds for believing that P has capacity in relation to the matter.

(2) Nothing in section 16(5) or 17 permits a deputy to be given power—
- (a) to prohibit a named person from having contact with P;
- (b) to direct a person responsible for P's health care to allow a different person to take over that responsibility.

(3) A deputy may not be given powers with respect to—
- (a) the settlement of any of P's property, whether for P's benefit or for the benefit of others,
- (b) the execution for P of a will, or
- (c) the exercise of any power (including a power to consent) vested in P whether beneficially or as trustee or otherwise.

(4) A deputy may not be given power to make a decision on behalf of P which is inconsistent with a decision made, within the scope of his authority and in accordance with this Act, by the donee of a lasting power of attorney granted by P (or, if there is more than one donee, by any of them).

(5) A deputy may not refuse consent to the carrying out or continuation of life sustaining treatment in relation to P.

(6) The authority conferred on a deputy is subject to the provisions of this Act and, in particular, sections 1 (the principles) and 4 (best interests).

(7) A deputy may not do an act that is intended to restrain P unless four conditions are satisfied.

(8) The first condition is that, in doing the act, the deputy is acting within the scope of an authority expressly conferred on him by the court.

(9) The second is that P lacks, or the deputy reasonably believes that P lacks, capacity in relation to the matter in question.

(10) The third is that the deputy reasonably believes that it is necessary to do the act in order to prevent harm to P.

(11) The fourth is that the act is a proportionate response to—
  (a) the likelihood of P's suffering harm, *or* [and]
  (b) the seriousness of that harm.

(12) For the purposes of this section, a deputy restrains P if he—
  (a) uses, or threatens to use, force to secure the doing of an act which P resists, or
  (b) restricts P's liberty of movement, whether or not P resists, or if he authorises another person to do any of those things.

(13) *But a deputy does more than merely restrain P if he deprives P of his liberty within the meaning of Article 5(1) of the Human Rights Convention (whether or not the deputy is a public authority).*

[Subsection (11) amended by section 51 of the 2007 Act: see Chapter 1 n 28 of this volume. Subsection (13) omitted by section 50(4)(c).]

21 Transfer of proceedings relating to people under 18

(1) The Lord Chief Justice, with the concurrence of the Lord Chancellor, may by order make provision as to the transfer of proceedings relating to a person under 18, in such circumstances as are specified in the order—
  (a) from the Court of Protection to a court having jurisdiction under the Children Act 1989 (c. 41), or
  (b) from a court having jurisdiction under that Act to the Court of Protection.

(2) The Lord Chief Justice may nominate any of the following to exercise his functions under this section—
  (a) the President of the Court of Protection;
  (b) a judicial officer holder (as defined in section 109(4) of the Constitutional Reform Act 2005).

[Powers of court in relation to Schedule A1]

21A Powers of court in relation to Schedule A1

(1) This section applies if either of the following has been given under Schedule A1—
  (a) a standard authorisation;
  (b) an urgent authorisation.

(2) Where a standard authorisation has been given, the court may determine any question relating to any of the following matters—
  (a) whether the relevant person meets one or more of the qualifying requirements;
  (b) the period during which the standard authorisation is to be in force;
  (c) the purpose for which the standard authorisation is given;
  (d) the conditions subject to which the standard authorisation is given.

(3) If the court determines any question under subsection (2), the court may make an order—
  (a) varying or terminating the standard authorisation, or
  (b) directing the supervisory body to vary or terminate the standard authorisation.

(4) Where an urgent authorisation has been given, the court may determine any question relating to any of the following matters—
  (a) whether the urgent authorisation should have been given;
  (b) the period during which the urgent authorisation is to be in force;
  (c) the purpose for which the urgent authorisation is given.

(5) Where the court determines any question under subsection (4), the court may make an order—
  (a) varying or terminating the urgent authorisation, or
  (b) directing the managing authority of the relevant hospital or care home to vary or terminate the urgent authorisation.

(6) Where the court makes an order under subsection (3) or (5), the court may make an order about a person's liability for any act done in connection with the standard or urgent authorisation before its variation or termination.

(7) An order under subsection (6) may, in particular, exclude a person from liability.]

[Section 21A inserted by paragraph 2 of Schedule 9 to the 2007 Act.]

Powers of the court in relation to lasting powers of attorney

22 Powers of court in relation to validity of lasting powers of attorney

(1) This section and section 23 apply if —
  (a) a person ('P') has executed or purported to execute an instrument with a view to creating a lasting power of attorney, or
  (b) an instrument has been registered as a lasting power of attorney conferred by P.

(2) The court may determine any question relating to—
  (a) whether one or more of the requirements for the creation of a lasting power of attorney have been met;
  (b) whether the power has been revoked or has otherwise come to an end.

(3) Subsection (4) applies if the court is satisfied—
  (a) that fraud or undue pressure was used to induce P—
    (i) to execute an instrument for the purpose of creating a lasting power of attorney, or
    (ii) to create a lasting power of attorney, or
  (b) that the donee (or, if more than one, any of them) of a lasting power of attorney—
    (i) has behaved, or is behaving, in a way that contravenes his authority or is not in P's best interests, or
    (ii) proposes to behave in a way that would contravene his authority or would not be in P's best interests.

(4) The court may—
  (a) direct that an instrument purporting to create the lasting power of attorney is not to be registered, or

(b) if P lacks capacity to do so, revoke the instrument or the lasting power of attorney.

(5) If there is more than one donee, the court may under subsection (4)(b) revoke the instrument or the lasting power of attorney so far as it relates to any of them.

(6) 'Donee' includes an intended donee.

23 Powers of court in relation to operation of lasting powers of attorney

(1) The court may determine any question as to the meaning or effect of a lasting power of attorney or an instrument purporting to create one.

(2) The court may—
   (a) give directions with respect to decisions—
      (i) which the donee of a lasting power of attorney has authority to make, and
      (ii) which P lacks capacity to make;
   (b) give any consent or authorisation to act which the donee would have to obtain from P if P had capacity to give it.

(3) The court may, if P lacks capacity to do so—
   (a) give directions to the donee with respect to the rendering by him of reports or accounts and the production of records kept by him for that purpose;
   (b) require the donee to supply information or produce documents or things in his possession as donee;
   (c) give directions with respect to the remuneration or expenses of the donee;
   (d) relieve the donee wholly or partly from any liability which he has or may have incurred on account of a breach of his duties as donee.

(4) The court may authorise the making of gifts which are not within section 12(2) (permitted gifts).

(5) Where two or more donees are appointed under a lasting power of attorney, this section applies as if references to the donee were to all or any of them.

Advance decisions to refuse treatment

24 Advance decisions to refuse treatment: general

(1) 'Advance decision' means a decision made by a person ('P'), after he has reached 18 and when he has capacity to do so, that if—
   (a) at a later time and in such circumstances as he may specify, a specified treatment is proposed to be carried out or continued by a person providing health care for him, and
   (b) at that time he lacks capacity to consent to the carrying out or continuation of the treatment,
   the specified treatment is not to be carried out or continued.

(2) For the purposes of subsection (1)(a), a decision may be regarded as specifying a treatment or circumstances even though expressed in layman's terms.

(3) P may withdraw or alter an advance decision at any time when he has capacity to do so.

(4) A withdrawal (including a partial withdrawal) need not be in writing.

(5) An alteration of an advance decision need not be in writing (unless section 25(5) applies in relation to the decision resulting from the alteration).

25 Validity and applicability of advance decisions

(1) An advance decision does not affect the liability which a person may incur for carrying out or continuing a treatment in relation to P unless the decision is at the material time—

(a) valid, and
(b) applicable to the treatment.

(2) An advance decision is not valid if P—
 (a) has withdrawn the decision at a time when he had capacity to do so,
 (b) has, under a lasting power of attorney created after the advance decision was made, conferred authority on the donee (or, if more than one, any of them) to give or refuse consent to the treatment to which the advance decision relates, or
 (c) has done anything else clearly inconsistent with the advance decision remaining his fixed decision.

(3) An advance decision is not applicable to the treatment in question if at the material time P has capacity to give or refuse consent to it.

(4) An advance decision is not applicable to the treatment in question if—
 (a) that treatment is not the treatment specified in the advance decision,
 (b) any circumstances specified in the advance decision are absent, or
 (c) there are reasonable grounds for believing that circumstances exist which P did not anticipate at the time of the advance decision and which would have affected his decision had he anticipated them.

(5) An advance decision is not applicable to life-sustaining treatment unless—
 (a) the decision is verified by a statement by P to the effect that it is to apply to that treatment even if life is at risk, and
 (b) the decision and statement comply with subsection (6).

(6) A decision or statement complies with this subsection only if—
 (a) it is in writing,
 (b) it is signed by P or by another person in P's presence and by P's direction,
 (c) the signature is made or acknowledged by P in the presence of a witness, and
 (d) the witness signs it, or acknowledges his signature, in P's presence.

(7) The existence of any lasting power of attorney other than one of a description mentioned in subsection (2)(b) does not prevent the advance decision from being regarded as valid and applicable.

26 Effect of advance decisions

(1) If P has made an advance decision which is—
 (a) valid, and
 (b) applicable to a treatment,
the decision has effect as if he had made it, and had had capacity to make it, at the time when the question arises whether the treatment should be carried out or continued.

(2) A person does not incur liability for carrying out or continuing the treatment unless, at the time, he is satisfied that an advance decision exists which is valid and applicable to the treatment.

(3) A person does not incur liability for the consequences of withholding or withdrawing a treatment from P if, at the time, he reasonably believes that an advance decision exists which is valid and applicable to the treatment.

(4) The court may make a declaration as to whether an advance decision—
 (a) exists;
 (b) is valid;
 (c) is applicable to a treatment.

(5) Nothing in an apparent advance decision stops a person—

(a) providing life-sustaining treatment, or

(b) doing any act he reasonably believes to be necessary to prevent a serious deterioration in P's condition,

while a decision as respects any relevant issue is sought from the court.

Excluded decisions

27 Family relationships etc.

(1) Nothing in this Act permits a decision on any of the following matters to be made on behalf of a person—

(a) consenting to marriage or a civil partnership,

(b) consenting to have sexual relations,

(c) consenting to a decree of divorce being granted on the basis of two years' separation,

(d) consenting to a dissolution order being made in relation to a civil partnership on the basis of two years' separation,

(e) consenting to a child's being placed for adoption by an adoption agency,

(f) consenting to the making of an adoption order,

(g) discharging parental responsibilities in matters not relating to a child's property,

(h) giving a consent under the Human Fertilisation and Embryology Act 1990 (c. 37).

(2) 'Adoption order' means—

(a) an adoption order within the meaning of the Adoption and Children Act 2002 (c. 38) (including a future adoption order), and

(b) an order under section 84 of that Act (parental responsibility prior to adoption abroad).

28 Mental Health Act matters

(1) Nothing in this Act authorises anyone—

(a) to give a patient medical treatment for mental disorder, or

(b) to consent to a patient's being given medical treatment for mental disorder, if, at the time when it is proposed to treat the patient, his treatment is regulated by Part 4 of the Mental Health Act.

[(1A) Subsection (1) does not apply in relation to any form of treatment to which section 58A of that Act (electro-convulsive therapy, etc.) applies if the patient comes within subsection (7) of that section (informal patient under 18 who cannot give consent).

(1B) Section 5 does not apply to an act to which section 64B of the Mental Health Act applies (treatment of community patients not recalled to hospital).]

(2) 'Medical treatment', 'mental disorder' and 'patient' have the same meaning as in that Act.

[Subsection (1A) inserted by section 28(10) of the 2007 Act. Subsection (1B) inserted by section 35(5).]

29 Voting rights

(1) Nothing in this Act permits a decision on voting at an election for any public office, or at a referendum, to be made on behalf of a person.

(2) 'Referendum' has the same meaning as in section 101 of the Political Parties, Elections and Referendums Act 2000 (c. 41).

Research

30 Research

(1) Intrusive research carried out on, or in relation to, a person who lacks capacity to consent to it is unlawful unless it is carried out—

   (a) as part of a research project which is for the time being approved by the appropriate body for the purposes of this Act in accordance with section 31, and

   (b) in accordance with sections 32 and 33.

(2) Research is intrusive if it is of a kind that would be unlawful if it was carried out—

   (a) on or in relation to a person who had capacity to consent to it, but

   (b) without his consent.

(3) A clinical trial which is subject to the provisions of clinical trials regulations is not to be treated as research for the purposes of this section.

(4) 'Appropriate body', in relation to a research project, means the person, committee or other body specified in regulations made by the appropriate authority as the appropriate body in relation to a project of the kind in question.

(5) 'Clinical trials regulations' means—

   (a) the Medicines for Human Use (Clinical Trials) Regulations 2004 (S.I. 2004/1031) and any other regulations replacing those regulations or amending them, and

   (b) any other regulations relating to clinical trials and designated by the Secretary of State as clinical trials regulations for the purposes of this section.

(6) In this section, section 32 and section 34, 'appropriate authority' means—

   (a) in relation to the carrying out of research in England, the Secretary of State, and

   (b) in relation to the carrying out of research in Wales, the National Assembly for Wales.

31 Requirements for approval

(1) The appropriate body may not approve a research project for the purposes of this Act unless satisfied that the following requirements will be met in relation to research carried out as part of the project on, or in relation to, a person who lacks capacity to consent to taking part in the project ('P').

(2) The research must be connected with—

   (a) an impairing condition affecting P, or

   (b) its treatment.

(3) 'Impairing condition' means a condition which is (or may be) attributable to, or which causes or contributes to (or may cause or contribute to), the impairment of, or disturbance in the functioning of, the mind or brain.

(4) There must be reasonable grounds for believing that research of comparable effectiveness cannot be carried out if the project has to be confined to, or relate only to, persons who have capacity to consent to taking part in it.

(5) The research must—

   (a) have the potential to benefit P without imposing on P a burden that is disproportionate to the potential benefit to P, or

   (b) be intended to provide knowledge of the causes or treatment of, or of the care of persons affected by, the same or a similar condition.

(6) If the research falls within paragraph (b) of subsection (5) but not within paragraph (a), there must be reasonable grounds for believing—

   (a) that the risk to P from taking part in the project is likely to be negligible, and

    (b) that anything done to, or in relation to, P will not—

        (i) interfere with P's freedom of action or privacy in a significant way, or

        (ii) be unduly invasive or restrictive.

(7) There must be reasonable arrangements in place for ensuring that the requirements of sections 32 and 33 will be met.

32 Consulting carers etc.

(1) This section applies if a person ('R')—

    (a) is conducting an approved research project, and

    (b) wishes to carry out research, as part of the project, on or in relation to a person ('P') who lacks capacity to consent to taking part in the project.

(2) R must take reasonable steps to identify a person who—

    (a) otherwise than in a professional capacity or for remuneration, is engaged in caring for P or is interested in P's welfare, and

    (b) is prepared to be consulted by R under this section.

(3) If R is unable to identify such a person he must, in accordance with guidance issued by the appropriate authority, nominate a person who—

    (a) is prepared to be consulted by R under this section, but

    (b) has no connection with the project.

(4) R must provide the person identified under subsection (2), or nominated under subsection (3), with information about the project and ask him—

    (a) for advice as to whether P should take part in the project, and

    (b) what, in his opinion, P's wishes and feelings about taking part in the project would be likely to be if P had capacity in relation to the matter.

(5) If, at any time, the person consulted advises R that in his opinion P's wishes and feelings would be likely to lead him to decline to take part in the project (or to wish to withdraw from it) if he had capacity in relation to the matter, R must ensure—

    (a) if P is not already taking part in the project, that he does not take part in it;

    (b) if P is taking part in the project, that he is withdrawn from it.

(6) But subsection (5)(b) does not require treatment that P has been receiving as part of the project to be discontinued if R has reasonable grounds for believing that there would be a significant risk to P's health if it were discontinued.

(7) The fact that a person is the donee of a lasting power of attorney given by P, or is P's deputy, does not prevent him from being the person consulted under this section.

(8) Subsection (9) applies if treatment is being, or is about to be, provided for P as a matter of urgency and R considers that, having regard to the nature of the research and of the particular circumstances of the case—

    (a) it is also necessary to take action for the purposes of the research as a matter of urgency, but

    (b) it is not reasonably practicable to consult under the previous provisions of this section.

(9) R may take the action if—

    (a) he has the agreement of a registered medical practitioner who is not involved in the organisation or conduct of the research project, or

    (b) where it is not reasonably practicable in the time available to obtain that agreement, he acts in accordance with a procedure approved by the appropriate body at the time when the research project was approved under section 31.

(10) But R may not continue to act in reliance on subsection (9) if he has reasonable grounds for believing that it is no longer necessary to take the action as a matter of urgency.

33 Additional safeguards

(1) This section applies in relation to a person who is taking part in an approved research project even though he lacks capacity to consent to taking part.

(2) Nothing may be done to, or in relation to, him in the course of the research—

    (a) to which he appears to object (whether by showing signs of resistance or otherwise) except where what is being done is intended to protect him from harm or to reduce or prevent pain or discomfort, or

    (b) which would be contrary to—

        (i) an advance decision of his which has effect, or

        (ii) any other form of statement made by him and not subsequently withdrawn, of which R is aware.

(3) The interests of the person must be assumed to outweigh those of science and society.

(4) If he indicates (in any way) that he wishes to be withdrawn from the project he must be withdrawn without delay.

(5) P must be withdrawn from the project, without delay, if at any time the person conducting the research has reasonable grounds for believing that one or more of the requirements set out in section 31(2) to (7) is no longer met in relation to research being carried out on, or in relation to, P.

(6) But neither subsection (4) nor subsection (5) requires treatment that P has been receiving as part of the project to be discontinued if R has reasonable grounds for believing that there would be a significant risk to P's health if it were discontinued.

34 Loss of capacity during research project

(1) This section applies where a person ('P')—

    (a) has consented to take part in a research project begun before the commencement of section 30, but

    (b) before the conclusion of the project, loses capacity to consent to continue to take part in it.

(2) The appropriate authority may by regulations provide that, despite P's loss of capacity, research of a prescribed kind may be carried out on, or in relation to, P if—

    (a) the project satisfies prescribed requirements,

    (b) any information or material relating to P which is used in the research is of a prescribed description and was obtained before P's loss of capacity, and

    (c) the person conducting the project takes in relation to P such steps as may be prescribed for the purpose of protecting him.

(3) The regulations may, in particular,—

    (a) make provision about when, for the purposes of the regulations, a project is to be treated as having begun;

    (b) include provision similar to any made by section 31, 32 or 33.

Independent Medical Capacity Advocates

35 Appointment of independent mental capacity advocates

(1) The appropriate authority must make such arrangements as it considers reasonable to enable persons ('independent mental capacity advocates') to be available to represent and support persons to whom acts or decisions proposed under sections 37, 38 and 39 relate [or persons who fall within section 39A, 39C or 39D].

(2) The appropriate authority may make regulations as to the appointment of independent mental capacity advocates.

(3) The regulations may, in particular, provide—

(a) that a person may act as an independent mental capacity advocate only in such circumstances, or only subject to such conditions, as may be prescribed;

(b) for the appointment of a person as an independent mental capacity advocate to be subject to approval in accordance with the regulations.

(4) In making arrangements under subsection (1), the appropriate authority must have regard to the principle that a person to whom a proposed act or decision relates should, so far as practicable, be represented and supported by a person who is independent of any person who will be responsible for the act or decision.

(5) The arrangements may include provision for payments to be made to, or in relation to, persons carrying out functions in accordance with the arrangements.

(6) For the purpose of enabling him to carry out his functions, an independent mental capacity advocate—

(a) may interview in private the person whom he has been instructed to represent, and

(b) may, at all reasonable times, examine and take copies of—

(i) any health record,

(ii) any record of, or held by, a local authority and compiled in connection with a social services function, and

(iii) any record held by a person registered under Part 2 of the Care Standards Act 2000 (c. 14), which the person holding the record considers may be relevant to the independent mental capacity advocate's investigation.

(7) In this section, section 36 and section 37, 'the appropriate authority' means—

(a) in relation to the provision of the services of independent mental capacity advocates in England, the Secretary of State, and

(b) in relation to the provision of the services of independent mental capacity advocates in Wales, the National Assembly for Wales.

[Subsection (1) amended by paragraph 3 of Schedule 9 to the 2007 Act.]

36 Functions of independent mental capacity advocates

(1) The appropriate authority may make regulations as to the functions of independent mental capacity advocates.

(2) The regulations may, in particular, make provision requiring an advocate to take such steps as may be prescribed for the purpose of—

(a) providing support to the person whom he has been instructed to represent ('P') so that P may participate as fully as possible in any relevant decision;

(b) obtaining and evaluating relevant information;

(c) ascertaining what P's wishes and feelings would be likely to be, and the beliefs and values that would be likely to influence P, if he had capacity;

(d) ascertaining what alternative courses of action are available in relation to P;

(e) obtaining a further medical opinion where treatment is proposed and the advocate thinks that one should be obtained.

(3) The regulations may also make provision as to circumstances in which the advocate may challenge, or provide assistance for the purpose of challenging, any relevant decision.

37 Provision of serious medical treatment by NHS body

(1) This section applies if an NHS body—

    (a) is proposing to provide, or secure the provision of, serious medical treatment for a person ('P') who lacks capacity to consent to the treatment, and

    (b) is satisfied that there is no person, other than one engaged in providing care or treatment for P in a professional capacity or for remuneration, whom it would be appropriate to consult in determining what would be in P's best interests.

(2) But this section does not apply if P's treatment is regulated by Part 4 [or 4A] of the Mental Health Act.

(3) Before the treatment is provided, the NHS body must instruct an independent mental capacity advocate to represent P.

(4) If the treatment needs to be provided as a matter of urgency, it may be provided even though the NHS body has not been able to comply with subsection (3).

(5) The NHS body must, in providing or securing the provision of treatment for P, take into account any information given, or submissions made, by the independent mental capacity advocate.

(6) 'Serious medical treatment' means treatment which involves providing, withholding or withdrawing treatment of a kind prescribed by regulations made by the appropriate authority.

(7) 'NHS body' has such meaning as may be prescribed by regulations made for the purposes of this section by—

    (a) the Secretary of State, in relation to bodies in England, or

    (b) the National Assembly for Wales, in relation to bodies in Wales.

[Words 'or 4A' inserted in subsection (2) by section 35(6) of the 2007 Act.]

38 Provision of accommodation by NHS body

(1) This section applies if an NHS body proposes to make arrangements—

    (a) for the provision of accommodation in a hospital or care home for a person ('P') who lacks capacity to agree to the arrangements, or

    (b) for a change in P's accommodation to another hospital or care home, and is satisfied that there is no person, other than one engaged in providing care or treatment for P in a professional capacity or for remuneration, whom it would be appropriate for it to consult in determining what would be in P's best interests.

(2) But this section does not apply if P is accommodated as a result of an obligation imposed on him under the Mental Health Act.

[(2A) And this section does not apply if—

    (a) an independent mental capacity advocate must be appointed under section 39A or 39C (whether or not by the NHS body) to represent P, and

    (b) the hospital or care home in which P is to be accommodated under the arrangements referred to in this section is the relevant hospital or care home under the authorisation referred to in that section.]

(3) Before making the arrangements, the NHS body must instruct an independent mental capacity advocate to represent P unless it is satisfied that—

    (a) the accommodation is likely to be provided for a continuous period which is less than the applicable period, or

    (b) the arrangements need to be made as a matter of urgency.

(4) If the NHS body—

    (a) did not instruct an independent mental capacity advocate to represent P before making the arrangements because it was satisfied that subsection (3)(a) or (b) applied, but

   (b) subsequently has reason to believe that the accommodation is likely to be provided for a continuous period—

     (i) beginning with the day on which accommodation was first provided in accordance with the arrangements, and

     (ii) ending on or after the expiry of the applicable period, it must instruct an independent mental capacity advocate to represent P.

(5) The NHS body must, in deciding what arrangements to make for P, take into account any information given, or submissions made, by the independent mental capacity advocate.

(6) 'Care home' has the meaning given in section 3 of the Care Standards Act 2000 (c. 14).

(7) 'Hospital' means—

   (a) a health service hospital as defined by section 275 of the National Health Service Act 2006 or section 206 of the National Health Service (Wales) Act 2006, or

   (b) an independent hospital as defined by section 2 of the Care Standards Act 2000.

(8) 'NHS body' has such meaning as may be prescribed by regulations made for the purposes of this section by—

   (a) the Secretary of State, in relation to bodies in England, or

   (b) the National Assembly for Wales, in relation to bodies in Wales.

(9) 'Applicable period' means—

   (a) in relation to accommodation in a hospital, 28 days, and

   (b) in relation to accommodation in a care home, 8 weeks.

[(10) For the purposes of subsection (1), a person appointed under Part 10 of Schedule A1 to be P's representative is not, by virtue of that appointment, engaged in providing care or treatment for P in a professional capacity or for remuneration.]

[Subsections (2A) and (10) inserted by paragraphs 4(2) and 4(3) respectively of Schedule 9 to the 2007 Act.]

39 Provision of accommodation by local authority

(1) This section applies if a local authority propose to make arrangements—

   (a) for the provision of residential accommodation for a person ('P') who lacks capacity to agree to the arrangements, or

   (b) for a change in P's residential accommodation, and are satisfied that there is no person, other than one engaged in providing care or treatment for P in a professional capacity or for remuneration, whom it would be appropriate for them to consult in determining what would be in P's best interests.

(2) But this section applies only if the accommodation is to be provided in accordance with—

   (a) section 21 or 29 of the National Assistance Act 1948 (c. 29), or

   (b) section 117 of the Mental Health Act, as the result of a decision taken by the local authority under section 47 of the National Health Service and Community Care Act 1990 (c. 19).

(3) This section does not apply if P is accommodated as a result of an obligation imposed on him under the Mental Health Act.

[(3A) And this section does not apply if—

   (a) an independent mental capacity advocate must be appointed under section 39A or 39C (whether or not by the local authority) to represent P, and

   (b) the place in which P is to be accommodated under the arrangements referred to in this section is the relevant hospital or care home under the authorisation referred to in that section.]

(4) Before making the arrangements, the local authority must instruct an independent mental capacity advocate to represent P unless they are satisfied that—
   (a) the accommodation is likely to be provided for a continuous period of less than 8 weeks, or
   (b) the arrangements need to be made as a matter of urgency.

(5) If the local authority—
   (a) did not instruct an independent mental capacity advocate to represent P before making the arrangements because they were satisfied that subsection (4)(a) or (b) applied, but
   (b) subsequently have reason to believe that the accommodation is likely to be provided for a continuous period that will end 8 weeks or more after the day on which accommodation was first provided in accordance with the arrangements, they must instruct an independent mental capacity advocate to represent P.

(6) The local authority must, in deciding what arrangements to make for P, take into account any information given, or submissions made, by the independent mental capacity advocate.

[(7) For the purposes of subsection (1), a person appointed under Part 10 of Schedule A1 to be P's representative is not, by virtue of that appointment, engaged in providing care or treatment for P in a professional capacity or for remuneration.]

[Subsections (3A) and (7) inserted by paragraphs 5(2) and (3) respectively of Schedule 9 to the 2007 Act.]

[39A Person becomes subject to Schedule A1

(1) This section applies if—
   (a) a person ('P') becomes subject to Schedule A1, and
   (b) the managing authority of the relevant hospital or care home are satisfied that there is no person, other than one engaged in providing care or treatment for P in a professional capacity or for remuneration, whom it would be appropriate to consult in determining what would be in P's best interests.

(2) The managing authority must notify the supervisory body that this section applies.

(3) The supervisory body must instruct an independent mental capacity advocate to represent P.

(4) Schedule A1 makes provision about the role of an independent mental capacity advocate appointed under this section.

(5) This section is subject to paragraph 161 of Schedule A1.

(6) For the purposes of subsection (1), a person appointed under Part 10 of Schedule A1 to be P's representative is not, by virtue of that appointment, engaged in providing care or treatment for P in a professional capacity or for remuneration.]

[Section 39A inserted by paragraph 6 of Schedule 9 to the 2007 Act.]

[39B Section 39A: supplementary provision

(1) This section applies for the purposes of section 39A.

(2) P becomes subject to Schedule A1 in any of the following cases.

(3) The first case is where an urgent authorisation is given in relation to P under paragraph 76(2) of Schedule A1 (urgent authorisation given before request made for standard authorisation).

(4) The second case is where the following conditions are met.

(5) The first condition is that a request is made under Schedule A1 for a standard authorisation to be given in relation to P ('the requested authorisation').

(6) The second condition is that no urgent authorisation was given under paragraph 76(2) of Schedule A1 before that request was made.

(7) The third condition is that the requested authorisation will not be in force on or before, or immediately after, the expiry of an existing standard authorisation.

(8) The expiry of a standard authorisation is the date when the authorisation is expected to cease to be in force.

(9) The third case is where, under paragraph 69 of Schedule 6, the supervisory body select a person to carry out an assessment of whether or not the relevant person is a detained resident.]

[Section 39B inserted by paragraph 6 of Schedule 9 to the 2007 Act.]

[39C Person unrepresented whilst subject to Schedule A1

(1) This section applies if—
   (a) an authorisation under Schedule A1 is in force in relation to a person ('P'),
   (b) the appointment of a person as P's representative ends in accordance with regulations made under Part 10 of Schedule A1, and
   (c) the managing authority of the relevant hospital or care home are satisfied that there is no person, other than one engaged in providing care or treatment for P in a professional capacity or for remuneration, whom it would be appropriate to consult in determining what would be in P's best interests.

(2) The managing authority must notify the supervisory body that this section applies.

(3) The supervisory body must instruct an independent mental capacity advocate to represent P.

(4) Paragraph 159 of Schedule A1 makes provision about the role of an independent mental capacity advocate appointed under this section.

(5) The appointment of an independent mental capacity advocate under this section ends when a new appointment of a person as P's representative is made in accordance with Part 10 of Schedule A1.

(6) For the purposes of subsection (1), a person appointed under Part 10 of Schedule A1 to be P's representative is not, by virtue of that appointment, engaged in providing care or treatment for P in a professional capacity or for remuneration.]

[Section 39C inserted by paragraph 6 of Schedule 9 to the 2007 Act.]

[39D Person subject to Schedule A1 without paid representative

(1) This section applies if—
   (a) an authorisation under Schedule A1 is in force in relation to aperson ('P'),
   (b) P has a representative ('R') appointed under Part 10 of Schedule A1, and
   (c) R is not being paid under regulations under Part 10 of Schedule A1 for acting as P's representative.

(2) The supervisory body must instruct an independent mental capacity advocate to represent P in any of the following cases.

(3) The first case is where P makes a request to the supervisory body to instruct an advocate.

(4) The second case is where R makes a request to the supervisory body to instruct an advocate.

(5) The third case is where the supervisory body have reason to believe one or more of the following—
   (a) that, without the help of an advocate, P and R would be unable to exercise one or both of the relevant rights;
   (b) that P and R have each failed to exercise a relevant right when it would have been reasonable to exercise it;
   (c) that P and R are each unlikely to exercise a relevant right when it would be reasonable to exercise it.

(6) The duty in subsection (2) is subject to section 39E.

(7) If an advocate is appointed under this section, the advocate is, in particular, to take such steps as are practicable to help P and R to understand the following matters—

  (a) the effect of the authorisation;

  (b) the purpose of the authorisation;

  (c) the duration of the authorisation;

  (d) any conditions to which the authorisation is subject;

  (e) the reasons why each assessor who carried out an assessment in connection with the request for the authorisation, or in connection with a review of the authorisation, decided that P met the qualifying requirement in question;

  (f) the relevant rights;

  (g) how to exercise the relevant rights.

(8) The advocate is, in particular, to take such steps as are practicable to help P or R—

  (a) to exercise the right to apply to court, if it appears to the advocate that P or R wishes to exercise that right, or

  (b) to exercise the right of review, if it appears to the advocate that P or R wishes to exercise that right.

(9) If the advocate helps P or R to exercise the right of review—

  (a) the advocate may make submissions to the supervisory body on the question of whether a qualifying requirement is reviewable;

  (b) the advocate may give information, or make submissions, to any assessor carrying out a review assessment.

(10) In this section—

  'relevant rights' means—

  (a) the right to apply to court, and

  (b) the right of review;

  'right to apply to court' means the right to make an application to the court to exercise its jurisdiction under section 21A;

  'right of review' means the right under Part 8 of Schedule A1 to request a review.]

[Section 39D inserted by paragraph 6 of Schedule 9 to the 2007 Act.]

[39E Limitation on duty to instruct advocate under section 39D

(1) This section applies if an advocate is already representing P in accordance with an instruction under section 39D.

(2) Section 39D(2) does not require another advocate to be instructed, unless the following conditions are met.

(3) The first condition is that the existing advocate was instructed—

  (a) because of a request by R, or

  (b) because the supervisory body had reason to believe one or more of the things in section 39D(5).

(4) The second condition is that the other advocate would be instructed because of a request by P.]

[Section 39E inserted by paragraph 6 of Schedule 9 to the 2007 Act.]

40 Exceptions

Sections 37(3), 38(3) and (4), and 39(4) and (5) do not apply if there is—

  (a) a person nominated by P (in whatever manner) as a person to be consulted in matters affecting his interests,

  (b) a donee of a lasting power of attorney created by P,

   (c) a deputy appointed by the court for P, or

   (d) a donee of an enduring power of attorney (within the meaning of Schedule 4) created by P.

[(1) The duty imposed by section 37(3), 38(3) or (4), 39(4) or 39(5), 39A(3), 39C(3) or 39D(2) does not apply where there is—

   (a) a person nominated by P (in whatever manner) as a person to be consulted on matters to which that duty relates,

   (b) a donee of a lasting power of attorney created by P who is authorised to make decisions in relation to those matters, or

   (c) a deputy appointed by the court for P with power to make decisions in relation to those matters.

(2) A person appointed under Part 10 of Schedule A1 to be P's representative is not, by virtue of that appointment, a person nominated by P as a person to be consulted in matters to which a duty mentioned in subsection (1) relates.]

[Subsection (1) inserted (unnumbered) by section 49 of the 2007 Act, but numbered and amended by paragraphs 7(2)&(3) respectively of Schedule 9. Subsection (2) inserted by paragraph 7(4) of that Schedule.]

41 Power to adjust role of independent mental capacity advocate

(1) The appropriate authority may make regulations—

   (a) expanding the role of independent mental capacity advocates in relation to persons who lack capacity, and

   (b) adjusting the obligation to make arrangements imposed by section 35.

(2) The regulations may, in particular—

   (a) prescribe circumstances (different to those set out in sections 37, 38 and 39) in which an independent mental capacity advocate must, or circumstances in which one may, be instructed by a person of a prescribed description to represent a person who lacks capacity, and

   (b) include provision similar to any made by section 37, 38, 39 or 40.

(3) 'Appropriate authority' has the same meaning as in section 35.

Miscellaneous and supplementary

42 Codes of practice ##

(1) The Lord Chancellor must prepare and issue one or more codes of practice—

   (a) for the guidance of persons assessing whether a person has capacity in relation to any matter,

   (b) for the guidance of persons acting in connection with the care or treatment of another person (see section 5),

   (c) for the guidance of donees of lasting powers of attorney,

   (d) for the guidance of deputies appointed by the court,

   (e) for the guidance of persons carrying out research in reliance on any provision made by or under this Act (and otherwise with respect to sections 30 to 34),

   (f) for the guidance of independent mental capacity advocates,

   [(fa) for the guidance of persons exercising functions under Schedule A1,

   (fb) for the guidance of representatives appointed under Part 10 of Schedule A1,]

   (g) with respect to the provisions of sections 24 to 26 (advance decisions and apparent advance decisions), and

   (h) with respect to such other matters concerned with this Act as he thinks fit.

(2) The Lord Chancellor may from time to time revise a code.

(3) The Lord Chancellor may delegate the preparation or revision of the whole or any part of a code so far as he considers expedient.

(4) It is the duty of a person to have regard to any relevant code if he is acting in relation to a person who lacks capacity and is doing so in one or more of the following ways—

    (a) as the donee of a lasting power of attorney,

    (b) as a deputy appointed by the court,

    (c) as a person carrying out research in reliance on any provision made by or under this Act (see sections 30 to 34),

    (d) as an independent mental capacity advocate,

    [(da) in the exercise of functions under Schedule A1,

    (db) as a representative appointed under Part 10 of Schedule A1,]

    (e) in a professional capacity,

    (f) for remuneration.

(5) If it appears to a court or tribunal conducting any criminal or civil proceedings that—

    (a) a provision of a code, or

    (b) a failure to comply with a code, is relevant to a question arising in the proceedings, the provision or failure must be taken into account in deciding the question.

(6) A code under subsection (1)(d) may contain separate guidance for deputies appointed by virtue of paragraph 1(2) of Schedule 5 (functions of deputy conferred on receiver appointed under the Mental Health Act).

(7) In this section and in section 43, 'code' means a code prepared or revised under this section.

[Sub-paragraphs (fa) and (fb) inserted into subsection (2) and sub-paragraphs (da) and (db) inserted into subsection (4) by paragraphs 8(2) and (3) respectively of Schedule 9 to the 2007 Act.]

43 Codes of practice: procedure

(1) Before preparing or revising a code, the Lord Chancellor must consult—

    (a) the National Assembly for Wales, and

    (b) such other persons as he considers appropriate.

(2) The Lord Chancellor may not issue a code unless—

    (a) a draft of the code has been laid by him before both Houses of Parliament, and

    (b) the 40 day period has elapsed without either House resolving not to approve the draft.

(3) The Lord Chancellor must arrange for any code that he has issued to be published in such a way as he considers appropriate for bringing it to the attention of persons likely to be concerned with its provisions.

(4) '40 day period', in relation to the draft of a proposed code, means—

    (a) if the draft is laid before one House on a day later than the day on which it is laid before the other House, the period of 40 days beginning with the later of the two days;

    (b) in any other case, the period of 40 days beginning with the day on which it is laid before each House.

(5) In calculating the period of 40 days, no account is to be taken of any period during which Parliament is dissolved or prorogued or during which both Houses are adjourned for more than 4 days.

44 Ill-treatment or neglect

(1) Subsection (2) applies if a person ('D')—

    (a) has the care of a person ('P') who lacks, or whom D reasonably believes to lack, capacity,

(b) is the donee of a lasting power of attorney, or an enduring power of attorney (within the meaning of Schedule 4), created by P, or

(c) is a deputy appointed by the court for P.

(2) D is guilty of an offence if he ill-treats or wilfully neglects P.

(3) A person guilty of an offence under this section is liable—

(a) on summary conviction, to imprisonment for a term not exceeding 12 months or a fine not exceeding the statutory maximum or both;

(b) on conviction on indictment, to imprisonment for a term not exceeding 5 years or a fine or both.

PART 2
THE COURT OF PROTECTION AND THE PUBLIC GUARDIAN

The Court of Protection

45 The Court of Protection

(1) There is to be a superior court of record known as the Court of Protection.

(2) The court is to have an official seal.

(3) The court may sit at any place in England and Wales, on any day and at any time.

(4) The court is to have a central office and registry at a place appointed by the Lord Chancellor, after consulting the Lord Chief Justice.

(5) The Lord Chancellor may, after consulting the Lord Chief Justice, designate as additional registries of the court any district registry of the High Court and any county court office.

(5A) The Lord Chief Justice may nominate any of the following to exercise his functions under this section-

(a) the President of the Court of Protection;

(b) a judicial officer holder (as defined in section 109(4) of the Constitutional Reform Act 2005).

(6) The office of the Supreme Court called the Court of Protection ceases to exist.

46 The judges of the Court of Protection

(1) Subject to Court of Protection Rules under section 51(2)(d), the jurisdiction of the court is exercisable by a judge nominated for that purpose by—

(a) the Lord Chief Justice, or

(b) where nominated by the Lord Chief Justice to act on his behalf under this subsection—

(i) the President of the Court of Protection;

(ii) a judicial officer holder (as defined in section 109(4) of the Constitutional Reform Act 2005).

(2) To be nominated, a judge must be—

(a) the President of the Family Division,

(b) the Vice-Chancellor,

(c) a puisne judge of the High Court,

(d) a circuit judge, or

(e) a district judge.

(3) The Lord Chief Justice, after consulting the Lord Chancellor, must—

(a) appoint one of the judges nominated by virtue of subsection (2)(a) to (c) to be President of the Court of Protection, an

(b) appoint another of those judges to be Vice-President of the Court of Protection.

(4) The Chief Justice, after consulting the Lord Chancellor, must appoint one of the judges nominated by virtue of subsection (2)(d) or (e) to be Senior Judge of the Court of Protection, having such administrative functions in relation to the court as the Lord Chancellor, after consulting the Lord Chief Justice, may direct.

Supplementary powers

47 General powers and effect of orders etc.

(1) The court has in connection with its jurisdiction the same powers, rights, privileges and authority as the High Court.

(2) Section 204 of the Law of Property Act 1925 (c. 20) (orders of High Court conclusive in favour of purchasers) applies in relation to orders and directions of the court as it applies to orders of the High Court.

(3) Office copies of orders made, directions given or other instruments issued by the court and sealed with its official seal are admissible in all legal proceedings as evidence of the originals without any further proof.

48 Interim orders and directions

The court may, pending the determination of an application to it in relation to a person ('P'), make an order or give directions in respect of any matter if—

(a) there is reason to believe that P lacks capacity in relation to the matter,

(b) the matter is one to which its powers under this Act extend, and

(c) it is in P's best interests to make the order, or give the directions, without delay.

49 Power to call for reports

(1) This section applies where, in proceedings brought in respect of a person ('P') under Part 1, the court is considering a question relating to P.

(2) The court may require a report to be made to it by the Public Guardian or by a Court of Protection Visitor.

(3) The court may require a local authority, or an NHS body, to arrange for a report to be made—

(a) by one of its officers or employees, or

(b) by such other person (other than the Public Guardian or a Court of Protection Visitor) as the authority, or the NHS body, considers appropriate.

(4) The report must deal with such matters relating to P as the court may direct.

(5) Court of Protection Rules may specify matters which, unless the court directs otherwise, must also be dealt with in the report.

(6) The report may be made in writing or orally, as the court may direct.

(7) In complying with a requirement, the Public Guardian or a Court of Protection Visitor may, at all reasonable times, examine and take copies of—

(a) any health record,

(b) any record of, or held by, a local authority and compiled in connection with a social services function, and

(c) any record held by a person registered under Part 2 of the Care Standards Act 2000 (c. 14), so far as the record relates to P.

(8) If the Public Guardian or a Court of Protection Visitor is making a visit in the course of complying with a requirement, he may interview P in private.

(9) If a Court of Protection Visitor who is a Special Visitor is making a visit in the course of complying with a requirement, he may if the court so directs carry out in private a medical, psychiatric or psychological examination of P's capacity and condition.

(10) 'NHS body' has the meaning given in section 148 of the Health and Social Care (Community Health and Standards) Act 2003 (c. 43).

(11) 'Requirement' means a requirement imposed under subsection (2) or (3).

Practice and procedure

50 Applications to the Court of Protection

(1) No permission is required for an application to the court for the exercise of any of its powers under this Act—
   (a) by a person who lacks, or is alleged to lack, capacity,
   (b) if such a person has not reached 18, by anyone with parental responsibility for him,
   (c) by the donor or a donee of a lasting power of attorney to which the application relates,
   (d) by a deputy appointed by the court for a person to whom the application relates, or
   (e) by a person named in an existing order of the court, if the application relates to the order.

[(1A) Nor is permission required for an application to the court under section 21A by the relevant person's representative.]

(2) But, subject to Court of Protection Rules and to paragraph 20(2) of Schedule 3 (declarations relating to private international law), permission is required for any other application to the court.

(3) In deciding whether to grant permission the court must, in particular, have regard to—
   (a) the applicant's connection with the person to whom the application relates,
   (b) the reasons for the application,
   (c) the benefit to the person to whom the application relates of a proposed order or directions, and
   (d) whether the benefit can be achieved in any other way.

(4) 'Parental responsibility' has the same meaning as in the Children Act 1989 (c. 41).

[Subsection (1A) inserted by paragraph 9 of Schedule 9 to the 2007 Act.]

51 Court of Protection Rules

(1) Rules of court with respect to the practice and procedure of the court (to be called 'Court of Protection Rules') may be made in accordance with Part 1 of Schedule 1 to the Constitutional Reform Act 2005.

(2) Court of Protection Rules may, in particular, make provision—
   (a) as to the manner and form in which proceedings are to be commenced;
   (b) as to the persons entitled to be notified of, and be made parties to, the proceedings;
   (c) for the allocation, in such circumstances as may be specified, of any specified description of proceedings to a specified judge or to specified descriptions of judges;
   (d) for the exercise of the jurisdiction of the court, in such circumstances as may be specified, by its officers or other staff;

(e) for enabling the court to appoint a suitable person (who may, with his consent, be the Official Solicitor) to act in the name of, or on behalf of, or to represent the person to whom the proceedings relate;

(f) for enabling an application to the court to be disposed of without a hearing;

(g) for enabling the court to proceed with, or with any part of, a hearing in the absence of the person to whom the proceedings relate;

(h) for enabling or requiring the proceedings or any part of them to be conducted in private and for enabling the court to determine who is to be admitted when the court sits in private and to exclude specified persons when it sits in public;

(i) as to what may be received as evidence (whether or not admissible apart from the rules) and the manner in which it is to be presented;

(j) for the enforcement of orders made and directions given in the proceedings.

(3) Court of Protection Rules may, instead of providing for any matter, refer to provision made or to be made about that matter by directions.

(4) Court of Protection Rules may make different provision for different areas.

52 Practice directions

(1) Directions as to the practice and procedure of the court may be given in accordance with Part 1 of Schedule 2 to the Constitutional Reform Act 2005.

(2) Practice directions given otherwise than under subsection (1) may not be given without the approval of –
(a) the Lord Chancellor, and
(b) the Lord Chief Justice.

(3) The Lord Chief Justice may nominate any of the following to exercise his functions under this section-
(a) the President of the Court of Protection;
(b) a judicial office holder (as defined in section 109(4) of the Constitutional Reform Act 2005.

53 Rights of appeal

(1) Subject to the provisions of this section, an appeal lies to the Court of Appeal from any decision of the court.

(2) Court of Protection Rules may provide that where a decision of the court is made by—
(a) a person exercising the jurisdiction of the court by virtue of rules made under section 51(2)(d),
(b) a district judge, or
(c) a circuit judge,
an appeal from that decision lies to a prescribed higher judge of the court and not to the Court of Appeal.

(3) For the purposes of this section the higher judges of the court are—
(a) in relation to a person mentioned in subsection (2)(a), a circuit judge or a district judge;
(b) in relation to a person mentioned in subsection (2)(b), a circuit judge;
(c) in relation to any person mentioned in subsection (2), one of the judges nominated by virtue of section 46(2)(a) to (c).

(4) Court of Protection Rules may make provision—
(a) that, in such cases as may be specified, an appeal from a decision of the court may not be made without permission;

(b) as to the person or persons entitled to grant permission to appeal;

(c) as to any requirements to be satisfied before permission is granted;

(d) that where a higher judge of the court makes a decision on an appeal, no appeal may be made to the Court of Appeal from that decision unless the Court of Appeal considers that—

    (i) the appeal would raise an important point of principle or practice, or

    (ii) there is some other compelling reason for the Court of Appeal to hear it;

(e) as to any considerations to be taken into account in relation to granting or refusing permission to appeal.

Fees and costs

54 Fees

(1) The Lord Chancellor may with the consent of the Treasury by order prescribe fees payable in respect of anything dealt with by the court.

(2) An order under this section may in particular contain provision as to—

    (a) scales or rates of fees;

    (b) exemptions from and reductions in fees;

    (c) remission of fees in whole or in part.

(3) Before making an order under this section, the Lord Chancellor must consult—

    (a) the President of the Court of Protection,

    (b) the Vice-President of the Court of Protection, and

    (c) the Senior Judge of the Court of Protection.

(4) The Lord Chancellor must take such steps as are reasonably practicable to bring information about fees to the attention of persons likely to have to pay them.

(5) Fees payable under this section are recoverable summarily as a civil debt.

55 Costs

(1) Subject to Court of Protection Rules, the costs of and incidental to all proceedings in the court are in its discretion.

(2) The rules may in particular make provision for regulating matters relating to the costs of those proceedings, including prescribing scales of costs to be paid to legal or other representatives.

(3) The court has full power to determine by whom and to what extent the costs are to be paid.

(4) The court may, in any proceedings—

    (a) disallow, or

    (b) order the legal or other representatives concerned to meet,

the whole of any wasted costs or such part of them as may be determined in accordance with the rules.

(5) 'Legal or other representative', in relation to a party to proceedings, means any person exercising a right of audience or right to conduct litigation on his behalf.

(6) 'Wasted costs' means any costs incurred by a party—

    (a) as a result of any improper, unreasonable or negligent act or omission on the part of any legal or other representative or any employee of such a representative, or

    (b) which, in the light of any such act or omission occurring after they were incurred, the court considers it is unreasonable to expect that party to pay.

56 Fees and costs: supplementary

(1) Court of Protection Rules may make provision—

(a) as to the way in which, and funds from which, fees and costs are to be paid;

(b) for charging fees and costs upon the estate of the person to whom the proceedings relate;

(c) for the payment of fees and costs within a specified time of the death of the person to whom the proceedings relate or the conclusion of the proceedings.

(2) A charge on the estate of a person created by virtue of subsection (1)(b) does not cause any interest of the person in any property to fail or determine or to be prevented from recommencing.

The Public Guardian

57 The Public Guardian

(1) For the purposes of this Act, there is to be an officer, to be known as the Public Guardian.

(2) The Public Guardian is to be appointed by the Lord Chancellor.

(3) There is to be paid to the Public Guardian out of money provided by Parliament such salary as the Lord Chancellor may determine.

(4) The Lord Chancellor may, after consulting the Public Guardian—

(a) provide him with such officers and staff, o

(b) enter into such contracts with other persons for the provision (by them or their sub-contractors) of officers, staff or services,

as the Lord Chancellor thinks necessary for the proper discharge of the Public Guardian's functions.

(5) Any functions of the Public Guardian may, to the extent authorised by him, be performed by any of his officers.

58 Functions of the Public Guardian

(1) The Public Guardian has the following functions—

(a) establishing and maintaining a register of lasting powers of attorney,

(b) establishing and maintaining a register of orders appointing deputies,

(c) supervising deputies appointed by the court,

(d) directing a Court of Protection Visitor to visit—

(i) a donee of a lasting power of attorney,

(ii) a deputy appointed by the court, or

(iii) the person granting the power of attorney or for whom the deputy is appointed ('P'), and to make a report to the Public Guardian on such matters as he may direct,

(e) receiving security which the court requires a person to give for the discharge of his functions,

(f) receiving reports from donees of lasting powers of attorney and deputies appointed by the court,

(g) reporting to the court on such matters relating to proceedings under this Act as the court requires,

(h) dealing with representations (including complaints) about the way in which a donee of a lasting power of attorney or a deputy appointed by the court is exercising his powers,

(i) publishing, in any manner the Public Guardian thinks appropriate, any information he thinks appropriate about the discharge of his functions.

(2) The functions conferred by subsection (1)(c) and (h) may be discharged in cooperation with any other person who has functions in relation to the care or treatment of P.

(3) The Lord Chancellor may by regulations make provision—
   (a) conferring on the Public Guardian other functions in connection with this Act;
   (b) in connection with the discharge by the Public Guardian of his functions.

(4) Regulations made under subsection (3)(b) may in particular make provision as to—
   (a) the giving of security by deputies appointed by the court and the enforcement and discharge of security so given;
   (b) the fees which may be charged by the Public Guardian;
   (c) the way in which, and funds from which, such fees are to be paid;
   (d) exemptions from and reductions in such fees;
   (e) remission of such fees in whole or in part;
   (f) the making of reports to the Public Guardian by deputies appointed by the court and others who are directed by the court to carry out any transaction for a person who lacks capacity.

(5) For the purpose of enabling him to carry out his functions, the Public Guardian may, at all reasonable times, examine and take copies of—
   (a) any health record,
   (b) any record of, or held by, a local authority and compiled in connection with a social services function, and
   (c) any record held by a person registered under Part 2 of the Care Standards Act 2000 (c. 14), so far as the record relates to P.

(6) The Public Guardian may also for that purpose interview P in private.

59 Public Guardian Board

(1) There is to be a body, to be known as the Public Guardian Board.

(2) The Board's duty is to scrutinise and review the way in which the Public Guardian discharges his functions and to make such recommendations to the Lord Chancellor about that matter as it thinks appropriate.

(3) The Lord Chancellor must, in discharging his functions under sections 57 and 58, give due consideration to recommendations made by the Board.

(5) The Board must have—
   (a) at least one member who is a judge of the court, and
   (b) at least four members who are persons appearing to the Lord Chancellor to have appropriate knowledge or experience of the work of the Public Guardian.

(5A) Where a person to be appointed as a member of the Board is a judge of the court, the appointment is to be made by the Lord Chief Justice after consulting the Lord Chancellor.

(5B) In any other case, the appointment of a person as a member of the Board is to be made by the Lord Chancellor.

(6) The Lord Chancellor may by regulations make provision as to—
   (a) the appointment of members of the Board (and, in particular, the procedures to be followed in connection with appointments);
   (b) the selection of one of the members to be the chairman;
   (c) the term of office of the chairman and members;
   (d) their resignation, suspension or removal;
   (e) the procedure of the Board (including quorum);
   (f) the validation of proceedings in the event of a vacancy among the members or a defect in the appointment of a member.

(7) Subject to any provision made in reliance on subsection (6)(c) or (d), a person is to hold and vacate office as a member of the Board in accordance with the terms of the instrument appointing him.

(8) The Lord Chancellor may make such payments to or in respect of members of the Board by way of reimbursement of expenses, allowances and remuneration as he may determine.

(9) The Board must make an annual report to the Lord Chancellor about the discharge of its functions.

(10) The Lord Chief Justice may nominate any of the following to exercise his functions under this section-

(a) the President of the Court of Protection

(b) a judicial office holder (as defined in section 109(4) of the Constitutional Reform Act 2005.)

60 Annual report

(1) The Public Guardian must make an annual report to the Lord Chancellor about the discharge of his functions.

(2) The Lord Chancellor must, within one month of receiving the report, lay a copy of it before Parliament.

Court of Protection Visitors

61 Court of Protection Visitors

(1) A Court of Protection Visitor is a person who is appointed by the Lord Chancellor to—

(a) a panel of Special Visitors, or

(b) a panel of General Visitors.

(2) A person is not qualified to be a Special Visitor unless he—

(a) is a registered medical practitioner or appears to the Lord Chancellor to have other suitable qualifications or training, and

(b) appears to the Lord Chancellor to have special knowledge of and experience in cases of impairment of or disturbance in the functioning of the mind or brain.

(3) A General Visitor need not have a medical qualification.

(4) A Court of Protection Visitor—

(a) may be appointed for such term and subject to such conditions, and

(b) may be paid such remuneration and allowances, as the Lord Chancellor may determine.

(5) For the purpose of carrying out his functions under this Act in relation to a person who lacks capacity ('P'), a Court of Protection Visitor may, at all reasonable times, examine and take copies of—

(a) any health record,

(b) any record of, or held by, a local authority and compiled in connection with a social services function, and

(c) any record held by a person registered under Part 2 of the Care Standards Act 2000 (c. 14),

so far as the record relates to P.

(6) A Court of Protection Visitor may also for that purpose interview P in private.

PART 3

MISCELLANEOUS AND GENERAL

Declaratory provision

62 Scope of the Act

For the avoidance of doubt, it is hereby declared that nothing in this Act is to be taken to affect the law relating to murder or manslaughter or the operation of section 2 of the Suicide Act 1961 (c. 60) (assisting suicide).

Private international law

63 International protection of adults

Schedule 3—

(a) gives effect in England and Wales to the Convention on the International Protection of Adults signed at the Hague on 13th January 2000 (Cm. 5881) (in so far as this Act does not otherwise do so), and

(b) makes related provision as to the private international law of England and Wales.

General

64 Interpretation ##

(1) In this Act—

'the 1985 Act' means the Enduring Powers of Attorney Act 1985 (c. 29),

'advance decision' has the meaning given in section 24(1),

['authorisation under Schedule A1' means either—

(a) a standard authorisation under that Schedule, or

(b) an urgent authorisation under that Schedule.]

'the court' means the Court of Protection established by section 45,

'Court of Protection Rules' has the meaning given in section 51(1),

'Court of Protection Visitor' has the meaning given in section 61,

'deputy' has the meaning given in section 16(2)(b),

'enactment' includes a provision of subordinate legislation (within the meaning of the Interpretation Act 1978 (c. 30)),

'health record' has the meaning given in section 68 of the Data Protection Act 1998 (c. 29) (as read with section 69 of that Act),

'the Human Rights Convention' has the same meaning as 'the Convention' in the Human Rights Act 1998 (c. 42),

'independent mental capacity advocate' has the meaning given in section 35(1),

'lasting power of attorney' has the meaning given in section 9,

'life-sustaining treatment' has the meaning given in section 4(10),

'local authority', [except in Schedule A1,] means—

(a) the council of a county in England in which there are no district councils,

(b) the council of a district in England,

(c) the council of a county or county borough in Wales,

(d) the council of a London borough,

(e) the Common Council of the City of London, or

(f) the Council of the Isles of Scilly,

'Mental Health Act' means the Mental Health Act 1983 (c. 20),

'prescribed', in relation to regulations made under this Act, means prescribed by those regulations,

'property' includes any thing in action and any interest in real or personal property,

'public authority' has the same meaning as in the Human Rights Act 1998,

'Public Guardian' has the meaning given in section 57,

'purchaser' and 'purchase' have the meaning given in section 205(1) of the Law of Property Act 1925 (c. 20),

'social services function' has the meaning given in section 1A of the Local Authority Social Services Act 1970 (c. 42),

'treatment' includes a diagnostic or other procedure

'trust corporation' has the meaning given in section 68(1) of the Trustee Act 1925 (c. 19), and

'will' includes codicil.

(2) In this Act, references to making decisions, in relation to a donee of a lasting power of attorney or a deputy appointed by the court, include, where appropriate, acting on decisions made.

(3) In this Act, references to the bankruptcy of an individual include a case where a bankruptcy restrictions order under the Insolvency Act 1986 (c. 45) has effect in respect of him.

(4) 'Bankruptcy restrictions order' includes an interim bankruptcy restrictions order.

[(5) In this Act, references to deprivation of a person's liberty have the same meaning as in Article 5(1) of the Human Rights Convention.

(6) For the purposes of such references, it does not matter whether a person is deprived of his liberty by a public authority or not.]

[Definition of 'authorisation under Schedule A1', additional words in definition of 'local authority' and new subsections (5) & (6) inserted by paragraphs 10(2), (3) and (4) respectively of Schedule 9 to the 2007 Act.]

65 Rules, regulations and orders

(1) Any power to make rules, regulations or orders under this Act, other than the power in section 21—

 (a) is exercisable by statutory instrument;

 (b) includes power to make supplementary, incidental, consequential, transitional or saving provision;

 (c) includes power to make different provision for different cases.

(2) Any statutory instrument containing rules, regulations or orders made by the Lord Chancellor or the Secretary of State under this Act, other than—

 (a) regulations under section 34 (loss of capacity during research project),

 (b) regulations under section 41 (adjusting role of independent mental capacity advocacy service),

 (c) regulations under paragraph 32(1)(b) of Schedule 3 (private international law relating to the protection of adults),

 (d) an order of the kind mentioned in section 67(6) (consequential amendments of primary legislation), or

 (e) an order under section 68 (commencement), is subject to annulment in pursuance of a resolution of either House of Parliament.

(3) A statutory instrument containing an Order in Council under paragraph 31 of Schedule 3 (provision to give further effect to Hague Convention) is subject to annulment in pursuance of a resolution of either House of Parliament.

(4) A statutory instrument containing regulations made by the Secretary of State under section 34 or 41, or by the Lord Chancellor under paragraph 32(1)(b) of Schedule 3 may not be made unless a draft has been laid before and approved by resolution of each House of Parliament.

[(4A) Subsection (2) does not apply to a statutory instrument containing regulations made by the Secretary of State under Schedule A1.

(4B) If such a statutory instrument contains regulations under paragraph 42(2)(b), 129, 162 or 164 of Schedule A1 (whether or not it also contains other regulations), the instrument may not be made unless a draft has been laid before and approved by resolution of each House of Parliament.

(4C) Subject to that, such a statutory instrument is subject to annulment in pursuance of a resolution of either House of Parliament.]

(5) An order under section 21—
   (a) may include supplementary, incidental, consequential, transitional or saving provision;
   (b) may make different provision for different cases;
   (c) is to be made in the form of a statutory instrument to which the Statutory Instruments Act 1946 applies as if the order were made by a Minister of the Crown; and
   (d) is subject to annulment in pursuance of a resolution of either House of Parliament.

[Subsections (4A) to (4C) inserted by paragraph 11(2) of Schedule 9 to the 2007 Act.]

66 Existing receivers and enduring powers of attorney etc.

(1) The following provisions cease to have effect—
   (a) Part 7 of the Mental Health Act,
   (b) the Enduring Powers of Attorney Act 1985 (c. 29).

(2) No enduring power of attorney within the meaning of the 1985 Act is to be created after the commencement of subsection (1)(b).

(3) Schedule 4 has effect in place of the 1985 Act in relation to any enduring power of attorney created before the commencement of subsection (1)(b).

(4) Schedule 5 contains transitional provisions and savings in relation to Part 7 of the Mental Health Act and the 1985 Act.

67 Minor and consequential amendments and repeals

(1) Schedule 6 contains minor and consequential amendments.

(2) Schedule 7 contains repeals.

(3) The Lord Chancellor may by order make supplementary, incidental, consequential, transitional or saving provision for the purposes of, in consequence of, or for giving full effect to a provision of this Act.

(4) An order under subsection (3) may, in particular—
   (a) provide for a provision of this Act which comes into force before another provision of this Act has come into force to have effect, until the other provision has come into force, with specified modifications;
   (b) amend, repeal or revoke an enactment, other than one contained in an Act or Measure passed in a Session after the one in which this Act is passed.

(5) The amendments that may be made under subsection (4)(b) are in addition to those made by or under any other provision of this Act.

(6) An order under subsection (3) which amends or repeals a provision of an Act or Measure may not be made unless a draft has been laid before and approved by resolution of each House of Parliament.

68 Commencement and extent

(1) This Act, other than sections 30 to 41, comes into force in accordance with provision made by order by the Lord Chancellor.

(2) Sections 30 to 41 come into force in accordance with provision made by order by—
    (a) the Secretary of State, in relation to England, and
    (b) the National Assembly for Wales, in relation to Wales.

(3) An order under this section may appoint different days for different provisions and different purposes.

(4) Subject to subsections (5) and (6), this Act extends to England and Wales only.

(5) The following provisions extend to the United Kingdom—
    (a) paragraph 16(1) of Schedule 1 (evidence of instruments and of registration of lasting powers of attorney),
    (b) paragraph 15(3) of Schedule 4 (evidence of instruments and of registration of enduring powers of attorney).

(6) Subject to any provision made in Schedule 6, the amendments and repeals made by Schedules 6 and 7 have the same extent as the enactments to which they relate.

69 Short title

This Act may be cited as the Mental Capacity Act 2005.

SCHEDULES

[SCHEDULE A1

HOSPITAL AND CARE HOME RESIDENTS: DEPRIVATION OF LIBERTY

PART 1
AUTHORISATION TO DEPRIVE RESIDENTS OF LIBERTY ETC.

Application of Part

1 (1) This Part applies if the following conditions are met.

(2) The first condition is that a person ('P') is detained in a hospital or care home—for the purpose of being given care or treatment—in circumstances which amount to deprivation of the person's liberty.

(3) The second condition is that a standard or urgent authorisation is in force.

(4) The third condition is that the standard or urgent authorisation relates—
    (a) to P, and
    (b) to the hospital or care home in which P is detained.]

[Authorisation to deprive P of liberty

2   The managing authority of the hospital or care home may deprive P of his liberty by detaining him as mentioned in paragraph 1(2).

No liability for acts done for purpose of depriving P of liberty

3 (1) This paragraph applies to any act which a person ('D') does for the purpose of detaining P as mentioned in paragraph 1(2).

(2) D does not incur any liability in relation to the act that he would not have incurred if P—
   (a) had had capacity to consent in relation to D's doing the act, and
   (b) had consented to D's doing the act.

No protection for negligent acts etc.

4 (1) Paragraphs 2 and 3 do not exclude a person's civil liability for loss or damage, or his criminal liability, resulting from his negligence in doing any thing.

(2) Paragraphs 2 and 3 do not authorise a person to do anything otherwise than for the purpose of the standard or urgent authorisation that is in force.

(3) In a case where a standard authorisation is in force, paragraphs 2 and 3 do not authorise a person to do anything which does not comply with the conditions (if any) included in the authorisation.

PART 2
INTERPRETATION: MAIN TERMS

Introduction

5 This Part applies for the purposes of this Schedule.

Detained resident

6 'Detained resident' means a person detained in a hospital or care home—for the purpose of being given care or treatment—in circumstances which amount to deprivation of the person's liberty.

Relevant person etc.

7 In relation to a person who is, or is to be, a detained resident—
   'relevant person' means the person in question;
   'relevant hospital or care home' means the hospital or care home in question;
   'relevant care or treatment' means the care or treatment in question.

Authorisations

8 'Standard authorisation' means an authorisation given under Part 4.]

[9 'Urgent authorisation' means an authorisation given under Part 5.

10 'Authorisation under this Schedule' means either of the following—

    (a) a standard authorisation;

    (b) an urgent authorisation.

11 (1) The purpose of a standard authorisation is the purpose which is stated in the authorisation in accordance with paragraph 55(1)(d).

(2) The purpose of an urgent authorisation is the purpose which is stated in the authorisation in accordance with paragraph 80(d).

PART 3
THE QUALIFYING REQUIREMENTS

The qualifying requirements

12 (1) These are the qualifying requirements referred to in this Schedule—

    (a) the age requirement;

    (b) the mental health requirement;

    (c) the mental capacity requirement;

    (d) the best interests requirement;

    (e) the eligibility requirement;

    (f) the no refusals requirement.

(2) Any question of whether a person who is, or is to be, a detained resident meets the qualifying requirements is to be determined in accordance with this Part.

(3) In a case where—

    (a) the question of whether a person meets a particular qualifying requirement arises in relation to the giving of a standard authorisation, and

    (b) any circumstances relevant to determining that question are expected to change between the time when the determination is made and the time when the authorisation is expected to come into force,

those circumstances are to be taken into account as they are expected to be at the later time.

The age requirement

13 The relevant person meets the age requirement if he has reached 18.

The mental health requirement

14 (1) The relevant person meets the mental health requirement if he is suffering from mental disorder (within the meaning of the Mental Health Act, but disregarding any exclusion for persons with learning disability).

(2) An exclusion for persons with learning disability is any provision of the Mental Health Act which provides for a person with learning disability not to be regarded as suffering from mental disorder for one or more purposes of that Act.]

[The mental capacity requirement

15 The relevant person meets the mental capacity requirement if he lacks capacity in relation to the question whether or not he should be accommodated in the relevant hospital or care home for the purpose of being given the relevant care or treatment.

The best interests requirement

16 (1) The relevant person meets the best interests requirement if all of the following conditions are met.

(2) The first condition is that the relevant person is, or is to be, a detained resident.

(3) The second condition is that it is in the best interests of the relevant person for him to be a detained resident.

(4) The third condition is that, in order to prevent harm to the relevant person, it is necessary for him to be a detained resident.

(5) The fourth condition is that it is a proportionate response to—
   (a) the likelihood of the relevant person suffering harm, and
   (b) the seriousness of that harm,
   for him to be a detained resident.

The eligibility requirement

17 (1) The relevant person meets the eligibility requirement unless he is ineligible to be deprived of liberty by this Act.

(2) Schedule 1A applies for the purpose of determining whether or not P is ineligible to be deprived of liberty by this Act.

The no refusals requirement

18 The relevant person meets the no refusals requirement unless there is a refusal within the meaning of paragraph 19 or 20.

19 (1) There is a refusal if these conditions are met—
   (a) the relevant person has made an advance decision;
   (b) the advance decision is valid;
   (c) the advance decision is applicable to some or all of the relevant treatment.

(2) Expressions used in this paragraph and any of sections 24, 25 or 26 have the same meaning in this paragraph as in that section.

20 (1) There is a refusal if it would be in conflict with a valid decision of a donee or deputy for the relevant person to be accommodated in the relevant hospital or care home for the purpose of receiving some or all of the relevant care or treatment—
   (a) in circumstances which amount to deprivation of the person's liberty, or
   (b) at all.

(2) A donee is a donee of a lasting power of attorney granted by the relevant person.

(3) A decision of a donee or deputy is valid if it is made—
   (a) within the scope of his authority as donee or deputy, and
   (b) in accordance with Part 1 of this Act.]

[PART 4
STANDARD AUTHORISATIONS

Supervisory body to give authorisation

21 Only the supervisory body may give a standard authorisation.

22 The supervisory body may not give a standard authorisation unless—
   (a) the managing authority of the relevant hospital or care home have requested it, or
   (b) paragraph 71 applies (right of third party to require consideration of whether authorisation needed).

23 The managing authority may not make a request for a standard authorisation unless—
   (a) they are required to do so by paragraph 24 (as read with paragraphs 27 to 29),
   (b) they are required to do so by paragraph 25 (as read with paragraph 28), or
   (c) they are permitted to do so by paragraph 30.

Duty to request authorisation: basic cases

24 (1) The managing authority must request a standard authorisation in any of the following cases.

   (2) The first case is where it appears to the managing authority that the relevant person—
       (a) is not yet accommodated in the relevant hospital or care home,
       (b) is likely—at some time within the next 28 days—to be a detained resident in the relevant hospital or care home, and
       (c) is likely—
           (i) at that time, or
           (ii) at some later time within the next 28 days,
       to meet all of the qualifying requirements.

   (3) The second case is where it appears to the managing authority that the relevant person—
       (a) is already accommodated in the relevant hospital or care home,
       (b) is likely — at some time within the next 28 days — to be a detained resident in the relevant hospital or care home, and
       (c) is likely—
           (i) at that time, or
           (ii) at some later time within the next 28 days,
       to meet all of the qualifying requirements.

   (4) The third case is where it appears to the managing authority that the relevant person—
       (a) is a detained resident in the relevant hospital or care home, and
       (b) meets all of the qualifying requirements, or is likely to do so at some time within the next 28 days.

   (5) This paragraph is subject to paragraphs 27 to 29.

Duty to request authorisation: change in place of detention

25 (1) The relevant managing authority must request a standard authorisation if it appears to them that these conditions are met.

   (2) The first condition is that a standard authorisation—
       (a) has been given, and
       (b) has not ceased to be in force.]

[(3) The second condition is that there is, or is to be, a change in the place of detention.

(4) This paragraph is subject to paragraph 28.

26 (1) This paragraph applies for the purposes of paragraph 25.

(2) There is a change in the place of detention if the relevant person—

  (a) ceases to be a detained resident in the stated hospital or care home, and

  (b) becomes a detained resident in a different hospital or care home ('the new hospital or care home').

(3) The stated hospital or care home is the hospital or care home to which the standard authorisation relates.

(4) The relevant managing authority are the managing authority of the new hospital or care home.

Other authority for detention: request for authorisation

27 (1) This paragraph applies if, by virtue of section 4A(3), a decision of the court authorises the relevant person to be a detained resident.

(2) Paragraph 24 does not require a request for a standard authorisation to be made in relation to that detention unless these conditions are met.

(3) The first condition is that the standard authorisation would be in force at a time immediately after the expiry of the other authority.

(4) The second condition is that the standard authorisation would not be in force at any time on or before the expiry of the other authority.

(5) The third condition is that it would, in the managing authority's view, be unreasonable to delay making the request until a time nearer the expiry of the other authority.

(6) In this paragraph—

  (a) the other authority is—

    (i) the decision mentioned in sub-paragraph (1), or

    (ii) any further decision of the court which, by virtue of section 4A(3), authorises, or is expected to authorise, the relevant person to be a detained resident;

  (b) the expiry of the other authority is the time when the other authority is expected to cease to authorise the relevant person to be a detained resident.

Request refused: no further request unless change of circumstances

28 (1) This paragraph applies if—

  (a) a managing authority request a standard authorisation under paragraph 24 or 25, and

  (b) the supervisory body are prohibited by paragraph 50(2) from giving the authorisation.

(2) Paragraph 24 or 25 does not require that managing authority to make a new request for a standard authorisation unless it appears to the managing authority that—

  (a) there has been a change in the relevant person's case, and

  (b) because of that change, the supervisory body are likely to give a standard authorisation if requested.

Authorisation given: request for further authorisation

29 (1) This paragraph applies if a standard authorisation—

  (a) has been given in relation to the detention of the relevant person, and] [(b) that authorisation ('the existing authorisation') has not ceased to be in force.

(2) Paragraph 24 does not require a new request for a standard authorisation ('the new authorisation') to be made unless these conditions are met.

(3) The first condition is that the new authorisation would be in force at a time immediately after the expiry of the existing authorisation.

(4) The second condition is that the new authorisation would not be in force at any time on or before the expiry of the existing authorisation.

(5) The third condition is that it would, in the managing authority's view, be unreasonable to delay making the request until a time nearer the expiry of the existing authorisation.

(6) The expiry of the existing authorisation is the time when it is expected to cease to be in force.

Power to request authorisation

30 (1) This paragraph applies if—

(a) a standard authorisation has been given in relation to the detention of the relevant person,

(b) that authorisation ('the existing authorisation') has not ceased to be in force,

(c) the requirement under paragraph 24 to make a request for a new standard authorisation does not apply, because of paragraph 29, and

(d) a review of the existing authorisation has been requested, or is being carried out, in accordance with Part 8.

(2) The managing authority may request a new standard authorisation which would be in force on or before the expiry of the existing authorisation; but only if it would also be in force immediately after that expiry.

(3) The expiry of the existing authorisation is the time when it is expected to cease to be in force.

(4) Further provision relating to cases where a request is made under this paragraph can be found in—

(a) paragraph 62 (effect of decision about request), and

(b) paragraph 134 (effect of request on Part 8 review).

Information included in request

31 A request for a standard authorisation must include the information (if any) required by regulations.

Records of requests

32 (1) The managing authority of a hospital or care home must keep a written record of—

(a) each request that they make for a standard authorisation, and

(b) the reasons for making each request.

(2) A supervisory body must keep a written record of each request for a standard authorisation that is made to them.]

[Relevant person must be assessed

33 (1) This paragraph applies if the supervisory body are requested to give a standard authorisation.

(2) The supervisory body must secure that all of these assessments are carried out in relation to the relevant person—

    (a) an age assessment;

    (b) a mental health assessment;

    (c) a mental capacity assessment;

    (d) a best interests assessment;

    (e) an eligibility assessment;

    (f) a no refusals assessment.

(3) The person who carries out any such assessment is referred to as the assessor.

(4) Regulations may be made about the period (or periods) within which assessors must carry out assessments.

(5) This paragraph is subject to paragraphs 49 and 133.

Age assessment

34 An age assessment is an assessment of whether the relevant person meets the age requirement.

Mental health assessment

35 A mental health assessment is an assessment of whether the relevant person meets the mental health requirement.

36 When carrying out a mental health assessment, the assessor must also—

    (a) consider how (if at all) the relevant person's mental health is likely to be affected by his being a detained resident, and

    (b) notify the best interests assessor of his conclusions.

Mental capacity assessment

37 A mental capacity assessment is an assessment of whether the relevant person meets the mental capacity requirement.

Best interests assessment

38 A best interests assessment is an assessment of whether the relevant person meets the best interests requirement.

39 (1) In carrying out a best interests assessment, the assessor must comply with the duties in sub-paragraphs (2) and (3).

(2) The assessor must consult the managing authority of the relevant hospital or care home.

(3) The assessor must have regard to all of the following—

    (a) the conclusions which the mental health assessor has notified to the best interests assessor in accordance with paragraph 36(b);

    (b) any relevant needs assessment;

    (c) any relevant care plan.]

[(4) A relevant needs assessment is an assessment of the relevant person's needs which—

    (a) was carried out in connection with the relevant person being accommodated in the relevant hospital or care home, and

    (b) was carried out by or on behalf of—

        (i) the managing authority of the relevant hospital or care home, or

        (ii) the supervisory body.

(5) A relevant care plan is a care plan which—

    (a) sets out how the relevant person's needs are to be met whilst he is accommodated in the relevant hospital or care home, and

    (b) was drawn up by or on behalf of—

        (i) the managing authority of the relevant hospital or care home, or

        (ii) the supervisory body.

(6) The managing authority must give the assessor a copy of—

    (a) any relevant needs assessment carried out by them or on their behalf, or

    (b) any relevant care plan drawn up by them or on their behalf.

(7) The supervisory body must give the assessor a copy of—

    (a) any relevant needs assessment carried out by them or on their behalf, or

    (b) any relevant care plan drawn up by them or on their behalf.

(8) The duties in sub-paragraphs (2) and (3) do not affect any other duty to consult or to take the views of others into account.

40 (1) This paragraph applies whatever conclusion the best interests assessment comes to.

(2) The assessor must state in the best interests assessment the name and address of every interested person whom he has consulted in carrying out the assessment.

41 Paragraphs 42 and 43 apply if the best interests assessment comes to the conclusion that the relevant person meets the best interests requirement.

42 (1) The assessor must state in the assessment the maximum authorisation period.

(2) The maximum authorisation period is the shorter of these periods—

    (a) the period which, in the assessor's opinion, would be the appropriate maximum period for the relevant person to be a detained resident under the standard authorisation that has been requested;

    (b) 1 year, or such shorter period as may be prescribed in regulations.

(3) Regulations under sub-paragraph (2)(b)—

    (a) need not provide for a shorter period to apply in relation to all standard authorisations;

    (b) may provide for different periods to apply in relation to different kinds of standard authorisations.

(4) Before making regulations under sub-paragraph (2)(b) the Secretary of State must consult all of the following—

    (a) each body required by regulations under paragraph 162 to monitor and report on the operation of this Schedule in relation to England;

    (b) such other persons as the Secretary of State considers it appropriate to consult.

(5) Before making regulations under sub-paragraph (2)(b) the National Assembly for Wales must consult all of the following—

    (a) each person or body directed under paragraph 163(2) to carry out any function of the Assembly of monitoring and reporting on the operation of this Schedule in relation to Wales;

    (b) such other persons as the Assembly considers it appropriate to consult.]

[43 The assessor may include in the assessment recommendations about conditions to which the standard authorisation is, or is not, to be subject in accordance with paragraph 53.

44 (1) This paragraph applies if the best interests assessment comes to the conclusion that the relevant person does not meet the best interests requirement.

(2) If, on the basis of the information taken into account in carrying out the assessment, it appears to the assessor that there is an unauthorised deprivation of liberty, he must include a statement to that effect in the assessment.

(3) There is an unauthorised deprivation of liberty if the managing authority of the relevant hospital or care home are already depriving the relevant person of his liberty without authority of the kind mentioned in section 4A.

45 The duties with which the best interests assessor must comply are subject to the provision included in appointment regulations under Part 10 (in particular, provision made under paragraph 146).

Eligibility assessment

46 An eligibility assessment is an assessment of whether the relevant person meets the eligibility requirement.

47 (1) Regulations may—

(a) require an eligibility assessor to request a best interests assessor to provide relevant eligibility information, and

(b) require the best interests assessor, if such a request is made, to provide such relevant eligibility information as he may have.

(2) In this paragraph—

'best interests assessor' means any person who is carrying out, or has carried out, a best interests assessment in relation to the relevant person;

'eligibility assessor' means a person carrying out an eligibility assessment in relation to the relevant person;

'relevant eligibility information' is information relevant to assessing whether or not the relevant person is ineligible by virtue of paragraph 5 of Schedule 1A.

No refusals assessment

48 A no refusals assessment is an assessment of whether the relevant person meets the no refusals requirement.

Equivalent assessment already carried out

49 (1) The supervisory body are not required by paragraph 33 to secure that a particular kind of assessment ('the required assessment') is carried out in relation to the relevant person if the following conditions are met.

(2) The first condition is that the supervisory body have a written copy of an assessment of the relevant person ('the existing assessment') that has already been carried out.

(3) The second condition is that the existing assessment complies with all requirements under this Schedule with which the required assessment would have to comply (if it were carried out).

(4) The third condition is that the existing assessment was carried out within the previous 12 months; but this condition need not be met if the required assessment is an age assessment.

(5) The fourth condition is that the supervisory body are satisfied that there is no reason why the existing assessment may no longer be accurate.]

[(6) If the required assessment is a best interests assessment, in satisfying themselves as mentioned in sub-paragraph (5), the supervisory body must take into account any information given, or submissions made, by—

(a) the relevant person's representative,

(b) any section 39C IMCA or

(c) any section 39D IMCA.

(7) It does not matter whether the existing assessment was carried out in connection with a request for a standard authorisation or for some other purpose.

(8) If, because of this paragraph, the supervisory body are not required by paragraph 33 to secure that the required assessment is carried out, the existing assessment is to be treated for the purposes of this Schedule—

(a) as an assessment of the same kind as the required assessment,

and

(b) as having been carried out under paragraph 33 in connection with the request for the standard authorisation.

Duty to give authorisation

50 (1) The supervisory body must give a standard authorisation if—

(a) all assessments are positive, and

(b) the supervisory body have written copies of all those assessments.

(2) The supervisory body must not give a standard authorisation except in accordance with sub-paragraph (1).

(3) All assessments are positive if each assessment carried out under paragraph 33 has come to the conclusion that the relevant person meets the qualifying requirement to which the assessment relates.

Terms of authorisation

51 (1) If the supervisory body are required to give a standard authorisation, they must decide the period during which the authorisation is to be in force.

(2) That period must not exceed the maximum authorisation period stated in the best interests assessment.

52 A standard authorisation may provide for the authorisation to come into force at a time after it is given.

53 (1) A standard authorisation may be given subject to conditions.

(2) Before deciding whether to give the authorisation subject to conditions, the supervisory body must have regard to any recommendations in the best interests assessment about such conditions.

(3) The managing authority of the relevant hospital or care home must ensure that any conditions are complied with.

Form of authorisation

54 A standard authorisation must be in writing.

55 (1) A standard authorisation must state the following things—

(a) the name of the relevant person;

(b) the name of the relevant hospital or care home;]

[(c) the period during which the authorisation is to be in force;

(d) the purpose for which the authorisation is given;

(e) any conditions subject to which the authorisation is given;

(f) the reason why each qualifying requirement is met.

(2) The statement of the reason why the eligibility requirement is met must be framed by reference to the cases in the table in paragraph 2 of Schedule 1A.

56 (1) If the name of the relevant hospital or care home changes, the standard authorisation is to be read as if it stated the current name of the hospital or care home.

(2) But sub-paragraph (1) is subject to any provision relating to the change of name which is made in any enactment or in any instrument made under an enactment.

Duty to give information about decision

57 (1) This paragraph applies if—

(a) a request is made for a standard authorisation, and

(b) the supervisory body are required by paragraph 50(1) to give the standard authorisation.

(2) The supervisory body must give a copy of the authorisation to each of the following—

(a) the relevant person's representative;

(b) the managing authority of the relevant hospital or care home;

(c) the relevant person;

(d) any section 39A IMCA;

(e) every interested person consulted by the best interests assessor.

(3) The supervisory body must comply with this paragraph as soon as practicable after they give the standard authorisation.

58 (1) This paragraph applies if—

(a) a request is made for a standard authorisation, and

(b) the supervisory body are prohibited by paragraph 50(2) from giving the standard authorisation.

(2) The supervisory body must give notice, stating that they are prohibited from giving the authorisation, to each of the following—

(a) the managing authority of the relevant hospital or care home;

(b) the relevant person;

(c) any section 39A IMCA;

(d) every interested person consulted by the best interests assessor.

(3) The supervisory body must comply with this paragraph as soon as practicable after it becomes apparent to them that they are prohibited from giving the authorisation.

Duty to give information about effect of authorisation

59 (1) This paragraph applies if a standard authorisation is given.

(2) The managing authority of the relevant hospital or care home must take such steps as are practicable to ensure that the relevant person understands all of the following—

(a) the effect of the authorisation;

(b) the right to make an application to the court to exercise its jurisdiction under section 21A;

(c) the right under Part 8 to request a review

(d) the right to have a section 39D IMCA appointed;

(e) how to have a section 39D IMCA appointed.]

[(3) Those steps must be taken as soon as is practicable after the authorisation is given.

(4) Those steps must include the giving of appropriate information both orally and in writing.

(5) Any written information given to the relevant person must also be given by the managing authority to the relevant person's representative.

(6) They must give the information to the representative as soon as is practicable after it is given to the relevant person.

(7) Sub-paragraph (8) applies if the managing authority is notified that a section 39D IMCA has been appointed.

(8) As soon as is practicable after being notified, the managing authority must give the section 39D IMCA a copy of the written information given in accordance with sub-paragraph (4).

Records of authorisations

60 A supervisory body must keep a written record of all of the following information—

(a) the standard authorisations that they have given;

(b) the requests for standard authorisations in response to which they have not given an authorisation;

(c) in relation to each standard authorisation given: the matters stated in the authorisation in accordance with paragraph 55.

Variation of an authorisation

61 (1) A standard authorisation may not be varied except in accordance with Part 7 or 8.

(2) This paragraph does not affect the powers of the Court of Protection or of any other court.

Effect of decision about request made under paragraph 25 or 30

62 (1) This paragraph applies where the managing authority request a new standard authorisation under either of the following—

(a) paragraph 25 (change in place of detention);

(b) paragraph 30 (existing authorisation subject to review).

(2) If the supervisory body are required by paragraph 50(1) to give the new authorisation, the existing authorisation terminates at the time when the new authorisation comes into force.

(3) If the supervisory body are prohibited by paragraph 50(2) from giving the new authorisation, there is no effect on the existing authorisation's continuation in force.

When an authorisation is in force

63 (1) A standard authorisation comes into force when it is given.

(2) But if the authorisation provides for it to come into force at a later time, it comes into force at that time.

64 (1) A standard authorisation ceases to be in force at the end of the period stated in the authorisation in accordance with paragraph 55(1)(c).

(2) But if the authorisation terminates before then in accordance with paragraph 62(2) or any other provision of this Schedule, it ceases to be in force when the termination takes effect.

(3) This paragraph does not affect the powers of the Court of Protection or of any other court.

65 (1) This paragraph applies if a standard authorisation ceases to be in force.]

[(2) The supervisory body must give notice that the authorisation has ceased to be in force.

(3) The supervisory body must give that notice to all of the following—
  (a) the managing authority of the relevant hospital or care home;
  (b) the relevant person;
  (c) the relevant person's representative;
  (d) every interested person consulted by the best interests assessor.

(4) The supervisory body must give that notice as soon as practicable after the authorisation ceases to be in force.

When a request for a standard authorisation is 'disposed of'

66 A request for a standard authorisation is to be regarded for the purposes of this Schedule as disposed of if the supervisory body have given—
  (a) a copy of the authorisation in accordance with paragraph 57, or
  (b) notice in accordance with paragraph 58.

Right of third party to require consideration of whether authorisation needed

67 For the purposes of paragraphs 68 to 73 there is an unauthorised deprivation of liberty if—
  (a) a person is already a detained resident in a hospital or care home,
  and
  (b) the detention of the person is not authorised as mentioned in section 4A

68 (1) If the following conditions are met, an eligible person may request the supervisory body to decide whether or not there is an unauthorised deprivation of liberty.

(2) The first condition is that the eligible person has notified the managing authority of the relevant hospital or care home that it appears to the eligible person that there is an unauthorised deprivation of liberty.

(3) The second condition is that the eligible person has asked the managing authority to request a standard authorisation in relation to the detention of the relevant person.

(4) The third condition is that the managing authority has not requested a standard authorisation within a reasonable period after the eligible person asks it to do so.

(5) In this paragraph 'eligible person' means any person other than the managing authority of the relevant hospital or care home.

69 (1) This paragraph applies if an eligible person requests the supervisory body to decide whether or not there is an unauthorised deprivation of liberty.

(2) The supervisory body must select and appoint a person to carry out an assessment of whether or not the relevant person is a detained resident.

(3) But the supervisory body need not select and appoint a person to carry out such an assessment in either of these cases.

(4) The first case is where it appears to the supervisory body that the request by the eligible person is frivolous or vexatious.

(5) The second case is where it appears to the supervisory body that—
  (a) the question of whether or not there is an unauthorised deprivation of liberty has already been decided, and
  (b) since that decision, there has been no change of circumstances which would merit the question being decided again.]

[(6) The supervisory body must not select and appoint a person to carry out an assessment under this paragraph unless it appears to the supervisory body that the person would be—
  (a) suitable to carry out a best interests assessment (if one were obtained in connection with a request for a standard authorisation relating to the relevant person), and
  (b) eligible to carry out such a best interests assessment.

(7) The supervisory body must notify the persons specified in sub-paragraph (8)—
  (a) that the supervisory body have been requested to decide whether or not there is an unauthorised deprivation of liberty;
  (b) of their decision whether or not to select and appoint a person to carry out an assessment under this paragraph;
  (c) if their decision is to select and appoint a person, of the person appointed.

(8) The persons referred to in sub-paragraph (7) are—
  (a) the eligible person who made the request under paragraph 68;
  (b) the person to whom the request relates;
  (c) the managing authority of the relevant hospital or care home;
  (d) any section 39A IMCA.

70 (1) Regulations may be made about the period within which an assessment under paragraph 69 must be carried out.

(2) Regulations made under paragraph 129(3) apply in relation to the selection and appointment of a person under paragraph 69 as they apply to the selection of a person under paragraph 129 to carry out a best interests assessment.

(3) The following provisions apply to an assessment under paragraph 69 as they apply to an assessment carried out in connection with a request for a standard authorisation—
  (a) paragraph 131 (examination and copying of records);
  (b) paragraph 132 (representations);
  (c) paragraphs 134 and 135(1) and (2) (duty to keep records and give copies).

(4) The copies of the assessment which the supervisory body are required to give under paragraph 135(2) must be given as soon as practicable after the supervisory body are themselves given a copy of the assessment.

71 (1) This paragraph applies if—
  (a) the supervisory body obtain an assessment under paragraph 69,
  (b) the assessment comes to the conclusion that the relevant person is a detained resident, and
  (c) it appears to the supervisory body that the detention of the person is not authorised as mentioned in section 4A.

(2) This Schedule (including Part 5) applies as if the managing authority of the relevant hospital or care home had, in accordance with Part 4, requested the supervisory body to give a standard authorisation in relation to the relevant person.

(3) The managing authority of the relevant hospital or care home must supply the supervisory body with the information (if any) which the managing authority would, by virtue of paragraph 31, have had to include in a request for a standard authorisation.

(4) The supervisory body must notify the persons specified in paragraph 69(8)—
  (a) of the outcome of the assessment obtained under paragraph 69, and
  (b) that this Schedule applies as mentioned in sub-paragraph (2).

72 (1) This paragraph applies if—
  (a) the supervisory body obtain an assessment under paragraph 69, and
  (b) the assessment comes to the conclusion that the relevant person is not a detained resident.]

[(2) The supervisory body must notify the persons specified in paragraph 69(8) of the outcome of the assessment.

73 (1) This paragraph applies if—

(a) the supervisory body obtain an assessment under paragraph 69,

(b) the assessment comes to the conclusion that the relevant person is a detained resident, and

(c) it appears to the supervisory body that the detention of the person is authorised as mentioned in section 4A.

(2) The supervisory body must notify the persons specified in paragraph 69(8)—

(a) of the outcome of the assessment, and

(b) that it appears to the supervisory body that the detention is authorised.

PART 5
URGENT AUTHORISATIONS

Managing authority to give authorisation

74 Only the managing authority of the relevant hospital or care home may give an urgent authorisation.

75 The managing authority may give an urgent authorisation only if they are required to do so by paragraph 76 (as read with paragraph 77).

Duty to give authorisation

76 (1) The managing authority must give an urgent authorisation in either of the following cases.

(2) The first case is where—

(a) the managing authority are required to make a request under paragraph 24 or 25 for a standard authorisation, and

(b) they believe that the need for the relevant person to be a detained resident is so urgent that it is appropriate for the detention to begin before they make the request.

(3) The second case is where—

(a) the managing authority have made a request under paragraph 24 or 25 for a standard authorisation, and

(b) they believe that the need for the relevant person to be a detained resident is so urgent that it is appropriate for the detention to begin before the request is disposed of.

(4) References in this paragraph to the detention of the relevant person are references to the detention to which paragraph 24 or 25 relates.

(5) This paragraph is subject to paragraph 77.

77 (1) This paragraph applies where the managing authority have given an urgent authorisation ('the original authorisation') in connection with a case where a person is, or is to be, a detained resident ('the existing detention').

(2) No new urgent authorisation is to be given under paragraph 76 in connection with the existing detention.

(3) But the managing authority may request the supervisory body to extend the duration of the original authorisation.

(4) Only one request under sub-paragraph (3) may be made in relation to the original authorisation.]

[(5) Paragraphs 84 to 86 apply to any request made under subparagraph (3).

Terms of authorisation

78 (1) If the managing authority decide to give an urgent authorisation, they must decide the period during which the authorisation is to be in force.

(2) That period must not exceed 7 days.

Form of authorisation

79 An urgent authorisation must be in writing.

80 An urgent authorisation must state the following things—
   (a) the name of the relevant person;
   (b) the name of the relevant hospital or care home;
   (c) the period during which the authorisation is to be in force;
   (d) the purpose for which the authorisation is given.

81 (1) If the name of the relevant hospital or care home changes, the urgent authorisation is to be read as if it stated the current name of the hospital or care home.

(2) But sub-paragraph (1) is subject to any provision relating to the change of name which is made in any enactment or in any instrument made under an enactment.

Duty to keep records and give copies

82 (1) This paragraph applies if an urgent authorisation is given.

(2) The managing authority must keep a written record of why they have given the urgent authorisation.

(3) As soon as practicable after giving the authorisation, the managing authority must give a copy of the authorisation to all of the following—
   (a) the relevant person;
   (b) any section 39A IMCA.

Duty to give information about authorisation

83 (1) This paragraph applies if an urgent authorisation is given.

(2) The managing authority of the relevant hospital or care home must take such steps as are practicable to ensure that the relevant person understands all of the following—
   (a) the effect of the authorisation;
   (b) the right to make an application to the court to exercise its jurisdiction under section 21A.

(3) Those steps must be taken as soon as is practicable after the authorisation is given.

(4) Those steps must include the giving of appropriate information both orally and in writing.

Request for extension of duration

84 (1) This paragraph applies if the managing authority make a request under paragraph 77 for the supervisory body to extend the duration of the original authorisation.]

[(2) The managing authority must keep a written record of why they have made the request.

(3) The managing authority must give the relevant person notice that they have made the request.

(4) The supervisory body may extend the duration of the original authorisation if it appears to them that—

(a) the managing authority have made the required request for a standard authorisation,

(b) there are exceptional reasons why it has not yet been possible for that request to be disposed of, and

(c) it is essential for the existing detention to continue until the request is disposed of.

(5) The supervisory body must keep a written record that the request has been made to them.

(6) In this paragraph and paragraphs 85 and 86—

(a) 'original authorisation' and 'existing detention' have the same meaning as in paragraph 77;

(b) the required request for a standard authorisation is the request that is referred to in paragraph 76(2) or (3).

85 (1) This paragraph applies if, under paragraph 84, the supervisory body decide to extend the duration of the original authorisation.

(2) The supervisory body must decide the period of the extension.

(3) That period must not exceed 7 days.

(4) The supervisory body must give the managing authority notice stating the period of the extension.

(5) The managing authority must then vary the original authorisation so that it states the extended duration.

(6) Paragraphs 82(3) and 83 apply (with the necessary modifications) to the variation of the original authorisation as they apply to the giving of an urgent authorisation.

(7) The supervisory body must keep a written record of—

(a) the outcome of the request, and

(b) the period of the extension.

86 (1) This paragraph applies if, under paragraph 84, the supervisory body decide not to extend the duration of the original authorisation.

(2) The supervisory body must give the managing authority notice stating—

(a) the decision, and

(b) their reasons for making it.

(3) The managing authority must give a copy of that notice to all of the following—

(a) the relevant person;

(b) any section 39A IMCA.

(4) The supervisory body must keep a written record of the outcome of the request.

No variation

87 (1) An urgent authorisation may not be varied except in accordance with paragraph 85.

(2) This paragraph does not affect the powers of the Court of Protection or of any other court.

When an authorisation is in force

88 An urgent authorisation comes into force when it is given.]

[89 (1) An urgent authorisation ceases to be in force at the end of the period stated in the authorisation in accordance with paragraph 80(c) (subject to any variation in accordance with paragraph 85).

(2) But if the required request is disposed of before the end of that period, the urgent authorisation ceases to be in force as follows.

(3) If the supervisory body are required by paragraph 50(1) to give the requested authorisation, the urgent authorisation ceases to be in force when the requested authorisation comes into force.

(4) If the supervisory body are prohibited by paragraph 50(2) from giving the requested authorisation, the urgent authorisation ceases to be in force when the managing authority receive notice under paragraph 58.

(5) In this paragraph—

'required request' means the request referred to in paragraph 76(2) or (3);

'requested authorisation' means the standard authorisation to which the required request relates.

(6) This paragraph does not affect the powers of the Court of Protection or of any other court.

90 (1) This paragraph applies if an urgent authorisation ceases to be in force.

(2) The supervisory body must give notice that the authorisation has ceased to be in force.

(3) The supervisory body must give that notice to all of the following—

(a) the relevant person;

(b) any section 39A IMCA.

(4) The supervisory body must give that notice as soon as practicable after the authorisation ceases to be in force.

PART 6
ELIGIBILITY REQUIREMENT NOT MET:
SUSPENSION OF STANDARD AUTHORISATION

91 (1) This Part applies if the following conditions are met.

(2) The first condition is that a standard authorisation—

(a) has been given, and

(b) has not ceased to be in force.

(3) The second condition is that the managing authority of the relevant hospital or care home are satisfied that the relevant person has ceased to meet the eligibility requirement.

(4) But this Part does not apply if the relevant person is ineligible by virtue of paragraph 5 of Schedule 1A (in which case see Part 8).

92 The managing authority of the relevant hospital or care home must give the supervisory body notice that the relevant person has ceased to meet the eligibility requirement.

93 (1) This paragraph applies if the managing authority give the supervisory body notice under paragraph 92.

(2) The standard authorisation is suspended from the time when the notice is given.

(3) The supervisory body must give notice that the standard authorisation has been suspended to the following persons—

(a) the relevant person;

(b) the relevant person's representative;

(c) the managing authority of the relevant hospital or care home.]

[94 (1) This paragraph applies if, whilst the standard authorisation is suspended, the managing authority are satisfied that the relevant person meets the eligibility requirement again.

(2) The managing authority must give the supervisory body notice that the relevant person meets the eligibility requirement again.

95 (1) This paragraph applies if the managing authority give the supervisory body notice under paragraph 94.

(2) The standard authorisation ceases to be suspended from the time when the notice is given.

(3) The supervisory body must give notice that the standard authorisation has ceased to be suspended to the following persons—

(a) the relevant person;

(b) the relevant person's representative;

(c) any section 39D IMCA;

(d) the managing authority of the relevant hospital or care home.

(4) The supervisory body must give notice under this paragraph as soon as practicable after they are given notice under paragraph 94.

96 (1) This paragraph applies if no notice is given under paragraph 94 before the end of the relevant 28 day period.

(2) The standard authorisation ceases to have effect at the end of the relevant 28 day period.

(3) The relevant 28 day period is the period of 28 days beginning with the day on which the standard authorisation is suspended under paragraph 93.

97 The effect of suspending the standard authorisation is that Part 1 ceases to apply for as long as the authorisation is suspended.

PART 7
STANDARD AUTHORISATIONS:
CHANGE IN SUPERVISORY RESPONSIBILITY

Application of this Part

98 (1) This Part applies if these conditions are met.

(2) The first condition is that a standard authorisation—

(a) has been given, and

(b) has not ceased to be in force.

(3) The second condition is that there is a change in supervisory responsibility.

(4) The third condition is that there is not a change in the place of detention (within the meaning of paragraph 25).

99 For the purposes of this Part there is a change in supervisory responsibility if—

(a) one body ('the old supervisory body') have ceased to be supervisory body in relation to the standard authorisation, and

(b) a different body ('the new supervisory body') have become supervisory body in relation to the standard authorisation.

Effect of change in supervisory responsibility

100 (1) The new supervisory body becomes the supervisory body in relation to the authorisation.]

[(2) Anything done by or in relation to the old supervisory body in connection with the authorisation has effect, so far as is necessary for continuing its effect after the change, as if done by or in relation to the new supervisory body.

(3) Anything which relates to the authorisation and which is in the process of being done by or in relation to the old supervisory body at the time of the change may be continued by or in relation to the new supervisory body.

(4) But—

    (a) the old supervisory body do not, by virtue of this paragraph, cease to be liable for anything done by them in connection with the authorisation before the change; and

    (b) the new supervisory body do not, by virtue of this paragraph, become liable for any such thing.

PART 8
STANDARD AUTHORISATIONS: REVIEW

Application of this Part

101 (1) This Part applies if a standard authorisation—

    (a) has been given, and

    (b) has not ceased to be in force.

(2) Paragraphs 102 to 122 are subject to paragraphs 123 to 125.

Review by supervisory body

102 (1) The supervisory body may at any time carry out a review of the standard authorisation in accordance with this Part.

(2) The supervisory body must carry out such a review if they are requested to do so by an eligible person.

(3) Each of the following is an eligible person—

    (a) the relevant person;

    (b) the relevant person's representative;

    (c) the managing authority of the relevant hospital or care home.

Request for review

103 (1) An eligible person may, at any time, request the supervisory body to carry out a review of the standard authorisation in accordance with this Part.

(2) The managing authority of the relevant hospital or care home must make such a request if one or more of the qualifying requirements appear to them to be reviewable.

Grounds for review

104 (1) Paragraphs 105 to 107 set out the grounds on which the qualifying requirements are reviewable.

(2) A qualifying requirement is not reviewable on any other ground.]

[Non-qualification ground

105 (1) Any of the following qualifying requirements is reviewable on the ground that the relevant person does not meet the requirement—
   (a) the age requirement;
   (b) the mental health requirement;
   (c) the mental capacity requirement;
   (d) the best interests requirement;
   (e) the no refusals requirement.
(2) The eligibility requirement is reviewable on the ground that the relevant person is ineligible by virtue of paragraph 5 of Schedule 1A.
(3) The ground in sub-paragraph (1) and the ground in sub-paragraph (2) are referred to as the non-qualification ground.

Change of reason ground

106 (1) Any of the following qualifying requirements is reviewable on the ground set out in sub-paragraph (2)—
   (a) the mental health requirement;
   (b) the mental capacity requirement;
   (c) the best interests requirement;
   (d) the eligibility requirement;
   (e) the no refusals requirement.
(2) The ground is that the reason why the relevant person meets the requirement is not the reason stated in the standard authorisation.
(3) This ground is referred to as the change of reason ground.

Variation of conditions ground

107 (1) The best interests requirement is reviewable on the ground that—
   (a) there has been a change in the relevant person's case, and
   (b) because of that change, it would be appropriate to vary the conditions to which the standard authorisation is subject.
(2) This ground is referred to as the variation of conditions ground.
(3) A reference to varying the conditions to which the standard authorisation is subject is a reference to—
   (a) amendment of an existing condition,
   (b) omission of an existing condition, or
   (c) inclusion of a new condition (whether or not there are already any existing conditions).

Notice that review to be carried out

108 (1) If the supervisory body are to carry out a review of the standard authorisation, they must give notice of the review to the following persons—
   (a) the relevant person;
   (b) the relevant person's representative;]

[(c) the managing authority of the relevant hospital or care home.
(2) The supervisory body must give the notice—
    (a) before they begin the review, or
    (b) if that is not practicable, as soon as practicable after they have begun it.
(3) This paragraph does not require the supervisory body to give notice to any person who has requested the review.

Starting a review

109 To start a review of the standard authorisation, the supervisory body must decide which, if any, of the qualifying requirements appear to be reviewable.

No reviewable qualifying requirements

110 (1) This paragraph applies if no qualifying requirements appear to be reviewable.
(2) This Part does not require the supervisory body to take any action in respect of the standard authorisation.

One or more reviewable qualifying requirements

111 (1) This paragraph applies if one or more qualifying requirements appear to be reviewable.
(2) The supervisory body must secure that a separate review assessment is carried out in relation to each qualifying requirement which appears to be reviewable.
(3) But sub-paragraph (2) does not require the supervisory body to secure that a best interests review assessment is carried out in a case where the best interests requirement appears to the supervisory body to be nonassessable.
(4) The best interests requirement is non-assessable if—
    (a) the requirement is reviewable only on the variation of conditions ground, and
    (b) the change in the relevant person's case is not significant.
(5) In making any decision whether the change in the relevant person's case is significant, regard must be had to—
    (a) the nature of the change, and
    (b) the period that the change is likely to last for.

Review assessments

112 (1) A review assessment is an assessment of whether the relevant person meets a qualifying requirement.
(2) In relation to a review assessment—
    (a) a negative conclusion is a conclusion that the relevant person does not meet the qualifying requirement to which the assessment relates;
    (b) a positive conclusion is a conclusion that the relevant person meets the qualifying requirement to which the assessment relates.
(3) An age review assessment is a review assessment carried out in relation to the age requirement.
(4) A mental health review assessment is a review assessment carried out in relation to the mental health requirement.]

[(5) A mental capacity review assessment is a review assessment carried out in relation to the mental capacity requirement.

(6) A best interests review assessment is a review assessment carried out in relation to the best interests requirement.

(7) An eligibility review assessment is a review assessment carried out in relation to the eligibility requirement.

(8) A no refusals review assessment is a review assessment carried out in relation to the no refusals requirement.

113 (1) In carrying out a review assessment, the assessor must comply with any duties which would be imposed upon him under Part 4 if the assessment were being carried out in connection with a request for a standard authorisation.

(2) But in the case of a best interests review assessment, paragraphs 43 and 44 do not apply.

(3) Instead of what is required by paragraph 43, the best interests review assessment must include recommendations about whether—and, if so, how—it would be appropriate to vary the conditions to which the standard authorisation is subject.

Best interests requirement reviewable but non-assessable

114 (1) This paragraph applies in a case where—
   (a) the best interests requirement appears to be reviewable, but
   (b) in accordance with paragraph 111(3), the supervisory body are not required to secure that a best interests review assessment is carried out.

(2) The supervisory body may vary the conditions to which the standard authorisation is subject in such ways (if any) as the supervisory body think are appropriate in the circumstances.

Best interests review assessment positive

115 (1) This paragraph applies in a case where—
   (a) a best interests review assessment is carried out, and
   (b) the assessment comes to a positive conclusion.

(2) The supervisory body must decide the following questions—
   (a) whether or not the best interests requirement is reviewable on the change of reason ground;
   (b) whether or not the best interests requirement is reviewable on the variation of conditions ground;
   (c) if so, whether or not the change in the person's case is significant.

(3) If the supervisory body decide that the best interests requirement is reviewable on the change of reason ground, they must vary the standard authorisation so that it states the reason why the relevant person now meets that requirement.

(4) If the supervisory body decide that—
   (a) the best interests requirement is reviewable on the variation of conditions ground, and
   (b) the change in the relevant person's case is not significant,
they may vary the conditions to which the standard authorisation is subject in such ways (if any) as they think are appropriate in the circumstances.

(5) If the supervisory body decide that—
   (a) the best interests requirement is reviewable on the variation of conditions ground, and]

[(b) the change in the relevant person's case is significant,

they must vary the conditions to which the standard authorisation is subject in such ways as they think are appropriate in the circumstances.

(6) If the supervisory body decide that the best interests requirement is not reviewable on—

(a) the change of reason ground, or

(b) the variation of conditions ground,

this Part does not require the supervisory body to take any action in respect of the standard authorisation so far as the best interests requirement relates to it.

Mental health, mental capacity, eligibility or no refusals review assessment positive

116 (1) This paragraph applies if the following conditions are met.

(2) The first condition is that one or more of the following are carried out—

(a) a mental health review assessment;

(b) a mental capacity review assessment;

(c) an eligibility review assessment;

(d) a no refusals review assessment.

(3) The second condition is that each assessment carried out comes to a positive conclusion.

(4) The supervisory body must decide whether or not each of the assessed qualifying requirements is reviewable on the change of reason ground.

(5) If the supervisory body decide that any of the assessed qualifying requirements is reviewable on the change of reason ground, they must vary the standard authorisation so that it states the reason why the relevant person now meets the requirement or requirements in question.

(6) If the supervisory body decide that none of the assessed qualifying requirements are reviewable on the change of reason ground, this Part does not require the supervisory body to take any action in respect of the standard authorisation so far as those requirements relate to it.

(7) An assessed qualifying requirement is a qualifying requirement in relation to which a review assessment is carried out.

One or more review assessments negative

117 (1) This paragraph applies if one or more of the review assessments carried out comes to a negative conclusion.

(2) The supervisory body must terminate the standard authorisation with immediate effect.

Completion of a review

118 (1) The review of the standard authorisation is complete in any of the following cases.

(2) The first case is where paragraph 110 applies.

(3) The second case is where—

(a) paragraph 111 applies, and

(b) paragraph 117 requires the supervisory body to terminate the standard authorisation.

(4) In such a case, the supervisory body need not comply with any of the other provisions of paragraphs 114 to 116 which would be applicable to the review (were it not for this sub-paragraph).

(5) The third case is where—

(a) paragraph 111 applies,]

[(b) paragraph 117 does not require the supervisory body to terminate the standard authorisation, and

(c) the supervisory body comply with all of the provisions of paragraphs 114 to 116 (so far as they are applicable to the review).

Variations under this Part

119 Any variation of the standard authorisation made under this Part must be in writing.

Notice of outcome of review

120 (1) When the review of the standard authorisation is complete, the supervisory body must give notice to all of the following—

(a) the managing authority of the relevant hospital or care home;

(b) the relevant person;

(c) the relevant person's representative;

(d) any section 39D IMCA.

(2) That notice must state—

(a) the outcome of the review, and

(b) what variation (if any) has been made to the authorisation under this Part.

Records

121 A supervisory body must keep a written record of the following information—

(a) each request for a review that is made to them;

(b) the outcome of each request;

(c) each review which they carry out;

(d) the outcome of each review which they carry out;

(e) any variation of an authorisation made in consequence of a review.

Relationship between review and suspension under Part 6

122 (1) This paragraph applies if a standard authorisation is suspended in accordance with Part 6.

(2) No review may be requested under this Part whilst the standard authorisation is suspended.

(3) If a review has already been requested, or is being carried out, when the standard authorisation is suspended, no steps are to be taken in connection with that review whilst the authorisation is suspended.

Relationship between review and request for new authorisation

123 (1) This paragraph applies if, in accordance with paragraph 24 (as read with paragraph 29), the managing authority of the relevant hospital or care home make a request for a new standard authorisation which would be in force after the expiry of the existing authorisation.

(2) No review may be requested under this Part until the request for the new standard authorisation has been disposed of.

(3) If a review has already been requested, or is being carried out, when the new standard authorisation is requested, no steps are to be taken in connection with that review until the request for the new standard authorisation has been disposed of.]

[124 (1) This paragraph applies if—

    (a) a review under this Part has been requested, or is being carried out, and

    (b) the managing authority of the relevant hospital or care home make a request under paragraph 30 for a new standard authorisation which would be in force on or before, and after, the expiry of the existing authorisation.

(2) No steps are to be taken in connection with the review under this Part until the request for the new standard authorisation has been disposed of.

125 In paragraphs 123 and 124—

    (a) the existing authorisation is the authorisation referred to in paragraph 101;

    (b) the expiry of the existing authorisation is the time when it is expected to cease to be in force.

PART 9
ASSESSMENTS UNDER THIS SCHEDULE

Introduction

126 This Part contains provision about assessments under this Schedule.

127 An assessment under this Schedule is either of the following—

    (a) an assessment carried out in connection with a request for a standard authorisation under Part 4;

    (b) a review assessment carried out in connection with a review of a standard authorisation under Part 8.

128 In this Part, in relation to an assessment under this Schedule—

'assessor' means the person carrying out the assessment;

'relevant procedure' means—

    (a) the request for the standard authorisation, or

    (b) the review of the standard authorisation;

'supervisory body' means the supervisory body responsible for securing that the assessment is carried out.

Supervisory body to select assessor

129 (1) It is for the supervisory body to select a person to carry out an assessment under this Schedule.

(2) The supervisory body must not select a person to carry out an assessment unless the person—

    (a) appears to the supervisory body to be suitable to carry out the assessment (having regard, in particular, to the type of assessment and the person to be assessed), and

    (b) is eligible to carry out the assessment.

(3) Regulations may make provision about the selection, and eligibility, of persons to carry out assessments under this Schedule.

(4) Sub-paragraphs (5) and (6) apply if two or more assessments are to be obtained for the purposes of the relevant procedure.

(5) In a case where the assessments to be obtained include a mental health assessment and a best interests assessment, the supervisory body must not select the same person to carry out both assessments.

(6) Except as prohibited by sub-paragraph (5), the supervisory body may select the same person to carry out any number of the assessments which the person appears to be suitable, and is eligible, to carry out.]

[130 (1) This paragraph applies to regulations under paragraph 129(3).

(2) The regulations may make provision relating to a person's—
  (a) qualifications,
  (b) skills,
  (c) training,
  (d) experience,
  (e) relationship to, or connection with, the relevant person or any other person,
  (f) involvement in the care or treatment of the relevant person,
  (g) connection with the supervisory body, or
  (h) connection with the relevant hospital or care home, or with any other establishment or undertaking.

(3) The provision that the regulations may make in relation to a person's training may provide for particular training to be specified by the appropriate authority otherwise than in the regulations.

(4) In sub-paragraph (3) the 'appropriate authority' means—
  (a) in relation to England: the Secretary of State;
  (b) in relation to Wales: the National Assembly for Wales.

(5) The regulations may make provision requiring a person to be insured in respect of liabilities that may arise in connection with the carrying out of an assessment.

(6) In relation to cases where two or more assessments are to be obtained for the purposes of the relevant procedure, the regulations may limit the number, kind or combination of assessments which a particular person is eligible to carry out.

(7) Sub-paragraphs (2) to (6) do not limit the generality of the provision that may be made in the regulations.

Examination and copying of records

131 An assessor may, at all reasonable times, examine and take copies of—
  (a) any health record,
  (b) any record of, or held by, a local authority and compiled in accordance with a social services function, and
  (c) any record held by a person registered under Part 2 of the Care Standards Act 2000,
  which the assessor considers may be relevant to the assessment which is being carried out.

Representations

132 In carrying out an assessment under this Schedule, the assessor must take into account any information given, or submissions made, by any of the following—
  (a) the relevant person's representative;
  (b) any section 39A IMCA;
  (c) any section 39C IMCA
  (d) any section 39D IMCA.

Assessments to stop if any comes to negative conclusion

133 (1) This paragraph applies if an assessment under this Schedule comes to the conclusion that the relevant person does not meet one of the qualifying requirements.]

[(2) This Schedule does not require the supervisory body to secure that any other assessments under this Schedule are carried out in relation to the relevant procedure.

(3) The supervisory body must give notice to any assessor who is carrying out another assessment in connection with the relevant procedure that they are to cease carrying out that assessment.

(4) If an assessor receives such notice, this Schedule does not require the assessor to continue carrying out that assessment.

Duty to keep records and give copies

134 (1) This paragraph applies if an assessor has carried out an assessment under this Schedule (whatever conclusions the assessment has come to).

(2) The assessor must keep a written record of the assessment.

(3) As soon as practicable after carrying out the assessment, the assessor must give copies of the assessment to the supervisory body.

135 (1) This paragraph applies to the supervisory body if they are given a copy of an assessment under this Schedule.

(2) The supervisory body must give copies of the assessment to all of the following—
  (a) the managing authority of the relevant hospital or care home;
  (b) the relevant person;
  (c) any section 39A IMCA;
  (d) the relevant person's representative.

(3) If—
  (a) the assessment is obtained in relation to a request for a standard authorisation, and
  (b) the supervisory body are required by paragraph 50(1) to give the standard authorisation, the supervisory body must give the copies of the assessment when they give copies of the authorisation in accordance with paragraph 57.

(4) If—
  (a) the assessment is obtained in relation to a request for a standard authorisation, and
  (b) the supervisory body are prohibited by paragraph 50(2) from giving the standard authorisation, the supervisory body must give the copies of the assessment when they give notice in accordance with paragraph 58.

(5) If the assessment is obtained in connection with the review of a standard authorisation, the supervisory body must give the copies of the assessment when they give notice in accordance with paragraph 120.

136 (1) This paragraph applies to the supervisory body if—
  (a) they are given a copy of a best interests assessment, and
  (b) the assessment includes, in accordance with paragraph 44(2), a statement that it appears to the assessor that there is an unauthorised deprivation of liberty.

(2) The supervisory body must notify all of the persons listed in sub-paragraph

(3) that the assessment includes such a statement.

(4) Those persons are—
  (a) the managing authority of the relevant hospital or care home;
  (b) the relevant parties;
  (c) any section 39A IMCA
  (d) any interested person consulted by the best interests assessor.

(5) The supervisory body must comply with this paragraph when (or at some time before) they comply with paragraph 135.]

[PART 10
RELEVANT PERSON'S REPRESENTATIVE

The representative

137 In this Schedule the relevant person's representative is the person appointed as such in accordance with this Part.

138 (1) Regulations may make provision about the selection and appointment of representatives.

(2) In this Part such regulations are referred to as 'appointment regulations'.

Supervisory body to appoint representative

139 (1) The supervisory body must appoint a person to be the relevant person's representative as soon as practicable after a standard authorisation is given.

(2) The supervisory body must appoint a person to be the relevant person's representative if a vacancy arises whilst a standard authorisation is in force.

(3) Where a vacancy arises, the appointment under sub-paragraph (2) is to be made as soon as practicable after the supervisory body becomes aware of the vacancy.

140 (1) The selection of a person for appointment under paragraph 139 must not be made unless it appears to the person making the selection that the prospective representative would, if appointed—

(a) maintain contact with the relevant person,

(b) represent the relevant person in matters relating to or connected with this Schedule, and

(c) support the relevant person in matters relating to or connected with this Schedule.

141 (1) Any appointment of a representative for a relevant person is in addition to, and does not affect, any appointment of a donee or deputy.

(2) The functions of any representative are in addition to, and do not affect—

(a) the authority of any donee,

(b) the powers of any deputy, or

(c) any powers of the court.

Appointment regulations

142 Appointment regulations may provide that the procedure for appointing a representative may begin at any time after a request for a standard authorisation is made (including a time before the request has been disposed of).

143 (1) Appointment regulations may make provision about who is to select a person for appointment as a representative.

(2) But regulations under this paragraph may only provide for the following to make a selection—

(a) the relevant person, if he has capacity in relation to the question of which person should be his representative;

(b) a donee of a lasting power of attorney granted by the relevant person, if it is within the scope of his authority to select a person;

(c) a deputy, if it is within the scope of his authority to select a person;

(d) a best interests assessor;

(e) the supervisory body.

(3) Regulations under this paragraph may provide that a selection by the relevant person, a donee or a deputy is subject to approval by a best interests assessor or the supervisory body.]

[(4) Regulations under this paragraph may provide that, if more than one selection is necessary in connection with the appointment of a particular representative—

(a) the same person may make more than one selection;

(b) different persons may make different selections.

(5) For the purposes of this paragraph a best interests assessor is a person carrying out a best interests assessment in connection with the standard authorisation in question (including the giving of that authorisation).

144 (1) Appointment regulations may make provision about who may, or may not, be—

(a) selected for appointment as a representative, or

(b) appointed as a representative.

(2) Regulations under this paragraph may relate to any of the following matters—

(a) a person's age;

(b) a person's suitability;

(c) a person's independence;

(d) a person's willingness;

(e) a person's qualifications.

145 Appointment regulations may make provision about the formalities of appointing a person as a representative.

146 In a case where a best interests assessor is to select a person to be appointed as a representative, appointment regulations may provide for the variation of the assessor's duties in relation to the assessment which he is carrying out.

Monitoring of representatives

147 Regulations may make provision requiring the managing authority of the relevant hospital or care home to—

(a) monitor, and

(b) report to the supervisory body on, the extent to which a representative is maintaining contact with the relevant person.

Termination

148 Regulations may make provision about the circumstances in which the appointment of a person as the relevant person's representative ends or may be ended.

149 Regulations may make provision about the formalities of ending the appointment of a person as a representative.

Suspension of representative's functions

150 (1) Regulations may make provision about the circumstances in which functions exercisable by, or in relation to, the relevant person's representative (whether under this Schedule or not) may be—

(a) suspended, and

(b) if suspended, revived.

(2) The regulations may make provision about the formalities for giving effect to the suspension or revival of a function.]

[(3) The regulations may make provision about the effect of the suspension or revival of a function.

Payment of representative

151 Regulations may make provision for payments to be made to, or in relation to, persons exercising functions as the relevant person's representative.

Regulations under this Part

152 The provisions of this Part which specify provision that may be made in regulations under this Part do not affect the generality of the power to make such regulations.

Effect of appointment of section 39C IMCA

153 Paragraphs 159 and 160 make provision about the exercise of functions by, or towards, the relevant person's representative during periods when—
   (a) no person is appointed as the relevant person's representative, but
   (b) a person is appointed as a section 39C IMCA.

PART 11
IMCAS

Application of Part

154 This Part applies for the purposes of this Schedule.

The IMCAs

155 A section 39A IMCA is an independent mental capacity advocate appointed under section 39A.
156 A section 39C IMCA is an independent mental capacity advocate appointed under section 39C.
157 A section 39D IMCA is an independent mental capacity advocate appointed under section 39D.
158 An IMCA is a section 39A IMCA or a section 39C IMCA or a section 39D IMCA.

Section 39C IMCA: functions

159 (1) This paragraph applies if, and for as long as, there is a section 39C IMCA.
(2) In the application of the relevant provisions, references to the relevant person's representative are to be read as references to the section 39C IMCA.
(3) But sub-paragraph (2) does not apply to any function under the relevant provisions for as long as the function is suspended in accordance with provision made under Part 10.
(4) In this paragraph and paragraph 160 the relevant provisions are—]

[(a) paragraph 102(3)(b) (request for review under Part 8);

(b) paragraph 108(1)(b) (notice of review under Part 8);

(c) paragraph 120(1)(c) (notice of outcome of review under Part 8).

160 (1) This paragraph applies if—

(a) a person is appointed as the relevant person's representative, and

(b) a person accordingly ceases to hold an appointment as a section 39C IMCA.

(2) Where a function under a relevant provision has been exercised by, or towards, the section 39C IMCA, there is no requirement for that function to be exercised again by, or towards, the relevant person's representative.

Section 39A IMCA: restriction of functions

161 (1) This paragraph applies if—

(a) there is a section 39A IMCA, and

(b) a person is appointed under Part 10 to be the relevant person's representative (whether or not that person, or any person subsequently appointed, is currently the relevant person's representative).

(2) The duties imposed on, and the powers exercisable by, the section 39A IMCA do not apply.

(3) The duties imposed on, and the powers exercisable by, any other person do not apply, so far as they fall to be performed or exercised towards the section 39A IMCA.

(4) But sub-paragraph (2) does not apply to any power of challenge exercisable by the section 39A IMCA.

(5) And sub-paragraph (3) does not apply to any duty or power of any other person so far as it relates to any power of challenge exercisable by the section 39A IMCA.

(6) Before exercising any power of challenge, the section 39A IMCA must take the views of the relevant person's representative into account.

(7) A power of challenge is a power to make an application to the court to exercise its jurisdiction under section 21A in connection with the giving of the standard authorisation.

PART 12

MISCELLANEOUS

Monitoring of operation of Schedule

162 (1) Regulations may make provision for, and in connection with, requiring one or more prescribed bodies to monitor, and report on, the operation of this Schedule in relation to England.

(2) The regulations may, in particular, give a prescribed body authority to do one or more of the following things—

(a) to visit hospitals and care homes;

(b) to visit and interview persons accommodated in hospitals and care homes;

(c) to require the production of, and to inspect, records relating to the care or treatment of persons.

(3) 'Prescribed' means prescribed in regulations under this paragraph.

163 (1) Regulations may make provision for, and in connection with, enabling the National Assembly for Wales to monitor, and report on, the operation of this Schedule in relation to Wales.]

[(2) The National Assembly may direct one or more persons or bodies to carry out the Assembly's functions under regulations under this paragraph.

Disclosure of information

164 (1) Regulations may require either or both of the following to disclose prescribed information to prescribed bodies—

(a) supervisory bodies;

(b) managing authorities of hospitals or care homes.

(2) 'Prescribed' means prescribed in regulations under this paragraph.

(3) Regulations under this paragraph may only prescribe information relating to matters with which this Schedule is concerned.

Directions by National Assembly in relation to supervisory functions

165 (1) The National Assembly for Wales may direct a Local Health Board to exercise in relation to its area any supervisory functions which are specified in the direction.

(2) Directions under this paragraph must not preclude the National Assembly from exercising the functions specified in the directions.

(3) In this paragraph 'supervisory functions' means functions which the National Assembly have as supervisory body, so far as they are exercisable in relation to hospitals (whether NHS or independent hospitals, and whether in Wales or England).

166 (1) This paragraph applies where, under paragraph 165, a Local Health Board ('the specified LHB') is directed to exercise supervisory functions ('delegated functions').

(2) The National Assembly for Wales may give directions to the specified LHB about the Board's exercise of delegated functions.

(3) The National Assembly may give directions for any delegated functions to be exercised, on behalf of the specified LHB, by a committee, subcommittee or officer of that Board.

(4) The National Assembly may give directions providing for any delegated functions to be exercised by the specified LHB jointly with one or more other Local Health Boards.

(5) Where, under sub-paragraph (4), delegated functions are exercisable jointly, the National Assembly may give directions providing for the functions to be exercised, on behalf of the Local Health Boards in question, by a joint committee or joint subcommittee.

167 (1) Directions under paragraph 165 must be given in regulations.

(2) Directions under paragraph 166 may be given—

(a) in regulations, or

(b) by instrument in writing.

168 The power under paragraph 165 or paragraph 166 to give directions includes power to vary or revoke directions given under that paragraph.

Notices

169 Any notice under this Schedule must be in writing.]

[*Regulations*

170 (1) This paragraph applies to all regulations under this Schedule, except regulations under paragraph 162, 163, 167 or 183.

(2) It is for the Secretary of State to make such regulations in relation to authorisations under this Schedule which relate to hospitals and care homes situated in England.

(3) It is for the National Assembly for Wales to make such regulations in relation to authorisations under this Schedule which relate to hospitals and care homes situated in Wales.

171 It is for the Secretary of State to make regulations under paragraph 162.

172 It is for the National Assembly for Wales to make regulations under paragraph 163 or 167.

173 (1) This paragraph applies to regulations under paragraph 183.

(2) It is for the Secretary of State to make such regulations in relation to cases where a question as to the ordinary residence of a person is to be determined by the Secretary of State.

(3) It is for the National Assembly for Wales to make such regulations in relation to cases where a question as to the ordinary residence of a person is to be determined by the National Assembly.

PART 13
INTERPRETATION

Introduction

174 This Part applies for the purposes of this Schedule.

Hospitals and their managing authorities

175 (1) 'Hospital' means—

(a) an NHS hospital, or

(b) an independent hospital.

(2) 'NHS hospital' means—

(a) a health service hospital as defined by section 275 of the National Health Service Act 2006 or section 206 of the National Health Service (Wales) Act 2006, or

(b) a hospital as defined by section 206 of the National Health Service (Wales) Act 2006 vested in a Local Health Board.

(3) 'Independent hospital' means a hospital as defined by section 2 of the Care Standards Act 2000 which is not an NHS hospital.

176 (1) 'Managing authority', in relation to an NHS hospital, means—

(a) if the hospital—

(i) is vested in the appropriate national authority for the purposes of its functions under the National Health Service Act 2006 or of the National Health Service (Wales) Act 2006, or

(ii) consists of any accommodation provided by a local authority and used as a hospital by or on behalf of the appropriate national authority under either of those Acts, the Primary Care Trust, Strategic Health Authority, Local Health Board or Special Health Authority responsible for the administration of the hospital;

(b) if the hospital is vested in a Primary Care Trust, National Health Service trust or NHS foundation trust, that trust;

(c) if the hospital is vested in a Local Health Board, that Board.]

[(2) For this purpose the appropriate national authority is—
    (a) in relation to England: the Secretary of State;
    (b) in relation to Wales: the National Assembly for Wales;
    (c) in relation to England and Wales: the Secretary of State and the National Assembly acting jointly.

177 'Managing authority', in relation to an independent hospital, means the person registered, or required to be registered, under Part 2 of the Care Standards Act 2000 in respect of the hospital.

Care homes and their managing authorities

178 'Care home' has the meaning given by section 3 of the Care Standards Act 2000.

179 'Managing authority', in relation to a care home, means the person registered, or required to be registered, under Part 2 of the Care Standards Act 2000 in respect of the care home.

Supervisory bodies: hospitals

180 (1) The identity of the supervisory body is determined under this paragraph in cases where the relevant hospital is situated in England.

(2) If a Primary Care Trust commissions the relevant care or treatment, that Trust is the supervisory body.

(3) If the National Assembly for Wales or a Local Health Board commission the relevant care or treatment, the National Assembly are the supervisory body.

(4) In any other case, the supervisory body are the Primary Care Trust for the area in which the relevant hospital is situated.

(5) If a hospital is situated in the areas of two (or more) Primary Care Trusts, it is to be regarded for the purposes of sub-paragraph (4) as situated in whichever of the areas the greater (or greatest) part of the hospital is situated.

181 (1) The identity of the supervisory body is determined under this paragraph in cases where the relevant hospital is situated in Wales.

(2) The National Assembly for Wales are the supervisory body.

(3) But if a Primary Care Trust commissions the relevant care or treatment, that Trust is the supervisory body.

Supervisory bodies: care homes

182 (1) The identity of the supervisory body is determined under this paragraph in cases where the relevant care home is situated in England or in Wales.

(2) The supervisory body are the local authority for the area in which the relevant person is ordinarily resident.

(3) But if the relevant person is not ordinarily resident in the area of a local authority, the supervisory body are the local authority for the area in which the care home is situated.

(4) In relation to England 'local authority' means—
    (a) the council of a county;
    (b) the council of a district for which there is no county council;
    (c) the council of a London borough;
    (d) the Common Council of the City of London;]

[(e) the Council of the Isles of Scilly.

(5) In relation to Wales 'local authority' means the council of a county or county borough.

(6) If a care home is situated in the areas of two (or more) local authorities, it is to be regarded for the purposes of sub-paragraph (3) as situated in whichever of the areas the greater (or greatest) part of the care home is situated.

183 (1) Subsections (5) and (6) of section 24 of the National Assistance Act 1948 (deemed place of ordinary residence) apply to any determination of where a person is ordinarily resident for the purposes of paragraph 182 as those subsections apply to such a determination for the purposes specified in those subsections.

(2) In the application of section 24(6) of the 1948 Act by virtue of subsection (1), section 24(6) is to be read as if it referred to a hospital vested in a Local Health Board as well as to hospitals vested in the Secretary of State and the other bodies mentioned in section 24(6).

(3) Any question arising as to the ordinary residence of a person is to be determined by the Secretary of State or by the National Assembly for Wales.

(4) The Secretary of State and the National Assembly must make and publish arrangements for determining which cases are to be dealt with by the Secretary of State and which are to be dealt with by the National Assembly.

(5) Those arrangements may include provision for the Secretary of State and the National Assembly to agree, in relation to any question that has arisen, which of them is to deal with the case.

(6) Regulations may make provision about arrangements that are to have effect before, upon, or after the determination of any question as to the ordinary residence of a person.

(7) The regulations may, in particular, authorise or require a local authority to do any or all of the following things—
   (a) to act as supervisory body even though it may wish to dispute that it is the supervisory body;
   (b) to become the supervisory body in place of another local authority;
   (c) to recover from another local authority expenditure incurred in exercising functions as the supervisory body.

Same body managing authority and supervisory body

184 (1) This paragraph applies if, in connection with a particular person's detention as a resident in a hospital or care home, the same body are both—
   (a) the managing authority of the relevant hospital or care home, and
   (b) the supervisory body.

(2) The fact that a single body are acting in both capacities does not prevent the body from carrying out functions under this Schedule in each capacity.

(3) But, in such a case, this Schedule has effect subject to any modifications contained in regulations that may be made for this purpose.

Interested persons

185 Each of the following is an interested person—
   (a) the relevant person's spouse or civil partner;
   (b) where the relevant person and another person of the opposite sex are not married to each other but are living together as husband and wife: the other person;]

[(c) where the relevant person and another person of the same sex are not civil partners of each other but are living together as if they were civil partners: the other person;

(d) the relevant person's children and step-children;

(e) the relevant person's parents and step-parents;

(f) the relevant person's brothers and sisters, half-brothers and halfsisters, and stepbrothers and stepsisters;

(g) the relevant person's grandparents;

(h) a deputy appointed for the relevant person by the court;

(i) a donee of a lasting power of attorney granted by the relevant person.

186 (1) An interested person consulted by the best interests assessor is any person whose name is stated in the relevant best interests assessment in accordance with paragraph 40 (interested persons whom the assessor consulted in carrying out the assessment).

(2) The relevant best interests assessment is the most recent best interests assessment carried out in connection with the standard authorisation in question (whether the assessment was carried out under Part 4 or Part 8).

186 Where this Schedule imposes on a person a duty towards an interested person, the duty does not apply if the person on whom the duty is imposed—

(a) is not aware of the interested person's identity or of a way of contacting him, and

(b) cannot reasonably ascertain it.

187 The following table contains an index of provisions defining or otherwise explaining expressions used in this Schedule—

age assessment	paragraph 34
age requirement	paragraph 13
age review assessment	paragraph 112(3)
appointment regulations	paragraph 138
assessment under this Schedule	paragraph 127
assessor (except in Part 9)	paragraph 33
assessor (in Part 9)	paragraphs 33 and 128
authorisation under this Schedule	paragraph 10
best interests (determination of)	section 4
best interests assessment	paragraph 38
best interests requirement	paragraph 16
best interests review assessment	paragraph 112(6)
care home	paragraph 178
change of reason ground	paragraph 106
complete (in relation to a review of a standard authorisation)	paragraph 118
deprivation of a person's liberty	section 64(5) and (6)
deputy	section 16(2)(b)
detained resident	paragraph 6
disposed of (in relation to a request for a standard authorisation)	paragraph 66
eligibility assessment	paragraph 46
eligibility requirement	paragraph 17
eligibility review assessment	paragraph 112(7)
eligible person (in relation to paragraphs 68 to 73)	paragraph 68
eligible person (in relation to Part 8)	paragraph 102(3)
expiry (in relation to an existing authorisation)	paragraph 125(b)]

[existing authorisation (in Part 8)	paragraph 125(a)
hospital	paragraph 175
IMCA	paragraph 158
in force (in relation to a standard authorisation)	paragraphs 63 and 64
in force (in relation to an urgent authorisation)	paragraphs 88 and 89
ineligible (in relation to the eligibility requirement)	Schedule 1A
interested person	paragraph 185
interested person consulted by the best interests assessor	paragraph 186
lack of capacity	section 2
lasting power of attorney	section 9
managing authority (in relation to a care home)	paragraph 179
managing authority (in relation to a hospital)	paragraph 176 or 177
maximum authorisation period	paragraph 42
mental capacity assessment	paragraph 37
mental capacity requirement	paragraph 15
mental capacity review assessment	paragraph 112(5)
mental health assessment	paragraph 35
mental health requirement	paragraph 14
mental health review assessment	paragraph 112(4)
negative conclusion	paragraph 112(2)(a)
new supervisory body	paragraph 99(b)
no refusals assessment	paragraph 48
no refusals requirement	paragraph 18
no refusals review assessment	paragraph 112(8)
non-qualification ground	paragraph 105
old supervisory body	paragraph 99(a)
positive conclusion	paragraph 112(2)(b)
purpose of a standard authorisation	paragraph 11(1)
purpose of an urgent authorisation	paragraph 11(2)
qualifying requirements	paragraph 12
refusal (for the purposes of the no refusals requirement)	paragraphs 19 and 20
relevant care or treatment	paragraph 7
relevant hospital or care home	paragraph 7
relevant managing authority	paragraph 26(4)
relevant person	paragraph 7
relevant person's representative	paragraph 137
relevant procedure	paragraph 128
review assessment	paragraph 112(1)
reviewable	paragraph 104
section 39A IMCA	paragraph 155
section 39C IMCA	paragraph 156
section 39D IMCA	paragraph 157
standard authorisation	paragraph 8
supervisory body (except in Part 8)	paragraph 180, 181 or 182
supervisory body (in Part 8)	paragraph 128 and paragraph 180, 181 or 182
unauthorised deprivation of liberty (in relation to paragraphs 68 to 73)	paragraph 67
urgent authorisation	paragraph 9
variation of conditions ground	paragraph 107]

[Schedule A1 inserted by section 50(5) and Schedule 7 to the 2007 Act.]

233

SCHEDULE 1
LASTING POWERS OF ATTORNEY: FORMALITIES

Section 9

PART 1
MAKING INSTRUMENTS

General requirements as to making instruments

1 (1) An instrument is not made in accordance with this Schedule unless—
    (a) it is in the prescribed form,
    (b) it complies with paragraph 2, and
    (c) any prescribed requirements in connection with its execution are satisfied.
(2) Regulations may make different provision according to whether—
    (a) the instrument relates to personal welfare or to property and affairs (or to both);
    (b) only one or more than one donee is to be appointed (and if more than one, whether jointly or jointly and severally).
(3) In this Schedule—
    (a) 'prescribed' means prescribed by regulations, and
    (b) 'regulations' means regulations made for the purposes of this Schedule by the Lord Chancellor.

Requirements as to content of instruments

2 (1) The instrument must include—
    (a) the prescribed information about the purpose of the instrument and the effect of a lasting power of attorney,
    (b) a statement by the donor to the effect that he—
        (i) has read the prescribed information or a prescribed part of it (or has had it read to him), and
        (ii) intends the authority conferred under the instrument to include authority to make decisions on his behalf in circumstances where he no longer has capacity,
    (c) a statement by the donor—
        (i) naming a person or persons whom the donor wishes to be notified of any application for the registration of the instrument, or
        (ii) stating that there are no persons whom he wishes to be notified of any such application,
    (d) a statement by the donee (or, if more than one, each of them) to the effect that he—
        (i) has read the prescribed information or a prescribed part of it (or has had it read to him), and
        (ii) understands the duties imposed on a donee of a lasting power of attorney under sections 1 (the principles) and 4 (best interests), and
    (e) a certificate by a person of a prescribed description that, in his opinion, at the time when the donor executes the instrument—
        (i) the donor understands the purpose of the instrument and the scope of the authority conferred under it,
        (ii) no fraud or undue pressure is being used to induce the donor to create a lasting power of attorney, and

     (iii) there is nothing else which would prevent a lasting power of attorney from being created by the instrument.

(2) Regulations may—

    (a) prescribe a maximum number of named persons;

    (b) provide that, where the instrument includes a statement under subparagraph (1)(c)(ii), two persons of a prescribed description must each give a certificate under sub-paragraph (1)(e).

(3) The persons who may be named persons do not include a person who is appointed as donee under the instrument.

(4) In this Schedule, 'named person' means a person named under subparagraph (1)(c).

(5) A certificate under sub-paragraph (1)(e)—

    (a) must be made in the prescribed form, and

    (b) must include any prescribed information.

(6) The certificate may not be given by a person appointed as donee under the instrument.

Failure to comply with prescribed form

3 (1) If an instrument differs in an immaterial respect in form or mode of expression from the prescribed form, it is to be treated by the Public Guardian as sufficient in point of form and expression.

(2) The court may declare that an instrument which is not in the prescribed form is to be treated as if it were, if it is satisfied that the persons executing the instrument intended it to create a lasting power of attorney.

PART 2
REGISTRATION

Applications and procedure for registration

4 (1) An application to the Public Guardian for the registration of an instrument intended to create a lasting power of attorney—

    (a) must be made in the prescribed form, and

    (b) must include any prescribed information.

(2) The application may be made—

    (a) by the donor,

    (b) by the donee or donees, or

    (c) if the instrument appoints two or more donees to act jointly and severally in respect of any matter, by any of the donees.

(3) The application must be accompanied by—

    (a) the instrument, and

    (b) any fee provided for under section 58(4)(b).

(4) A person who, in an application for registration, makes a statement which he knows to be false in a material particular is guilty of an offence and is liable—

    (a) on summary conviction, to imprisonment for a term not exceeding 12 months or a fine not exceeding the statutory maximum or both;

    (b) on conviction on indictment, to imprisonment for a term not exceeding 2 years or a fine or both.

5 Subject to paragraphs 11 to 14, the Public Guardian must register the instrument as a lasting power of attorney at the end of the prescribed period.

Notification requirements

6 (1) A donor about to make an application under paragraph 4(2)(a) must notify any named persons that he is about to do so.

(2) The donee (or donees) about to make an application under paragraph 4(2)(b) or (c) must notify any named persons that he is (or they are) about to do so.

7 As soon as is practicable after receiving an application by the donor under paragraph 4(2)(a), the Public Guardian must notify the donee (or donees) that the application has been received.

8 (1) As soon as is practicable after receiving an application by a donee (or donees) under paragraph 4(2)(b), the Public Guardian must notify the donor that the application has been received.

(2) As soon as is practicable after receiving an application by a donee under paragraph 4(2)(c), the Public Guardian must notify—

(a) the donor, and

(b) the donee or donees who did not join in making the application, that the application has been received.

9 (1) A notice under paragraph 6 must be made in the prescribed form.

(2) A notice under paragraph 6, 7 or 8 must include such information, if any, as may be prescribed.

Power to dispense with notification requirements

10 The court may—

(a) on the application of the donor, dispense with the requirement to notify under paragraph 6(1), or

(b) on the application of the donee or donees concerned, dispense with the requirement to notify under paragraph 6(2), if satisfied that no useful purpose would be served by giving the notice.

Instrument not made properly or containing ineffective provision

11 (1) If it appears to the Public Guardian that an instrument accompanying an application under paragraph 4 is not made in accordance with this Schedule, he must not register the instrument unless the court directs him to do so.

(2) Sub-paragraph (3) applies if it appears to the Public Guardian that the instrument contains a provision which—

(a) would be ineffective as part of a lasting power of attorney, or

(b) would prevent the instrument from operating as a valid lasting power of attorney.

(3) The Public Guardian—

(a) must apply to the court for it to determine the matter under section 23(1), and

(b) pending the determination by the court, must not register the instrument.

(4) Sub-paragraph (5) applies if the court determines under section 23(1) (whether or not on an application by the Public Guardian) that the instrument contains a provision which—

(a) would be ineffective as part of a lasting power of attorney, or

(b) would prevent the instrument from operating as a valid lasting power of attorney.

(5) The court must—

    (a) notify the Public Guardian that it has severed the provision, or

    (b) direct him not to register the instrument.

(6) Where the court notifies the Public Guardian that it has severed a provision, he must register the instrument with a note to that effect attached to it.

Deputy already appointed

12 (1) Sub-paragraph (2) applies if it appears to the Public Guardian that—

    (a) there is a deputy appointed by the court for the donor, and

    (b) the powers conferred on the deputy would, if the instrument were registered, to any extent conflict with the powers conferred on the attorney.

(2) The Public Guardian must not register the instrument unless the court directs him to do so.

Objection by donee or named person

13 (1) Sub-paragraph (2) applies if a donee or a named person—

    (a) receives a notice under paragraph 6, 7 or 8 of an application for the registration of an instrument, and

    (b) before the end of the prescribed period, gives notice to the Public Guardian of an objection to the registration on the ground that an event mentioned in section 13(3) or (6)(a) to (d) has occurred which has revoked the instrument.

(2) If the Public Guardian is satisfied that the ground for making the objection is established, he must not register the instrument unless the court, on the application of the person applying for the registration—

    (a) is satisfied that the ground is not established, and

    (b) directs the Public Guardian to register the instrument.

(3) Sub-paragraph (4) applies if a donee or a named person—

    (a) receives a notice under paragraph 6, 7 or 8 of an application for the registration of an instrument, and

    (b) before the end of the prescribed period—

        (i) makes an application to the court objecting to the registration on a prescribed ground, and

        (ii) notifies the Public Guardian of the application.

(4) he Public Guardian must not register the instrument unless the court directs him to do so.

Objection by donor

14 (1) This paragraph applies if the donor—

    (a) receives a notice under paragraph 8 of an application for the registration of an instrument, and

    (b) before the end of the prescribed period, gives notice to the Public Guardian of an objection to the registration.

(2) The Public Guardian must not register the instrument unless the court, on the application of the donee or, if more than one, any of them—

    (a) is satisfied that the donor lacks capacity to object to the registration, and

    (b) directs the Public Guardian to register the instrument.

Notification of registration

15 Where an instrument is registered under this Schedule, the Public Guardian must give notice of the fact in the prescribed form to—

    (a) the donor, and

    (b) the donee or, if more than one, each of them.

Evidence of registration

16 (1) A document purporting to be an office copy of an instrument registered under this Schedule is, in any part of the United Kingdom, evidence of—

    (a) the contents of the instrument, and

    (b) the fact that it has been registered.

(2) Sub-paragraph (1) is without prejudice to—

    (a) section 3 of the Powers of Attorney Act 1971 (c. 27) (proof by certified copy), and

    (b) any other method of proof authorised by law.

PART 3
CANCELLATION OF REGISTRATION AND NOTIFICATION OF SEVERANCE

17 (1) The Public Guardian must cancel the registration of an instrument as a lasting power of attorney on being satisfied that the power has been revoked—

    (a) as a result of the donor's bankruptcy, or

    (b) on the occurrence of an event mentioned in section 13(6)(a) to (d).

(2) If the Public Guardian cancels the registration of an instrument he must notify—

    (a) the donor, and

    (b) the donee or, if more than one, each of them.

18 The court must direct the Public Guardian to cancel the registration of an instrument as a lasting power of attorney if it—

    (a) determines under section 22(2)(a) that a requirement for creating the power was not met,

    (b) determines under section 22(2)(b) that the power has been revoked or has otherwise come to an end, or

    (c) revokes the power under section 22(4)(b) (fraud etc.).

19 (1) Sub-paragraph (2) applies if the court determines under section 23(1) that a lasting power of attorney contains a provision which—

    (a) is ineffective as part of a lasting power of attorney, or

    (b) prevents the instrument from operating as a valid lasting power of attorney.

(2) The court must—

    (a) notify the Public Guardian that it has severed the provision, or

    (b) direct him to cancel the registration of the instrument as a lasting power of attorney.

20 On the cancellation of the registration of an instrument, the instrument and any office copies of it must be delivered up to the Public Guardian to be cancelled.

PART 4

RECORDS OF ALTERATIONS IN REGISTERED POWERS

Partial revocation or suspension of power as a result of bankruptcy

21 If in the case of a registered instrument it appears to the Public Guardian that under section 13 a lasting power of attorney is revoked, or suspended, in relation to the donor's property and affairs (but not in relation to other matters), the Public Guardian must attach to the instrument a note to that effect.

Termination of appointment of donee which does not revoke power

22 If in the case of a registered instrument it appears to the Public Guardian that an event has occurred—
    (a) which has terminated the appointment of the donee, but
    (b) which has not revoked the instrument, the Public Guardian must attach to the instrument a note to that effect.

Replacement of donee

23 If in the case of a registered instrument it appears to the Public Guardian that the donee has been replaced under the terms of the instrument the Public Guardian must attach to the instrument a note to that effect.

Severance of ineffective provisions

24 If in the case of a registered instrument the court notifies the Public Guardian under paragraph 19(2)(a) that it has severed a provision of the instrument, the Public Guardian must attach to it a note to that effect.

Notification of alterations

25 If the Public Guardian attaches a note to an instrument under paragraph 21, 22, 23 or 24 he must give notice of the note to the donee or donees of the power (or, as the case may be, to the other donee or donees of the power).

[SCHEDULE 1A

PERSONS INELIGIBLE TO BE DEPRIVED OF LIBERTY BY THIS ACT

PART 1

INELIGIBLE PERSONS

Application

1 This Schedule applies for the purposes of—
   (a) section 16A, and
   (b) paragraph 17 of Schedule A1.]

[Determining ineligibility

2   A person ('P') is ineligible to be deprived of liberty by this Act ('ineligible') if—
   (a) P falls within one of the cases set out in the second column of the following table, and
   (b) the corresponding entry in the third column of the table — or the provision, or one of the provisions, referred to in that entry — provides that he is ineligible.

	Status of P	*Determination of ineligibility*
Case A	P is— (a) subject to the hospital treatment regime, and (b) detained in a hospital under that regime.	P is ineligible.
Case B	P is— (a) subject to the hospital treatment regime, but (b) not detained in a hospital under that regime.	See paragraphs 3 and 4.
Case C	P is subject to the community treatment regime.	See paragraphs 3 and 4.
Case D	P is subject to the guardianship regime.	See paragraphs 3 and 5.
Case E	P is— (a) within the scope of the Mental Health Act, but (b) not subject to any of the mental health regimes.	See paragraph 5.

Authorised course of action not in accordance with regime

3 (1) This paragraph applies in cases B, C and D in the table in paragraph 2.
(2) P is ineligible if the authorised course of action is not in accordance with a requirement which the relevant regime imposes.
(3) That includes any requirement as to where P is, or is not, to reside.
(4) The relevant regime is the mental health regime to which P is subject.

Treatment for mental disorder in a hospital

4 (1) This paragraph applies in cases B and C in the table in paragraph.
(2) P is ineligible if the relevant care or treatment consists in whole or in part of medical treatment for mental disorder in a hospital.

P objects to being a mental health patient etc

5 (1) This paragraph applies in cases D and E in the table in paragraph 2.
(2) P is ineligible if the following conditions are met.
(3) The first condition is that the relevant instrument authorises P to be a mental health patient.
(4) The second condition is that P objects—
   (a) to being a mental health patient, or
   (b) to being given some or all of the mental health treatment.
(5) The third condition is that a donee or deputy has not made a valid decision to consent to each matter to which P objects.
(6) In determining whether or not P objects to something, regard must be had to all the circumstances (so far as they are reasonably ascertainable), including the following—]

[(a) P's behaviour;
  (b) P's wishes and feelings;
  (c) P's views, beliefs and values.
(7) But regard is to be had to circumstances from the past only so far as it is still appropriate to have regard to them.

PART 2
INTERPRETATION

Application

6 This Part applies for the purposes of this Schedule.

Mental health regimes

7 The mental health regimes are—
  (a) the hospital treatment regime,
  (b) the community treatment regime, and
  (c) the guardianship regime.

Hospital treatment regime

8 (1) P is subject to the hospital treatment regime if he is subject to—
  (a) a hospital treatment obligation under the relevant enactment, or
  (b) an obligation under another England and Wales enactment which has the same effect as a hospital treatment obligation.
(2) But where P is subject to any such obligation, he is to be regarded as not subject to the hospital treatment regime during any period when he is subject to the community treatment regime.
(3) A hospital treatment obligation is an application, order or direction of a kind listed in the first column of the following table.
(4) In relation to a hospital treatment obligation, the relevant enactment is the enactment in the Mental Health Act which is referred to in the corresponding entry in the second column of the following table.

Hospital treatment obligation	*Relevant enactment*
Application for admission for assessment	Section 2
Application for admission for assessment	Section 4
Application for admission for treatment	Section 3
Order for remand to hospital	Section 35
Order for remand to hospital	Section 36
Hospital order	Section 37
Interim hospital order	Section 38
Order for detention in hospital	Section 44
Hospital direction	Section 45A
Transfer direction	Section 47
Transfer direction	Section 48
Hospital order	Section 51]

[Community treatment regime

9   P is subject to the community treatment regime if he is subject to—
   (a) a community treatment order under section 17A of the Mental Health Act, or
   (b) an obligation under another England and Wales enactment which has the same effect as a community treatment order.

Guardianship regime

10   P is subject to the guardianship regime if he is subject to—
   (a) a guardianship application under section 7 of the Mental Health Act,
   (b) a guardianship order under section 37 of the Mental Health Act, or
   (c) an obligation under another England and Wales enactment which has the same effect as a guardianship application or guardianship order.

England and Wales enactments

11 (1) An England and Wales enactment is an enactment which extends to England and Wales (whether or not it also extends elsewhere).
   (2) It does not matter if the enactment is in the Mental Health Act or not.

P within scope of Mental Health Act

12 (1) P is within the scope of the Mental Health Act if—
   (a) an application in respect of P could be made under section 2 or 3 of the Mental Health Act, and
   (b) P could be detained in a hospital in pursuance of such an application, were one made.
   (2) The following provisions of this paragraph apply when determining whether an application in respect of P could be made under section 2 or 3 of the Mental Health Act.
   (3) If the grounds in section 2(2) of the Mental Health Act are met in P's case, it is to be assumed that the recommendations referred to in section 2(3) of that Act have been given.
   (4) If the grounds in section 3(2) of the Mental Health Act are met in P's case, it is to be assumed that the recommendations referred to in section 3(3) of that Act have been given.
   (5) In determining whether the ground in section 3(2)(c) of the Mental Health Act is met in P's case, it is to be assumed that the treatment referred to in section 3(2)(c) cannot be provided under this Act.

Authorised course of action, relevant care or treatment & relevant instrument

13   In a case where this Schedule applies for the purposes of section 16A—
      'authorised course of action' means any course of action amounting to deprivation of liberty which the order under section 16(2)(a) authorises;]

['relevant care or treatment' means any care or treatment which—

    (a) comprises, or forms part of, the authorised course of action, or

    (b) is to be given in connection with the authorised course of action;

'relevant instrument' means the order under section 16(2)(a).

14   In a case where this Schedule applies for the purposes of paragraph 17 of Schedule A1—

    'authorised course of action' means the accommodation of the relevant person in the relevant hospital or care home for the purpose of being given the relevant care or treatment;

    'relevant care or treatment' has the same meaning as in Schedule A1;

    'relevant instrument' means the standard authorisation under Schedule A1.

15 (1) This paragraph applies where the question whether a person is ineligible to be deprived of liberty by this Act is relevant to either of these decisions—

    (a) whether or not to include particular provision ('the proposed provision') in an order under section 16(2)(a);

    (b) whether or not to give a standard authorisation under Schedule A1.

  (2) A reference in this Schedule to the authorised course of action or the relevant care or treatment is to be read as a reference to that thing as it would be if—

    (a) the proposed provision were included in the order, or

    (b) the standard authorisation were given.

  (3) A reference in this Schedule to the relevant instrument is to be read as follows—

    (a) where the relevant instrument is an order under section 16(2)(a): as a reference to the order as it would be if the proposed provision were included in it;

    (b) where the relevant instrument is a standard authorisation: as a reference to the standard authorisation as it would be if it were given.

Expressions used in paragraph 5

16 (1) These expressions have the meanings given—

    'donee' means a donee of a lasting power of attorney granted by P;

    'mental health patient' means a person accommodated in a hospital for the purpose of being given medical treatment for mental disorder;

    'mental health treatment' means the medical treatment for mental disorder referred to in the definition of 'mental health patient'.

  (2) A decision of a donee or deputy is valid if it is made—

    (a) within the scope of his authority as donee or deputy, and

    (b) in accordance with Part 1 of this Act.

Expressions with same meaning as in Mental Health Act

17 (1) 'Hospital' has the same meaning as in Part 2 of the Mental Health Act.

  (2) 'Medical treatment' has the same meaning as in the Mental Health Act.

  (3) 'Mental disorder' has the same meaning as in Schedule A1 (see paragraph 14).]

[Schedule 1A inserted by section 50(6) and Schedule 8 to the 2007 Act.]

SCHEDULE 2
PROPERTY AND AFFAIRS: SUPPLEMENTARY PROVISIONS

Section 18(4)

Wills: general

1 Paragraphs 2 to 4 apply in relation to the execution of a will, by virtue of section 18, on behalf of P.

Provision that may be made in will

2 The will may make any provision (whether by disposing of property or exercising a power or otherwise) which could be made by a will executed by P if he had capacity to make it.

Wills: requirements relating to execution

3 (1) Sub-paragraph (2) applies if under section 16 the court makes an order or gives directions requiring or authorising a person ('the authorised person') to execute a will on behalf of P.
(2) Any will executed in pursuance of the order or direction—
    (a) must state that it is signed by P acting by the authorised person,
    (b) must be signed by the authorised person with the name of P and his own name, in the presence of two or more witnesses present at the same time,
    (c) must be attested and subscribed by those witnesses in the presence of the authorised person, and
    (d) must be sealed with the official seal of the court.

Wills: effect of execution

4 (1) This paragraph applies where a will is executed in accordance with paragraph 3.
(2) The Wills Act 1837 (c. 26) has effect in relation to the will as if it were signed by P by his own hand, except that—
    (a) section 9 of the 1837 Act (requirements as to signing and attestation) does not apply, and
    (b) in the subsequent provisions of the 1837 Act any reference to execution in the manner required by the previous provisions is to be read as a reference to execution in accordance with paragraph 3.
(3) The will has the same effect for all purposes as if—
    (a) P had had the capacity to make a valid will, and
    (b) the will had been executed by him in the manner required by the 1837 Act.
(4) But sub-paragraph (3) does not have effect in relation to the will—
    (a) in so far as it disposes of immovable property outside England and Wales, or
    (b) in so far as it relates to any other property or matter if, when the will is executed—
        (i) P is domiciled outside England and Wales, and
        (ii) the condition in sub-paragraph (5) is met.
(5) The condition is that, under the law of P's domicile, any question of his testamentary capacity would fall to be determined in accordance with the law of a place outside England and Wales.

Vesting orders ancillary to settlement etc.

5 (1) If provision is made by virtue of section 18 for—
  (a) the settlement of any property of P, or
  (b) the exercise of a power vested in him of appointing trustees or retiring from a trust,
  the court may also make as respects the property settled or the trust property such consequential vesting or other orders as the case may require.
(2) The power under sub-paragraph (1) includes, in the case of the exercise of such a power, any order which could have been made in such a case under Part 4 of the Trustee Act 1925 (c. 19).

Variation of settlements

6 (1) If a settlement has been made by virtue of section 18, the court may by order vary or revoke the settlement if—
  (a) the settlement makes provision for its variation or revocation,
  (b) the court is satisfied that a material fact was not disclosed when the settlement was made, or
  (c) the court is satisfied that there has been a substantial change of circumstances.
(2) Any such order may give such consequential directions as the court thinks fit.

7 (1) Sub-paragraph (2) applies if the court is satisfied—
  (a) that under the law prevailing in a place outside England and Wales a person ('M') has been appointed to exercise powers in respect of the property or affairs of P on the ground (however formulated) that P lacks capacity to make decisions with respect to the management and administration of his property and affairs, and
  (b) that, having regard to the nature of the appointment and to the circumstances of the case, it is expedient that the court should exercise its powers under this paragraph.
(2) The court may direct—
  (a) any stocks standing in the name of P, or
  (b) the right to receive dividends from the stocks, to be transferred into M's name or otherwise dealt with as required by M, and may give such directions as the court thinks fit for dealing with accrued dividends from the stocks.
(3) 'Stocks' includes—
  (a) shares, and
  (b) any funds, annuity or security transferable in the books kept by any body corporate or unincorporated company or society or by an instrument of transfer either alone or accompanied by other formalities, and 'dividends' is to be construed accordingly.

Preservation of interests in property disposed of on behalf of person lacking capacity

8 (1) Sub-paragraphs (2) and (3) apply if—
  (a) P's property has been disposed of by virtue of section 18,
  (b) under P's will or intestacy, or by a gift perfected or nomination taking effect on his death, any other person would have taken an interest in the property but for the disposal, and
  (c) on P's death, any property belonging to P's estate represents the property disposed of.
(2) The person takes the same interest, if and so far as circumstances allow, in the property representing the property disposed of.
(3) If the property disposed of was real property, any property representing it is to be treated, so long as it remains part of P's estate, as if it were real property.

(4) The court may direct that, on a disposal of P's property—

    (a) which is made by virtue of section 18, and

    (b) which would apart from this paragraph result in the conversion of personal property into real property,

property representing the property disposed of is to be treated, so long as it remains P's property or forms part of P's estate, as if it were personal property.

(5) References in sub-paragraphs (1) to (4) to the disposal of property are to—

    (a) the sale, exchange, charging of or other dealing (otherwise than by will) with property other than money;

    (b) the removal of property from one place to another;

    (c) the application of money in acquiring property;

    (d) the transfer of money from one account to another;

and references to property representing property disposed of are to be construed accordingly and as including the result of successive disposals.

(6) The court may give such directions as appear to it necessary or expedient for the purpose of facilitating the operation of sub-paragraphs (1) to (3), including the carrying of money to a separate account and the transfer of property other than money.

9 (1) Sub-paragraph (2) applies if the court has ordered or directed the expenditure of money—

    (a) for carrying out permanent improvements on any of P's property, or

    (b) otherwise for the permanent benefit of any of P's property.

(2) The court may order that—

    (a) the whole of the money expended or to be expended, or

    (b) any part of it,

is to be a charge on the property either without interest or with interest at a specified rate.

(3) An order under sub-paragraph (2) may provide for excluding or restricting the operation of paragraph 8(1) to (3).

(4) A charge under sub-paragraph (2) may be made in favour of such person as may be just and, in particular, where the money charged is paid out of P's general estate, may be made in favour of a person as trustee for P.

(5) No charge under sub-paragraph (2) may confer any right of sale or foreclosure during P's lifetime.

Powers as patron of benefice

10 (1) Any functions which P has as patron of a benefice may be discharged only by a person ('R') appointed by the court.

(2) R must be an individual capable of appointment under section 8(1)(b) of the 1986 Measure (which provides for an individual able to make a declaration of communicant status, a clerk in Holy Orders, etc. to be appointed to discharge a registered patron's functions).

(3) The 1986 Measure applies to R as it applies to an individual appointed by the registered patron of the benefice under section 8(1)(b) or (3) of that Measure to discharge his functions as patron.

(4) 'The 1986 Measure' means the Patronage (Benefices) Measure 1986 (No.3).

SCHEDULE 3
INTERNATIONAL PROTECTION OF ADULTS

Section 63

PART 1
PRELIMINARY

Introduction

1 This Part applies for the purposes of this Schedule.

The Convention

2 (1) 'Convention' means the Convention referred to in section 63.

(2) 'Convention country' means a country in which the Convention is in force.

(3) A reference to an Article or Chapter is to an Article or Chapter of the Convention.

(4) An expression which appears in this Schedule and in the Convention is to be construed in accordance with the Convention.

Countries, territories and nationals

3 (1) 'Country' includes a territory which has its own system of law.

(2) Where a country has more than one territory with its own system of law, a reference to the country, in relation to one of its nationals, is to the territory with which the national has the closer, or the closest, connection.

Adults with incapacity

4 'Adult' means a person who—

(a) as a result of an impairment or insufficiency of his personal faculties, cannot protect his interests, and

(b) has reached 16.

Protective measures

5 (1) 'Protective measure' means a measure directed to the protection of the person or property of an adult; and it may deal in particular with any of the following—

(a) the determination of incapacity and the institution of a protective regime,

(b) placing the adult under the protection of an appropriate authority,

(c) guardianship, curatorship or any corresponding system,

(d) the designation and functions of a person having charge of the adult's person or property, or representing or otherwise helping him,

(e) placing the adult in a place where protection can be provided,

(f) administering, conserving or disposing of the adult's property,

(g) authorising a specific intervention for the protection of the person or property of the adult.

(2) Where a measure of like effect to a protective measure has been taken in relation to a person before he reaches 16, this Schedule applies to the measure in so far as it has effect in relation to him once he has reached 16.

Central Authority

6 (1) Any function under the Convention of a Central Authority is exercisable in England and Wales by the Lord Chancellor.

(2) A communication may be sent to the Central Authority in relation to England and Wales by sending it to the Lord Chancellor.

PART 2
JURISDICTION OF COMPETENT AUTHORITY

Scope of jurisdiction

7 (1) The court may exercise its functions under this Act (in so far as it cannot otherwise do so) in relation to—
   (a) an adult habitually resident in England and Wales,
   (b) an adult's property in England and Wales,
   (c) an adult present in England and Wales or who has property there, if the matter is urgent, or
   (d) an adult present in England and Wales, if a protective measure which is temporary and limited in its effect to England and Wales is proposed in relation to him.

(2) An adult present in England and Wales is to be treated for the purposes of this paragraph as habitually resident there if—
   (a) his habitual residence cannot be ascertained,
   (b) he is a refugee, or
   (c) he has been displaced as a result of disturbance in the country of his habitual residence.

8 (1) The court may also exercise its functions under this Act (in so far as it cannot otherwise do so) in relation to an adult if sub-paragraph (2) or (3) applies in relation to him.

(2) This sub-paragraph applies in relation to an adult if—
   (a) he is a British citizen,
   (b) he has a closer connection with England and Wales than with Scotland or Northern Ireland, and
   (c) Article 7 has, in relation to the matter concerned, been complied with.

(3) This sub-paragraph applies in relation to an adult if the Lord Chancellor, having consulted such persons as he considers appropriate, agrees to a request under Article 8 in relation to the adult.

Exercise of jurisdiction

9 (1) This paragraph applies where jurisdiction is exercisable under this Schedule in connection with a matter which involves a Convention country other than England and Wales.

(2) Any Article on which the jurisdiction is based applies in relation to the matter in so far as it involves the other country (and the court must, accordingly, comply with any duty conferred on it as a result).

(3) Article 12 also applies, so far as its provisions allow, in relation to the matter in so far as it involves the other country.

10 A reference in this Schedule to the exercise of jurisdiction under this Schedule is to the exercise of functions under this Act as a result of this Part of this Schedule.

PART 3
APPLICABLE LAW

Applicable law

11 In exercising jurisdiction under this Schedule, the court may, if it thinks that the matter has a substantial connection with a country other than England and Wales, apply the law of that other country.

12 Where a protective measure is taken in one country but implemented in another, the conditions of implementation are governed by the law of the other country.

Lasting powers of attorney, etc.

13 (1) If the donor of a lasting power is habitually resident in England and Wales at the time of granting the power, the law applicable to the existence, extent, modification or extinction of the power is—
(a) the law of England and Wales, or
(b) if he specifies in writing the law of a connected country for the purpose, that law.

(2) If he is habitually resident in another country at that time, but England and Wales is a connected country, the law applicable in that respect is—
(a) the law of the other country, or
(b) if he specifies in writing the law of England and Wales for the purpose, that law.

(3) A country is connected, in relation to the donor, if it is a country—
(a) of which he is a national,
(b) in which he was habitually resident, or
(c) in which he has property.

(4) Where this paragraph applies as a result of sub-paragraph (3)(c), it applies only in relation to the property which the donor has in the connected country.

(5) The law applicable to the manner of the exercise of a lasting power is the law of the country where it is exercised.

(6) In this Part of this Schedule, 'lasting power' means—
(a) a lasting power of attorney (see section 9),
(b) an enduring power of attorney within the meaning of Schedule 4, or
(c) any other power of like effect.

14 (1) Where a lasting power is not exercised in a manner sufficient to guarantee the protection of the person or property of the donor, the court, in exercising jurisdiction under this Schedule, may disapply or modify the power.

(2) Where, in accordance with this Part of this Schedule, the law applicable to the power is, in one or more respects, that of a country other than England and Wales, the court must, so far as possible, have regard to the law of the other country in that respect (or those respects).

15 Regulations may provide for Schedule 1 (lasting powers of attorney: formalities) to apply with modifications in relation to a lasting power which comes within paragraph 13(6)(c) above.

Protection of third parties

16 (1) This paragraph applies where a person (a 'representative') in purported exercise of an authority to act on behalf of an adult enters into a transaction with a third party.

(2) The validity of the transaction may not be questioned in proceedings, nor may the third party be held liable, merely because—

  (a) where the representative and third party are in England and Wales when entering into the transaction, sub-paragraph (3) applies;

  (b) here they are in another country at that time, sub-paragraph (4) applies.

(3) This sub-paragraph applies if—

  (a) the law applicable to the authority in one or more respects is, as a result of this Schedule, the law of a country other than England and Wales, and

  (b) the representative is not entitled to exercise the authority in that respect (or those respects) under the law of that other country.

(4) This sub-paragraph applies if—

  (a) the law applicable to the authority in one or more respects is, as a result of this Part of this Schedule, the law of England and Wales, and

  (b) the representative is not entitled to exercise the authority in that respect (or those respects) under that law.

(5) This paragraph does not apply if the third party knew or ought to have known that the applicable law was—

  (a) in a case within sub-paragraph (3), the law of the other country;

  (b) in a case within sub-paragraph (4), the law of England and Wales.

Mandatory rules

17 Where the court is entitled to exercise jurisdiction under this Schedule, the mandatory provisions of the law of England and Wales apply, regardless of any system of law which would otherwise apply in relation to the matter.

Public policy

18 Nothing in this Part of this Schedule requires or enables the application in England and Wales of a provision of the law of another country if its application would be manifestly contrary to public policy.

PART 4
RECOGNITION AND ENFORCEMENT

Recognition

19 (1) A protective measure taken in relation to an adult under the law of a country other than England and Wales is to be recognised in England and Wales if it was taken on the ground that the adult is habitually resident in the other country.

(2) A protective measure taken in relation to an adult under the law of a Convention country other than England and Wales is to be recognised in England and Wales if it was taken on a ground mentioned in Chapter 2 (jurisdiction).

(3) But the court may disapply this paragraph in relation to a measure if it thinks that—
  (a) the case in which the measure was taken was not urgent,
  (b) the adult was not given an opportunity to be heard, and
  (c) that omission amounted to a breach of natural justice.

(4) It may also disapply this paragraph in relation to a measure if it thinks that—
  (a) recognition of the measure would be manifestly contrary to public policy,
  (b) the measure would be inconsistent with a mandatory provision of the law of England and Wales, or
  (c) the measure is inconsistent with one subsequently taken, or recognised, in England and Wales in relation to the adult.

(5) And the court may disapply this paragraph in relation to a measure taken under the law of a Convention country in a matter to which Article 33 applies, if the court thinks that that Article has not been complied with in connection with that matter.

20 (1) An interested person may apply to the court for a declaration as to whether a protective measure taken under the law of a country other than England and Wales is to be recognised in England and Wales.

(2) No permission is required for an application to the court under this paragraph.

21 For the purposes of paragraphs 19 and 20, any finding of fact relied on when the measure was taken is conclusive.

Enforcement

22 (1) An interested person may apply to the court for a declaration as to whether a protective measure taken under the law of, and enforceable in, a country other than England and Wales is enforceable, or to be registered, in England and Wales in accordance with Court of Protection Rules.

(2) The court must make the declaration if—
  (a) the measure comes within sub-paragraph (1) or (2) of paragraph 19, and
  (b) the paragraph is not disapplied in relation to it as a result of subparagraph (3), (4) or (5).

(3) A measure to which a declaration under this paragraph relates is enforceable in England and Wales as if it were a measure of like effect taken by the court.

Measures taken in relation to those aged under 16

23 (1) This paragraph applies where—
  (a) provision giving effect to, or otherwise deriving from, the Convention in a country other than England and Wales applies in relation to a person who has not reached 16, and

(b) a measure is taken in relation to that person in reliance on that provision.

(2) This Part of this Schedule applies in relation to that measure as it applies in relation to a protective measure taken in relation to an adult under the law of a Convention country other than England and Wales.

Supplementary

24 The court may not review the merits of a measure taken outside England and Wales except to establish whether the measure complies with this Schedule in so far as it is, as a result of this Schedule, required to do so.

25 Court of Protection Rules may make provision about an application under paragraph 20 or 22.

PART 5
CO-OPERATION

Proposal for cross-border placement

26 (1) This paragraph applies where a public authority proposes to place an adult in an establishment in a Convention country other than England and Wales.

(2) The public authority must consult an appropriate authority in that other country about the proposed placement and, for that purpose, must send it—

(a) a report on the adult, and

(b) a statement of its reasons for the proposed placement.

(3) If the appropriate authority in the other country opposes the proposed placement within a reasonable time, the public authority may not proceed with it.

27 A proposal received by a public authority under Article 33 in relation to an adult is to proceed unless the authority opposes it within a reasonable time.

Adult in danger etc.

28 (1) This paragraph applies if a public authority is told that an adult—

(a) who is in serious danger, and

(b) in relation to whom the public authority has taken, or is considering taking, protective measures

is, or has become resident, in a Convention country other than England and Wales.

(2) The public authority must tell an appropriate authority in that other country about—

(a) the danger, and

(b) the measures taken or under consideration.

29 A public authority may not request from, or send to, an appropriate authority in a Convention country information in accordance with Chapter 5 (cooperation) in relation to an adult if it thinks that doing so—

(a) would be likely to endanger the adult or his property, or

(b) would amount to a serious threat to the liberty or life of a member of the adult's family.

PART 6
GENERAL

Certificates

30 A certificate given under Article 38 by an authority in a Convention country other than England and Wales is, unless the contrary is shown, proof of the matters contained in it.

Powers to make further provision as to private international law

31 Her Majesty may by Order in Council confer on the Lord Chancellor, the court or another public authority functions for enabling the Convention to be given effect in England and Wales.

32 (1) Regulations may make provision—

(a) giving further effect to the Convention, or

(b) otherwise about the private international law of England and Wales in relation to the protection of adults.

(2) The regulations may—

(a) confer functions on the court or another public authority;

(b) amend this Schedule;

(c) provide for this Schedule to apply with specified modifications;

(d) make provision about countries other than Convention countries.

Exceptions

33 Nothing in this Schedule applies, and no provision made under paragraph 32 is to apply, to any matter to which the Convention, as a result of Article 4, does not apply.

Regulations and orders

34 A reference in this Schedule to regulations or an order (other than an Order in Council) is to regulations or an order made for the purposes of this Schedule by the Lord Chancellor.

Commencement

35 The following provisions of this Schedule have effect only if the Convention is in force in accordance with Article 57—

(a) paragraph 8,

(b) paragraph 9,

(c) paragraph 19(2) and (5),

(d) Part 5,

(e) paragraph 30.

SCHEDULE 4
PROVISIONS APPLYING TO EXISTING ENDURING POWERS OF ATTORNEY

Section 66(3)

PART 1
ENDURING POWERS OF ATTORNEY

Enduring power of attorney to survive mental incapacity of donor

1 (1) Where an individual has created a power of attorney which is an enduring power within the meaning of this Schedule—
  (a) the power is not revoked by any subsequent mental incapacity of his,
  (b) upon such incapacity supervening, the donee of the power may not do anything under the authority of the power except as provided by sub-paragraph (2) unless or until the instrument creating the power is registered under paragraph 13, and
  (c) if and so long as paragraph (b) operates to suspend the donee's authority to act under the power, section 5 of the Powers of Attorney Act 1971 (c. 27) (protection of donee and third persons), so far as applicable, applies as if the power had been revoked by the donor's mental incapacity,
  and, accordingly, section 1 of this Act does not apply.
(2) Despite sub-paragraph (1)(b), where the attorney has made an application for registration of the instrument then, until it is registered, the attorney may take action under the power—
  (a) to maintain the donor or prevent loss to his estate, or
  (b) to maintain himself or other persons in so far as paragraph 3(2) permits him to do so.
(3) Where the attorney purports to act as provided by sub-paragraph (2) then, in favour of a person who deals with him without knowledge that the attorney is acting otherwise than in accordance with sub-paragraph (2)(a) or (b), the transaction between them is as valid as if the attorney were acting in accordance with sub-paragraph (2)(a) or (b).

Characteristics of an enduring power of attorney

2 (1) Subject to sub-paragraphs (5) and (6) and paragraph 20, a power of attorney is an enduring power within the meaning of this Schedule if the instrument which creates the power—
  (a) is in the prescribed form,
  (b) was executed in the prescribed manner by the donor and the attorney, and
  (c) incorporated at the time of execution by the donor the prescribed explanatory information.
(2) In this paragraph, 'prescribed' means prescribed by such of the following regulations as applied when the instrument was executed—
  (a) the Enduring Powers of Attorney (Prescribed Form) Regulations 1986 (S.I. 1986/126),
  (b) the Enduring Powers of Attorney (Prescribed Form) Regulations 1987 (S.I. 1987/1612),
  (c) the Enduring Powers of Attorney (Prescribed Form) Regulations 1990 (S.I. 1990/1376),

(d) the Enduring Powers of Attorney (Welsh Language Prescribed Form) Regulations 2000 (S.I. 2000/289).

(3) An instrument in the prescribed form purporting to have been executed in the prescribed manner is to be taken, in the absence of evidence to the contrary, to be a document which incorporated at the time of execution by the donor the prescribed explanatory information.

(4) If an instrument differs in an immaterial respect in form or mode of expression from the prescribed form it is to be treated as sufficient in point of form and expression.

(5) A power of attorney cannot be an enduring power unless, when he executes the instrument creating it, the attorney is—

(a) an individual who has reached 18 and is not bankrupt, or

(b) a trust corporation.

(6) A power of attorney which gives the attorney a right to appoint a substitute or successor cannot be an enduring power.

(7) An enduring power is revoked by the bankruptcy of the donor or attorney.

(8) But where the donor or attorney is bankrupt merely because an interim bankruptcy restrictions order has effect in respect of him, the power is suspended for so long as the order has effect.

(9) An enduring power is revoked if the court—

(a) exercises a power under sections 16 to 20 in relation to the donor, and

(b) directs that the enduring power is to be revoked.

(10) No disclaimer of an enduring power, whether by deed or otherwise, is valid unless and until the attorney gives notice of it to the donor or, where paragraph 4(6) or 15(1) applies, to the Public Guardian.

Scope of authority etc. of attorney under enduring power

3 (1) If the instrument which creates an enduring power of attorney is expressed to confer general authority on the attorney, the instrument operates to confer, subject to—

(a) the restriction imposed by sub-paragraph (3), and

(b) any conditions or restrictions contained in the instrument,

authority to do on behalf of the donor anything which the donor could lawfully do by an attorney at the time when the donor executed the instrument.

(2) Subject to any conditions or restrictions contained in the instrument, an attorney under an enduring power, whether general or limited, may (without obtaining any consent) act under the power so as to benefit himself or other persons than the donor to the following extent but no further—

(a) he may so act in relation to himself or in relation to any other person if the donor might be expected to provide for his or that person's needs respectively, and

(b) he may do whatever the donor might be expected to do to meet those needs.

(3) Without prejudice to sub-paragraph (2) but subject to any conditions or restrictions contained in the instrument, an attorney under an enduring power, whether general or limited, may (without obtaining any consent) dispose of the property of the donor by way of gift to the following extent but no further—

(a) he may make gifts of a seasonal nature or at a time, or on an anniversary, of a birth, a marriage or the formation of a civil partnership, to persons (including himself) who are related to or connected with the donor, and

(b) he may make gifts to any charity to whom the donor made or might be expected to make gifts,

provided that the value of each such gift is not unreasonable having regard to all the circumstances and in particular the size of the donor's estate.

PART 2
ACTION ON ACTUAL OR IMPENDING INCAPACITY OF DONOR

Duties of attorney in event of actual or impending incapacity of donor

4 (1) Sub-paragraphs (2) to (6) apply if the attorney under an enduring power has reason to believe that the donor is or is becoming mentally incapable.

(2) The attorney must, as soon as practicable, make an application to the Public Guardian for the registration of the instrument creating the power.

(3) Before making an application for registration the attorney must comply with the provisions as to notice set out in Part 3 of this Schedule.

(4) An application for registration—
  (a) must be made in the prescribed form, and
  (b) must contain such statements as may be prescribed.

(5) The attorney—
  (a) may, before making an application for the registration of the instrument, refer to the court for its determination any question as to the validity of the power, and
  (b) must comply with any direction given to him by the court on that determination.

(6) No disclaimer of the power is valid unless and until the attorney gives notice of it to the Public Guardian; and the Public Guardian must notify the donor if he receives a notice under this sub-paragraph.

(7) A person who, in an application for registration, makes a statement which he knows to be false in a material particular is guilty of an offence and is liable—
  (a) on summary conviction, to imprisonment for a term not exceeding 12 months or a fine not exceeding the statutory maximum or both;
  (b) on conviction on indictment, to imprisonment for a term not exceeding 2 years or a fine or both.

(8) In this paragraph, 'prescribed' means prescribed by regulations made for the purposes of this Schedule by the Lord Chancellor.

PART 3
NOTIFICATION PRIOR TO REGISTRATION

Duty to give notice to relatives

5 Subject to paragraph 7, before making an application for registration the attorney must give notice of his intention to do so to all those persons (if any) who are entitled to receive notice by virtue of paragraph 6.

6 (1) Subject to sub-paragraphs (2) to (4), persons of the following classes ('relatives') are entitled to receive notice under paragraph 5—
  (a) the donor's spouse or civil partner,

   (b) the donor's children,

   (c) the donor's parents,

   (d) the donor's brothers and sisters, whether of the whole or half blood,

   (e) the widow, widower or surviving civil partner of a child of the donor,

   (f) the donor's grandchildren,

   (g) the children of the donor's brothers and sisters of the whole blood,

   (h) the children of the donor's brothers and sisters of the half blood,

   (i) the donor's uncles and aunts of the whole blood,

   (j) the children of the donor's uncles and aunts of the whole blood.

(2) A person is not entitled to receive notice under paragraph 5 if—

   (a) his name or address is not known to the attorney and cannot be reasonably ascertained by him, or

   (b) the attorney has reason to believe that he has not reached 18 or is mentally incapable.

(3) Except where sub-paragraph (4) applies—

   (a) no more than 3 persons are entitled to receive notice under paragraph 5, and

   (b) in determining the persons who are so entitled, persons falling within the class in sub-paragraph (1)(a) are to be preferred to persons falling within the class in sub-paragraph (1)(b), those falling within the class in sub-paragraph (1)(b) are to be preferred to those falling within the class in sub-paragraph (1)(c), and so on.

(4) Despite the limit of 3 specified in sub-paragraph (3), where—

   (a) there is more than one person falling within any of classes (a) to (j) of sub-paragraph (1), and

   (b) at least one of those persons would be entitled to receive notice under paragraph 5,

then, subject to sub-paragraph (2), all the persons falling within that class are entitled to receive notice under paragraph 5.

7 (1) An attorney is not required to give notice under paragraph 5—

   (a) to himself, or

   (b) to any other attorney under the power who is joining in making the application,

even though he or, as the case may be, the other attorney is entitled to receive notice by virtue of paragraph 6.

(2) In the case of any person who is entitled to receive notice by virtue of paragraph 6, the attorney, before applying for registration, may make an application to the court to be dispensed from the requirement to give him notice; and the court must grant the application if it is satisfied—

   (a) that it would be undesirable or impracticable for the attorney to give him notice, or

   (b) that no useful purpose is likely to be served by giving him notice.

Duty to give notice to donor

8 (1) Subject to sub-paragraph (2), before making an application for registration the attorney must give notice of his intention to do so to the donor.

(2) Paragraph 7(2) applies in relation to the donor as it applies in relation to a person who is entitled to receive notice under paragraph 5.

Contents of notices

9 A notice to relatives under this Part of this Schedule must—

   (a) be in the prescribed form,

(b) state that the attorney proposes to make an application to the Public Guardian for the registration of the instrument creating the enduring power in question,

(c) inform the person to whom it is given of his right to object to the registration under paragraph 13(4), and

(d) specify, as the grounds on which an objection to registration may be made, the grounds set out in paragraph 13(9).

10 A notice to the donor under this Part of this Schedule—

(a) must be in the prescribed form,

(b) must contain the statement mentioned in paragraph 9(b), and

(c) must inform the donor that, while the instrument remains registered, any revocation of the power by him will be ineffective unless and until the revocation is confirmed by the court.

Duty to give notice to other attorneys

11 (1) Subject to sub-paragraph (2), before making an application for registration an attorney under a joint and several power must give notice of his intention to do so to any other attorney under the power who is not joining in making the application; and paragraphs 7(2) and 9 apply in relation to attorneys entitled to receive notice by virtue of this paragraph as they apply in relation to persons entitled to receive notice by virtue of paragraph 6.

(2) An attorney is not entitled to receive notice by virtue of this paragraph if—

(a) his address is not known to the applying attorney and cannot reasonably be ascertained by him, or

(b) the applying attorney has reason to believe that he has not reached 18 or is mentally incapable.

Supplementary

12 Despite section 7 of the Interpretation Act 1978 (c. 30) (construction of references to service by post), for the purposes of this Part of this Schedule a notice given by post is to be regarded as given on the date on which it was posted.

PART 4
REGISTRATION

Registration of instrument creating power

13 (1) If an application is made in accordance with paragraph 4(3) and (4) the Public Guardian must, subject to the provisions of this paragraph, register the instrument to which the application relates.

(2) If it appears to the Public Guardian that—

(a) there is a deputy appointed for the donor of the power created by the instrument, and

    (b) the powers conferred on the deputy would, if the instrument were registered, to any extent conflict with the powers conferred on the attorney,

the Public Guardian must not register the instrument except in accordance with the court's directions.

(3) The court may, on the application of the attorney, direct the Public Guardian to register an instrument even though notice has not been given as required by paragraph 4(3) and Part 3 of this Schedule to a person entitled to receive it, if the court is satisfied—

    (a) that it was undesirable or impracticable for the attorney to give notice to that person, or

    (b) that no useful purpose is likely to be served by giving him notice.

(4) Sub-paragraph (5) applies if, before the end of the period of 5 weeks beginning with the date (or the latest date) on which the attorney gave notice under paragraph 5 of an application for registration, the Public Guardian receives a valid notice of objection to the registration from a person entitled to notice of the application.

(5) The Public Guardian must not register the instrument except in accordance with the court's directions.

(6) Sub-paragraph (7) applies if, in the case of an application for registration—

    (a) it appears from the application that there is no one to whom notice has been given under paragraph 5, or

    (b) the Public Guardian has reason to believe that appropriate inquiries might bring to light evidence on which he could be satisfied that one of the grounds of objection set out in sub-paragraph (9) was established.

(7) The Public Guardian—

    (a) must not register the instrument, and

    (b) must undertake such inquiries as he thinks appropriate in all the circumstances.

(8) If, having complied with sub-paragraph (7)(b), the Public Guardian is satisfied that one of the grounds of objection set out in sub-paragraph (9) is established—

    (a) the attorney may apply to the court for directions, and

    (b) the Public Guardian must not register the instrument except in accordance with the court's directions.

(9) A notice of objection under this paragraph is valid if made on one or more of the following grounds—

    (a) that the power purported to have been created by the instrument was not valid as an enduring power of attorney,

    (b) that the power created by the instrument no longer subsists,

    (c) that the application is premature because the donor is not yet becoming mentally incapable,

    (d) that fraud or undue pressure was used to induce the donor to create the power,

    (e) that, having regard to all the circumstances and in particular the attorney's relationship to or connection with the donor, the attorney is unsuitable to be the donor's attorney.

(10) If any of those grounds is established to the satisfaction of the court it must direct the Public Guardian not to register the instrument, but if not so satisfied it must direct its registration.

(11) If the court directs the Public Guardian not to register an instrument because it is satisfied that the ground in sub-paragraph (9)(d) or (e) is established, it must by order revoke the power created by the instrument.

(12) If the court directs the Public Guardian not to register an instrument because it is satisfied that any ground in sub-paragraph (9) except that in paragraph (c) is established, the instrument must be delivered up to be cancelled unless the court otherwise directs.

Register of enduring powers

14   The Public Guardian has the function of establishing and maintaining a register of enduring powers for the purposes of this Schedule.

PART 5
LEGAL POSITION AFTER REGISTRATION

Effect and proof of registration

15   (1)   The effect of the registration of an instrument under paragraph 13 is that—

(a)   no revocation of the power by the donor is valid unless and until the court confirms the revocation under paragraph 16(3);

(b)   no disclaimer of the power is valid unless and until the attorney gives notice of it to the Public Guardian;

(c)   the donor may not extend or restrict the scope of the authority conferred by the instrument and no instruction or consent given by him after registration, in the case of a consent, confers any right and, in the case of an instruction, imposes or confers any obligation or right on or creates any liability of the attorney or other persons having notice of the instruction or consent.

(2)   Sub-paragraph (1) applies for so long as the instrument is registered under paragraph 13 whether or not the donor is for the time being mentally incapable.

(3)   A document purporting to be an office copy of an instrument registered under this Schedule is, in any part of the United Kingdom, evidence of—

(a)   the contents of the instrument, and

(b)   the fact that it has been so registered.

(4)   Sub-paragraph (3) is without prejudice to section 3 of the Powers of Attorney Act 1971 (c. 27) (proof by certified copies) and to any other method of proof authorised by law.

Functions of court with regard to registered power

16   (1)   Where an instrument has been registered under paragraph 13, the court has the following functions with respect to the power and the donor of and the attorney appointed to act under the power.

(2)   The court may—

(a)   determine any question as to the meaning or effect of the instrument;

(b)   give directions with respect to—

(i)   the management or disposal by the attorney of the property and affairs of the donor;

(ii)   the rendering of accounts by the attorney and the production of the records kept by him for the purpose;

(iii)   the remuneration or expenses of the attorney whether or not in default of or in accordance with any provision made by the instrument, including directions for the repayment of excessive or the payment of additional remuneration;

(c) require the attorney to supply information or produce documents or things in his possession as attorney;

(d) give any consent or authorisation to act which the attorney would have to obtain from a mentally capable donor;

(e) authorise the attorney to act so as to benefit himself or other persons than the donor otherwise than in accordance with paragraph 3(2) and (3) (but subject to any conditions or restrictions contained in the instrument);

(f) relieve the attorney wholly or partly from any liability which he has or may have incurred on account of a breach of his duties as attorney.

(3) On application made for the purpose by or on behalf of the donor, the court must confirm the revocation of the power if satisfied that the donor—

(a) has done whatever is necessary in law to effect an express revocation of the power, and

(b) was mentally capable of revoking a power of attorney when he did so (whether or not he is so when the court considers the application).

(4) The court must direct the Public Guardian to cancel the registration of an instrument registered under paragraph 13 in any of the following circumstances—

(a) on confirming the revocation of the power under sub-paragraph (3),

(b) on directing under paragraph 2(9)(b) that the power is to be revoked,

(c) on being satisfied that the donor is and is likely to remain mentally capable,

(d) on being satisfied that the power has expired or has been revoked by the mental incapacity of the attorney,

(e) on being satisfied that the power was not a valid and subsisting enduring power when registration was effected,

(f) on being satisfied that fraud or undue pressure was used to induce the donor to create the power,

(g) on being satisfied that, having regard to all the circumstances and in particular the attorney's relationship to or connection with the donor, the attorney is unsuitable to be the donor's attorney.

(5) If the court directs the Public Guardian to cancel the registration of an instrument on being satisfied of the matters specified in sub-paragraph (4)(f) or (g) it must by order revoke the power created by the instrument.

(6) If the court directs the cancellation of the registration of an instrument under sub-paragraph (4) except paragraph (c) the instrument must be delivered up to the Public Guardian to be cancelled, unless the court otherwise directs.

Cancellation of registration by Public Guardian

17 The Public Guardian must cancel the registration of an instrument creating an enduring power of attorney—

(a) on receipt of a disclaimer signed by the attorney;

(b) if satisfied that the power has been revoked by the death or bankruptcy of the donor or attorney or, if the attorney is a body corporate, by its winding up or dissolution;

(c) on receipt of notification from the court that the court has revoked the power;

(d) on confirmation from the court that the donor has revoked the power.

PART 6

PROTECTION OF ATTORNEY AND THIRD PARTIES

Protection of attorney and third persons where power is invalid or revoked

18 (1) Sub-paragraphs (2) and (3) apply where an instrument which did not create a valid power of attorney has been registered under paragraph 13 (whether or not the registration has been cancelled at the time of the act or transaction in question).

(2) An attorney who acts in pursuance of the power does not incur any liability (either to the donor or to any other person) because of the non-existence of the power unless at the time of acting he knows—

   (a) that the instrument did not create a valid enduring power,

   (b) that an event has occurred which, if the instrument had created a valid enduring power, would have had the effect of revoking the power, or

   (c) that, if the instrument had created a valid enduring power, the power would have expired before that time.

(3) Any transaction between the attorney and another person is, in favour of that person, as valid as if the power had then been in existence, unless at the time of the transaction that person has knowledge of any of the matters mentioned in sub-paragraph (2).

(4) If the interest of a purchaser depends on whether a transaction between the attorney and another person was valid by virtue of sub-paragraph (3), it is conclusively presumed in favour of the purchaser that the transaction was valid if—

   (a) the transaction between that person and the attorney was completed within 12 months of the date on which the instrument was registered, or

   (b) that person makes a statutory declaration, before or within 3 months after the completion of the purchase, that he had no reason at the time of the transaction to doubt that the attorney had authority to dispose of the property which was the subject of the transaction.

(5) For the purposes of section 5 of the Powers of Attorney Act 1971 (c. 27) (protection where power is revoked) in its application to an enduring power the revocation of which by the donor is by virtue of paragraph 15 invalid unless and until confirmed by the court under paragraph 16—

   (a) knowledge of the confirmation of the revocation is knowledge of the revocation of the power, but

   (b) knowledge of the unconfirmed revocation is not.

Further protection of attorney and third persons

19 (1) If—

   (a) an instrument framed in a form prescribed as mentioned in paragraph 2(2) creates a power which is not a valid enduring power, and

   (b) the power is revoked by the mental incapacity of the donor, subparagraphs

(2) and (3) apply, whether or not the instrument has been registered.

(2) An attorney who acts in pursuance of the power does not, by reason of the revocation, incur any liability (either to the donor or to any other person) unless at the time of acting he knows—

   (a) that the instrument did not create a valid enduring power, and

   (b) that the donor has become mentally incapable.

(3) Any transaction between the attorney and another person is, in favour of that person, as valid as if the power had then been in existence, unless at the time of the transaction that person knows—

(a) that the instrument did not create a valid enduring power, and

(b) that the donor has become mentally incapable.

(4) Paragraph 18(4) applies for the purpose of determining whether a transaction was valid by virtue of sub-paragraph (3) as it applies for the purpose or determining whether a transaction was valid by virtue of paragraph 18(3).

PART 7
JOINT AND JOINT AND SEVERAL ATTORNEYS

Application to joint and joint and several attorneys

20 (1) An instrument which appoints more than one person to be an attorney cannot create an enduring power unless the attorneys are appointed to act—

(a) jointly, or

(b) jointly and severally.

(2) This Schedule, in its application to joint attorneys, applies to them collectively as it applies to a single attorney but subject to the modifications specified in paragraph 21.

(3) This Schedule, in its application to joint and several attorneys, applies with the modifications specified in sub-paragraphs (4) to (7) and in paragraph 22.

(4) A failure, as respects any one attorney, to comply with the requirements for the creation of enduring powers—

(a) prevents the instrument from creating such a power in his case, but

(b) does not affect its efficacy for that purpose as respects the other or others or its efficacy in his case for the purpose of creating a power of attorney which is not an enduring power.

(5) If one or more but not both or all the attorneys makes or joins in making an application for registration of the instrument—

(a) an attorney who is not an applicant as well as one who is may act pending the registration of the instrument as provided in paragraph 1(2),

(b) notice of the application must also be given under Part 3 of this Schedule to the other attorney or attorneys, and

(c) objection may validly be taken to the registration on a ground relating to an attorney or to the power of an attorney who is not an applicant as well as to one or the power of one who is an applicant.

(6) The Public Guardian is not precluded by paragraph 13(5) or (8) from registering an instrument and the court must not direct him not to do so under paragraph 13(10) if an enduring power subsists as respects some attorney who is not affected by the ground or grounds of the objection in question; and where the Public Guardian registers an instrument in that case, he must make against the registration an entry in the prescribed form.

(7) Sub-paragraph (6) does not preclude the court from revoking a power in so far as it confers a power on any other attorney in respect of whom the ground in paragraph 13(9)(d) or (e) is established; and where any ground in paragraph 13(9) affecting any other attorney is established the court must direct the Public Guardian to make against the registration an entry in the prescribed form.

(8) In sub-paragraph (4), 'the requirements for the creation of enduring powers' means the provisions of—

(a) paragraph 2 other than sub-paragraphs (8) and (9), and

(b) the regulations mentioned in paragraph 2.

Joint attorneys

21 (1) In paragraph 2(5), the reference to the time when the attorney executes the instrument is to be read as a reference to the time when the second or last attorney executes the instrument.

(2) In paragraph 2(6) to (8), the reference to the attorney is to be read as a reference to any attorney under the power.

(3) Paragraph 13 has effect as if the ground of objection to the registration of the instrument specified in sub-paragraph (9)(e) applied to any attorney under the power.

(4) In paragraph 16(2), references to the attorney are to be read as including references to any attorney under the power.

(5) In paragraph 16(4), references to the attorney are to be read as including references to any attorney under the power.

(6) In paragraph 17, references to the attorney are to be read as including references to any attorney under the power.

Joint and several attorneys

22 (1) In paragraph 2(7), the reference to the bankruptcy of the attorney is to be read as a reference to the bankruptcy of the last remaining attorney under the power; and the bankruptcy of any other attorney under the power causes that person to cease to be an attorney under the power.

(2) In paragraph 2(8), the reference to the suspension of the power is to be read as a reference to its suspension in so far as it relates to the attorney in respect of whom the interim bankruptcy restrictions order has effect.

(3) The restriction upon disclaimer imposed by paragraph 4(6) applies only to those attorneys who have reason to believe that the donor is or is becoming mentally incapable.

PART 8
INTERPRETATION

23 (1) In this Schedule—

'enduring power' is to be construed in accordance with paragraph 2,

'mentally incapable' or 'mental incapacity', except where it refers to revocation at common law, means in relation to any person, that he is incapable by reason of mental disorder *(within the meaning of the Mental Health Act)* of managing and administering his property and affairs and 'mentally capable' and 'mental capacity' are to be construed accordingly,

'notice' means notice in writing, and

'prescribed', except for the purposes of paragraph 2, means prescribed by regulations made for the purposes of this Schedule by the Lord Chancellor.

[(1A) In sub-paragraph (1), 'mental disorder' has the same meaning as in the Mental Health Act but disregarding the amendments made to that Act by the Mental Health Act 2007.]

(2) Any question arising under or for the purposes of this Schedule as to what the donor of the power might at any time be expected to do is to be determined by assuming that he had full mental capacity at the time but otherwise by reference to the circumstances existing at that time.

[Words omitted from sub-paragraph (1) and new sub-paragraph (1A) inserted by paragraphs 23(2) and (3) respectively of Schedule 1 to the 2007 Act.]

SCHEDULE 5
TRANSITIONAL PROVISIONS AND SAVINGS

Section 66(4)

PART 1
REPEAL OF PART 7 OF THE MENTAL HEALTH ACT 1983

Existing receivers

1 (1) This paragraph applies where, immediately before the commencement day, there is a receiver ('R') for a person ('P') appointed under section 99 of the Mental Health Act.

(2) On and after that day—

 (a) this Act applies as if R were a deputy appointed for P by the court, but with the functions that R had as receiver immediately before that day, and

 (b) a reference in any other enactment to a deputy appointed by the court includes a person appointed as a deputy as a result of paragraph (a).

(3) On any application to it by R, the court may end R's appointment as P's deputy.

(4) Where, as a result of section 20(1), R may not make a decision on behalf of P in relation to a relevant matter, R must apply to the court.

(5) If, on the application, the court is satisfied that P is capable of managing his property and affairs in relation to the relevant matter—

 (a) it must make an order ending R's appointment as P's deputy in relation to that matter, but

 (b) it may, in relation to any other matter, exercise in relation to P any of the powers which it has under sections 15 to 19.

(6) If it is not satisfied, the court may exercise in relation to P any of the powers which it has under sections 15 to 19.

(7) R's appointment as P's deputy ceases to have effect if P dies.

(8) 'Relevant matter' means a matter in relation to which, immediately before the commencement day, R was authorised to act as P's receiver.

(9) In sub-paragraph (1), the reference to a receiver appointed under section 99 of the Mental Health Act includes a reference to a person who by virtue of Schedule 5 to that Act was deemed to be a receiver appointed under that section.

Orders, appointments etc.

2 (1) Any order or appointment made, direction or authority given or other thing done which has, or by virtue of Schedule 5 to the Mental Health Act was deemed to have, effect under Part 7 of the Act immediately before the commencement day is to continue to have effect despite the repeal of Part 7.

(2) In so far as any such order, appointment, direction, authority or thing could have been made, given or done under sections 15 to 20 if those sections had then been in force—

   (a) it is to be treated as made, given or done under those sections, and

   (b) the powers of variation and discharge conferred by section 16(7) apply accordingly.

(3) Sub-paragraph (1)—

   (a) does not apply to nominations under section 93(1) or (4) of the Mental Health Act, and

   (b) as respects receivers, has effect subject to paragraph 1.

(4) This Act does not affect the operation of section 109 of the Mental Health Act (effect and proof of orders etc.) in relation to orders made and directions given under Part 7 of that Act.

(5) This paragraph is without prejudice to section 16 of the Interpretation Act 1978 (c. 30) (general savings on repeal).

Pending proceedings

3 (1) Any application for the exercise of a power under Part 7 of the Mental Health Act which is pending immediately before the commencement day is to be treated, in so far as a corresponding power is exercisable under sections 16 to 20, as an application for the exercise of that power.

(2) For the purposes of sub-paragraph (1) an application for the appointment of a receiver is to be treated as an application for the appointment of a deputy.

Appeals

4 (1) Part 7 of the Mental Health Act and the rules made under it are to continue to apply to any appeal brought by virtue of section 105 of that Act which has not been determined before the commencement day.

(2) If in the case of an appeal brought by virtue of section 105(1) (appeal to nominated judge) the judge nominated under section 93 of the Mental Health Act has begun to hear the appeal, he is to continue to do so but otherwise it is to be heard by a puisne judge of the High Court nominated under section 46.

Fees

5 All fees and other payments which, having become due, have not been paid to the former Court of Protection before the commencement day, are to be paid to the new Court of Protection.

Court records

6 (1) The records of the former Court of Protection are to be treated, on and after the commencement day, as records of the new Court of Protection and are to be dealt with accordingly under the Public Records Act 1958 (c. 51).

(2) On and after the commencement day, the Public Guardian is, for the purpose of exercising any of his functions, to be given such access as he may require to such of the records mentioned

in sub-paragraph (1) as relate to the appointment of receivers under section 99 of the Mental Health Act.

Existing charges

7   This Act does not affect the operation in relation to a charge created before the commencement day of—

(a)   so much of section 101(6) of the Mental Health Act as precludes a charge created under section 101(5) from conferring a right of sale or foreclosure during the lifetime of the patient, or

(b)   section 106(6) of the Mental Health Act (charge created by virtue of section 106(5) not to cause interest to fail etc.).

Preservation of interests on disposal of property

8   Paragraph 8(1) of Schedule 2 applies in relation to any disposal of property (within the meaning of that provision) by a person living on 1st November 1960, being a disposal effected under the Lunacy Act 1890 (c. 5) as it applies in relation to the disposal of property effected under sections 16 to 20.

Accounts

9   Court of Protection Rules may provide that, in a case where paragraph 1 applies, R is to have a duty to render accounts—

(a)   while he is receiver;

(b)   after he is discharged.

Interpretation

10   In this Part of this Schedule—

(a)   'the commencement day' means the day on which section 66(1)(a) (repeal of Part 7 of the Mental Health Act) comes into force,

(b)   'the former Court of Protection' means the office abolished by section 45, and

(c)   'the new Court of Protection' means the court established by that section.

PART 2
REPEAL OF THE ENDURING POWERS OF ATTORNEY ACT 1985

Orders, determinations, etc.

11   (1)   Any order or determination made, or other thing done, under the 1985 Act which has effect immediately before the commencement day continues to have effect despite the repeal of that Act.

(2)   In so far as any such order, determination or thing could have been made or done under Schedule 4 if it had then been in force—

(a)   it is to be treated as made or done under that Schedule, and

(b)   the powers of variation and discharge exercisable by the court apply accordingly.

(3) Any instrument registered under the 1985 Act is to be treated as having been registered by the Public Guardian under Schedule 4.

(4) This paragraph is without prejudice to section 16 of the Interpretation Act 1978 (c. 30) (general savings on repeal).

Pending proceedings

12 (1) An application for the exercise of a power under the 1985 Act which is pending immediately before the commencement day is to be treated, in so far as a corresponding power is exercisable under Schedule 4, as an application for the exercise of that power.

(2) For the purposes of sub-paragraph (1)—

   (a) a pending application under section 4(2) of the 1985 Act for the registration of an instrument is to be treated as an application to the Public Guardian under paragraph 4 of Schedule 4 and any notice given in connection with that application under Schedule 1 to the 1985 Act is to be treated as given under Part 3 of Schedule 4,

   (b) a notice of objection to the registration of an instrument is to be treated as a notice of objection under paragraph 13 of Schedule 4, and

   (c) pending proceedings under section 5 of the 1985 Act are to be treated as proceedings on an application for the exercise by the court of a power which would become exercisable in relation to an instrument under paragraph 16(2) of Schedule 4 on its registration.

Appeals

13 (1) The 1985 Act and, so far as relevant, the provisions of Part 7 of the Mental Health Act and the rules made under it as applied by section 10 of the 1985 Act are to continue to have effect in relation to any appeal brought by virtue of section 10(1)(c) of the 1985 Act which has not been determined before the commencement day.

(2) If, in the case of an appeal brought by virtue of section 105(1) of the Mental Health Act as applied by section 10(1)(c) of the 1985 Act (appeal to nominated judge), the judge nominated under section 93 of the Mental Health Act has begun to hear the appeal, he is to continue to do so but otherwise the appeal is to be heard by a puisne judge of the High Court nominated under section 46.

Exercise of powers of donor as trustee

14 (1) Section 2(8) of the 1985 Act (which prevents a power of attorney under section 25 of the Trustee Act 1925 (c. 19) as enacted from being an enduring power) is to continue to apply to any enduring power—

   (a) created before 1st March 2000, and

   (b) having effect immediately before the commencement day.

(2) S ection 3(3) of the 1985 Act (which entitles the donee of an enduring power to exercise the donor's powers as trustee) is to continue to apply to any enduring power to which, as a result of the provision mentioned in subparagraph (3), it applies immediately before the commencement day.

(3) The provision is section 4(3)(a) of the Trustee Delegation Act 1999 (c. 15) (which provides for section 3(3) of the 1985 Act to cease to apply to an enduring power when its registration is cancelled, if it was registered in response to an application made before 1st March 2001).

(4) Even though section 4 of the 1999 Act is repealed by this Act, that section is to continue to apply in relation to an enduring power—
  (a) to which section 3(3) of the 1985 Act applies as a result of subparagraph (2), or
  (b) to which, immediately before the repeal of section 4 of the 1999 Act, section 1 of that Act applies as a result of section 4 of it.
(5) The reference in section 1(9) of the 1999 Act to section 4(6) of that Act is to be read with sub-paragraphs (2) to (4).

Interpretation

15 In this Part of this Schedule, 'the commencement day' means the day on which section 66(1)(b) (repeal of the 1985 Act) comes into force.

SCHEDULE 6
MINOR AND CONSEQUENTIAL AMENDMENTS

Section 67(1)

Fines and Recoveries Act 1833 (c. 74)

1 (1) The Fines and Recoveries Act 1833 (c. 74) is amended as follows.
(2) In section 33 (case where protector of settlement lacks capacity to act), for the words from 'shall be incapable' to 'is incapable as aforesaid' substitute
'lacks capacity (within the meaning of the Mental Capacity Act 2005) to manage his property and affairs, the Court of Protection is to take his place as protector of the settlement while he lacks capacity'.
(3) In sections 48 and 49 (mental health jurisdiction), for each reference to the judge having jurisdiction under Part 7 of the Mental Health Act substitute a reference to the Court of Protection.
2 In section 68 of the Improvement of Land Act 1864 (c. 114) (apportionment of rent charges)—
  (a) for ', curator, or receiver of' substitute 'or curator of, or a deputy with powers in relation to property and affairs appointed by the Court of Protection for,', and
  (b) for 'or patient within the meaning of Part VII of the Mental Health Act 1983' substitute 'person who lacks capacity (within the meaning of the Mental Capacity Act 2005) to receive the notice'.

Trustee Act 1925 (c. 19)

3 (1) The Trustee Act 1925 (c. 19) is amended as follows.
(2) In section 36 (appointment of new trustee)—
  (a) in subsection (6C), for the words from 'a power of attorney' to the end, substitute 'an enduring power of attorney or lasting power of attorney registered under the Mental Capacity Act 2005', and
  (b) in subsection (9)—
    (i) for the words from 'is incapable' to 'exercising' substitute 'lacks capacity to exercise', and
    (ii) for the words from 'the authority' to the end substitute 'the Court of Protection'.

(3) In section 41(1) (power of court to appoint new trustee) for the words from 'is incapable' to 'exercising' substitute 'lacks capacity to exercise'.

(4) In section 54 (mental health jurisdiction)—

    (a) for subsection (1) substitute—

'(1) Subject to subsection (2), the Court of Protection may not make an order, or give a direction or authority, in relation to a person who lacks capacity to exercise his functions as trustee, if the High Court may make an order to that effect under this Act.',

    (b) in subsection (2)—

        (i) for the words from the beginning to 'of a receiver' substitute 'Where a person lacks capacity to exercise his functions as a trustee and a deputy is appointed for him by the Court of Protection or an application for the appointment of a deputy',

        (ii) for 'the said authority', in each place, substitute 'the Court of Protection', and

        (iii) f or 'the patient', in each place, substitute 'the person concerned', and

    (c) omit subsection (3).

(5) In section 55 (order made on particular allegation to be conclusive evidence of it)—

    (a) for the words from 'Part VII' to 'Northern Ireland' substitute

'sections 15 to 20 of the Mental Capacity Act 2005 or any corresponding provisions having effect in Northern Ireland', and

    (b) for paragraph (a) substitute—

'(a) that a trustee or mortgagee lacks capacity in relation to the matter in question;'.

(6) In section 68 (definitions), at the end add—

'(3) Any reference in this Act to a person who lacks capacity in relation to a matter is to a person—

    (a) who lacks capacity within the meaning of the Mental Capacity Act 2005 in relation to that matter, or

    (b) in respect of whom the powers conferred by section 48 of that Act are exercisable and have been exercised in relation to that matter.'.

Law of Property Act 1925 (c. 20)

4 (1) The Law of Property Act 1925 (c. 20) is amended as follows.

(2) In section 22 (conveyances on behalf of persons who lack capacity)—

    (a) in subsection (1)—

        (i) for the words from 'in a person suffering' to 'is acting' substitute ', either solely or jointly with any other person or persons, in a person lacking capacity (within the meaning of the Mental Capacity Act 2005) to convey or create a legal estate, a deputy appointed for him by the Court of Protection or (if no deputy is appointed', and

        (ii) for 'the authority having jurisdiction under Part VII of the Mental Health Act 1983' substitute 'the Court of Protection',

    (b) in subsection (2), for 'is incapable, by reason of mental disorder, of exercising' substitute 'lacks capacity (within the meaning of that Act) to exercise', and

    (c) in subsection (3), for the words from 'an enduring power' to the end substitute 'an enduring power of attorney or lasting power of attorney (within the meaning of the 2005 Act) is entitled to act for the trustee who lacks capacity in relation to the dealing.'.

(3) In section 205(1) (interpretation), omit paragraph (xiii).

Administration of Estates Act 1925 (c. 23)

5 (1) The Administration of Estates Act 1925 (c. 23) is amended as follows.

(2) In section 41(1) (powers of personal representatives to appropriate), in the proviso—
  (a) in paragraph (ii)—
      (i) for the words from 'is incapable' to 'the consent' substitute 'lacks capacity (within the meaning of the Mental Capacity Act 2005) to give the consent, it', and
      (ii) for 'or receiver' substitute 'or a person appointed as deputy for him by the Court of Protection', and
  (b) in paragraph (iv), for 'no receiver is acting for a person suffering from mental disorder' substitute 'no deputy is appointed for a person who lacks capacity to consent'.

(3) Omit section 55(1)(viii) (definitions of 'person of unsound mind' and 'defective').

National Assistance Act 1948 (c. 29)

6 In section 49 of the National Assistance Act 1948 (c. 29) (expenses of council officers acting for persons who lack capacity)—
  (a) for the words from 'applies' to 'affairs of a patient' substitute 'applies for appointment by the Court of Protection as a deputy', and
  (b) for 'such functions' substitute 'his functions as deputy'.

U.S.A. Veterans' Pensions (Administration) Act 1949 (c. 45)

7 In section 1 of the U.S.A. Veterans' Pensions (Administration) Act 1949 (c. 45) (administration of pensions)—
  (a) in subsection (4), omit the words from 'or for whom' to '1983', and
  (b) after subsection (4), insert—
  '(4A) An agreement under subsection (1) is not to be made in relation to a person who lacks capacity (within the meaning of the Mental Capacity Act 2005) for the purposes of this Act if—
  (a) there is a donee of an enduring power of attorney or lasting power of attorney (within the meaning of the 2005 Act), or a deputy appointed for the person by the Court of Protection, and
  (b) the donee or deputy has power in relation to the person for the purposes of this Act.
  (4B) The proviso at the end of subsection (4) also applies in relation to subsection (4A).'.

Intestates' Estates Act 1952 (c. 64)

8 In Schedule 2 to the Intestates' Estates Act 1952 (c. 64) (rights of surviving spouse or civil partner in relation to home), for paragraph 6(1) substitute—
  '(1) Where the surviving spouse or civil partner lacks capacity (within the meaning of the Mental Capacity Act 2005) to make a requirement or give a consent under this Schedule, the requirement or consent may be made or given by a deputy appointed by the Court of Protection with power in that respect or, if no deputy has that power, by that court.'.

Variation of Trusts Act 1958 (c. 53)

9 In section 1 of the Variation of Trusts Act 1958 (c. 53) (jurisdiction of courts to vary trusts)—

(a) in subsection (3), for the words from 'shall be determined' to the end substitute 'who lacks capacity (within the meaning of the Mental Capacity Act 2005) to give his assent is to be determined by the Court of Protection', and

(b) in subsection (6), for the words from 'the powers' to the end substitute 'the powers of the Court of Protection'.

Administration of Justice Act 1960 (c. 65)

10 In section 12(1)(b) of the Administration of Justice Act 1960 (c. 65) (contempt of court to publish information about proceedings in private relating to persons with incapacity) for the words from 'under Part VIII' to
'that Act' substitute 'under the Mental Capacity Act 2005, or under any provision of the Mental Health Act 1983'.

Industrial and Provident Societies Act 1965 (c. 12)

11 In section 26 of the Industrial and Provident Societies Act 1965 (c. 12) (payments for mentally incapable people), for subsection (2) substitute—
'(2) Subsection (1) does not apply where the member or person concerned lacks capacity (within the meaning of the Mental Capacity Act 2005) for the purposes of this Act and—
(a) there is a donee of an enduring power of attorney or lasting power of attorney (within the meaning of the 2005 Act), or a deputy appointed for the member or person by the Court of Protection, and
(b) the donee or deputy has power in relation to the member or person for the purposes of this Act.'.

Compulsory Purchase Act 1965 (c. 56)

12 In Schedule 1 to the Compulsory Purchase Act 1965 (c. 56) (persons without power to sell their interests), for paragraph 1(2)(b) substitute—
'(b) do not have effect in relation to a person who lacks capacity (within the meaning of the Mental Capacity Act 2005) for the purposes of this Act if—
(i) there is a donee of an enduring power of attorney or lasting power of attorney (within the meaning of the 2005 Act), or a deputy appointed for the person by the Court of Protection, and
(ii) the donee or deputy has power in relation to the person for the purposes of this Act.'

Leasehold Reform Act 1967 (c. 88)

13 (1) For section 26(2) of the Leasehold Reform Act 1967 (c. 88) (landlord lacking capacity) substitute—
'(2) Where a landlord lacks capacity (within the meaning of the Mental Capacity Act 2005) to exercise his functions as a landlord, those functions are to be exercised—

(a) by a donee of an enduring power of attorney or lasting power of attorney (within the meaning of the 2005 Act), or a deputy appointed for him by the Court of Protection, with power to exercise those functions, or

(b) if no donee or deputy has that power, by a person authorised in that respect by that court.'.

(2) That amendment does not affect any proceedings pending at the commencement of this paragraph in which a receiver or a person authorised under Part 7 of the Mental Health Act is acting on behalf of the landlord.

Medicines Act 1968 (c. 67)

14 In section 72 of the Medicines Act 1968 (c. 67) (pharmacist lacking capacity)—

(a) in subsection (1)(c), for the words from 'a receiver' to '1959' substitute 'he becomes a person who lacks capacity (within the meaning of the Mental Capacity Act 2005) to carry on the business',

(b) after subsection (1) insert—

'(1A) In subsection (1)(c), the reference to a person who lacks capacity to carry on the business is to a person—

(a) in respect of whom there is a donee of an enduring power of attorney or lasting power of attorney (within the meaning of the Mental Capacity Act 2005), or

(b) for whom a deputy is appointed by the Court of Protection, and in relation to whom the donee or deputy has power for the purposes of this Act.',

(c) In subsection (3)(d)—

(i) for 'receiver' substitute 'deputy', and

(ii) after 'guardian' insert 'or from the date of registration of the instrument appointing the donee', and

(d) in subsection (4)(c), for 'receiver' substitute 'donee, deputy'.

Family Law Reform Act 1969 (c. 46)

15 For section 21(4) of the Family Law Reform Act 1969 (c. 46) (consent required for taking of bodily sample from person lacking capacity), substitute—

'(4) A bodily sample may be taken from a person who lacks capacity (within the meaning of the Mental Capacity Act 2005) to give his consent, if consent is given by the court giving the direction under section 20 or by—

(a) a donee of an enduring power of attorney or lasting power of attorney (within the meaning of that Act), or

(b) a deputy appointed, or any other person authorised, by the Court of Protection, with power in that respect.'.

Local Authority Social Services Act 1970 (c. 42)

16 (1) Schedule 1 to the Local Authority Social Services Act 1970 (c. 42) (enactments conferring functions assigned to social services committee) is amended as follows.

(2) In the entry for section 49 of the National Assistance Act 1948 (expenses of local authority officer appointed for person who lacks capacity) for 'receiver' substitute 'deputy'.

(3) At the end, insert—

'Mental Capacity Act 2005

Section 39	Instructing independent mental capacity advocate before providing accommodation for person lacking capacity.
Section 49	Reports in proceedings.'

Courts Act 1971 (c. 23)

17 In Part 1A of Schedule 2 to the Courts Act 1971 (c. 23) (office-holders eligible for appointment as circuit judges), omit the reference to a Master of the Court of Protection.

Local Government Act 1972 (c. 70)

18 (1) Omit section 118 of the Local Government Act 1972 (c. 70) (payment of pension etc. where recipient lacks capacity).

(2) Sub-paragraph (3) applies where, before the commencement of this paragraph, a local authority has, in respect of a person referred to in that section as 'the patient', made payments under that section—

(a) to an institution or person having the care of the patient, or

(b) in accordance with subsection (1)(a) or (b) of that section.

(3) The local authority may, in respect of the patient, continue to make payments under that section to that institution or person, or in accordance with subsection (1)(a) or (b) of that section, despite the repeal made by subparagraph (1).

Matrimonial Causes Act 1973 (c. 18)

19 In section 40 of the Matrimonial Causes Act 1973 (c. 18) (payments to person who lacks capacity) (which becomes subsection (1))—

(a) for the words from 'is incapable' to 'affairs' substitute '('P') lacks capacity (within the meaning of the Mental Capacity Act 2005) in relation to the provisions of the order',

(b) for 'that person under Part VIII of that Act' substitute 'P under that Act',

(c) for the words from 'such persons' to the end substitute 'such person ('D') as it may direct', and

(d) at the end insert—

'(2) In carrying out any functions of his in relation to an order made under subsection (1), D must act in P's best interests (within the meaning of that Act).'.

Juries Act 1974 (c. 23)

20 In Schedule 1 to the Juries Act 1974 (c. 23) (disqualification for jury service), for paragraph 3 substitute—

'3 A person who lacks capacity, within the meaning of the Mental Capacity Act 2005, to serve as a juror.'.

Consumer Credit Act 1974 (c. 39)

21 For section 37(1)(c) of the Consumer Credit Act 1974 (c. 39) (termination of consumer credit licence if holder lacks capacity) substitute—
'(c) becomes a person who lacks capacity (within the meaning of the Mental Capacity Act 2005) to carry on the activities covered by the licence.'.

Solicitors Act 1974 (c. 47)

22 (1) The Solicitors Act 1974 (c. 47) is amended as follows.

(2) For section 12(1)(j) (application for practising certificate by solicitor lacking capacity) substitute—
'(j) while he lacks capacity (within the meaning of the Mental Capacity Act 2005) to act as a solicitor and powers under sections 15 to 20 or section 48 of that Act are exercisable in relation to him;'.

(3) In section 62(4) (contentious business agreements made by clients) for paragraphs (c) and (d) substitute—
'(c) as a deputy for him appointed by the Court of Protection with powers in relation to his property and affairs, or (d) as another person authorised under that Act to act on his behalf.'.

(4) In paragraph 1(1) of Schedule 1 (circumstances in which Law Society may intervene in solicitor's practice), for paragraph (f) substitute—
'(f) a solicitor lacks capacity (within the meaning of the Mental Capacity Act 2005) to act as a solicitor and powers under sections 15 to 20 or section 48 of that Act are exercisable in relation to him;'.

Local Government (Miscellaneous Provisions) Act 1976 (c. 57)

23 In section 31 of the Local Government (Miscellaneous Provisions) Act 1976 (c. 57) (the title to which becomes 'Indemnities for local authority officers appointed as deputies or administrators'), for the words from 'as a receiver' to '1959' substitute 'as a deputy for a person by the Court of Protection'.

Sale of Goods Act 1979 (c. 54)

24 In section 3(2) of the Sale of Goods Act 1979 (c. 54) (capacity to buy and sell) the words 'mental incapacity or' cease to have effect in England and Wales.

Limitation Act 1980 (c. 58)

25 In section 38 of the Limitation Act 1980 (c. 58) (interpretation) substitute—
(a) in subsection (2) for 'of unsound mind' substitute 'lacks capacity (within the meaning of the Mental Capacity Act 2005) to conduct legal proceedings', and (b) omit subsections (3) and (4).

Public Passenger Vehicles Act 1981 (c. 14)

26 In section 57(2)(c) of the Public Passenger Vehicles Act 1981 (c. 14) (termination of public service vehicle licence if holder lacks capacity) for the words from 'becomes a patient' to 'or' substitute 'becomes a person who lacks capacity (within the meaning of the Mental Capacity Act 2005) to use a vehicle under the licence, or'.

Judicial Pensions Act 1981 (c. 20)

27 In Schedule 1 to the Judicial Pensions Act 1981 (c. 20) (pensions of Supreme Court officers, etc.), in paragraph 1, omit the reference to a Master of the Court of Protection except in the case of a person holding that office immediately before the commencement of this paragraph or who had previously retired from that office or died.

Supreme Court Act 1981 (c. 54)

28 In Schedule 2 to the Senior Courts Act 19811 (c. 54) (qualifications for appointment to office in Supreme Court), omit paragraph 11 (Master of the Court of Protection).

Mental Health Act 1983 (c. 20)

29 (1) The Mental Health Act is amended as follows.
(2) In section 134(3) (cases where correspondence of detained patients may not be withheld) for paragraph (b) substitute—
   '(b) any judge or officer of the Court of Protection, any of the Court of Protection Visitors or any person asked by that Court for a report under section 49 of the Mental Capacity Act 2005 concerning the patient;'.
(3) In section 139 (protection for acts done in pursuance of 1983 Act), in subsection (1), omit from 'or in, or in pursuance' to 'Part VII of this Act,'.
(4) Section 142 (payment of pension etc. where recipient lacks capacity) ceases to have effect in England and Wales.
(5) Sub-paragraph (6) applies where, before the commencement of subparagraph (4), an authority has, in respect of a person referred to in that section as 'the patient', made payments under that section—
   (a) to an institution or person having the care of the patient, or
   (b) in accordance with subsection (2)(a) or (b) of that section.
(6) The authority may, in respect of the patient, continue to make payments under that section to that institution or person, or in accordance with subsection (2)(a) or (b) of that section, despite the amendment made by subparagraph (4).
(7) In section 145(1) (interpretation), in the definition of 'patient', omit '(except in Part VII of this Act)'.
(8) In section 146 (provisions having effect in Scotland), omit from '104(4)' to 'section),'.
(9) In section 147 (provisions having effect in Northern Ireland), omit from '104(4)' to 'section),'.

Administration of Justice Act 1985 (c. 61)

30 In section 18(3) of the Administration of Justice Act 1985 (c. 61) (licensed conveyancer who lacks capacity), for the words from 'that person' to the end substitute 'he becomes a person who lacks capacity (within the meaning of the Mental Capacity Act 2005) to practise as a licensed conveyancer.'.

Insolvency Act 1986 (c. 45)

31 (1) The Insolvency Act 1986 (c. 45) is amended as follows.

(2) In section 389A (people not authorised to act as nominee or supervisor in voluntary arrangement), in subsection (3)—
   (a) omit the 'or' immediately after paragraph (b),
   (b) in paragraph (c), omit 'Part VII of the Mental Health Act 1983 or', and
   (c) after that paragraph, insert ', or (d) he lacks capacity (within the meaning of the Mental Capacity Act 2005) to act as nominee or supervisor'.

(3) In section 390 (people not qualified to be insolvency practitioners), in subsection (4)—
   (a) omit the 'or' immediately after paragraph (b),
   (b) in paragraph (c), omit 'Part VII of the Mental Health Act 1983 or', and
   (c) after that paragraph, insert ', or
   (d) he lacks capacity (within the meaning of the Mental Capacity Act 2005) to act as an insolvency practitioner.'.

Building Societies Act 1986 (c. 53)

32 In section 102D(9) of the Building Societies Act 1986 (c. 53) (references to a person holding an account on trust for another)—
   (a) in paragraph (a), for 'Part VII of the Mental Health Act 1983' substitute 'the Mental Capacity Act 2005', and
   (b) for paragraph (b) substitute—
      '(b) to an attorney holding an account for another person under—
      (i) an enduring power of attorney or lasting power of attorney registered under the Mental Capacity Act 2005, or
      (ii) an enduring power registered under the Enduring Powers of Attorney (Northern Ireland) Order 1987;'.

Public Trustee and Administration of Funds Act 1986 (c. 57)

33 In section 3 of the Public Trustee and Administration of Funds Act 1986 (c. 57) (functions of the Public Trustee)—
   (a) for subsections (1) to (5) substitute—
      '(1) The Public Trustee may exercise the functions of a deputy appointed by the Court of Protection.',
   (b) in subsection (6), for 'the 1906 Act' substitute 'the Public Trustee Act 1906', and
   (c) omit subsection (7).

Patronage (Benefices) Measure 1986 (No.3)

34 (1) The Patronage (Benefices) Measure 1986 (No. 3) is amended as follows.

(2) In section 5 (rights of patronage exercisable otherwise than by registered patron), after subsection (3) insert—

'(3A) The reference in subsection (3) to a power of attorney does not include an enduring power of attorney or lasting power of attorney (within the meaning of the Mental Capacity Act 2005).'

(3) In section 9 (information to be sent to designated officer when benefice becomes vacant), after subsection (5) insert—

'(5A) Subsections (5B) and (5C) apply where the functions of a registered patron are, as a result of paragraph 10 of Schedule 2 to the Mental Capacity Act 2005 (patron's loss of capacity to discharge functions), to be discharged by an individual appointed by the Court of Protection.

(5B) If the individual is a clerk in Holy Orders, subsection (5) applies to him as it applies to the registered patron.

(5C) If the individual is not a clerk in Holy Orders, subsection (1) (other than paragraph (b)) applies to him as it applies to the registered patron.'

Courts and Legal Services Act 1990 (c. 41)

35 (1) The Courts and Legal Services Act 1990 (c. 41) is amended as follows.

(2) In Schedule 11 (judges etc. barred from legal practice), for the reference to a Master of the Court of Protection substitute a reference to each of the following—

(a) Senior Judge of the Court of Protection,

(b) President of the Court of Protection,

(c) Vice-President of the Court of Protection.

(3) In paragraph 5(3) of Schedule 14 (exercise of powers of intervention in registered foreign lawyer's practice), for paragraph (f) substitute—

'(f) he lacks capacity (within the meaning of the Mental Capacity Act 2005) to act as a registered foreign lawyer and powers under sections 15 to 20 or section 48 are exercisable in relation to him;'.

Child Support Act 1991 (c. 48)

36 In section 50 of the Child Support Act 1991 (c. 48) (unauthorised disclosure of information)—

(a) in subsection (8)—

(i) immediately after paragraph (a), insert 'or',

(ii) omit paragraphs (b) and (d) and the 'or' immediately after paragraph (c), and

(iii) for ', receiver, custodian or appointee' substitute 'or custodian', and

(b) after that subsection, insert—

'(9) Where the person to whom the information relates lacks capacity (within the meaning of the Mental Capacity Act 2005) to consent to its disclosure, the appropriate person is—

(a) a donee of an enduring power of attorney or lasting power of attorney (within the meaning of that Act), or

(b) a deputy appointed for him, or any other person authorised, by the Court of Protection, with power in that respect.'.

Social Security Administration Act 1992 (c. 5)

37 In section 123 of the Social Security Administration Act 1992 (c. 5) (unauthorised disclosure of information)—

(a) In subsection (10), omit—

(i) in paragraph (b), 'a receiver appointed under section 99 of the Mental Health Act 1983 or',

(ii) in paragraph (d)(i), 'sub-paragraph (a) of rule 41(1) of the Court of Protection Rules 1984 or',

(iii) in paragraph (d)(ii), 'a receiver ad interim appointed under sub-paragraph (b) of the said rule 41(1) or', and

(iv) 'receiver,', and

(b) after that subsection, insert—

'(11) Where the person to whom the information relates lacks capacity (within the meaning of the Mental Capacity Act 2005) to consent to its disclosure, the appropriate person is—

(a) a donee of an enduring power of attorney or lasting power of attorney (within the meaning of that Act), or

(b) a deputy appointed for him, or any other person authorised, by the Court of Protection, with power in that respect.'.

Judicial Pensions and Retirement Act 1993 (c. 8)

38 (1) The Judicial Pensions and Retirement Act 1993 (c. 8) is amended as follows.

(2) In Schedule 1 (qualifying judicial offices), in Part 2, under the cross-heading 'Court officers', omit the reference to a Master of the Court of Protection except in the case of a person holding that office immediately before the commencement of this sub-paragraph or who had previously retired from that office or died.

(3) In Schedule 5 (retirement: the relevant offices), omit the entries relating to the Master and Deputy or temporary Master of the Court of Protection, except in the case of a person holding any of those offices immediately before the commencement of this sub-paragraph.

(4) In Schedule 7 (retirement: transitional provisions), omit paragraph 5(5)(i)(g) except in the case of a person holding office as a deputy or temporary Master of the Court of Protection immediately before the commencement of this sub-paragraph.

Leasehold Reform, Housing and Urban Development Act 1993 (c. 28)

39 (1) For paragraph 4 of Schedule 2 to the Leasehold Reform, Housing and Urban Development Act 1993 (c. 28) (landlord under a disability), substitute—

'4 (1) This paragraph applies where a Chapter I or Chapter II landlord lacks capacity (within the meaning of the Mental Capacity Act 2005) to exercise his functions as a landlord.

(2) For the purposes of the Chapter concerned, the landlord's place is to be taken—

(a) by a donee of an enduring power of attorney or lasting power of attorney (within the meaning of the 2005 Act), or a deputy appointed for him by the Court of Protection, with power to exercise those functions, or

(b) if no deputy or donee has that power, by a person authorised in that respect by that court.'.

(2) That amendment does not affect any proceedings pending at the commencement of this paragraph in which a receiver or a person authorised under Part 7 of the Mental Health Act 1983 (c. 20) is acting on behalf of the landlord.

Goods Vehicles (Licensing of Operators) Act 1995 (c. 23)

40 (1) The Goods Vehicles (Licensing of Operators) Act 1995 (c. 23) is amended as follows.
(2) In section 16(5) (termination of licence), for 'he becomes a patient within the meaning of Part VII of the Mental Health Act 1983' substitute 'he becomes a person who lacks capacity (within the meaning of the Mental Capacity Act 2005) to use a vehicle under the licence'.
(3) In section 48 (licence not to be transferable, etc.)—
   (a) in subsection (2)—
      (i) for 'or become a patient within the meaning of Part VII of the Mental Health Act 1983' substitute ', or become a person who lacks capacity (within the meaning of the Mental Capacity Act 2005) to use a vehicle under the licence,', and
      (ii) in paragraph (a), for 'became a patient' substitute 'became a person who lacked capacity in that respect', and
   (b) in subsection (5), for 'a patient within the meaning of Part VII of the Mental Health Act 1983' substitute 'a person lacking capacity'.

Disability Discrimination Act 1995 (c. 50)

41 In section 20(7) of the Disability Discrimination Act 1995 (c. 50) (regulations to disapply provisions about incapacity), in paragraph (b), for 'Part VII of the Mental Health Act 1983' substitute 'the Mental Capacity Act 2005'.

Trusts of Land and Appointment of Trustees Act 1996 (c. 47)

42 (1) The Trusts of Land and Appointment of Trustees Act 1996 (c. 47) is amended as follows.
(2) In section 9 (delegation by trustees), in subsection (6), for the words from 'an enduring power' to the end substitute 'an enduring power of attorney or lasting power of attorney within the meaning of the Mental Capacity Act 2005'.
(3) In section 20 (the title to which becomes 'Appointment of substitute for trustee who lacks capacity')—
   (a) In subsection (1)(a), for 'is incapable by reason of mental disorder of exercising' substitute 'lacks capacity (within the meaning of the Mental Capacity Act 2005) to exercise', and
   (b) In subsection (2)—
      (i) for paragraph (a) substitute—
      '(a) a deputy appointed for the trustee by the Court of Protection,',
      (ii) in paragraph (b), for the words from 'a power of attorney' to the end substitute 'an enduring power of attorney or lasting power of attorney registered under the Mental Capacity Act 2005', and
      (iii) in paragraph (c), for the words from 'the authority' to the end substitute 'the Court of Protection'.

Human Rights Act 1998 (c. 42)

43 In section 4(5) of the Human Rights Act 1998 (c. 42) (courts which may make declarations of incompatibility), after paragraph (e) insert—
'(f) the Court of Protection, in any matter being dealt with by the President of the Family Division, the Vice-Chancellor or a puisne judge of the High Court.'

Access to Justice Act 1999 (c. 22)

44 In paragraph 1 of Schedule 2 to the Access to Justice Act 1999 (c. 22) (services excluded from the Community Legal Service), after paragraph (e) insert—
'(ea) the creation of lasting powers of attorney under the Mental Capacity Act 2005, (eb) the making of advance decisions under that Act,'.

Adoption and Children Act 2002 (c. 38)

45 In section 52(1)(a) of the Adoption and Children Act 2002 (c. 38) (parental consent to adoption), for 'is incapable of giving consent' substitute 'lacks capacity (within the meaning of the Mental Capacity Act 2005) to give consent'.

Licensing Act 2003 (c. 17)

46 (1) The Licensing Act 2003 (c.17) is amended as follows.
(2) In section 27(1) (lapse of premises licence), for paragraph (b) substitute—
'(b) becomes a person who lacks capacity (within the meaning of the Mental Capacity Act 2005) to hold the licence,'.
(3) In section 47 (interim authority notice in relation to premises licence)—
(a) in subsection (5), for paragraph (b) substitute—
'(b) the former holder lacks capacity (within the meaning of the Mental Capacity Act 2005) to hold the licence and that person acts for him under an enduring power of attorney or lasting power of attorney registered under that Act,',
and (b) in subsection (10), omit the definition of 'mentally incapable'.

Courts Act 2003 (c. 39)

47 (1) The Courts Act 2003 (c. 39) is amended as follows.
(2) In section 1(1) (the courts in relation to which the Lord Chancellor must discharge his general duty), after paragraph (a) insert—
'(aa) the Court of Protection,'.
(3) In section 64(2) (judicial titles which the Lord Chancellor may by order alter)—
(a) omit the reference to a Master of the Court of Protection, and
(b) at the appropriate place insert a reference to each of the following—
(i) Senior Judge of the Court of Protection,
(ii) President of the Court of Protection,
(iii) Vice-president of the Court of Protection.

SCHEDULE 7
REPEALS

Section 67(2)

Short title and chapter	Extent of repeal
Trustee Act 1925 (c. 19)	Section 54(3).
Law of Property Act 1925 (c. 20)	Section 205(1)(xiii).
Administration of Estates Act 1925 (c. 23)	Section 55(1)(viii)
U.S.A. Veterans' Pensions (Administration) Act 1949 (c. 45)	In section 1(4), the words from 'or for whom' to '1983'.
Mental Health Act 1959 (c. 72)	In Schedule 7, in Part 1, the entries relating to— • section 33 of the Fines and Recoveries Act 1833, • section 68 of the Improvement of Land Act 1864, • section 55 of the Trustee Act 1925, • section 205(1) of the Law of Property Act 1925, • section 49 of the National Assistance Act 1948, and • section 1 of the Variation of Trusts Act 1958
Courts Act 1971 (c. 23)	In Schedule 2, in Part 1A, the words 'Master of the Court of Protection'.
Local Government Act 1972 (c. 70)	Section 118.
Limitation Act 1980 (c. 58)	Section 38(3) and (4).
Supreme Courts Act 1981 (c. 54)	In Schedule 2, in Part 2, paragraph 11.
Mental Health Act 1983 (c. 20)	Part 7. In section 139(1) the words from 'or in, or in pursuance' to 'Part VII of this Act,'. In section 145(1), in the definition of 'patient' the words '(except in Part VII of this Act)'. In sections 146 and 147 the words from '104(4)' to 'section),'. Schedule 3. In Schedule 4, paragraphs 1, 2, 4, 5, 7, 9, 14, 20, 22, 25, 32, 38, 55 and 56. In Schedule 5, paragraphs 26, 43, 44 and 45.
Enduring Powers of Attorney Act 1985 (c. 29)	The whole Act
Insolvency Act 1986 (c. 45)	In section 389A(3)— • the 'or' immediately after paragraph (b), and in paragraph (c), the words 'Part VII of the Mental Health Act 1983 or'. In section 390(4)— • the 'or' immediately after paragraph (b), and in paragraph (c), the words 'Part VII of the Mental Health Act 1983 or'.
Public Trustee and Administration of Funds Act 1986 (c. 57)	Section 2. Section 3(7).

Short title and chapter	Extent of repeal
Child Support Act 1991 (c. 48)	In section 50(8)— • paragraphs (b) and (d), and the 'or' immediately after paragraph (c).
Social Security Administration Act 1992 (c. 5)	In section 123(10)— • in paragraph (b), 'a receiver appointed under section 99 of the Mental Health Act 1983 or', • in paragraph (d)(i), 'sub-paragraph (a) of rule 41(1) of the Court of Protection Rules Act 1984 or', • in paragraph (d)(ii), 'a receiver ad interim appointed under sub-paragraph (b) of the said rule 41(1) or', and • 'receiver,'.
Trustee Delegation Act 1999 (c. 15)	Section 4. Section 6. In section 7(3), the words 'in accordance with section 4 above'.
Care Standards Act 2000 (c. 14)	In Schedule 4, paragraph 8.
Licensing Act 2003 (c. 17)	In section 47(10), the definition of 'mentally incapable'.
Courts Act 2003 (c. 64)	In section 64(2), the words 'Master of the Court of Protection'.

Mental Capacity Act 2005 Code of Practice

FOREWORD BY LORD FALCONER

The Mental Capacity Act 2005 is a vitally important piece of legislation, and one that will make a real difference to the lives of people who may lack mental capacity. It will empower people to make decisions for themselves wherever possible, and protect people who lack capacity by providing a flexible framework that places individuals at the very heart of the decision-making process. It will ensure that they participate as much as possible in any decisions made on their behalf, and that these are made in their best interests. It also allows people to plan ahead for a time in the future when they might lack the capacity, for any number of reasons, to make decisions for themselves. The Act covers a wide range of decisions and circumstances, but legislation alone is not the whole story. We have always recognised that the Act needs to be supported by practical guidance, and the Code of Practice is a key part of this. It explains how the Act will operate on a day-to-day basis and offers examples of best practice to carers and practitioners. Many individuals and organisations have read and commented upon earlier drafts of the Code of Practice and I am very grateful to all those who contributed to this process. This Code of Practice is a better document as a result of this input.

A number of people will be under a formal duty to have regard to the Code: professionals and paid carers for example, or people acting as attorneys or as deputies appointed by the Court of Protection. But for many people, the most important relationships will be with the wide range of less formal carers, the close family and friends who know the person best, some of whom will have been caring for them for many years. The Code is also here to provide help and guidance for them. It will be crucial to the Code's success that all those relying upon it have a document that is clear and that they can understand. I have been particularly keen that we do all we can to achieve this.

The Code of Practice will be important in shaping the way the Mental Capacity Act 2005 is put into practice and I strongly encourage you to take the time to read and digest it.

Lord Falconer of Thoroton

INTRODUCTION

The Mental Capacity Act 2005, covering England and Wales, provides a statutory framework for people who lack capacity to make decisions for themselves, or who have capacity and want to make preparations for a time when they may lack capacity in the future. It sets out who can take decisions, in which situations, and how they should go about this. The Act received Royal Assent on 7 April 2005 and will come into force during 2007.

The legal framework provided by the Mental Capacity Act 2005 is supported by this Code of Practice (the Code), which provides guidance and information about how the Act works in practice. Section 42 of the Act requires the Lord Chancellor to produce a Code of Practice for the guidance of a range of people with different duties and functions under the Act. Before the Code is prepared, section 43 requires that the Lord Chancellor must have consulted the National Assembly for Wales and such other persons as he considers appropriate. The Code is also subject to the approval of Parliament and must have been placed before both Houses of Parliament for a 40-day period without either House voting against it. This Code of Practice has been produced in accordance with these requirements.

The Code has statutory force, which means that certain categories of people have a legal duty to have regard to it when working with or caring for adults who may lack capacity to make decisions for themselves. These categories of people are listed below.

How should the Code of Practice be used?

The Code of Practice provides guidance to anyone who is working with and/ or caring for adults who may lack capacity to make particular decisions. It describes their responsibilities when acting or making decisions on behalf of individuals who lack the capacity to act or make these decisions for themselves. In particular, the Code of Practice focuses on those who have a duty of care to someone who lacks the capacity to agree to the care that is being provided.

Who is the Code of Practice for?

The Act does not impose a legal duty on anyone to 'comply' with the Code—it should be viewed as guidance rather than instruction. But if they have not followed relevant guidance contained in the Code then they will be expected to give good reasons why they have departed from it. Certain categories of people are legally required to 'have regard to' relevant guidance in the Code of Practice. That means they must be aware of the Code of Practice when acting or making decisions on behalf of someone who lacks capacity to make a decision for themselves, and they should be able to explain how they have had regard to the Code when acting or making decisions.

The categories of people that are required to have regard to the Code of Practice include anyone who is:
- an attorney under a Lasting Power of Attorney (LPA) (see chapter 7)
- a deputy appointed by the new Court of Protection (see chapter 8)
- acting as an Independent Mental Capacity Advocate (see chapter 10)
- carrying out research approved in accordance with the Act (see chapter 11)
- acting in a professional capacity for, or in relation to, a person who lacks capacity working
- being paid for acts for or in relation to a person who lacks capacity.
- The last two categories cover a wide range of people. People acting in a professional capacity may include:
- a variety of healthcare staff (doctors, dentists, nurses, therapists, radiologists, paramedics etc)
- social care staff (social workers, care managers, etc)
- others who may occasionally be involved in the care of people who lack capacity to make the decision in question, such as ambulance crew, housing workers, or police officers.

People who are being paid for acts for or in relation to a person who lacks capacity may include:
- care assistants in a care home
- care workers providing domiciliary care services, and
- others who have been contracted to provide a service to people who lack capacity to consent to that service.

However, the Act applies more generally to everyone who looks after, or cares for, someone who lacks capacity to make particular decisions for themselves. This includes family carers or other carers. Although these carers are not legally required to have regard to the Code of Practice, the guidance given in the Code will help them to understand the Act and apply it. They should follow the guidance in the Code as far as they are aware of it.

What does 'lacks capacity' mean?

One of the most important terms in the Code is 'a person who lacks capacity'.

Whenever the term 'a person who lacks capacity' is used, it **means a person who lacks capacity to make a particular decision or take a particular action for themselves at the time the decision or action needs to be taken.**

This reflects the fact that people may lack capacity to make some decisions for themselves, but will have capacity to make other decisions. For example, they may have capacity to make small decisions about everyday issues such as what to wear or what to eat, but lack capacity to make more complex decisions about financial matters.

It also reflects the fact that a person who lacks capacity to make a decision for themselves at a certain time may be able to make that decision at a later date. This may be because they have an illness or condition that means their capacity changes. Alternatively, it may be because at the time the decision needs to be made, they are unconscious or barely conscious whether due to an accident or being under anaesthetic or their ability to make a decision may be affected by the influence of alcohol or drugs.

Finally, it reflects the fact that while some people may always lack capacity to make some types of decisions—for example, due to a condition or severe learning disability that has affected them from birth—others may learn new skills that enable them to gain capacity and make decisions for themselves.

Chapter 4 provides a full definition of what is meant by 'lacks capacity'.

What does the Code of Practice actually cover?

The Code explains the Act and its key provisions.
- **Chapter 1** introduces the Mental Capacity Act 2005.
- **Chapter 2** sets out the five statutory principles behind the Act and the way they affect how it is put in practice.
- **Chapter 3** explains how the Act makes sure that people are given the right help and support to make their own decisions.
- **Chapter 4** explains how the Act defines 'a person who lacks capacity to make a decision' and sets out a single clear test for assessing whether a person lacks capacity to make a particular decision at a particular time.
- **Chapter 5** explains what the Act means by acting in the best interests of someone lacking capacity to make a decision for themselves, and describes the checklist set out in the Act for working out what is in someone's best interests.
- **Chapter 6** explains how the Act protects people providing care or treatment for someone who lacks the capacity to consent to the action being taken.
- **Chapter 7** shows how people who wish to plan ahead for the possibility that they might lack the capacity to make particular decisions for themselves in the future are able to grant Lasting Powers of Attorney (LPAs) to named individuals to make certain decisions on their behalf, and how attorneys appointed under an LPA should act.
- **Chapter 8** describes the role of the new Court of Protection, established under the Act, to make a decision or to appoint a decision-maker on someone's behalf in cases where there is no other

way of resolving a matter affecting a person who lacks capacity to make the decision in question.

- **Chapter 9** explains the procedures that must be followed if someone wishes to make an advance decision to refuse medical treatment to come into effect when they lack capacity to refuse the specified treatment.
- **Chapter 10** describes the role of Independent Mental Capacity Advocates appointed under the Act to help and represent particularly vulnerable people who lack capacity to make certain significant decisions. It also sets out when they should be instructed.
- **Chapter 11** provides guidance on how the Act sets out specific safeguards and controls for research involving, or in relation to, people lacking capacity to consent to their participation.
- **Chapter 12** explains those parts of the Act which can apply to children and young people and how these relate to other laws affecting them.
- **Chapter 13** explains how the Act relates to the Mental Health Act 1983.
- **Chapter 14** sets out the role of the Public Guardian, a new public office established by the Act to oversee attorneys and deputies and to act as a single point of contact for referring allegations of abuse in relation to attorneys and deputies to other relevant agencies.
- **Chapter 15** examines the various ways that disputes over decisions made under the Act or otherwise affecting people lacking capacity to make relevant decisions can be resolved.
- **Chapter 16** summarises how the laws about data protection and freedom of information relate to the provisions of the Act.

What is the legal status of the Code?

Where does it apply?

The Act and therefore this Code applies to everyone it concerns who is habitually resident or present in England and Wales. However, it will also be possible for the Court of Protection to consider cases which involve persons who have assets or property outside this jurisdiction, or who live abroad but have assets or property in England or Wales.

What happens if people don't comply with it?

There are no specific sanctions for failure to comply with the Code. But a failure to comply with the Code can be used in evidence before a court or tribunal in any civil or criminal proceedings, if the court or tribunal considers it to be relevant to those proceedings. For example, if a court or tribunal believes that anyone making decisions for someone who lacks capacity has not acted in the best interests of the person they care for, the court can use the person's failure to comply with the Code as evidence. That's why it's important that anyone working with or caring for a person who lacks capacity to make specific decisions should become familiar with the Code.

Where can I find out more?

The Code of Practice is not an exhaustive guide or complete statement of the law. Other materials have been produced by the Department for Constitutional Affairs, the Department of Health and the Office of the Public Guardian to help explain aspects of the Act from different perspectives and for people in different situations. These include guides for family carers and other carers and basic information of interest to the general public. Professional organisations may also produce specialist information and guidance for their members.

The Code also provides information on where to get more detailed guidance from other sources. A list of contact details is provided in Annex A and further information appears in the footnotes to each chapter. References made and any links provided to material or organisations do not form part of the Code and do not attract the same legal status. Signposts to further information are provided for assistance only and references made should not suggest that the Department for Constitutional Affairs endorses such material.

Using the code

References in the Code of Practice

Throughout the Code of Practice, the Mental Capacity Act 2005 is referred to as 'the Act' and any sections quoted refer to this Act unless otherwise stated. References are shown as follows: section 4(1). This refers to the section of the Act. The subsection number is in brackets. Where reference is made to provisions from other legislation, the full title of the relevant Act will be set out, for example 'the Mental Health Act 1983', unless otherwise stated. (For example, in chapter 13, the Mental Health Act 1983 is referred to as MHA and the Mental Capacity Act as MCA.) The Code of Practice is sometimes referred to as the Code.

Scenarios used in the Code of Practice

The Code includes many boxes within the text in which there are scenarios, using imaginary characters and situations. These are intended to help illustrate what is meant in the main text. The scenarios should not in any way be taken as templates for decisions that need to be made in similar situations.

Alternative formats and further information

The Code is also available in Welsh and can be made available in other formats on request.

CONTENTS

3. How should people be helped to make their own decisions?
Quick summary

How can someone be helped to make a decision?

What happens in emergency situations?

What information should be provided to people and how should it be provided?

What steps should be taken to put a person at ease?

What other ways are there to enable decision-making?

4. How does the Act define a person's capacity to make a decision and how should capacity be assessed?
Quick summary

What is mental capacity?

What does the Act mean by 'lack of capacity'?

What safeguards does the Act provide around assessing someone's capacity?

What proof of lack of capacity does the Act require?

What is the test of capacity?

What does the Act mean by 'inability to make a decision'?

What other issues might affect capacity?

When should capacity be assessed?

Who should assess capacity?

What is 'reasonable belief' of lack of capacity?

What other factors might affect an assessment of capacity?

What practical steps should be taken when assessing capacity?

When should professionals be involved?

Are assessment processes confidential?

What if someone refuses to be assessed?

Who should keep a record of assessments?

How can someone challenge a finding of lack of capacity?

5. What does the Act mean when it talks about 'best interests'?
Quick summary

What is the best interests principle and who does it apply to?

What does the Act mean by best interests?

Who can be a decision-maker?

What must be taken into account when trying to work out someone's best interests?

What safeguards does the Act provide around working out someone's best interests?

How does a decision-maker work out what 'all relevant circumstances' are?

How should the person who lacks capacity be involved in working out their best interests?

How do the chances of someone regaining and developing capacity affect working out what is in their best interests?

How should someone's best interests be worked out when making decisions about life-sustaining treatment?

How do a person's wishes and feelings, beliefs and values affect working out what is in their best interests?

Who should be consulted when working out someone's best interests?

How can decision-makers respect confidentiality?

When does the best interests principle apply?

What problems could arise when working out someone's best interests?

6. What protection does the Act offer for people providing care or treatment?
Quick summary
What protection do people have when caring for those who lack capacity to consent?
What type of actions might have protection from liability?
Who is protected from liability by section 5?
What steps should people take to be protected from liability?
What happens in emergency situations?
What happens in cases of negligence?
What is the effect of an advance decision to refuse treatment?
What limits are there on protection from liability?
How does section 5 apply to attorneys and deputies?
Who can pay for goods or services?

7. What does the Act say about Lasting Powers of Attorney?
Quick summary
What is a Lasting Power of Attorney (LPA)?
How does a donor create an LPA?
Who can be an attorney?
How should somebody register and use an LPA?
What guidance should an attorney follow?
What decisions can an LPA attorney make?
Are there any other restrictions on attorneys' powers?
What powers does the Court of Protection have over LPAs?
What responsibilities do attorneys have?
What duties does the Act impose?
What are an attorney's other duties?
How does the Act protect donors from abuse?
What happens to existing EPAs once the Act comes into force?

8. What is the role of the Court of Protection and court-appointed deputies?
Quick summary
What is the Court of Protection?
How can somebody make an application to the Court of Protection?
What powers does the Court of Protection have?
What decisions can the court make?
What are the rules for appointing deputies?
When might a deputy need to be appointed?
Who can be a deputy?
Can the court protect people lacking capacity from financial loss?
Are there any restrictions on a deputy's powers?
What responsibilities do deputies have?
What duties does the Act impose?
What are a deputy's other duties?
Who is responsible for supervising deputies?

9. What does the Act say about advance decisions to refuse treatment?
Quick summary
How can someone make an advance decision to refuse treatment?
Who can make an advance decision to refuse treatment?
What should people include in an advance decision?

What rules apply to advance decisions to refuse life-sustaining treatment?
When should someone review or update an advance decision?
How can someone withdraw an advance decision?
How can someone make changes to an advance decision?
How do advance decisions relate to other rules about decision-making?
How can somebody decide on the existence, validity and applicability of advance decisions?
What should healthcare professionals do if an advance decision is not valid or applicable?
What happens to decisions made before the Act comes into force?
What implications do advance decisions have for healthcare professionals?
When can healthcare professionals be found liable?
What if a healthcare professional has a conscientious objection to stopping or providing life-sustaining treatment?
What happens if there is a disagreement about an advance decision?

10. What is the new Independent Mental Capacity Advocate service and how does it work?
Quick summary
What is the IMCA service?
Who is responsible for delivering the service?
Who can be an IMCA?
What is an IMCA's role?
What happens if the IMCA disagrees with the decision-maker?
What decisions require an IMCA?
When can a local authority or NHS body decide to instruct an IMCA? 196
Who qualifies for an IMCA?

11. How does the Act affect research projects involving a person who lacks capacity?
Quick summary
Why does the Act cover research?
What is 'research'?
What assumptions can a researcher make about capacity?
What research does the Act cover?
How can research get approval?
What responsibilities do researchers have?
What happens if urgent decisions are required during the research project?
What happens for research involving human tissue?
What should happen to research that started before the Act came into force?

12. How does the Act apply to children and young people?
Quick summary
Does the Act apply to children?
Does the Act apply to young people aged 16–17?
Do any parts of the Act not apply to young people aged 16 or 17?
What does the Act say about care or treatment of young people aged 16 or 17?
What powers do the courts have in cases involving young people?

13. What is the relationship between the Mental Capacity Act and the Mental Health Act 1983?
Quick summary
Who does the MHA apply to?
What are the MCA's limits?
When can a person be detained under the MHA?

How does the MCA apply to a patient subject to guardianship under the MHA?

How does the MCA apply to a patient subject to after-care under supervision under the MHA?

How does the Mental Capacity Act affect people covered by the Mental Health Act?

What are the implications for people who need treatment for a mental disorder?

How does the Mental Health Act affect advance decisions to refuse treatment?

Does the MHA affect the duties of attorneys and deputies?

Does the MHA affect when Independent Mental Capacity Advocates must be instructed?

What is the effect of section 57 of the Mental Health Act on the MCA?

What changes does the Government plan to make to the MHA and the MCA?

14. What means of protection exist for people who lack capacity to make decisions for themselves?

Quick summary

What is abuse?

How does the Act protect people from abuse?

How does the Public Guardian oversee LPAs?

How does the Public Guardian supervise deputies?

What happens if someone says they are worried about an attorney or deputy?

How does the Act deal with ill treatment and wilful neglect?

What other measures protect people from abuse?

Who should check that staff are safe to work with vulnerable adults?

Who is responsible for monitoring the standard of care providers?

What is an appointee, and who monitors them?

Are there any other means of protection that people should be aware of?

15. What are the best ways to settle disagreements and disputes about issues covered in the Act?

Quick summary

What options are there for settling disagreements?

When is an advocate useful?

When is mediation useful?

How can someone complain about healthcare?

How can somebody complain about social care?

What if a complaint covers healthcare and social care?

Who can handle complaints about other welfare issues?

What is the best way to handle disagreement about a person's finances?

How can the Court of Protection help?

Will public legal funding be available?

16. What rules govern access to information about a person who lacks capacity?

Quick summary

What laws and regulations affect access to information?

What information do people generally have a right to see?

When can attorneys and deputies ask to see personal information?

When can someone see information about healthcare or social care?

What financial information can carers ask to see?

Is information still confidential after someone shares it?

What is the best way to settle a disagreement about personal information?

Key words and phrases used in the Code

Annex A

1. WHAT IS THE MENTAL CAPACITY ACT 2005?

1.1 The Mental Capacity Act 2005 (the Act) provides the legal framework for acting and making decisions on behalf of individuals who lack the mental capacity to make particular decisions for themselves. Everyone working with and/or caring for an adult who may lack capacity to make specific decisions must comply with this Act when making decisions or acting for that person, when the person lacks the capacity to make a particular decision for themselves. The same rules apply whether the decisions are life-changing events or everyday matters.

1.2 The Act's starting point is to confirm in legislation that it should be assumed that an adult (aged 16 or over) has full legal capacity to make decisions for themselves (the right to autonomy) unless it can be shown that they lack capacity to make a decision for themselves at the time the decision needs to be made. This is known as the presumption of capacity. The Act also states that people must be given all appropriate help and support to enable them to make their own decisions or to maximise their participation in any decision-making process.

1.3 The underlying philosophy of the Act is to ensure that any decision made, or action taken, on behalf of someone who lacks the capacity to make the decision or act for themselves is made in their best interests.

1.4 The Act is intended to assist and support people who may lack capacity and to discourage anyone who is involved in caring for someone who lacks capacity from being overly restrictive or controlling. But the Act also aims to balance an individual's right to make decisions for themselves with their right to be protected from harm if they lack capacity to make decisions to protect themselves.

1.5 The Act sets out a legal framework of how to act and make decisions on behalf of people who lack capacity to make specific decisions for themselves. It sets out some core principles and methods for making decisions and carrying out actions in relation to personal welfare, healthcare and financial matters affecting people who may lack capacity to make specific decisions about these issues for themselves.

1.6 Many of the provisions in the Act are based upon existing common law principles (i.e. principles that have been established through decisions made by courts in individual cases). The Act clarifies and improves upon these principles and builds on current good practice which is based on the principles.

1.7 The Act introduces several new roles, bodies and powers, all of which will support the Act's provisions. These include:
  • Attorneys appointed under Lasting Powers of Attorney (see chapter 7)
  • The new Court of Protection, and court-appointed deputies (see chapter 8)
  • Independent Mental Capacity Advocates (see chapter 10).
The roles, bodies and powers are all explained in more depth in the specific chapters of the Code highlighted above.

What decisions are covered by the Act, and what decisions are excluded?

1.8 The Act covers a wide range of decisions made, or actions taken, on behalf of people who may lack capacity to make specific decisions for themselves. These can be decisions about day-to-day matters—like what to wear, or what to buy when doing the weekly shopping—or decisions about major life-changing events, such as whether the person should move into a care home or undergo a major surgical operation.

1.9 There are certain decisions which can never be made on behalf of a person who lacks capacity to make those specific decisions. This is because they are either so personal to the individual concerned, or governed by other legislation.

Sections 27–29 and 62 of the Act set out the specific decisions which can never be made or 1.10 actions which can never be carried out under the Act, whether by family members, carers, professionals, attorneys or the Court of Protection. These are summarised below.

Decisions concerning family relationships (section 27)

Nothing in the Act permits a decision to be made on someone else's behalf on any of the following matters:
- consenting to marriage or a civil partnership
- consenting to have sexual relations
- consenting to a decree of divorce on the basis of two years' separation
- consenting to the dissolution of a civil partnership
- consenting to a child being placed for adoption or the making of an adoption order
- discharging parental responsibility for a child in matters not relating to the child's property, or
- giving consent under the Human Fertilisation and Embryology Act 1990.

Mental Health Act matters (section 28)

Where a person who lacks capacity to consent is currently detained and being treated under Part 4 of the Mental Health Act 1983, nothing in the Act authorises anyone to:
- give the person treatment for mental disorder, or
- consent to the person being given treatment for mental disorder.

Further guidance is given in chapter 13 of the Code.

Voting rights (section 29)

Nothing in the Act permits a decision on voting, at an election for any public office or at a referendum, to be made on behalf of a person who lacks capacity to vote.

Unlawful killing or assisting suicide (section 62)

For the avoidance of doubt, nothing in the Act is to be taken to affect the law relating to murder, manslaughter or assisting suicide.

Although the Act does not allow anyone to make a decision about these matters on behalf of 1.11 someone who lacks capacity to make such a decision for themselves (for example, consenting to have sexual relations), this does not prevent action being taken to protect a vulnerable person from abuse or exploitation.

How does the Act relate to other legislation?

The Mental Capacity Act 2005 will apply in conjunction with other legislation affecting people 1.12 who may lack capacity in relation to specific matters. This means that healthcare and social care staff acting under the Act should also be aware of their obligations under other legislation, including (but not limited to) the:
- Care Standards Act 2000
- Data Protection Act 1998
- Disability Discrimination Act 1995
- Human Rights Act 1998
- Mental Health Act 1983
- National Health Service and Community Care Act 1990
- Human Tissue Act 2004.

What does the Act say about the Code of Practice?

1.13 Section 42 of the Act sets out the purpose of the Code of Practice, which is to provide guidance for specific people in specific circumstances. Section 43 explains the procedures that had to be followed in preparing the Code and consulting on its contents, and for its consideration by Parliament. Section 42, subsections (4) and (5), set out the categories of people who are placed under a legal duty to 'have regard to' the Code and gives further information about the status of the Code. More details can be found in the Introduction, which explains the legal status of the Code

2. WHAT ARE THE STATUTORY PRINCIPLES AND HOW SHOULD THEY BE APPLIED?

Section 1 of the Act sets out the five 'statutory principles'—the values that underpin the legal requirements in the Act. The Act is intended to be enabling and supportive of people who lack capacity, not restricting or controlling of their lives. It aims to protect people who lack capacity to make particular decisions, but also to maximise their ability to make decisions, or to participate in decision-making, as far as they are able to do so.

The five statutory principles are:

1. A person must be assumed to have capacity unless it is established that they lack capacity.
2. A person is not to be treated as unable to make a decision unless all practicable steps to help him to do so have been taken without success.
3. A person is not to be treated as unable to make a decision merely because he makes an unwise decision.
4. An act done, or decision made, under this Act for or on behalf of a person who lacks capacity must be done, or made, in his best interests.
5. Before the act is done, or the decision is made, regard must be had to whether the purpose for which it is needed can be as effectively achieved in a way that is less restrictive of the person's rights and freedom of action.

This chapter provides guidance on how people should interpret and apply the statutory principles when using the Act. Following the principles and applying them to the Act's framework for decision-making will help to ensure not only that appropriate action is taken in individual cases, but also to point the way to solutions in difficult or uncertain situations.

In this chapter, as throughout the Code, a person's capacity (or lack of capacity) refers specifically to their capacity to make a particular decision at the time it needs to be made.

Quick summary

- Every adult has the right to make their own decisions if they have the capacity to do so. Family carers and healthcare or social care staff must assume that a person has the capacity to make decisions, unless it can be established that the person does not have capacity.
- People should receive support to help them make their own decisions. Before concluding that individuals lack capacity to make a particular decision, it is important to take all possible steps to try to help them reach a decision themselves.
- People have the right to make decisions that others might think are unwise. A person who makes a decision that others think is unwise should not automatically be labelled as lacking the capacity to make a decision.

- Any act done for, or any decision made on behalf of, someone who lacks capacity must be in their best interests.
- Any act done for, or any decision made on behalf of, someone who lacks capacity should be an option that is less restrictive of their basic rights and freedoms – as long as it is still in their best interests.

What is the role of the statutory principles?

The statutory principles aim to: 2.1
- protect people who lack capacity and
- help them take part, as much as possible, in decisions that affect them.

They aim to assist and support people who may lack capacity to make particular decisions, not to restrict or control their lives.

The statutory principles apply to any act done or decision made under the Act. When followed   2.2
and applied to the Act's decision-making framework, they will help people take appropriate action in individual cases. They will also help people find solutions in difficult or uncertain situations.

How should the statutory principles be applied?

Principle 1: *'A person must be assumed to have capacity unless it is established that he lacks capacity.'*
(section1(2))

This principle states that every adult has the right to make their own decisions – unless there is   2.3
proof that they lack the capacity to make a particular decision when it needs to be made. This has been a fundamental principle of the common law for many years and it is now set out in the Act.

It is important to balance people's right to make a decision with their right to safety and   2.4
protection when they can't make decisions to protect themselves. But the starting assumption must always be that an individual has the capacity, until there is proof that they do not. Chapter 4 explains the Act's definition of 'lack of capacity' and the processes involved in assessing capacity.

Scenario: Assessing a person's capacity to make decisions

When planning for her retirement, Mrs Arnold made and registered a Lasting Power of Attorney (LPA)—a legal process that would allow her son to manage her property and financial affairs if she ever lacked capacity to manage them herself. She has now been diagnosed with dementia, and her son is worried that she is becoming confused about money. Her son must assume that his mother has capacity to manage her affairs. Then he must consider each of Mrs Arnold's financial decisions as she makes them, giving her any help and support she needs to make these decisions herself. Mrs Arnold's son goes shopping with her, and he sees she is quite capable of finding goods and making sure she gets the correct change. But when she needs to make decisions about her investments, Mrs Arnold gets confused—even though she has made such decisions in the past. She still doesn't understand after her son explains the different options. Her son concludes that she has capacity to deal with everyday financial matters but not more difficult affairs at this time. Therefore, he is able to use the LPA for the difficult financial decisions his mother can't make. But Mrs Arnold can continue to deal with her other affairs for as long as she has capacity to do so.

Some people may need help to be able to make a decision or to communicate their decision.   2.5
However, this does not necessarily mean that they cannot make that decision—unless there is proof that they do lack capacity to do so. Anyone who believes that a person lacks capacity should be able to prove their case. Chapter 4 explains the standard of proof required.

Principle 2: *'A person is not to be treated as unable to make a decision unless all practicable steps to help him to do so have been taken without success.' (section1(3))*

2.6   It is important to do everything practical (the Act uses the term 'practicable') to help a person make a decision for themselves before concluding that they lack capacity to do so. People with an illness or disability affecting their ability to make a decision should receive support to help them make as many decisions as they can. This principle aims to stop people being automatically labelled as lacking capacity to make particular decisions. Because it encourages individuals to play as big a role as possible in decision-making, it also helps prevent unnecessary interventions in their lives.

2.7   The kind of support people might need to help them make a decision varies. It depends on personal circumstances, the kind of decision that has to be made and the time available to make the decision. It might include:
- using a different form of communication (for example, non-verbal communication)
- providing information in a more accessible form (for example, photographs, drawings, or tapes)
- treating a medical condition which may be affecting the person's capacity or
- having a structured programme to improve a person's capacity to make particular decisions (for example, helping a person with learning disabilities to learn new skills).

Chapter 3 gives more information on ways to help people make decisions for themselves.

Scenario: Taking steps to help people make decisions for themselves

Mr Jackson is brought into hospital following a traffic accident. He is conscious but in shock. He cannot speak and is clearly in distress, making noises and gestures. From his behaviour, hospital staff conclude that Mr Jackson currently lacks the capacity to make decisions about treatment for his injuries, and they give him urgent treatment. They hope that after he has recovered from the shock they can use an advocate to help explain things to him. However, one of the nurses thinks she recognises some of his gestures as sign language, and tries signing to him. Mr Jackson immediately becomes calmer, and the doctors realise that he can communicate in sign language. He can also answer some written questions about his injuries. The hospital brings in a qualified sign-language interpreter and concludes that Mr Jackson has the capacity to make decisions about any further treatment.

2.8   Anyone supporting a person who may lack capacity should not use excessive persuasion or 'undue pressure'.[1] This might include behaving in a manner which is overbearing or dominating, or seeking to influence the person's decision, and could push a person into making a decision they might not otherwise have made. However, it is important to provide appropriate advice and information.

Scenario: Giving appropriate advice and support

Sara, a young woman with severe depression, is getting treatment from mental health services. Her psychiatrist determines that she has capacity to make decisions about treatment, if she gets advice and support. Her mother is trying to persuade Sara to agree to electro-convulsive therapy (ECT), which helped her mother when she had clinical depression in the past. However, a friend has told Sara that ECT is 'barbaric'. The psychiatrist provides factual information about the different types of treatment available and explains their advantages and disadvantages. She also describes how

---

[1] Undue influence in relation to consent to medical treatment was considered in *Re T* (*Adult: Refusal of Treatment*) [1992] 4 All ER 649, 662 and in financial matters in *Royal Bank of Scotland v Etridge* [2001] UKHL 44.

different people experience different reactions or side effects. Sara is then able to consider what treatment is right for her, based on factual information rather than the personal opinions of her mother and friend.

In some situations treatment cannot be delayed while a person gets support to make a decision. This can happen in emergency situations or when an urgent decision is required (for example, immediate medical treatment). In these situations, the only practical and appropriate steps might be to keep a person informed of what is happening and why.

2.9

Principle 3: *'A person is not to be treated as unable to make a decision merely because he makes an unwise decision.' (section 1(4))*

Everybody has their own values, beliefs, preferences and attitudes. A person should not be assumed to lack the capacity to make a decision just because other people think their decision is unwise. This applies even if family members, friends or healthcare or social care staff are unhappy with a decision.

2.10

Scenario: Allowing people to make decisions that others think are unwise

Mr Garvey is a 40-year-old man with a history of mental health problems. He sees a Community Psychiatric Nurse (CPN) regularly. Mr Garvey decides to spend £2,000 of his savings on a camper van to travel around Scotland for six months. His CPN is concerned that it will be difficult to give Mr Garvey continuous support and treatment while travelling, and that his mental health might deteriorate as a result. However, having talked it through with his CPN, it is clear that Mr Garvey is fully aware of these concerns and has the capacity to make this particular decision. He has decided he would like to have a break and thinks this will be good for him. Just because, in the CPN's opinion, continuity of care might be a wiser option, it should not be assumed that Mr Garvey lacks the capacity to make this decision for himself.

There may be cause for concern if somebody:

2.11

* repeatedly makes unwise decisions that put them at significant risk of harm or exploitation or
* makes a particular unwise decision that is obviously irrational or out of character.

These things do not necessarily mean that somebody lacks capacity. But there might be need for further investigation, taking into account the person's past decisions and choices. For example, have they developed a medical condition or disorder that is affecting their capacity to make particular decisions? Are they easily influenced by undue pressure? Or do they need more information to help them understand the consequences of the decision they are making?

Scenario: Decisions that cause concern

Cyril, an elderly man with early signs of dementia, spends nearly £300 on fresh fish from a door-to-door salesman. He has always been fond of fish and has previously bought small amounts in this way. Before his dementia, Cyril was always very careful with his money and would never have spent so much on fish in one go. This decision alone may not automatically mean Cyril now lacks capacity to manage all aspects of his property and affairs. But his daughter makes further enquiries and discovers Cyril has overpaid his cleaner on several occasions—something he has never done in the past. He has also made payments from his savings that he cannot account for. His daughter decides it is time to use the registered Lasting Power of Attorney her father made in the past. This gives her the authority to manage Cyril's property and affairs whenever he lacks the capacity to manage them himself. She takes control of Cyril's chequebook to protect him from possible exploitation, but she can still ensure he has enough money to spend on his everyday needs.

Principle 4: *'An act done, or decision made, under this Act for or on behalf of a person who lacks capacity must be done, or made, in his best interests.' (section 1(5))*

2.12   The principle of acting or making a decision in the best interests of a person who lacks capacity to make the decision in question is a well-established principle in the common law.[2] This principle is now set out in the Act, so that a person's best interests must be the basis for all decisions made and actions carried out on their behalf in situations where they lack capacity to make those particular decisions for themselves. The only exceptions to this are around research (see chapter 11) and advance decisions to refuse treatment (see chapter 9) where other safeguards apply.

2.13   It is impossible to give a single description of what 'best interests' are, because they depend on individual circumstances. However, section 4 of the Act sets out a checklist of steps to follow in order to determine what is in the best interests of a person who lacks capacity to make the decision in question each time someone acts or makes a decision What are on that person's behalf. See chapter 5 for detailed guidance and examples.

Principle 5: *'Before the act is done, or the decision is made, regard must be had to whether the purpose for which it is needed can be as effectively achieved in a way that is less restrictive of the person's rights and freedom of action.' (section 1(6))*

2.14   Before somebody makes a decision or acts on behalf of a person who lacks capacity to make that decision or consent to the act, they must always question if they can do something else that would interfere less with the person's basic rights and freedoms. This is called finding the 'less restrictive alternative'. It includes considering whether there is a need to act or make a decision at all.

2.15   Where there is more than one option, it is important to explore ways that would be less restrictive or allow the most freedom for a person who lacks capacity to make the decision in question. However, the final decision must always allow the original purpose of the decision or act to be achieved.

2.16   Any decision or action must still be in the best interests of the person who lacks capacity. So sometimes it may be necessary to choose an option that is not the least restrictive alternative if that option is in the person's best interests. In practice, the process of choosing a less restrictive option and deciding what is in the person's best interests will be combined. But both principles must be applied each time a decision or action may be taken on behalf of a person who lacks capacity to make the relevant decision.

Scenario: Finding a less restrictive option

Sunil, a young man with severe learning disabilities, also has a very severe and unpredictable form of epilepsy that is associated with drop attacks. These can result in serious injury. A neurologist has advised that, to limit the harm that might come from these attacks, Sunil should either be under constant close observation, or wear a protective helmet. After assessment, it is decided that Sunil lacks capacity to decide on the most appropriate course of action for himself. But through his actions and behaviour, Sunil makes it clear he doesn't like to be too closely observed – even though he likes having company. The staff of the home where he lives consider various options, such as providing a special room for him with soft furnishings, finding ways to keep him under close observation or getting him to wear a helmet. In discussion with Sunil's parents, they agree that the option that is in his best interests, and is less restrictive, will be the helmet—as it will enable him to go out, and prevent further harm.

---

[2] See for example *Re MB (Medical Treatment)* [1997] 2 FLR 426, CA; *Re A (Male Sterilisation)* [2000] 1 FLR 549; *Re S (Sterilisation: Patient's Best Interests)* [2000] 2 FLR 389; *Re F (Adult Patient: Sterilisation)* [2001] Fam 15.

3. HOW SHOULD PEOPLE BE HELPED TO MAKE THEIR OWN DECISIONS?

Before deciding that someone lacks capacity to make a particular decision, it is important to take all practical and appropriate steps to enable them to make that decision themselves (statutory principle 2, see chapter 2). In addition, as section 3(2) of the Act underlines, these steps (such as helping individuals to communicate) must be taken in a way which reflects the person's individual circumstances and meets their particular needs. This chapter provides practical guidance on how to support people to make decisions for themselves, or play as big a role as possible in decision-making.

In this chapter, as throughout the Code, a person's capacity (or lack of capacity) refers specifically to their capacity to make a particular decision at the time it needs to be made.

Quick summary

To help someone make a decision for themselves, check the following points:

Providing relevant information
- Does the person have all the relevant information they need to make a particular decision?
- If they have a choice, have they been given information on all the alternatives?

Communicating in an appropriate way
- Could information be explained or presented in a way that is easier for the person to understand (for example, by using simple language or visual aids)?
- Have different methods of communication been explored if required, including non-verbal communication?
- Could anyone else help with communication (for example, a family member, support worker, interpreter, speech and language therapist or advocate)?

Making the person feel at ease
- Are there particular times of day when the person's understanding is better?
- Are there particular locations where they may feel more at ease?
- Could the decision be put off to see whether the person can make the decision at a later time when circumstances are right for them?

Supporting the person
- Can anyone else help or support the person to make choices or express a view?

How can someone be helped to make a decision?

There are several ways in which people can be helped and supported to enable them to make a decision for themselves. These will vary depending on the decision to be made, the time-scale for making the decision and the individual circumstances of the person making it.   3.1

The Act applies to a wide range of people with different conditions that may affect their capacity to make particular decisions. So, the appropriate steps to take will depend on: 3.2
- a person's individual circumstances (for example, somebody with learning difficulties may need a different approach to somebody with dementia)
- the decision the person has to make and
- the length of time they have to make it.

Significant, one-off decisions (such as moving house) will require different considerations from day-to-day decisions about a person's care and welfare. However, the same general processes should apply to each decision.   3.3

3.4   In most cases, only some of the steps described in this chapter will be relevant or appropriate, and the list included here is not exhaustive. It is up to the people (whether family carers, paid carers, healthcare staff or anyone else) caring for or supporting an individual to consider what is possible and appropriate in individual cases. In all cases it is extremely important to find the most effective way of communicating with the person concerned. Good communication is essential for explaining relevant information in an appropriate way and for ensuring that the steps being taken meet an individual's needs.

3.5   Providing appropriate help with decision-making should form part of care planning processes for people receiving health or social care services. Examples include:
- Person Centred Planning for people with learning disabilities
- the Care Programme Approach for people with mental disorders
- the Single Assessment Process for older people in England, and
- the Unified Assessment Process in Wales.

What happens in emergency situations?

3.6   Clearly, in emergency medical situations (for example, where a person collapses with a heart attack or for some unknown reason and is brought unconscious into a hospital), urgent decisions will have to be made and immediate action taken in the person's best interests. In these situations, it may not be practical or appropriate to delay the treatment while trying to help the person make their own decisions, or to consult with any known attorneys or deputies. However, even in emergency situations, healthcare staff should try to communicate with the person and keep them informed of what is happening.

What information should be provided to people and how should it be provided?

3.7   Providing relevant information is essential in all decision-making. For example, to make a choice about what they want for breakfast, people need to know what food is available. If the decision concerns medical treatment, the doctor must explain the purpose and effect of the course of treatment and the likely consequences of accepting or refusing treatment.

3.8   All practical and appropriate steps must be taken to help people to make a decision for themselves. Information must be tailored to an individual's needs and abilities. It must also be in the easiest and most appropriate form of communication for the person concerned.

What information is relevant?

3.9   The Act cannot state exactly what information will be relevant in each case. Anyone helping someone to make a decision for themselves should therefore follow these steps.
- Take time to explain anything that might help the person make a decision. It is important that they have access to all the information they need to make an informed decision.
- Try not to give more detail than the person needs – this might confuse them. In some cases, a simple, broad explanation will be enough. But it must not miss out important information.
- What are the risks and benefits? Describe any foreseeable consequences of making the decision, and of not making any decision at all.
- Explain the effects the decision might have on the person and those close to them – including the people involved in their care.
- If they have a choice, give them the same information in a balanced way for all the options.

- For some types of decisions, it may be important to give access to advice from elsewhere. This may be independent or specialist advice (for example, from a medical practitioner or a financial or legal adviser). But it might simply be advice from trusted friends or relatives.

Communication—general guidance

3.10 To help someone make a decision for themselves, all possible and appropriate means of communication should be tried.

- Ask people who know the person well about the best form of communication (try speaking to family members, carers, day centre staff or support workers). They may also know somebody the person can communicate with easily, or the time when it is best to communicate with them.
- Use simple language. Where appropriate, use pictures, objects or illustrations to demonstrate ideas.
- Speak at the right volume and speed, with appropriate words and sentence structure. It may be helpful to pause to check understanding or show that a choice is available.
- Break down difficult information into smaller points that are easy to understand. Allow the person time to consider and understand each point before continuing.
- It may be necessary to repeat information or go back over a point several times.
- Is help available from people the person trusts (relatives, friends, GP, social worker, religious or community leaders)? If so, make sure the person's right to confidentiality is respected.
- Be aware of cultural, ethnic or religious factors that shape a person's way of thinking, behaviour or communication. For example, in some cultures it is important to involve the community in decision-making. Some religious beliefs (for example, those of Jehovah's Witnesses or Christian Scientists) may influence the person's approach to medical treatment and information about treatment decisions.
- If necessary, consider using a professional language interpreter. Even if a person communicated in English or Welsh in the past, they may have lost some verbal skills (for example, because of dementia). They may now prefer to communicate in their first language. It is often more appropriate to use a professional interpreter rather than to use family members.
- If using pictures to help communication, make sure they are relevant and the person can understand them easily. For example, a red bus may represent a form of transport to one person but a day trip to another.
- Would an advocate (someone who can support and represent the person) improve communication in the current situation? (See chapters 10 and 15 for more information about advocates.)3

Scenario: Providing relevant information

Mrs Thomas has Alzheimer's disease and lives in a care home. She enjoys taking part in the activities provided at the home. Today there is a choice between going to a flower show, attending her usual pottery class or watching a DVD. Although she has the capacity to choose, having to decide is making her anxious. The care assistant carefully explains the different options. She tells Mrs Thomas about the DVD she could watch, but Mrs Thomas doesn't like the sound of it. The care assistant shows her a leaflet about the flower show. She explains the plans for the day, where the show is being held and how long it will take to get there in the mini-van. She has to repeat this information several times, as Mrs Thomas keeps asking whether they will be back in time for supper. She also tells Mrs Thomas that one of her friends is going on the trip. At first, Mrs Thomas is reluctant to disturb her usual routine. But the care assistant reassures her she will not lose her place at pottery if she misses a class. With this information, Mrs Thomas can therefore choose whether or not to go on the day trip.

Helping people with specific communication or cognitive problems

3.11   Where people have specific communication or cognitive problems, the following steps can help:
  • Find out how the person is used to communicating. Do they use picture boards or Makaton (signs and symbols for people with communication or learning difficulties)? Or do they have a way of communicating that is only known to those close to them?
  • If the person has hearing difficulties, use their preferred method of communication (for example, visual aids, written messages or sign language). Where possible, use a qualified interpreter.
  • Are mechanical devices such as voice synthesisers, keyboards or other computer equipment available to help?
  • If the person does not use verbal communication skills, allow more time to learn how to communicate effectively.
  • For people who use non-verbal methods of communication, their behaviour (in particular, changes in behaviour) can provide indications of their feelings.
  • Some people may prefer to use non-verbal means of communication and can communicate most effectively in written form using computers or other communication technologies. This is particularly true for those with autistic spectrum disorders.
  • For people with specific communication difficulties, consider other types of professional help (for example, a speech and language therapist or an expert in clinical neuropsychology).3

Scenario: Helping people with specific communication difficulties

David is a deafblind man with learning disabilities who has no formal ommunication. He lives in a specialist home. He begins to bang his head against the wall and repeats this behaviour throughout the day. He has not done this before. The staff in the home are worried and discuss ways to reduce the risk of injury. They come up with a range of possible interventions, aimed at engaging him with activities and keeping him away from objects that could injure him. They assess these as less restrictive ways to ensure he is safe. But David lacks the capacity to make a decision about which would the best option. The staff call in a specialist in challenging behaviour, who says that David's behaviour is communicative. After investigating this further, staff discover he is in pain because of tooth decay. They consult a dentist about how to resolve this, and the dentist decides it is in David's best interests to get treatment for the tooth decay. After treatment, David's head-banging stops.

What steps should be taken to put a person at ease?

3.12   To help put someone at ease and so improve their ability to make a decision, careful consideration should be given to both location and timing.

Location

3.13   In terms of location, consider the following:
  • Where possible, choose a location where the person feels most at ease. For example, people are usually more comfortable in their own home than at a doctor's surgery.
  • Would the person find it easier to make their decision in a relevant location? For example, could you help them decide about medical treatment by taking them to hospital to see what is involved?
  • Choose a quiet location where the discussion can't be easily interrupted.
  • Try to eliminate any background noise or distractions (for example, the television or radio, or people talking).
  • Choose a location where the person's privacy and dignity can be properly respected.

Timing

In terms of timing, consider the following:

3.14

- Try to choose the time of day when the person is most alert—some people are better in the mornings, others are more lively in the afternoon or early evening. It may be necessary to try several times before a decision can be made.
- If the person's capacity is likely to improve in the foreseeable future, wait until it has done so—if practical and appropriate. For example, this might be the case after treatment for depression or a psychotic episode. Obviously, this may not be practical and appropriate if the decision is urgent.
- Some medication could affect a person's capacity (for example, medication which causes drowsiness or affects memory). Can the decision be delayed until side effects have subsided?
- Take one decision at a time—be careful to avoid making the person tired or confused.
- Don't rush—allow the person time to think things over or ask for clarification, where that is possible and appropriate.
- Avoid or challenge time limits that are unnecessary if the decision is not urgent. Delaying the decision may enable further steps to be taken to assist people to make the decision for themselves.

Scenario: Getting the location and timing right

Luke, a young man, was seriously injured in a road traffic accident and suffered permanent brain damage. He has been in hospital several months, and has made good progress, but he gets very frustrated at his inability to concentrate or do things for himself. Luke now needs surgical treatment on his leg. During the early morning ward round, the surgeon tries to explain what is involved in the operation. She asks Luke to sign a consent form, but he gets angry and says he doesn't want to talk about it. His key nurse knows that Luke becomes more alert and capable later in the day. After lunch, she asks him if he would like to discuss the operation again. She also knows that he responds better one-to-one than in a group. So she takes Luke into a private room and repeats the information that the surgeon gave him earlier. He understands why the treatment is needed, what is involved and the likely consequences. Therefore, Luke has the capacity to make a decision about the operation.

Support from other people

In some circumstances, individuals will be more comfortable making decisions when someone else is there to support them.

3.15

- Might the person benefit from having another person present? Sometimes having a relative or friend nearby can provide helpful support and reduce anxiety. However, some people might find this intrusive, and it could increase their anxiety or affect their ability to make a free choice. Find ways of getting the person's views on this, for example, by watching their behaviour towards other people.
- Always respect a person's right to confidentiality.

Scenario: Getting help from other people

Jane has a learning disability. She expresses herself using some words, facial expressions and body language. She has lived in her current community home all her life, but now needs to move to a new group home. She finds it difficult to discuss abstract ideas or things she hasn't experienced. Staff conclude that she lacks the capacity to decide for herself which new group home she should move to. The staff involve an advocate to help Jane express her views. Jane's advocate spends time with her in different environments. The advocate uses pictures, symbols and Makaton to find out the things that are important to Jane, and speaks to people who know Jane to find out what they think she likes. She then supports Jane to show their work to her care manager, and checks that the new homes suggested for her are able to meet Jane's needs and preferences. When the care manager has found some suitable places, Jane's advocate visits the homes with Jane. They take photos of the houses to help her distinguish between them. The advocate then uses the photos to help Jane work out which home she prefers. Jane's own feelings can now play an important part in deciding what is in her best interests—and so in the final decision about where she will live.

What other ways are there to enable decision-making?

3.16   There are other ways to help someone make a decision for themselves.
- Many people find it helpful to talk things over with people they trust—or people who have been in a similar situation or faced similar dilemmas. For example, people with learning difficulties may benefit from the help of a designated support worker or being part of a support network.
- If someone is very distressed (for example, following a death of someone close) or where there are long-standing problems that affect someone's ability to understand an issue, it may be possible to delay a decision so that the person can have psychological therapy, if needed.
- Some organisations have produced materials to help people who need support to make decisions and for those who support them. Some of this material is designed to help people with specific conditions, such as Alzheimer's disease or profound learning disability.
- It may be important to provide access to technology. For example, some people who appear not to communicate well verbally can do so very well using computers.

Scenario: Making the most of technology

Ms Patel has an autistic spectrum disorder. Her family and care staff find it difficult to communicate with her. She refuses to make eye contact, and gets very upset and angry when her carers try to encourage her to speak. One member of staff notices that Ms Patel is interested in the computer equipment. He shows her how to use the keyboard, and they are able to have a conversation using the computer. An IT specialist works with her to make sure she can make the most of her computing skills to communicate her feelings and decisions.

4. HOW DOES THE ACT DEFINE A PERSON'S CAPACITY TO MAKE A DECISION AND HOW SHOULD CAPACITY BE ASSESSED?

This chapter explains what the Act means by 'capacity' and 'lack of capacity'. It provides guidance on how to assess whether someone has the capacity to make a decision, and suggests when professionals should be involved in the assessment.

In this chapter, as throughout the Code, a person's capacity (or lack of capacity) refers specifically to their capacity to make a particular decision at the time it needs to be made.

Quick summary

This checklist is a summary of points to consider when assessing a person's capacity to make a specific decision. Readers should also refer to the more detailed guidance in this chapter and chapters 2 and 3.

Presuming someone has capacity
- The starting assumption must always be that a person has the capacity to make a decision, unless it can be established that they lack capacity.

Understanding what is meant by capacity and lack of capacity
- A person's capacity must be assessed specifically in terms of their capacity to make a particular decision at the time it needs to be made.

Treating everyone equally
- A person's capacity must not be judged simply on the basis of their age, appearance, condition or an aspect of their behaviour.

Supporting the person to make the decision for themselves
- It is important to take all possible steps to try to help people make a decision for themselves (see chapter 2, principle 2, and chapter 3).

Assessing capacity
Anyone assessing someone's capacity to make a decision for themselves should use the two-stage test of capacity.
- Does the person have an impairment of the mind or brain, or is there some sort of disturbance affecting the way their mind or brain works? (It doesn't matter whether the impairment or disturbance is temporary or permanent.)
- If so, does that impairment or disturbance mean that the person is unable to make the decision in question at the time it needs to be made?

Assessing ability to make a decision
- Does the person have a general understanding of what decision they need to make and why they need to make it?
- Does the person have a general understanding of the likely consequences of making, or not making, this decision?
- Is the person able to understand, retain, use and weigh up the information relevant to this decision?
- Can the person communicate their decision (by talking, using sign language or any other means)? Would the services of a professional (such as a speech and language therapist) be helpful?

Assessing capacity to make more complex or serious decisions
- Is there a need for a more thorough assessment (perhaps by involving a doctor or other professional expert)?

What is mental capacity?

Mental capacity is the ability to make a decision. 4.1
- This includes the ability to make a decision that affects daily life—such as when to get up, what to wear or whether to go to the doctor when feeling ill—as well as more serious or significant decisions.
- It also refers to a person's ability to make a decision that may have legal consequences—for them or others. Examples include agreeing to have medical treatment, buying goods or making a will.

The starting point must always be to assume that a person has the capacity to make a specific 4.2 decision (see chapter 2, principle 1). Some people may need help to be able to make or communicate a decision (see chapter 3). But this does not necessarily mean that they lack capacity to do so.

What matters is their ability to carry out the processes involved in making the decision—and not the outcome.

What does the Act mean by 'lack of capacity'?

4.3   Section 2(1) of the Act states:

'For the purposes of this Act, a person lacks capacity in relation to a matter if at the material time he is unable to make a decision for himself in relation to the matter because of an impairment of, or a disturbance in the functioning of, the mind or brain.'

This means that a person lacks capacity if:

- they have an impairment or disturbance (for example, a disability, condition or trauma) that affects the way their mind or brain works, and
- the impairment or disturbance means that they are unable to make a specific decision at the time it needs to be made.

4.4   An assessment of a person's capacity must be based on their ability to make a specific decision at the time it needs to be made, and not their ability to make decisions in general. Section 3 of the Act defines what it means to be unable to make a decision (this is explained in paragraph 4.14 below).

4.5   Section 2(2) states that the impairment or disturbance does not have to be permanent. A person can lack capacity to make a decision at the time it needs to be made even if:

- the loss of capacity is partial
- the loss of capacity is temporary
- their capacity changes over time.

A person may also lack capacity to make a decision about one issue but not about others.

4.6   The Act generally applies to people who are aged 16 or older. Chapter 12 explains how the Act affects children and young people—in particular those aged 16 and 17 years.

What safeguards does the Act provide around assessing someone's capacity?

4.7   An assessment that a person lacks capacity to make a decision must never be based simply on:

- their age
- their appearance
- assumptions about their condition, or
- any aspect of their behaviour. (section 2(3))

4.8   The Act deliberately uses the word 'appearance', because it covers all aspects of the way people look. So for example, it includes the physical characteristics of certain conditions (for example, scars, features linked to Down's syndrome or muscle spasms caused by cerebral palsy) as well as aspects of appearance like skin colour, tattoos and body piercings, or the way people dress (including religious dress).

4.9   The word 'condition' is also wide-ranging. It includes physical disabilities, learning difficulties and disabilities, illness related to age, and temporary conditions (for example, drunkenness or unconsciousness). Aspects of behaviour might include extrovert (for example, shouting or gesticulating) and withdrawn behaviour (for example, talking to yourself or avoiding eye contact).

Scenario: Treating everybody equally

Tom, a man with cerebral palsy, has slurred speech. Sometimes he also falls over for no obvious reason. One day Tom falls in the supermarket. Staff call an ambulance, even though he says he is fine. They think he may need treatment after his fall. When the ambulance comes, the ambulance crew know they must not make assumptions about Tom's capacity to decide about treatment, based simply on his condition and the effects of his disability. They talk to him and find that he is capable of making healthcare decisions for himself.

What proof of lack of capacity does the Act require?

Anybody who claims that an individual lacks capacity should be able to provide proof. They need to be able to show, on the balance of probabilities, that the individual lacks capacity to make a particular decision, at the time it needs to be made (section 2(4)). This means being able to show that it is more likely than not that the person lacks capacity to make the decision in question.   4.10

What is the test of capacity?

To help determine if a person lacks capacity to make particular decisions, the Act sets out a two-stage test of capacity.

Stage 1: Does the person have an impairment of, or a disturbance in the functioning of, their mind or brain?

Stage 1 requires proof that the person has an impairment of the mind or brain, or some sort of disturbance that affects the way their mind or brain works. If a person does not have such an impairment or disturbance of the mind or brain, they will not lack capacity under the Act.   4.11

Examples of an impairment or disturbance in the functioning of the mind or brain may include the following: 4.12

* conditions associated with some forms of mental illness
* dementia
* significant learning disabilities
* the long-term effects of brain damage
* physical or medical conditions that cause confusion, drowsiness or loss of consciousness
* delirium
* concussion following a head injury, and
* the symptoms of alcohol or drug use.

Scenario: Assessing whether an impairment or disturbance is affecting someone's ability to make a decision

Mrs Collins is 82 and has had a stroke. This has weakened the left-hand side of her body. She is living in a house that has been the family home for years. Her son wants her to sell her house and live with him. Mrs Collins likes the idea, but her daughter does not. She thinks her mother will lose independence and her condition will get worse. She talks to her mother's consultant to get information that will help stop the sale. But he says that although Mrs Collins is anxious about the physical effects the stroke has had on her body, it has not caused any mental impairment or affected her brain, so she still has capacity to make her own decision about selling her house.

Stage 2: Does the impairment or disturbance mean that the person is unable to make a specific decision when they need to?

For a person to lack capacity to make a decision, the Act says their impairment or disturbance must affect their ability to make the specific decision when they need to. But first people must be given all practical and appropriate support to help them make the decision for themselves (see chapter 2, principle 2). Stage 2 can only apply if all practical and appropriate support to help   4.13

the person make the decision has failed. See chapter 3 for guidance on ways of helping people to make their own decisions.

What does the Act mean by 'inability to make a decision'?

4.14 A person is unable to make a decision if they cannot:
1. understand information about the decision to be made (the Act calls this 'relevant information')
2. retain that information in their mind
3. use or weigh that information as part of the decision-making process, or
4. communicate their decision (by talking, using sign language or any other means). See section 3(1).

4.15 These four points are explained in more detail below. The first three should be applied together. If a person cannot do any of these three things, they will be treated as unable to make the decision. The fourth only applies in situations where people cannot communicate their decision in any way.

Understanding information about the decision to be made

4.16 It is important not to assess someone's understanding before they have been given relevant information about a decision. Every effort must be made to provide information in a way that is most appropriate to help the person to understand. Quick or inadequate explanations are not acceptable unless the situation is urgent (see chapter 3 for some practical steps). Relevant information includes:
- the nature of the decision
- the reason why the decision is needed, and
- the likely effects of deciding one way or another, or making no decision at all.

4.17 Section 3(2) outlines the need to present information in a way that is appropriate to meet the individual's needs and circumstances. It also stresses the importance of explaining information using the most effective form of communication for that person (such as simple language, sign language, visual representations, computer support or any other means).

4.18 For example:
- a person with a learning disability may need somebody to read information to them. They might also need illustrations to help them to understand what is happening. Or they might stop the reader to ask what things mean. It might also be helpful for them to discuss information with an advocate.
- a person with anxiety or depression may find it difficult to reach a decision about treatment in a group meeting with professionals. They may prefer to read the relevant documents in private. This way they can come to a conclusion alone, and ask for help if necessary.
- someone who has a brain injury might need to be given information several times. It will be necessary to check that the person understands the information. If they have difficulty understanding, it might be useful to present information in a different way (for example, different forms of words, pictures or diagrams). Written information, audiotapes, videos and posters can help people remember important facts.

4.19 Relevant information must include what the likely consequences of a decision would be (the possible effects of deciding one way or another)—and also the likely consequences of making no decision at all (section 3(4)). In some cases, it may be enough to give a broad explanation using simple language. But a person might need more detailed information or access to advice, depending on the decision that needs to be made. If a decision could have serious or grave consequences, it is even more important that a person understands the information relevant to that decision.

Scenario: Providing relevant information in an appropriate format

Mr Leslie has learning disabilities and has developed an irregular heartbeat. He has been prescribed medication for this, but is anxious about having regular blood tests to check his medication levels. His doctor gives him a leaflet to explain:

- the reason for the tests
- what a blood test involves
- the risks in having or not having the tests, and
- that he has the right to decide whether or not to have the test.

The leaflet uses simple language and photographs to explain these things. Mr Leslie's carer helps him read the leaflet over the next few days, and checks that he understands it. Mr Leslie goes back to tell the doctor that, even though he is scared of needles, he will agree to the blood tests so that he can get the right medication. He is able to pick out the equipment needed to do the blood test. So the doctor concludes that Mr Leslie can understand, retain and use the relevant information and therefore has the capacity to make the decision to have the test. should capacity be assessed?

Retaining information

The person must be able to hold the information in their mind long enough to use it to make an   4.20
effective decision. But section 3(3) states that people who can only retain information for a short while must not automatically be assumed to lack the capacity to decide – it depends on what is necessary for the decision in question. Items such as notebooks, photographs, posters, videos and voice recorders can help people record and retain information.

Scenario: Assessing a person's ability to retain information

Walter, an elderly man, is diagnosed with dementia and has problems remembering things in the short term. He can't always remember his great-grandchildren's names, but he recognises them when they come to visit. He can also pick them out on photographs. Walter would like to buy premium bonds (a type of financial investment) for each of his great-grandchildren. He asks his solicitor to make the arrangements. After assessing his capacity to make financial decisions, the solicitor is satisfied that Walter has capacity to make this decision, despite his short-term memory problems.

Using or weighing information as part of the decision-making process

For someone to have capacity, they must have the ability to weigh up information and use it to   4.21
arrive at a decision. Sometimes people can understand information but an impairment or disturbance stops them using it. In other cases, the impairment or disturbance leads to a person making a specific decision without understanding or using the information they have been given.[3]

For example, a person with the eating disorder anorexia nervosa may understand information   4.22
about the consequences of not eating. But their compulsion not to eat might be too strong for them to ignore. Some people who have serious brain damage might make impulsive decisions regardless of information they have been given or their understanding of it.

---

[3] This issue has been considered in a number of court cases, including *Re MB* [1997] 2 FLR 426; *R v Collins and Ashworth Hospital Authority ex p Brady* [2001] 58 BMLR 173.

Inability to communicate a decision in any way

4.23 Sometimes there is no way for a person to communicate. This will apply to very few people, but it does include:

- people who are unconscious or in a coma, or
- those with the very rare condition sometimes known as 'locked-in syndrome', who are conscious but cannot speak or move at all.

If a person cannot communicate their decision in any way at all, the Act says they should be treated as if they are unable to make that decision.

4.24 Before deciding that someone falls into this category, it is important to make all practical and appropriate efforts to help them communicate. This might call for the involvement of speech and language therapists, specialists in non-verbal communication or other professionals. Chapter 3 gives advice for communicating with people who have specific disabilities or cognitive problems.

4.25 Communication by simple muscle movements can show that somebody can communicate and may have capacity to make a decision.[4] For example, a person might blink an eye or squeeze a hand to say 'yes' or 'no'. In these cases, assessment must use the first three points listed in paragraph 4.14, which are explained in more depth in paragraphs 4.16–4.22.

What other issues might affect capacity?

People with fluctuating or temporary capacity

4.26 Some people have fluctuating capacity—they have a problem or condition that gets worse occasionally and affects their ability to make decisions. For example, someone who has manic depression may have a temporary manic phase which causes them to lack capacity to make financial decisions, leading them to get into debt even though at other times they are perfectly able to manage their money. A person with a psychotic illness may have delusions that affect their capacity to make decisions at certain times but disappear at others. Temporary factors may also affect someone's ability to make decisions. Examples include acute illness, severe pain, the effect of medication, or distress after a death or shock. More guidance on how to support someone with fluctuating or temporary capacity to make a decision can be found in chapter 3, particularly paragraphs 3.12–3.16. More information about factors that may indicate that a person may regain or develop capacity in the future can be found at paragraph 5.28.

4.27 As in any other situation, an assessment must only examine a person's capacity to make a particular decision when it needs to be made. It may be possible to put off the decision until the person has the capacity to make it (see also guidance on best interests in chapter 5).

Ongoing conditions that may affect capacity

4.28 Generally, capacity assessments should be related to a specific decision. But there may be people with an ongoing condition that affects their ability to make certain decisions or that may affect other decisions in their life. One decision on its own may make sense, but may give cause for concern when considered alongside others.

4.29 Again, it is important to review capacity from time to time, as people can improve their decision-making capabilities. In particular, someone with an ongoing condition may become able to make some, if not all, decisions. Some people (for example, people with learning disabilities) will learn

---

[4] This was demonstrated in the case *Re AK (Adult Patient) (Medical Treatment: Consent)* [2001] 1 FLR 129.

new skills throughout their life, improving their capacity to make certain decisions. So assessments should be reviewed from time to time. Capacity should always be reviewed:

- whenever a care plan is being developed or reviewed
- at other relevant stages of the care planning process, and
- as particular decisions need to be made.

It is important to acknowledge the difference between: 4.30

- unwise decisions, which a person has the right to make (chapter 2, principle 3), and
- decisions based on a lack of understanding of risks or inability to weigh up the information about a decision.

Information about decisions the person has made based on a lack of understanding of risks or inability to weigh up the information can form part of a capacity assessment—particularly if someone repeatedly makes decisions that put them at risk or result in harm to them or someone else.

Scenario: Ongoing conditions

Paul had an accident at work and suffered severe head injuries. He was awarded compensation to pay for care he will need throughout his life as a result of his head injury. An application was made to the Court of Protection to consider how the award of compensation should be managed, including whether to appoint a deputy to manage Paul's financial affairs. Paul objected as he believed he could manage his life and should be able to spend his money however he liked. He wrote a list of what he intended to spend his money on. This included fully-staffed luxury properties and holiday villas, cars with chauffeurs, jewellery and various other items for himself and his family. But spending money on all these luxury items would not leave enough money to cover the costs of his care in future years. The court judged that Paul had capacity to make day-to-day financial decisions, but he did not understand why he had received compensation and what the money was supposed to be used for. Nor did he understand how buying luxuries now could affect his future care. The court therefore decided Paul lacked capacity to manage large amounts of money and appointed a deputy to make ongoing financial decisions relating to his care. But it gave him access to enough funds to cover everyday needs and occasional treats.

What other legal tests of capacity are there?

The Act makes clear that the definition of 'lack of capacity' and the two-stage test for capacity set   4.31
out in the Act are 'for the purposes of this Act'. This means that the definition and test are to be used in situations covered by this Act. Schedule 6 of the Act also amends existing laws to ensure that the definition and test are used in other areas of law not covered directly by this Act.

For example, Schedule 6, paragraph 20 allows a person to be disqualified from jury service if they lack the capacity (using this Act's definition) to carry out a juror's tasks.

There are several tests of capacity that have been produced following judgments in court cases   4.32
(known as common law tests).[5] These cover:

- capacity to make a will[6]
- capacity to make a gift[7]
- capacity to enter into a contract[8]

---

[5] For details, see British Medical Association & Law Society, *Assessment of Mental Capacity: Guidance for Doctors and Lawyers* (Second edition) (London: BMJ Books, 2004).

[6] *Banks v Goodfellow* (1870) LR 5 QB 549.

[7] *Re Beaney (deceased)* [1978] 2 All ER 595.

[8] *Boughton v Knight* (1873) LR 3 PD 64.

- capacity to litigate (take part in legal cases),[9] and
- capacity to enter into marriage.[10]

4.33   The Act's new definition of capacity is in line with the existing common law tests, and the Act does not replace them. When cases come before the court on the above issues, judges can adopt the new definition if they think it is appropriate. The Act will apply to all other cases relating to financial, healthcare or welfare decisions.

When should capacity be assessed?

4.34   Assessing capacity correctly is vitally important to everyone affected by the Act. Someone who is assessed as lacking capacity may be denied their right to make a specific decision—particularly if others think that the decision would not be in their best interests or could cause harm. Also, if a person lacks capacity to make specific decisions, that person might make decisions they do not really understand. Again, this could cause harm or put the person at risk. So it is important to carry out an assessment when a person's capacity is in doubt. It is also important that the person who does an assessment can justify their conclusions. Many organisations will provide specific professional guidance for members of their profession.[11]

4.35   There are a number of reasons why people may question a person's capacity to make a specific decision:

- the person's behaviour or circumstances cause doubt as to whether they have the capacity to make a decision
- somebody else says they are concerned about the person's capacity, or
- the person has previously been diagnosed with an impairment or disturbance that affects the way their mind or brain works (see paragraphs 4.11–4.12 above), and it has already been shown they lack capacity to make other decisions in their life.

4.36   The starting assumption must be that the person has the capacity to make the specific decision. If, however, anyone thinks a person lacks capacity, it is important to then ask the following questions:

- Does the person have all the relevant information they need to make the decision?
- If they are making a decision that involves choosing between alternatives, do they have information on all the different options?
- Would the person have a better understanding if information was explained or presented in another way?
- Are there times of day when the person's understanding is better?
- Are there locations where they may feel more at ease?
- Can the decision be put off until the circumstances are different and the person concerned may be able to make the decision?
- Can anyone else help the person to make choices or express a view (for example, a family member or carer, an advocate or someone to help with communication)?

---

[9] *Masterman-Lister v Brutton & Co and Jewell & Home Counties Dairies* [2003] 3 All ER 162 (CA).

[10] *Sheffield City Council v E & S* [2005] 1 FLR 965.

[11] See for example, British Medical Association & Law Society, *Assessment of Mental Capacity: Guidance for Doctors and Lawyers* (Second edition) (London: BMJ Books, 2004); the Joint Royal Colleges Ambulance Service Liaison Committee Clinical Practice Guidelines (JRCALC, available online at www2.warwick.ac.uk/fac/med/research/hsri/emergencycare/jrcalc_2006/clinical_guidelines_2006.pdf) and British Psychological Society, *Guidelines on assessing capacity* (BPS, 2006 available online at www.bps.org.uk).

Chapter 3 describes ways to deal with these questions and suggest steps which may help people make their own decisions. If all practical and appropriate steps fail, an assessment will then be needed of the person's capacity to make the decision that now needs to be made. 4.37

Who should assess capacity?

The person who assesses an individual's capacity to make a decision will usually be the person who is directly concerned with the individual at the time the decision needs to be made. This means that different people will be involved in assessing someone's capacity to make different decisions at different times. 4.38

For most day-to-day decisions, this will be the person caring for them at the time a decision must be made. For example, a care worker might need to assess if the person can agree to being bathed. Then a district nurse might assess if the person can consent to have a dressing changed.

For acts of care or treatment (see chapter 6), the assessor must have a 'reasonable belief' that the person lacks capacity to agree to the action or decision to be taken (see paragraphs 4.44–4.45 for a description of reasonable belief). 4.39

If a doctor or healthcare professional proposes treatment or an examination, they must assess the person's capacity to consent. In settings such as a hospital, this can involve the multi-disciplinary team (a team of people from different professional backgrounds who share responsibility for a patient). But ultimately, it is up to the professional responsible for the person's treatment to make sure that capacity has been assessed. 4.40

For a legal transaction (for example, making a will), a solicitor or legal practitioner must assess the client's capacity to instruct them. They must assess whether the client has the capacity to satisfy any relevant legal test. In cases of doubt, they should get an opinion from a doctor or other professional expert. 4.41

More complex decisions are likely to need more formal assessments (see paragraph 4.54 below). A professional opinion on the person's capacity might be necessary. This could be, for example, from a psychiatrist, psychologist, a speech and language therapist, occupational therapist or social worker. But the final decision about a person's capacity must be made by the person intending to make the decision or carry out the action on behalf of the person who lacks capacity – not the professional, who is there to advise. 4.42

Any assessor should have the skills and ability to communicate effectively with the person (see chapter 3). If necessary, they should get professional help to communicate with the person. 4.43

Scenario: Getting help with assessing capacity

Ms Dodd suffered brain damage in a road accident and is unable to speak. At first, her family thought she was not able to make decisions. But they soon discovered that she could choose by pointing at things, such as the clothes she wants to wear or the food she prefers. Her behaviour also indicates that she enjoys attending a day centre, but she refuses to go swimming. Her carers have assessed her as having capacity to make these decisions. Ms Dodd needs hospital treatment but she gets distressed when away from home. Her mother feels that Ms Dodd is refusing treatment by her behaviour, but her father thinks she lacks capacity to say no to treatment that could improve her condition. The clinician who is proposing the treatment will have to assess Ms Dodd's capacity to consent. He gets help from a member of staff at the day centre who knows Ms Dodd's communication well and also discusses things with her parents. Over several meetings the clinician explains the treatment options to Ms Dodd with the help of the staff member. The final decision about Ms Dodd's capacity rests with the clinician, but he will need to use information from the staff member and others who know Ms Dodd well to make this assessment.

What is 'reasonable belief' of lack of capacity?

4.44   Carers (whether family carers or other carers) and care workers do not have to be experts in assessing capacity. But to have protection from liability when providing care or treatment (see chapter 6), they must have a 'reasonable belief' that the person they care for lacks capacity to make relevant decisions about their care or treatment (section 5 (1)). To have this reasonable belief, they must have taken 'reasonable' steps to establish that that the person lacks capacity to make a decision or consent to an act at the time the decision or consent is needed. They must also establish that the act or decision is in the person's best interests (see chapter 5).

They do not usually need to follow formal processes, such as involving a professional to make an assessment. However, if somebody challenges their assessment (see paragraph 4.63 below), they must be able to describe the steps they have taken. They must also have objective reasons for believing the person lacks capacity to make the decision in question.

4.45   The steps that are accepted as 'reasonable' will depend on individual circumstances and the urgency of the decision. Professionals, who are qualified in their particular field, are normally expected to undertake a fuller assessment, reflecting their higher degree of knowledge and experience, than family members or other carers who have no formal qualifications. See paragraph 4.36 for a list of points to consider when assessing someone's capacity. The following may also be helpful:

- Start by assuming the person has capacity to make the specific decision. Is there anything to prove otherwise?
- Does the person have a previous diagnosis of disability or mental disorder? Does that condition now affect their capacity to make this decision? If there has been no previous diagnosis, it may be best to get a medical opinion.
- Make every effort to communicate with the person to explain what is happening.
- Make every effort to try to help the person make the decision in question.
- See if there is a way to explain or present information about the decision in a way that makes it easier to understand. If the person has a choice, do they have information about all the options?
- Can the decision be delayed to take time to help the person make the decision, or to give the person time to regain the capacity to make the decision for themselves?
- Does the person understand what decision they need to make and why they need to make it?
- Can they understand information about the decision? Can they retain it, use it and weigh it to make the decision?
- Be aware that the fact that a person agrees with you or assents to what is proposed does not necessarily mean that they have capacity to make the decision.

What other factors might affect an assessment of capacity?

4.46   It is important to assess people when they are in the best state to make the decision, if possible. Whether this is possible will depend on the nature and urgency of the decision to be made. Many of the practical steps suggested in chapter 3 will help to create the best environment for assessing capacity. The assessor must then carry out the two stages of the test of capacity (see paragraphs 4.11–4.25 above).

4.47   In many cases, it may be clear that the person has an impairment or disturbance in the functioning of their mind or brain which could affect their ability to make a decision. For example, there might be a past diagnosis of a disability or mental disorder, or there may be signs that an illness is returning. Old assumptions about an illness or condition should be reviewed. Sometimes an illness develops gradually (for example, dementia), and it is hard to know when it starts to affect capacity. Anyone assessing someone's capacity may need to ask for a medical opinion as to whether a person has an illness or condition that could affect their capacity to make a decision in this specific case.

Scenario: Getting a professional opinion

Mr Elliott is 87 years old and lives alone. He has poor short-term memory, and he often forgets to eat. He also sometimes neglects his personal hygiene. His daughter talks to him about the possibility of moving into residential care. She decides that he understands the reasons for her concerns as well as the risks of continuing to live alone and, having weighed these up, he has the capacity to decide to stay at home and accept the consequences. Two months later, Mr Elliott has a fall and breaks his leg. While being treated in hospital, he becomes confused and depressed. He says he wants to go home, but the staff think that the deterioration in his mental health has affected his capacity to make this decision at this time. They think he cannot understand the consequences or weigh up the risks he faces if he goes home. They refer him to a specialist in old age psychiatry, who assesses whether his mental health is affecting his capacity to make this decision. The staff will then use the specialist's opinion to help their assessment of Mr Elliott's capacity.

Anyone assessing someone's capacity must not assume that a person lacks capacity simply 4.48 because they have a particular diagnosis or condition. There must be proof that the diagnosed illness or condition affects the ability to make a decision when it needs to be made. The person assessing capacity should ask the following questions:
- Does the person have a general understanding of what decision they need to make and why they need to make it?
- Do they understand the likely consequences of making, or not making, this decision?
- Can they understand and process information about the decision? And can they use it to help them make a decision?

In borderline cases, or where there is doubt, the assessor must be able to show that it is more likely than not that the answer to these questions is 'no'.

What practical steps should be taken when assessing capacity?

Anyone assessing someone's capacity will need to decide which of these steps are relevant to their 4.49 situation.
- They should make sure that they understand the nature and effect of the decision to be made themselves. They may need access to relevant documents and background information (for example, details of the person's finances if assessing capacity to manage affairs). See chapter 16 for details on access to information.
- They may need other relevant information to support the assessment (for example, healthcare records or the views of staff involved in the person's care).
- Family members and close friends may be able to provide valuable background information (for example, the person's past behaviour and abilities and the types of decisions they can currently make). But their personal views and wishes about what they would want for the person must not influence the assessment.
- They should again explain to the person all the information relevant to the decision. The explanation must be in the most appropriate and effective form of communication for that person.

- Check the person's understanding after a few minutes. The person should be able to give a rough explanation of the information that was explained. There are different methods for people who use nonverbal means of communication (for example, observing behaviour or their ability to recognise objects or pictures).
- Avoid questions that need only a 'yes' or 'no' answer (for example, did you understand what I just said?). They are not enough to assess the person's capacity to make a decision. But there may be no alternative in cases where there are major communication difficulties. In these cases, check the response by asking questions again in a different way.
- Skills and behaviour do not necessarily reflect the person's capacity to make specific decisions. The fact that someone has good social or language skills, polite behaviour or good manners doesn't necessarily mean they understand the information or are able to weigh it up.
- Repeating these steps can help confirm the result.

4.50 For certain kinds of complex decisions (for example, making a will), there are specific legal tests (see paragraph 4.32 above) in addition to the two-stage test for capacity. In some cases, medical or psychometric tests may also be helpful tools (for example, for assessing cognitive skills) in assessing a person's capacity to make particular decisions, but the relevant legal test of capacity must still be fulfilled.

When should professionals be involved?

4.51 Anyone assessing someone's capacity may need to get a professional opinion when assessing a person's capacity to make complex or major decisions. In some cases this will simply involve contacting the person's general practitioner (GP) or family doctor. If the person has a particular condition or disorder, it may be appropriate to contact a specialist (for example, consultant psychiatrist, psychologist or other professional with experience of caring for patients with that condition). A speech and language therapist might be able to help if there are communication difficulties. In some cases, a multi-disciplinary approach is best. This means combining the skills and expertise of different professionals.

4.52 Professionals should never express an opinion without carrying out a proper examination and assessment of the person's capacity to make the decision. They must apply the appropriate test of capacity. In some cases, they will need to meet the person more than once—particularly if the person has communication difficulties. Professionals can get background information from a person's family and carers. But the personal views of these people about what they want for the person who lacks capacity must not influence the outcome of that assessment.

4.53 Professional involvement might be needed if:
- the decision that needs to be made is complicated or has serious consequences
- an assessor concludes a person lacks capacity, and the person challenges the finding
- family members, carers and/or professionals disagree about a person's capacity
- there is a conflict of interest between the assessor and the person being assessed
- the person being assessed is expressing different views to different people – they may be trying to please everyone or telling people what they think they want to hear
- somebody might challenge the person's capacity to make the decision – either at the time of the decision or later (for example, a family member might challenge a will after a person has died on the basis that the person lacked capacity when they made the will)
- somebody has been accused of abusing a vulnerable adult who may lack capacity to make decisions that protect them
- a person repeatedly makes decisions that put them at risk or could result in suffering or damage.

Scenario: Involving professional opinion

Ms Ledger is a young woman with learning disabilities and some autistic spectrum disorders. Recently she began a sexual relationship with a much older man, who is trying to persuade her to move in with him and come off the pill. There are rumours that he has been violent towards her and has taken her bankbook. Ms Ledger boasts about the relationship to her friends. But she has admitted to her key worker that she is sometimes afraid of the man. Staff at her sheltered accommodation decide to make a referral under the local adult protection procedures. They arrange for a clinical psychologist to assess Ms Ledger's understanding of the relationship and her capacity to consent to it.

In some cases, it may be a legal requirement, or good professional practice, to undertake a 4.54
formal assessment of capacity. These cases include:
- where a person's capacity to sign a legal document (for example, a will), could later be challenged, in which case an expert should be asked for an opinion[12]
- to establish whether a person who might be involved in a legal case needs the assistance of the Official Solicitor or other litigation friend (somebody to represent their views to a court and give instructions to their legal representative) and there is doubt about the person's capacity to instruct a solicitor or take part in the case[13]
- whenever the Court of Protection has to decide if a person lacks capacity in a certain matter
- if the courts are required to make a decision about a person's capacity in other legal proceedings[14]
- if there may be legal consequences of a finding of capacity (for example, deciding on financial compensation following a claim for personal injury).

Are assessment processes confidential?

People involved in assessing capacity will need to share information about a person's circumstances. 4.55
But there are ethical codes and laws that require professionals to keep personal information confidential. As a general rule, professionals must ask their patients or clients if they can reveal information to somebody else – even close relatives. But sometimes information may be disclosed without the consent of the person who the information concerns (for example, to protect the person or prevent harm to other people).[15]

Anyone assessing someone's capacity needs accurate information concerning the person being 4.56
assessed that is relevant to the decision the person has to make. So professionals should, where possible, make relevant information available. They should make every effort to get the person's permission to reveal relevant information. They should give a full explanation of why this is necessary, and they should tell the person about the risks and consequences of revealing, and not revealing information. If the person is unable to give permission, the professional might still be allowed to provide information that will help make an accurate assessment of the person's capacity to make the specific decision. Chapter 16 has more detail on how to access information.

---

[12] *Kenward v Adams*, The Times, 29 November 1975.
[13] Civil Procedure Rules 1998, r 21.1.
[14] *Masterman-Lister v Brutton & Co and Jewell & Home Counties Dairies* [2002] EWCA Civ 1889, CA at 54.
[15] For example, in the circumstances discussed in *W v Egdell and others* [1990] 1 All ER 835 at 848; *S v Plymouth City Council and C* [2002] EWCA Civ 388 at 49.

What if someone refuses to be assessed?

4.57   There may be circumstances in which a person whose capacity is in doubt refuses to undergo an assessment of capacity or refuses to be examined by a doctor or other professional. In these circumstances, it might help to explain to someone refusing an assessment why it is needed and what the consequences of refusal are. But threats or attempts to force the person to agree to an assessment are not acceptable.

4.58   If the person lacks capacity to agree or refuse, the assessment can normally go ahead, as long as the person does not object to the assessment, and it is in their best interests (see chapter 5).

4.59   Nobody can be forced to undergo an assessment of capacity. If someone refuses to open the door to their home, it cannot be forced. If there are serious worries about the person's mental health, it may be possible to get a warrant to force entry and assess the person for treatment in hospital—but the situation must meet the requirements of the Mental Health Act 1983 (section 135). But simply refusing an assessment of capacity is in no way sufficient grounds for an assessment under the Mental Health Act 1983 (see chapter 13).

Who should keep a record of assessments?

4.60   Assessments of capacity to take day-to-day decisions or consent to care require no formal assessment procedures or recorded documentation. Paragraphs 4.44–4.45 above explain the steps to take to reach a 'reasonable belief' that someone lacks capacity to make a particular decision. It is good practice for paid care workers to keep a record of the steps they take when caring for the person concerned.

Professional records

4.61   It is good practice for professionals to carry out a proper assessment of a person's capacity to make particular decisions and to record the findings in the relevant professional records.
- A doctor or healthcare professional proposing treatment should carry out an assessment of the person's capacity to consent (with a multi-disciplinary team, if appropriate) and record it in the patient's clinical notes.
- Solicitors should assess a client's capacity to give instructions or carry out a legal transaction (obtaining a medical or other professional opinion, if necessary) and record it on the client's file.
- An assessment of a person's capacity to consent or agree to the provision of services will be part of the care planning processes for health and social care needs, and should be recorded in the relevant documentation. This includes:
- Person Centred Planning for people with learning disabilities
- the Care Programme Approach for people with mental illness
- the Single Assessment Process for older people in England, and
- the Unified Assessment Process in Wales.

Formal reports or certificates of capacity

4.62   In some cases, a more detailed report or certificate of capacity may be required, for example,
- for use in court or other legal processes
- as required by Regulations, Rules or Orders made under the Act.

How can someone challenge a finding of lack of capacity?

There are likely to be occasions when someone may wish to challenge the results of an assessment of capacity. The first step is to raise the matter with the person who carried out the assessment. If the challenge comes from the individual who is said to lack capacity, they might need support from family, friends or an advocate. Ask the assessor to: **4.63**

- give reasons why they believe the person lacks capacity to make the decision, and
- provide objective evidence to support that belief.

The assessor must show they have applied the principles of the Mental Capacity Act (see chapter 2). Attorneys, deputies and professionals will need to show that they have also followed guidance in this chapter. **4.64**

It might be possible to get a second opinion from an independent professional or another expert in assessing capacity. Chapter 15 has other suggestions for dealing with disagreements. But if a disagreement cannot be resolved, the person who is challenging the assessment may be able to apply to the Court of Protection. The Court of Protection can rule on whether a person has capacity to make the decision covered by the assessment (see chapter 8). **4.65**

5. WHAT DOES THE ACT MEAN WHEN IT TALKS ABOUT 'BEST INTERESTS'?

One of the key principles of the Act is that any act done for, or any decision made on behalf of a person who lacks capacity must be done, or made, in that person's best interests. That is the same whether the person making the decision or acting is a family carer, a paid care worker, an attorney, a court-appointed deputy, or a healthcare professional, and whether the decision is a minor issue—like what to wear—or a major issue, like whether to provide particular healthcare.

As long as these acts or decisions are in the best interests of the person who lacks capacity to make the decision for themselves, or to consent to acts concerned with their care or treatment, then the decision-maker or carer will be protected from liability.

There are exceptions to this, including circumstances where a person has made an advance decision to refuse treatment (see chapter 9) and, in specific circumstances, the involvement of a person who lacks capacity in research (see chapter 11). But otherwise the underpinning principle of the Act is that all acts and decisions should be made in the best interests of the person without capacity.

Working out what is in someone else's best interests may be difficult, and the Act requires people to follow certain steps to help them work out whether a particular act or decision is in a person's best interests. In some cases, there may be disagreement about what someone's best interests really are. As long as the person who acts or makes the decision has followed the steps to establish whether a person has capacity, and done everything they reasonably can to work out what someone's best interests are, the law should protect them.

This chapter explains what the Act means by 'best interests' and what things should be considered when trying to work out what is in someone's best interests. It also highlights some of the difficulties that might come up in working out what the best interests of a person who lacks capacity to make the decision actually are.

In this chapter, as throughout the Code, a person's capacity (or lack of capacity) refers specifically to their capacity to make a particular decision at the time it needs to be made.

Quick summary

A person trying to work out the best interests of a person who lacks capacity to make a particular decision ('lacks capacity') should:

Encourage participation
- do whatever is possible to permit and encourage the person to take part, or to improve their ability to take part, in making the decision

Identify all relevant circumstances
- try to identify all the things that the person who lacks capacity would take into account if they were making the decision or acting for themselves

Find out the person's views
- try to find out the views of the person who lacks capacity, including:
  —the person's past and present wishes and feelings – these may have been expressed verbally, in writing or through behaviour or habits.
  — any beliefs and values (e.g. religious, cultural, moral or political) that would be likely to influence the decision in question.
  — any other factors the person themselves would be likely to consider if they were making the decision or acting for themselves.

Avoid discrimination
- not make assumptions about someone's best interests simply on the basis of the person's age, appearance, condition or behaviour.

Assess whether the person might regain capacity
- consider whether the person is likely to regain capacity (e.g. after receiving medical treatment). If so, can the decision wait until then?

If the decision concerns life-sustaining treatment
- not be motivated in any way by a desire to bring about the person's death. They should not make assumptions about the person's quality of life.

Consult others
- if it is practical and appropriate to do so, consult other people for their views about the person's best interests and to see if they have any information about the person's wishes and feelings, beliefs and values. In particular, try to consult:
  — anyone previously named by the person as someone to be consulted on either the decision in question or on similar issues
  — anyone engaged in caring for the person
  — close relatives, friends or others who take an interest in the person's welfare
  — any attorney appointed under a Lasting Power of Attorney or Enduring Power of Attorney made by the person
  — any deputy appointed by the Court of Protection to make decisions for the person.
- For decisions about major medical treatment or where the person should live and where there is no-one who fits into any of the above categories, an Independent Mental Capacity Advocate (IMCA) must be consulted. (See chapter 10 for more information about IMCAs.)
- When consulting, remember that the person who lacks the capacity to make the decision or act for themselves still has a right to keep their affairs private—so it would not be right to share every piece of information with everyone.

Avoid restricting the person's rights
- see if there are other options that may be less restrictive of the person's rights.

Take all of this into account
- weigh up all of these factors in order to work out what is in the person's best interests.

What is the best interests principle and who does it apply to?

The best interests principle underpins the Mental Capacity Act. It is set out in section 1(5) of the Act. **5.1**

'An act done, or decision made, under this Act for or on behalf of a person who lacks capacity must be done, or made, in his best interests.'

The concept has been developed by the courts in cases relating to people who lack capacity to make specific decisions for themselves, mainly decisions concerned with the provision of medical treatment or social care.

This principle covers all aspects of financial, personal welfare and healthcare decision-making and actions. It applies to anyone making decisions or acting under the provisions of the Act, including: **5.2**
- family carers, other carers and care workers
- healthcare and social care staff
- attorneys appointed under a Lasting Power of Attorney or registered Enduring Power of Attorney
- deputies appointed by the court to make decisions on behalf of someone who lacks capacity, and
- the Court of Protection.

However, as chapter 2 explained, the Act's first key principle is that people must be assumed to have capacity to make a decision or act for themselves unless it is established that they lack it. That means that working out a person's best interests is only relevant when that person has been assessed as lacking, or is reasonably believed to lack, capacity to make the decision in question or give consent to an act being done. **5.3**

People with capacity are able to decide for themselves what they want to do. When they do this, they might choose an option that other people don't think is in their best interests. That is their choice and does not, in itself, mean that they lack capacity to make those decisions.

Exceptions to the best interests principle

There are two circumstances when the best interests principle will not apply. The first is where someone has previously made an advance decision to refuse medical treatment while they had the capacity to do so. Their advance decision should be respected when they lack capacity, even if others think that the decision to refuse treatment is not in their best interests (guidance on advance decisions is given in chapter 9). **5.4**

The second concerns the involvement in research, in certain circumstances, of someone lacking capacity to consent (see chapter 11).

What does the Act mean by best interests?

The term 'best interests' is not actually defined in the Act. This is because so many different types of decisions and actions are covered by the Act, and so many different people and circumstances are affected by it. **5.5**

Section 4 of the Act explains how to work out the best interests of a person who lacks capacity to make a decision at the time it needs to be made. This section sets out a checklist of common **5.6** factors that must always be considered by anyone who needs to decide what is in the best interests of a person who lacks capacity in any particular situation. This checklist is only the starting point: in many cases, extra factors will need to be considered.

5.7   When working out what is in the best interests of the person who lacks capacity to make a decision or act for themselves, decision-makers must take into account all relevant factors that it would be reasonable to consider, not just those that they think are important. They must not act or make a decision based on what they would want to do if they were the person who lacked capacity.

Scenario: Whose best interests?

Pedro, a young man with a severe learning disability, lives in a care home. He has dental problems which cause him a lot of pain, but refuses to open his mouth for his teeth to be cleaned. The staff suggest that it would be a good idea to give Pedro an occasional general anaesthetic so that a dentist can clean his teeth and fill any cavities. His mother is worried about the effects of an anaesthetic, but she hates to see him distressed and suggests instead that he should be given strong painkillers when needed. While the views of Pedro's mother and carers are important in working out what course of action would be in his best interests, the decision must not be based on what would be less stressful for them. Instead, it must focus on Pedro's best interests. Having talked to others, the dentist tries to find ways of involving Pedro in the decision, with the help of his key worker and an advocate, to try to find out the cause and location of the problem and to explain to him that they are trying to stop the pain. The dentist tries to find out if any other forms of dental care would be better, such as a mouthwash or dental gum. The dentist concludes that it would be in Pedro's best interests for:

- a proper investigation to be carried out under anaesthetic so that immediate treatment can be provided
- options for his future dental care to be reviewed by the care team, involving Pedro as far as possible.

Who can be a decision-maker?

5.8   Under the Act, many different people may be required to make decisions or act on behalf of someone who lacks capacity to make decisions for themselves. The person making the decision is referred to throughout this chapter, and in other parts of the Code, as the 'decision-maker', and it is the decision-maker's responsibility to work out what would be in the best interests of the person who lacks capacity.

- For most day-to-day actions or decisions, the decision-maker will be the carer most directly involved with the person at the time.
- Where the decision involves the provision of medical treatment, the doctor or other member of healthcare staff responsible for carrying out the particular treatment or procedure is the decision-maker.
- Where nursing or paid care is provided, the nurse or paid carer will be the decision-maker.
- If a Lasting Power of Attorney (or Enduring Power of Attorney) has been made and registered, or a deputy has been appointed under a court order, the attorney or deputy will be the decision-maker, for decisions within the scope of their authority.

5.9   What this means is that a range of different decision-makers may be involved with a person who lacks capacity to make different decisions.

5.10   In some cases, the same person may make different types of decision for someone who lacks capacity to make decisions for themselves. For instance, a family carer may carry out certain acts in caring for the person on a day-to-day basis, but if they are also an attorney, appointed under a Lasting Power of Attorney (LPA), they may also make specific decisions concerning the person's property and affairs or their personal welfare (depending on what decisions the LPA has been set up to cover).

There are also times when a joint decision might be made by a number of people. For example, when a care plan for a person who lacks capacity to make relevant decisions is being put together, different healthcare or social care staff might be involved in making decisions or recommendations about the person's care package. Sometimes these decisions will be made by a team of healthcare or social care staff as a whole. At other times, the decision will be made by a specific individual within the team. A different member of the team may then implement that decision, based on what the team has worked out to be the person's best interests. **5.11**

No matter who is making the decision, the most important thing is that the decision-maker tries to work out what would be in the best interests of the person who lacks capacity. **5.12**

Scenario: Coming to a joint decision

Jack, a young man with a brain injury, lacks capacity to agree to a rehabilitation programme designed to improve his condition. But the healthcare and social care staff who are looking after him believe that he clearly needs the programme, and have obtained the necessary funding from the Primary Care Trust. However, Jack's family want to take him home from hospital as they believe they can provide better care for him at home. A 'best interests' case conference is held, involving Jack, his parents and other family members and the relevant professionals, in order to decide what course of action would be in the Jack's best interests. A plan is developed to enable Jack to live at home, but attend the day hospital every weekday. Jack seems happy with the proposals and both the family carers and the healthcare and social care staff are satisfied that the plan is in his best interests.

What must be taken into account when trying to work out someone's best interests?

Because every case—and every decision—is different, the law can't set out all the factors that will need to be taken into account in working out someone's best interests. But section 4 of the Act sets out some common factors that must always be considered when trying to work out someone's best interests. These factors are summarised in the checklist here: **5.13**

- Working out what is in someone's best interests cannot be based simply on someone's age, appearance, condition or behaviour. (see paragraphs 5.16–5.17).
- All relevant circumstances should be considered when working out someone's best interests (paragraphs 5.18–5.20).
- Every effort should be made to encourage and enable the person who lacks capacity to take part in making the decision (paragraphs 5.21–5.24).
- If there is a chance that the person will regain the capacity to make a particular decision, then it may be possible to put off the decision until later if it is not urgent (paragraphs 5.25–5.28).
- Special considerations apply to decisions about life-sustaining treatment (paragraphs 5.29–5.36).
- The person's past and present wishes and feelings, beliefs and values should be taken into account (paragraphs 5.37–5.48).
- The views of other people who are close to the person who lacks capacity should be considered, as well as the views of an attorney or deputy (paragraphs 5.49–5.55).

It's important not to take shortcuts in working out best interests, and a proper and objective assessment must be carried out on every occasion. If the decision is urgent, there may not be time to examine all possible factors, but the decision must still be made in the best interests of the person who lacks capacity. Not all the factors in the checklist will be relevant to all types of decisions or actions, and in many cases other factors will have to be considered as well, even though some of them may then not be found to be relevant.

5.14   What is in a person's best interests may well change over time. This means that even where similar actions need to be taken repeatedly in connection with the person's care or treatment, the person's best interests should be regularly reviewed.

5.15   Any staff involved in the care of a person who lacks capacity should make sure a record is kept of the process of working out the best interests of that person for each relevant decision, setting out:

- how the decision about the person's best interests was reached
- what the reasons for reaching the decision were
- who was consulted to help work out best interests, and
- what particular factors were taken into account.
- This record should remain on the person's file.

For major decisions based on the best interests of a person who lacks capacity, it may also be useful for family and other carers to keep a similar kind of record.

What safeguards does the Act provide around working out someone's best interests?

5.16   Section 4(1) states that anyone working out someone's best interests must not make unjustified assumptions about what their best interests might be simply on the basis of the person's age, appearance, condition or any aspect of their behaviour. In this way, the Act ensures that people who lack capacity to make decisions for themselves are not subject to discrimination or treated any less favourably than anyone else.

5.17   'Appearance' is a broad term and refers to all aspects of physical appearance, including skin colour, mode of dress and any visible medical problems, disfiguring scars or other disabilities. A person's 'condition' also covers a range of factors including physical disabilities, learning difficulties or disabilities, age-related illness or temporary conditions (such as drunkenness or unconsciousness). 'Behaviour' refers to behaviour that might seem unusual to others, such as talking too loudly or laughing inappropriately.

Scenario: Following the checklist

Martina, an elderly woman with dementia, is beginning to neglect her appearance and personal hygiene and has several times been found wandering in the street unable to find her way home. Her care workers are concerned that Martina no longer has capacity to make appropriate decisions relating to her daily care. Her daughter is her personal welfare attorney and believes the time has come to act under the Lasting Power of Attorney (LPA). She assumes it would be best for Martina to move into a care home, since the staff would be able to help her wash and dress smartly and prevent her from wandering. However, it cannot be assumed simply on the basis of her age, condition, appearance or behaviour either that Martina lacks capacity to make such a decision or that such a move would be in her best interests. Instead, steps must be taken to assess her capacity. If it is then agreed that Martina lacks the capacity to make this decision, all the relevant factors in the best interests' checklist must be considered to try to work out what her best interests would be. Her daughter must therefore consider:

- Martina's past and present wishes and feelings
- the views of the people involved in her care
- any alternative ways of meeting her care needs effectively which might be less restrictive of Martina's rights and freedoms, such as increased provision of home care or attendance at a day centre.

By following this process, Martina's daughter can then take decisions on behalf of her mother and in her best interests, when her mother lacks the capacity to make them herself, on any matters that fall under the authority of the LPA.

How does a decision-maker work out what 'all relevant circumstances' are?

When trying to work out someone's best interests, the decision-maker should try to identify all the issues that would be most relevant to the individual who lacks capacity and to the particular decision, as well as those in the 'checklist'. Clearly, it is not always possible or practical to investigate in depth every issue which may have some relevance to the person who lacks capacity or the decision in question. So relevant circumstances are defined in section 4(11) of the Act as those: '(a) of which the person making the determination is aware, and (b) which it would be reasonable to regard as relevant.' 5.18

The relevant circumstances will of course vary from case to case. For example, when making a decision about major medical treatment, a doctor would need to consider the clinical needs of the patient, the potential benefits and burdens of the treatment on the person's health and life expectancy and any other factors relevant to making a professional judgement.[16] But it would not be reasonable to consider issues such as life expectancy when working out whether it would be in someone's best interests to be given medication for a minor problem. 5.19

Financial decisions are another area where the relevant circumstances will vary. For example, if a person had received a substantial sum of money as compensation for an accident resulting in brain injury, the decision-maker would have to consider a wide range of circumstances when making decisions about how the money is spent or invested, such as: 5.20
- whether the person's condition is likely to change
- whether the person needs professional care, and
- whether the person needs to live somewhere else to make it easier for them.

These kinds of issues can only be decided on a case-by-case basis.

How should the person who lacks capacity be involved in working out their best interests?

Wherever possible, the person who lacks capacity to make a decision should still be involved in the decision-making process (section 4(4)). 5.21

Even if the person lacks capacity to make the decision, they may have views on matters affecting the decision, and on what outcome would be preferred. Their involvement can help work out what would be in their best interests. 5.22

The decision-maker should make sure that all practical means are used to enable and encourage the person to participate as fully as possible in the decision-making process and any action taken as a result, or to help the person improve their ability to participate. 5.23

Consulting the person who lacks capacity will involve taking time to explain what is happening and why a decision needs to be made. Chapter 3 includes a number of practical steps to assist and enable decision-making which may be also be helpful in encouraging greater participation. These include: 5.24
- using simple language and/or illustrations or photographs to help the person understand the options

---

[16] An *Hospital NHS Trust v S* [2003] EWHC 365 (Fam), paragraph 47.

- asking them about the decision at a time and location where the person feels most relaxed and at ease
- breaking the information down into easy-to-understand points
- using specialist interpreters or signers to communicate with the person.

This may mean that other people are required to communicate with the person to establish their views. For example, a trusted relative or friend, a full-time carer or an advocate may be able to help the person to express wishes or aspirations or to indicate a preference between different options.

More information on all of these steps can be found in chapter 3.

Scenario: Involving someone in working out their best interests

The parents of Amy, a young woman with learning difficulties, are going through a divorce and are arguing about who should continue to care for their daughter. Though she cannot understand what is happening, attempts are made to see if Amy can give some indication of where she would prefer to live. An advocate is appointed to work with Amy to help her understand the situation and to find out her likes and dislikes and matters which are important to her. With the advocate's help, Amy is able to participate in decisions about her future care.

How do the chances of someone regaining and developing capacity affect working out what is in their best interests?

5.25　There are some situations where decisions may be deferred, if someone who currently lacks capacity may regain the capacity to make the decision for themselves. Section 4(3) of the Act requires the decision-maker to consider:
- whether the individual concerned is likely to regain the capacity to make that particular decision in the future, and
- if so, when that is likely to be.

It may then be possible to put off the decision until the person can make it for themselves.

5.26　In emergency situations—such as when urgent medical treatment is needed—it may not be possible to wait to see if the person may regain capacity so they can decide for themselves whether or not to have the urgent treatment.

5.27　Where a person currently lacks capacity to make a decision relating to their day-to-day care, the person may—over time and with the right support—be able to develop the skills to do so. Though others may need to make the decision on the person's behalf at the moment, all possible support should be given to that person to enable them to develop the skills so that they can make the decision for themselves in the future.

Scenario: Taking a short-term decision for someone who may regain capacity

Mr Fowler has suffered a stroke leaving him severely disabled and unable to speak. Within days, he has shown signs of improvement, so with intensive treatment there is hope he will recover over time. But at present both his wife and the hospital staff find it difficult to communicate with him and have been unable to find out his wishes. He has always looked after the family finances, so Mrs Fowler suddenly discovers she has no access to his personal bank account to provide the family with money to live on or pay the bills. Because the decision can't be put off while efforts are made to find effective means of communicating with Mr Fowler, an application is made to the Court of Protection for an order that allows Mrs Fowler to access Mr Fowler's money. The decision about longer-term arrangements, on the other hand, can be delayed until alternative methods of communication have been tried and the extent of Mr Fowler's recovery is known.

Some factors which may indicate that a person may regain or develop capacity in the future are: 5.29
- the cause of the lack of capacity can be treated, either by medication or some other form of treatment or therapy
- the lack of capacity is likely to decrease in time (for example, where it is caused by the effects of medication or alcohol, or following a sudden shock)
- a person with learning disabilities may learn new skills or be subject to new experiences which increase their understanding and ability to make certain decisions
- the person may have a condition which causes capacity to come and go at various times (such as some forms of mental illness) so it may be possible to arrange for the decision to be made during a time when they do have capacity
- a person previously unable to communicate may learn a new form of communication (see chapter 3).

How should someone's best interests be worked out when making decisions about life-sustaining treatment?

A special factor in the checklist applies to decisions about treatment which is necessary to keep the 5.29 person alive ('life-sustaining treatment') and this is set out in section 4(5) of the Act. The fundamental rule is that anyone who is deciding whether or not life-sustaining treatment is in the best interests of someone who lacks capacity to consent to or refuse such treatment must not be motivated by a desire to bring about the person's death.

Whether a treatment is 'life-sustaining' depends not only on the type of treatment, but also on 5.30 the particular circumstances in which it may be prescribed. For example, in some situations giving antibiotics may be life-sustaining, whereas in other circumstances antibiotics are used to treat a non-life-threatening condition. It is up to the doctor or healthcare professional providing treatment to assess whether the treatment is life-sustaining in each particular situation.

All reasonable steps which are in the person's best interests should be taken to prolong their life. 5.31 There will be a limited number of cases where treatment is futile, overly burdensome to the patient or where there is no prospect of recovery. In circumstances such as these, it may be that an assessment of best interests leads to the conclusion that it would be in the best interests of the patient to withdraw or withhold life-sustaining treatment, even if this may result in the person's death. The decision-maker must make a decision based on the best interests of the person who lacks capacity. They must not be motivated by a desire to bring about the person's death for whatever reason, even if this is from a sense of compassion. Healthcare and social care staff should also refer to relevant professional guidance when making decisions regarding life-sustaining treatment.

As with all decisions, before deciding to withdraw or withhold life-sustaining treatment, the 5.32 decision-maker must consider the range of treatment options available to work out what would be in the person's best interests. All the factors in the best interests checklist should be considered, and in particular, the decision-maker should consider any statements that the person has previously made about their wishes and feelings about life-sustaining treatment.

Importantly, section 4(5) cannot be interpreted to mean that doctors are under an obligation to 5.33 provide, or to continue to provide, life-sustaining treatment where that treatment is not in the best interests of the person, even where the person's death is foreseen. Doctors must apply the best interests' checklist and use their professional skills to decide whether life-sustaining treatment is in the person's best interests. If the doctor's assessment is disputed, and there is no other way of resolving the dispute, ultimately the Court of Protection may be asked to decide what is in the person's best interests.

5.34   Where a person has made a written statement in advance that requests particular medical treatments, such as artificial nutrition and hydration (ANH), these requests should be taken into account by the treating doctor in the same way as requests made by a patient who has the capacity to make such decisions. Like anyone else involved in making this decision, the doctor must weigh written statements alongside all other relevant factors to decide whether it is in the best interests of the patient to provide or continue life-sustaining treatment.

5.35   If someone has made an advance decision to refuse life-sustaining treatment, specific rules apply. More information about these can be found in chapter 9 and in paragraph 5.45 below.

5.36   As mentioned in paragraph 5.33 above, where there is any doubt about the patient's best interests, an application should be made to the Court of Protection for a decision as to whether withholding or withdrawing life-sustaining treatment is in the patient's best interests.

How do a person's wishes and feelings, beliefs and values affect working out what is in their best interests?

5.37   Section 4(6) of the Act requires the decision-maker to consider, as far as they are 'reasonably ascertainable':

'(a) the person's past and present wishes and feelings (and in particular, any relevant written statements made by him when he had capacity),

(b) the beliefs and values that would be likely to influence his decision if he had capacity, and

(c) the other factors that he would be likely to consider if he were able to do so.'

Paragraphs 5.38–5.48 below give further guidance on each of these factors.

5.38   In setting out the requirements for working out a person's 'best interests', section 4 of the Act puts the person who lacks capacity at the centre of the decision to be made. Even if they cannot make the decision, their wishes and feelings, beliefs and values should be taken fully into account – whether expressed in the past or now. What does the But their wishes and feelings, beliefs and values will not necessarily Act mean when it talks about 'best interests'?be the deciding factor in working out their best interests. Any such assessment must consider past and current wishes and feelings, beliefs and values alongside all other factors, but the final decision must be based entirely on what is in the person's best interests.

Scenario: Considering wishes and feelings as part of best interests

Andre, a young man with severe learning disabilities who does not use any formal system of communication, cuts his leg while outdoors. There is some earth in the wound. A doctor wants to give him a tetanus jab, but Andre appears scared of the needle and pushes it away. Assessments have shown that he is unable to understand the risk of infection following his injury, or the consequences of rejecting the injection. The doctor decides that it is in the Andre's best interests to give the vaccination. She asks a nurse to comfort Andre, and if necessary, restrain him while she gives the injection. She has objective reasons for believing she is acting in Andre's best interests, and for believing that Andre lacks capacity to make the decision for himself. So she should be protected from liability under section 5 of the Act (see chapter 6).

What is 'reasonably ascertainable'?

5.39   How much someone can learn about a person's past and present views will depend on circumstances and the time available. 'Reasonably ascertainable' means considering all possible information in the time available. What is available in an emergency will be different to what is available in a non-emergency. But even in an emergency, there may still be an opportunity to try to communicate with the person or his friends, family or carers (see chapter 3 for guidance on helping communication).

What role do a person's past and present wishes and feelings play?

People who cannot express their current wishes and feelings in words may express themselves through their behaviour. Expressions of pleasure or distress and emotional responses will also be relevant in working out what is in their best interests. It is also important to be sure that other people have not influenced a person's views. An advocate could help the person make choices and express their views.

The person may have held strong views in the past which could have a bearing on the decision now to be made. All reasonable efforts must be made to find out whether the person has expressed views in the past that will shape the decision to be made. This could have been through verbal communication, writing, behaviour or habits, or recorded in any other way (for example, home videos or audiotapes).

Section 4(6)(a) places special emphasis on written statements the person might have made before losing capacity. These could provide a lot of information about a person's wishes. For example, these statements could include information about the type of medical treatment they would want in the case of future illness, where they would prefer to live, or how they wish to be cared for.

The decision-maker should consider written statements carefully. If their decision does not follow something a person has put in writing, they must record the reasons why. They should be able to justify their reasons if someone challenges their decision.

A doctor should take written statements made by a person before losing capacity which request specific treatments as seriously as those made by people who currently have capacity to make treatment decisions. But they would not have to follow a written request if they think the specific treatment would be clinically unnecessary or not appropriate for the person's condition, so not in the person's best interests.

It is important to note the distinction between a written statement expressing treatment preferences and a statement which constitutes an advance decision to refuse treatment. This is covered by section 24 of the Act, and it has a different status in law. Doctors cannot ignore a written statement that is a valid advance decision to refuse treatment. An advance decision to refuse treatment must be followed if it meets the Act's requirements and applies to the person's circumstances. In these cases, the treatment must not be given (see chapter 9 for more information). If there is not a valid and applicable advance decision, treatment should be provided based on the person's best interests.

What role do beliefs and values play?

Everybody's values and beliefs influence the decisions they make. They may become especially important for someone who lacks capacity to make a decision because of a progressive illness such as dementia, for example. Evidence of a person's beliefs and values can be found in things like their:

- cultural background
- religious beliefs
- political convictions, or
- past behaviour or habits.

Some people set out their values and beliefs in a written statement while they still have capacity.

5.40

5.41

5.42

5.43

5.44

5.45

5.46

Scenario: Considering beliefs and values

Anita, a young woman, suffers serious brain damage during a car accident. The court appoints her father as deputy to invest the compensation she received. As the decision-maker he must think about her wishes, beliefs and values before deciding how to invest the money. Anita had worked for an overseas charity. Her father talks to her former colleagues. They tell him how Anita's political beliefs shaped her work and personal beliefs, so he decides not to invest in the bonds that a financial adviser had recommended, because they are from companies Anita would not have approved of. Instead, he employs an ethical investment adviser to choose appropriate companies in line with her beliefs.

What other factors should a decision-maker consider?

5.47   Section 4(6)(c) of the Act requires decision-makers to consider any other factors the person who lacks capacity would consider if they were able to do so. This might include the effect of the decision on other people, obligations to dependants or the duties of a responsible citizen.

5.48   The Act allows actions that benefit other people, as long as they are in the best interests of the person who lacks capacity to make the decision. For example, having considered all the circumstances of the particular case, a decision might be made to take a blood sample from a person who lacks capacity to consent, to check for a genetic link to cancer within the family, because this might benefit someone else in the family. But it might still be in the best interests of the person who lacks capacity. 'Best interests' goes beyond the person's medical interests.

For example, courts have previously ruled that possible wider benefits to a person who lacks capacity to consent, such as providing or gaining emotional support from close relationships, are important factors in working out the person's own best interests.[17] If it is likely that the person who lacks capacity would have considered these factors themselves, they can be seen as part of the person's best interests.

Who should be consulted when working out someone's best interests?

5.49   The Act places a duty on the decision-maker to consult other people close to a person who lacks capacity, where practical and appropriate, on decisions affecting the person and what might be in the person's best interests. This also applies to those involved in caring for the person and interested in the person's welfare. Under section 4(7), the decision-maker has a duty to take into account the views of the following people, where it is practical and appropriate to do so:
- anyone the person has previously named as someone they want to be consulted
- anyone involved in caring for the person
- anyone interested in their welfare (for example, family carers, other close relatives, or an advocate already working with the person)
- an attorney appointed by the person under a Lasting Power of Attorney, and
- a deputy appointed for that person by the Court of Protection.

5.50   If there is no-one to speak to about the person's best interests, in some circumstances the person may qualify for an Independent Mental Capacity Advocate (IMCA). For more information on IMCAs, see chapter 10.

---

[17] See for example *Re Y (Mental Incapacity: Bone marrow transplant)* [1996] 2 FLR 787; *Re A (Male Sterilisation)* [2000] 1 FLR 549.

Decision-makers must show they have thought carefully about who to speak to. If it is practical   5.51
and appropriate to speak to the above people, they must do so and must take their views into
account. They must be able to explain why they did not speak to a particular person—it is good
practice to have a clear record of their reasons. It is also good practice to give careful consideration
to the views of family carers, if it is possible to do so.

It is also good practice for healthcare and social care staff to record at the end of the process why   5.52
they think a specific decision is in the person's best interests. This is particularly important if
healthcare and social care staff go against the views of somebody who has been consulted while
working out the person's best interests.

The decision-maker should try to find out: 5.53
• what the people consulted think is in the person's best interests in this matter, and
• if they can give information on the person's wishes and feelings, beliefs and values.

This information may be available from somebody the person named before they lost capacity   5.54
as someone they wish to be consulted. People who are close to the person who lacks capacity, such
as close family members, are likely to know them best. They may also be able to help with
communication or interpret signs that show the person's present wishes and feelings. Everybody's
views are equally important—even if they do not agree with each other. They must be considered
alongside the views of the person who lacks capacity and other factors. See paragraphs 5.62–5.69
below for guidance on dealing with conflicting views.

Scenario: Considering other people's views

Lucia, a young woman with severe brain damage, is cared for at home by her parents and attends
a day centre a couple of days each week. The day centre staff would like to take some of the service
users on holiday. They speak to Lucia's parents as part of the process of assessing whether the
holiday would be in her best interests. The parents think that the holiday would be good for her,
but they are worried that Lucia gets very anxious if she is surrounded by strangers who don't know
how to communicate with her. Having tried to seek Lucia's views and involve her in the decision,
the staff and parents agree that a holiday would be in her best interests, as long as her care assistant
can go with her to help with communication.

Where an attorney has been appointed under a Lasting Power of Attorney or Enduring Power   5.55
of Attorney, or a deputy has been appointed by a court, they must make the decisions on any
matters they have been appointed to deal with. Attorneys and deputies should also be consulted,
if practical and appropriate, on other issues affecting the person who lacks capacity.

For instance, an attorney who is appointed only to look after the person's property and affairs
may have information about the person's beliefs and values, wishes and feelings, that could help
work out what would be in the person's best interests regarding healthcare or treatment decisions.
(See chapters 7 and 8 for more information about the roles of attorneys and deputies.)

How can decision-makers respect confidentiality?

Decision-makers must balance the duty to consult other people with the right to confidentiality   5.56
of the person who lacks capacity. So if confidential information is to be discussed, they should
only seek the views of people who it is appropriate to consult, where their views are relevant to the
decision to be made and the particular circumstances.

There may be occasions where it is in the person's best interests for personal information (for   5.57
example, about their medical condition, if the decision concerns the provision of medical
treatment) to be revealed to the people consulted as part of the process of working out their best
interests (further guidance on this is given in chapter 16). Healthcare and social care staff who are

trying to determine a person's best interests must follow their professional guidance, as well as other relevant guidance, about confidentiality.

When does the best interests principle apply?

5.58 Section 1(5) of the Act confirms that the principle applies to any act done, or any decision made, on behalf of someone where there is reasonable belief that the person lacks capacity under the Act. This covers informal day-to-day decisions and actions as well as decisions made by the courts.

Reasonable belief about a person's best interests

5.59 Section 4(9) confirms that if someone acts or makes a decision in the reasonable belief that what they are doing is in the best interests of the person who lacks capacity, then—provided they have followed the checklist in section 4—they will have complied with the best interests principle set out in the Act. Coming to an incorrect conclusion about a person's capacity or best interests does not necessarily mean that the decision-maker would not get protection from liability (this is explained in chapter 6). But they must be able to show that it was reasonable for them to think that the person lacked capacity and that they were acting in the person's best interests at the time they made their decision or took action.

5.60 Where there is a need for a court decision, the court is likely to require formal evidence of what might be in the person's best interests. This will include evidence from relevant professionals (for example, psychiatrists or social workers). But in most day-to-day situations, there is no need for such formality. In emergency situations, it may not be practical or possible to gather formal evidence.

5.61 Where the court is not involved, people are still expected to have reasonable grounds for believing that they are acting in somebody's best interests. This does not mean that decision-makers can simply impose their own views. They must have objective reasons for their decisions – and they must be able to demonstrate them. They must be able to show they have considered all relevant circumstances and applied all elements of the best interests checklist.

Scenario: Demonstrating reasonable belief

Mrs Prior is mugged and knocked unconscious. She is brought to hospital without any means of identification. She has head injuries and a stab wound, and has lost a lot of blood. In casualty, a doctor arranges an urgent blood transfusion. Because this is necessary to save her life, the doctor believes this is in her best interests. When her relatives are contacted, they say that Mrs Prior's beliefs meant that she would have refused all blood products. But since Mrs Prior's handbag had been stolen, the doctor had no idea who the woman was nor what her beliefs her. He needed to make an immediate decision and Mrs Prior lacked capacity to make the decision for herself. Therefore he had reasonable grounds for believing that his action was in his patient's best interests—and so was protected from liability. Now that the doctor knows Mrs Prior's beliefs, he can take them into account in future decisions about her medical treatment if she lacks capacity to make them for herself. He can also consult her family, now that he knows where they are.

What problems could arise when working out someone's best interests?

5.62 It is important that the best interests principle and the statutory checklist are flexible. Without flexibility, it would be impossible to prioritise factors in different cases—and it would be difficult to ensure that the outcome is the best possible for the person who lacks capacity to make the particular decision. Some cases will be straightforward. Others will require decision-makers to balance the pros and cons of all relevant factors.[18] But this flexibility could lead to problems in reaching a conclusion about a person's best interests.

What happens when there are conflicting concerns?

A decision-maker may be faced with people who disagree about a person's best interests. Family members, partners and carers may disagree between themselves. Or they might have different memories about what views the person expressed in the past. Carers and family might disagree with a professional's view about the person's care or treatment needs.   5.63

The decision-maker will need to find a way of balancing these concerns or deciding between them. The first approach should be to review all elements of the best interests checklist with everyone involved. They should include the person who lacks capacity (as much as they are able to take part) and anyone who has been involved in earlier discussions. It may be possible to reach an agreement at a meeting to air everyone's concerns. But an agreement in itself might not be in the person's best interests. Ultimate responsibility for working out best interests lies with the decision-maker.   5.64

Scenario: Dealing with disagreement

Some time ago, Mr Graham made a Lasting Power of Attorney (LPA) appointing his son and daughter as joint attorneys to manage his finances and property. He now has Alzheimer's disease and has moved into private residential care. The son and daughter have to decide what to do with Mr Graham's house. His son thinks it is in their father's best interests to sell it and invest the money for Mr Graham's future care. But his daughter thinks it is in Mr Graham's best interests to keep the property, because he enjoys visiting and spending time in his old home. After making every effort to get Mr Graham's views, the family meets to discuss all the issues involved. After hearing other family views, the attorneys agree that it would be in their father's best interests to keep the property for so long as he is able to enjoy visiting it.

Family, partners and carers who are consulted

If disagreement continues, the decision-maker will need to weigh up the views of different parties. This will depend entirely upon the circumstances of each case, the people involved and their relationship with the person who lacks capacity. Sometimes the decision-maker will find that carers have an insight into how to interpret a person's wishes and feelings that can help them reach a decision.   5.65

At the same time, paid care workers and voluntary sector support workers may have specialist knowledge about up-to-date care options or treatments. Some may also have known the person for many years.   5.66

People with conflicting interests should not be cut out of the process (for example, those who stand to inherit from the person's will may still have a right to be consulted about the person's care or medical treatment). But decision-makers must always ensure that the interests of those consulted do not overly influence the process of working out a person's best interests. In weighing up different contributions, the decision-maker should consider: 5.67

- how long an individual has known the person who lacks capacity, and
- what their relationship is.

---

[18] *Re A (Male Sterilisation)* [2000] 1 FLR 549.

Scenario: Settling disagreements

Robert is 19 and has learning disabilities and autism. He is about to leave his residential special school. His parents want Robert to go to a specialist unit run by a charitable organisation, but he has been offered a place in a local supported living scheme. The parents don't think Robert will get appropriate care there. The school sets up a 'best interests' meeting. People who attend include Robert, his parents, teachers from his school and professionals involved in preparing Robert's care plan. Robert's parents and teachers know him best. They set out their views and help Robert to communicate where he would like to live. Social care staff identify some different placements within the county. Robert visits these with his parents. After further discussion, everyone agrees that a community placement near his family home would be in Robert's best interests.

Settling disputes about best interests

5.68 If someone wants to challenge a decision-maker's conclusions, there are several options:
- Involve an advocate to act on behalf of the person who lacks capacity to make the decision (see paragraph 5.69 below).
- Get a second opinion.
- Hold a formal or informal 'best interests' case conference.
- Attempt some form of mediation (see chapter 15).
- Pursue a complaint through the organisation's formal procedures.

Ultimately, if all other attempts to resolve the dispute have failed, the court might need to decide what is in the person's best interests. Chapter 8 provides more information about the Court of Protection.

Advocacy

5.69 An advocate might be useful in providing support for the person who lacks capacity to make a decision in the process of working out their best interests, if:
- the person who lacks capacity has no close family or friends to take an interest in their welfare, and they do not qualify for an Independent Mental Capacity Advocate (see chapter 10)
- family members disagree about the person's best interests
- family members and professionals disagree about the person's best Act mean when interests
- there is a conflict of interest for people who have been consulted in the best interests assessment (for example, the sale of a family property where the person lives)
- the person who lacks capacity is already in contact with an advocate
- the proposed course of action may lead to the use of restraint or other restrictions on the person who lacks capacity
- there is a concern about the protection of a vulnerable adult.

6. WHAT PROTECTION DOES THE ACT OFFER FOR PEOPLE PROVIDING CARE OR TREATMENT?

Section 5 of the Act allows carers, healthcare and social care staff to carry out certain tasks without fear of liability. These tasks involve the personal care, healthcare or treatment of people who lack capacity to consent to them. The aim is to give legal backing for acts that need to be carried out in the best interests of the person who lacks capacity to consent.[19]

This chapter explains:

- how the Act provides protection from liability
- how that protection works in practice
- where protection is restricted or limited, and
- when a carer can use a person's money to buy goods or services without formal permission.

In this chapter, as throughout the Code, a person's capacity (or lack of capacity) refers specifically to their capacity to make a particular decision at the time it needs to be made.

Quick summary

The following steps list all the things that people providing care or treatment should bear in mind to ensure they are protected by the Act.

Acting in connection with the care or treatment of someone who lacks capacity to consent

- Is the action to be carried out in connection with the care or treatment of a person who lacks capacity to give consent to that act?
- Does it involve major life changes for the person concerned? If so, it will need special consideration.
- Who is carrying out the action? Is it appropriate for that person to do so at the relevant time?

Checking whether the person has capacity to consent

- Have all possible steps been taken to try to help the person make a decision for themselves about the action?
- Has the two-stage test of capacity been applied?
- Are there reasonable grounds for believing the person lacks capacity to give permission?

Acting in the person's best interests

- Has the best interests checklist been applied and all relevant circumstances considered?
- Is a less restrictive option available?
- Is it reasonable to believe that the proposed act is in the person's best interests?

Understanding possible limitations on protection from liability

- If restraint is being considered, is it necessary to prevent harm to the person who lacks capacity, and is it a proportionate response to the likelihood of the person suffering harm—and to the seriousness of that harm?
- Could the restraint be classed as a 'deprivation of the person's liberty'?
- Does the action conflict with a decision that has been made by an attorney or deputy under their powers?

Paying for necessary goods and services

- If someone wishes to use the person's money to buy goods or pay for services for someone who lacks capacity to do so themselves, are those goods or services necessary and in the person's best interests?
- Is it necessary to take money from the person's bank or building society account or to sell the person's property to pay for goods or services? If so, formal authority will be required.

---

[19] The provisions of section 5 are based on the common law 'doctrine of necessity' as set out in *Re F (Mental Patient: Sterilisation)* [1990] 2 AC 1.

What protection do people have when caring for those who lack capacity to consent?

6.1 Every day, millions of acts are done to and for people who lack capacity either to:
- take decisions about their own care or treatment, or
- consent to someone else caring for them.

Such acts range from everyday tasks of caring (for example, helping someone to wash) to life-changing events (for example, serious medical treatment or arranging for someone to go into a care home).

In theory, many of these actions could be against the law. Legally, people have the right to stop others from interfering with their body or property unless they give permission. But what happens if someone lacks capacity to give permission? Carers who dress people who cannot dress themselves are potentially interfering with someone's body without their consent, so could theoretically be prosecuted for assault. A neighbour who enters and cleans the house of a person who lacks capacity could be trespassing on the person's property.

6.2 Section 5 of the Act provides 'protection from liability'. In other words, it protects people who carry out these actions. It stops them being prosecuted for acts that could otherwise be classed as civil wrongs or crimes. By protecting family and other carers from liability, the Act allows necessary caring acts or treatment to take place as if a person who lacks capacity to consent had consented to them. People providing care of this sort do not therefore need to get formal authority to act.

6.3 Importantly, section 5 does not give people caring for or treating someone the power to make any other decisions on behalf of those who lack capacity to make their own decisions. Instead, it offers protection from liability so that they can act in connection with the person's care or treatment. The power to make decisions on behalf of someone who lacks capacity can be granted through other parts of the Act (such as the powers granted to attorneys and deputies, which are explained in chapters 7 and 8).

What type of actions might have protection from liability?

6.4 Section 5(1) provides possible protection for actions carried out in connection with care or treatment. The action may be carried out on behalf of someone who is believed to lack capacity to give permission for the action, so long as it is in that person's best interests (see chapter 5). The Act does not define 'care' or 'treatment'. They should be given their normal meaning. However, section 64(1) makes clear that treatment includes diagnostic or other procedures.

6.5 Actions that might be covered by section 5 include:

Personal care
- helping with washing, dressing or personal hygiene
- helping with eating and drinking
- helping with communication
- helping with mobility (moving around)
- helping someone take part in education, social or leisure activities
- going into a person's home to drop off shopping or to see if they are alright
- doing the shopping or buying necessary goods with the person's money
- arranging household services (for example, arranging repairs or maintenance for gas and electricity supplies)
- providing services that help around the home (such as homecare or meals on wheels)
- undertaking actions related to community care services (for example, day care, residential accommodation or nursing care) – but see also paragraphs 6.7–6.14 below
- helping someone to move home (including moving property and clearing the former home).

Healthcare and treatment
- carrying out diagnostic examinations and tests (to identify an illness, condition or other problem)
- providing professional medical, dental and similar treatment
- giving medication
- taking someone to hospital for assessment or treatment
- providing nursing care (whether in hospital or in the community)
- carrying out any other necessary medical procedures (for example, taking a blood sample) or therapies (for example, physiotherapy or chiropody)
- providing care in an emergency.

6.6 These actions only receive protection from liability if the person is reasonably believed to lack capacity to give permission for the action. The action must also be in the person's best interests and follow the Act's principles (see paragraph 6.26 onwards).

6.7 Some acts in connection with care or treatment may cause major life changes with significant consequences for the person concerned. Those requiring particularly careful consideration include a change of residence, perhaps into a care home or nursing home, or major decisions about healthcare and medical treatment. These are described in the following paragraphs.

A change of residence

6.8 Sometimes a person cannot get sufficient or appropriate care in their own home, and they may have to move—perhaps to live with relatives or to go into a care home or nursing home. If the person lacks capacity to consent to a move, the decision-maker(s) must consider whether the move is in the person's best interests (by referring to the best interests checklist in chapter 5 and in particular the person's past and present wishes and feelings, as well as the views of other relevant people). The decision-maker(s) must also consider whether there is a less restrictive option (see chapter 2, principle 5).

This may involve speaking to:
- anyone currently involved in the person's care
- family carers and other family members close to the person and interested in their welfare
- others who have an interest in the person's welfare
- anyone the person has previously named as someone to be consulted, and
- an attorney or deputy who has been legally appointed to make particular decisions on their behalf.

6.9 Some cases will require an Independent Mental Capacity Advocate (IMCA). The IMCA represents and supports the person who lacks capacity and they will provide information to make sure the final decision is in the person's best interests (see chapter 10). An IMCA is needed when there is no-one close to the person who lacks capacity to give an opinion about what is best for them, and:
- an NHS body is proposing to provide serious medical treatment or
- an NHS body or local authority is proposing to arrange accommodation in hospital or a care home or other longer-term accommodation and
  —the person will stay in hospital longer than 28 days, or
  —they will stay in a care home for more than eight weeks.

There are also some circumstances where an IMCA may be appointed on a discretionary basis. More guidance is available in chapter 10.

6.10 Sometimes the final outcome may not be what the person who lacks capacity wanted. For example, they might want to stay at home, but those caring for them might decide a move is in their best interests. In all cases, those making the decision must first consider other options that might restrict the person's rights and freedom of action less (see chapter 2, principle 5).

6.11 In some cases, there may be no alternative but to move the person. Such a move would normally require the person's formal consent if they had capacity to give, or refuse, it. In cases where a person lacks capacity to consent, section 5 of the Act allows carers to carry out actions relating to the move—as long as the Act's principles and the requirements for working out best interests have been followed. This applies even if the person continues to object to the move.

However, section 6 places clear limits on the use of force or restraint by only permitting restraint to be used (for example, to transport the person to their new home) where this is necessary to protect the person from harm and is a proportionate response to the risk of harm (see paragraphs 6.40–6.53). Any action taken to move the person concerned or their property could incur liability unless protected under section 5.

6.12 If there is a serious disagreement about the need to move the person that cannot be settled in any other way, the Court of Protection can be asked to decide what the person's best interests are and where they should live. For example, this could happen if members of a family disagree over what is best for a relative who lacks capacity to give or deny permission for a move.

6.13 In some circumstances, being placed in a hospital or care home may deprive the person of their liberty (see paragraphs 6.49–6.53). If this is the case, there is no protection from liability—even if the placement was considered to be in the best interests of the person (section 6(5)). It is up to the decision-maker to first look at a range of alternative and less restrictive options to see if there is any way of avoiding taking away the person's liberty.

6.14 If there is no alternative way of caring for the person, specific authority will be required to keep the person in a situation which deprives them of their liberty. For instance, sometimes the Court of Protection might be prepared to grant an order of which a consequence is the deprivation of a person's liberty—if it is satisfied that this is in the person's best interests. In other cases, if the person needs treatment for a mental disorder and meets the criteria for detention under the Mental Health Act 1983, this may be used to admit or keep the person in hospital (see chapter 13).

Healthcare and treatment decisions

6.15 Section 5 also allows actions to be taken to ensure a person who lacks capacity to consent receives necessary medical treatment. This could involve taking the person to hospital for out-patient treatment or arranging for admission to hospital. Even if a person who lacks capacity to consent objects to the proposed treatment or admission to hospital, the action might still be allowed under section 5 (but see paragraphs 6.20 and 6.22 below). But there are limits about whether force or restraint can be used to impose treatment (see paragraphs 6.40–6.53).

6.16 Major healthcare and treatment decisions – for example, major surgery or a decision that no attempt is to be made to resuscitate the patient (known as 'DNR' decisions)—will also need special consideration. Unless there is a valid and applicable advance decision to refuse the specific treatment, healthcare staff must carefully work out what would be in the person's best interests (see chapter 5). As part of the process of working this out, they will need to consider (where practical and appropriate):

- the past and present wishes and feelings, beliefs and values of the person who lacks capacity to make the treatment decision, including any advance statement the person wrote setting out their wishes when they had capacity
- the views of anyone previously named by the person as someone to be consulted
- the views of anyone engaged in caring for the person
- the views of anyone interested in their welfare, and
- the views of any attorney or deputy appointed for the person.

In specific cases where there is no-one else available to consult about the person's best interests, an IMCA must be appointed to support and represent the person (see paragraph 6.9 above and chapter 10).

Healthcare staff must also consider whether there are alternative treatment options that might be less intrusive or restrictive (see chapter 2, principle 5). When deciding about the provision or withdrawal of life-sustaining treatment, anyone working out what is in the best interests of a person who lacks capacity must not be motivated by a desire to bring about the person's death (see chapter 5).

6.17 Multi-disciplinary meetings are often the best way to decide on a person's best interests. They bring together healthcare and social care staff with different skills to discuss the person's options and may involve those who are closest to the person concerned. But final responsibility for deciding what is in a person's best interest lies with the member of healthcare staff responsible for the person's treatment. They should record their decision, how they reached it and the reasons for it in the person's clinical notes. As long as they have recorded objective reasons to show that the decision is in the person's best interests, and the other requirements of section 5 of the Act are met, all healthcare staff taking actions in connection with the particular treatment will be protected from liability.

6.18 Some treatment decisions are so serious that the court has to make them—unless the person has previously made a Lasting Power of Attorney appointing an attorney to make such healthcare decisions for them (see chapter 7) or they have made a valid advance decision to refuse the proposed treatment (see chapter 9). The Court of Protection must be asked to make decisions relating to:[20]

- the proposed withholding or withdrawal of artificial nutrition and hydration (ANH) from a patient in a permanent vegetative state (PVS)
- cases where it is proposed that a person who lacks capacity to consent should donate an organ or bone marrow to another person
- the proposed non-therapeutic sterilisation of a person who lacks capacity to consent (for example, for contraceptive purposes)
- cases where there is a dispute about whether a particular treatment will be in a person's best interests.

See paragraphs 8.18–8.24 for more details on these types of cases.

6.19 This last category may include cases that introduce ethical dilemmas concerning untested or innovative treatments (for example, new treatments for variant Creutzfeldt-Jakob Disease (CDJ)) where it is not known if the treatment will be effective, or certain cases involving a termination of pregnancy. It may also include cases where there is conflict between professionals or between professionals and family members which cannot be resolved in any other way.

Where there is conflict, it is advisable for parties to get legal advice, though they may not necessarily be able to get legal aid to pay for this advice. Chapter 8 gives more information about the need to refer cases to court for a decision.

Who is protected from liability by section 5?

6.20 Section 5 of the Act is most likely to affect:

- family carers and other kinds of carers
- care workers
- healthcare and social care staff, and

---

[20] The procedures resulting from those court judgements are set out in a Practice Note from the Official Solicitor (available at www.officialsolicitor.gov.uk) and will be set out in a Practice Direction from the new Court of Protection.

- others who may occasionally be involved in the care or treatment of a person who lacks capacity to consent (for example, ambulance staff, housing workers, police officers and volunteer support workers).

6.21 At any time, it is likely that several people will be carrying out tasks that are covered by section 5 of the Act. Section 5 does not:
- give one person more rights than another to carry out tasks
- specify who has the authority to act in a specific instance
- allow somebody to make decisions relating to subjects other than the care or treatment of the person who lacks capacity, or
- allow somebody to give consent on behalf of a person who lacks capacity to do so.

6.22 To receive protection from liability under section 5, all actions must be related to the care or treatment of the person who lacks capacity to consent. Before taking action, carers must first reasonably believe that:
- the person lacks the capacity to make that particular decision at the time it needs to be made, and
- the action is in the person's best interests.

This is explained further in paragraphs 6.26–6.34 below.

Scenario: Protecting multiple carers

Mr Rose, an older man with dementia, gets help from several people. His sister sometimes cooks meals for him. A district nurse visits him to change the dressing on a pressure sore, and a friend often takes Mr Rose to the park, guiding him when they cross the road. Each of these individuals would be protected from liability under section 5 of the Act—but only if they take reasonable steps to check that he lacks capacity to consent to the actions they take and hold a reasonable belief that the actions are in Mr Rose's best interests.

6.23 Section 5 may also protect carers who need to use the person's money to pay for goods or services that the person needs but lacks the capacity to purchase for themselves. However, there are strict controls over who may have access to another person's money. See paragraphs 6.56–6.66 for more information.

6.24 Carers who provide personal care services must not carry out specialist procedures that are normally done by trained healthcare staff. If the action involves medical treatment, the doctor or other member of healthcare staff with responsibility for the patient will be the decision-maker who has to decide whether the proposed treatment is in the person's best interests (see chapter 5). A doctor can delegate responsibility for giving the treatment to other people in the clinical team who have the appropriate skills or expertise. People who do more than their experience or qualifications allow may not be protected from liability.

Care planning

6.25 Decisions about a person's care or treatment are often made by a multi-disciplinary team (a team of professionals with different skills that contribute to a person's care), by drawing up a care plan for the person. The preparation of a care plan should always include an assessment of the person's capacity to consent to the actions covered by the care plan, and confirm that those actions are agreed to be in the person's best interests. Healthcare and social care staff may then be able to assume that any actions they take under the care plan are in the person's best interests, and therefore receive protection from liability under section 5. But a person's capacity and best interests must still be reviewed regularly.

What steps should people take to be protected from liability?

As well as taking the following steps, somebody who wants to be protected from liability should bear in mind the statutory principles set out in section 1 of the Act (see chapter 2). 6.26

First, reasonable steps must be taken to find out whether a person has the capacity to make a decision about the proposed action (section 5(1)(a)). If the person has capacity, they must give their consent for anyone to take an action on their behalf, so that the person taking the action is protected from liability. For guidance on what is classed as 'reasonable steps', see paragraphs 6.29–6.34. But reasonable steps must always include: 6.27

- taking all practical and appropriate steps to help people to make a decision about an action themselves, and
- applying the two-stage test of capacity (see chapter 4).

The person who is going to take the action must have a 'reasonable belief' that the individual lacks capacity to give consent for the action at the time it needs to be taken.

Secondly, the person proposing to take action must have reasonable grounds for believing that the action is in the best interests of the person who lacks capacity. They should apply all elements of the best interests checklist (see chapter 5), and in particular 6.28

- consider whether the person is likely to regain capacity to make this decision in the future. Can the action wait until then?
- consider whether a less restrictive option is available (chapter 2, principle 5), and
- have objective reasons for thinking an action is in the best interests of the person who lacks capacity to consent to it.

What is 'reasonable'?

As explained in chapter 4, anyone assessing a person's capacity to make decisions for themselves or give consent must focus wholly on whether the person has capacity to make a specific decision at the time it needs to be made and not the person's capacity to make decisions generally. For example, a carer helping a person to dress can assess a person's capacity to agree to their help by explaining the different options (getting dressed or staying in nightclothes), and the consequences (being able to go out, or staying in all day). 6.29

Carers do not have to be experts in assessing capacity. But they must be able to show that they have taken reasonable steps to find out if the person has the capacity to make the specific decision. Only then will they have reasonable grounds for believing the person lacks capacity in relation to that particular matter. See paragraphs 4.44–4.45 for guidance on what is classed as 'reasonable'—although this will vary, depending on circumstances. 6.30

For the majority of decisions, formal assessment processes are unlikely to be required. But in some circumstances, professional practice requires some formal procedures to be carried out (for example, where consent to medical treatment is required, the doctor will need to assess—and record the person's capacity to consent). Under section 5, carers and professionals will be protected from liability as long as they are able to provide some objective reasons that explain why they believe that the person lacks capacity to consent to the action. If somebody challenges their belief, both carers and professionals will be protected from liability as long as they can show that they took steps to find out whether the person has capacity and that they have a reasonable belief that the person lacks capacity. 6.31

Similarly, carers, relatives and others involved in caring for someone who lacks capacity must have reasonable grounds for believing that their action is in the person's best interests. They must not simply impose their own views. They must be able to show that they considered all relevant circumstances and applied the best interests checklist. This includes showing that they have tried 6.32

to involve the person who lacks capacity, and find out their wishes and feelings, beliefs and values. They must also have asked other people's opinions, where practical and appropriate. If somebody challenges their decision, they will be protected from liability if they can show that it was reasonable for them to believe that their action was in the person's best interests—in all the circumstances of that particular case.

6.33   If healthcare and social care staff are involved, their skills and knowledge will affect what is classed as 'reasonable'. For example, a doctor assessing somebody's capacity to consent to treatment must demonstrate more skill than someone without medical training. They should also record in the person's healthcare record the steps they took and the reasons for the finding. Healthcare and social care staff should apply normal clinical and professional standards when deciding what treatments to offer. They must then decide whether the proposed treatment is in the best interests of the person who lacks capacity to consent. This includes considering all relevant circumstances and applying the best interests checklist (see chapter 5).

6.34   Healthcare and social care staff can be said to have 'reasonable grounds for believing' that a person lacks capacity if:
• they are working to a person's care plan, and
• the care planning process involved an assessment of the person's capacity to make a decision about actions in the care plan.
It is also reasonable for them to assume that the care planning process assessed a person's best interests. But they should still make every effort to communicate with the person to find out if they still lack capacity and the action is still in their best interests.

Scenario: Working with a care plan

Margaret, an elderly woman, has serious mental health and physical problems. She lives in a nursing home and a care plan has been prepared by the multi-disciplinary team, in consultation with her relatives in deciding what course of action would be in Margaret's best interests. The care plan covers the medication she has been prescribed, the physiotherapy she needs, help with her personal care and other therapeutic activities such as art therapy. Although attempts were made to involve Margaret in the care planning process, she has been assessed by the doctor responsible for her care as lacking capacity to consent to most aspects of her care plan. The care plan can be relied on by the nurse or care assistant who administers the medication, by the physiotherapist and art therapist, and also by the care assistant who helps with Margaret's personal care, providing them with reasonable grounds for believing that they are acting in her best interests. However, as each act is performed, they must all take reasonable steps to communicate with Margaret to explain what they are doing and to ascertain whether she has the capacity to consent to the act in question. If they think she does, they must stop the treatment unless or until Margaret agrees that it should continue.

What happens in emergency situations?

6.35   Sometimes people who lack capacity to consent will require emergency medical treatment to save their life or prevent them from serious harm. In these situations, what steps are 'reasonable' will differ to those in non-urgent cases. In emergencies, it will almost always be in the person's best interests to give urgent treatment without delay. One exception to this is when the healthcare staff giving treatment are satisfied that an advance decision to refuse treatment exists (see paragraph 6.37).

What happens in cases of negligence?

Section 5 does not provide a defence in cases of negligence—either in carrying out a particular act or by failing to act where necessary. For example, a doctor may be protected against a claim of battery for carrying out an operation that is in a person's best interests. But if they perform the operation negligently, they are not protected from a charge of negligence. So the person who lacks capacity has the same rights in cases of negligence as someone who has consented to the operation. **6.36**

What is the effect of an advance decision to refuse treatment?

Sometimes people will make an advance decision to refuse treatment while they still have capacity to do so and before they need that particular treatment. Healthcare staff must respect this decision if it is valid and applies to the proposed treatment. **6.37**

If healthcare staff are satisfied that an advance decision is valid and applies to the proposed treatment, they are not protected from liability if they give any treatment that goes against it. But they are protected from liability if they did not know about an advance decision or they are not satisfied that the advance decision is valid and applies in the current circumstances (section 26(2)). See chapter 9 for further guidance. **6.38**

What limits are there on protection from liability?

Section 6 imposes some important limitations on acts which can be carried out with protection from liability under section 5 (as described in the first part of this chapter). The key areas where acts might not be protected from liability are where there is inappropriate use of restraint or where a person who lacks capacity is deprived of their liberty. **6.39**

Using restraint

Section 6(4) of the Act states that someone is using restraint if they: **6.40**
- use force—or threaten to use force—to make someone do something that they are resisting, or
- restrict a person's freedom of movement, whether they are resisting or not.

Any action intended to restrain a person who lacks capacity will not attract protection from liability unless the following two conditions are met: **6.41**
- the person taking action must reasonably believe that restraint is necessary to prevent harm to the person who lacks capacity, and
- the amount or type of restraint used and the amount of time it lasts must be a proportionate response to the likelihood and seriousness of harm.

See paragraphs 6.44–6.48 for more explanation of the terms necessary, harm and a proportionate response.

Healthcare and social care staff should also refer to: **6.42**
- professional and other guidance on restraint or physical intervention, such as that issued by the Department of Health[21] or Welsh Assembly Government,[22] and

---

[21] For guidance on using restraint with people with learning disabilities and autistic spectrum disorder, see *Guidance for restrictive physical interventions* (published by the Department of Health and Department for Education and Skills and available at www.dh.gov.uk/ assetRoot/04/06/84/61/04068461.pdf).

[22] In Wales, the relevant guidance is the Welsh Assembly Government's *Framework for restrictive physical intervention policy and practice* (available at www.childrenfirst.wales. gov.uk/content/framework/ phys-int-e.pdf).

- limitations imposed by regulations and standards, such as the national minimum standards for care services (see chapter 14).

6.43 In addition to the requirements of the Act, the common law imposes a duty of care on healthcare and social care staff in respect of all people to whom they provide services. Therefore if a person who lacks capacity to consent has challenging behaviour, or is in the acute stages of illness causing them to act in way which may cause harm to others, staff may, under the common law, take appropriate and necessary action to restrain or remove the person, in order to prevent harm, both to the person concerned and to anyone else.

However, within this context, the common law would not provide sufficient grounds for an action that would have the effect of depriving someone of their liberty (see paragraphs 6.49–6.53).

When might restraint be 'necessary'?

6.44 Anybody considering using restraint must have objective reasons to justify that restraint is necessary. They must be able to show that the person being cared for is likely to suffer harm unless proportionate restraint is used. A carer or professional must not use restraint just so that they can do something more easily. If restraint is necessary to prevent harm to the person who lacks capacity, it must be the minimum amount of force for the shortest time possible.

Scenario: Appropriate use of restraint

Derek, a man with learning disabilities, has begun to behave in a challenging way. Staff at his care home think he might have a medical condition that is causing him distress. They take him to the doctor, who thinks that Derek might have a hormone imbalance. But the doctor needs to take a blood test to confirm this, and when he tries to take the test Derek attempts to fight him off. The results might be negative—so the test might not be necessary. But the doctor decides that a test is in Derek's best interests, because failing to treat a problem like a hormone imbalance might make it worse. It is therefore in Derek's best interests to restrain him to take the blood test. The temporary restraint is in proportion to the likely harm caused by failing to treat a possible medical condition.

What is 'harm'?

6.45 The Act does not define 'harm', because it will vary depending on the situation. For example,
- a person with learning disabilities might run into a busy road without warning, if they do not understand the dangers of cars
- a person with dementia may wander away from home and get lost, if they cannot remember where they live
- a person with manic depression might engage in excessive spending during a manic phase, causing them to get into debt
- a person may also be at risk of harm if they behave in a way that encourages others to assault or exploit them (for example, by behaving in a dangerously provocative way).

6.46 Common sense measures can often help remove the risk of harm (for example, by locking away poisonous chemicals or removing obstacles). Also, care planning should include risk assessments and set out appropriate actions to try to prevent possible risks. But it is impossible to remove all risk, and a proportionate response is needed when the risk of harm does arise.

What is a 'proportionate response'?

6.47 A 'proportionate response' means using the least intrusive type and minimum amount of restraint to achieve a specific outcome in the best interests of the person who lacks capacity. On occasions when the use of force may be necessary, carers and healthcare and social care staff should use the minimum amount of force for the shortest possible time.

For example, a carer may need to hold a person's arm while they cross the road, if the person does not understand the dangers of roads. But it would not be a proportionate response to stop the person going outdoors at all. It may be appropriate to have a secure lock on a door that faces a busy road, but it would not be a proportionate response to lock someone in a bedroom all the time to prevent them from attempting to cross the road.

Carers and healthcare and social care staff should consider less restrictive options before using restraint. Where possible, they should ask other people involved in the person's care what action they think is necessary to protect the person from harm. For example, it may be appropriate to get an advocate to work with the person to see if they can avoid or minimise the need for restraint to be used.   6.48

Scenario: Avoiding restraint

Oscar has learning disabilities. People at the college he attends sometimes cannot understand him, and he gets frustrated. Sometimes he hits the wall and hurts himself. Staff don't want to take Oscar out of class, because he says he enjoys college and is learning new skills. They have allowed his support worker to sit with him, but he still gets upset. The support worker could try to hold Oscar back. But she thinks this is too forceful, even though it would stop him hurting himself. Instead, she gets expert advice from members of the local community team. Observation helps them understand Oscar's behaviour better. They come up with a support strategy that reduces the risk of harmful behaviour and is less restrictive of his freedom.

When are acts seen as depriving a person of their liberty?

Although section 5 of the Act permits the use of restraint where it is necessary under the above conditions, section 6(5) confirms that there is no protection under the Act for actions that result in someone being deprived of their liberty (as defined by Article 5(1) of the European Convention on Human Rights). This applies not only to public authorities covered by the Human Rights Act 1998 but to everyone who might otherwise get protection under section 5 of the Act. It also applies to attorneys or deputies—they cannot give permission for an action that takes away a person's liberty.   6.49

Sometimes there is no alternative way to provide care or treatment other than depriving the person of their liberty. In this situation, some people may be detained in hospital under the Mental Health Act 1983—but this only applies to people who require hospital treatment for a mental disorder (see chapter 13). Otherwise, actions that amount to a deprivation of liberty will not be lawful unless formal authorisation is obtained.   6.50

In some cases, the Court of Protection might grant an order that permits the deprivation of a person's liberty, if it is satisfied that this is in a person's best interests.   6.51

It is difficult to define the difference between actions that amount to a restriction of someone's liberty and those that result in a deprivation of liberty. In recent legal cases, the European Court of Human Rights said that the difference was 'one of degree or intensity, not one of nature or substance'.[23] There must therefore be particular factors in the specific situation of the person concerned which provide the 'degree' or 'intensity' to result in a deprivation of liberty. In practice, this can relate to: 6.52

- the type of care being provided
- how long the situation lasts
- its effects, or

---

[23] *HL v The United Kingdom* (Application no, 45508/99). Judgement 5 October 2004, paragraph 89.

- the way in a particular situation came about.[24]

The European Court of Human Rights has identified the following as factors contributing to deprivation of liberty in its judgments on cases to date:
- restraint was used, including sedation, to admit a person who is resisting
- professionals exercised complete and effective control over care and movement for a significant period
- professionals exercised control over assessments, treatment, contacts and residence
- the person would be prevented from leaving if they made a meaningful attempt to do so
- a request by carers for the person to be discharged to their care was refused
- the person was unable to maintain social contacts because of restrictions placed on access to other people
- the person lost autonomy because they were under continuous supervision and control.[25]

6.53   The Government has announced that it intends to amend the Act to introduce new procedures and provisions for people who lack capacity to make relevant decisions but who need to be deprived of their liberty, in their best interests, otherwise than under the Mental Health Act 1983 (the so-called 'Bournewood provisions'). This chapter will be fully revised in due course to reflect those changes. Information about the Government's current proposals in respect of the Bournewood safeguards is available on the Department of Health website. This information includes draft illustrative Code of Practice guidance about the proposed safeguards. See paragraphs 13.52–13.55 for more details.

How does section 5 apply to attorneys and deputies?

6.54   Section 5 does not provide protection for actions that go against the decision of someone who has been authorised to make decisions for a person who lacks capacity to make such decision for themselves. For instance, if someone goes against the decision of an attorney acting under a Lasting Power of Attorney (LPA) (see chapter 7) or a deputy appointed by the Court of Protection (see chapter 8), they will not be protected under section 5.

6.55   Attorneys and deputies must only make decisions within the scope of the authority of the LPA or court order. Sometimes carers or healthcare and social care staff might feel that an attorney or deputy is making decisions they should not be making, or that are not in a person's best interests. If this is the case, and the disagreement cannot be settled any other way, either the carers, the staff or the attorney or deputy can apply to the Court of Protection. If the dispute concerns the provision of medical treatment, medical staff can still give life-sustaining treatment, or treatment which stops a person's condition getting seriously worse, while the court is coming to a decision (section 6(6)).

---

[24] *In HL v UK* (also known as the 'Bournewood' case), the European Court said that 'the key factor in the present case [is] that the health care professionals treating and managing the applicant exercised complete and effective control over his care and movements'. They found 'the concrete situation was that the applicant was under continuous supervision and control and was not free to leave.'

[25] These are listed in the Department of Health's draft illustrative Code of Practice guidance about the proposed safeguards. www.dh.gov.uk/assetRoot/04/14/17/64/04141764.pdf.

Who can pay for goods or services?

Carers may have to spend money on behalf of someone who lacks capacity to purchase necessary goods or services. For example, they may need to pay for a milk delivery or for a chiropodist to provide a service at the person's home. In some cases, they might have to pay for more costly arrangements such as house repairs or organising a holiday. Carers are likely to be protected from liability if their actions are properly taken under section 5, and in the best interests of the person who lacks capacity. **6.56**

In general, a contract entered into by a person who lacks capacity to make the contract cannot be enforced if the other person knows, or must be taken to have known, of the lack of capacity. Section 7 of the Act modifies this rule and states that where the contract is for 'necessary' goods or services for a person who lacks capacity to make the arrangements for themselves, that person must pay a reasonable price for them. **6.57**

What are necessary goods and services?

'Necessary' means something that is suitable to the person's condition in life (their place in society, rather than any mental or physical condition) and their actual requirements when the goods or services are provided (section 7(2)). The aim is to make sure that people can enjoy a similar standard of living and way of life to those they had before lacking capacity. For example, if a person who now lacks capacity previously chose to buy expensive designer clothes, these are still necessary goods—as long as they can still afford them. But they would not be necessary for a person who always wore cheap clothes, no matter how wealthy they were. **6.58**

Goods are not necessary if the person already has a sufficient supply of them. For example, buying one or two new pairs of shoes for a person who lacks capacity could be necessary. But a dozen pairs would probably not be necessary. **6.59**

How should payments be arranged?

If a person lacks capacity to arrange for payment for necessary goods and services, sections 5 and 8 allow a carer to arrange payment on their behalf. **6.60**

The carer must first take reasonable steps to check whether a person can arrange for payment themselves, or has the capacity to consent to the carer doing it for them. If the person lacks the capacity to consent or pay themselves, the carer must decide what goods or services would be necessary for the person and in their best interests. The carer can then lawfully deal with payment for those goods and services in one of three ways: **6.61**

- If neither the carer nor the person who lacks capacity can produce the necessary funds, the carer may promise that the person who lacks capacity will pay. A supplier may not be happy with this, or the carer may be worried that they will be held responsible for any debt. In such cases, the carer must follow the formal steps in paragraphs 6.62–6.66 below.
- If the person who lacks capacity has cash, the carer may use that money to pay for goods or services (for example, to pay the milkman or the hairdresser).
- The carer may choose to pay for the goods or services with their own money. The person who lacks capacity must pay them back. This may involve using cash in the person's possession or running up an IOU. (This is not appropriate for paid care workers, whose contracts might stop them handling their clients' money.) The carer must follow formal steps to get money held in a bank or building society account (see paragraphs 6.63–6.66 below).

Carers should keep bills, receipts and other proof of payment when paying for goods and services. They will need these documents when asking to get money back. Keeping appropriate **6.62** financial records and documentation is a requirement of the national minimum standards for care homes or domiciliary care agencies.

Access to a person's assets

6.63   The Act does not give a carer or care worker access to a person's income or assets. Nor does it allow them to sell the person's property.

6.64   Anyone wanting access to money in a person's bank or building society will need formal legal authority. They will also need legal authority to sell a person's property. Such authority could be given in a Lasting Power of Attorney (LPA) appointing an attorney to deal with property and affairs, or in an order of the Court of Protection (either a single decision of the court or an order appointing a deputy to make financial decisions for the person who lacks capacity to make such decisions).

Scenario: Being granted access to a person's assets

A storm blew some tiles off the roof of a house owned by Gordon, a man with Alzheimer's disease. He lacks capacity to arrange for repairs and claim on his insurance. The repairs are likely to be costly. Gordon's son decides to organise the repairs, and he agrees to pay because his father doesn't have enough cash available. The son could then apply to the Court of Protection for authority to claim insurance on his father's behalf and for him to be reimbursed from his father's bank account to cover the cost of the repairs once the insurance payment had been received.

6.65   Sometimes another person will already have legal control of the finances and property of a person who lacks capacity to manage their own affairs. This could be an attorney acting under a registered EPA or an appropriate LPA (see chapter 7) or a deputy appointed by the Court of Protection (see chapter 8). Or it could be someone (usually a carer) that has the right to act as an 'appointee' (under Social Security Regulations) and claim benefits for a person who lacks capacity to make their own claim and use the money on the person's behalf. But an appointee cannot deal with other assets or savings from sources other than benefits.

6.66   Section 6(6) makes clear that a family carer or other carer cannot make arrangements for goods or services to be supplied to a person who lacks capacity if this conflicts with a decision made by someone who has formal powers over the person's money and property, such as an attorney or deputy acting within the scope of their authority. Where there is no conflict and the carer has paid for necessary goods and services the carer may ask for money back from an attorney, a deputy or where relevant, an appointee.

7. WHAT DOES THE ACT SAY ABOUT LASTING POWERS OF ATTORNEY?

This chapter explains what Lasting Powers of Attorney (LPAs) are and how they should be used. It also sets out:

- how LPAs differ from Enduring Powers of Attorney (EPAs)
- the types of decisions that people can appoint attorneys to make (attorneys are also called 'donees' in the Act)
- situations in which an LPA can and cannot be used
- the duties and responsibilities of attorneys
- the standards required of attorneys, and
- measures for dealing with attorneys who don't meet appropriate standards.

This chapter also explains what should happen to EPAs that were made before the Act comes into force.

In this chapter, as throughout the Code, a person's capacity (or lack of capacity) refers specifically to their capacity to make a particular decision at the time it needs to be made.

Quick summary

Anyone asked to be an attorney should:
- consider whether they have the skills and ability to act as an attorney (especially if it is for a property and affairs LPA)
- ask themselves whether they actually want to be an attorney and take on the duties and responsibilities of the role.

Before acting under an LPA, attorneys must:
- make sure the LPA has been registered with the Public Guardian
- take all practical and appropriate steps to help the donor make the particular decision for themselves.

When acting under an LPA:
- make sure that the Act's statutory principles are followed
- check whether the person has the capacity to make that particular decision for themselves. If they do:
  - a personal welfare LPA cannot be used
  - the person must make the decision
  - a property and affairs LPA can be used even if the person has capacity to make the decision, unless they have stated in the LPA that they should make decisions for themselves when they have capacity to do so.

At all times, remember:
- anything done under the authority of the LPA must be in the person's best interests
- anyone acting as an attorney must have regard to guidance in this Code of Practice that is relevant to the decision that is to be made
- attorneys must fulfil their responsibilities and duties to the person who lacks capacity.

What is a Lasting Power of Attorney (LPA)?

7.1 Sometimes one person will want to give another person authority to make a decision on their behalf. A power of attorney is a legal document that allows them to do so. Under a power of attorney, the chosen person (the attorney or donee) can make decisions that are as valid as one made by the person (the donor).

7.2 Before the Enduring Powers of Attorney Act 1985, every power of attorney automatically became invalid as soon as the donor lacked the capacity to make their own decision. But that Act introduced the Enduring Power of Attorney (EPA). An EPA allows an attorney to make decisions about property and financial affairs even if the donor lacks capacity to manage their own affairs.

7.3 The Mental Capacity Act replaces the EPA with the Lasting Power of Attorney (LPA). It also increases the range of different types of decisions that people can authorise others to make on their behalf. As well as property and affairs (including financial matters), LPAs can also cover personal welfare (including healthcare and consent to medical treatment) for people who lack capacity to make such decisions for themselves.

7.4   The donor can choose one person or several to make different kinds of decisions. See paragraphs 7.21–7.31 for more information about personal welfare LPAs. See paragraphs 7.32–7.42 for more information about LPAs on property and affairs.

How do LPAs compare to EPAs?

7.5   There are a number of differences between LPAs and EPAs. These are summarised as follows:
- EPAs only cover property and affairs. LPAs can also cover personal welfare.
- Donors must use the relevant specific form (prescribed in regulations) to make EPAs and LPAs. There are different forms for EPAs, personal welfare LPAs and property and affairs LPAs.
- EPAs must be registered with the Public Guardian when the donor can no longer manage their own affairs (or when they start to lose capacity). But LPAs can be registered at any time before they are used – before or after the donor lacks capacity to make particular decisions that the LPA covers. If the LPA is not registered, it can't be used.
- EPAs can be used while the donor still has capacity to manage their own property and affairs, as can property and affairs LPAs, so long as the donor does not say otherwise in the LPA. But personal welfare LPAs can only be used once the donor lacks capacity to make the welfare decision in question.
- Once the Act comes into force, only LPAs can be made but existing EPAs will continue to be valid. There will be different laws and procedures for EPAs and LPAs.
- Attorneys making decisions under a registered EPA or LPA must follow the Act's principles and act in the best interests of the donor.
- The duties under the law of agency apply to attorneys of both EPAs and LPAs (see paragraphs 7.58–7.68 below).
- Decisions that the courts have made about EPAs may also affect how people use LPAs.
- Attorneys acting under an LPA have a legal duty to have regard to the guidance in this Code of Practice. EPA attorneys do not. But the Code's guidance will still be helpful to them.

How does a donor create an LPA?

7.6   The donor must also follow the right procedures for creating and registering an LPA, as set out below. Otherwise the LPA might not be valid. It is not always necessary to get legal advice. But it is a good idea for certain cases (for example, if the donor's circumstances are complicated).

7.7   Only adults aged 18 or over can make an LPA, and they can only make an LPA if they have the capacity to do so. For an LPA to be valid:
- the LPA must be a written document set out in the statutory form prescribed by regulations[26]
- the document must include prescribed information about the nature and effect of the LPA (as set out in the regulations)
- the donor must sign a statement saying that they have read the prescribed information (or somebody has read it to them) and that they want the LPA to apply when they no longer have capacity
- the document must name people (not any of the attorneys) who should be told about an application to register the LPA, or it should say that there is no-one they wish to be told
- the attorneys must sign a statement saying that they have read the prescribed information and that they understand their duties—in particular the duty to act in the donor's best interests

---

[26] The prescribed forms will be available from the Office of the Public Guardian (OPG) or from legal stationers.

- the document must include a certificate completed by an independent third party,[27] confirming that:
  - — in their opinion, the donor understands the LPA's purpose
  - — nobody used fraud or undue pressure to trick or force the donor into making the LPA and
  - — there is nothing to stop the LPA being created.

Who can be an attorney?

A donor should think carefully before choosing someone to be their attorney. An attorney should be someone who is trustworthy, competent and reliable. They should have the skills and ability to carry out the necessary tasks.   7.8

Attorneys must be at least 18 years of age. For property and affairs LPAs, the attorney could be either: 7.9

- an individual (as long as they are not bankrupt at the time the LPA is made), or
- a trust corporation (often parts of banks or other financial institutions).

If an attorney nominated under a property and affairs LPA becomes bankrupt at any point, they will no longer be allowed to act as an attorney for property and affairs. People who are bankrupt can still act as an attorney for personal welfare LPAs.

The donor must name an individual rather than a job title in a company or organisation, (for example, 'The Director of Adult Services' or 'my solicitor' would not be sufficient). A paid care worker (such as a care home manager) should not agree to act as an attorney, apart from in unusual circumstances (for example, if they are the only close relative of the donor).   7.10

Section 10(4) of the Act allows the donor to appoint two or more attorneys and to specify whether they should act 'jointly', 'jointly and severally', or 'jointly in respect of some matters and jointly and severally in respect of others'.   7.11

- Joint attorneys must always act together. All attorneys must agree decisions and sign any relevant documents.
- Joint and several attorneys can act together but may also act independently if they wish. Any action taken by any attorney alone is as valid as if they were the only attorney.

The donor may want to appoint attorneys to act jointly in some matters but jointly and severally in others. For example, a donor could choose to appoint two or more financial attorneys jointly and severally. But they might say then when selling the donor's house, the attorneys must act jointly. The donor may appoint welfare attorneys to act jointly and severally but specify that they must act jointly in relation to giving consent to surgery. If a donor who has appointed two or more attorneys does not specify how they should act, they must always act jointly (section 10(5)).   7.12

Section 10(8) says that donors may choose to name replacement attorneys to take over the duties in certain circumstances (for example, in the event of an attorney's death). The donor may name a specific attorney to be replaced, or the replacements can take over from any attorney, if necessary. Donors cannot give their attorneys the right to appoint a substitute or successor.   7.13

How should somebody register and use an LPA?

An LPA must be registered with the Office of the Public Guardian (OPG) before it can be used. An unregistered LPA will not give the attorney any legal powers to make a decision for the donor.   7.14

---

[27] Details of who may and who may not be a certificate provider will be available in regulations. The OPG will produce guidance for certificate providers on their role.

The donor can register the LPA while they are still capable, or the attorney can apply to register the LPA at any time.

7.15 There are advantages in registering the LPA soon after the donor makes it (for example, to ensure that there is no delay when the LPA needs to be used). But if this has not been done, an LPA can be registered after the donor lacks the capacity to make a decision covered by the LPA.

7.16 If an LPA is unregistered, attorneys must register it before making any decisions under the LPA. If the LPA has been registered but not used for some time, the attorney should tell the OPG when they begin to act under it—so that the attorney can be sent relevant, up-to-date information about the rules governing LPAs.

7.17 While they still have capacity, donors should let the OPG know of permanent changes of address for the donor or the attorney or any other changes in circumstances. If the donor no longer has capacity to do this, attorneys should report any such changes to the OPG. Examples include an attorney of a property and affairs LPA becoming bankrupt or the ending of a marriage between the donor and their attorney. This will help keep OPG records up to date, and will make sure that attorneys do not make decisions that they no longer have the authority to make.

What guidance should an attorney follow?

7.18 Section 9(4) states that attorneys must meet the requirements set out in the Act. Most importantly, they have to follow the statutory principles (section 1) and make decisions in the best interests of the person who lacks capacity (section 4). They must also respect any conditions or restrictions that the LPA document contains. See chapter 2 for guidance on how to apply the Act's principles.

7.19 Chapter 3 gives suggestions of ways to help people make their own decisions in accordance with the Act's second principle . Attorneys should also refer to the guidance in chapter 4 when assessing the donor's capacity to make particular decisions, and in particular, should follow the steps suggested for establishing a 'reasonable belief' that the donor lacks capacity (see paragraphs 4.44–4.45). Assessments of capacity or best interests must not be based merely on:
- a donor's age or appearance, or
- unjustified assumptions about any condition they might have or their behaviour.

7.20 When deciding what is in the donor's best interests, attorneys should refer to the guidance in chapter 5. In particular, they must consider the donor's past and present wishes and feelings, beliefs and values. Where practical and appropriate, they should consult with:
- anyone involved in caring for the donor
- close relatives and anyone else with an interest in their welfare
- other attorneys appointed by the donor.

See paragraphs 7.52–7.68 for a description of an attorney's duties.

Scenario: Making decisions in a donor's best interests

Mr Young has been a member of the Green Party for a long time. He has appointed his solicitor as his attorney under a property and affairs LPA. But Mr Young did not state in the LPA that investments made on his behalf must be ethical investments. When the attorney assesses his client's best interests, however, the attorney considers the donor's past wishes, values and beliefs. He makes sure that he only invests in companies that are socially and environmentally responsible.

What decisions can an LPA attorney make?

Personal welfare LPAs

LPAs can be used to appoint attorneys to make decisions about personal welfare, which can 7.21 include healthcare and medical treatment decisions. Personal welfare LPAs might include decisions about:

- where the donor should live and who they should live with
- the donor's day-to-day care, including diet and dress
- who the donor may have contact with
- consenting to or refusing medical examination and treatment on the donor's behalf
- arrangements needed for the donor to be given medical, dental or optical treatment
- assessments for and provision of community care services
- whether the donor should take part in social activities, leisure activities, education or training
- the donor's personal correspondence and papers
- rights of access to personal information about the donor, or
- complaints about the donor's care or treatment.

The standard form for personal welfare LPAs allows attorneys to make decisions about anything 7.22 that relates to the donor's personal welfare. But donors can add restrictions or conditions to areas where they would not wish the attorney to have the power to act. For example, a donor might only want an attorney to make decisions about their social care and not their healthcare. There are particular rules for LPAs authorising an attorney to make decisions about life-sustaining treatment (see paragraphs 7.30–7.31 below).

A general personal welfare LPA gives the attorney the right to make all of the decisions set out 7.23 above although this is not a full list of the actions they can take or decisions they can make. However, a personal welfare LPA can only be used at a time when the donor lacks capacity to make a specific welfare decision.

Scenario: Denying attorneys the right to make certain decisions

Mrs Hutchison is in the early stages of Alzheimer's disease. She is anxious to get all her affairs in order while she still has capacity to do so. She makes a personal welfare LPA, appointing her daughter as attorney. But Mrs Hutchison knows that her daughter doesn't always get on with some members of the family – and she wouldn't want her daughter to stop those relatives from seeing her. She states in the LPA that her attorney does not have the authority to decide who can contact her or visit her. If her daughter wants to prevent anyone having contact with Mrs Hutchison, she must ask the Court of Protection to decide.

Before making a decision under a personal welfare LPA, the attorney must be sure that: 7.24
- the LPA has been registered with the OPG
- the donor lacks the capacity to make the particular decision or the attorney reasonably believes that the donor lacks capacity to take the decisions covered by the LPA (having applied the Act's principles), and
- they are making the decision in the donor's best interests.

When healthcare or social care staff are involved in preparing a care plan for someone who has 7.25 appointed a personal welfare attorney, they must first assess whether the donor has capacity to agree to the care plan or to parts of it. If the donor lacks capacity, professionals must then consult the attorney and get their agreement to the care plan. They will also need to consult the attorney when considering what action is in the person's best interests.

Personal welfare LPAs that authorise an attorney to make healthcare decisions

7.26 A personal welfare LPA allows attorneys to make decisions to accept or refuse healthcare or treatment unless the donor has stated clearly in the LPA that they do not want the attorney to make these decisions.

7.27 Even where the LPA includes healthcare decisions, attorneys do not have the right to consent to or refuse treatment in situations where:

- the donor has capacity to make the particular healthcare decision (section 11(7)(a)) An attorney has no decision-making power if the donor can make their own treatment decisions.
- the donor has made an advance decision to refuse the proposed treatment (section 11(7)(b))
- An attorney cannot consent to treatment if the donor has made a valid and applicable advance decision to refuse a specific treatment (see chapter 9). But if the donor made an LPA after the advance decision, and gave the attorney the right to consent to or refuse the treatment, the attorney can choose not to follow the advance decision.
- a decision relates to life-sustaining treatment (section 11(7)(c))
- An attorney has no power to consent to or refuse life-sustaining treatment, unless the LPA document expressly authorises this (See paragraphs 7.30–7.31 below.)
- the donor is detained under the Mental Health Act (section 28) An attorney cannot consent to or refuse treatment for a mental disorder for a patient detained under the Mental Health Act 1983 (see also chapter 13).7

7.28 LPAs cannot give attorneys the power to demand specific forms of medical treatment that healthcare staff do not believe are necessary or appropriate for the donor's particular condition.

7.29 Attorneys must always follow the Act's principles and make decisions in the donor's best interests. If healthcare staff disagree with the attorney's assessment of best interests, they should discuss the case with other medical experts and/or get a formal second opinion. Then they should discuss the matter further with the attorney. If they cannot settle the disagreement, they can apply to the Court of Protection (see paragraphs 7.45–7.49 below). While the court is coming to a decision, healthcare staff can give life-sustaining treatment to prolong the donor's life or stop their condition getting worse.

Personal welfare LPAs that authorise an attorney to make decisions about life-sustaining treatment

7.30 An attorney can only consent to or refuse life-sustaining treatment on behalf of the donor if, when making the LPA, the donor has specifically stated in the LPA document that they want the attorney to have this authority.

7.31 As with all decisions, an attorney must act in the donor's best interests when making decisions about such treatment. This will involve applying the best interests checklist (see chapter 5) and consulting with carers, family members and others interested in the donor's welfare. In particular, the attorney must not be motivated in any way by the desire to bring about the donor's death (see paragraphs 5.29–5.36). Anyone who doubts that the attorney is acting in the donor's best interests can apply to the Court of Protection for a decision.

Scenario: Making decisions about life-sustaining treatment

Mrs Joshi has never trusted doctors. She prefers to rely on alternative therapies. Because she saw her father suffer after invasive treatment for cancer, she is clear that she would refuse such treatment herself. She is diagnosed with cancer and discusses her wishes with her husband. Mrs Joshi knows that he would respect her wishes if he ever had to make a decision about her treatment. She makes a personal welfare LPA appointing him as her attorney with authority to make all her welfare and healthcare decisions. She includes a specific statement authorising him to consent to or refuse life-sustaining treatment. He will then be able to consider her views and make decisions about treatment in her best interests if she later lacks capacity to make those decisions herself.

Property and affairs LPAs

A donor can make an LPA giving an attorney the right to make decisions about property and affairs (including financial matters). Unless the donor states otherwise, once the LPA is registered, the attorney is allowed to make all decisions about the donor's property and affairs even if the donor still has capacity to make the decisions for themselves. In this situation, the LPA will continue to apply when the donor no longer has capacity.

7.32

Alternatively a donor can state in the LPA document that the LPA should only apply when they lack capacity to make a relevant decision. It is the donor's responsibility to decide how their capacity should then be assessed. For example, the donor may trust the attorney to carry out an assessment, or they may say that the LPA only applies if their GP or another doctor confirms in writing that they lack capacity to make specific decisions about property or finances. Financial institutions may wish to see the written confirmation before recognising the attorney's authority to act under the LPA.

7.33

The fact that someone has made a property and affairs LPA does not mean that they cannot continue to carry out financial transactions for themselves. The donor may have full capacity, but perhaps anticipates that they may lack capacity at some future time. Or they may have fluctuating or partial capacity and therefore be able to make some decisions (or at some times), but need an attorney to make others (or at other times). The attorney should allow and encourage the donor to do as much as possible, and should only act when the donor asks them to or to make those decisions the donor lacks capacity to make. However, in other cases, the donor may wish to hand over responsibility for all decisions to the attorney, even those they still have capacity to make.

7.34

If the donor restricts the decisions an attorney can make, banks may ask the attorney to sign a declaration that protects the bank from liability if the attorney misuses the account.[28]

7.35

If a donor does not restrict decisions the attorney can make, the attorney will be able to decide on any or all of the person's property and financial affairs. This might include:

7.36

- buying or selling property
- opening, closing or operating any bank, building society or other account
- giving access to the donor's financial information
- claiming, receiving and using (on the donor's behalf) all benefits, pensions, allowances and rebates (unless the Department for Work and Pensions has already appointed someone and everyone is happy for this to continue)
- receiving any income, inheritance or other entitlement on behalf of the donor
- dealing with the donor's tax affairs
- paying the donor's mortgage, rent and household expenses
- insuring, maintaining and repairing the donor's property
- investing the donor's savings
- making limited gifts on the donor's behalf (but see paragraphs 7.40–7.42 below)
- paying for private medical care and residential care or nursing home fees
- applying for any entitlement to funding for NHS care, social care or adaptations
- using the donor's money to buy a vehicle or any equipment or other help they need
- repaying interest and capital on any loan taken out by the donor.

---

[28] See British Banking Association's guidance for bank staff on *'Banking for mentally incapacitated and learning disabled customers'*.

7.37   A general property and affairs LPA will allow the attorney to carry out any or all of the actions above (although this is not a full list of the actions they can take). However, the donor may want to specify the types of powers they wish the attorney to have, or to exclude particular types of decisions. If the donor holds any assets as trustee, they should get legal advice about how the LPA may affect this.

7.38   The attorney must make these decisions personally and cannot generally give someone else authority to carry out their duties (see paragraphs 7.61–7.62 below). But if the donor wants the attorney to be able to give authority to a specialist to make specific decisions, they need to state this clearly in the LPA document (for example, appointing an investment manager to make particular investment decisions).

7.39   Donors may like to appoint someone (perhaps a family member or a professional) to go through their accounts with the attorney from time to time. This might help to reassure donors that somebody will check their financial affairs when they lack capacity to do so. It may also be helpful for attorneys to arrange a regular check that everything is being done properly. The donor should ensure that the person is willing to carry out this role and is prepared to ask for the accounts if the attorney does not provide them. They should include this arrangement in the signed LPA document. The LPA should also say whether the person can charge a fee for this service.

What gifts can an attorney make under a property and affairs LPA?

7.40   An attorney can only make gifts of the donor's money or belongings to people who are related to or connected with the donor (including the attorney) on specific occasions, including:
- births or birthdays
- weddings or wedding anniversaries
- civil partnership ceremonies or anniversaries, or
- any other occasion when families, friends or associates usually give presents (section 12(3)(b)).

7.41   If the donor previously made donations to any charity regularly or from time to time, the attorney can make donations from the person's funds. This also applies if the donor could have been expected to make such payments (section 12(2)(b)). But the value of any gift or donation must be reasonable and take into account the size of the donor's estate. For example, it would not be reasonable to buy expensive gifts at Christmas if the donor was living on modest means and had to do without essential items in order to pay for them.

7.42   The donor cannot use the LPA to make more extensive gifts than those allowed under section 12 of the Act. But they can impose stricter conditions or restrictions on the attorney's powers to make gifts. They should state these restrictions clearly in the LPA document when they are creating it. When deciding on appropriate gifts, the attorney should consider the donor's wishes and feelings to work out what would be in the donor's best interests. The attorney can apply to the Court of Protection for permission to make gifts that are not included in the LPA (for example, for tax planning purposes).

Are there any other restrictions on attorneys' powers?

7.43   Attorneys are not protected from liability if they do something that is intended to restrain the donor, unless:
- the attorney reasonably believes that the donor lacks capacity to make the decision in question, and
- the attorney reasonably believes that restraint is necessary to prevent harm to the donor, and
- the type of restraint used is in proportion to the likelihood and the seriousness of the harm.

If an attorney needs to make a decision or take action which may involve the use of restraint, they should take account of the guidance set out in chapter 6.

Attorneys have no authority to take actions that result in the donor being deprived of their liberty. Any deprivation of liberty will only be lawful if this has been properly authorised and there is other protection available for the person who lacks capacity. An example would be the protection around detention under the Mental Health Act 1983 (see chapter 13) or a court ruling. Chapter 6 gives more guidance on working out whether an action is restraint or a deprivation of liberty. 7.44

What powers does the Court of Protection have over LPAs?

The Court of Protection has a range of powers to: 7.45
- determine whether an LPA is valid
- give directions about using the LPA, and
- to remove an attorney (for example, if the attorney does not act in the best interests of the donor).

Chapter 8 gives more information about the Court of Protection's powers.

If somebody has doubts over whether an LPA is valid, they can ask the court to decide whether 7.46 the LPA:
- meets the Act's requirements
- has been revoked (cancelled) by the donor, or
- has come to an end for any other reason.

The court can also stop somebody registering an LPA or rule that an LPA is invalid if: 7.47
- the donor made the LPA as a result of undue pressure or fraud, or
- the attorney behaves, has behaved or is planning to behave in a way that goes against their duties or is not in the donor's best interests.

The court can also clarify an LPA's meaning, if it is not clear, and it can tell attorneys how they 7.48 should use an LPA. If an attorney thinks that an LPA does not give them enough powers, they can ask the court to extend their powers—if the donor no longer has capacity to authorise this. The court can also authorise an attorney to give a gift that the Act does not normally allow (section 12(2)), if it is in the donor's best interests.

All attorneys should keep records of their dealings with the donor's affairs (see also paragraph 7.67 7.49 below). The court can order attorneys to produce records (for example, financial accounts) and to provide specific reports, information or documentation. If somebody has concerns about an attorney's payment or expenses, the court could resolve the matter.

What responsibilities do attorneys have?

A donor cannot insist on somebody agreeing to become an attorney. It is down to the proposed 7.50 attorney to decide whether to take on this responsibility. When an attorney accepts the role by signing the LPA document, this is confirmation that they are willing to act under the LPA once it is registered. An attorney can withdraw from the appointment if they ever become unable or unwilling to act, but if the LPA has been registered they must follow the correct procedures for withdrawing. (see paragraph 7.66 below).

Once the attorney starts to act under an LPA, they must meet certain standards. If they don't 7.51 carry out the duties below, they could be removed from the role. In some circumstances they could face charges of fraud or negligence.

7.52 Attorneys acting under an LPA have a duty to:
- follow the Act's statutory principles (see chapter 2)
- make decisions in the donor's best interests
- have regard to the guidance in the Code of Practice
- only make those decisions the LPA gives them authority to make.

Principles and best interests

7.53 Attorneys must act in accordance with the Act's statutory principles (section 1) and in the best interests of the donor (the steps for working out best interests are set out in section 4). In particular, attorneys must consider whether the donor has capacity to make the decision for themselves. If not, they should consider whether the donor is likely to regain capacity to make the decision in the future. If so, it may be possible to delay the decision until the donor can make it.

The Code of Practice

7.54 As well as this chapter, attorneys should pay special attention to the following guidance set out in the Code:
- chapter 2, which sets out how the Act's principles should be applied
- chapter 3, which describes the steps which can be taken to try to help the person make decisions for themselves
- chapter 4, which describes the Act's definition of lack of capacity and gives guidance on assessing capacity, and
- chapter 5, which gives guidance on working out the donor's best interests.

7.55 In some circumstances, attorneys might also find it useful to refer to guidance in:
- chapter 6, which explains when attorneys who have caring responsibilities may have protection from liability and gives guidance on the few circumstances when the Act allows restraint in connection with care and treatment
- chapter 8, which gives a summary of the Court of Protection's powers relating to LPAs
- chapter 9, which explains how LPAs may be affected if the donor has made an advance decision to refuse treatment, and
- chapter 15, which describes ways to settle disagreements.

Only making decisions covered by an LPA

7.56 A personal welfare attorney has no authority to make decisions about a donor's property and affairs (such as their finances). A property and affairs attorney has no authority in decisions about a donor's personal care. (But the same person could be appointed in separate LPAs to carry out both these roles.) Under any LPA, the attorney will have authority in a wide range of decisions. But if a donor includes restrictions in the LPA document, this will limit the attorney's authority (section 9(4)(b)). If the attorney thinks that they need greater powers, they can apply to the Court of Protection which may decide to give the attorney the authority required or alternatively to appoint the attorney as a deputy with the necessary powers (see chapter 8).

7.57 It is good practice for decision-makers to consult attorneys about any decision or action, whether or not it is covered by the LPA. This is because an attorney is likely to have known the donor for some time and may have important information about their wishes and feelings. Researchers can also consult attorneys if they are thinking about involving the donor in research (see chapter 11).

Scenario: Consulting attorneys

Mr Varadi makes a personal welfare LPA appointing his son and daughter as his joint attorneys. He also makes a property and affairs LPA, appointing his son and his solicitor to act jointly and severally. He registers the property and affairs LPA straight away, so his attorneys can help with financial decisions. Two years later, Mr Varadi has a stroke, is unable to speak and has difficulty communicating his wishes. He also lacks the capacity to make decisions about treatment. The attorneys apply to register the personal welfare LPA. Both feel that they should delay decisions about Mr Varadi's future care, because he might regain capacity to make the decisions himself. But they agree that some decisions cannot wait. Although the solicitor has no authority to make welfare decisions, the welfare attorneys consult him about their father's best interests. They speak to him about immediate treatment decisions and their suggestion to delay making decisions about his future care. Similarly, the property and affairs attorneys consult the daughter about the financial decisions that Mr Varadi does not have the capacity to make himself.

What are an attorney's other duties?

An attorney appointed under an LPA is acting as the chosen agent of the donor and therefore, under the law of agency, the attorney has certain duties towards the donor. An attorney takes on a role which carries a great deal of power, which they must use carefully and responsibly. They have a duty to: 7.58

- apply certain standards of care and skill (duty of care) when making decisions
- carry out the donor's instructions
- not take advantage of their position and not benefit themselves, but benefit the donor (fiduciary duty)
- not delegate decisions, unless authorised to do so
- act in good faith
- respect confidentiality
- comply with the directions of the Court of Protection
- not give up the role without telling the donor and the court.
  In relation to property and affairs LPAs, they have a duty to:
- keep accounts
- keep the donor's money and property separate from their own.

Duty of care

'Duty of care' means applying a certain standard of care and skill—depending on whether the attorney is paid for their services or holds relevant professional qualifications.   7.59

- Attorneys who are not being paid must apply the same care, skill and diligence they would use to make decisions about their own life. An attorney who claims to have particular skills or qualifications must show greater skill in those particular areas than someone who does not make such claims.
- If attorneys are being paid for their services, they should demonstrate a higher degree of care and skill.
- Attorneys who undertake their duties in the course of their professional work (such as solicitors or corporate trustees) must display professional competence and follow their profession's rules and standards.

Fiduciary duty

7.60 A fiduciary duty means attorneys must not take advantage of their position. Nor should they put themselves in a position where their personal interests conflict with their duties. They also must not allow any other influences to affect the way in which they act as an attorney. Decisions should always benefit the donor, and not the attorney. Attorneys must not profit or get any personal benefit from their position, apart from receiving gifts where the Act allows it, whether or not it is at the donor's expense.

Duty not to delegate

7.61 Attorneys cannot usually delegate their authority to someone else. They must carry out their duties personally. The attorney may seek professional or expert advice (for example, investment advice from a financial adviser or advice on medical treatment from a doctor). But they cannot, as a general rule, allow someone else to make a decision that they have been appointed to make, unless this has been specifically authorised by the donor in the LPA.

7.62 In certain circumstances, attorneys may have limited powers to delegate (for example, through necessity or unforeseen circumstances, or for specific tasks which the donor would not have expected the attorney to attend to personally). But attorneys cannot usually delegate any decisions that rely on their discretion.

Duty of good faith

7.63 Acting in good faith means acting with honesty and integrity. For example, an attorney must try to make sure that their decisions do not go against a decision the donor made while they still had capacity (unless it would be in the donor's best interests to do so).

Duty of confidentiality

7.64 Attorneys have a duty to keep the donor's affairs confidential, unless:
- before they lost capacity to do so, the donor agreed that some personal or financial information may be revealed for a particular purpose (for example, they have named someone they want to check their financial accounts), or
- there is some other good reason to release it (for example, it is in the public interest or the best interests of the person who lacks capacity, or there is a risk of harm to the donor or others).

In the latter circumstances, it may be advisable for the attorney to get legal advice. Chapter 16 gives more information about confidentiality.

Duty to comply with the directions of the Court of Protection

7.65 Under sections 22 and 23 of the Act, the Court of Protection has wide-ranging powers to decide on issues relating to the operation or validity of an LPA. It can also:
- give extra authority to attorneys
- order them to produce records (for example, financial accounts), or
- order them to provide specific information or documentation to the court.

Attorneys must comply with any decision or order that the court makes.

Duty not to disclaim without notifying the donor and the OPG

7.66 Once someone becomes an attorney, they cannot give up that role without notifying the donor and the OPG. If they decide to give up their role, they must follow the relevant guidance available from the OPG.

Duty to keep accounts

Property and affairs attorneys must keep accounts of transactions carried out on the donor's behalf. 7.67
Sometimes the Court of Protection will ask to see accounts. If the attorney is not a financial expert
and the donor's affairs are relatively straightforward, a record of the donor's income and expenditure
(for example, through bank statements) may be enough. The more complicated the donor's affairs,
the more detailed the accounts may need to be.

Duty to keep the donor's money and property separate

Property and affairs attorneys should usually keep the donor's money and property separate from 7.68
their own or anyone else's. There may be occasions where donors and attorneys have agreed in the
past to keep their money in a joint bank account (for example, if a husband is acting as his wife's
attorney). It might be possible to continue this under the LPA. But in most circumstances,
attorneys must keep finances separate to avoid any possibility of mistakes or confusion.

How does the Act protect donors from abuse?

What should someone do if they think an attorney is abusing their position?

Attorneys are in a position of trust, so there is always a risk of them abusing their position. Donors 7.69
can help prevent abuse by carefully choosing a suitable and trustworthy attorney. But others have
a role to play in looking out for possible signs of abuse or exploitation, and reporting any concerns
to the OPG. The OPG will then follow this up in co-operation with relevant agencies.

Signs that an attorney may be exploiting the donor (or failing to act in the donor's best interests) 7.70
include:

- stopping relatives or friends contacting the donor – for example, the attorney may prevent
  contact or the donor may suddenly refuse visits or telephone calls from family and friends for
  no reason
- sudden unexplained changes in living arrangements (for example, someone moves in to care for
  a donor they've had little contact with)
- not allowing healthcare or social care staff to see the donor
- taking the donor out of hospital against medical advice, while the donor is having necessary
  medical treatment
- unpaid bills (for example, residential care or nursing home fees)
- an attorney opening a credit card account for the donor
- spending money on things that are not obviously related to the donor's needs
- the attorney spending money in an unusual or extravagant way
- transferring financial assets to another country.

Somebody who suspects abuse should contact the OPG immediately. The OPG may direct a 7.71
Court of Protection Visitor to visit an attorney to investigate. In cases of suspected physical or
sexual abuse, theft or serious fraud, the person should contact the police. They might also be able
to refer the matter to the relevant local adult protection authorities.

In serious cases, the OPG will refer the matter to the Court of Protection. The court may revoke 7.72
(cancel) the LPA or (through the OPG) prevent it being registered, if it decides that:

- the LPA does not meet the legal requirements for creating an LPA
- the LPA has been revoked or come to an end for any other reason
- somebody used fraud or undue pressure to get the donor to make the LPA
- the attorney has done something that they do not have authority to do, or

- the attorney has behaved or is planning to behave in a way that is not in the donor's best interests.

The court might then consider whether the authority previously given to an attorney can be managed by:

- the court making a single decision, or
- appointing a deputy.

What should an attorney do if they think someone else is abusing the donor?

7.73   An attorney who thinks someone else is abusing or exploiting the donor should report it to the OPG and ask for advice on what action they should take. They should contact the police if they suspect physical or sexual abuse, theft or serious fraud. They might also be able to refer the matter to local adult protection authorities.

7.74   Chapter 13 gives more information about protecting vulnerable people from abuse, ill treatment or neglect. It also discusses the duties and responsibilities of the various agencies involved, including the OPG and local authorities. In particular, it is a criminal offence (with a maximum penalty of five years' imprisonment, a fine, or both) for anyone (including attorneys) to wilfully neglect or ill-treat a person in their care who lacks capacity to make decisions for themselves (section 44).

What happens to existing EPAs once the Act comes into force?

7.75   Once the Act comes into force, it will not be possible to make new EPAs. Only LPAs can then be made.

7.76   Some donors will have created EPAs before the Act came into force with the expectation that their chosen attorneys will manage their property and affairs in the future, whether or not they have capacity to do so themselves.

7.77   If donors still have capacity after the Act comes into force, they can cancel the EPA and make an LPA covering their property and affairs. They should also notify attorneys and anyone else aware of the EPA (for example, a bank) that they have cancelled it.

7.78   Some donors will choose not to cancel their EPA or they may already lack the capacity to do so. In such cases, the Act allows existing EPAs, whether registered or not, to continue to be valid so that attorneys can meet the donor's expectations (Schedule 4). An EPA must be registered with the OPG when the attorney thinks the donor lacks capacity to manage their own affairs, or is beginning to lack capacity to do so.

7.79   EPA attorneys may find guidance in this chapter helpful. In particular, all attorneys must comply with the duties described in paragraphs 7.58–7.68 above. EPA attorneys can also be found liable under section 44 of the new Act, which sets out the new criminal offences of ill treatment and wilful neglect. The OPG has produced guidance on EPAs (see Annex A for details of publications and contact information).

8. WHAT IS THE ROLE OF THE COURT OF PROTECTION AND COURT-APPOINTED DEPUTIES?

This chapter describes the role of the Court of Protection and the role of court-appointed deputies. It explains the powers that the court has and how to make an application to the court. It also looks at how the court appoints a deputy to act and make decisions on behalf of someone who lacks capacity to make those decisions. In particular, it gives guidance on a deputy's duties and the consequences of not carrying them out responsibly.

The Office of the Public Guardian (OPG) produces detailed guidance for deputies. See the Annex for more details of the publications and how to get them. Further details on the court's procedures are given in the Court of Protection Rules and Practice Directions issued by the court.

In this chapter, as throughout the Code, a person's capacity (or lack of capacity) refers specifically to their capacity to make a particular decision at the time it needs to be made.

Quick summary

The Court of Protection has powers to:
- decide whether a person has capacity to make a particular decision for themselves
- make declarations, decisions or orders on financial or welfare matters affecting people who lack capacity to make such decisions
- appoint deputies to make decisions for people lacking capacity to make those decisions
- decide whether an LPA or EPA is valid, and
- remove deputies or attorneys who fail to carry out their duties.

Before accepting an appointment as a deputy, a person the court nominates should consider whether:
- they have the skills and ability to carry out a deputy's duties (especially in relation to property and affairs)
- they actually want to take on the duties and responsibilities.

Anyone acting as a deputy must:
- make sure that they only make those decisions that they are authorised to make by the order of the court
- make sure that they follow the Act's statutory principles, including:
  — considering whether the person has capacity to make a particular decision for themselves. If they do, the deputy should allow them to do so unless the person agrees that the deputy should make the decision
  — taking all possible steps to try to help a person make the particular decision
- always make decisions in the person's best interests
- have regard to guidance in the Code of Practice that is relevant to the situation
- fulfil their duties towards the person concerned (in particular the duty of care and fiduciary duties to respect the degree of trust placed in them by the court).

What is the Court of Protection?

Section 45 of the Act sets up a specialist court, the Court of Protection, to deal with decision-making for adults (and children in a few cases) who may lack capacity to make specific decisions for themselves. The new Court of Protection replaces the old court of the same name, which only

8.1

dealt with decisions about the property and financial affairs of people lacking capacity to manage their own affairs. As well as property and affairs, the new court also deals with serious decisions affecting healthcare and personal welfare matters. These were previously dealt with by the High Court under its inherent jurisdiction.

8.2 The new Court of Protection is a superior court of record and is able to establish precedent (it can set examples for future cases) and build up expertise in all issues related to lack of capacity. It has the same powers, rights, privileges and authority as the High Court. When reaching any decision, the court must apply all the statutory principles set out in section 1 of the Act. In particular, it must make a decision in the best interests of the person who lacks capacity to make the specific decision. There will usually be a fee for applications to the court.[29]

How can somebody make an application to the Court of Protection?

8.3 In most cases concerning personal welfare matters, the core principles of the Act and the processes set out in chapters 5 and 6 will be enough to:
- help people take action or make decisions in the best interests of someone who lacks capacity to make decisions about their own care or treatment, or
- find ways of settling disagreements about such actions or decisions.

But an application to the Court of Protection may be necessary for:
- particularly difficult decisions
- disagreements that cannot be resolved in any other way (see chapter 15), or
- situations where ongoing decisions may need to be made about the personal welfare of a person who lacks capacity to make decisions for themselves.

8.4 An order of the court will usually be necessary for matters relating to the property and affairs (including financial matters) of people who lack capacity to make specific financial decisions for themselves, unless:
- their only income is state benefits (see paragraph 8.36 below), or
- they have previously made an Enduring Power of Attorney (EPA) or a Lasting Power of Attorney (LPA) to give somebody authority to manage their property and affairs (see chapter 7).

8.5 Receivers appointed by the court before the Act commences will be treated as deputies. But they will keep their existing powers and duties. They must meet the requirements set out in the Act and, in particular, follow the statutory principles and act in the best interests of the person for whom they have been appointed. They must also have regard to guidance in this chapter and other parts of the Code of Practice. Further guidance for receivers is available from the OPG.

Cases involving young people aged 16 or 17

8.6 Either a court dealing with family proceedings or the Court of Protection can hear cases involving people aged 16 or 17 who lack capacity. In some cases, the Court of Protection can hear cases involving people younger than 16 (for example, when somebody needs to be appointed to make longer-term decisions about their financial affairs). Under section 21 of the Mental Capacity Act, the Court of Protection can transfer cases concerning children to a court that has powers under the Children Act 1989. Such a court can also transfer cases to the Court of Protection, if necessary. Chapter 12 gives more detail on cases where this might apply.

---

[29] Details of the fees charged by the court, and the circumstances in which the fees may be waived or remitted, are available from the Office of the Public Guardian (OPG).

Who should make the application?

The person making the application will vary, depending on the circumstances. For example, a **8.7** person wishing to challenge a finding that they lack capacity may apply to the court, supported by others where necessary. Where there is a disagreement among family members, for example, a family member may wish to apply to the court to settle the disagreement—bearing in mind the need, in most cases, to get permission beforehand (see paragraphs 8.11–8.12 below).

For cases about serious or major decisions concerning medical treatment (see paragraphs 8.18– **8.8** 8.24 below), the NHS Trust or other organisation responsible for the patient's care will usually make the application. If social care staff are concerned about a decision that affects the welfare of a person who lacks capacity, the relevant local authority should make the application.

For decisions about the property and affairs of someone who lacks capacity to manage their own **8.9** affairs, the applicant will usually be the person (for example, family carer) who needs specific authority from the court to deal with the individual's money or property.

If the applicant is the person who is alleged to lack capacity, they will always be a party to the **8.10** court proceedings. In all other cases, the court will decide whether the person who lacks, or is alleged to lack, capacity should be involved as a party to the case. Where the person is a party to the case, the court may appoint the Official Solicitor to act for them.

Who must ask the court for permission to make an application?

As a general rule, potential applicants must get the permission of the Court of Protection before **8.11** making an application (section 50). People who the Act says do not need to ask for permission include:

- a person who lacks, or is alleged to lack, capacity in relation to a specific decision or action (or anyone with parental responsibility, if the person is under 18 years)
- the donor of the LPA an application relates to—or their attorney
- a deputy who has been appointed by the court to act for the person concerned, and
- a person named in an existing court order relating to the application. The Court of Protection Rules also set out specific types of cases where permission is not required.

When deciding whether to give permission for an application, the court must consider: **8.12**

- the applicant's connection to the person the application is about
- the reasons for the application
- whether a proposed order or direction of the court will benefit the person the application is about, and
- whether it is possible to get that benefit another way.

Scenario: Considering whether to give permission for an application

Sunita, a young Asian woman, has always been close to her older brother, who has severe learning disabilities and lives in a care home. Two years ago, Sunita married a non-Asian man, and her family cut off contact with her. She still wants to visit her brother and to be consulted about his care and what is in his best interests. But the family is not letting her. The Court of Protection gives Sunita permission to apply to the court for an order allowing her contact with her brother.

What powers does the Court of Protection have?

The Court of Protection may: **8.13**

- make declarations, decisions and orders on financial and welfare matters affecting people who lack, or are alleged to lack, capacity (the lack of capacity must relate to the particular issue being presented to the court)

- appoint deputies to make decisions for people who lack capacity to make those decisions
- remove deputies or attorneys who act inappropriately.

The Court can also hear cases about LPAs and EPAs. The court's powers concerning EPAs are set out in Schedule 4 of the Act.

8.14   The court must always follow the statutory principles set out in section 1 of the Act (see chapter 2) and make the decision in the best interests of the person concerned (see chapter 5).

What declarations can the court make?

8.15   Section 15 of the Act provides the court with powers to make a declaration (a ruling) on specific issues. For example, it can make a declaration as to whether a person has capacity to make a particular decision or give consent for or take a particular action. The court will require evidence of any assessment of the person's capacity and may wish to see relevant written evidence (for example, a diary, letters or other papers). If the court decides the person has capacity to make that decision, they will not take the case further. The person can now make the decision for themselves.

8.16   Applications concerning a person's capacity are likely to be rare—people can usually settle doubts and disagreements informally (see chapters 4 and 15). But an application may be relevant if:

- a person wants to challenge a decision that they lack capacity
- professionals disagree about a person's capacity to make a specific (usually serious) decision
- there is a dispute over whether the person has capacity (for example, between family members).

8.17   The court can also make a declaration as to whether a specific act relating to a person's care or treatment is lawful (either where somebody has carried out the action or is proposing to). Under section 15, this can include an omission or failure to provide care or treatment that the person needs.

This power to decide on the lawfulness of an act is particularly relevant for major medical treatment cases where there is doubt or disagreement over whether the treatment would be in the person's best interests. Healthcare staff can still give life-sustaining treatment, or treatment which stops a person's condition getting seriously worse, while the court is coming to a decision.

Serious healthcare and treatment decisions

8.18   Prior to the Act coming into force, the courts decided that some decisions relating to the provision of medical treatment were so serious that in each case, an application should be made to the court for a declaration that the proposed action was lawful before that action was taken. Cases involving any of the following decisions should therefore be brought before a court:

- decisions about the proposed withholding or withdrawal of artificial nutrition and hydration (ANH) from patients in a permanent vegetative state (PVS)
- cases involving organ or bone marrow donation by a person who lacks capacity to consent
- cases involving the proposed non-therapeutic sterilisation of a person who lacks capacity to consent to this (e.g. for contraceptive purposes) and
- all other cases where there is a doubt or dispute about whether a particular treatment will be in a person's best interests.

8.19   The case law requirement to seek a declaration in cases involving the withholding or withdrawing of artificial nutrition and hydration to people in a permanent vegetative state is unaffected by the Act[30] and as a matter of practice, these cases should be put to the Court of Protection for approval.

---

[30] *Airedale NHS Trust v Bland* [1993] AC 789 31.

Cases involving organ or bone marrow donation by a person who lacks capacity to consent should also be referred to the Court of Protection. Such cases involve medical procedures being performed on a person who lacks capacity to consent but which would benefit a third party (though would not necessarily directly or physically benefit the person who lacks capacity). However, sometimes such procedures may be in the person's overall best interests (see chapter 5). For example, the person might receive emotional, social and psychological benefits as a result of the help they have given, and in some cases the person may experience only minimal physical discomfort. 8.20

A prime example of this is the case of *Re Y*[31] where it was found to be in Y's best interests for her to donate bone marrow to her sister. The court decided that it was in Y's best interests to continue to receive strong emotional support from her mother, which might be diminished if her sister's health were to deteriorate further, or she were to die. 8.21

Further details on this area are available in Department of Health or Welsh Assembly guidance.[32]

Non-therapeutic sterilisation is the sterilisation for contraceptive purposes of a person who cannot consent. Such cases will require a careful assessment of whether such sterilisation would be in the best interests of the person who lacks capacity and such cases should continue to be referred to the court.[33] The court has also given guidance on when certain termination of pregnancy cases should be brought before the court.[34] 8.22

Other cases likely to be referred to the court include those involving ethical dilemmas in untested areas (such as innovative treatments for variant CJD), or where there are otherwise irresolvable conflicts between healthcare staff, or between staff and family members. 8.23

There are also a few types of cases that should generally be dealt with by the court, since other dispute resolution methods are unlikely to be appropriate (see chapter 15). This includes, for example, cases where it is unclear whether proposed serious and/or invasive medical treatment is likely to be in the best interests of the person who lacks capacity to consent. 8.24

What powers does the court have to make decisions and appoint deputies?

In cases of serious dispute, where there is no other way of finding a solution or when the authority of the court is needed in order to make a particular decision or take a particular action, the court can be asked to make a decision to settle the matter using its powers under section 16. 8.25

However, if there is a need for ongoing decision-making powers and there is no relevant EPA or LPA, the court may appoint a deputy to make future decisions. It will also state what decisions the deputy has the authority to make on the person's behalf.

In deciding what type of order to make, the court must apply the Act's principles and the best interests checklist. In addition, it must follow two further principles, intended to make any intervention as limited as possible: 8.26

• Where possible, the court should make the decision itself in preference to appointing a deputy.

---

[31] *Re Y (Mental Incapacity: Bone marrow transplant)* [1996] 2 FLR 787.

[32] Reference Guide to Consent for Examination or Treatment, Department of Health, March 2001 www. dh.gov.uk/PublicationsAndStatistics/Publications/PublicationsPolicyAndGuidance/PublicationsPolicyAndG uidanceArticle/fs/en?CONTENT_ ID=4006757&chk=snmdw8.

[33] See e.g. *Re A (medical treatment: male sterilisation)* (1999) 53 BMLR 66 where a mother applied for a declaration that a vasectomy was in the best interests of A, her son, (who had Down's syndrome and was borderline between significant and severe impairment of intelligence), in the absence of his consent. After balancing the burdens and benefits of the proposed vasectomy to A, the Court of Appeal held that the vasectomy would not be in A's best interests.

[34] *D v An NHS Trust (Medical Treatment: Consent: Termination)* [2004] 1 FLR 1110 144.

- If a deputy needs to be appointed, their appointment should be as limited in scope and for as short a time as possible.

What decisions can the court make?

8.27   In some cases, the court must make a decision, because someone needs specific authority to act and there is no other route for getting it. These include cases where:
- there is no EPA or property and affairs LPA in place and someone needs to make a financial decision for a person who lacks capacity to make that decision (for example, the decision to terminate a tenancy agreement), or
- it is necessary to make a will, or to amend an existing will, on behalf of a person who lacks capacity to do so.

8.28   Examples of other types of cases where a court decision might be appropriate include cases where:
- there is genuine doubt or disagreement about the existence, validity or applicability of an advance decision to refuse treatment (see chapter 9)
- there is a major disagreement regarding a serious decision (for example, about where a person who lacks capacity to decide for themselves should live)
- a family carer or a solicitor asks for personal information about someone who lacks capacity to consent to that information being revealed (for example, where there have been allegations of abuse of a person living in a care home)
- someone suspects that a person who lacks capacity to make decisions to protect themselves is at risk of harm or abuse from a named individual (the court could stop that individual contacting the person who lacks capacity).

8.29   Anyone carrying out actions under a decision or order of the court must still also follow the Act's principles.

Scenario: Making a decision to settle disagreements

Mrs Worrell has Alzheimer's disease. Her son and daughter argue over which care home their mother should move to. Although Mrs Worrell lacks the capacity to make this decision herself, she has enough money to pay the fees of a care home. Her solicitor acts as attorney in relation to her financial affairs under a registered EPA. But he has no power to get involved in this family dispute—nor does he want to get involved. The Court of Protection makes a decision in Mrs Worrell's best interests, and decides which care home can best meet her needs. Once this matter is resolved, there is no need to appoint a deputy.

What powers does the court have in relation to LPAs?

8.30   The Court of Protection can determine the validity of an LPA or EPA and can give directions as to how an attorney should use their powers under an LPA (see chapter 7). In particular, the court can cancel an LPA and end the attorney's appointment. The court might do this if the attorney was not carrying out their duties properly or acting in the best interests of the donor. The court must then decide whether it is necessary to appoint a deputy to take over the attorney's role.

What are the rules for appointing deputies?

8.31   Sometimes it is not practical or appropriate for the court to make a single declaration or decision. In such cases, if the court thinks that somebody needs to make future or ongoing decisions for someone whose condition makes it likely they will lack capacity to make some further decisions in the future, it can appoint a deputy to act for and make decisions for that person. A deputy's authority should be as limited in scope and duration as possible (see paragraphs 8.35–8.39 below).

How does the court appoint deputies?

It is for the court to decide who to appoint as a deputy. Different skills may be required depending on whether the deputy's decisions will be about a person's welfare (including healthcare), their finances or both. The court will decide whether the proposed deputy is reliable and trustworthy and has an appropriate level of skill and competence to carry out the necessary tasks.   8.32

In the majority of cases, the deputy is likely to be a family member or someone who knows the person well. But in some cases the court may decide to appoint a deputy who is independent of the family (for example, where the person's affairs or care needs are particularly complicated). This could be, for example, the Director of Adult Services in the relevant local authority (but see paragraph 8.60 below) or a professional deputy. The OPG has a panel of professional deputies (mainly solicitors who specialise in this area of law) who may be appointed to deal with property and affairs if the court decides that would be in the person's best interests.   8.33

When might a deputy need to be appointed?

Whether a person who lacks capacity to make specific decisions needs a deputy will depend on: 8.34
- the individual circumstances of the person concerned
- whether future or ongoing decisions are likely to be necessary, and
- whether the appointment is for decisions about property and affairs or personal welfare.

Property and affairs

The court will appoint a deputy to manage a person's property and affairs (including financial matters) in similar circumstances to those in which they would have appointed a receiver in the past. If a person who lacks capacity to make decisions about property and affairs has not made an EPA or LPA, applications to the court are necessary: 8.35
- for dealing with cash assets over a specified amount that remain after any debts have been paid
- for selling a person's property, or
- where the person has a level of income or capital that the court thinks a deputy needs to manage.

If the only income of a person who lacks capacity is social security benefits and they have no property or savings, there will usually be no need for a deputy to be appointed. This is because the person's benefits can be managed by an *appointee*, appointed by the Department for Work and Pensions to receive and deal with the benefits of a person who lacks capacity to do this for themselves. Although appointees are not covered by the Act, they will be expected to act in the person's best interests and must do so if they are involved in caring for the person. If the court does appoint a property and affairs deputy for someone who has an appointee, it is likely that the deputy would take over the appointee's role.   8.36

Anybody considered for appointment as a property and affairs deputy will need to sign a declaration giving details of their circumstances and ability to manage financial affairs. The declaration will include details of the tasks and duties the deputy must carry out. The deputy must assure the court that they have the skills, knowledge and commitment to carry them out.   8.37

Personal welfare (including healthcare)

8.38 Deputies for personal welfare decisions will only be required in the most difficult cases where:
- important and necessary actions cannot be carried out without the court's authority, or
- there is no other way of settling the matter in the best interests of the person who lacks capacity to make particular welfare decisions.

8.39 Examples include when:
- someone needs to make a series of linked welfare decisions over time and it would not be beneficial or appropriate to require all of those decisions to be made by the court. For example, someone (such as a family carer) who is close to a person with profound and multiple learning disabilities might apply to be appointed as a deputy with authority to make such decisions
- the most appropriate way to act in the person's best interests is to have a deputy, who will consult relevant people but have the final authority to make decisions
- there is a history of serious family disputes that could have a detrimental effect on the person's future care unless a deputy is appointed to make necessary decisions
- the person who lacks capacity is felt to be at risk of serious harm if left in the care of family members. In these rare cases, welfare decisions may need to be made by someone independent of the family, such as a local authority officer. There may even be a need for an additional court order prohibiting those family members from having contact with the person.

Who can be a deputy?

8.40 Section 19(1) states that deputies must be at least 18 years of age. Deputies with responsibility for property and affairs can be either an individual or a trust corporation (often parts of banks or other financial institutions). No-one can be appointed as a deputy without their consent.

8.41 Paid care workers (for example, care home managers) should not agree to act as a deputy because of the possible conflict of interest—unless there are exceptional circumstances (for example, if the care worker is the only close relative of the person who lacks capacity). But the court can appoint someone who is an office-holder or in a specified position (for example, the Director of Adult Services of the relevant local authority). In this situation, the court will need to be satisfied that there is no conflict of interest before making such an appointment (see paragraphs 8.58–8.60).

8.42 The court can appoint two or more deputies and state whether they should act 'jointly', 'jointly and severally' or 'jointly in respect of some matters and jointly and severally in respect of others' (section 19 (4)(c)).
- Joint deputies must always act together. They must all agree decisions or actions, and all sign any relevant documents.
- Joint and several deputies can act together, but they may also act independently if they wish. Any action taken by any deputy alone is as valid as if that person were the only deputy.

8.43 Deputies may be appointed jointly for some issues and jointly and severally for others. For example, two deputies could be appointed jointly and severally for most decisions, but the court might rule that they act jointly when selling property.

Scenario: Acting jointly and severally

Toby had a road accident and suffered brain damage and other disabilities. He gets financial compensation but lacks capacity to manage this amount of money or make decisions about his future care. His divorced parents are arguing about where their son should live and how his compensation money should be used. Toby has always been close to his sister, who is keen to be involved but is anxious about dealing with such a large amount of money. The court decides where

Toby will live. It also appoints his sister and a solicitor as joint and several deputies to manage his property and affairs. His sister can deal with any day-to-day decisions that Toby lacks capacity to make, and the solicitor can deal with more complicated matters.

What happens if a deputy can no longer carry out their duties?

When appointing a deputy, the court can also appoint someone to be a successor deputy (someone who can take over the deputy's duties in certain situations). The court will state the circumstances under which this could occur. In some cases it will also state a period of time in which the successor deputy can act. Appointment of a successor deputy might be useful if the person appointed as deputy is already elderly and wants to be sure that somebody will take over their duties in the future, if necessary. **8.44**

Scenario: Appointing a successor deputy

Neil, a man with Down's syndrome, inherits a lot of money and property. His parents were already retired when the court appointed them as joint deputies to manage Neil's property and affairs. They are worried about what will happen to Neil when they cannot carry out their duties as deputies any more. The court agrees to appoint other relatives as successor deputies. They will then be able to take over as deputies after the parents' death or if his parents are no longer able to carry out the deputy's role.

Can the court protect people lacking capacity from financial loss?

Under section 19(9)(a) of the Act the court can ask a property and affairs deputy to provide some form of security (for example, a guarantee bond) to the Public Guardian to cover any loss as a result of the deputy's behaviour in carrying out their role. The court can also ask a deputy to provide reports and accounts to the Public Guardian, as it sees fit. **8.45**

Are there any restrictions on a deputy's powers?

Section 20 sets out some specific restrictions on a deputy's powers. In particular, a deputy has no authority to make decisions or take action: **8.46**
- if they do something that is intended to restrain the person who lacks capacity—apart from under certain circumstances (guidance on the circumstances when restraint might be permitted is given in chapter 6)[35]
- if they think that the person concerned has capacity to make the particular decision for themselves
- if their decision goes against a decision made by an attorney acting under a Lasting Power of Attorney granted by the person before they lost capacity, or
- to refuse the provision or continuation of life-sustaining treatment for a person who lacks capacity to consent—such decisions must be taken by the court.

If a deputy thinks their powers are not enough for them to carry out their duties effectively, they can apply to the court to change their powers. See paragraph 8.54 below.

[35] It is worth noting that there is a drafting error in section 20 of the Act. The word 'or' in section 20(11)(a) should have been 'and' in order to be consistent with sections 6(3)(a) and 11(4)(a). The Government will make the necessary amendment to correct this error at the earliest available legislative opportunity.

What responsibilities do deputies have?

8.47 Once a deputy has been appointed by the court, the order of appointment will set out their specific powers and the scope of their authority. On taking up the appointment, the deputy will assume a number of duties and responsibilities and will be required to act in accordance with certain standards. Failure to comply with the duties set out below could result in the Court of Protection revoking the order appointing the deputy and, in some circumstances, the deputy could be personally liable to claims for negligence or criminal charges of fraud.

8.48 Deputies should always inform any third party they are dealing with that the court has appointed them as deputy. The court will give the deputy official documents to prove their appointment and the extent of their authority.

8.49 A deputy must act whenever a decision or action is needed and it falls within their duties as set out in the court order appointing them. A deputy who fails to act at all in such situations could be in breach of duty.

What duties does the Act impose?

8.50 Deputies must:
- follow the Act's statutory principles (see chapter 2)
- make decisions or act in the best interests of the person who lacks capacity
- have regard to the guidance in this Code of Practice
- only make decisions the Court has given them authority to make.

Principles and best interests

8.51 Deputies must act in accordance with the Act's statutory principles (section 1) and in particular the best interests of the person who lacks capacity (the steps for working out best interests are set out in section 4). In particular, deputies must consider whether the person has capacity to make the decision for themselves. If not, they should consider whether the person is likely to regain capacity to make the decision in the future. If so, it may be possible to delay the decision until the person can make it.

The Code of Practice

8.52 As well as this chapter, deputies should pay special attention to the following guidance set out in the Code:
- chapter 2, which sets out how the Act's principles should be applied
- chapter 3, which describes the steps which can be taken to try to help the person make decisions for themselves
- chapter 4, which describes the Act's definition of lack of capacity and gives guidance on assessing capacity, and
- chapter 5, which gives guidance on working out someone's best interests.

8.53 In some situations, deputies might also find it useful to refer to guidance in:
- chapter 6, which explains when deputies who have caring responsibilities may have protection from liability and gives guidance on the few circumstances when the Act allows restraint in connection with care and treatment, and
- chapter 15, which describes ways to settle disagreements.

Only making decisions the court authorises a deputy to make

A deputy has a duty to act only within the scope of the actual powers given by the court, which   8.54
are set out in the order of appointment. It is possible that a deputy will think their powers are not
enough for them to carry out their duties effectively. In this situation, they must apply to the court
either to:
- ask the court to make the decision in question, or
- ask the court to change the deputy's powers.

What are a deputy's other duties?

Section 19(6) states that a deputy is to be treated as 'the agent' of the person who lacks capacity   8.55
when they act on their behalf. Being an agent means that the deputy has legal duties (under the
law of agency) to the person they are representing. It also means that when they carry out tasks
within their powers, they are not personally liable to third parties.

Deputies must carry out their duties carefully and responsibly. They have a duty to: 8.56
- act with due care and skill (duty of care)
- not take advantage of their situation (fiduciary duty)
- indemnify the person against liability to third parties caused by the deputy's negligence
- not delegate duties unless authorised to do so
- act in good faith
- respect the person's confidentiality, and
- comply with the directions of the Court of Protection.

Property and affairs deputies also have a duty to:
- keep accounts, and
- keep the person's money and property separate from own finances.

Duty of care

'Duty of care' means applying a certain standard of care and skill—depending on whether the   8.57
deputy is paid for their services or holds relevant professional qualifications.
- Deputies who are not being paid must use the same care, skill and diligence they would use
  when making decisions for themselves or managing their own affairs. If they do not, they could
  be held liable for acting negligently. A deputy who claims to have particular skills or qualifications
  must show greater skill in those particular areas than a person who does not make such claims.
- If deputies are being paid for their services, they are expected to demonstrate a higher degree of
  care or skill when carrying out their duties.
- Deputies whose duties form part of their professional work (for example, solicitors or
  accountants) must display normal professional competence and follow their profession's rules
  and standards.

Fiduciary duty

A fiduciary duty means deputies must not take advantage of their position. Nor should they put   8.58
themselves in a position where their personal interests conflict with their duties. For example,
deputies should not buy property that they are selling for the person they have been appointed to
represent. They should also not accept a third party commission in any transactions. Deputies
must not allow anything else to influence their duties. They cannot use their position for any
personal benefit, whether or not it is at the person's expense.

8.59　　In many cases, the deputy will be a family member. In rare situations, this could lead to potential conflicts of interests. When making decisions, deputies should follow the Act's statutory principles and apply the best interests checklist and not allow their own personal interests to influence the decision.

8.60　　Sometimes the court will consider appointing the Director of Adult Services in England or Director of Social Services in Wales of the relevant local authority as a deputy. The court will need to be satisfied that the authority has arrangements to avoid possible conflicts of interest. For example where the person for whom a financial deputy is required receives community care services from the local authority, the court will wish to be satisfied that decisions about the person's finances will be made in the best interests of that person, regardless of any implications for the services provided.

Duty not to delegate

8.61　A deputy may seek professional or expert advice (for example, investment advice from a financial adviser or a second medical opinion from a doctor). But they cannot give their decision-making responsibilities to someone else. In certain circumstances, the court will authorise the delegation of specific tasks (for example, appointing a discretionary investment manager for the conduct of investment business).

8.62　　In certain circumstances, deputies may have limited powers to delegate (for example, through necessity or unforeseen circumstances, or for specific tasks which the court would not have expected the deputy to attend to personally). But deputies cannot usually delegate any decisions that rely on their discretion. If the deputy is the Director of Adult Services in England or Director of Social Services in Wales, or a solicitor, they can delegate specific tasks to other staff. But the deputy is still responsible for any actions or decisions taken, and can therefore be held accountable for any errors that are made.

Duty of good faith

8.63　Acting in good faith means acting with honesty and integrity. For example, a deputy must try to make sure that their decisions do not go against a decision the person made while they still had capacity (unless it would be in the person's best interests to do so).

Duty of confidentiality

8.64　Deputies have a duty to keep the person's affairs confidential, unless:
- before they lost capacity to do so, the person agreed that information could be revealed where necessary
- there is some other good reason to release information (for example, it is in the public interest or in the best interests of the person who lacks capacity, or where there is a risk of harm to the person concerned or to other people).

In the latter circumstances, it is advisable for the deputy to contact the OPG for guidance or get legal advice. See chapter 16 for more information about revealing personal information.

Duty to comply with the directions of the Court of Protection

8.65　The Court of Protection may give specific directions to deputies about how they should use their powers. It can also order deputies to provide reports (for example, financial accounts or reports on the welfare of the person who lacks capacity) to the Public Guardian at any time or at such intervals as the court directs. Deputies must comply with any direction of the court or request from the Public Guardian.

Duty to keep accounts

A deputy appointed to manage property and affairs is expected to keep, and periodically submit to the Public Guardian, correct accounts of all their dealings and transactions on the person's behalf.

8.66

Duty to keep the person's money and property separate

Property and affairs deputies should usually keep the person's money and property separate from their own or anyone else's. This is to avoid any possibility of mistakes or confusion in handling the person's affairs. Sometimes there may be good reason not to do so (for example, a husband might be his wife's deputy and they might have had a joint account for many years).

8.67

Changes of contact details

A deputy should inform the OPG of any changes of contact details or circumstances (for the deputy or the person they are acting for). This will help make sure that the OPG has up-to-date records. It will also allow the court to discharge people who are no longer eligible to act as deputies.

8.68

Who is responsible for supervising deputies?

Deputies are accountable to the Court of Protection. The court can cancel a deputy's appointment at any time if it decides the appointment is no longer in the best interests of the person who lacks capacity.

8.69

The OPG is responsible for supervising and supporting deputies. But it must also protect people lacking capacity from possible abuse or exploitation. Anybody who suspects that a deputy is abusing their position should contact the OPG immediately. The OPG may instruct a Court of Protection Visitor to visit a deputy to investigate any matter of concern. It can also apply to the court to cancel a deputy's appointment.

8.70

The OPG will consider carefully any concerns or complaints against deputies. But if somebody suspects physical or sexual abuse or serious fraud, they should contact the police and/or social services immediately, as well as informing the OPG. Chapter 14 gives more information about the role of the OPG. It also discusses the protection of vulnerable people from abuse, ill treatment or wilful neglect and the responsibilities of various relevant agencies.

8.71

9. WHAT DOES THE ACT SAY ABOUT ADVANCE DECISIONS TO REFUSE TREATMENT?

This chapter explains what to do when somebody has made an advance decision to refuse treatment. It sets out:

- what the Act means by an 'advance decision'
- guidance on making, updating and cancelling advance decisions
- how to check whether an advance decision exists
- how to check that an advance decision is valid and that it applies to current circumstances

- the responsibilities of healthcare professionals when an advance decision exists
- how to handle disagreements about advance decisions.

In this chapter, as throughout the Code, a person's capacity (or lack of capacity) refers specifically to their capacity to make a particular decision at the time it needs to be made.

Quick summary

- An advance decision enables someone aged 18 and over, while still capable, to refuse specified medical treatment for a time in the future when they may lack the capacity to consent to or refuse that treatment.
- An advance decision to refuse treatment must be valid and applicable to current circumstances. If it is, it has the same effect as a decision that is made by a person with capacity: healthcare professionals must follow the decision.
- Healthcare professionals will be protected from liability if they:
  — stop or withhold treatment because they reasonably believe that an advance decision exists, and that it is valid and applicable
  — treat a person because, having taken all practical and appropriate steps to find out if the person has made an advance decision to refuse treatment, they do not know or are not satisfied that a valid and applicable advance decision exists.
- People can only make an advance decision under the Act if they are 18 or over and have the capacity to make the decision. They must say what treatment they want to refuse, and they can cancel their decision – or part of it – at any time.
- If the advance decision refuses life-sustaining treatment, it must: What does the Act say
  — be in writing (it can be written by a someone else or recorded in about advance healthcare notes)
  — be signed and witnessed, and decisions to refuse treatment?
  — state clearly that the decision applies even if life is at risk.
- To establish whether an advance decision is valid and applicable, healthcare professionals must try to find out if the person:
  — has done anything that clearly goes against their advance decision
  — has withdrawn their decision
  — has subsequently conferred the power to make that decision on an attorney, or
  — would have changed their decision if they had known more about the current circumstances.
- Sometimes healthcare professionals will conclude that an advance decision does not exist, is not valid and/or applicable—but that it is an expression of the person's wishes. The healthcare professional must then consider what is set out in the advance decision as an expression of previous wishes when working out the person's best interests (see chapter 5).
- Some healthcare professionals may disagree in principle with patients' decisions to refuse life-sustaining treatment. They do not have to act against their beliefs. But they must not simply abandon patients or act in a way that that affects their care.
- Advance decisions to refuse treatment for mental disorder may not apply if the person who made the advance decision is or is liable to be detained under the Mental Health Act 1983.

How can someone make an advance decision to refuse treatment?

What is an advance decision to refuse treatment?

It is a general principle of law and medical practice that people have a right to consent to or refuse   9.1
treatment. The courts have recognised that adults have the right to say in advance that they want
to refuse treatment if they lose capacity in the future—even if this results in their death. A valid
and applicable advance decision to refuse treatment has the same force as a contemporaneous
decision. This has been a fundamental principle of the common law for many years and it is now
set out in the Act. Sections 24–26 of the Act set out the when a person can make an advance
decision to refuse treatment. This applies if:

- the person is 18 or older, and
- they have the capacity to make an advance decision about treatment.

Information on advance decisions to refuse treatment made by young people (under the age of 18)
will be available at www.dh.gov.uk/consent

Healthcare professionals must follow an advance decision if it is valid and applies to the   9.2
particular circumstances. If they do not, they could face criminal prosecution (they could be
charged for committing a crime) or civil liability (somebody could sue them).

Advance decisions can have serious consequences for the people who make them. They can also   9.3
have an important impact on family and friends, and professionals involved in their care. Before
healthcare professionals can apply an advance decision, there must be proof that the decision:

- exists
- is valid, and
- is applicable in the current circumstances.

These tests are legal requirements under section 25(1). Paragraphs 9.38–9.44 explain the standard
of proof the Act requires.

Who can make an advance decision to refuse treatment?

It is up to individuals to decide whether they want to refuse treatment in advance. They are   9.4
entitled to do so if they want, but there is no obligation to do so. Some people choose to make
advance decisions while they are still healthy, even if there is no prospect of illness. This might be
because they want to keep some control over what might happen to them in the future. Others
may think of an advance decision as part of their preparations for growing older (similar to making
a will). Or they might make an advance decision after they have been told they have a specific
disease or condition.

Many people prefer not to make an advance decision, and instead leave healthcare professionals
to make decisions in their best interests at the time a decision needs to be made. Another option
is to make a Lasting Power of Attorney. This allows a trusted family member or friend to make
personal welfare decisions, such as those around What does treatment, on someone's behalf, and
in their best interests if they ever the Act say lose capacity to make those decisions themselves (see
paragraph 9.33 about advance decisions to refuse treatment?below and chapter 7).

People can only make advance decisions to *refuse* treatment. Nobody has the legal right to   9.5
demand specific treatment, either at the time or in advance. So no-one can insist (either at the
time or in advance) on being given treatments that healthcare professionals consider to be clinically
unnecessary, futile or inappropriate. But people can make a request or state their wishes and
preferences in advance. Healthcare professionals should then consider the request when deciding
what is in a patient's best interests (see chapter 5) if the patient lacks capacity.

9.6   Nobody can ask for and receive procedures that are against the law (for example, help with committing suicide). As section 62 sets out, the Act does not change any of the laws relating to murder, manslaughter or helping someone to commit suicide.

Capacity to make an advance decision

9.7   For most people, there will be no doubt about their capacity to make an advance decision. Even those who lack capacity to make some decisions may have the capacity to make an advance decision. In some cases it may be helpful to get evidence of a person's capacity to make the advance decision (for example, if there is a possibility that the advance decision may be challenged in the future). It is also important to remember that capacity can change over time, and a person who lacks capacity to make a decision now might be able to make it in the future.

Chapter 3 explains how to assess a person's capacity to make a decision.

Scenario: Respecting capacity to make an advance decision

Mrs Long's family has a history of polycystic ovary syndrome. She has made a written advance decision refusing any treatment or procedures that might affect her fertility. The document states that her ovaries and uterus must not be removed. She is having surgery to treat a blocked fallopian tube and, during the consent process, she told her doctor about her advance decision. During surgery the doctor discovers a solid mass that he thinks might be cancerous. In his clinical judgement, he thinks it would be in Mrs Long's best interests for him to remove the ovary. But he knows that Mrs Long had capacity when she made her valid and applicable advance decision, so he must respect her rights and follow her decision. After surgery, he can discuss the matter with Mrs Long and advise her about treatment options.

9.8   In line with principle 1 of the Act, that 'a person must be assumed to have capacity unless it is established that he lacks capacity', healthcare professionals should always start from the assumption that a person who has made an advance decision had capacity to make it, *unless* they are aware of reasonable grounds to doubt the person had the capacity to make the advance decision at the time they made it. If a healthcare professional is not satisfied that the person had capacity at the time they made the advance decision, or if there are doubts about its existence, validity or applicability, they can treat the person without fear of liability. It is good practice to record their decisions and the reasons for them. The Act does not require them to record their assessment of the person's capacity at the time the decision was made, but it would be good practice to do so.

9.9   Healthcare professionals may have particular concerns about the capacity of someone with a history of suicide attempts or suicidal thoughts who has made an advance decision. It is important to remember that making an advance decision which, if followed, may result in death does not necessarily mean a person is or feels suicidal. Nor does it necessarily mean the person lacks capacity to make the advance decision. If the person is clearly suicidal, this may raise questions about their capacity to make an advance decision at the time they made it.

What should people include in an advance decision?

9.10   There are no particular formalities about the format of an advance decision. It can be written or verbal, unless it deals with life-sustaining treatment, in which case it must be written and specific rules apply (see paragraphs 9.24–9.28 below).

9.11   An advance decision to refuse treatment:
- must state precisely what treatment is to be refused—a statement giving a general desire not to be treated is not enough

- may set out the circumstances when the refusal should apply – it is helpful to include as much detail as possible
- will only apply at a time when the person lacks capacity to consent to or refuse the specific treatment.

Specific rules apply to life-sustaining treatment.

People can use medical language or everyday language in their advance decision. But they must make clear what their wishes are and what treatment they would like to refuse. **9.12**

An advance decision refusing all treatment in any situation (for example, where a person explains that their decision is based on their religion or personal beliefs) may be valid and applicable. **9.13**

It is recommended that people who are thinking about making an advance decision get advice from: **9.14**

- healthcare professionals (for example, their GP or the person most closely involved with current healthcare or treatment), or
- an organisation that can provide advice on specific conditions or situations (they might have their own format for recording an advance decision).

But it is up to the person whether they want to do this or not. Healthcare professionals should record details of any discussion on healthcare records.

Some people may also want to get legal advice. This will help them make sure that they express their decision clearly and accurately. It will also help to make sure that people understand their advance decision in the future. **9.15**

It is a good idea to try to include possible future circumstances in the advance decision. For example, a woman may want to state in the advance decision whether or not it should still apply if she later becomes pregnant. If the document does not anticipate a change in circumstance, healthcare professionals may decide that it is not applicable if those particular circumstances arise. **9.16**

If an advance decision is recorded on a patient's healthcare records, it is confidential. Some patients will tell others about their advance decision (for example, they might tell healthcare professionals, friends or family). Others will not. People who do not ask for their advance decision to be recorded on their healthcare record will need to think about where it should be kept and how they are going to let people know about their decision. **9.17**

Written advance decisions

A written document can be evidence of an advance decision. It is helpful to tell others that the document exists and where it is. A person may want to carry it with them in case of emergency, or carry a card, bracelet or other indication that they have made an advance decision and explaining where it is kept. **9.18**

There is no set form for written advance decisions, because contents will vary depending on a person's wishes and situation. But it is helpful to include the following information: **9.19**

- full details of the person making the advance decision, including date of birth, home address and any distinguishing features (in case healthcare professionals need to identify an unconscious person, for example)
- the name and address of the person's GP and whether they have a copy of the document
- a statement that the document should be used if the person ever lacks capacity to make treatment decisions
- a clear statement of the decision, the treatment to be refused and the circumstances in which the decision will apply
- the date the document was written (or reviewed)

- the person's signature (or the signature of someone the person has asked to sign on their behalf and in their presence)
- the signature of the person witnessing the signature, if there is one (or a statement directing somebody to sign on the person's behalf).

See paragraphs 9.24–9.28 below if the advance decision deals with life-sustaining treatment.

9.20 Witnessing the person's signature is not essential, except in cases where the person is making an advance decision to refuse life-sustaining treatment. But if there is a witness, they are witnessing the signature and the fact that it confirms the wishes set out in the advance decision. It may be helpful to give a description of the relationship between the witness and person making the advance decision. The role of the witness is to witness the person's signature, it is not to certify that the person has the capacity to make the advance decision—even if the witness is a healthcare professional or knows the person.

9.21 It is possible that a professional acting as a witness will also be the person who assesses the person's capacity. If so, the professional should also make a record of the assessment, because acting as a witness does not prove that there has been an assessment.

Verbal advance decisions

9.22 There is no set format for verbal advance decisions. This is because they will vary depending on a person's wishes and situation. Healthcare professionals will need to consider whether a verbal advance decision exists and whether it is valid and applicable (see paragraphs 9.38– 9.44).

9.23 Where possible, healthcare professionals should record a verbal advance decision to refuse treatment in a person's healthcare record. This will produce a written record that could prevent confusion about the decision in the future. The record should include:
- a note that the decision should apply if the person lacks capacity to make treatment decisions in the future
- a clear note of the decision, the treatment to be refused and the circumstances in which the decision will apply
- details of someone who was present when the oral advance decision was recorded and the role in which they were present (for example, healthcare professional or family member), and
- whether they heard the decision, took part in it or are just aware that it exists.

What rules apply to advance decisions to refuse life-sustaining treatment?

9.24 The Act imposes particular legal requirements and safeguards on the making of advance decisions to refuse life-sustaining treatment. Advance decisions to refuse life-sustaining treatment *must* meet specific requirements:
- They must be put in writing. If the person is unable to write, someone else should write it down for them. For example, a family member can write down the decision on their behalf, or a healthcare professional can record it in the person's healthcare notes.
- The person must sign the advance decision. If they are unable to sign, they can direct someone to sign on their behalf in their presence.
- The person making the decision must sign in the presence of a witness to the signature. The witness must then sign the document in the presence of the person making the advance decision. If the person making the advance decision is unable to sign, the witness can witness them directing someone else to sign on their behalf. The witness must then sign to indicate that they have witnessed the nominated person signing the document in front of the person making the advance decision.

- The advance decision must include a clear, specific written statement from the person making the advance decision that the advance decision is to apply to the specific treatment even if life is at risk.
- If this statement is made at a different time or in a separate document to the advance decision, the person making the advance decision (or someone they have directed to sign) must sign it in the presence of a witness, who must also sign it.

Section 4(10) states that life-sustaining treatment is treatment which a healthcare professional who is providing care to the person regards as necessary to sustain life. This decision will not just depend on the type of treatment. It will also depend on the circumstances in which the healthcare professional is giving it. For example, in some situations antibiotics may be life-sustaining, but in others they can be used to treat conditions that do not threaten life. 9.25

Artificial nutrition and hydration (ANH) has been recognised as a form of medical treatment. ANH involves using tubes to provide nutrition and fluids to someone who cannot take them by mouth. It bypasses the natural mechanisms that control hunger and thirst and requires clinical monitoring. An advance decision can refuse ANH. Refusing ANH in an advance decision is likely to result in the person's death, if the advance decision is followed. 9.26

It is very important to discuss advance decisions to refuse life-sustaining treatment with a healthcare professional. But it is not compulsory. A healthcare professional will be able to explain: 9.27
- what types of treatment may be life-sustaining treatment, and in what circumstances
- the implications and consequences of refusing such treatment (see also paragraph 9.14).

An advance decision cannot refuse actions that are needed to keep a person comfortable (sometimes called basic or essential care). Examples include warmth, shelter, actions to keep a person clean and the offer of food and water by mouth. Section 5 of the Act allows healthcare professionals to carry out these actions in the best interests of a person who lacks capacity to consent (see chapter 6). An advance decision can refuse artificial nutrition and hydration. 9.28

When should someone review or update an advance decision?

Anyone who has made an advance decision is advised to regularly review and update it as necessary. Decisions made a long time in advance are not automatically invalid or inapplicable, but they may raise doubts when deciding whether they are valid and applicable. A written decision that is regularly reviewed is more likely to be valid and applicable to current circumstances—particularly for progressive illnesses. This is because it is more likely to have taken on board changes that have occurred in a person's life since they made their decision. 9.29

Views and circumstances may change over time. A new stage in a person's illness, the development of new treatments or a major change in personal circumstances may be appropriate times to review and update an advance decision. 9.30

How can someone withdraw an advance decision?

Section 24(3) allows people to cancel or alter an advance decision at any time while they still have capacity to do so. There are no formal processes to follow. People can cancel their decision verbally or in writing, and they can destroy any original written document. Where possible, the person who made the advance decision should tell anybody who knew about their advance decision that it has been cancelled. They can do this at any time. For example, they can do this on their way to the operating theatre or immediately before being given an anaesthetic. Healthcare professionals 9.31

should record a verbal cancellation in healthcare records. This then forms a written record for future reference.

How can someone make changes to an advance decision?

9.32   People can makes changes to an advance decision verbally or in writing (section 24(3)) whether or not the advance decision was made in writing. It is good practice for healthcare professionals to record a change of decision in the person's healthcare notes. But if the person wants to change an advance decision to include a refusal of life-sustaining treatment, they must follow the procedures described in paragraphs 9.24–9.28.

How do advance decisions relate to other rules about decision-making?

9.33   A valid and applicable advance decision to refuse treatment is as effective as a refusal made when a person has capacity. Therefore, an advance decision overrules:
* the decision of any personal welfare Lasting Power of Attorney (LPA) made before the advance decision was made. So an attorney cannot give consent to treatment that has been refused in an advance decision made after the LPA was signed
* the decision of any court-appointed deputy (so a deputy cannot give consent to treatment that has been refused in an advance decision which is valid and applicable)
* the provisions of section 5 of the Act, which would otherwise allow healthcare professionals to give treatment that they believe is in a person's best interests.

9.34   An LPA made after an advance decision will make the advance decision invalid, if the LPA gives the attorney the authority to make decisions about the same treatment (see paragraph 9.40).

9.35   The Court of Protection may make declarations as to the existence, validity and applicability of an advance decision, but it has no power to overrule a valid and applicable advance decision to refuse treatment.

9.36   Where an advance decision is being followed, the best interests principle (see chapter 5) does not apply. This is because an advance decision reflects the decision of an adult with capacity who has made the decision for themselves. Healthcare professionals must follow a valid and applicable advance decision, even if they think it goes against a person's best interests.

Advance decisions regarding treatment for mental disorder

9.37   Advance decisions can refuse any kind of treatment, whether for a physical or mental disorder. But generally an advance decision to refuse treatment for mental disorder can be overruled if the person is detained in hospital under the Mental Health Act 1983, when treatment could be given compulsorily under Part 4 of that Act. Advance decisions to refuse treatment for other illnesses or conditions are not affected by the fact that the person is detained in hospital under the Mental Health Act. For further information see chapter 13.

How can somebody decide on the existence, validity and applicability of advance decisions?

Deciding whether an advance decision exists

9.38   It is the responsibility of the person making the advance decision to make sure their decision will be drawn to the attention of healthcare professionals when it is needed. Some people will want their decision to be recorded on their healthcare records. Those who do not will need to find other ways of alerting people that they have made an advance decision and where somebody will find any written document and supporting evidence. Some people carry a card or wear a bracelet. It is also useful to share this information with family and friends, who may alert healthcare professionals to the existence of an advance decision. But it is not compulsory. Providing their GP with a copy of the written document will allow them to record the decision in the person's healthcare records.

It is important to be able to establish that the person making the advance decision was 18 or over when they made their decision, and that they had the capacity to make that decision when they made it, in line with the two-stage test for capacity set out in chapter 3. But as explained in paragraphs 9.7–9.9 above, healthcare professionals should always start from the assumption that the person had the capacity to make the advance decision. **9.39**

Deciding whether an advance decision is valid

An existing advance decision must still be valid at the time it needs to be put into effect. Healthcare professionals must consider the factors in section 25 of the Act before concluding that an advance decision is valid. Events that would make an advance decision invalid include those where: **9.40**
- the person withdrew the decision while they still had capacity to do so
- after making the advance decision, the person made a Lasting Power of Attorney (LPA) giving an attorney authority to make treatment decisions that are the same as those covered by the advance decision (see also paragraph 9.33)
- the person has done something that clearly goes against the advance decision which suggests that they have changed their mind.

Scenario: Assessing whether an advance decision is valid

A young man, Angus, sees a friend die after prolonged hospital treatment. Angus makes a signed and witnessed advance decision to refuse treatment to keep him alive if he is ever injured in this way. The advance decision includes a statement that this will apply even if his life is at risk. A few years later, Angus is seriously injured in a road traffic accident. He is paralysed from the neck down and cannot breathe without the help of a machine. At first he stays conscious and gives permission to be treated. He takes part in a rehabilitation programme. Some months later he loses consciousness. At this point somebody finds his written advance decision, even though Angus has not mentioned it during his treatment. His actions before his lack of capacity obviously go against the advance decision. Anyone assessing the advance decision needs to consider very carefully the doubt this has created about the validity of the advance decision, and whether the advance decision is valid and applicable as a result.

Deciding whether an advance decision is applicable

To be applicable, an advance decision must apply to the situation in question and in the current circumstances. Healthcare professionals must first determine if the person still has capacity to accept or refuse treatment at the relevant time (section 25(3)). If the person has capacity, they can refuse treatment there and then. Or they can change their decision and accept treatment. The advance decision is not applicable in such situations. **9.41**

The advance decision must also apply to the proposed treatment. It is not applicable to the treatment in question if (section 25(4)): **9.42**
- the proposed treatment is not the treatment specified in the advance decision
- the circumstances are different from those that may have been set out in the advance decision, or

- there are reasonable grounds for believing that there have been changes in circumstance, which would have affected the decision if the person had known about them at the time they made the advance decision.

9.43 So when deciding whether an advance decision applies to the proposed treatment, healthcare professionals must consider:
- how long ago the advance decision was made, and
- whether there have been changes in the patient's personal life (for example, the person is pregnant, and this was not anticipated when they made the advance decision) that might affect the validity of the advance decision, and
- whether there have been developments in medical treatment that the person did not foresee (for example, new medications, treatment or therapies).

9.44 For an advance decision to apply to life-sustaining treatment, it must meet the requirements set out in paragraphs 9.24–9.28.

Scenario: Assessing if an advance decision is applicable

Mr Moss is HIV positive. Several years ago he began to have AIDS-related symptoms. He has accepted general treatment, but made an advance decision to refuse specific retro-viral treatments, saying he didn't want to be a 'guinea pig' for the medical profession. Five years later, he is admitted to hospital seriously ill and keeps falling unconscious. The doctors treating Mr Moss examine his advance decision. They are aware that there have been major developments in retro-viral treatment recently. They discuss this with Mr Moss's partner and both agree that there are reasonable grounds to believe that Mr Moss may have changed his advance decision if he had known about newer treatment options. So the doctors decide the advance decision does not apply to the new retro-virals and give him treatment. If Mr Moss regains his capacity, he can change his advance decision and accept or refuse future treatment.

What should healthcare professionals do if an advance decision is not valid or applicable?

9.45 If an advance decision is not valid or applicable to current circumstances:
- healthcare professionals must consider the advance decision as part of their assessment of the person's best interests (see chapter 5) if they have reasonable grounds to think it is a true expression of the person's wishes, and
- they must not assume that because an advance decision is either invalid or not applicable, they should always provide the specified treatment (including life-sustaining treatment)—they must base this decision on what is in the person's best interests.

What happens to decisions made before the Act comes into force?

9.46 Advance decisions made before the Act comes into force may still be valid and applicable. Healthcare professionals should apply the rules in the Act to advance decisions made before the Act comes into force, subject to the transitional protections that will apply to advance decisions that refuse life-sustaining treatment. Further guidance will be available at www.dh.gov.uk/consent.

What implications do advance decisions have for healthcare professionals?

What are healthcare professionals' responsibilities?

Healthcare professionals should be aware that: 9.47
- a patient they propose to treat may have refused treatment in advance, and
- valid and applicable advance decisions to refuse treatment have the same legal status as decisions made by people with capacity at the time of treatment.

Where appropriate, when discussing treatment options with people who have capacity, 9.48 healthcare professionals should ask if there are any specific types of treatment they do not wish to receive if they ever lack capacity to consent in the future.

If somebody tells a healthcare professional that an advance decision exists for a patient who now 9.49 lacks capacity to consent, they should make reasonable efforts to find out what the decision is. Reasonable efforts might include having discussions with relatives of the patient, looking in the patient's clinical notes held in the hospital or contacting the patient's GP.

Once they know a verbal or written advance decision exists, healthcare professionals must 9.50 determine whether:
- it is valid (see paragraph 9.40), and
- it is applicable to the proposed treatment (see paragraphs 9.41–9.44).

When establishing whether an advance decision applies to current circumstances, healthcare 9.51 professionals should take special care if the decision does not seem to have been reviewed or updated for some time. If the person's current circumstances are significantly different from those when the decision was made, the advance decision may not be applicable. People close to the person concerned, or anyone named in the advance decision, may be able to help explain the person's prior wishes.

If healthcare professionals are satisfied that an advance decision to refuse treatment exists, is 9.52 valid and is applicable, they must follow it and not provide the treatment refused in the advance decision.

If healthcare professionals are not satisfied that an advance decision exists that is both valid and 9.53 applicable, they can treat the person without fear of liability. But treatment must be in the person's best interests (see chapter 5). They should make clear notes explaining why they have not followed an advance decision which they consider to be invalid or not applicable.

Sometimes professionals can give or continue treatment while they resolve doubts over an 9.54 advance decision. It may be useful to get information from someone who can provide information about the person's capacity when they made the advance decision. The Court of Protection can settle disagreements about the existence, validity or applicability of an advance decision. Section 26 of the Act allows healthcare professionals to give necessary treatment, including life-sustaining treatment, to stop a person's condition getting seriously worse while the court decides.

Do advance decisions apply in emergencies?

A healthcare professional must provide treatment in the patient's best interests, unless they are 9.55 satisfied that there is a advance decision that is:
- valid, and
- applicable in the circumstances.

Healthcare professionals should not delay emergency treatment to look for an advance decision 9.56 if there is no clear indication that one exists. But if it is clear that a person has made an advance decision that is likely to be relevant, healthcare professionals should assess its validity and applicability as soon as possible. Sometimes the urgency of treatment decisions will make this difficult.

When can healthcare professionals be found liable?

9.57 Healthcare professionals must follow an advance decision if they are satisfied that it exists, is valid and is applicable to their circumstances. Failure to follow an advance decision in this situation could lead to a claim for damages for battery or a criminal charge of assault.

9.58 But they are protected from liability if they are not:
- aware of an advance decision, or
- satisfied that an advance decision exists, is valid and is applicable to the particular treatment and the current circumstances (section 26(2)).

If healthcare professionals have genuine doubts, and are therefore not 'satisfied', about the existence, validity or applicability of the advance decision, treatment can be provided without incurring liability.

9.59 Healthcare professionals will be protected from liability for failing to provide treatment if they 'reasonably believe' that a valid and applicable advance decision to refuse that treatment exists. But they must be able to demonstrate that their belief was reasonable (section 26(3)) and point to reasonable grounds showing why they believe this. Healthcare professionals can only base their decision on the evidence that is available at the time they need consider an advance decision.

9.60 Some situations might be enough in themselves to raise concern about the existence, validity or applicability of an advance decision to refuse treatment. These could include situations when:
- a disagreement between relatives and healthcare professionals about whether verbal comments were really an advance decision
- evidence about the person's state of mind raises questions about their capacity at the time they made the decision (see paragraphs 9.7–9.9)
- evidence of important changes in the person's behaviour before they lost capacity that might suggest a change of mind.

9.61 In cases where serious doubt remains and cannot be resolved in any other way, it will be possible to seek a declaration from the court.

What if a healthcare professional has a conscientious objection to stopping or providing life-sustaining treatment?

9.62 Some healthcare professionals may disagree in principle with patients' rights to refuse life-sustaining treatment. The Act does not change the current legal situation. They do not have to do something that goes against their beliefs. But they must not simply abandon patients or cause their care to suffer.

Healthcare professionals should make their views clear to the patient and the healthcare team as soon as someone raises the subject of withholding, stopping or providing life-sustaining treatment. Patients who still have capacity should then have the option of transferring their care to another healthcare professional, if it is possible to do this without affecting their care.

9.63 In cases where the patient now lacks capacity but has made a valid and applicable advance decision to refuse treatment which a doctor or health professional cannot, for reasons of conscience, comply with, arrangements should be made for the management of the patient's care to be transferred to another healthcare professional.[36] Where a transfer cannot be agreed, the Court of Protection can direct those responsible for the person's healthcare (for example, a Trust, doctor or other health professional) to make arrangements to take over responsibility for the person's healthcare (section 17(1)(e)).

What happens if there is a disagreement about an advance decision?

It is ultimately the responsibility of the healthcare professional who is in charge of the person's care when the treatment is required to decide whether there is an advance decision which is valid and applicable in the circumstances. In the event of disagreement about an advance decision between healthcare professionals, or between healthcare professionals and family members or others close to the person, the senior clinician must consider all the available evidence. This is likely to be a hospital consultant or the GP where the person is being treated in the community.   9.64

The senior clinician may need to consult with relevant colleagues and others who are close to or familiar with the patient. All staff involved in the person's care should be given the opportunity to express their views. If the person is in hospital, their GP may also have relevant information.   9.65

The point of such discussions should not be to try to overrule the person's advance decision but rather to seek evidence concerning its validity and to confirm its scope and its applicability to the current circumstances. Details of these discussions should be recorded in the person's healthcare records. Where the senior clinician has a reasonable belief that an advance decision to refuse medical treatment is both valid and applicable, the person's advance decision should be complied with.   9.66

When can somebody apply to the Court of Protection?

The Court of Protection can make a decision where there is genuine doubt or disagreement about an advance decision's existence, validity or applicability. But the court does not have the power to overturn a valid and applicable advance decision.   9.67

The court has a range of powers (sections 16–17) to resolve disputes concerning the personal care and medical treatment of a person who lacks capacity (see chapter 8). It can decide whether: 9.68
- a person has capacity to accept or refuse treatment at the time it is proposed
- an advance decision to refuse treatment is valid
- an advance decision is applicable to the proposed treatment in the current circumstances.

While the court decides, healthcare professionals can provide life-sustaining treatment or treatment to stop a serious deterioration in their condition. The court has emergency procedures which operate 24 hours a day to deal with urgent cases quickly. See chapter 8 for guidance on applying to the court.   9.69

10. WHAT IS THE NEW INDEPENDENT MENTAL CAPACITY ADVOCATE SERVICE AND HOW DOES IT WORK?

This chapter describes the new Independent Mental Capacity Advocate (IMCA) service created under the Act. The purpose of the IMCA service is to help particularly vulnerable people who lack the capacity to make important decisions about serious medical treatment and changes of

---

[36] *Re B (Adult: Refusal of Medical Treatment)* [2002] EWHC 429 (Fam) at paragraph 100(viii).

accommodation, and who have no family or friends that it would be appropriate to consult about those decisions. IMCAs will work with and support people who lack capacity, and represent their views to those who are working out their best interests.

The chapter provides guidance both for IMCAs and for everyone who may need to instruct an IMCA. It explains how IMCAs should be appointed. It also explains the IMCA's duties and the situations when an IMCA should be instructed. Both IMCAs and decision-makers are required to have regard to the Code of Practice.

In this chapter, as throughout the Code, a person's capacity (or lack of capacity) refers specifically to their capacity to make a particular decision at the time it needs to be made.

Quick summary

Understanding the role of the IMCA service
- The aim of the IMCA service is to provide independent safeguards for people who lack capacity to make certain important decisions and, at the time such decisions need to be made, have no-one else (other than paid staff) to support or represent them or be consulted.
- IMCAs must be independent.

Instructing and consulting an IMCA
- An IMCA *must* be instructed, and then consulted, for people lacking capacity who have no-one else to support them (other than paid staff), whenever:
  — an NHS body is proposing to provide serious medical treatment, or
  — an NHS body or local authority is proposing to arrange accommodation (or a change of accommodation) in hospital or a care home, and
  — the person will stay in hospital longer than 28 days, or
  — they will stay in the care home for more than eight weeks.
- An IMCA *may* be instructed to support someone who lacks capacity to make decisions concerning:
  — care reviews, where no-one else is available to be consulted
  — adult protection cases, whether or not family, friends or others are involved
  — *Ensuring an IMCA's views are taken into consideration*
- The IMCA's role is to support and represent the person who lacks capacity. Because of this, IMCAs have the right to see relevant healthcare and social care records.
- Any information or reports provided by an IMCA must be taken into account as part of the process of working out whether a proposed decision is in the person's best interests.

What is the IMCA service?

10.1 Sections 35–41 of the Act set up a new IMCA service that provides safeguards for people who:
- lack capacity to make a specified decision at the time it needs to be made
- are facing a decision on a long-term move or about serious medical treatment and
- have nobody else who is willing and able to represent them or be consulted in the process of working out their best interests.

10.2 Regulations made under the Act also state that IMCAs may be involved in other decisions, concerning:
- a care review, or
- an adult protection case.

In adult protection cases, an IMCA may be appointed even where family members or others are available to be consulted.

Most people who lack capacity to make a specific decision will have people to support them (for example, family members or friends who take an interest in their welfare). Anybody working out a person's best interests must consult these people, where possible, and take their views into account (see chapter 5). But if a person who lacks capacity has nobody to represent them or no-one who it is appropriate to consult, an IMCA must be instructed in prescribed circumstances. The prescribed circumstances are: **10.3**

- providing, withholding or stopping serious medical treatment
- moving a person into long-term care in hospital or a care home (see 10.11 for definition), or
- moving the person to a different hospital or care home.

The only exception to this can be in situations where an urgent decision is needed. Further details on the situations where there is a duty to instruct an IMCA are given in paragraphs 10.40–10.58.

In other circumstances, an IMCA *may* be appointed for the person (see paragraphs 10.59–10.68). These include:

- care reviews or
- adult protection cases.

The IMCA will: **10.4**

- be independent of the person making the decision
- provide support for the person who lacks capacity
- represent the person without capacity in discussions to work out whether the proposed decision is in the person's best interests
- provide information to help work out what is in the person's best interests (see chapter 5), and
- raise questions or challenge decisions which appear not to be in the best interests of the person.

The information the IMCA provides must be taken into account by decision-makers whenever they are working out what is in a person's best interests. See paragraphs 10.20–10.39 for more information on an IMCA's role. For more information on who is a decision-maker, see chapter 5.

The IMCA service will build on good practice in the independent advocacy sector. But IMCAs have a different role from many other advocates. They: **10.5**

- provide statutory advocacy
- are instructed to support and represent people who lack capacity to make decisions on specific issues
- have a right to meet in private the person they are supporting
- are allowed access to relevant healthcare records and social care records
- provide support and representation specifically while the decision is being made, and
- act quickly so their report can form part of decision-making.

Who is responsible for delivering the service?

The IMCA service is available in England and Wales. Both countries have regulations for setting up and managing the service. **10.6**

- England's regulations[37] are available at www.opsi.gov.uk/si/si200618.htm and www.opsi.gov.uk/si/dsis2006.htm.
- The regulations for Wales[38] are available at www.new.wales.gov.uk/ consultations/closed/healandsoccarecloscons/.

Guidance has been issued to local health boards and local authorities involved in commissioning IMCA services for their area.

10.7   In England the Secretary of State for Health delivers the service through local authorities, who work in partnership with NHS organisations. Local authorities have financial responsibility for the service. In Wales the National Assembly for Wales delivers the service through local health boards, who have financial responsibility for the service and work in partnership with local authority social services departments and other NHS organisations. The service is commissioned from independent organisations, usually advocacy organisations.

10.8   Local authorities or NHS organisations are responsible for instructing an IMCA to represent a person who lacks capacity. In these circumstances they are called the 'responsible body'.

10.9   For decisions about serious medical treatment, the responsible body will be the NHS organisation providing the person's healthcare or treatment. But if the person is in an independent or voluntary sector hospital, the responsible body will be the NHS organisation arranging and funding the person's care, which should have arrangements in place with the independent or voluntary sector hospital to ensure an IMCA is appointed promptly.

10.10   For decisions about admission to accommodation in hospital for 28 days or more, the responsible body will be the NHS body that manages the hospital. For admission to an independent or voluntary sector hospital for 28 days or more, the responsible body will be the NHS organisation arranging and funding the person's care. The independent or voluntary hospital must have arrangements in place with the NHS organisation to ensure that an IMCA can be appointed without delay.

10.11   For decisions about moves into long-term accommodation[39] (for eight weeks or longer), or about a change of accommodation, the responsible body will be either:
- the NHS body that proposes the move or change of accommodation (e.g. a nursing home), or
- the local authority that has carried out an assessment of the person under the NHS and Community Care Act 1990 and decided the move may be necessary.

---

37 *The Mental Capacity Act 2005 (Independent Mental Capacity Advocate) (General) Regulations 2006 SI: 2006 /No 1832.* The 'General Regulations'. These regulations set out the details on how the IMCA will be appointed, the functions of the IMCA, including their role in challenging the decision-maker and include definitions of 'serious medical treatment' and 'NHS body'.

The Mental Capacity Act 2005 (Independent Mental Capacity Advocate) (Expansion of Role) Regulations 2006 SI: 2883. The 'Expansion Regulations'. These regulations specify the circumstances in which local authorities and NHS bodies may provide the IMCA service on a discretionary basis. These include involving the IMCA in a care review and in adult protection cases.

38 *The Mental Capacity Act 2005 (Independent Mental Capacity Advocate) (Wales) Regulations 2007 SI: /No (W.).* These regulations will remain in draft form until they are made by the National Assembly for Wales. The target coming into force date is 1 October 2007. Unlike the two sets of English regulations there will be one set only for Wales. Although the Welsh regulations will remain in draft form until the coming into force date, these have been drafted to give effect to similar and corresponding provisions to the regulations in England.

39 This may be accommodation in a care home, nursing home, ordinary and sheltered housing, housing association or other registered social housing or in private sector housing provided by a local authority or in hostel accommodation.

Sometimes NHS organisations and local authorities will make decisions together about moving a person into long-term care. In these cases, the organisation that must instruct the IMCA is the one that is ultimately responsible for the decision to move the person. The IMCA to be instructed is the one who works wherever the person is at the time that the person needs support and representation. 10.12

What are the responsible body's duties?

The responsible body: 10.13

- *must* instruct an IMCA to support and represent a person in the situations set out in paragraphs 10.40–10.58
- *may* decide to instruct an IMCA in situations described in paragraphs 10.59–10.68
- *must*, in all circumstances when an IMCA is instructed, take properly into account the information that the IMCA provides when working out whether the particular decision (such as giving, withholding or stopping treatment, changing a person's accommodation, or carrying out a recommendation following a care review or an allegation requiring adult protection) is in the best interests of the person who lacks capacity.

The responsible body should also have procedures, training and awareness programmes to make sure that: 10.14

- all relevant staff know when they need to instruct an IMCA and are able to do so promptly
- all relevant staff know how to get in touch with the IMCA service and know the procedure for instructing an IMCA
- they record an IMCA's involvement in a case and any information the IMCA provides to help decision-making
- they also record how a decision-maker has taken into account the IMCA's report and information as part of the process of working out the person's best interests (this should include reasons for disagreeing with that advice, if relevant)
- they give access to relevant records when requested by an IMCA under section 35(6)(b) of the Act
- the IMCA gets information about changes that may affect the support and representation the IMCA provides
- decision-makers let all relevant people know when an IMCA is working on a person's case, and
- decision-makers inform the IMCA of the final decision taken and the reason for it.

Sometimes an IMCA and staff working for the responsible body might disagree. If this happens, they should try to settle the disagreement through discussion and negotiation as soon as possible. If they cannot do this, they should then follow the responsible body's formal procedures for settling disputes or complaints (see paragraphs 10.34 to 10.39 below). 10.15

In some situations the IMCA may challenge a responsible body's decision, or they may help somebody who is challenging a decision. The General Regulations in England and the Regulations in Wales set out when this may happen (see also chapter 15). If there is no other way of resolving the disagreement, the decision may be challenged in the Court of Protection. 10.16

Who can be an IMCA?

In England, a person can only be an IMCA if the local authority approves their appointment. In Wales, the local health board will provide approval. Qualified employees of an approved organisation can act as IMCAs. Local authorities and health boards will usually commission 10.17

independent advocacy organisations to provide the IMCA service. These organisations will work to appropriate organisational standards set through the contracting/commissioning process.

10.18 Individual IMCAs must:
- have specific experience
- have IMCA training
- have integrity and a good character, and
- be able to act independently.

All IMCAs must complete the IMCA training in order that they can work as an independent mental capacity advocate. A national advocacy qualification is also being developed, which will include the IMCA training.

Before a local authority or health board appoints an IMCA, they must carry out checks with the Criminal Records Bureau (CRB) to get a criminal record certificate or enhanced criminal record certificate for that individual.[40]

10.19 IMCAs must be independent. People cannot act as IMCAs if they:
- care for or treat (in a paid or professional capacity) the person they will be representing (this does not apply if they are an existing advocate acting for that person), or
- have links to the person instructing them, to the decision-maker or to other individuals involved in the person's care or treatment that may affect their independence.

What is an IMCA's role?

10.20 An IMCA must decide how best to represent and support the person who lacks capacity that they are helping. They:
- must confirm that the person instructing them has the authority to do so
- should interview or meet in private the person who lacks capacity, if possible
- must act in accordance with the principles of the Act (as set out in section 1 of the Act and chapter 2 of the Code) and take account of relevant guidance in the Code
- may examine any relevant records that section 35(6) of the Act gives them access to
- should get the views of professionals and paid workers providing care or treatment for the person who lacks capacity
- should get the views of anybody else who can give information about the wishes and feelings, beliefs or values of the person who lacks capacity
- should get hold of any other information they think will be necessary
- must find out what support a person who lacks capacity has had to help them make the specific decision
- must try to find out what the person's wishes and feelings, beliefs and values would be likely to be if the person had capacity
- should find out what alternative options there are
- should consider whether getting another medical opinion would help the person who lacks capacity, and
- must write a report on their findings for the local authority or NHS body.

---

[40] IMCAs were named as a group that is subject to mandatory checking under the new vetting and barring system in the Safeguarding Vulnerable Groups Act 2006. Roll-out of the bulk of the scheme will take place in 2008.

Where possible, decision-makers should make decisions based on a full understanding of a person's past and present wishes. The IMCA should provide the decision-maker with as much of this information as possible—and anything else they think is relevant. The report they give the decision-maker may include questions about the proposed action or may include suggested alternatives, if they think that these would be better suited to the person's wishes and feelings. **10.21**

Another important part of the IMCA's role is communicating their findings. Decision-makers should find the most effective way to enable them to do this. In some of the IMCA pilot areas,[41] hospital discharge teams added a 'Need to instruct an IMCA?' question on their patient or service user forms. This allowed staff to identify the need for an IMCA as early as possible, and to discuss the timetable for the decision to be made. Some decisions need a very quick IMCA response, others will allow more time. In the pilot areas, IMCA involvement led to better informed discharge planning, with a clearer focus on the best interests of a person who lacked capacity. It did not cause additional delays in the hospital discharge. **10.22**

Representing and supporting the person who lacks capacity

IMCAs should take account of the guidance in chapter 5. **10.23**
- IMCAs should find out whether the decision-maker has given all practical and appropriate support to help the person who lacks capacity to be involved as much as possible in decision-making. If the person has communication difficulties, the IMCA should also find out if the decision-maker has obtained any specialist help (for example, from a speech and language therapist).
- Sometimes an IMCA may find information to suggest a person might regain capacity in the future, either so they can make the decision themselves or be more involved in decision-making. In such a situation, the IMCA can ask the decision-maker to delay the decision, if it is not urgent.
- The IMCA will need to get as much information as possible about the person's wishes, feelings, beliefs and values—both past and present. They should also consider the person's religion and any cultural factors that may influence the decision.

Sometimes a responsible body will not have time to instruct an IMCA (for example in an emergency or if a decision is urgent). If this is the case, this should be recorded, with the reason an IMCA has not been instructed. Where the decision concerns a move of accommodation, the local authority must appoint an IMCA as soon as possible afterwards. Sometimes the IMCA will not have time to carry out full investigations. In these situations, the IMCA must make a judgement about what they can achieve in the time available to support and represent the person who lacks capacity. **10.24**

Sometimes an IMCA might not be able to get a good picture of what the person might want. They should still try to make sure the decision-maker considers all relevant information by: **10.25**
- raising relevant issues and questions, and
- providing additional, relevant information to help the final decision.

Finding and evaluating information

Section 35(6) provides IMCAs with certain powers to enable them to carry out their duties. These include: **10.26**
- the right to have an interview in private with the person who lacks capacity, and

---

[41] For further information see www.dh.gov.uk/imca

- the right to examine, and take copies of, any records that the person holding the record thinks are relevant to the investigation (for example, clinical records, care plans, social care assessment documents or care home records).

10.27   The IMCA may also need to meet professionals or paid carers providing care or treatment for the person who lacks capacity. These people can help assess the information in case records or other sources. They can also comment on possible alternative courses of action. Ultimately, it is the decision-maker's responsibility to decide whether a proposed course of action is in the person's best interests. However, the Act requires the decision-maker to take account of the reports made and information given by the IMCA. In most cases a decision on the person's best interests will be made through discussion involving all the relevant people who are providing care or treatment, as well as the IMCA.

Finding out the person's wishes and feelings, beliefs and values

10.28   The IMCA needs to try and find out what the person's wishes and feelings might be, and what their underlying beliefs and values might also be. The IMCA should try to communicate both verbally and non-verbally with the person who may lack capacity, as appropriate. For example, this might mean using pictures or photographs. But there will be cases where the person cannot communicate at all (for example, if they are unconscious). The IMCA may also talk to other professionals or paid carers directly involved in providing present or past care or treatment. The IMCA might also need to examine health and social care records and any written statements of preferences the person may have made while they still had capacity to do so. Chapter 5 contains further guidance on finding out the views of people who lack capacity. Chapter 3 contains further guidance on helping someone to make their own decision.

Considering alternative courses of action

10.29   The IMCA will need to check whether the decision-maker has considered all possible options. They should also ask whether the proposed option is less restrictive of the person's rights or future choices or would allow them more freedom (chapter 2, principle 5).

10.30   The IMCA may wish to discuss possible options with other professionals or paid carers directly involved in providing care or treatment for the person. But they must respect the confidentiality of the person they are representing.

Scenario: Using an IMCA

Mrs Nolan has dementia. She is being discharged from hospital. She has no close family or friends. She also lacks the capacity to decide whether she should return home or move to a care home. The local authority instructs an IMCA. Mrs Nolan tells the IMCA that she wants to go back to her own home, which she can remember and describe. But the hospital care team thinks she needs additional support, which can only be provided in a care home. The IMCA reviewed all the assessments of Mrs Nolan's needs, spoke to people involved in her care and wrote a report stating that Mrs Nolan had strong and clear wishes. The IMCA also suggested that a care package could be provided to support Mrs Nolan if she were allowed to return home. The care manager now has to decide what is in Mrs Nolan's best interests. He must consider the views of the hospital care team and the IMCA's report.

Getting a second medical opinion

10.31   For decisions about serious medical treatment, the IMCA may consider seeking a second medical opinion from a doctor with appropriate expertise. This puts a person who lacks the capacity to make a specific decision in the same position as a person who has capacity, who has the right to request a second opinion.

What happens if the IMCA disagrees with the decision-maker?

The IMCA's role is to support and represent their client. They may do this through asking questions, raising issues, offering information and writing a report. They will often take part in a meeting involving different healthcare and social care staff to work out what is in the person's best interests. There may sometimes be cases when an IMCA thinks that a decision-maker has not paid enough attention to their report and other relevant information and is particularly concerned about the decision made. They may then need to challenge the decision. **10.32**

An IMCA has the same rights to challenge a decision as any other person caring for the person or interested in his welfare. The right of challenge applies both to decisions about lack of capacity and a person's best interests. **10.33**

Chapter 15 sets out how disagreements can be settled. The approach will vary, depending on the type and urgency of the disagreement. It could be a formal or informal approach. **10.34**

Disagreements about health care or treatment
• Consult the Patient Advice and Liaison Service (England)
• Consult the Community Health Council (Wales)
• Use the NHS Complaints Procedure
• Refer the matter to the local continuing care review panel
• Engage the services of the Independent Complaints Advocacy Service (England) or another advocate.

Disagreements about social care
• Use the care home's complaints procedure (if the person is in a care home)
• Use the local authority complaints procedure.

Before using these formal methods, the IMCA and the decision-maker should discuss the areas they disagree about—particularly those that might have a serious impact on the person the IMCA is representing. The IMCA and decision-maker should make time to listen to each other's views and to understand the reason for the differences. Sometimes these discussions can help settle a disagreement. **10.35**

Sometimes an IMCA service will have a steering group, with representatives from the local NHS organisations and the local authority. These representatives can sometimes negotiate between two differing views. Or they can clarify policy on a certain issue. They should also be involved if an IMCA believes they have discovered poor practice on an important issue. **10.36**

IMCAs may use complaints procedures as necessary to try to settle a disagreement—and they can pursue a complaint as far as the relevant ombudsman if needed. In particularly serious or urgent cases, an IMCA may seek permission to refer a case to the Court of Protection for a decision. The Court will make a decision in the best interests of the person who lacks capacity. **10.37**

The first step in making a formal challenge is to approach the Official Solicitor (OS) with the facts of the case. The OS can decide to apply to the court as a litigation friend (acting on behalf of the person the IMCA is representing). If the OS decides not to apply himself, the IMCA can ask for permission to apply to the Court of Protection. The OS can still be asked to act as a litigation friend for the person who lacks capacity. **10.38**

In extremely serious cases, the IMCA might want to consider an application for judicial review in the High Court. This might happen if the IMCA thinks there are very serious consequences to **10.39** a decision that has been made by a public authority. There are time limits for making an application, and the IMCA would have to instruct solicitors—and may be liable for the costs of the case going to court. So IMCAs should get legal advice before choosing this approach. The IMCA can also ask the OS to consider making the claim.

What decisions require an IMCA?

10.40   There are three types of decisions which require an IMCA to be instructed for people who lack capacity. These are:
- decisions about providing, withholding or stopping serious medical treatment
- decisions about whether to place people into accommodation (for example a care home or a long stay hospital), and
- decisions about whether to move people to different long stay accommodation.

For these decisions all local authorities and all health bodies must refer the same kinds of decisions to an IMCA for anyone who lacks capacity and qualifies for the IMCA service.

10.41   There are two further types of decisions where the responsible body has the power to instruct an IMCA for a person who lacks capacity. These are decisions relating to:
- care reviews and
- adult protection cases.

In such cases, the relevant local authority or NHS body must decide in each individual case whether it would be of particular benefit to the person who lacks capacity to have an IMCA to support them. The factors which should be considered are explained in paragraphs 10.59–10.68.[42]

Decisions about serious medical treatment

10.42   Where a serious medical treatment decision is being considered for a person who lacks the capacity to consent, and who qualifies for additional safeguards, section 37 of the Act imposes a duty on the NHS body to instruct an IMCA. NHS bodies must instruct an IMCA whenever they are proposing to take a decision about 'serious medical treatment', or proposing that another organisation (such as a private hospital) carry out the treatment on their behalf, if:
- the person concerned does not have the capacity to make a decision about the treatment, and
- there is no-one appropriate to consult about whether the decision is in the person's best interests, other than paid care staff.

10.43   Regulations for England and Wales set out the definition of 'serious medical treatment' for decisions that require an IMCA. It includes treatments for both mental and physical conditions.
Serious medical treatment is defined as treatment which involves giving new treatment, stopping treatment that has already started or withholding treatment that could be offered in circumstances where:
- if a single treatment is proposed there is a fine balance between the likely benefits and the burdens to the patient and the risks involved
- a decision between a choice of treatments is finely balanced, or
- what is proposed is likely to have serious consequences for the patient.

---

[42] See chapter 11 for information about the role of 'consultees' when research is proposed involving a person who lacks capacity to make a decision about whether to agree to take part in research. In certain situations IMCAs may be involved as consultees for research purposes.

'Serious consequences' are those which could have a serious impact on the patient, either from the effects of the treatment itself or its wider implications. This may include treatments which: **10.44**

- cause serious and prolonged pain, distress or side effects
- have potentially major consequences for the patient (for example, stopping life-sustaining treatment or having major surgery such as heart surgery), or
- have a serious impact on the patient's future life choices (for example, interventions for ovarian cancer).

It is impossible to set out all types of procedures that may amount to 'serious medical treatment',   **10.45**
although some examples of medical treatments that might be considered serious include:

- chemotherapy and surgery for cancer
- electro-convulsive therapy
- therapeutic sterilisation
- major surgery (such as open-heart surgery or brain/neuro-surgery)
- major amputations (for example, loss of an arm or leg)
- treatments which will result in permanent loss of hearing or sight
- withholding or stopping artificial nutrition and hydration, and
- termination of pregnancy.

These are illustrative examples only, and whether these or other procedures are considered serious medical treatment in any given case, will depend on the circumstances and the consequences for the patient. There are also many more treatments which will be defined as serious medical treatments under the Act's regulations. Decision-makers who are not sure whether they need to instruct an IMCA should consult their colleagues.

The only situation in which the duty to instruct an IMCA need not be followed, is when an   **10.46**
urgent decision is needed (for example, to save the person's life). This decision must be recorded with the reason for the non-referral. Responsible bodies will however still need to instruct an IMCA for any serious treatment that follows the emergency treatment.

While a decision-maker is waiting for the IMCA's report, they must still act in the person's best   **10.47**
interests (for example, to give treatment that stops the person's condition getting worse).

Scenario: Using an IMCA for serious medical treatment

Mr Jones had a fall and suffered serious head injuries. Hospital staff could not find any family or friends. He needed urgent surgery, but afterwards still lacked capacity to accept or refuse medical treatment. The hospital did not involve an IMCA in the decision to operate, because it needed to make an emergency decision. But it did instruct an IMCA when it needed to carry out further serious medical treatment. The IMCA met with Mr Jones looked at his case notes and reviewed the options with the consultant. The decision-maker then made the clinical decision about Mr Jones' best interests taking into account the IMCA's report.

Some decisions about medical treatment are so serious that the courts need to make them (see   **10.48**
chapter 8). But responsible bodies should still instruct an IMCA in these cases. The OS may be involved as a litigation friend of the person who lacks capacity.

Responsible bodies do not have to instruct an IMCA for patients detained under the Mental   **10.49**
Health Act 1983, if:

- the treatment is for mental disorder, and
- they can give it without the patient's consent under that Act.

If serious medical treatment proposed for the detained patient is not for their mental disorder, the   **10.50**
patient then has a right to an IMCA—as long as they meet the Mental Capacity Act's requirements.

So a detained patient without capacity to consent to cancer treatment, for example, should qualify for an IMCA if there are no family or friends whom it would be appropriate to consult.

Decisions about accommodation or changes of residence

10.51 The Act imposes similar duties on NHS bodies and local authorities who are responsible for long-term accommodation decisions for a person who lacks the capacity to agree to the placement and who qualifies for the additional safeguard of an IMCA. The right to an IMCA applies to decisions about long-term accommodation in a hospital or care home if it is:
- provided or arranged by the NHS, or
- residential care that is provided or arranged by the local authority or provided under section 117 of the Mental Health Act 1983, or
- a move between such accommodation.

10.52 Responsible bodies have a duty to instruct an IMCA if:
- an NHS organisation proposes to place a person who lacks capacity in a hospital—or to move them to another hospital—for longer than 28 days, or
- an NHS organisation proposes to place a person who lacks capacity in a care home—or to move them to a different care home—for what is likely to be longer than eight weeks.

In either situation the other qualifying conditions apply. So, if the accommodation is for less than 28 days in a hospital or less than 8 weeks in a care home, then an IMCA need not be appointed.

10.53 The duty also applies if a local authority carries out an assessment under section 47 of the NHS and Community Care Act 1990, and it decides to:
- provide care services for a person who lacks capacity in the form of residential accommodation in a care home or its equivalent (see paragraph 10.11) which is likely to be longer than eight weeks, or
- move a person who lacks capacity to another care home or its equivalent for a period likely to exceed eight weeks.

10.54 In some cases, a care home may decide to de-register so that they can provide accommodation and care in a different way. If a local authority makes the new arrangements, then an IMCA should still be instructed if a patient lacks capacity and meets the other qualifying conditions.

10.55 Sometimes a person's placement will be longer than expected. The responsible body should involve an IMCA as soon as they realise the stay will be longer than 28 days or eight weeks, as appropriate.

10.56 People who fund themselves in long-term accommodation have the same rights to an IMCA as others, if the local authority:
- carries out an assessment under section 47 of the NHS and Community Care Act 1990, and
- decides it has a duty to the person (under either section 21 or 29 of the National Assistance Act 1947 or section 117 of the Mental Health Act 1983).

10.57 Responsible bodies can only put aside the duty to involve an IMCA if the placement or move is urgent (for example, an emergency admission to hospital or possible homelessness). The decision-maker must involve an IMCA as soon as possible after making an emergency decision, if:
- the person is likely to stay in hospital for longer than 28 days, or
- they will stay in other accommodation for longer than eight weeks.

10.58 Responsible bodies do not have to involve IMCAs if the person in question is going to be required to stay in the accommodation under the Mental Health Act 1983. But if a person is discharged from detention, they have a right to an IMCA in future accommodation decisions (if they meet the usual conditions set out in the Act).

The Expansion Regulations have given local authorities and NHS bodies the power to apply the   **10.59**
IMCA role to two further types of decisions:

- a care review, and
- adult protection cases that involve vulnerable people.

In these situations, the responsible body must consider in each individual case whether to instruct   **10.60**
an IMCA. Where an IMCA is instructed:

- the decision-maker must be satisfied that having an IMCA will be of particular benefit to the person who lacks capacity
- the decision-maker must also follow the best interests checklist, including getting the views of anyone engaged in caring for a person when assessing their best interests, and
- the decision-maker must consider the IMCA's report and related information when making a decision.

Responsible bodies are expected to take a strategic approach in deciding when they will use   **10.61**
IMCAs in these two additional situations. They should establish a policy locally for determining
these decisions, setting out the criteria for appointing an IMCA including the issues to be taken
into account when deciding if an IMCA will be of particular benefit to the person concerned.
However, decision-makers will need to consider each case separately to see if the criteria are met.
Local authorities or NHS bodies may want to publish their approach for ease of access, setting out
the ways they intend to use these additional powers and review it periodically.

Involving an IMCA in care reviews

A responsible body can instruct an IMCA to support and represent a person who lacks capacity   **10.62**
when:

- they have arranged accommodation for that person
- they aim to review the arrangements (as part of a care plan or otherwise), and
- there are no family or friends who it would be appropriate to consult.

Section 7 of the Local Authority Social Services Act 1970 sets out current requirements for   **10.63**
care reviews. It states that there should be a review 'within three months of help being provided
or major changes made to services'. There should then be a review every year—or more often, if
needed.

Reviews should relate to decisions about accommodation: **10.64**

- for someone who lacks capacity to make a decision about accommodation
- that will be provided for a continuous period of more than 12 weeks
- that are not the result of an obligation under the Mental Health Act 1983, and
- that do not relate to circumstances where sections 37 to 39 of the Act would apply.

Where the person is to be detained or required to live in accommodation under the Mental Health   **10.65**
Act 1983, an IMCA will not be needed since the safeguards available under that Act will apply.

Involving IMCAs in adult protection cases

Responsible bodies have powers to instruct an IMCA to support and represent a person who lacks   **10.66**
capacity where it is alleged that:

- the person is or has been abused or neglected by another person, or
- the person is abusing or has abused another person.

The responsible bodies can only instruct an IMCA if they propose to take, or have already taken, protective measures. This is in accordance with adult protection procedures set up under statutory guidance.[43]

10.67   In adult protection cases (and no other cases), access to IMCAs is not restricted to people who have no-one else to support or represent them. People who lack capacity who have family and friends can still have an IMCA to support them in the adult protection procedures.

10.68   In some situations, a case may start out as an adult protection case where a local authority may consider whether or not to involve an IMCA under the criteria they have set—but may then become a case where the allegations or evidence give rise to the question of whether the person should be moved in their best interests. In these situations the case has become one where an IMCA must be involved if there is no-one else appropriate to support and represent the person in this decision.

Who qualifies for an IMCA?

10.69   Apart from the adult protection cases discussed above, IMCAs are only available to people who:
- lack capacity to make a specific decision about serious medical treatment or long-term accommodation, *and*
- have no family or friends who are available and appropriate to support or represent them apart from professionals or paid workers providing care or treatment, *and*
- have not previously named someone who could help with a decision, *and*
- have not made a Lasting Power of Attorney or Enduring Power of Attorney (see paragraph 10.70 below).

10.70   The Act says that IMCAs cannot be instructed if:
- a person who now lacks capacity previously named a person that should be consulted about decisions that affect them, and that person is available and willing to help
- the person who lacks capacity has appointed an attorney, either under a Lasting Power of Attorney or an Enduring Power of Attorney, and the attorney continues to manage the person's affairs
- the Court of Protection has appointed a deputy, who continues to act on the person's behalf.

10.71   However, where a person has no family or friends to represent them, but does have an attorney or deputy who has been appointed solely to deal with their property and affairs, they should not be denied access to an IMCA. The Government is seeking to amend the Act at the earliest opportunity to ensure that, in such circumstances, an IMCA should always be appointed to represent the person's views when they lack the capacity to make decisions relating to serious medical treatment or long-term accommodation moves.

---

[43] Published guidance: *No secrets: Guidance on developing and implementing multi-agency policies and procedures to protect vulnerable adults from abuse* for England (on the Department of Health website) and *In safe hands* in Wales.

No secrets applies to adults aged 18 or over. The Children Act 1989 applies to 16 and 17 year olds who may be facing abuse. Part V of the Act covers the Protection of Children, which includes at section 47 the duty to investigate by a local authority in order to decide whether they should take any action to safeguard or promote a child's welfare where he or she requires protection or may suffer harm. See also chapter 12 of this Code.

A responsible body can still instruct an IMCA if the Court of Protection is deciding on a   10.72
deputy, but none is in place when a decision needs to be made.

Scenario: Qualifying for an IMCA

Ms Lewis, a woman with a history of mental health problems has lived in a care home for several years. Her home will soon close, and she has no-one who could help her. She has become very anxious and now lacks capacity to make a decision about future accommodation. The local authority instructs an IMCA to support her. The IMCA visits Ms Lewis, talks to staff who have been involved in her care and reviews her case notes. In his report, the IMCA includes the information that Ms Lewis is very close to another client in the care home. The IMCA notes that they could move together—if it is also in the interests of the other client. The local authority now has to decide on the best interests of the client, considering the information that the IMCA has provided.

Will IMCAs be available to people in prisons?

IMCAs should be available to people who are in prison and lack capacity to make decisions about   10.73
serious medical treatment or long-term accommodation.

Who is it 'appropriate to consult'?

The IMCA is a safeguard for those people who lack capacity, who have no-one close to them who   10.74
'it would be appropriate to consult'. (This is apart from adult protection cases where this criterion does not apply.) The safeguard is intended to apply to those people who have little or no network of support, such as close family or friends, who take an interest in their welfare or no-one willing or able to be formally consulted in decision-making processes.

The Act does not define those 'whom it would be appropriate to consult' and the evaluation of   10.75
the IMCA pilots reported that decision-makers in the local authority and in the NHS, whose decision it is to determine this, sometimes found it difficult to establish when an IMCA was required.[44] Section 4(7) provides that consultation about a person's best interests shall include among others, anyone:

- named by the person as someone to be consulted on a relevant decision
- engaged in caring for them, or
- interested in their welfare (see chapter 4).

The decision-maker must determine if it is possible and practical to speak to these people, and   10.76
those described in paragraph 10.70 when working out whether the proposed decision is in the person's best interests. If it is not possible, practical and appropriate to consult anyone, an IMCA should be instructed.

There may be situations where a person who lacks capacity has family or friends, but it is not   10.77
practical or appropriate to consult them. For example, an elderly person with dementia may have an adult child who now lives in Australia, or an older person may have relatives who very rarely visit. Or, a family member may simply refuse to be consulted. In such cases, decision-makers must instruct an IMCA—for serious medical treatment and care moves and record the reason for the decision.

The person who lacks capacity may have friends or neighbours who know their wishes and   10.78
feelings but are not willing or able to help with the specific decision to be made. They may think

---

[44] See www.dh.gov.uk/PolicyAndGuidance/HealthAndSocialCareTopics/SocialCare/IMCA/fs/en

it is too much of a responsibility. If they are elderly and frail themselves, it may be too difficult for them to attend case conferences and participate formally. In this situation, the responsible body should instruct an IMCA, and the IMCA may visit them and enable them to be involved more informally.

10.79   If a family disagrees with a decision-maker's proposed action, this is not grounds for concluding that there is nobody whose views are relevant to the decision.

10.80   A person who lacks capacity and already has an advocate may still be entitled to an IMCA. The IMCA would consult with the advocate. Where that advocate meets the appointment criteria for the IMCA service, they may be appointed to fulfil the IMCA role for this person in addition to their other duties.

11. HOW DOES THE ACT AFFECT RESEARCH PROJECTS INVOLVING A PERSON WHO LACKS CAPACITY?

It is important that research involving people who lack capacity can be carried out, and that is carried out properly. Without it, we would not improve our knowledge of what causes a person to lack or lose capacity, and the diagnosis, treatment, care and needs of people who lack capacity.

This chapter gives guidance on involving people who lack capacity to consent to take part in research. It sets out:

• what the Act means by 'research'
• the requirements that people must meet if their research project involves somebody who lacks capacity
• the specific responsibilities of researchers, and
• how the Act applies to research that started before the Act came into force.

This chapter only deals with research in relation to adults. Further guidance will be provided on how the Act applies in relation to research involving those under the age of 18.

In this chapter, as throughout the Code, a person's capacity (or lack of capacity) refers specifically to their capacity to make a particular decision at the time it needs to be made.

Quick summary

The Act's rules for research that includes people who lack capacity to consent to their involvement cover:

• when research can be carried out
• the ethical approval process
• respecting the wishes and feelings of people who lack capacity
• other safeguards to protect people who lack capacity
• how to engage with a person who lacks capacity
• how to engage with carers and other relevant people.

This chapter also explains:

• the specific rules that apply to research involving human tissue and
• what to do if research projects have already been given the go-ahead.

The Act applies to all research that is intrusive. 'Intrusive' means research that would be unlawful if it involved a person who had capacity but had not consented to take part. The Act does not apply to research involving clinical trials (testing new drugs).

Why does the Act cover research?

Because the Act is intended to assist and support people who may lack capacity, the Act protects people who take part in research projects but lack capacity to make decisions about their involvement. It makes sure that researchers respect their wishes and feelings. The Act does not apply to research that involves clinical trials of medicines—because these are covered by other rules.[45]

11.1

How can research involving people who lack capacity help?

A high percentage of patients with Down's syndrome lack capacity to agree or refuse to take part in research. Research involving patients with Down's syndrome has shown that they are more likely than other people to get pre-senile dementia. Research has also shown that when this happens the pathological changes that occur in a person with Down's syndrome (changes affecting their body and brain) are similar to those that occur in someone with Alzheimer's disease. This means that we now know that treatment similar to that used for memory disorders in patients with Alzheimer's is appropriate to treat dementia in those with Down's syndrome.

What is 'research'?

The Act does not have a specific definition for 'research'. The Department of Health and National Assembly for Wales publications *Research governance framework for health and social care* both state:

11.2

'research can be defined as the attempt to derive generalisable new knowledge by addressing clearly defined questions with systematic and rigorous methods.'[46]

Research may:

• provide information that can be applied generally to an illness, disorder or condition
• demonstrate how effective and safe a new treatment is
• add to evidence that one form of treatment works better than another
• add to evidence that one form of treatment is safer than another, or
• examine wider issues (for example, the factors that affect someone's capacity to make a decision).

Researchers must state clearly if an activity is part of someone's care and not part of the research. Sometimes experimental medicine or treatment may be performed for the person's benefit and be the best option for their care. But in these cases, it may be difficult to decide whether treatment is research or care. Where there is doubt, the researcher should seek legal advice.

11.3

What assumptions can a researcher make about capacity?

Researchers should assume that a person has capacity, unless there is proof that they lack capacity to make a specific decision (see chapter 3). The person must also receive support to try to help them make their own decision (see chapter 2). The person whose capacity is in question has the

11.4

---

45 The Medicines for Human Use (Clinical Trials) Regulations 2004.

46 www.dh.gov.uk/PublicationsAndStatistics/Publications/PublicationsPolicyAndGuidance/Publications PolicyAndGuidanceArticle/fs/en?CONTENT_ID=4008777&chk=dMRd/5 and www.word.wales.gov.uk/content/ governance/governance-e.htm

right to make decisions that others might not agree with, and they have the right not to take part in research.

What research does the Act cover?

11.5 It is expected that most of the researchers who ask for their research to be approved under the Act will be medical or social care researchers. However, the Act can cover more than just medical and social care research. Intrusive research which does not meet the requirements of the Act cannot be carried out lawfully in relation to people who lack capacity.

11.6 The Act applies to research that:
- is 'intrusive' (if a person taking part had capacity, the researcher would need to get their consent to involve them)
- involves people who have an impairment of, or a disturbance in the functioning of, their mind or brain which makes them unable to decide whether or not to agree to take part in the research (i.e. they lack capacity to consent), and
- is not a clinical trial covered under the Medicines for Human Use (Clinical Trials) Regulations 2004.

11.7 There are circumstances where no consent is needed to lawfully involve a person in research. These apply to all persons, whether they have capacity or not:
- Sometimes research only involves data that has been anonymised (it cannot be traced back to individuals). Confidentiality and data protection laws do not apply in this case.
- Under the Human Tissue Act 2004, research that deals only with human tissue that has been anonymised does not require consent (see paragraphs 11.37–11.40). This applies to both those who have capacity and those who do not. But the research must have ethical approval, and the tissue must come from a living person.[47]
- If researchers collected human tissue samples before 31 August 2006, they do not need a person's consent to work on them. But they will normally have to get ethical approval.
- Regulations[48] made under section 251 of the NHS Act 2006 (formerly known as section 60 of the Health and Social Care Act 2001)[49] allow people to use confidential patient information without breaking the law on confidentiality by applying to the Patient Information Advisory Group for approval on behalf of the Secretary of State.[50]

Who is responsible for making sure research meets the Act's requirements?

11.8 Responsibility for meeting the Act's requirements lies with:
- the 'appropriate body', as defined in regulations made by the Secretary of State (for regulations applying in England) or the National Assembly for Wales (for regulations applying in Wales) (see paragraph 11.10), and
- the researchers carrying out the research (see paragraphs 11.20–11.40).

---

[47] Human Tissue Act 2004 section 1(9).

[48] Health Service (Control of Patient Information) Regulations 2002 Section I. 2002/1438.

[49] Section 60 of the Health and Social Care Act 2001 was included in the NHS Act 2006 which consolidated all the previous health legislation still in force.

[50] The Patient Information Advisory Group considers applications on behalf of the Secretary of State to allow the common law duty of confidentiality to be aside. It was established under section 61of the Health and Social Care Act 2006 (now known as section 252 of the NHS Act 2006). Further information can be found at www.advisorybodies.doh.gov.uk/PIAG.

How can research get approval?

Research covered by the Act cannot include people who lack capacity to consent to the research 11.9
unless:
- it has the approval of 'the appropriate body', and
- it follows other requirements in the Act to:

  —consider the views of carers and other relevant people
  —treat the person's interests as more important than those of science and society, and
  —respect any objections a person who lacks capacity makes during research.

An 'appropriate body' is an organisation that can approve research projects. In England, the 11.10
'appropriate body' must be a research ethics committee recognised by the Secretary of State.[51] In
Wales, the 'appropriate body' must be a research ethics committee recognised by the Welsh
Assembly Government.

The appropriate body can only approve a research project if the research is linked to: 11.11
- an impairing condition that affects the person who lacks capacity, or
- the treatment of that condition (see paragraph 11.17)

and:
- there are reasonable grounds for believing that the research would be less effective if only people
  with capacity are involved, and
- the research project has made arrangements to consult carers and to follow the other requirements
  of the Act.

Research must also meet one of two requirements: 11.12
1. The research must have some chance of benefiting the person who lacks capacity, as set out in
   paragraph 11.14 below. The benefit must be in proportion to any burden caused by taking
   part, or
2. The aim of the research must be to provide knowledge about the cause of, or treatment or care
   of people with, the same impairing condition—or a similar condition.

If researchers are relying on the second requirement, the Act sets out further requirements that
must be met:
- the risk to the person who lacks capacity must be negligible
- there must be no significant interference with the freedom of action or privacy of the person
  who lacks capacity, and
- nothing must be done to or in relation to the person who lacks capacity which is unduly invasive
  or restrictive (see paragraphs 11.16–11.19 below).

An impairing condition: 11.13
- is caused by (or may be caused by) an impairment of, or disturbance in the functioning of, the
  person's mind or brain
- causes (or may cause) an impairment or disturbance of the mind or brain, or
- contributes to (or may contribute to) an impairment or disturbance of the mind or brain.

Balancing the benefit and burden of research

Potential benefits of research for a person who lacks capacity could include: 11.14
- developing more effective ways of treating a person or managing their condition
- improving the quality of healthcare, social care or other services that they have access to

---

[51] Mental Capacity Act 2005 (Appropriate Body) (England) Regulations 2006.

- discovering the cause of their condition, if they would benefit from that knowledge, or
- reducing the risk of the person being harmed, excluded or disadvantaged.

11.15   Benefits may be direct or indirect (for example, the person might benefit at a later date if policies or care packages affecting them are changed because of the research). It might be that participation in the research itself will be of benefit to the person in particular circumstances. For example, if the research involves interviews and the person has the opportunity to express their views, this could be considered of real benefit to a particular individual.

Providing knowledge about causes, treatment or care of people with the same impairing condition or a similar condition

11.16   It is possible for research to be carried out which doesn't actually benefit the person taking part, as long as it aims to provide knowledge about the causes, treatment or care of people with the same impairing condition, or a similar condition. '*Care*' and '*treatment*' are not limited to medical care and treatment. For example, research could examine how day-to-day life in prison affects prisoners with mental health conditions.

11.17   It is the person's actual condition that must be the same or similar in research, not the underlying cause. A '*similar condition*' may therefore have a different cause to that suffered by the participant. For example, research into ways of supporting people with learning disabilities to live more independently might involve a person with a learning disability caused by a head trauma. But its findings might help people with similar learning disabilities that have different causes.

Scenario: Research that helps find a cause or treatment

Mr Neal has Down's syndrome. For many years he has lived in supported housing and worked in a local supermarket. But several months ago, he became aggressive, forgetful and he started to make mistakes at work. His consultant believes that this may indicate the start of Alzheimer's disease. Mr Neal's condition is now so bad that he does not have capacity to consent to treatment or make other decisions about his care. A research team is researching the cause of dementia in people with Down's syndrome. They would like to involve Mr Neal. The research satisfies the Act's requirement that it is intended to provide knowledge of the causes or treatment of that condition, even though it may not directly benefit Mr Neal. So the approving body might give permission – if the research meets other requirements.

11.18   Any risk to people involved in this category of research must be 'negligible' (minimal). This means that a person should suffer no harm or distress by taking part. Researchers must consider risks to psychological wellbeing as well as physical wellbeing. This is particularly relevant for research related to observations or interviews.

11.19   Research in this category also must not affect a person's freedom of action or privacy in a significant way, and it should not be unduly invasive or restrictive. What will be considered as unduly invasive will be different for different people and different types of research. For example, in psychological research some people may think a specific question is intrusive, but others would not. Actions will not usually be classed as unduly invasive if they do not go beyond the experience of daily life, a routine medical examination or a psychological examination.

Scenario: Assessing the risk to research participants

A research project is studying:
- how well people with a learning disability make financial decisions, and
- communication techniques that may improve their decision-making capacity.

Some of the participants lack capacity to agree to take part. The Research Ethics Committee is satisfied that some of these participants may benefit from the study because their capacity to make financial decisions may be improved. For those who will not gain any personal benefit, the Committee is satisfied that:

- the research meets the other conditions of the Act
- the research methods (psychological testing and different communication techniques) involve no risk to participants, and
- the research could not have been carried out as effectively with people who have capacity.

What responsibilities do researchers have?

Before starting the research, the research team must make arrangements to: 11.20

- obtain approval for the research from the 'appropriate body'
- get the views of any carers and other relevant people before involving a person who lacks capacity in research (see paragraphs 11.22–11.28). There is an exception to this consultation requirement in situations where urgent treatment needs to be given or is about to be given
- respect the objections, wishes and feelings of the person, and
- place more importance on the person's interests than on those of science and society.

The research proposal must give enough information about what the team will do if a person 11.21 who lacks capacity needs urgent treatment during research and it is not possible to speak to the person's carer or someone else who acts or makes decisions on behalf of the person (see paragraphs 11.32–11.36).

Consulting carers

Once it has been established that a person lacks capacity to agree to participate, then before they 11.22 are included in research the researcher must consult with specified people in accordance with section 32 of the Act to determine whether the person should be included in the research.

Who can researchers consult?

The researcher should as a matter of good practice take reasonable steps to identify someone to 11.23 consult. That person (the consultee) must be involved in the person's care, interested in their welfare and must be willing to help. They must not be a professional or paid care worker. They will probably be a family member, but could be another person.

The researcher must take into account previous wishes and feelings that the person might have 11.24 expressed about who they would, or would not, like involved in future decisions.

A person is not prevented from being consulted if they are an attorney authorised under a 11.25 registered Lasting Power of Attorney or are a deputy appointed by the Court of Protection. But that person must not be acting in a professional or paid capacity (for example, person's solicitor).

Where there is no-one who meets the conditions mentioned at paragraphs 11.23 and 11.25, the 11.26 researcher must nominate a person to be the consulted. In this situation, they must follow guidance from the Secretary of State for Health in England or the National Assembly for Wales (the guidance will be available from mid-2007). The person who is nominated must have no connection with the research project.

The researcher must provide the consultee with information about the research project and ask 11.27 them:

- for advice about whether the person who lacks capacity should take part in the project, and
- what they think the person's feelings and wishes would be, if they had capacity to decide whether to take part.

11.28   Sometimes the consultee will say that the person would probably not take part in the project or that they would ask to be withdrawn. In this situation, the researcher must not include the person in the project, or they should withdraw them from it. But if the project has started, and the person is getting treatment as part of the research, the researcher may decide that the person should not be withdrawn if the researcher reasonably believes that this would cause a significant risk to the person's health. The researcher may decide that the person should continue with the research while the risk exists. But they should stop any parts of the study that are not related to the risk to the person's health.

What other safeguards does the Act require?

11.29   Even when a consultee agrees that a person can take part in research, the researcher must still consider the person's wishes and feelings.

11.30   Researchers must not do anything the person who lacks capacity objects to. They must not do anything to go against any advance decision to refuse treatment or other statement the person has previously made expressing preferences about their care or treatment. They must assume that the person's interests in this matter are more important than those of science and society.

11.31   A researcher must withdraw someone from a project if:
- they indicate in any way that they want to be withdrawn from the project (for example, if they become upset or distressed), or
- any of the Act's requirements are no longer met.

What happens if urgent decisions are required during the research project?

11.32   Anyone responsible for caring for a person must give them urgent treatment if they need it. In some circumstances, it may not be possible to separate the research from the urgent treatment.

11.33   A research proposal should explain to the appropriate body how researchers will deal with urgent decisions which may occur during the project, when there may not be time to carry out the consultations required under the Act. For example, after a patient has arrived in intensive care, the doctor may want to chart the course of an injury by taking samples or measurements immediately and then taking further samples after some type of treatment to compare with the first set.

11.34   Special rules apply where a person who lacks capacity is getting, or about to get, urgent treatment and researchers want to include them in a research project. If in these circumstances a researcher thinks that it is necessary to take urgent action for the purposes of the research, and they think it is not practical to consult someone about it, the researcher can take that action if:
- they get agreement from a registered medical practitioner not involved with the research, or
- they follow a procedure that the appropriate body agreed to at approval stage.

11.35   The medical practitioner may have a connection to the person who lacks capacity (for example, they might be their doctor). But they must not be involved in the research project in any way. This is to avoid conflicts of interest.

11.36   This exception to the duty to consult only applies:
- for as long as the person needs urgent treatment, and
- when the researcher needs to take action urgently for research to be valid.

It is likely to be limited to research into procedures or treatments used in emergencies. It does not apply where the researcher simply wants to act quickly.

What happens for research involving human tissue?

A person with capacity has to give their permission for someone to remove tissue from their body (for example, taking a biopsy (a sample) for diagnosis or removal of tissue in surgery). The Act allows the removal of tissue from the body of a person who lacks capacity, if it is in their best interests (see chapter 5). **11.37**

People with capacity must also give permission for the storage or use of tissue for certain purposes, set out in the Human Tissue Act 2004, (for example, transplants and research). But there are situations in which permission is not required by law: **10.38**

- research where the samples are anonymised and the research has ethical approval[52]
- clinical audit
- education or training relating to human health
- performance assessment
- public health monitoring, and
- quality assurance.

If an adult lacks capacity to consent, the Human Tissue Act 2004 says that tissue can be stored or used without seeking permission if the storage or use is: **11.39**

- to get information relevant to the health of another individual (for example, before conducting a transplant), as long as the researcher or healthcare professional storing or using the human tissue believes they are doing it in the best interests of the person who lacks capacity to consent
- for a clinical trial approved and carried out under the Medicines for Human Use (Clinical Trials) Regulations 2004, or
- for intrusive research:
  — after the Mental Capacity Act comes into force
  — that meets the Act's requirements, and
  — that has ethical approval.

Tissue samples that were obtained before 31 August 2006 are existing holdings under the Human Tissue Act. Researchers can work with these tissues without seeking permission. But they will still need to get ethical approval. Guidance is available in the Human Tissue Authority Code of Practice on consent.[53] **11.40**

What should happen to research that started before the Act came into force?

What if a person has capacity when research starts but loses capacity?

Some people with capacity will agree to take part in research but may then lose capacity before the end of the project. In this situation, researchers will be able to continue research as long as they comply with the conditions set out in the Mental Capacity Act 2005 (Loss of Capacity During Research Project) (England) Regulations 2007 or equivalent Welsh regulations. **11.41**

The regulations only apply to tissue and data collected before the loss of capacity from a person who gave consent before 31 March 2008 to join a project that starts before 1 October 2007.

The regulations do not cover research involving direct intervention (for example, taking of further blood pressure readings) or the taking of further tissue after loss of capacity. Such research must comply with sections 30 to 33 of the Act to be lawful. **11.42**

---

[52] Section 1(9) of the Human Tissue Act 2004.

[53] www.hta.gov.uk

11.43   Where the regulations do apply, research can only continue if the project already has procedures to deal with people who lose capacity during the project. An appropriate body must have approved the procedures. The researcher must follow the procedures that have been approved.

11.44   The researcher must also:

• seek out the views of someone involved in the person's care or interested in their welfare and if a carer can't be found they must nominate a consultee (see paragraphs 11.22–11.28)

• respect advance decisions and expressed preferences, wishes or objections that the person has made in the past, and

• treat the person's interests as more important than those of science and society.

The appropriate body must be satisfied that the research project has reasonable arrangements to meet these requirements.

11.45   If at any time the researcher believes that procedures are no longer in place or the appropriate body no longer approves the research, they must stop research on the person immediately.

11.46   Where regulations do apply, research does not have to:

• be linked to an impairing condition of the person

• have the potential to benefit that person, or

• aim to provide knowledge relevant to others with the same or a similar condition.

What happens to existing projects that a person never had capacity to agree to?

11.47   There are no regulations for projects that:

• started before the Act comes into force, and

• a person never had the capacity to agree to.

Projects that already have ethical approval will need to obtain approval from an appropriate body under sections 30 and 31 of the Mental Capacity Act and to comply with the requirements of sections 32 and 33 of that Act by 1 October 2008. Research that does not have ethical approval must get approval from an appropriate body by 1 October 2007 to continue lawfully. This is the case in England and it is expected that similar arrangements will apply in Wales.

12. HOW DOES THE ACT APPLY TO CHILDREN AND YOUNG PEOPLE?

This chapter looks at the few parts of the Act that may affect children under 16 years of age. It also explains the position of young people aged 16 and 17 years and the overlapping laws that affect them.

This chapter does not deal with research. Further guidance will be provided on how the Act applies in relation to research involving those under the age of 18.

Within this Code of Practice, 'children' refers to people aged below 16. 'Young people' refers to people aged 16–17. This differs from the Children Act 1989 and the law more generally, where the term 'child' is used to refer to people aged under 18.

In this chapter, as throughout the Code, a person's capacity (or lack of capacity) refers specifically to their capacity to make a particular decision at the time it needs to be made.

Quick summary

Children under 16

• The Act does not generally apply to people under the age of 16.

- There are two exceptions:
  - —The Court of Protection can make decisions about a child's property or finances (or appoint a deputy to make these decisions) if the child lacks capacity to make such decisions within section 2(1) of the Act and is likely to still lack capacity to make financial decisions when they reach the age of 18 (section 18(3)).
  - —Offences of ill treatment or wilful neglect of a person who lacks capacity within section 2(1) can also apply to victims younger than 16 (section 44).

Young people aged 16–17 years
- Most of the Act applies to young people aged 16–17 years, who may lack capacity within section 2(1) to make specific decisions.
- There are three exceptions:
  - —Only people aged 18 and over can make a Lasting Power of Attorney (LPA).
  - —Only people aged 18 and over can make an advance decision to refuse medical treatment.
  - —The Court of Protection may only make a statutory will for a person aged 18 and over.

Care or treatment for young people aged 16–17
- People carrying out acts in connection with the care or treatment of a young person aged 16–17 who lacks capacity to consent within section 2(1) will generally have protection from liability (section 5), as long as the person carrying out the act:
  - —has taken reasonable steps to establish that the young person lacks capacity
  - — reasonably believes that the young person lacks capacity and that the act is in the young person's best interests, and
  - —follows the Act's principles.
- When assessing the young person's best interests (see chapter 5), the person providing care or treatment must consult those involved in the young person's care and anyone interested in their welfare—if it is practical and appropriate to do so. This may include the young person's parents. Care should be taken not to unlawfully breach the young person's right to confidentiality (see chapter 16).
- Nothing in section 5 excludes a person's civil liability for loss or damage, or his criminal liability, resulting from his negligence in carrying out the act.

Legal proceedings involving young people aged 16-17
- Sometimes there will be disagreements about the care, treatment or welfare of a young person aged 16 or 17 who lacks capacity to make relevant decisions. Depending on the circumstances, the case may be heard in the family courts or the Court of Protection.
- The Court of Protection may transfer a case to the family courts, and vice versa.

Does the Act apply to children?

Section 2(5) of the Act states that, with the exception of section 2(6), as explained below, no powers under the Act may be exercised in relation to a child under 16.   12.1

Care and treatment of children under the age of 16 is generally governed by common law principles. Further information is provide at www.dh.gov.uk/consent.   12.2

Can the Act help with decisions about a child's property or finances?

Section 2(6) makes an exception for some decisions about a child's property and financial affairs. The Court of Protection can make decisions about property and affairs of those under 16 in cases   12.3

where the person is likely to still lack capacity to make financial decisions after reaching the age of 18. The court's ruling will still apply when the person reaches the age of 18, which means there will not be a need for further court proceedings once the person reaches the age of 18.

12.4 The Court of Protection can:

- make an order (for example, concerning the investment of an award of compensation for the child), and/or
- appoint a deputy to manage the child's property and affairs and to make ongoing financial decisions on the child's behalf.

In making a decision, the court must follow the Act's principles and decide in the child's best interests as set out in chapter 5 of the Code.

Scenario: Applying the Act to children

Tom was nine when a drunk driver knocked him off his bicycle. He suffered severe head injuries and permanent brain damage. He received a large amount of money in compensation. He is unlikely to recover enough to be able to make financial decisions when he is 18. So the Court of Protection appoints Tom's father as deputy to manage his financial affairs in order to pay for the care Tom will need in the future.

What if somebody mistreats or neglects a child who lacks capacity?

12.5 Section 44 covers the offences of ill treatment or wilful neglect of a person who lacks capacity to make relevant decisions (see chapter 14). This section also applies to children under 16 and young people aged 16 or 17. But it only applies if the child's lack of capacity to make a decision for themselves is caused by an impairment or disturbance that affects how their mind or brain works (see chapter 4). If the lack of capacity is solely the result of the child's youth or immaturity, then the ill treatment or wilful neglect would be dealt with under the separate offences of child cruelty or neglect.

Does the Act apply to young people aged 16–17?

12.6 Most of the Act applies to people aged 16 years and over. There is an overlap with the Children Act 1989. For the Act to apply to a young person, they must lack capacity to make a particular decision (in line with the Act's definition of lack of capacity described in chapter 4).

In such situations either this Act or the Children Act 1989 may apply, depending upon the particular circumstances.

However, there may also be situations where neither of these Acts provides an appropriate solution. In such cases, it may be necessary to look to the powers available under the Mental Health Act 1983 or the High Court's inherent powers to deal with cases involving young people.

12.7 There are currently no specific rules for deciding when to use either the Children Act 1989 or the Mental Capacity Act 2005 or when to apply to the High Court. But, the examples below show circumstances where this Act may be the most appropriate (see also paragraphs 12.21–12.23 below).

- In unusual circumstances it might be in a young person's best interests for the Court of Protection to make an order and/or appoint a property and affairs deputy. For example, this might occur when a young person receives financial compensation and the court appoints a parent or a solicitor as a property and affairs deputy.
- It may be appropriate for the Court of Protection to make a welfare decision concerning a young person who lacks capacity to decide for themselves (for example, about where the young

person should live) if the court decides that the parents are not acting in the young person's best interests.

- It might be appropriate to refer a case to the Court of Protection where there is disagreement between a person interested in the care and welfare of a young person and the young person's medical team about the young person's best interests or capacity.

Do any parts of the Act not apply to young people aged 16 or 17?

LPAs

Only people aged 18 or over can make a Lasting Power of Attorney (LPA) (section 9(2)(c)).   12.8

Advance decisions to refuse treatment

Information on decisions to refuse treatment made in advance by young people under the age of 18 will be available at www.dh.gov.uk/consent.   12.9

Making a will

The law generally does not allow anyone below the age of 18 to make a will. So section 18(2) confirms that the Court of Protection can only make a statutory will on behalf of those aged 18 and over.   12.10

What does the Act say about care or treatment of young people aged 16 or 17?

Background information concerning competent young people

The Family Law Reform Act 1969 presumes that young people have the legal capacity to agree to surgical, medical or dental treatment.[54] This also applies to any associated procedures (for example, investigations, anaesthesia or nursing care).   12.11

It does not apply to some rarer types of procedure (for example, organ donation or other procedures which are not therapeutic for the young person) or research. In those cases, anyone under 18 is presumed to lack legal capacity, subject to the test of 'Gillick competence' (testing whether they are mature and intelligent enough to understand a proposed treatment or procedure).[55]   12.12

Even where a young person is presumed to have legal capacity to consent to treatment, they may not necessarily be able to make the relevant decision. As with adults, decision-makers should assess the young person's capacity to consent to the proposed care or treatment (see chapter 4). If a young person lacks capacity to consent within section 2(1) of the Act because of an impairment of, or a disturbance in the functioning of, the mind or brain then the Mental Capacity Act will apply in the same way as it does to those who are 18 and over. If however they are unable to make the decision for some other reason, for example because they are overwhelmed by the implications of the decision, the Act will not apply to them and the legality of any treatment should be assessed under common law principles.   12.13

---

[54] Family Law Reform Act 1969, section 8(1).

[55] In the case of *Gillick v West Norfolk and Wisbech Area Health Authority* [1986] 1 AC 112 the court found that a child below 16 years of age will be competent to consent to medical treatment if they have sufficient intelligence and understanding to understand what is proposed. This test applies in relation to all people under 18 where there is no presumption of competence in relation to the procedure—for example where the procedure is not one referred to in section 8 of the Family Law Reform Act 1969, e.g. organ donation.

12.14   If a young person has capacity to agree to treatment, their decision to consent must be respected. Difficult issues can arise if a young person has legal and mental capacity and refuses consent— especially if a person with parental responsibility wishes to give consent on the young person's behalf. The Family Division of the High Court can hear cases where there is disagreement. The Court of Protection has no power to settle a dispute about a young person who is said to have the mental capacity to make the specific decision.

12.15   It may be unclear whether a young person lacks capacity within section 2(1) of the Act. In those circumstances, it would be prudent for the person providing care or treatment for the young person to seek a declaration from the court.

If the young person lacks capacity to make care or treatment decisions

12.16   Under the common law, a person with parental responsibility for a young person is generally able to consent to the young person receiving care or medical treatment where they lack capacity under section 2(1) of the Act. They should act in the young person's best interests.

12.17   However if a young person lacks the mental capacity to make a specific care or treatment decision within section 2(1) of the Act, healthcare staff providing treatment, or a person providing care to the young person, can carry out treatment or care with protection from liability (section 5) whether or not a person with parental responsibility consents.[56] They must follow the Act's principles and make sure that the actions they carry out are in the young person's best interests. They must make every effort to work out and consider the young person's wishes, feelings, beliefs and values—both past and present—and consider all other factors in the best interests checklist (see chapter 5).

12.18   When assessing a young person's best interests, healthcare staff must take into account the views of anyone involved in caring for the young person and anyone interested in their welfare, where it is practical and appropriate to do so. This may include the young person's parents and others with parental responsibility for the young person. Care should be taken not to unlawfully breach the young person's right to confidentiality (see chapter 16).

12.19   If a young person has said they do not want their parents to be consulted, it may not be appropriate to involve them (for example, where there have been allegations of abuse).

12.20   If there is a disagreement about whether the proposed care or treatment is in the best interests of a young person, or there is disagreement about whether the young person lacks capacity and there is no other way of resolving the matter, it would be prudent for those in disagreement to seek a declaration or other order from the appropriate court (see paragraphs 12.23–12.25 below).

Scenario: Working out a young person's best interests

Mary is 16 and has Down's syndrome. Her mother wants Mary to have dental treatment that will improve her appearance but is not otherwise necessary. To be protected under section 5 of the Act, the dentist must consider whether Mary has capacity to agree to the treatment and what would be in her best interests. He decides that she is unable to understand what is involved or the possible consequences of the proposed treatment and so lacks capacity to make the decision. But Mary seems to want the treatment, so he takes her views into account in deciding whether the treatment is in her best interests. He also consults with both her parents and with her teacher and GP to see if there are other relevant factors to take into account. He decides that the treatment is likely to improve Mary's confidence and self-esteem and is in her best interests.

---

[56] Nothing in section 5 excludes a person's civil liability for loss or damage, or his criminal liability, resulting from his negligence in doing the Act.

There may be particular difficulties where young people with mental health problems require in-patient psychiatric treatment, and are treated informally rather than detained under the Mental Health Act 1983. The Mental Capacity Act and its principles apply to decisions related to the care and treatment of young people who lack mental capacity to consent, including treatment for mental disorder. As with any other form of treatment, somebody assessing a young person's best interests should consult anyone involved in caring for the young person or anyone interested in their welfare, as far as is practical and appropriate. This may include the young person's parents or those with parental responsibility for the young person. 12.21

But the Act does not allow any actions that result in a young person being deprived of their liberty (see chapter 6). In such circumstances, detention under the Mental Health Act 1983 and the safeguards provided under that Act might be appropriate (see also chapter 13).

People may disagree about a young person's capacity to make the specific decision or about their best interests, or it may not be clear whether they lack capacity within section 2(1) or for some other reason. In this situation, legal proceedings may be necessary if there is no other way of settling the disagreement (see chapters 8 and 15). If those involved in caring for the young person or who are interested in the young person's welfare do not agree with the proposed treatment, it may be necessary for an interested party to make an application to the appropriate court. 12.22

What powers do the courts have in cases involving young people?

A case involving a young person who lacks mental capacity to make a specific decision could be heard in the family courts (probably in the Family Division of the High Court) or in the Court of Protection. 12.23

If a case might require an ongoing order (because the young person is likely to still lack capacity when they are 18), it may be more appropriate for the Court of Protection to hear the case. For one-off cases not involving property or finances, the Family Division may be more appropriate. 12.24

So that the appropriate court hears a case, the Court of Protection can transfer cases to the family courts, and vice versa (section 21). 12.25

Scenario: Hearing cases in the appropriate court

Shola is 17. She has serious learning disabilities and lacks the capacity to decide where she should live. Her parents are involved in a bitter divorce. They cannot agree on several issues concerning Shola's care—including where she should live. Her mother wants to continue to look after Shola at home. But her father wants Shola to move into a care home. In this case, it may be more appropriate for the Court of Protection to deal with the case. This is because an order made in the Court of Protection could continue into Shola's adulthood. However an order made by the family court under the Children Act 1989 would end on Shola's eighteenth birthday.

13. WHAT IS THE RELATIONSHIP BETWEEN THE MENTAL CAPACITY ACT AND THE MENTAL HEALTH ACT 1983?

This chapter explains the relationship between the Mental Capacity Act 2005 (MCA) and the Mental Health Act 1983 (MHA). It:

- sets out when it may be appropriate to detain someone under the MHA rather than to rely on the MCA
- describes how the MCA affects people lacking capacity who are also subject to the MHA

- explains when doctors cannot give certain treatments for a mental disorder (in particular, psychosurgery) to someone who lacks capacity to consent to it, and
- sets out changes that the Government is planning to make to both Acts.

It does not provide a full description of the MHA. The MHA has its own Memorandum to explain the Act and its own Code of Practice to guide people about how to use it.[57]

In this chapter, as throughout the Code, a person's capacity (or lack of capacity) refers specifically to their capacity to make a particular decision at the time it needs to be made.

Quick summary

- Professionals may need to think about using the MHA to detain and treat somebody who lacks capacity to consent to treatment (rather than use the MCA), if:
  — it is not possible to give the person the care or treatment they need without doing something that might deprive them of their liberty
  — the person needs treatment that cannot be given under the MCA (for example, because the person has made a valid and applicable advance decision to refuse an essential part of treatment)
  — the person may need to be restrained in a way that is not allowed under the MCA
  — it is not possible to assess or treat the person safely or effectively without treatment being compulsory (perhaps because the person is expected to regain capacity to consent, but might then refuse to give consent)
  — the person lacks capacity to decide on some elements of the treatment but has capacity to refuse a vital part of it—and they have done so, or
  — there is some other reason why the person might not get treatment, and they or somebody else might suffer harm as a result.
- Before making an application under the MHA, decision-makers should consider whether they could achieve their aims safely and effectively by using the MCA instead.
- Compulsory treatment under the MHA is not an option if:
  — the patient's mental disorder does not justify detention in hospital, or
  — the patient needs treatment only for a physical illness or disability.
- The MCA applies to people subject to the MHA in the same way as it applies to anyone else, with four exceptions:
  — if someone is detained under the MHA, decision-makers cannot normally rely on the MCA to give treatment for mental disorder or make decisions about that treatment on that person's behalf
  — if somebody can be treated for their mental disorder without their consent because they are detained under the MHA, healthcare staff can treat them even if it goes against an advance decision to refuse that treatment
  — if a person is subject to guardianship, the guardian has the exclusive right to take certain decisions, including where the person is to live, and
  — Independent Mental Capacity Advocates do not have to be involved in decisions about serious medical treatment or accommodation, if those decisions are made under the MHA.

---

[57] Department of Health & Welsh Office, Mental Health Act 1983 Code of Practice (TSO, 1999), www. dh.gov.uk/assetRoot/04/07/49/61/04074961.pdf

- Healthcare staff cannot give psychosurgery (i.e. neurosurgery for mental disorder) to a person who lacks capacity to agree to it. This applies whether or not the person is otherwise subject to the MHA.

Who does the MHA apply to?

The MHA provides ways of assessing, treating and caring for people who have a serious mental disorder that puts them or other people at risk. It sets out when: **13.1**
- people with mental disorders can be detained in hospital for assessment or treatment
- people who are detained can be given treatment for their mental disorder without their consent (it also sets out the safeguards people must get in this situation), and
- people with mental disorders can be made subject to guardianship or after-care under supervision to protect them or other people.

Most of the MHA does not distinguish between people who have the capacity to make decisions and those who do not. Many people covered by the MHA have the capacity to make decisions for themselves. Most people who lack capacity to make decisions about their treatment will never be affected by the MHA, even if they need treatment for a mental disorder.   **13.2**

But there are cases where decision-makers will need to decide whether to use the MHA or MCA, or both, to meet the needs of people with mental health problems who lack capacity to make decisions about their own treatment.   **13.3**

What are the MCA's limits?

Section 5 of the MCA provides legal protection for people who care for or treat someone who lacks capacity (see chapter 6). But they must follow the Act's principles and may only take action that is in a person's best interests (see chapter 5). This applies to care or treatment for physical and mental conditions. So it can apply to treatment for people with mental disorders, however serious those disorders are.   **13.4**

But section 5 does have its limits. For example, somebody using restraint only has protection if the restraint is: **13.5**
- necessary to protect the person who lacks capacity from harm, and
- in proportion to the likelihood and seriousness of that harm.

There is no protection under section 5 for actions that deprive a person of their liberty (see chapter 6 for guidance). Similarly, the MCA does not allow giving treatment that goes against a valid and applicable advance decision to refuse treatment (see chapter 9).   **13.6**

None of these restrictions apply to treatment for mental disorder given under the MHA—but other restrictions do.   **13.7**

When can a person be detained under the MHA?

A person may be taken into hospital and detained for assessment under section 2 of the MHA for up to 28 days if: **13.8**
- they have a mental disorder that is serious enough for them to be detained in a hospital for assessment (or for assessment followed by treatment) for at least a limited period, and
- they need to be detained to protect their health or safety, or to protect others.

13.9   A patient may be admitted to hospital and detained for treatment under section 3 of the MHA if:

- they have a mental illness, severe mental impairment, psychopathic disorder or mental impairment (the MHA sets out definitions for these last three terms)
- their mental disorder is serious enough to need treatment in hospital
- treatment is needed for the person's health or safety, or for the protection of other people—and it cannot be provided without detention under this section, and
- (if the person has a mental impairment or psychopathic disorder) treatment is likely to improve their condition or stop it getting worse.

13.10   Decision-makers should consider using the MHA if, in their professional judgment, they are not sure it will be possible, or sufficient, to rely on the MCA. They do not have to ask the Court of Protection to rule that the MCA does not apply before using the MHA.

13.11   If a clinician believes that they can safely assess or treat a person under the MCA, they do not need to consider using the MHA. In this situation, it would be difficult to meet the requirements of the MHA anyway.

13.12   It might be necessary to consider using the MHA rather than the MCA if:

- it is not possible to give the person the care or treatment they need without carrying out an action that might deprive them of their liberty
- the person needs treatment that cannot be given under the MCA (for example, because the person has made a valid and applicable advance decision to refuse all or part of that treatment)
- the person may need to be restrained in a way that is not allowed under the MCA
- it is not possible to assess or treat the person safely or effectively without treatment being compulsory (perhaps because the person is expected to regain capacity to consent, but might then refuse to give consent)
- the person lacks capacity to decide on some elements of the treatment but has capacity to refuse a vital part of it—and they have done so, or
- there is some other reason why the person might not get the treatment they need, and they or somebody else might suffer harm as a result.

13.13   But it is important to remember that a person cannot be treated under the MHA unless they meet the relevant criteria for being detained. Unless they are sent to hospital under Part 3 of the MHA in connection with a criminal offence, people can only be detained where:

- the conditions summarised in paragraph 13.8 or 13.9 are met
- the relevant people agree that an application is necessary (normally two doctors and an approved social worker), and
- (in the case of section 3) the patient's nearest relative has not objected to the application.

'Nearest relative' is defined in section 26 of the MHA. It is usually, but not always, a family member.

Scenario: Using the MHA

Mr Oliver has a learning disability. For the last four years, he has had depression from time to time, and has twice had treatment for it at a psychiatric hospital. He is now seriously depressed and his care workers are worried about him. Mr Oliver's consultant has given him medication and is considering electro-convulsive therapy. The consultant thinks this care plan will only work if Mr Oliver is detained in hospital. This will allow close observation and Mr Oliver will be stopped if he tries to leave. The consultant thinks an application should be made under section 3 of the MHA. The consultant also speaks to Mr Oliver's nearest relative, his mother. She asks why Mr Oliver needs to be detained when he has not needed to be in the past. But after she hears the consultant's reasons, she does not object to the application. An approved social worker makes the application and obtains a second medical recommendation. Mr Oliver is then detained and taken to hospital for his treatment for depression to begin.

Compulsory treatment under the MHA is not an option if: 13.14

- the patient's mental disorder does not justify detention in hospital, or
- the patient needs treatment only for a physical illness or disability.

There will be some cases where a person who lacks capacity cannot be treated either under the 13.15 MHA or the MCA—even if the treatment is for mental disorder.

Scenario: Deciding whether to use the MHA or MCA

Mrs Carter is in her 80s and has dementia. Somebody finds her wandering in the street, very confused and angry. A neighbour takes her home and calls her doctor. At home, it looks like she has been deliberately smashing things. There are cuts on her hands and arms, but she won't let the doctor touch them, and she hasn't been taking her medication. Her doctor wants to admit her to hospital for assessment. Mrs Carter gets angry and says that they'll never keep her in hospital. So the doctor thinks that it might be necessary to use the MHA. He arranges for an approved social worker to visit. The social worker discovers that Mrs Carter was expecting her son this morning, but he has not turned up. They find out that he has been delayed, but could not call because Mrs Carter's telephone has become unplugged. When she is told that her son is on his way, Mrs Carter brightens up. She lets the doctor treat her cuts—which the doctor thinks it is in her best interests to do as soon as possible. When Mrs Carter's son arrives, the social worker explains the doctor is very worried, especially that Mrs Carter is not taking her medication. The son explains that he will help his mother take it in future. It is agreed that the MCA will allow him to do that. The social worker arranges to return a week later and calls the doctor to say that she thinks Mrs Carter can get the care she needs without being detained under the MHA. The doctor agrees.

How does the MCA apply to a patient subject to guardianship under the MHA?

Guardianship gives someone (usually a local authority social services department) the exclusive 13.16 right to decide where a person should live—but in doing this they cannot deprive the person of their liberty. The guardian can also require the person to attend for treatment, work, training or education at specific times and places, and they can demand that a doctor, approved social worker or another relevant person have access to the person wherever they live. Guardianship can apply whether or not the person has the capacity to make decisions about care and treatment. It does not give anyone the right to treat the person without their permission or to consent to treatment on their behalf.

An application can be made for a person who has a mental disorder to be received into guardianship 13.17 under section 7 of the MHA when:

- the situation meets the conditions summarised in paragraph 13.18
- the relevant people agree an application for guardianship should be made (normally two doctors and an approved social worker), and
- the person's nearest relative does not object.

An application can be made in relation to any person who is 16 years or over if: 13.18

- they have a mental illness, severe mental impairment, psychopathic disorder or mental impairment that is serious enough to justify guardianship (see paragraph 13.20 below), and
- guardianship is necessary in the interests of the welfare of the patient or to protect other people.

13.19   Applicants (usually approved social workers) and doctors supporting the application will need to determine whether they could achieve their aims without guardianship. For patients who lack capacity, the obvious alternative will be action under the MCA.

13.20   But the fact that the person lacks capacity to make relevant decision is not the only factor that applicants need to consider. They need to consider all the circumstances of the case. They may conclude that guardianship is the best option for a person with a mental disorder who lacks capacity to make those decisions if, for example:

- they think it is important that one person or authority should be in charge of making decisions about where the person should live (for example, where there have been long-running or difficult disagreements about where the person should live)
- they think the person will probably respond well to the authority and attention of a guardian, and so be more prepared to accept treatment for the mental disorder (whether they are able to consent to it or it is being provided for them under the MCA), or
- they need authority to return the person to the place they are to live (for example, a care home) if they were to go absent.

Decision-makers must never consider guardianship as a way to avoid applying the MCA.

13.21   A guardian has the exclusive right to decide where a person lives, so nobody else can use the MCA to arrange for the person to live elsewhere. Somebody who knowingly helps a person leave the place a guardian requires them to stay may be committing a criminal offence under the MHA. A guardian also has the exclusive power to require the person to attend set times and places for treatment, occupation, education or training. This does not stop other people using the MCA to make similar arrangements or to treat the person in their best interests. But people cannot use the MCA in any way that conflicts with decisions which a guardian has a legal right to make under the MHA. See paragraph 13.16 above for general information about a guardian's powers.

How does the MCA apply to a patient subject to after-care under supervision under the MHA?

13.22   When people are discharged from detention for medical treatment under the MHA, their responsible medical officer may decide to place them on after-care under supervision. The responsible medical officer is usually the person's consultant psychiatrist. Another doctor and an approved social worker must support their application.

13.23   After-care under supervision means:

- the person can be required to live at a specified place (where they can be taken to and returned, if necessary)
- the person can be required to attend for treatment, occupation, education or training at a specific time and place (where they can be taken, if necessary), and
- their supervisor, any doctor or approved social worker or any other relevant person must be given access to them wherever they live.

13.24   Responsible medical officers can apply for after-care under supervision under section 25A of the MHA if:

- the person is 16 or older and is liable to be detained in a hospital for treatment under section 3 (and certain other sections) of the MHA
- the person has a mental illness, severe mental impairment, psychopathic disorder or mental impairment
- without after-care under supervision the person's health or safety would be at risk of serious harm, they would be at risk of serious exploitation, or other people's safety would be at risk of serious harm, and

- after-care under supervision is likely to help make sure the person gets the after-care services they need.

'Liable to be detained' means that a hospital is allowed to detain them. Patients who are liable to be detained are not always actually in hospital, because they may have been given permission to leave hospital for a time.

After-care under supervision can be used whether or not the person lacks capacity to make 13.25 relevant decisions. But if a person lacks capacity, decision-makers will need to decide whether action under the MCA could achieve their aims before making an application. The kinds of cases in which after-care under supervision might be considered for patients who lack capacity to take decisions about their own care and treatment are similar to those for guardianship.

How does the Mental Capacity Act affect people covered by the Mental Health Act?

There is no reason to assume a person lacks capacity to make their own decisions just because they 13.26 are subject (under the MHA) to:
- detention
- guardianship, or
- after-care under supervision.

People who lack capacity to make specific decisions are still protected by the MCA even if they 13.27 are subject to the MHA (this includes people who are subject to the MHA as a result of court proceedings). But there are four important exceptions:
- if someone is liable to be detained under the MHA, decision-makers cannot normally rely on the MCA to give mental health treatment or make decisions about that treatment on someone's behalf
- if somebody can be given mental health treatment without their consent because they are liable to be detained under the MHA, they can also be given mental health treatment that goes against an advance decision to refuse treatment
- if a person is subject to guardianship, the guardian has the exclusive right to take certain decisions, including where the person is to live, and
- Independent Mental Capacity Advocates do not have to be involved in decisions about serious medical treatment or accommodation, if those decisions are made under the MHA.

What are the implications for people who need treatment for a mental disorder?

Subject to certain conditions, Part 4 of the MHA allows doctors to give patients who are liable to 13.28 be detained treatment for mental disorders without their consent—whether or not they have the capacity to give that consent. Paragraph 13.31 below lists a few important exceptions.

Where Part 4 of the MHA applies, the MCA cannot be used to give medical treatment for a 13.29 mental disorder to patients who lack capacity to consent. Nor can anyone else, like an attorney or a deputy, use the MCA to give consent for that treatment. This is because Part 4 of the MHA already allows clinicians, if they comply with the relevant rules, to give patients medical treatment for mental disorder even though they lack the capacity to consent. In this context, medical treatment includes nursing and care, habilitation and rehabilitation under medical supervision.

But clinicians treating people for mental disorder under the MHA cannot simply ignore a 13.30 person's capacity to consent to treatment. As a matter of good practice (and in some cases in order to comply with the MHA) they will always need to assess and record:
- whether patients have capacity to consent to treatment, and

- if so, whether they have consented to or refused that treatment.

For more information, see the MHA Code of Practice.

13.31   Part 4 of the MHA does not apply to patients:
- admitted in an emergency under section 4(4)(a) of the MHA, following a single medical recommendation and awaiting a second recommendation
- temporarily detained (held in hospital) under section 5 of the MHA while awaiting an application for detention under section 2 or section 3
- remanded by a court to hospital for a report on their medical condition under section 35 of the MHA
- detained under section 37(4), 135 or 136 of the MHA in a place of safety, or
- who have been conditionally discharged by the Mental Health Review Tribunal (and not recalled to hospital).

13.32   Since the MHA does not allow treatment for these patients without their consent, the MCA applies in the normal way, even if the treatment is for mental disorder.

13.33   Even when the MHA allows patients to be treated for mental disorders, the MCA applies in the normal way to treatment for physical disorders. But sometimes healthcare staff may decide to focus first on treating a detained patient's mental disorder in the hope that they will get back the capacity to make a decision about treatment for the physical disorder.

13.34   Where people are subject to guardianship or after-care under supervision under the MHA, the MCA applies as normal to all treatment. Guardianship and after-care under supervision do not give people the right to treat patients without consent.

Scenario: Using the MCA to treat a patient who is detained under the MHA

Mr Peters is detained in hospital under section 3 of the MHA and is receiving treatment under Part 4 of the MHA. Mr Peters has paranoid schizophrenia, delusions, hallucinations and thought disorder. He refuses all medical treatment. Mr Peters has recently developed blood in his urine and staff persuaded him to have an ultrasound scan. The scan revealed suspected renal carcinoma. His consultant believes that he needs a CT scan and treatment for the carcinoma. But Mr Peters refuses a general anaesthetic and other medical procedures. The consultant assesses Mr Peters as lacking capacity to consent to treatment under the MCA's test of capacity. The MHA is not relevant here, because the CT scan is not part of Mr Peters' treatment for mental disorder. Under section 5 of the MCA, doctors can provide treatment without consent. But they must follow the principles of the Act and believe that treatment is in Mr Peters' best interests.

How does the Mental Health Act affect advance decisions to refuse treatment?

13.35   The MHA does not affect a person's advance decision to refuse treatment, unless Part 4 of the MHA means the person can be treated for mental disorder without their consent. In this situation healthcare staff can treat patients for their mental disorder, even if they have made an advance decision to refuse such treatment.

13.36   But even then healthcare staff must treat a valid and applicable advance decision as they would a decision made by a person with capacity at the time they are asked to consent to treatment. For example, they should consider whether they could use a different type of treatment which the patient has not refused in advance. If healthcare staff do not follow an advance decision, they should record in the patient's notes why they have chosen not to follow it.

13.37   Even if a patient is being treated without their consent under Part 4 of the MHA, an advance decision to refuse other forms of treatment is still valid. Being subject to guardianship or after-care under supervision does not affect an advance decision in any way. See chapter 9 for further guidance on advance decisions to refuse treatment.

Scenario: Deciding on whether to follow an advance decision to refuse treatment

Miss Khan gets depression from time to time and has old physical injuries that cause her pain. She does not like the side effects of medication, and manages her health through diet and exercise. She knows that healthcare staff might doubt her decision-making capacity when she is depressed. So she makes an advance decision to refuse all medication for her physical pain and depression. A year later, she gets major depression and is detained under the MHA. Her GP (family doctor) tells her responsible medical officer (RMO) at the hospital about her advance decision. But Miss Khan's condition gets so bad that she will not discuss treatment. So the RMO decides to prescribe medication for her depression, despite her advance decision. This is possible because Miss Khan is detained under the MHA. The RMO also believes that Miss Khan now lacks capacity to consent to medication for her physical pain. He assesses the validity of the advance decision to refuse medication for the physical pain. Her GP says that Miss Khan seemed perfectly well when she made the decision and seemed to understand what it meant. In the GP's view, Miss Khan had the capacity to make the advance decision. The RMO decides that the advance decision is valid and applicable, and does not prescribe medication for Miss Khan's pain – even though he thinks it would be in her best interests. When Miss Khan's condition improves, the consultant will be able to discuss whether she would like to change her mind about treatment for her physical pain.

Does the MHA affect the duties of attorneys and deputies?

13.38 In general, the MHA does not affect the powers of attorneys and deputies. But there are two exceptions:
- they will not be able to give consent on a patient's behalf for treatment under Part 4 of the MHA, where the patient is liable to be detained under the MHA (see 13.28–13.34 above), and
- they will not be able to take decisions:
  —about where a person subject to guardianship should live, or
  —that conflict with decisions that a guardian has a legal right to make.

13.39 Being subject to the MHA does not stop patients creating new Lasting Powers of Attorney (if they have the capacity to do so). Nor does it stop the Court of Protection from appointing a deputy for them.

13.40 In certain cases, people subject to the MHA may be required to meet the specific conditions relating to:
- leave of absence from hospital
- after-care under supervision, or
- conditional discharge.

Conditions vary from case to case, but could include a requirement to:
- live in a particular place
- maintain contact with health services, or
- avoid a particular area.

13.41 If an attorney or deputy takes a decision that goes against one of these conditions, the patient will be taken to have gone against the condition. The MHA sets out the actions that could be taken in such circumstances. In the case of leave of absence or conditional discharge, this might involve the patient being recalled to hospital.

13.42   Attorneys and deputies are able to exercise patients' rights under the MHA on their behalf, if they have the relevant authority. In particular, some personal welfare attorneys and deputies may be able to apply to the Mental Health Review Tribunal (MHRT) for the patient's discharge from detention, guardianship or after-care under supervision.

13.43   The MHA also gives various rights to a patient's nearest relative. These include the right to:
- insist that a local authority social services department instructs an approved social worker to consider whether the patient should be made subject to the MHA
- apply for the patient to be admitted to hospital or guardianship
- object to an application for admission for treatment
- order the patient's discharge from hospital (subject to certain conditions) and
- order the patient's discharge from guardianship.

13.44   Attorneys and deputies may not exercise these rights, unless they are themselves the nearest relative. If the nearest relative and an attorney or deputy disagree, it may be helpful for them to discuss the issue, perhaps with the assistance of the patient's clinicians or social worker. But ultimately they have different roles and both must act as they think best. An attorney or deputy must act in the patient's best interests.

13.45   It is good practice for clinicians and others involved in the assessment or treatment of patients under the MHA to try to find out if the person has an attorney or deputy. But this may not always be possible. So attorneys and deputies should contact either:
- the healthcare professional responsible for the patient's treatment (generally known as the patient's RMO)
- the managers of the hospital where the patient is detained
- the person's guardian (normally the local authority social services department), or
- the person's supervisor (if the patient is subject to after-care under supervision).

Hospitals that treat detained patients normally have a Mental Health Act Administrator's office, which may be a useful first point of contact.

Does the MHA affect when Independent Mental Capacity Advocates must be instructed?

13.46   As explained in chapter 10, there is no duty to instruct an Independent Mental Capacity Advocate (IMCA) for decisions about serious medical treatment which is to be given under Part 4 of the MHA. Nor is there a duty to do so in respect of a move into accommodation, or a change of accommodation, if the person in question is to be required to live in it because of an obligation under the MHA. That obligation might be a condition of leave of absence or conditional discharge from hospital or a requirement imposed by a guardian or a supervisor.

13.47   However, the rules for instructing an IMCA for patients subject to the MHA who might undergo serious medical treatment not related to their mental disorder are the same as for any other patient.

13.48   The duty to instruct an IMCA would also apply as normal if accommodation is being planned as part of the after-care under section 117 of the MHA following the person's discharge from detention (and the person is not going to be required to live in it as a condition of after-care under supervision). This is because the person does not have to accept that accommodation.

What is the effect of section 57 of the Mental Health Act on the MCA?

13.49   Section 57 of the MHA states that psychosurgery (neurosurgery for mental disorder) requires:
- the consent of the patient, and

- the approval of an independent doctor and two other people appointed by the Mental Health Act Commission.

Psychosurgery is any surgical operation that destroys brain tissue or the function of brain tissue.

The same rules apply to other treatments specified in regulations under section 57. Currently, the only treatment included in regulations is the surgical implantation of hormones to reduce a man's sex drive. **13.50**

The combined effect of section 57 of the MHA and section 28 of the MCA is, effectively, that a person who lacks the capacity to consent to one of these treatments for mental disorder may never be given it. Healthcare staff cannot use the MCA as an alternative way of giving these kinds of treatment. Nor can an attorney or deputy give permission for them on a person's behalf. **13.51**

What changes does the Government plan to make to the MHA and the MCA?

The Government has introduced a Mental Health Bill into Parliament in order to modernise the MHA. Among the changes it proposes to make are: **13.52**
- some amendments to the criteria for detention, including a new requirement that appropriate medical treatment be available for patients before they can be detained for treatment
- the introduction of supervised treatment in the community for suitable patients following a period of detention and treatment in hospital. This will help make sure that patients get the treatment they need and help stop them relapsing and returning to hospital
- the replacement of the approved social worker with the approved mental health professional. This will open up the possibility of approved mental healthcare professionals being drawn from other disciplines as well as social work. Other changes will open up the possibility of clinicians who are not doctors being approved to take on the role of the responsible medical officer. This role will be renamed the responsible clinician.
- provisions to make it possible for patients to apply to the county court for an unsuitable nearest relative to be replaced, and
- the abolition of after-care under supervision.

The Bill will also amend the MCA to introduce new procedures and provisions to make relevant decisions but who need to be deprived of their liberty, in their best interests, otherwise than under the Mental Health Act 1983 (the so-called 'Bournewood provisions').[58] **13.53**

This chapter, as well as chapter 6, will be fully revised in due course to reflect those changes. Information about the Government's current proposals in respect of the Bournewood safeguards is available on the Department of Health website. This information includes draft illustrative Code of Practice guidance about the proposed safeguards.[59] **13.54**

In the meantime, people taking decisions under both the MCA and the MHA must base those decisions on the Acts as they stand now. **13.55**

---

[58] This refers to the European Court of Human Rights judgement (5 October 2004) in the case of *HL v The United Kingdom* (Application no, 45508/99).

[59] See www.dh.gov.uk/PublicationsAndStatistics/Publications/PublicationsPolicyAndGuidance/Publications PolicyAndGuidanceArticle/fs/en?CONTENT_ ID=4141656&chk=jlw07L

14. WHAT MEANS OF PROTECTION EXIST FOR PEOPLE WHO LACK CAPACITY TO MAKE DECISIONS FOR THEMSELVES?

This chapter describes the different agencies that exist to help make sure that adults who lack capacity to make decisions for themselves are protected from abuse. It also explains the services those agencies provide and how they supervise people who provide care for or make decisions on behalf of people who lack capacity. Finally, it explains what somebody should do if they suspect that somebody is abusing a vulnerable adult who lacks capacity.

In this chapter, as throughout the Code, a person's capacity (or lack of capacity) refers specifically to their capacity to make a particular decision at the time it needs to be made.

Quick summary

- Always report suspicions of abuse of a person who lacks capacity to the relevant agency.

Concerns about an appointee

- When someone is concerned about the collection or use of social security benefits by an appointee on behalf a person who lacks capacity, they should contact the local Jobcentre Plus. If the appointee is for someone who is over the age of 60, contact The Pension Service.

Concerns about an attorney or deputy

- If someone is concerned about the actions of an attorney or deputy, they should contact the Office of the Public Guardian.

Concerns about a possible criminal offence

- If there is a good reason to suspect that someone has committed a crime against a vulnerable person, such as theft or physical or sexual assault, contact the police.
- In addition, social services should also be contacted, so that they can support the vulnerable person during the investigation.

Concerns about possible ill-treatment or wilful neglect

- The Act introduces new criminal offences of ill treatment or wilful neglect of a person who lacks capacity to make relevant decisions (section 44).
- If someone is not being looked after properly, contact social services.
- In serious cases, contact the police.

Concerns about care standards

- In cases of concern about the standard of care in a care home or an adult placement scheme, or about the care provided by a home care worker, contact social services.
- It may also be appropriate to contact the Commission for Social Care Inspection (in England) or the Care and Social Services Inspectorate for Wales.

Concerns about healthcare or treatment

- If someone is concerned about the care or treatment given to the person in any NHS setting (such as an NHS hospital or clinic) contact the managers of the service.
- It may also be appropriate to make a formal complaint through the NHS complaints procedure (see chapter 15).

What is abuse?

14.1 The word 'abuse' covers a wide range of actions. In some cases, abuse is clearly deliberate and intentionally unkind. But sometimes abuse happens because somebody does not know how to act correctly—or they haven't got appropriate help and support. It is important to prevent abuse, wherever possible. If somebody is abused, it is important to investigate the abuse and take steps to stop it happening.

Abuse is anything that goes against a person's human and civil rights. This includes sexual, physical, verbal, financial and emotional abuse. Abuse can be: 14.2

- a single act
- a series of repeated acts
- a failure to provide necessary care, or
- neglect.

Abuse can take place anywhere (for example, in a person's own home, a care home or a hospital).

The main types of abuse are: 14.3

Type of abuse	Examples
Financial	• theft • fraud • undue pressure • misuse of property, possessions or benefits • dishonest gain of property, possessions or benefits.
Physical	• slapping, pushing, kicking or other forms of violence • misuse of medication (for example, increasing dosage to make someone drowsy) • inappropriate punishments (for example, not giving someone a meal because they have been 'bad').
Sexual	• rape • sexual assault • sexual acts without consent (this includes if a person is not able to give consent or the abuser used pressure).
Psychological	• emotional abuse • threats of harm, restraint or abandonment • refusing contact with other people • intimidation • threats to restrict someone's liberty.
Neglect and acts of omission	• ignoring the person's medical or physical care needs • failing to get healthcare or social care • withholding medication, food or heating.

The Department of Health and the National Assembly for Wales have produced separate guidance on protecting vulnerable adults from abuse. *No secrets*[60] (England) and *in safe hands*[61] (Wales) both define vulnerable adults as people aged 18 and over who: 14.4

- need community care services due to a mental disability, other disability, age or illness, and
- may be unable to take care of themselves or protect themselves against serious harm or exploitation.

---

[60] Department of Health and Home Office, *No secrets: Guidance on developing and implementing multi-agency policies and procedures to protect vulnerable adults from abuse*, (2000) www.dh.gov.uk/assetRoot/04/07/45/40/04074540.pdf

[61] National Assembly for Wales, *In safe hands: Implementing adult protection procedures in Wales* (2000), http://new.wales.gov.uk.about.departments/dhss/publications/social_services_publications/reports/insafehands?lang=en

This description applies to many people who lack capacity to make decisions for themselves.

14.5   Anyone who thinks that someone might be abusing a vulnerable adult who lacks capacity should:

- contact the local social services (see paragraphs 14.27–14.28 below)
- contact the Office of the Public Guardian (see paragraph 14.8 below), or
- seek advice from a relevant telephone helpline[62] or through the Community Legal Service.[63]

Full contact details are provided in Annex A.

14.6   In most cases, local adult protection procedures will say who should take action (see paragraphs 14.28–14.29 below). But some abuse will be a criminal offence, such as physical assault, sexual assault or rape, theft, fraud and some other forms of financial exploitation. In these cases, the person who suspects abuse should contact the police urgently. The criminal investigation may take priority over all other forms of investigation. So all agencies will have to work together to plan the best way to investigate possible abuse.

14.7   The Fraud Act 2006 (due to come into force in 2007) creates a new offence of 'fraud by abuse of position'. This new offence may apply to a range of people, including:

- attorneys under a Lasting Power of Attorney (LPA) or an Enduring Power of Attorney (EPA), or
- deputies appointed by the Court of Protection to make financial decisions on behalf of a person who lacks capacity. Attorneys and deputies may be guilty of fraud if they dishonestly abuse their position, intend to benefit themselves or others, and cause loss or expose a person to the risk of loss. People who suspect fraud should report the case to the police.

How does the Act protect people from abuse?

The Office of the Public Guardian

14.8   Section 57 of the Act creates a new Public Guardian, supported by staff of the Office of the Public Guardian (OPG). The Public Guardian helps protect people who lack capacity by:

- setting up and managing a register of LPAs
- setting up and managing a register of EPAs
- setting up and managing a register of court orders that appoint deputies
- supervising deputies, working with other relevant organisations (for example, social services, if the person who lacks capacity is receiving social care)
- sending Court of Protection Visitors to visit people who may lack capacity to make particular decisions and those who have formal powers to act on their behalf (see paragraphs 14.10–14.11 below)
- receiving reports from attorneys acting under LPAs and from deputies
- providing reports to the Court of Protection, as requested, and
- dealing with representations (including complaints) about the way in which attorneys or deputies carry out their duties.

14.9   Section 59 of the Act creates a Public Guardian Board to oversee and review how the Public Guardian carries out these duties.

---

[62] For example, the Action on Elder Abuse (0808 808 8141), Age Concern (0800 009966) or CarersLine (0808 808 7777).

[63] Community Legal Service Direct www.clsdirect.org.uk

Court of Protection Visitors

The role of a Court of Protection Visitor is to provide independent advice to the court and the   **14.10**
Public Guardian. They advise on how anyone given power under the Act should be, and is, carrying out their duties and responsibilities. There are two types of visitor: General Visitors and Special Visitors. Special visitors are registered medical practitioners with relevant expertise. The court or Public Guardian can send whichever type of visitor is most appropriate to visit and interview a person who may lack capacity. Visitors can also interview attorneys or deputies and inspect any relevant healthcare or social care records. Attorneys and deputies must co-operate with the visitors and provide them with all relevant information. If attorneys or deputies do not co-operate, the court can cancel their appointment, where it thinks that they have not acted in the person's best interests.

Scenario: Using a General Visitor

Mrs Quinn made an LPA appointing her nephew, Ian, as her financial attorney. She recently lost capacity to make her own financial decisions, and Ian has registered the LPA. He has taken control of Mrs Quinn's financial affairs. But Mrs Quinn's niece suspects that Ian is using Mrs Quinn's money to pay off his own debts. She contacts the OPG, which sends a General Visitor to visit Mrs Quinn and Ian. The visitor's report will assess the facts. It might suggest the case go to court to consider whether Ian has behaved in a way which:

• goes against his authority under the LPA, or
• is not in Mrs Quinn's best interests.

The Public Guardian will decide whether the court should be involved in the matter. The court will then decide if it requires further evidence. If it thinks that Ian is abusing his position, the court may cancel the LPA.

Court of Protection Visitors have an important part to play in investigating possible abuse. But   **14.11**
their role is much wider than this. They can also check on the general wellbeing of the person who lacks capacity, and they can give support to attorneys and deputies who need help to carry out their duties.

How does the Public Guardian oversee LPAs?

An LPA is a private arrangement between the donor and the attorney (see chapter 7). Donors   **14.12**
should only choose attorneys that they can trust. The OPG provides information to help potential donors understand:

• the impact of making an LPA
• what they can give an attorney authority to do
• what to consider when choosing an attorney.

The Public Guardian must make sure that an LPA meets the Act's requirements. Before registering   **14.13**
an LPA, the OPG will check documentation. For property and affairs LPAs, it will check whether an attorney appointed under the LPA is bankrupt since this would revoke the authority.

The Public Guardian will not usually get involved once somebody has registered an LPA—   **14.14**
unless someone is worried about how an attorney is carrying out their duties. If concerns are raised about an attorney, the OPG works closely with organisations such as local authorities and NHS Trusts to carry out investigations.

How does the Public Guardian supervise deputies?

14.15   Individuals do not choose who will act as a deputy for them. The court will make the decision. There are measures to make sure that the court appoints an appropriate deputy. The OPG will then supervise deputies and support them in carrying out their duties, while also making sure they do not abuse their position.

14.16   When a case comes before the Court of Protection, the Act states that the court should make a decision to settle the matter rather than appoint a deputy, if possible. Deputies are most likely to be needed for financial matters where someone needs continued authority to make decisions about the person's money or other assets. It will be easier for the courts to make decisions in cases where a one-off decision is needed about a person's welfare, so there are likely to be fewer personal welfare deputies. But there will be occasions where ongoing decisions about a person's welfare will be required, and so the court will appoint a personal welfare deputy (see chapter 8).

Scenario: Appointing deputies

Peter was in a motorbike accident that left him permanently and seriously brain-damaged. He has minimal awareness of his surroundings and an assessment has shown that he lacks capacity to make most decisions for himself. Somebody needs to make several decisions about what treatment Peter needs and where he should be treated. His parents feel that healthcare staff do not always consider their views in decisions about what treatment is in Peter's best interests. So they make an application to the court to be appointed as joint personal welfare deputies. There will be many care or treatment decisions for Peter in the future. The court decides it would not be practical to make a separate decision on each of them. It also thinks Peter needs some continuity in decision-making. So it appoints Peter's parents as joint personal welfare deputies.

14.17   The OPG may run checks on potential deputies if requested to by the court. It will carry out a risk assessment to determine what kind of supervision a deputy will need once they are appointed.

14.18   Deputies are accountable to the court. The OPG supervises the deputy's actions on the court's behalf, and the court may want the deputy to provide financial accounts or other reports to the OPG. The Public Guardian deals with complaints about the way deputies carry out their duties. It works with other relevant agencies to investigate them. Chapter 8 gives detailed information about the responsibilities of deputies.

What happens if someone says they are worried about an attorney or deputy?

14.19   Many people who lack capacity are likely to get care or support from a range of agencies. Even when an attorney or deputy is acting on behalf of a person who lacks capacity, the other carers still have a responsibility to the person to provide care and act in the person's best interests. Anybody who is caring for a person who lacks capacity, whether in a paid or unpaid role, who is worried about how attorneys or deputies carry out their duties should contact the Public Guardian.

14.20   The OPG will not always be the most appropriate organisation to investigate all complaints. It may investigate a case jointly with:

- healthcare or social care professionals
- social services
- NHS bodies
- the Commission for Social Care Inspection in England or the Care and Social Services Inspectorate for Wales (CSSIW)[64]

---

[64] In April 2007, the Care Standards Inspectorate for Wales (CSIW) and the Social Services Inspectorate for Wales (SSIW) came together to form the Care and Social Services Inspectorate for Wales.

- the Healthcare Commission in England or the Healthcare Inspectorate for Wales, and
- in some cases, the police.

The OPG will usually refer concerns about personal welfare LPAs or personal welfare deputies 14.21
to the relevant agency. In certain circumstances it will alert the police about a case. When it makes
a referral, the OPG will make sure that the relevant agency keeps it informed of the action it takes.
It will also make sure that the court has all the information it needs to take possible action against
the attorney or deputy.

Examples of situations in which a referral might be necessary include where: 14.22
- someone has complained that a welfare attorney is physically abusing a donor—the OPG would
  refer this case to the relevant local authority adult protection procedures and possibly the
  police
- the OPG has found that a solicitor appointed as a financial deputy for an elderly woman has
  defrauded her estate—the OPG would refer this case to the police and the Law Society
  Consumer Complaints Service.

How does the Act deal with ill treatment and wilful neglect?

The Act introduces two new criminal offences: ill treatment and wilful neglect of a person who 14.23
lacks capacity to make relevant decisions (section 44). The offences may apply to:
- anyone caring for a person who lacks capacity – this includes family carers, healthcare and social
  care staff in hospital or care homes and those providing care in a person's home
- an attorney appointed under an LPA or an EPA, or
- a deputy appointed for the person by the court.

These people may be guilty of an offence if they ill-treat or wilfully neglect the person they 14.24
care for or represent. Penalties will range from a fine to a sentence of imprisonment of up to five
years—or both.

Ill treatment and neglect are separate offences.[65] For a person to be found guilty of ill treatment, 14.25
they must either:
- have deliberately ill-treated the person, or
- be reckless in the way they were ill-treating the person or not.

It does not matter whether the behaviour was likely to cause, or actually caused, harm or damage
to the victim's health.

The meaning of 'wilful neglect' varies depending on the circumstances. But it usually means 14.26
that a person has deliberately failed to carry out an act they knew they had a duty to do.

Scenario: Reporting abuse

Norma is 95 and has Alzheimer's disease. Her son, Brendan, is her personal welfare attorney under
an LPA. A district nurse has noticed that Norma has bruises and other injuries. She suspects
Brendan may be assaulting his mother when he is drunk. She alerts the police and the local Adult
Protection Committee. Following a criminal investigation, Brendan is charged with ill-treating his
mother. The Public Guardian applies to the court to cancel the LPA. Social services start to make
alternative arrangements for Norma's care.

---

[65] *R v Newington* (1990) 91 Cr App R 247, CA.

What other measures protect people from abuse?

14.27 Local agencies have procedures that allow them to work together (called multi-agency working) to protect vulnerable adults—in care settings and elsewhere. Most areas have Adult Protection Committees. These committees:
- create policy (including reporting procedures)
- oversee investigations and other activity between agencies
- carry out joint training, and
- monitor and review progress.

Other local authorities have developed multi-agency Adult Protection Procedures, which are managed by a dedicated Adult Protection Co-ordinator.

14.28 Adult Protection Committees and Procedures (APCP) involve representatives from the NHS, social services, housing, the police and other relevant agencies. In England, they are essential points of contact for anyone who suspects abuse or ill treatment of a vulnerable adult. They can also give advice to the OPG if it is uncertain whether an intervention is necessary in a case of suspected abuse. In Wales, APCPs are not necessarily points of contact themselves, but they publish details of points of contact.

Who should check that staff are safe to work with vulnerable adults?

14.29 Under the Safeguarding Vulnerable Groups Act 2006, criminal record checks are now compulsory for staff who:
- have contact with service users in registered care homes
- provide personal care services in someone's home, and
- are involved in providing adult placement schemes.

14.30 Potential employers must carry out a pre-employment criminal record check with the Criminal Records Bureau (CRB) for all potential new healthcare and social care staff. This includes nursing agency staff and home care agency staff.
See Annex A for sources of more detailed information.

14.31 The Protection of Vulnerable Adults (POVA) list has the names of people who have been barred from working with vulnerable adults (in England and Wales). Employers providing care in a residential setting or a person's own home must check whether potential employees are on the list.[66] If they are on the list, they must:
- refuse to employ them, or
- employ them in a position that does not give them regular contact with vulnerable adults.

It is an offence for anyone on the list to apply for a care position. In such cases, the employer should report the person making the application.

Who is responsible for monitoring the standard of care providers?

14.32 All care providers covered by the Care Standards Act 2000 must register with the Commission for Social Care Inspection in England (CSCI) or the Care and Social Services Inspectorate for Wales

---

[66] www.dh.gov.uk/PublicationsAndStatistics/Publications/PublicationsPolicyAndGuidance/
PublicationsPolicyAndGuidanceArticle/fs/en?CONTENT_ID=4085855&chk=p0kQeS

(CSSIW).[67] These agencies make sure that care providers meet certain standards. They require care providers to have procedures to protect people from harm or abuse. These agencies can take action if they discover dangerous or unsafe practices that could place people at risk.

Care providers must also have effective complaints procedures. If providers cannot settle complaints, CSCI or CSSIW can look into them.   14.33

CSCI or CSSIW assesses the effectiveness of local adult protection procedures. They will also monitor the arrangements local councils make in response to the Care Standards Act.   14.34

What is an appointee, and who monitors them?

The Department for Work and Pensions (DWP) can appoint someone (an appointee) to claim and spend benefits on a person's behalf[68] if that person: 14.35

- gets social security benefits or pensions
- lacks the capacity to act for themselves
- has not made a property and affairs LPA or an EPA, and
- the court has not appointed a property and affairs deputy.

The DWP checks that an appointee is trustworthy. It also investigates any allegations that an appointee is not acting appropriately or in the person's interests. It can remove an appointee who abuses their position. Concerns about appointees should be raised with the relevant DWP agency (the local Jobcentre Plus, or if the person is aged 60 or over, The Pension Service).   14.36

Are there any other means of protection that people should be aware of?

There are a number of additional means that exist to protect people who lack capacity to make decisions for themselves. Healthcare and social care staff, attorneys and deputies should be aware of: 14.37

- National Minimum Standards (for example, for healthcare, care homes, and home care agencies) which apply to both England and Wales (see paragraph 14.38)
- National Service Frameworks, which set out national standards for specific health and care services for particular groups (for example, for mental health services[69] or services for older people)[70]
- complaints procedures for all NHS bodies and local councils (see chapter 15)
- Stop Now Orders (also known as Enforcement Orders) that allow consumer protection bodies to apply for court orders to stop poor trading practices (for example, unfair door-step selling or rogue traders).[71]
- The Public Interest Disclosure Act 1998, which encourages people to report malpractice in the workplace and protects people who report malpractice from being sacked or victimised.

---

[67] See note 64 above regarding the merger of the Care Standards Inspectorate for Wales and the Social Services Inspectorate for Wales.

[68] www.dwp.gov.uk/publications/dwp/2005/gl21_apr.pdf

[69] www.dh.gov.uk/assetRoot/04/07/72/09/04077209.pdf and www.wales.nhs.uk/sites3/page.cfm?orgid=438&pid=11071

[70] www.dh.gov.uk/assetRoot/04/07/12/83/04071283.pdf and www.wales.nhs.uk/sites3/home.cfm?orgid=439&redirect=yes&CFID=298511&CFTOKEN=6985382

[71] www.oft.gov.uk/Business/Legal/Stop+Now+Regulations.htm

14.38   Information about all national minimum standards are available on the CSCI[72] and Healthcare Commission websites[73] and the Welsh Assembly Government website. Chapter 15 gives guidance on complaints procedures. Individual local authorities will have their own complaints system in place.

15. WHAT ARE THE BEST WAYS TO SETTLE DISAGREEMENTS AND DISPUTES ABOUT ISSUES COVERED IN THE ACT?

Sometimes people will disagree about:
- a person's capacity to make a decision
- their best interests
- a decision someone is making on their behalf, or
- an action someone is taking on their behalf.

It is in everybody's interests to settle disagreements and disputes quickly and effectively, with minimal stress and cost. This chapter sets out the different options available for settling disagreements. It also suggests ways to avoid letting a disagreement become a serious dispute. Finally, it sets out when it might be necessary to apply to the Court of Protection and when somebody can get legal funding.

In this chapter, as throughout the Code, a person's capacity (or lack of capacity) refers specifically to their capacity to make a particular decision at the time it needs to be made.

Quick summary

- When disagreements occur about issues that are covered in the Act, it is usually best to try and settle them before they become serious.
- Advocates can help someone who finds it difficult to communicate their point of view. (This may be someone who has been assessed as lacking capacity.)
- Some disagreements can be effectively resolved by mediation.
- Where there is a concern about healthcare or social care provided to a person who lacks capacity, there are formal and informal ways of complaining about the care or treatment.
- The Health Service Ombudsman or the Local Government Ombudsman (in England) or the Public Services Ombudsman (in Wales) can be asked to investigate some problems that have not been resolved through formal complaints procedures.
- Disputes about the finances of a person who lacks capacity should usually be referred to the Office of the Public Guardian (OPG).
- When other methods of resolving disagreements are not appropriate, the matter can be referred to the Court of Protection.
- There are some decisions that are so serious that the Court of Protection should always make them.

---

[72] www.csci.org.uk/information_for_service_providers/national_minimum_standards/ default.htm
[73] www.healthcarecommission.org.uk/_db/_documents/The_annual_health_check_in_2006_2007_
assessing_and_rating_the_NHS_200609225143.pdf

What options are there for settling disagreements?

Disagreements about healthcare, social or other welfare services may be between: 15.1
- people who have assessed a person as lacking capacity to make a decision and the person they have assessed (see chapter 4 for how to challenge an assessment of lack of capacity)
- family members or other people concerned with the care and welfare of a person who lacks capacity
- family members and healthcare or social care staff involved in providing care or treatment
- healthcare and social care staff who have different views about what is in the best interests of a person who lacks capacity.

In general, disagreements can be resolved by either formal or informal procedures, and there 15.2 is more information on both in this chapter. However, there are some disagreements and some subjects that are so serious they can only be resolved by the Court of Protection.

It is usually best to try and settle disagreements before they become serious disputes. Many 15.3 people settle them by communicating effectively and taking the time to listen and to address worries. Disagreements between family members are often best settled informally, or sometimes through mediation. When professionals are in disagreement with a person's family, it is a good idea to start by:
- setting out the different options in a way that is easy to understand
- inviting a colleague to talk to the family and offer a second opinion offering to get independent expert advice
- using an advocate to support and represent the person who lacks capacity
- arranging a case conference or meeting to discuss matters in detail
- listening to, acknowledging and addressing worries, and
- where the situation is not urgent, allowing the family time to think it over.

Further guidance on how to deal with problems without going to court may also be found in the Community Legal Services Information Leaflet 'Alternatives to Court'.[74]

When is an advocate useful?

An advocate helps communicate the feelings and views of someone who has communication 15.4 difficulties. The definition of advocacy set out in the Advocacy Charter adopted by most advocacy schemes is as follows: 'Advocacy is taking action to help people say what they want, secure their rights, represent their interests and obtain services they need. Advocates and advocacy schemes work in partnership with the people they support and take their side. Advocacy promotes social inclusion, equality and social justice.'[75]

An advocate may be able to help settle a disagreement simply by presenting a person's feelings to their family, carers or professionals. Most advocacy services are provided by the voluntary sector and are arranged at a local level. They have no link to any agency involved with the person.

Using advocates can help people who find it difficult to communicate (including those who 15.5 have been assessed as lacking capacity) to:
- say what they want
- claim their rights

---

[74] CLS (Community Legal Services) Direct Information Leaflet Number 23, www.clsdirect.org.uk/legalhelp/leaflet23.jsp?lang=en

[75] Advocacy across London, *Advocacy Charter* (2002).

- represent their interests, and
- get the services they need.

15.6   Advocates may also be involved in supporting the person during mediation (see paragraphs 15.7–15.13 below) or helping with complaints procedures. Sometimes people who lack capacity or have been assessed as lacking capacity have a legal right to an advocate, for example:
  - when making a formal complaint against the NHS (see paragraph 15.18), and
  - where the Act requires the involvement of an Independent Mental Capacity Advocate (IMCA) (see chapter 10).

When is mediation useful?

15.7   A mediator helps people to come to an agreement that is acceptable to all parties. Mediation can help solve a problem at an early stage. It offers a wider range of solutions than the court can – and it may be less stressful for all parties, more cost-effective and quicker. People who come to an agreement through mediation are more likely to keep to it, because they have taken part in decision-making.

15.8   Mediators are independent. They have no personal interest in the outcome of a case. They do not make decisions or impose solutions. The mediator will decide whether the case is suitable for mediation. They will consider the likely chances of success and the need to protect the interests of the person who lacks capacity.

15.9   Any case that can be settled through negotiation is likely to benefit from mediation. It is most suitable when people are not communicating well or not understanding each other's point of view. It can improve relationships and stop future disputes, so it is a good option when it is in the person's interests for people to have a good relationship in the future.

Scenario: Using mediation

Mrs Roberts has dementia and lacks capacity to decide where she should live. She currently lives with her son. But her daughter has found a care home where she thinks her mother will get better care. Her brother disagrees. Mrs Roberts is upset by this family dispute, and so her son and daughter decide to try mediation. The mediator believes that Mrs Roberts is able to communicate her feelings and agrees to take on the case. During the sessions, the mediator helps them to focus on their mother's best interests rather than imposing their own views. In the end, everybody agrees that Mrs Roberts should continue to live with her son. But they agree to review the situation again in six months to see if the care home might then be better for her.

15.10   In mediation, everybody needs to take part as equally as possible so that a mediator can help everyone involved to focus on the person's best interests. It might also be appropriate to involve an advocate to help communicate the wishes of the person who lacks capacity.

15.11   The National Mediation Helpline[76] helps callers to identify an effective means of resolving their difficulty without going to court. It will arrange an appointment with a trained and accredited mediator. The Family Mediation Helpline[77] can provide information on family mediation and referrals to local family mediation services. Family mediators are trained to deal with the emotional, practical and financial needs of those going through relationship breakdown.

---

[76] National Mediation Helpline, Tel: 0845 60 30 809, www.nationalmediationhelpline.com
[77] Family Mediation Helpline, Tel: 0845 60 26 627, www.familymediationhelpline.co.uk

Healthcare and social care staff may also take part in mediation processes. But it may be more appropriate to follow the relevant healthcare or social care complaints procedures (see paragraphs 15.14–15.32).

15.12

In certain situations (mainly family mediation), legal aid may be available to fund mediation for people who meet the qualifying criteria (see paragraphs 15.38–15.44).

15.13

How can someone complain about healthcare?

There are formal and informal ways of complaining about a patient's healthcare or treatment. Healthcare staff and others need to know which methods are suitable in which situations.

15.14

In England, the Patient Advice and Liaison Service (PALS) provides an informal way of dealing with problems before they reach the complaints stage. PALS operate in every NHS and Primary Care Trust in England. They provide advice and information to patients (or their relatives or carers) to try to solve problems quickly. They can direct people to specialist support services (for example, advocates, mental health support teams, social services or interpreting services). PALS do not investigate complaints. Their role is to explain complaints procedures and direct people to the formal NHS complaints process, if necessary. NHS complaints procedures deal with complaints about something that happened in the past that requires an apology or explanation. A court cannot help in this situation, but court proceedings may be necessary in some clinical negligence cases (see paragraph 15.22).

15.15

In Wales, complaints advocates based at Community Health Councils provide advice and support to anyone with concerns about treatment they have had.

15.16

Disagreements about proposed treatments

If a case is not urgent, the supportive atmosphere of the PALS may help settle it. In Wales, the local Community Health Council may be able to help. But urgent cases about proposed serious treatment may need to go to the Court of Protection (see paragraphs 15.35–15.36).

15.17

Scenario: Disagreeing about treatment or an assessment

Mrs Thompson has Alzheimer's and does not want a flu jab. Her daughter thinks she should have the injection. The doctor does not want to go against the wishes of his patient, because he believes she has capacity to refuse treatment. Mrs Thompson's daughter goes to PALS. A member of staff gives her information and advice about what is meant by capacity to consent to or refuse treatment, and tells her how to find out about the flu jab. The PALS staff speak to the doctor, and then they explain his clinical assessment to Mrs Thompson's daughter. The daughter is still unhappy. PALS staff advise her that the Independent Complaints Advocacy Service can help if she wishes to make a formal complaint.

The formal NHS complaints procedure

The formal NHS complaints procedure deals with complaints about NHS services provided by NHS organisations or primary care practitioners. As a first step, people should try to settle a disagreement through an informal discussion between:

15.18

- the healthcare staff involved
- the person who may lack capacity to make the decision in question (with support if necessary)
- their carers, and
- any appropriate relatives.

If the person who is complaining is not satisfied, the Independent Complaints Advocacy Service (ICAS) may help. In Wales, the complaints advocates based at Community Health Councils will support and advise anyone who wants to make a complaint.

15.19   In England, if the person is still unhappy after a local investigation, they can ask for an independent review by the Healthcare Commission. If the patient involved in the complaint was or is detained under the Mental Health Act 1983, the Mental Health Act Commission can be asked to look into the complaint. If people are still unhappy after this stage, they can go to the Health Service Ombudsman. More information on how to make a complaint in England is available from the Department of Health.

15.20   In Wales, if patients are still unhappy after a local investigation, they can ask for an independent review of their complaint by independent lay reviewers. After this, they can take their case to the Public Services Ombudsman for Wales. People can take their complaint direct to the Ombudsman if:

• the complaint is about care or treatment that took place after 1 April 2006, and
• they have tried to settle the problem locally first.

The Mental Health Act Commission may also investigate complaints about the care or treatment of detained patients in Wales, if attempts have been made to settle the complaint locally without success.

15.21   Regulations about first trying to settle complaints locally do not apply to NHS Foundation Trusts. But these Trusts are covered by the independent review stage operated by the Healthcare Commission and by the Health Service Ombudsman. People who have a complaint about an NHS Foundation Trust should contact the Trust for advice on how to make a complaint.

Cases of clinical negligence

15.22   The NHS Litigation Authority oversees all clinical negligence cases brought against the NHS in England. It actively encourages people to try other forms of settling complaints before going to court. The National Assembly for Wales also encourages people to try other forms of settling complaints before going to court.

How can somebody complain about social care?

15.23   The social services complaints procedure has been reformed. The reformed procedure came into effect on 1 September 2006 in England and on 1 April 2006 in Wales.

15.24   A service provider's own complaints procedure should deal with complaints about:

• the way in which care services are delivered
• the type of services provided, or
• a failure to provide services.

15.25   Care agencies contracted by local authorities or registered with the Commission for Social Care Inspection (CSCI) in England or Care and Social Services Inspectorate for Wales (CSSIW) are legally obliged to have their own written complaints procedures. This includes residential homes, agencies providing care in people's homes, nursing agencies and adult placement schemes. The procedures should set out how to make a complaint and what to do with a complaint that cannot be settled locally.

Local authority complaints procedures

For services contracted by a local authority, it may be more appropriate to use the local authority's 15.26 complaints procedure. A simple example would be a situation where a local authority places a person in a care home and the person's family are not happy with the placement. If their complaint is not about the services the home provides (for example, it might be about the local authority's assessment of the person's needs), it might be more appropriate to use the local authority's complaints procedure.

As a first step, people should try to settle a disagreement through an informal discussion, 15.27 involving:

- the professionals involved
- the person who may lack capacity to make the decision in question (with support if necessary)
- their carers, and
- any appropriate relatives.

If the person making the complaint is not satisfied, the local authority will carry out a formal 15.28 investigation using its complaints procedure. In England, after this stage, a social service Complaints Review Panel can hear the case. In Wales complaints can be referred to the National Assembly for Wales for hearing by an independent panel.

Other complaints about social care

People can take their complaint to the CSCI in England or the CSSIW in Wales, if: 15.29
- the complaint is about regulations or national minimum standards not being met, and
- the complainants are not happy with the provider's own complaints procedure or the response to their complaint.

If a complaint is about a local authority's administration, it may be referred to the Commission for 15.30 Local Administration in England (the Local Government Ombudsman) or the Public Services Ombudsman for Wales.

What if a complaint covers healthcare and social care?

Taking a complaint through NHS or local authority complaints procedures can be a complicated 15.31 process – especially if the complaint covers a number of service providers or both healthcare and social care. In such situations, local authorities and the NHS must work together and agree which organisation will lead in handling the complaint. If a person is not happy with the outcome, they can take their case to the Health Service Ombudsman or to the Local Government Ombudsman (in England). There is guidance which sets out how organisations should work together to handle complaints that cover healthcare and social care (in England *Learning from Complaints* and in Wales *Listening and learning*). The Public Services Ombudsman for Wales handles complaints that cover both healthcare and social care.

Who can handle complaints about other welfare issues?

The Independent Housing Ombudsman deals with complaints about registered social landlords 15.32 in England. This applies mostly to housing associations. But it also applies to many landlords who manage homes that were formerly run by local authorities and some private landlords. In Wales, the Public Services Ombudsman for Wales deals with complaints about registered social landlords. Complaints about local authorities may be referred to the Local Government Ombudsman in

England or the Public Services Ombudsman for Wales. They look at complaints about decisions on council housing, social services, Housing Benefit and planning applications. More information about complaints to an Ombudsman is available on the relevant websites (see Annex A).

What is the best way to handle disagreement about a person's finances?

15.33 Some examples of disagreements about a person's finances are:
- disputes over the amount of money a person who lacks capacity should pay their carer
- disputes over whether a person who lacks capacity should sell their house
- somebody questioning the actions of a carer, who may be using the money of a person who lacks capacity inappropriately or without proper authority
- somebody questioning the actions of an attorney appointed under a Lasting Power of Attorney or an Enduring Power of Attorney or a deputy appointed by the court.

15.34   In all of the above circumstances, the most appropriate action would usually be to contact the Office of the Public Guardian (OPG) for guidance and advice. See chapter 14 for further details on the role of the OPG.

How can the Court of Protection help?

15.35 The Court of Protection deals with all areas of decision-making for adults who lack capacity to make particular decisions for themselves (see chapter 8 for more information about its roles and responsibilities). But the court is not always the right place to settle problems involving people who lack capacity. Other forms of settling disagreements may be more appropriate and less distressing.

15.36   There are some decisions that are so serious that the court should always make them. There are also other types of cases that the court should deal with when another method would generally not be suitable. See chapter 8 for more information about both kinds of cases.

Right of Appeal

15.37 Section 53 of the Act describes the rights of appeal against any decision taken by the Court of Protection. There are further details in the Court of Protection Rules. It may be advisable for anyone who wishes to appeal a decision made by the court to seek legal advice.

Will public legal funding be available?

15.38 Depending on their financial situation, once the Act comes into force people may be entitled to:
- publicly funded legal advice from accredited solicitors or advice agencies
- legal representation before the new Court of Protection (in the most serious cases).

Information about solicitors and organisations who give advice on different areas of law is available from Community Legal Services Direct (CLS Direct).[78] Further information about legal aid and public funding can be obtained from the Legal Services Commission.[79] See Annex A for full contact details.

---

[78] CLS Direct, Tel: 0845 345 4 345, www.clsdirect.org.uk

[79] www.legalservices.gov.uk

People who lack capacity to instruct a solicitor or conduct their own case will need a litigation 15.39
friend. This person could be a relative, friend, attorney or the Official Solicitor (when no-one else
is available). The litigation friend is able to instruct the solicitor and conduct the case on behalf of
a person who lacks capacity to give instructions. If the person qualifies for public legal funding,
the litigation friend can claim funding on their behalf.

When can someone get legal help?

Legal help is a type of legal aid (public funding) that pays for advice and assistance on legal issues, 15.40
including those affecting a person who lacks capacity. But it does not provide representation for a
full court hearing, although there is a related form of funding called 'help at court' under which a
legal representative can speak in court on a client's behalf on an informal basis. To qualify for legal
help, applicants must show that:
• they get specific social security benefits, or they earn less than a specific amount and do not have
  savings or other financial assets in excess of a specific amount
• they would benefit sufficiently from legal advice to justify the amount it costs, and
• they cannot get another form of funding.

Legal help can include: 15.41
• help from a solicitor or other representative in writing letters
• in exceptional circumstances, getting a barrister's opinion, and
• assistance in preparing for Court of Protection hearings.

People cannot get legal help for making a Lasting Power of Attorney or an advance decision to 15.42
refuse treatment. But they can get general help and information from the OPG. The OPG cannot
give legal or specialist advice. For example, they will not be able to advise someone on what powers
they should delegate to their attorney under an LPA.

When can someone get legal representation?

Public funding for legal representation in the Court of Protection will be available from solicitors 15.43
with a relevant contract—but only for the most serious cases. To qualify, applicants will normally
face the same test as for legal help to qualify financially (paragraph 15.40). They will generally
have to satisfy more detailed criteria than applicants for legal help, relating, for instance, to their
prospects of being successful, to whether legal representation is necessary and to the cost benefit of
being represented. They will also have to establish that the case could not be brought or funded in
another way and that there are not alternatives to court proceedings that should be explored first.

Serious personal welfare cases that were previously heard by the High Court will continue to 15.44
have public funding for legal representation when they are transferred to the Court of Protection.
These cases will normally be related to personal liberty, serious welfare decisions or medical
treatment for a person who lacks capacity. But legal representation may also be available in other
types of cases, depending on the particular circumstances.

16. WHAT RULES GOVERN ACCESS TO INFORMATION ABOUT A PERSON WHO LACKS CAPACITY?

This chapter gives guidance on:
• what personal information about someone who lacks capacity people involved in their care have
  the right to see, and
• how they can get hold of that information.

This chapter is only a general guide. It does not give detailed information about the law. Nor does it replace professional guidance or the guidance of the Information Commissioner's Office on the Data Protection Act 1998 (this guidance is available on its website, see Annex A). Where necessary, people should take legal advice.

This chapter is mainly for people such as family carers and other carers, deputies and attorneys, who care for or represent someone who lacks capacity to make specific decisions and in particular, lacks capacity to allow information about them to be disclosed. Professionals have their own codes of conduct, and they may have the support of experts in their organisations.

In this chapter, as throughout the Code, a person's capacity (or lack of capacity) refers specifically to their capacity to make a particular decision at the time it needs to be made.

Quick summary

Questions to ask when requesting personal information about someone who may lack capacity
- Am I acting under a Lasting Power of Attorney or as a deputy with specific authority?
- Does the person have capacity to agree that information can be disclosed? Have they previously agreed to disclose the information?
- What information do I need?
- Why do I need it?
- Who has the information?
- Can I show that:
  — I need the information to make a decision that is in the best interests of the person I am acting for, and
  — the person does not have the capacity to act for themselves?
- Do I need to share the information with anyone else to make a decision that is in the best interests of the person who lacks capacity?
- Should I keep a record of my decision or action?
- How long should I keep the information for?
- Do I have the right to request the information under section 7 of the Data Protection Act 1998?

Questions to ask when considering whether to disclose information
- Is the request covered by section 7 of the Data Protection Act 1998? Is the request being made by a formally authorised representative?
If not:
- Is the disclosure legal?
- Is the disclosure justified, having balanced the person's best interests and the public interest against the person's right to privacy?

Questions to ask to decide whether the disclosure is legal or justified
- Do I (or does my organisation) have the information?
- Am I satisfied that the person concerned lacks capacity to agree to disclosure?
- Does the person requesting the information have any formal authority to act on behalf of the person who lacks capacity?
- Am I satisfied that the person making the request:
  — is acting in the best interests of the person concerned?
  — needs the information to act properly?
  — will respect confidentiality?
  — will keep the information for no longer than necessary?
- Should I get written confirmation of these things?

What laws and regulations affect access to information?

People caring for, or managing the finances of, someone who lacks capacity may need informa- 16.1
tion to:
- assess the person's capacity to make a specific decision
- determine the person's best interests, and
- make appropriate decisions on the person's behalf.

The information they need varies depending on the circumstances. For example: 16.2
- a daughter providing full-time care for an elderly parent will make decisions based on her own experience and knowledge of her parent
- a deputy may need information from other people. For instance, if they were deciding whether a person needs to move into a care home or whether they should sell the person's home, they might need information from family members, the family doctor, the person's bank and their solicitor to make sure they are making the decision in the person's best interests.

Much of the information needed to make decisions under the Act is sensitive or confidential. It 16.3
is regulated by:
- the Data Protection Act 1998
- the common law duty of confidentiality
- professional codes of conduct on confidentiality, and
- the Human Rights Act 1998 and European Convention on Human Rights, in particular Article 8 (the right to respect for private and family life), which means that it is only lawful to reveal someone's personal information if:
  —there is a legitimate aim in doing so
  —a democratic society would think it necessary to do so, and
  —the kind and amount of information disclosed is in relation to the need.

What information do people generally have a right to see?

Section 7 of the Data Protection Act 1998 gives everyone the right to see personal information 16.4
that an organisation holds about them. They may also authorise someone else to access their information on their behalf. The person holding the information has a legal duty to release it. So, where possible, it is important to try to get a person's consent before requesting to see information about them.

A person may have the capacity to agree to someone seeing their personal information, even if 16.5
they do not have the capacity to make other decisions. In some situations, a person may have previously given consent (while they still had capacity) for someone to see their personal information in the future.

Doctors and lawyers cannot share information about their clients, or that clients have given 16.6
them, without the client's consent. Sometimes it is fair to assume that a doctor or lawyer already has someone's consent (for example, patients do not usually expect healthcare staff or legal professionals to get consent every time they share information with a colleague—but staff may choose to get clients' consent in writing when they begin treating or acting for that person). But in other circumstances, doctors and lawyers must get specific consent to 'disclose' information (share it with someone else).

If someone's capacity changes from time to time, the person needing the information may want 16.7
to wait until that person can give their consent. Or they may decide that it is not necessary to get access to information at all, if the person will be able to make a decision on their own in the future.

445

16.8   If someone lacks the capacity to give consent, someone else might still be able to see their personal information. This will depend on:

- whether the person requesting the information is acting as an agent (a representative recognised by the law, such as a deputy or attorney) for the person who lacks capacity
- whether disclosure is in the best interests of the person who lacks capacity, and
- what type of information has been requested.

When can attorneys and deputies ask to see personal information?

16.9   An attorney acting under a valid LPA or EPA (and sometimes a deputy) can ask to see information concerning the person they are representing, as long as the information applies to decisions the attorney has the legal right to make.

16.10   In practice, an attorney or deputy may only require limited information and may not need to make a formal request. In such circumstances, they can approach the information holder informally. Once satisfied that the request comes from an attorney or deputy (having seen appropriate authority), the person holding information should be able to release it. The attorney or deputy can still make a formal request for information in the future.

16.11   The attorney or deputy must treat the information confidentially. They should be extremely careful to protect it. If they fail to do so, the court can cancel the LPA or deputyship.

16.12   Before the Act came into effect, only a few receivers were appointed with the general authority to manage a person's property and affairs. So they needed specific authority from the Court of Protection to ask for access to the person's personal information. Similarly, a deputy who only has authority to act in specific areas only has the right to ask for information relating to decisions in those specific areas. For information relating to other areas, the deputy will need to apply to the Court of Protection.

16.13   Requests for personal information must be in writing, and there might be a fee. Information holders should release it promptly (always within 40 calendar days). Fees may be particularly high for getting copies of healthcare records – particularly where information may be in unusual formats (for example, x-rays). The maximum fee is currently £50. Complaints about a failure to comply with the Data Protection Act 1998 should be directed to the Information Commissioner's Office (see Annex A for contact details).

What limitations are there?

16.14   Attorneys and deputies should only ask for information that will help them make a decision they need to make on behalf of the person who lacks capacity. For example, if the attorney needs to know when the person should take medication, they should not ask to see the entire healthcare record. The person who releases information must make sure that an attorney or deputy has official authority (they may ask for proof of identity and appointment). When asking to see personal information, attorneys and deputies should bear in mind that their decision must always be in the best interests of the person who lacks capacity to make that decision.

16.15   The attorney or deputy may not know the kind of information that someone holds about the person they are representing. So sometimes it might be difficult for them to make a specific request. They might even need to see all the information to make a decision. But again, the 'best interests' principle applies.

Scenario: Giving attorneys access to personal information

Mr Yapp is in the later stages of Alzheimer's disease. His son is responsible for Mr Yapp's personal welfare under a Lasting Power of Attorney. Mr Yapp has been in residential care for a number of years. But his son does not think that the home is able to meet his father's current needs as his condition has recently deteriorated. The son asks to see his father's records. He wants specific information about his father's care, so that he can make a decision about his father's best interests. But the manager of the care home refuses, saying that the Data Protection Act stops him releasing personal information. Mr Yapp's son points out that he can see his father's records, because he is his personal welfare attorney and needs the information to make a decision. The Data Protection Act 1998 requires the care home manager to provide access to personal data held on Mr Yapp.

The deputy or attorney may find that some information is held back (for example, when this contains references to people other than the person who lacks capacity). This might be to protect another person's privacy, if that person is mentioned in the records. It is unlikely that information relating to another person would help an attorney make a decision on behalf of the person who lacks capacity. The information holder might also be obliged to keep information about the other person confidential. There might be another reason why the person does not want information about them to be released. Under these circumstances, the attorney does not have the right to see that information. 16.16

An information holder should not release information if doing so would cause serious physical or mental harm to anyone—including the person the information is about. This applies to information on health, social care and education records. 16.17

The Information Commissioner's Office can give further details on: 16.18
- how to request personal information
- restrictions on accessing information, and
- how to appeal against a decision not to release information.

When can someone see information about healthcare or social care?

Healthcare and social care staff may disclose information about somebody who lacks capacity only when it is in the best interests of the person concerned to do so, or when there is some other, lawful reason for them to do so. 16.19

The Act's requirement to consult relevant people when working out the best interests of a person who lacks capacity will encourage people to share the information that makes a consultation meaningful. But people who release information should be sure that they are acting lawfully and that they can justify releasing the information. They need to balance the person's right to privacy with what is in their best interests or the wider public interest (see paragraphs 16.24–16.25 below). 16.20

Sometimes it will be fairly obvious that staff should disclose information. For example, a doctor would need to tell a new care worker about what drugs a person needs or what allergies the person has. This is clearly in the person's best interests. 16.21

Other information may need to be disclosed as part of the process of working out someone's best interests. A social worker might decide to reveal information about someone's past when discussing their best interests with a close family member. But staff should always bear in mind that the Act requires them to consider the wishes and feelings of the person who lacks capacity. 16.22

In both these cases, staff should only disclose as much information as is relevant to the decision to be made. 16.23

Scenario: Sharing appropriate information

Mr Jeremy has learning disabilities. His care home is about to close down. His care team carries out a careful assessment of his needs. They involve him as much as possible, and use the support of an Independent Mental Capacity Advocate. Following the assessment, he is placed with carers under an adult placement scheme. The carers ask to see Mr Jeremy's case file, so that they can provide him with appropriate care in his best interests. The care manager seeks Mr Jeremy's consent to disclosure of his notes, but believes that Mr Jeremy lacks capacity to make this decision. She recognises that it is appropriate to provide the carers with sufficient information to enable them to act in Mr Jeremy's best interests. But it is not appropriate for them to see all the information on the case file. Much of it is not relevant to his current care needs. The care manager therefore only passes on relevant information from the file.

16.24   Sometimes a person's right to confidentiality will conflict with broader public concerns. Information can be released if it is in the public interest, even if it is not in the best interests of the person who lacks capacity. It can be difficult to decide in these cases, and information holders should consider each case on its merits. The NHS Code on Confidentiality gives examples of when disclosure is in the public interest. These include situations where disclosing information could prevent, or aid investigation of, serious crimes, or to prevent serious harm, such as spread of an infectious disease. It is then necessary to judge whether the public good that would be achieved by the disclosure outweighs *both* the obligation of confidentiality to the individual concerned *and* the broader public interest in the provision of a confidential service.

16.25   For disclosure to be in the public interest, it must be proportionate and limited to the relevant details. Healthcare or social care staff faced with this decision should seek advice from their legal advisers. It is not just things for 'the public's benefit' that are in the public interest – disclosure for the benefit of the person who lacks capacity can also be in the public interest (for example, to stop a person who lacks capacity suffering physical or mental harm).

What financial information can carers ask to see?

16.26   It is often more difficult to get financial information than it is to get information on a person's welfare. A bank manager, for example, is less likely to:

• know the individual concerned
• be able to make an assessment of the person's capacity to consent to disclosure, and
• be aware of the carer's relationship to the person.

So they are less likely than a doctor or social worker to be able to judge what is in a person's best interests and are bound by duties to keep clients' affairs confidential. It is likely that someone wanting financial information will need to apply to the Court of Protection for access to that information. This clearly does not apply to an attorney or a deputy appointed to manage the person's property and affairs, who will generally have the authority (because of their appointment) to obtain all relevant information about the person's property and affairs.

Is information still confidential after someone shares it?

16.27   Whenever a carer gets information, they should treat the information in confidence, and they should not share it with anyone else (unless there is a lawful basis for doing so). In some circumstances, the information holder might ask the carer to give a formal confirmation that they will keep information confidential.

16.28   Where the information is in written form, carers should store it carefully and not keep it for longer than necessary. In many cases, the need to keep the information will be temporary. So the carer should be able to reassure the information holder that they will not keep a permanent record of the information.

What is the best way to settle a disagreement about personal information?

A carer should always start by trying to get consent from the person whose information they are trying to access. If the person lacks capacity to consent, the carer should ask the information holder for the relevant information and explain why they need it. They may need to remind the information holder that they have to make a decision in the person's best interests and cannot do so without the relevant information. **16.29**

This can be a sensitive area and disputes will inevitably arise. Healthcare and social care staff have a difficult judgement to make. They might feel strongly that disclosing the information would not be in the best interests of the person who lacks capacity and would amount to an invasion of their privacy. This may be upsetting for the carer who will probably have good motives for wanting the information. In all cases, an assessment of the interests and needs of the person who lacks capacity should determine whether staff should disclose information. **16.30**

If a discussion fails to settle the matter, and the carer still is not happy, there are other ways to settle the disagreement (see chapter 15). The carer may need to use the appropriate complaints procedure. Since the complaint involves elements of data protection and confidentiality, as well as best interests, relevant experts should help deal with the complaint. **16.31**

In cases where carers and staff cannot settle their disagreement, the carer can apply to the Court of Protection for the right to access to the specific information. The court would then need to decide if this was in the best interests of the person who lacks capacity to consent. In urgent cases, it might be necessary for the carer to apply directly to the court without going through the earlier stages. **16.32**

KEY WORDS AND PHRASES USED IN THE CODE

The table below is not a full index or glossary. Instead, it is a list of key terms used in the Code or the Act, and the main references to them. References in bold indicate particularly valuable content for that term.

Acts in connection with care or treatment	Tasks carried out by carers, healthcare or social care staff which involve the personal care, healthcare or medical treatment of people who lack capacity to consent to them—referred to in the Act as 'section 5 acts'.	**Chapter 6** 2.13–2.14, 4.39 Best interests and 5.10, 5,39 Deprivation of liberty and _ 6.39. 6.49–6.52
Advance decision to refuse treatment	A decision to refuse specified treatment made in advance by a person who has capacity to do so. This decision will then apply at a future time when that person lacks capacity to consent to, or refuse, the specified treatment. This is set out in Section 24(1) of the Act. Specific rules apply to advance decisions to refuse life-sustaining treatment.	**Chapter 9 (all)** Best interests and _ 5.5, 5.35, 5.45 Protection from liability and _ 6.37–6.38 LPAs and _ 7.55 Deputies and _ 8.28 Research and 11.30 Young people and _ 12.9 Mental Health Act 13.35–13.37
Adult protection procedures	Procedures devised by local authorities, in conjunction with other relevant agencies, to investigate and deal with allegations of abuse or ill treatment of vulnerable adults, and to put in place safeguards to provide protection from abuse.	**Chapter 14** 14.6, 14.22, 14.27–28, 14.34 IMCAs and _ 10.66–10.67

After-care under supervision	Arrangements for supervision in the community following discharge from hospital of certain patients previously detained under the Mental Health Act 1983.	**Chapter 13** 13.22–13.25, 13.34, 13.37, 13.40, 13.42, 13.45, 13.48, 13.52
Agent	A person authorised to act on behalf of another person under the law of agency. Attorneys appointed under an LPA or EPA are agents and court-appointed deputies are deemed to be agents and must undertake certain duties as agents.	LPAs and _ 7.58–7.68 Deputies and _ 8.55–8.68
Appointee	Someone appointed under Social Security Regulations to claim and collect social security benefits or pensions on behalf of a person who lacks capacity to manage their own benefits. An appointee is permitted to use the money claimed to meet the person's needs.	Role of _ 6:65–6.66 Deputies and _ 8.56 Concerns about _ 14:35–14.36
Appropriate body	A committee which is established to advise on, or on matters which include, the ethics of intrusive research in relation to people who lack capacity to consent to it, and is recognised for those purposes by the Secretary of State (in England) or the National Assembly for Wales (in Wales).	**Chapter 11** 11.8–11.11, 11.20, 11.33–11.34, 11.43–11.47.
Approved Social Worker (ASW)	A specially trained social worker with responsibility for assessing a person's needs for care and treatment under the Mental Health Act 1983. In particular, an ASW assesses whether the person should be admitted to hospital for assessment and/or treatment.	**Chapter 13** 13.16, 13.22–13.23, 13.43, 13.52
Artificial Nutrition and Hydration (ANH)	Artificial nutrition and hydration (ANH) has been recognised as a form of medical treatment. ANH involves using tubes to provide nutrition and fluids to someone who cannot take them by mouth. It bypasses the natural mechanisms that controlhunger and thirst and requires clinical monitoring.	9.26 5.34 6.18 8.18

Attorney	Someone appointed under either a Lasting Power of Attorney (LPA) or an Enduring Power of Attorney (EPA), who has the legal right to make decisions within the scope of their authority on behalf of the person (the donor) who made the Power of Attorney.	**Chapter 7** Best interests principle and _ 5.2, 5.13, 5.49, 5.55 Protection from liability as _ 6.54–6.55 Court of Protection and _ 8.30 Advance decisions and _ 9.33 Mental Health Act and _ 13.38–13.45 Public Guardian and _ 14.7–14.14 Legal help and _ 15.39–15.42 Accessing personal information as _16.9–16.16
Best interests	Any decisions made, or anything done for a person who lacks capacity to make specific decisions, must be in the person's best interests. There are standard minimum steps to follow when working out someone's best interests. These are set out in section 4 of the Act, and in the non-exhaustive checklist in 5.13.	**Chapter 2 (Principle 4)** **Chapter 5** Protection from liability and _ 6.4–6.18 Reasonable belief and _ 6.32–6.36 Deprivation of liberty and _ 6.51–6.53 Acting as an attorney and _ 7.19–7.20, 7.29, 7.53 Court of Protection and _ 8.14–8.26 Acting as a deputy and _ 8.50–8.52 Advance decisions and _ 9.4–9.5
Bournewood provisions	A name given to some proposed new procedures and safeguards for people who lack capacity to make relevant decisions but who need to be deprived of their liberty, in their best interests, otherwise than under the Mental Health Act 1983. The name refers to a case which was eventually decided by the European Court of Human Rights.	6.53–6.54 13.53–13.54
Capacity	The ability to make a decision about a particular matter at the time the decision needs to be made. The legal definition of a person who lacks capacity is set out in section 2 of the Act.	Chapter 4

Carer	Someone who provides *unpaid* care by looking after a friend or neighbour who needs support because of sickness, age or disability. In this document, the role of the carer is different from the role of a professional care worker.	**Acting as decision-maker 5.8–5.10 Protection from liability 6.20–6.24** Assessing capacity as _ 4.44–4.45 Acting with reasonable belief 6.29–6.34 Paying for goods and services 6.56–6.66 Accessing information 16.26–16.32
Care worker	Someone employed to provide personal care for people who need help because of sickness, age or disability. They could be employed by the person themselves, by someone acting on the person's behalf or by a care agency.	Assessing capacity as _4.38, 4.44–4.45 Protection from liability 6.20 Paying for goods and services 6.56–6.66 Acting as an attorney 7.10 Acting as a deputy 8.41
Children Act 1989	A law relating to children and those with parental responsibility for children.	**Chapter 12**
Complaints Review Panel	A panel of people set up to review and reconsider complaints about health or social care services which have not been resolved under the first stage of the relevant complaints procedure.	15.28
Consultee	A person who is consulted, for example about the involvement in a research project of a person who lacks capacity to consent to their participation in the research.	11.23, 11.28–29, 11.44
Court of Protection	The specialist Court for all issues relating to people who lack capacity to make specific decisions. The Court of Protection is established under section 45 of the Act.	**Chapter 8** _ must always make decisions about these issues 6.18 Decisions about life-sustaining treatment 5.33–5.36 LPAs and _7.45–7.49 Advance decisions and _ 9.35, 9.54, 9.67–9.69 Decisions regarding children and young people 12.3–12.4, 12.7, 12.10, 12.23–12.25 Access to legal help 15.40–15.44
Court of Protection Visitor	Someone who is appointed to report to the Court of Protection on how attorneys or deputies are carrying out their duties. Court of Protection Visitors are established under section 61 of the Act. They can also be directed by the Public Guardian to visit donors, attorney and deputies under section 58 (1) (d).	**14.10–14.11** Attorneys and _ 7.71 Deputies and _ 8.71

Criminal Records Bureau (CRB)	An Executive Agency of the Home Office which provides access to criminal record information. Organisations in the public, private and voluntary sectors can ask for the CRB to check candidates for jobs to see if they have any criminal records which would make them unsuitable for certain work, especially that involves children or vulnerable adults. For some jobs, a CRB check is mandatory.	Checking healthcare and social care staff 14.29–14.30 Checking IMCAs 10.18
Data Protection Act 1998	A law controlling the handling of, and access to, personal information, such as medical records, files held by public bodies and financial information held by credit reference agencies.	Chapter 16
Decision-maker	Under the Act, many different people may be required to make decisions or act on behalf of someone who lacks capacity to make decisions for themselves. The person making the decision is referred to throughout the Code, as the 'decision-maker', and it is the decision-maker's responsibility to work out what would be in the best interests of the person who lacks capacity.	**Chapter 5** Working with IMCAs 10.4, 10.21–10.29 Applying the MHA 13.3, 13.10, 13.27
Declaration	A kind of order made by the Court of Protection. For example, a declaration could say whether a person has or lacks capacity to make a particular decision, or declaring that a particular act would or would not be lawful. The Court's power to make declarations is set out in section 15 of the Act.	**8.13–8.19** Advance decisions and _ 9.35
Deprivation of liberty	Deprivation of liberty is a term used in the European Convention on Human Rights about circumstances when a person's freedom is taken away. Its meaning in practice is being defined through case law.	**6.49–6.54** Protection from liability 6.13–6.14 Attorneys and _ 7.44 Mental Health Act and _ 13.12, 13.16
Deputy	Someone appointed by the Court of Protection with ongoing legal authority as prescribed by the Court to make decisions on behalf of a person who lacks capacity to make particular decisions as set out in Section 16(2) of the Act.	**Chapter 8** Best interests principle and _ 5.2, 5.13, 5.49, 5.55 Protection from liability as _ 6.54–6.55 Attorneys becoming _ 7.56 Advance decisions and _ 9.33 IMCAs and _10.70–72 Acting for children and young people 12.4, 12.7 Public Guardian and _ 14.15–14.18 Complaints about 14.19–14.25 Accessing personal information as _16.9–16.16
Donor	A person who makes a Lasting Power of Attorney or Enduring Power of Attorney.	Chapter 7

Enduring Power of Attorney (EPA)	A Power of Attorney created under the Enduring Powers of Attorney Act 1985 appointing an attorney to deal with the donor's property and financial affairs. Existing EPAs will continue to operate under Schedule 4 of the Act, which replaces the EPA Act 1985.	**Chapter 7** See also LPA
Family carer	A family member who looks after a relative who needs support because of sickness, age or disability. It does not mean a professional care-worker employed by a disabled person or a care assistant in a nursing home, for example.	See carer
Family Division of the High Court	The Division of the High Court that has the jurisdiction to deal with all matrimonial and civil partnership matters, family disputes, matters relating to children and some disputes about medical treatment.	12.14, 12.23
Fiduciary duty	Anyone acting under the law of agency will have this duty. In essence, it means that any decision taken or act done as an agent (such as an attorney or deputy) must not benefit themselves, but must benefit the person for whom they are acting.	_ for attorneys 7.58 _ for deputies 8.58
Guardianship	Arrangements, made under the Mental Health Act 1983, for a guardian to be appointed for a person with mental disorder to help ensure that the person gets the care they need in the community.	**13.16–13.21** 13.1, 13.25–13.27, 13.54
Health Service Ombudsman	An independent person whose organisation investigates complaints about National Health Service (NHS) care or treatment in England which have not been resolved through the NHS complaints procedure.	15.19, 15.21, 15.31
Human Rights Act 1998	A law largely incorporating into UK law the substantive rights set out in the European Convention on Human Rights.	6.49 16.3
Human Tissue Act 2004	A law to regulate issues relating to whole body donation and the taking, storage and use of human organs and tissue.	11.7 11.38–11.39
Ill treatment	Section 44 of the Act introduces a new offence of ill treatment of a person who lacks capacity by someone who is caring for them, or acting as a deputy or attorney for them. That person can be guilty of ill treatment if they have deliberately ill-treated a person who lacks capacity, or been reckless as to whether they were ill-treating the person or not. It does not matter whether the behaviour was likely to cause, or actually caused, harm or damage to the victim's health.	14.23–14.26

Independent Complaints Advocacy Service (ICAS)	In England, a service to support patients and their carers who wish to pursue a complaint about their NHS treatment or care.	15.18
Independent Mental Capacity Advocate (IMCA)	Someone who provides support and representation for a person who lacks capacity to make specific decisions, where the person has no-one else to support them. The IMCA service is established under section 35 of the Act and the functions of IMCAs are set out in section 36. It is not the same as an ordinary advocacy service.	**Chapter 10** Consulting to work out best interests 5.51 Involvement in changes of residence 6.9 Involvement in serious medical decisions 6.16 MHA and _13.46–13.48
Information Commissioner's Office	An independent authority set up to promote access to official information and to protect personal information. It has powers to ensure that the laws about information, such as the Data Protection Act 1998, are followed.	16.13 16.18
Lasting Power of Attorney (LPA)	A Power of Attorney created under the Act (see Section 9(1)) appointing an attorney (or attorneys) to make decisions about the donor's personal welfare (including healthcare) and/or deal with the donor's property and affairs.	**Chapter 7** Best interests principle and _ 5.2, 5.13, 5.49, 5.55 Protection from liability as _ 6.54–6.55 Court of Protection and _ 8.30 Advance decisions and _ 9.33 Mental Health Act and _ 13.38–13.45 Public Guardian and _ 14.7–14.14 Legal help and _ 15.39–15.42 Accessing personal information as _16.9–16.16
Life-sustaining treatment	Treatment that, in the view of the person providing healthcare, is necessary to keep a person alive See Section 4(10) of the Act.	**Providing or stopping _ in best interests 5.29–5.36 Advance decisions to refuse _ 9.10–9.11, 9.19–9.20, 9.24–9.28** Protection from liability when providing _ 6.16, 6.55 Attorneys and _ 7.22, 7.27, 7.29-7.30 Deputies and _ 8.17, 8.46 Conscientious objection to stopping _ 9.61–9.63 IMCAs and _ 10.44
Litigation friend	A person appointed by the court to conduct legal proceedings on behalf of, and in the name of, someone who lacks capacity to conduct the litigation or to instruct a lawyer themselves.	4.54 10.38 15.39

Local Government Ombudsman	In England, an independent organisation that investigates complaints about councils and local authorities on most council matters including housing, planning, education and social services.	15.30–15.32
Makaton	A language programme using signs and symbols, for the teaching of communication, language and literacy skills for people with communication and learning difficulties.	3.11
Mediation	A process for resolving disagreements in which an impartial third party (the mediator) helps people in dispute to find a mutually acceptable resolution.	15.7–15.13
Mental capacity	See capacity	
Mental Health Act 1983	A law mainly about the compulsory care and treatment of patients with mental health problems. In particular, it covers detention in hospital for mental health treatment.	**Chapter 13** Deprivation of liberty other than in line with _ 6.50–6.53, 7.44 Attorneys and _ 7.27 Advance decisions and _9.37 IMCAs and 10.44, 10.51, 10.56–10.58 Children and young people and _ 12.6, 12.21 Complaints regarding _ 15.19
Mental Health Review Tribuna	An independent judicial body with powers to direct the discharge of patients who are detained under the Mental Health Act 1983.	13.31 13.42
NHS Litigation Authority	A Special Health Authority (part of the NHS), responsible for handling negligence claims made against NHS bodies in England.	15.22
Office of the Public Guardian (OPG)	The Public Guardian is an officer established under Section 57 of the Act. The Public Guardian will be supported by the Office of the Public Guardian, which will supervise deputies, keep a register of deputies, Lasting Powers of Attorney and Enduring Powers of Attorney, check on what attorneys are doing, and investigate any complaints about attorneys or deputies. The OPG replaces the Public Guardianship Office (PGO) that has been in existence for many years.	**14.8–14.22** Registering LPAs with _ 7.14– 7.17 Supervision of attorneys by _ 7.69–7.74 Registering EPAs with _ 7.78 Guidance for EPAs _ 7.79 Guidance for receivers_ 8.5 Panel of deputies of _ 8.35 Supervision of deputies by _ 8.69–8.77
Official Solicitor	Provides legal services for vulnerable persons, or in the interests of achieving justice. The Official Solicitor represents adults who lack capacity to conduct litigation in county court or High Court proceedings in England and Wales, and in the Court of Protection.	Helping with formal assessment of capacity 4.54 Acting in applications to the Court of Protection 8.10 Acting as litigation friend 10.38, 15.39

Patient Advice and Liaison Service (PALS)	In England, a service providing information, advice and support to help NHS patients, their families and carers. PALS act on behalf of service users when handling patient and family concerns and can liaise with staff, managers and, where appropriate, other relevant organisations, to find solutions.	15.15–15.17
Permanent vegetative state (PVS)	A condition caused by catastrophic brain damage whereby patients in PVS have a permanent and irreversible lack of awareness of their surroundings and no ability to interact at any level with those around them.	6.18 8.18
Personal welfare	Personal welfare decisions are any decisions about person's healthcare, where they live, what clothes they wear, what they eat and anything needed for their general care and well-being. Attorneys and deputies can be appointed to make decisions about personal welfare on behalf of a person who lacks capacity. Many acts of care are to do with personal welfare.	_ LPAs 7.21–7.31 _ deputies 8.38–8.39 Advance decisions about _ 9.4, 9.35 Role of High Court in decisions about _15.44
Property and affairs	Any possessions owned by a person (such as a house or flat, jewellery or other possessions), the money they have in income, savings or investments and any expenditure. Attorneys and deputies can be appointed to make decisions about property and affairs on behalf of a person who lacks capacity.	_ LPAs 7.32–7.42 _ deputies 8.34–8.37 Restrictions on _ LPA 7.56 Duties of _ attorney 7.58, 7.67–7.68 _ EPAs 7.76–7.77 OPG panel of _deputies 8.35 Duties of _ deputy 8.56, 8.67–8.68 _ of children and young people 12.3–12.4, 12.7
Protection from liability	Legal protection, granted to anyone who has acted or made decisions in line with the Act's principles.	Chapter 6
Protection of Vulnerable Adults (POVA) list	A register of individuals who have abused, neglected or otherwise harmed vulnerable adults in their care or placed vulnerable adults at risk of harm. Providers of care must not offer such individuals employment in care positions.	14.31
Public Services Ombudsman for Wales	An independent body that investigates complaints about local government and NHS organisations in Wales, and the National Assembly for Wales, concerning matters such as housing, planning, education, social services and health services.	15.20 15.30–15.32
Receiver	Someone appointed by the former Court of Protection to manage the property and affairs of a person lacking capacity to manage their own affairs. Existing receivers continue as deputies with legal authority to deal with the person's property and affairs.	8.5 8.35

Restraint	See Section 6(4) of the Act. The use or threat of force to help do an act which the person resists, or the restriction of the person's liberty of movement, whether or not they resist. Restraint may only be used where it is necessary to protect the person from harm and is proportionate to the risk of harm.	**6.39–6.44, 6.47–53** Use of _ in moves between accommodation 6.11 Use of _ in healthcare and treatment decisions 6.15 Attorneys and _ 7.43-7.44 Deputies and _ 8.46 MHA and _ 13.5
Statutory principles	The five key principles are set out in Section 1 of the Act. They are designed to emphasise the fundamental concepts and core values of the Act and to provide a benchmark to guide decision-makers, professionals and carers acting under the Act's provisions. The principles generally apply to all actions and decisions taken under the Act.	**Chapter 2**
Two-stage test of capacity	Using sections 2 and 3 of the Act to assess whether or not a person has capacity to make a decision for themselves at that time.	**4.10–4.13** Protection from liability 6.27 Applying _ to advance decisions 9.39
Wilful neglect	An intentional or deliberate omission or failure to carry out an act of care by someone who has care of a person who lacks (or whom the person reasonably believes lacks) capacity to care for themselves. Section 44 introduces a new offence of wilful neglect of a person who lacks capacity.	14.23–14.26
Written statements of wishes and feelings	Written statements the person might have made before losing capacity about their wishes and feelings regarding issues such as the type of medical treatment they would want in the case of future illness, where they would prefer to live, or how they wish to be cared for. They should be used to help find out what someone's wishes and feelings might be, as part of working out their best interests. They are not the same as advance decisions to refuse treatment and are not binding.	5.34 5.37 5.42–5.44

ANNEX A

The following list provides contact details for some organisations that provide information, guidance or materials related to the Code of Practice and the Mental Capacity Act. The list is not exhaustive: many other organisations may also produce their own materials.

British Banking Association

Provides guidance for bank staff on 'Banking for mentally incapacitated and learning disabled customers'.

Available from www.bba.org.uk/bba/jsp/polopoly.jsp?d=146&a=5757, price £10 (members) /£12 (non-members). Not inclusive of VAT.
web: www.bba.org.uk **telephone:** 020 7216 8800

British Medical Association

Co-authors (with the Law Society) of *Assessment of Mental Capacity: Guidance for Doctors and Lawyers* (Second edition) (London: BMJ Books, 2004). www.bma.org.uk/ap.nsf/Content/Assess mentmental?OpenDocument& Highlight=2,mental, capacity
Available from BMJ Books (www.bmjbookshop.com), price £20.99
web: www.bma.org.uk **telephone:** 020 7387 4499

British Psychological Society

Publishers of *Guidelines on assessing capacity*—professional guidance available online to members.
web: www.bps.org.uk **telephone:** (0)116 254 9568

Commission for Social Care Inspection

The Commission for Social Care Inspection (CSCI) registers, inspects and reports on social care services in England.
web: www.csci.org.uk **telephone:** 0845 015 0120 / 0191 233 3323 **textphone:** 0845 015 2255 / 0191 233 3588

Community Legal Services Direct

Provides free legal information to people living in England and Wales to help them deal with legal problems.
web: www.clsdirect.org.uk **telephone (helpline):** 0845 345 4 345

Criminal Records Bureau (CRB)

The CRB runs criminal records checks on people who apply for jobs working with children and vulnerable adults.
web: www.crb.org.uk **telephone:** 0870 90 90 811

Department for Constitutional Affairs

The government department with responsibility for the Mental Capacity Act and the Code of Practice. Also publishes guidance for specific audiences www.dca.gov.uk/legal-policy/mental-capacity/guidance.htm

Department of Health

Publishes guidance for healthcare and social care staff in England. Key publications referenced in the Code include:
* on using restraint with people with learning disabilities and autistic spectrum disorder, see *Guidance for restrictive physical interventions* www.dh.gov.uk/assetRoot/04/06/84/61/04068461.pdf
* on adult protection procedures, see *No secrets: Guidance on developing and implementing multi-agency policies and procedures to protect vulnerable adults from abuse* www.dh.gov.uk/assetRoot/04/07/45/44/04074544.pdf

- on consent to examination and treatment, including advance decisions to refuse treatment www.dh/gov.uk/consent
- on the proposed Bournewood safeguards, a draft illustrative Code of Practice www.dh.gov.uk/assetRoot/04/14/17/64/04141764.pdf
- on IMCAs and the IMCA pilots www.dh.gov.uk/imca

DH also is responsible for the *Mental Health Act 1983 Code of Practice* (TSO 1999) www.dh.gov.uk/assetRoot/04/07/49/61/04074961.pdf

Family Mediation Helpline

Provides general information on family mediation and contact details for mediation services in your local area.

web: www.familymediationhelpline.co.uk **telephone:** 0845 60 26 627

Healthcare Commission

The health watchdog in England, undertaking reviews and investigations into the provision of NHS and private healthcare services.

web:
www.healthcarecommission.org.uk
telephone helpline:
0845 601 3012
switchboard:
020 7448 9200

Healthcare Inspectorate for Wales

Undertakes reviews and investigations into the provision of NHS funded care, either by or for Welsh NHS organisations.

web: www.hiw.org.uk email: hiw@wales.gsi.gov.uk **telephone:** 029 2092 8850

Housing Ombudsman Service

The Housing Ombudsman Service considers complaints against member organisations, and deals with other housing disputes.

web: www.ihos.org.uk email: info@housing-ombudsman.org.uk **telephone:** 020 7421 3800

Information Commissioner's Office

The Information Commissioner's Office is the UK's independent authority set up to promote access to official information and to protect personal information.

web: www.ico.gov.uk **telephone helpline:** 08456 30 60 60

Legal Services Commission

Looks after legal aid in England and Wales, and provides information, advice and legal representation.

web: www.legalservices.gov.uk See also Community Legal Services Direct.

Local Government Ombudsman

The Local Government Ombudsmen investigate complaints about councils and certain other bodies.

web: www.lgo.org.uk **telephone:** 0845 602 1983

National Mediation Helpline

Provides access to a simple, low cost method of resolving a wide range of disputes. The National Mediation Helpline is operated on behalf of the Department for Constitutional Affairs (DCA) in conjunction with the Civil Mediation Council (CMC).

web: www.nationalmediationhelpline.com **telephone:** 0845 60 30 809

Office of the Public Guardian

The new Public Guardian is established under the Act and will be supported by the Office of the Public Guardian, which will replace the current Public Guardianship Office (PGO). The OPG will be an executive agency of the Department for Constitutional Affairs. Amongst its other roles, it provides forms for LPAs and EPAs.

web: From October 2007, a new website will be created at www.publicguardian.gov.uk

Official Solicitor

Provides legal services for vulnerable people and is able to represent people who lack capacity and act as a litigation friend. web: www.officialsolicitor.gov.uk telephone: 020 7911 7127

Patient Advice and Liaison Service (PALS)

Provides information about the NHS and help resolve concerns or problems with the NHS, including support when making complaints.

web: www.pals.nhs.uk

The site includes contact details for local PALS offices around the country.

Patient Information Advisory Group

Considers applications on behalf of the Secretary of State to allow the common law duty of confidentiality to be aside.

web: www.advisorybodies.doh.gov.uk/PIAG

Public Service Ombudsman for Wales

Investigates complaints about local authorities and NHS organisations in Wales, and about the National Assembly Government for Wales.

web: www.ombudsman-wales.org.uk **telephone:** 01656 641 150

Welsh Assembly Government

Produces key pieces of guidance for healthcare and social care staff, including:

- *In safe hands—Implementing Adult Protection Procedures in Wales* (July 2000) http://new.wales. gov.uk/about/departments—dhss/publications/social_services_publications/reports/ insafehands?lang=en
- *Framework for restrictive physical intervention policy and practice* (available at www.childrenfirst. wales.gov.uk/content/framework/ phys-int-e.pdf)

Copies of this publication can be downloaded from www.guardianship.gsi.gov.uk

Hard copies of this publication are available from TSO

For more information on the Mental Capacity Act contact the
Public Guardianship Office:
9am – 5pm, Mon – Fri

Telephone:
0845 330 2900 (local call rate)
or
+44 207 664 7000 (for callers outside UK)
Text Phone:
020 7664 7755
Fax:
0870 739 5780 (UK callers)
Email:
custserv@guardianship.gsi.gov.uk
Website:
www.guardianship.gsi.gov.uk
Post:
Public Guardianship Office
Archway Tower
2 Junction Road
London N19 5SZ

APPENDIX 3

The Lasting Powers of Attorney, Enduring Powers of Attorney and Public Guardian Regulations 2007

STATUTORY INSTRUMENTS
2007 NO. 1253
MENTAL CAPACITY, ENGLAND AND WALES

The Lasting Powers of Attorney, Enduring Powers of Attorney and Public Guardian Regulations

Made – – – – 16th April 2007
Laid before Parliament 17th April 2007
Coming into force – – 1st October 2007

CONTENTS

PART 1
PRELIMINARY

PART 2
LASTING POWERS OF ATTORNEY

Instruments intended to create a lasting power of attorney

The Lord Chancellor makes the following Regulations in exercise of the powers conferred by sections 13(6)(a), 58(3) and 64(1) of, and Schedules 1 and 4 to, the Mental Capacity Act 2005.[1]

PART 1
PRELIMINARY

Citation and commencement

1.—

(1) These Regulations may be cited as the Lasting Powers of Attorney, Enduring Powers of Attorney and Public Guardian Regulations 2007.

(2) These Regulations shall come into force on 1 October 2007.

---

[1] 2005 c.9. Paragraph 1(3) of Schedule 1 is cited because of the meaning there given to 'prescribed' and 'regulations'.

Interpretation

2.—

(1) In these Regulations—

'the Act' means the Mental Capacity Act 2005;

'court' means the Court of Protection;

'LPA certificate', in relation to an instrument made with a view to creating a lasting power of attorney, means the certificate which is required to be included in the instrument by virtue of paragraph 2(1)(e) of Schedule 1 to the Act;

'named person', in relation to an instrument made with a view to creating a lasting power of attorney, means a person who is named in the instrument as being a person to be notified of any application for the registration of the instrument;

'prescribed information', in relation to any instrument intended to create a lasting power of attorney, means the information contained in the form used for the instrument which appears under the heading 'prescribed information'.

Minimal differences from forms prescribed in these Regulations

3.—

(1) In these Regulations, any reference to a form—

    (a) in the case of a form set out in Schedules 1 to 7 to these Regulations, is to be regarded as including a Welsh version of that form; and

    (b) in the case of a form set out in Schedules 2 to 7 to these Regulations, is to be regarded as also including—

        (i) a form to the same effect but which differs in an immaterial respect in form or mode of expression;

        (ii) a form to the same effect but with such variations as the circumstances may require or the court or the Public Guardian may approve; or

        (iii) a Welsh version of a form within (i) or (ii).

Computation of time

4.—

(1) This regulation shows how to calculate any period of time which is specified in these Regulations.

(2) A period of time expressed as a number of days must be computed as clear days.

(3) Where the specified period is 7 days or less, and would include a day which is not a business day, that day does not count.

(4) When the specified period for doing any act at the office of the Public Guardian ends on a day on which the office is closed, that act will be done in time if done on the next day on which the office is open.

(5) In this regulation—

'business day' means a day other than—

    (a) a Saturday, Sunday, Christmas Day or Good Friday; or

    (b) a bank holiday under the Banking and Financial Dealings Act 1971(a), in England and Wales; and

'clear days' means that in computing the number of days—

    (a) the day on which the period begins, and

    (b) if the end of the period is defined by reference to an event, the day on which that event occurs, are not included.

PART 2
LASTING POWERS OF ATTORNEY

Instruments intended to create a lasting power of attorney

Forms for lasting powers of attorney

5. The forms set out in Parts 1 and 2 of Schedule 1 to these Regulations are the forms which, in the circumstances to which they apply, are to be used for instruments intended to create a lasting power of attorney.

Maximum number of named persons

6. The maximum number of named persons that the donor of a lasting power of attorney may specify in the instrument intended to create the power is 5.

Requirement for two LPA certificates where instrument has no named persons

7. Where an instrument intended to create a lasting power of attorney includes a statement by the donor that there are no persons whom he wishes to be notified of any application for the registration of the instrument—
    (a) the instrument must include two LPA certificates; and
    (b) each certificate must be completed and signed by a different person.

Persons who may provide an LPA certificate

8.—

(1) Subject to paragraph (3), the following persons may give an LPA certificate—
    (a) a person chosen by the donor as being someone who has known him personally for the period of at least two years which ends immediately before the date on which that person signs the LPA certificate;
    (b) a person chosen by the donor who, on account of his professional skills and expertise, reasonably considers that he is competent to make the judgments necessary to certify the matters set out in paragraph (2)(1)(e) of Schedule 1 to the Act.
(2) The following are examples of persons within paragraph (1)(b)—
    (a) a registered health care professional;
    (b) a barrister, solicitor or advocate called or admitted in any part of the United Kingdom;
    (c) a registered social worker; or
    (d) an independent mental capacity advocate.
(3) A person is disqualified from giving an LPA certificate in respect of any instrument intended to create a lasting power of attorney if that person is—
    (a) a family member of the donor;
    (b) a donee of that power;
    (c) a donee of—
        (i) any other lasting power of attorney, or
        (ii) an enduring power of attorney, which has been executed by the donor (whether or not it has been revoked);
    (d) a family member of a donee within sub-paragraph (b);
    (e) a director or employee of a trust corporation acting as a donee within sub-paragraph (b);

(f) a business partner or employee of—

    (i) the donor, or

    (ii) a donee within sub-paragraph (b);

(g) an owner, director, manager or employee of any care home in which the donor is living when the instrument is executed; or

(h) a family member of a person within sub-paragraph (g).

(4) In this regulation—

'care home' has the meaning given in section 3 of the Care Standards Act 2000;[2]

'registered health care professional' means a person who is a member of a profession regulated by a body mentioned in section 25(3) of the National Health Service Reform and Health Care Professions Act 2002;[3] and

'registered social worker' means a person registered as a social worker in a register maintained by—

(a) the General Social Care Council;

(b) the Care Council for Wales;

(c) the Scottish Social Services Council; or

(d) the Northern Ireland Social Care Council.

Execution of instrument

9.—

(1) An instrument intended to create a lasting power of attorney must be executed in accordance with this regulation.

(2) The donor must read (or have read to him) all the prescribed information.

(3) As soon as reasonably practicable after the steps required by paragraph (2) have been taken, the donor must—

(a) complete the provisions of Part A of the instrument that apply to him (or direct another person to do so); and

(b) subject to paragraph (7), sign Part A of the instrument in the presence of a witness.

(4) As soon as reasonably practicable after the steps required by paragraph (3) have been taken—

(a) the person giving an LPA certificate, or

(b) if regulation 7 applies (two LPA certificates required), each of the persons giving a certificate, must complete the LPA certificate at Part B of the instrument and sign it.

(5) As soon as reasonably practicable after the steps required by paragraph (4) have been taken—

(a) the donee, or

(b) if more than one, each of the donees, must read (or have read to him) all the prescribed information.

(6) As soon as reasonably practicable after the steps required by paragraph (5) have been taken, the donee or, if more than one, each of them—

(a) must complete the provisions of Part C of the instrument that apply to him (or direct another person to do so); and

(b) subject to paragraph (7), must sign Part C of the instrument in the presence of a witness.

(7) If the instrument is to be signed by any person at the direction of the donor, or at the direction of any donee, the signature must be done in the presence of two witnesses.

---

[2] 2000 c.14.

[3] 2002 c.17.

(8) For the purposes of this regulation—
- (a) the donor may not witness any signature required for the power;
- (b) a donee may not witness any signature required for the power apart from that of another donee.

(9) A person witnessing a signature must—
- (a) sign the instrument; and
- (b) give his full name and address.

(10) Any reference in this regulation to a person signing an instrument (however expressed) includes his signing it by means of a mark made on the instrument at the appropriate place.

Registering the instrument

Notice to be given by a person about to apply for registration of lasting power of attorney

10. Schedule 2 to these Regulations sets out the form of notice ('LPA 001') which must be given by a donor or donee who is about to make an application for the registration of an instrument intended to create a lasting power of attorney.

Application for registration

11.—

(1) Schedule 3 to these Regulations sets out the form ('LPA 002') which must be used for making an application to the Public Guardian for the registration of an instrument intended to create a lasting power of attorney.

(2) Where the instrument to be registered which is sent with the application is neither—
- (a) the original instrument intended to create the power, nor
- (b) a certified copy of it, the Public Guardian must not register the instrument unless the court directs him to do so.

(3) In paragraph (2) 'a certified copy' means a photographic or other facsimile copy which is certified as an accurate copy by—
- (a) the donor; or
- (b) a solicitor or notary.

Period to elapse before registration in cases not involving objection or defect

12. The period at the end of which the Public Guardian must register an instrument in accordance with paragraph 5 of Schedule 1 to the Act is the period of 6 weeks beginning with—
- (a) the date on which the Public Guardian gave the notice or notices under paragraph 7 or 8 of Schedule 1 to the Act of receipt of an application for registration; or
- (b) if notices were given on more than one date, the latest of those dates.

Notice of receipt of application for registration

13.—

(1) Part 1 of Schedule 4 to these Regulations sets out the form of notice ('LPA 003A') which the Public Guardian must give to the donee (or donees) when the Public Guardian receives an application for the registration of a lasting power of attorney.

(2) Part 2 of Schedule 4 sets out the form of notice ('LPA 003B') which the Public Guardian must give to the donor when the Public Guardian receives such an application.

(3) Where it appears to the Public Guardian that there is good reason to do so, the Public Guardian must also provide (or arrange for the provision of) an explanation to the donor of—
  (a) the notice referred to in paragraph (2) and what the effect of it is; and
  (b) why it is being brought to his attention.

(4) Any information provided under paragraph (3) must be provided—
  (a) to the donor personally; and
  (b) in a way that is appropriate to the donor's circumstances (for example using simple language, visual aids or other appropriate means).

Objection to registration: notice to Public Guardian

14.—

(1) This regulation deals with any objection to the registration of an instrument as a lasting power of attorney which is to be made to the Public Guardian.

(2) Where any person—
  (a) is entitled to receive notice under paragraph 6, 7 or 8 of Schedule 1 to the Act of an application for the registration of the instrument, and
  (b) wishes to object to registration on a ground set out in paragraph 13(1) of Schedule 1 to the Act, he must do so before the end of the period of 5 weeks beginning with the date on which the notice is given.

(3) A notice of objection must be given in writing, setting out—
  (a) the name and address of the objector;
  (b) if different, the name and address of the donor of the power;
  (c) if known, the name and address of the donee (or donees); and
  (d) the ground for making the objection.

(4) The Public Guardian must notify the objector as to whether he is satisfied that the ground of the objection is established.

(5) At any time after receiving the notice of objection and before giving the notice required by paragraph (4), the Public Guardian may require the objector to provide such further information, or produce such documents, as the Public Guardian reasonably considers necessary to enable him to determine whether the ground for making the objection is established.

(6) Where—
  (a) the Public Guardian is satisfied that the ground of the objection is established, but
  (b) by virtue of section 13(7) of the Act, the instrument is not revoked, the notice under paragraph (4) must contain a statement to that effect.

(7) Nothing in this regulation prevents an objector from making a further objection under paragraph 13 of Schedule 1 to the Act where—
  (a) the notice under paragraph (4) indicates that the Public Guardian is not satisfied that the particular ground of objection to which that notice relates is established; and
  (b) the period specified in paragraph (2) has not expired.

Objection to registration: application to the court

15.—

(1) This regulation deals with any objection to the registration of an instrument as a lasting power of attorney which is to be made to the court.

(2) The grounds for making an application to the court are—
  (a) that one or more of the requirements for the creation of a lasting power of attorney have not been met;

(b) that the power has been revoked, or has otherwise come to an end, on a ground other than the grounds set out in paragraph 13(1) of Schedule 1 to the Act;

(c) any of the grounds set out in paragraph (a) or (b) of section 22(3) of the Act.

(3) Where any person—

(a) is entitled to receive notice under paragraph 6, 7 or 8 of Schedule 1 to the Act of an application for the registration of the instrument, and

(b) wishes to object to registration on one or more of the grounds set out in paragraph (2),

he must make an application to the court before the end of the period of 5 weeks beginning with the date on which the notice is given.

(4) The notice of an application to the court, which a person making an objection to the court is required to give to the Public Guardian under paragraph 13(3)(b)(ii) of Schedule 1 to the Act, must be in writing.

Notifying applicants of non-registration of lasting power of attorney

16. Where the Public Guardian is prevented from registering an instrument as a lasting power of attorney by virtue of—

(a) paragraph 11(1) of Schedule 1 to the Act (instrument not made in accordance with Schedule),

(b) paragraph 12(2) of that Schedule (deputy already appointed),

(c) paragraph 13(2) of that Schedule (objection by donee or named person on grounds of bankruptcy, disclaimer, death etc),

(d) paragraph 14(2) of that Schedule (objection by donor), or

(e) regulation 11(2) of these Regulations (application for registration not accompanied by original instrument or certified copy),

he must notify the person (or persons) who applied for registration of that fact.

Notice to be given on registration of lasting power of attorney

17.—

(1) Where the Public Guardian registers an instrument as a lasting power of attorney, he must—

(a) retain a copy of the instrument; and

(b) return to the person (or persons) who applied for registration the original instrument, or the certified copy of it, which accompanied the application for registration.

(2) Schedule 5 to these Regulations sets out the form of notice ('LPA 004') which the Public Guardian must give to the donor and donee (or donees) when the Public Guardian registers an instrument.

(3) Where it appears to the Public Guardian that there is good reason to do so, the Public Guardian must also provide (or arrange for the provision of) an explanation to the donor of—

(a) the notice referred to in paragraph (2) and what the effect of it is; and

(b) why it is being brought to his attention.

(4) Any information provided under paragraph (3) must be provided—

(a) to the donor personally; and

(b) in a way that is appropriate to the donor's circumstances (for example using simple language, visual aids or other appropriate means).

(5) 'Certified copy' is to be construed in accordance with regulation 11(3).

Post-registration

Changes to instrument registered as lasting power of attorney

18.—

(1) This regulation applies in any case where any of paragraphs 21 to 24 of Schedule 1 to the Act requires the Public Guardian to attach a note to an instrument registered as a lasting power of attorney.

(2) The Public Guardian must give a notice to the donor and the donee (or, if more than one, each of them) requiring him to deliver to the Public Guardian—

    (a) the original of instrument which was sent to the Public Guardian for registration;

    (b) any office copy of that registered instrument; and

    (c) any certified copy of that registered instrument.

(3) On receipt of the document, the Public Guardian must—

    (a) attach the required note; and

    (b) return the document to the person from whom it was obtained.

Loss or destruction of instrument registered as lasting power of attorney

19.—

(1) This regulation applies where—

    (a) a person is required by or under the Act to deliver up to the Public Guardian any of the following documents—

        (i) an instrument registered as a lasting power of attorney;

        (ii) an office copy of that registered instrument;

        (iii) a certified copy of that registered instrument; and

    (b) the document has been lost or destroyed.

(2) The person required to deliver up the document must provide to the Public Guardian in writing—

    (a) if known, the date of the loss or destruction and the circumstances in which it occurred;

    (b) otherwise, a statement of when he last had the document in his possession.

Disclaimer of appointment by a donee of lasting power of attorney

20.—(1) Schedule 6 to these Regulations sets out the form ('LPA 005') which a donee of an instrument registered as a lasting power of attorney must use to disclaim his appointment as donee.

(2) The donee must send—

    (a) the completed form to the donor; and

    (b) a copy of it to—

        (i) the Public Guardian; and

        (ii) any other donee who, for the time being, is appointed under the power.

Revocation by donor of lasting power of attorney

21.—

(1) A donor who revokes a lasting power to attorney must—

    (a) notify the Public Guardian that he has done so; and

    (b) notify the donee (or, if more than one, each of them) of the revocation.

(2) Where the Public Guardian receives a notice under paragraph (1)(a), he must cancel the registration of the instrument creating the power if he is satisfied that the donor has taken such steps as are necessary in law to revoke it.

(3) The Public Guardian may require the donor to provide such further information, or produce such documents, as the Public Guardian reasonably considers necessary to enable him to determine whether the steps necessary for revocation have been taken.

(4) Where the Public Guardian cancels the registration of the instrument he must notify—
   (a) the donor; and
   (b) the donee or, if more than one, each of them.

Revocation of a lasting power of attorney on death of donor

22.—

(1) The Public Guardian must cancel the registration of an instrument as a lasting power of attorney if he is satisfied that the power has been revoked as a result of the donor's death.

(2) Where the Public Guardian cancels the registration of an instrument he must notify the donee or, if more than one, each of them.

PART 3

ENDURING POWERS OF ATTORNEY

Notice of intention to apply for registration of enduring power of attorney

23.—

(1) Schedule 7 to these Regulations sets out the form of notice ('EP1PG') which an attorney (or attorneys) under an enduring power of attorney must give of his intention to make an application for the registration of the instrument creating the power.

(2) In the case of the notice to be given to the donor, the attorney must also provide (or arrange for the provision of) an explanation to the donor of—
   (a) the notice and what the effect of it is; and
   (b) why it is being brought to his attention.

(3) The information provided under paragraph (2) must be provided—
   (a) to the donor personally; and
   (b) in a way that is appropriate to the donor's circumstances (for example using simple language, visual aids or other appropriate means).

Application for registration

24.—

(1) Schedule 8 to these Regulations sets out the form ('EP2PG') which must be used for making an application to the Public Guardian for the registration of an instrument creating an enduring power of attorney.

(2) Where the instrument to be registered which is sent with the application is neither—
   (a) the original instrument creating the power, nor
   (b) a certified copy of it,
   the Public Guardian must not register the instrument unless the court directs him to do so.

(3) 'Certified copy', in relation to an enduring power of attorney, means a copy certified in accordance with section 3 of the Powers of Attorney Act 1971.[4]

---

[4] 1971 c.27

Notice of objection to registration

25.—

(1) This regulation deals with any objection to the registration of an instrument creating an enduring power of attorney which is to be made to the Public Guardian under paragraph 13(4) of Schedule 4 to the Act.

(2) A notice of objection must be given in writing, setting out—

    (a) the name and address of the objector;

    (b) if different, the name and address of the donor of the power;

    (c) if known, the name and address of the attorney (or attorneys); and

    (d) the ground for making the objection.

Notifying applicants of non-registration of enduring power of attorney

26. Where the Public Guardian is prevented from registering an instrument creating an enduring power of attorney by virtue of—

    (a) paragraph 13(2) of Schedule 4 to the Act (deputy already appointed),

    (b) paragraph 13(5) of that Schedule (receipt by Public Guardian of valid notice of objection from person entitled to notice of application to register),

    (c) paragraph 13(7) of that Schedule (Public Guardian required to undertake appropriate enquiries in certain circumstances), or

    (d) regulation 24(2) of these Regulations (application for registration not accompanied by original instrument or certified copy),

he must notify the person (or persons) who applied for registration of that fact.

Registration of instrument creating an enduring power of attorney

27.—

(1) Where the Public Guardian registers an instrument creating an enduring power of attorney, he must—

    (a) retain a copy of the instrument; and

    (b) return to the person (or persons) who applied for registration the original instrument, or the certified copy of it, which accompanied the application.

(2) 'Certified copy' has the same meaning as in regulation 24(3).

Objection or revocation not applying to all joint and several attorneys

28. In a case within paragraph 20(6) or (7) of Schedule 4 to the Act, the form of the entry to be made in the register in respect of an instrument creating the enduring power of attorney is a stamp bearing the following words (inserting the information indicated, as appropriate)—
'THE REGISTRATION OF THIS ENDURING POWER OF ATTORNEY IS QUALIFIED AND EXTENDS TO THE APPOINTMENT OF ....(insert name of attorney(s) not affected by ground(s) of objection or revocation) ONLY AS THE ATTORNEY(S) OF .... (insert name of donor)'.

Loss or destruction of instrument registered as enduring power of attorney

29.—

(1) This regulation applies where—

    (a) a person is required by or under the Act to deliver up to the Public Guardian any of the following documents—

        (i) an instrument registered as an enduring power of attorney;

(ii) an office copy of that registered instrument; or

(iii) a certified copy of that registered instrument; and

(b) the document has been lost or destroyed.

(2) The person who is required to deliver up the document must provide to the Public Guardian in writing—

(a) if known, the date of the loss or destruction and the circumstances in which it occurred;

(b) otherwise, a statement of when he last had the document in his possession.

PART 4
FUNCTIONS OF THE PUBLIC GUARDIAN

The registers

Establishing and maintaining the registers

30.—

(1) In this Part 'the registers' means—

(a) the register of lasting powers of attorney,

(b) the register of enduring powers of attorney, and

(c) the register of court orders appointing deputies,

which the Public Guardian must establish and maintain.

(2) On each register the Public Guardian may include—

(a) such descriptions of information about a registered instrument or a registered order as the Public Guardian considers appropriate; and

(b) entries which relate to an instrument or order for which registration has been cancelled.

Disclosure of information on a register: search by the Public Guardian

31.—

(1) Any person may, by an application made under paragraph (2), request the Public Guardian to carry out a search of one or more of the registers.

(2) An application must—

(a) state—

(i) the register or registers to be searched;

(ii) the name of the person to whom the application relates; and

(iii) such other details about that person as the Public Guardian may require for the purpose of carrying out the search; and

(b) be accompanied by any fee provided for under section 58(4)(b) of the Act.

(3) The Public Guardian may require the applicant to provide such further information, or produce such documents, as the Public Guardian reasonably considers necessary to enable him to carry out the search.

(4) As soon as reasonably practicable after receiving the application—

(a) the Public Guardian must notify the applicant of the result of the search; and

(b) in the event that it reveals one or more entries on the register, the Public Guardian must disclose to the applicant all the information appearing on the register in respect of each entry.

Disclosure of additional information held by the Public Guardian

32.—

(1) This regulation applies in any case where, as a result of a search made under regulation 31, a person has obtained information relating to a registered instrument or a registered order which confers authority to make decisions about matters concerning a person ('P').

(2) On receipt of an application made in accordance with paragraph (4), the Public Guardian may, if he considers that there is good reason to do so, disclose to the applicant such additional information as he considers appropriate.

(3) 'Additional information' means any information relating to P—

    (a) which the Public Guardian has obtained in exercising the functions conferred on him under the Act; but

    (b) which does not appear on the register.

(4) An application must state—

    (a) the name of P;

    (b) the reasons for making the application; and

    (c) what steps, if any, the applicant has taken to obtain the information from P.

(5) The Public Guardian may require the applicant to provide such further information, or produce such documents, as the Public Guardian reasonably considers necessary to enable him to determine the application.

(6) In determining whether to disclose any additional information to P, the Public Guardian must, in particular, have regard to—

    (a) the connection between P and the applicant;

    (b) the reasons for requesting the information (in particular, why the information cannot or should not be obtained directly from P);

    (c) the benefit to P, or any detriment he may suffer, if a disclosure is made; and

    (d) any detriment that another person may suffer if a disclosure is made.

Security for discharge of functions

Persons required to give security for the discharge of their functions

33.—

(1) This regulation applies in any case where the court orders a person ('S') to give to the Public Guardian security for the discharge of his functions.

(2) The security must be given by S—

    (a) by means of a bond which is entered into in accordance with regulation 34; or

    (b) in such other manner as the court may direct.

(3) For the purposes of paragraph (2)(a), S complies with the requirement to give the security only if—

    (a) the endorsement required by regulation 34(2) has been provided; and

    (b) the person who provided it has notified the Public Guardian of that fact.

(4) For the purposes of paragraph (2)(b), S complies with the requirement to give the security—

    (a) in any case where the court directs that any other endorsement must be provided, only if—

        (i) that endorsement has been provided; and

        (ii) the person who provided it has notified the Public Guardian of that fact;

    (b) in any case where the court directs that any other requirements must be met in relation to the giving of the security, only if the Public Guardian is satisfied that those other requirements have been met.

Security given under regulation 33(2)(a): requirement for endorsement

34.—

(1) This regulation has effect for the purposes of regulation 33(2)(a).

(2) A bond is entered into in accordance with this regulation only if it is endorsed by—

(a) an authorised insurance company; or

(b) an authorised deposit-taker.

(3) A person may enter into the bond under—

(a) arrangements made by the Public Guardian; or

(b) other arrangements which are made by the person entering into the bond or on his behalf.

(4) The Public Guardian may make arrangements with any person specified in paragraph (2) with a view to facilitating the provision by them of bonds which persons required to give security to the Public Guardian may enter into.

(5) In this regulation—

'authorised insurance company' means—

(a) a person who has permission under Part 4 of the Financial Services and Markets Act 2000[5] to effect or carry out contracts of insurance;

(b) an EEA firm of the kind mentioned in paragraph 5(d) of Schedule 3 to that Act, which has permission under paragraph 15 of that Schedule to effect or carry out contracts of insurance;

(c) a person who carries on insurance market activity (within the meaning given in section 316(3) of that Act); and

'authorised deposit-taker' means—

(a) a person who has permission under Part 4 of the Financial Services and Markets Act 2000 to accept deposits;

(b) an EEA firm of the kind mentioned in paragraph 5(d) of Schedule 3 to that Act, which has permission under paragraph 15 of that Schedule to accept deposits.

(6) The definitions of 'authorised insurance company' and 'authorised deposit-taker' must be read with—

(a) section 22 of the Financial Services and Markets Act 2000;

(b) any relevant order[6] under that section; and

(c) Schedule 2 to that Act.

Security given under regulation 33(2)(a): maintenance or replacement

35.—

(1) This regulation applies to any security given under regulation 33(2)(a).

(2) At such times or at such intervals as the Public Guardian may direct by notice in writing, any person ('S') who has given the security must satisfy the Public Guardian that any premiums payable in respect of it have been paid.

(3) Where S proposes to replace a security already given by him, the new security is not to be regarded as having been given until the Public Guardian is satisfied that—

(a) the requirements set out in sub-paragraphs (a) and (b) of regulation 33(3) have been met in relation to it; and

(b) no payment is due from S in connection with the discharge of his functions.

---

[5] 2000 c.8.

[6] S.I. 2001/544, as amended by S.I. 2001/3544, 2002/682, 1310, 1776 and 1777, 2003/1475, 1476 and 2822, 2004/1610 and 2737, 2005/593, 1518 and 2967 and 2006/1969, 2383 and 3221.

Enforcement following court order of any endorsed security

36.—

(1) This regulation applies to any security given to the Public Guardian in respect of which an endorsement has been provided.

(2) Where the court orders the enforcement of the security, the Public Guardian must—
   (a) notify any person who endorsed the security of the contents of the order; and
   (b) notify the court when payment has been made of the amount secured.

Discharge of any endorsed security

37.—

(1) This regulation applies to any security given by a person ('S') to the Public Guardian in respect of which an endorsement has been provided.

(2) The security may be discharged if the court makes an order discharging it.

(3) In any other case, the security may not be discharged until the end of the period of 7 years commencing with whichever of the following dates first occurs—
   (a) if the person on whose behalf S was appointed to act dies, the date of his death;
   (b) if S dies, the date of his death;
   (c) if the court makes an order which discharges S but which does not also discharge the security under paragraph (2), the date of the order;
   (d) the date when S otherwise ceases to be under a duty to discharge the functions in respect of which he was ordered to give security.

(4) For the purposes of paragraph (3), if a person takes any step with a view to discharging the security before the end of the period specified in that paragraph, the security is to be treated for all purposes as if it were still in place.

Deputies

Application for additional time to submit a report

38.—

(1) This regulation applies where the court requires a deputy to submit a report to the Public Guardian and specifies a time or interval for it to be submitted.

(2) A deputy may apply to the Public Guardian requesting more time for submitting a particular report.

(3) An application must—
   (a) state the reason for requesting more time; and
   (b) contain or be accompanied by such information as the Public Guardian may reasonably require to determine the application.

(4) In response to an application, the Public Guardian may, if he considers it appropriate to do so, undertake that he will not take steps to secure performance of the deputy's duty to submit the report at the relevant time on the condition that the report is submitted on or before such later date as he may specify.

Content of reports

39.—

(1) Any report which the court requires a deputy to submit to the Public Guardian must include such material as the court may direct.

(2) The report must also contain or be accompanied by—
- (a) specified information or information of a specified description; or
- (b) specified documents or documents of a specified description.

(3) But paragraph (2)—
- (a) extends only to information or documents which are reasonably required in connection with the exercise by the Public Guardian of functions conferred on him under the Act; and
- (b) is subject to paragraph (1) and to any other directions given by the court.

(4) Where powers as respects a person's property and affairs are conferred on a deputy under section 16 of the Act, the information specified by the Public Guardian under paragraph (2) may include accounts which—
- (a) deal with specified matters; and
- (b) are provided in a specified form.

(5) The Public Guardian may require—
- (a) any information provided to be verified in such manner, or
- (b) any document produced to be authenticated in such manner,

as he may reasonably require.

(6) 'Specified' means specified in a notice in writing given to the deputy by the Public Guardian.

Power to require final report on termination of appointment

40.—

(1) This regulation applies where—
- (a) the person on whose behalf a deputy was appointed to act has died;
- (b) the deputy has died;
- (c) the court has made an order discharging the deputy; or
- (d) the deputy otherwise ceases to be under a duty to discharge the functions to which his appointment relates.

(2) The Public Guardian may require the deputy (or, in the case of the deputy's death, his personal representatives) to submit a final report on the discharge of his functions.

(3) A final report must be submitted—
- (a) before the end of such reasonable period as may be specified; and
- (b) at such place as may be specified.

(4) The Public Guardian must consider the final report, together with any other information that he may have relating to the discharge by the deputy of his functions.

(5) Where the Public Guardian is dissatisfied with any aspect of the final report he may apply to the court for an appropriate remedy (including enforcement of security given by the deputy).

(6) 'Specified' means specified in a notice in writing given to the deputy or his personal representatives by the Public Guardian.

Power to require information from deputies

41.—

(1) This regulation applies in any case where—
- (a) the Public Guardian has received representations (including complaints) about—
  - (i) the way in which a deputy is exercising his powers; or
  - (ii) any failure to exercise them; or
- (b) it appears to the Public Guardian that there are other circumstances which—
  - (i) give rise to concerns about, or dissatisfaction with, the conduct of the deputy (including any failure to act); or

      (ii) otherwise constitute good reason to seek information about the deputy's discharge of his functions.
(2) The Public Guardian may require the deputy—
    (a) to provide specified information or information of a specified description; or
    (b) to produce specified documents or documents of a specified description.
(3) The information or documents must be provided or produced—
    (a) before the end of such reasonable period as may be specified; and
    (b) at such place as may be specified.
(4) The Public Guardian may require—
    (a) any information provided to be verified in such manner, or
    (b) any document produced to be authenticated in such manner,
    as he may reasonably require.
(5) 'Specified' means specified in a notice in writing given to the deputy by the Public Guardian.

Right of deputy to require review of decisions made by the Public Guardian

42.—
(1) A deputy may require the Public Guardian to reconsider any decision he has made in relation to the deputy.
(2) The right under paragraph (1) is exercisable by giving notice of exercise of the right to the Public Guardian before the end of the period of 14 days beginning with the date on which notice of the decision is given to the deputy.
(3) The notice of exercise of the right must—
    (a) state the grounds on which reconsideration is required; and
    (b) contain or be accompanied by any relevant information or documents.
(4) At any time after receiving the notice and before reconsidering the decision to which it relates, the Public Guardian may require the deputy to provide him with such further information, or to produce such documents, as he reasonably considers necessary to enable him to reconsider the matter.
(5) The Public Guardian must give to the deputy—
    (a) written notice of his decision on reconsideration, and
    (b) if he upholds the previous decision, a statement of his reasons.

Miscellaneous functions

Applications to the Court of Protection

43. The Public Guardian has the function of making applications to the court in connection with his functions under the Act in such circumstances as he considers it necessary or appropriate to do so.

Visits by the Public Guardian or by Court of Protection Visitors at his direction

44.—
(1) This regulation applies where the Public Guardian visits, or directs a Court of Protection Visitor to visit, any person under any provision of the Act or these Regulations.
(2) The Public Guardian must notify (or make arrangements to notify) the person to be visited of—
    (a) the date or dates on which it is proposed that the visit will take place;

(b) to the extent that it is practicable to do so, any specific matters likely to be covered in the course of the visit; and

(c) any proposal to inform any other person that the visit is to take place.

(3) Where the visit is to be carried out by a Court of Protection Visitor—

(a) the Public Guardian may—

(i) give such directions to the Visitor, and

(ii) provide him with such information concerning the person to be visited,

as the Public Guardian considers necessary for the purposes of enabling the visit to take place and the Visitor to prepare any report the Public Guardian may require; and

(b) the Visitor must seek to carry out the visit and take all reasonable steps to obtain such other information as he considers necessary for the purpose of preparing a report.

(4) A Court of Protection Visitor must submit any report requested by the Public Guardian in accordance with any timetable specified by the Public Guardian.

(5) If he considers it appropriate to do so, the Public Guardian may, in relation to any person interviewed in the course of preparing a report—

(a) disclose the report to him; and

(b) invite him to comment on it.

Functions in relation to persons carrying out specific transactions

45.—

(1) This regulation applies where, in accordance with an order made under section 16(2)(a) of the Act, a person ('T') has been authorised to carry out any transaction for a person who lacks capacity.

(2) The Public Guardian has the functions of—

(a) receiving any reports from T which the court may require;

(b) dealing with representations (including complaints) about—

(i) the way in which the transaction has been or is being carried out; or

(ii) any failure to carry it out.

(3) Regulations 38 to 41 have effect in relation to T as they have effect in relation a deputy.

Power to require information from donees of lasting power of attorney

46.—

(1) This regulation applies where it appears to the Public Guardian that there are circumstances suggesting that the donee of a lasting power of attorney may—

(a) have behaved, or may be behaving, in a way that contravenes his authority or is not in the best interests of the donor of the power,

(b) be proposing to behave in a way that would contravene that authority or would not be inthe donor's best interests, or

(c) have failed to comply with the requirements of an order made, or directions given, by the court.

(2) The Public Guardian may require the donee—

(a) to provide specified information or information of a specified description; or

(b) to produce specified documents or documents of a specified description.

(3) The information or documents must be provided or produced—

(a) before the end of such reasonable period as may be specified; and

(b) at such place as may be specified.

(4) The Public Guardian may require—

(a) any information provided to be verified in such manner, or

(b) any document produced to be authenticated in such manner, as he may reasonably require.

(5) 'Specified' means specified in a notice in writing given to the donee by the Public Guardian.

Power to require information from attorneys under enduring power of attorney

47.—

(1) This regulation applies where it appears to the Public Guardian that there are circumstances suggesting that, having regard to all the circumstances (and in particular the attorney's relationship to or connection with the donor) the attorney under a registered enduring power of attorney may be unsuitable to be the donor's attorney.

(2) The Public Guardian may require the attorney—
   (a) to provide specified information or information of a specified description; or
   (b) to produce specified documents or documents of a specified description.

(3) The information or documents must be provided or produced—
   (a) before the end of such reasonable period as may be specified; and
   (b) at such place as may be specified.

(4) The Public Guardian may require—
   (a) any information provided to be verified in such manner, or
   (b) any document produced to be authenticated in such manner, as he may reasonably require.

(5) 'Specified' means specified in a notice in writing given to the attorney by the Public Guardian.

Other functions in relation to enduring powers of attorney

48. The Public Guardian has the following functions—
   (a) directing a Court of Protection Visitor—
       (i) to visit an attorney under a registered enduring power of attorney, or
       (ii) to visit the donor of a registered enduring power of attorney,
       and to make a report to the Public Guardian on such matters as he may direct;
   (b) dealing with representations (including complaints) about the way in which an attorney under a registered enduring power of attorney is exercising his powers.

Signed by authority of the Lord Chancellor.
Cathy Ashton,
Parliamentary Under-Secretary of State,
16th April 2007 Department for Constitutional Affairs

SCHEDULES 1–8

[Not reproduced here, can be found at
<http.//www.opsi.gov.uk/si/si2007/uksi_20071253_en_1>]

EXPLANATORY NOTE
(This note is not part of the Regulations)

These Regulations supplement the requirements set out in Schedule 1 to the Mental Capacity Act 2005 (c. 9) ('the Act') which apply to the making and registration of lasting powers of attorney and the requirements set out in Schedule 4 to the Act which apply to the registration of enduring powers or attorney. The Regulations also confer functions on the Public Guardian and make other provision in connection with functions conferred on him by the Act or by these Regulations.

Part 1 of the Regulations is general and contains a number of definitions and interpretative provisions.

Part 2 of, and Schedules 1 to 6 to, the Regulations deal with lasting powers of attorney. Under section 9(2)(b) of the Act, a lasting power of attorney is not created unless it has (amongst other things) been made and registered in accordance with Schedule 1 to the Act. Regulation 5 (and Schedule 1) set out the forms of instruments to be used to make a lasting power of attorney. A different form must be used according to whether the instrument is intended to confer authority to make decisions about the donor's personal welfare, or about his property and affairs. Regulations 6 to 8 make detailed provision about the content of the instrument. Regulation 9 specifies the steps that must be taken to execute the instrument and the sequence in which those steps must be taken.

Regulations 10 to 17 make provision about the procedure for registering an instrument as a lasting power of attorney, and Schedules 2 to 5 set out the application form and the form of notices to be used at different stages of the process. There are also certain other requirements specified which relate to the registration process.

Regulations 18 to 22 contain a number of miscellaneous provisions that apply to instruments which have been registered as lasting powers of attorney. These provisions specify steps to be taken if an instrument is changed, revoked, lost or destroyed.

Regulation 20 (and Schedule 6) set out the form to be used by the donee of a lasting power when he wishes to disclaim his appointment.

Part 3 of, and Schedules 7 and 8 to, the Regulations deal with enduring powers of attorney. No new enduring power of attorney may be created after the commencement of section 66(1)(b) of the Act, but Schedules 4 and 5 to the Act apply to any power that was created before then. Regulation 23 (and Schedule 7) set out the form of notice to be given to the donor, and to his relatives, when an attorney under an enduring power intends to apply for registration. Regulation 23 also requires that the notice be given to the donor personally, together with an explanation of its effect.

Regulations 24 to 28 (and Schedule 8) specify certain other requirements applying to the registration process and regulation 29 specifies steps to be taken if an instrument creating an enduring power of attorney is lost or destroyed after it has been registered.

Part 4 of the Regulations confers a number of specific functions on the Public Guardian. It also makes provision in connection with functions conferred on him by the Act or by these Regulations.

Additional functions are conferred by regulations 43, 45 and 48. Regulation 43 deals with the making of applications to the Court of Protection, regulation 45 sets out functions in relation to persons who are authorised to carry out a particular transaction and regulation 48 sets out functions in relation to enduring powers of attorney.

There are also provisions relating to the registers which the Public Guardian is required to maintain under the Act (regulations 30 to 32); relating to the giving of any security and the replacement, maintenance, enforcement or discharge of a security which has been endorsed (regulations 33 to 37); relating to the information that a deputy appointed by the Court of Protection must give to the Public Guardian (regulations 38 to 41); and relating to the review of a decision made by the Public Guardian in relation to a deputy (regulation 42). Regulations 44, 46 and 47 make provision in connection with a number of other areas where the Public Guardian has functions, including the requirements to be met when visits on any person are carried out by, or at the direction of, the Public Guardian (regulation 48).

APPENDIX 4

Court of Protection Rules 2007

STATUTORY INSTRUMENTS
2007 NO. 1744 (L. 12)

MENTAL CAPACITY, ENGLAND AND WALES
The Court of Protection Rules 2007

Made – – – – 25th June 2007
Laid before Parliament 4th July 2007
Coming into force – – 1st October 2007

CONTENTS

PART 1
PRELIMINARY

PART 2
THE OVERRIDING OBJECTIVE

PART 3
INTERPRETATION AND GENERAL PROVISIONS

PART 4
COURT DOCUMENTS

PART 5
GENERAL CASE MANAGEMENT POWERS

PART 6
SERVICE OF DOCUMENTS

Service generally

PART 9
HOW TO START PROCEEDINGS

Initial steps

Steps following issue of application form

Responding to an application

The parties to the proceedings

PART 10
APPLICATIONS WITHIN PROCEEDINGS

Interim Remedies

PART 14

ADMISSIONS, EVIDENCE AND DEPOSITIONS

PART 15
EXPERTS

PART 16
DISCLOSURE

PART 17
LITIGATION FRIEND

PART 18
CHANGE OF SOLICITOR

PART 19
COSTS

PART 20
APPEALS

The President of the Family Division of the High Court (the judicial office holder nominated by the Lord Chief Justice) with the agreement of the Lord Chancellor, makes the following Rules in exercise of the powers conferred by sections 49(5), 50(2), 51, 53(2) and (4), 55, 56 and 65(1) of the Mental Capacity Act 2005,[1] and in accordance with Part 1 of Schedule 1 to the Constitutional Reform Act 2005.[2]

PART 1
PRELIMINARY

Title and commencement

1. These Rules may be cited as the Court of Protection Rules 2007 and come into force on 1 October 2007.

Revocations

2. The following rules are revoked—

(a) the Court of Protection Rules 2001;[3] and

(b) the Court of Protection (Enduring Powers of Attorney) Rules 2001.[4]

PART 2
THE OVERRIDING OBJECTIVE

The overriding objective

3.—

(1) These Rules have the overriding objective of enabling the court to deal with a case justly, having regard to the principles contained in the Act.

(2) The court will seek to give effect to the overriding objective when it—

(a) exercises any power under these Rules; or

(b) interprets any rule or practice direction.

(3) Dealing with a case justly includes, so far as is practicable—

(a) ensuring that it is dealt with expeditiously and fairly;

(b) ensuring that P's interests and position are properly considered;

(c) dealing with the case in ways which are proportionate to the nature, importance and complexity of the issues;

(d) ensuring that the parties are on an equal footing;

(e) saving expense; and

(f) allotting to it an appropriate share of the court's resources, while taking account of the need to allot resources to other cases.

The duty of the parties

4. The parties are required to help the court to further the overriding objective.

---

[1] (a) 2005 c.9, as amended by article 2 of, and paragraphs 30 and 34 of Schedule 1 to, the Lord Chancellor (Transfer of Functions and Supplementary Provisions) (No. 2) Order 2006 (S.I. 2006/1016).

[2] (b) 2005 c.4.

[3] S.I. 2001/824, as amended by S.I. 2001/2977, S.I. 2002/833, S.I. 2003/1733, S.I. 2004/1291, S.I. 2005/667 and S.I. 2006/653.

[4] S.I. 2001/825, as amended by S.I. 2002/832, S.I. 2002/1944, S.I. 2005/668 and S.I. 2005/3126.

Court's duty to manage cases

5.—

(1) The court will further the overriding objective by actively managing cases.

(2) Active case management includes—

   (a) encouraging the parties to co-operate with each other in the conduct of the proceedings;

   (b) identifying at an early stage—

      (i) the issues; and

      (ii) who should be a party to the proceedings;

   (c) deciding promptly—

      (i) which issues need a full investigation and hearing and which do not; and

      (ii) the procedure to be followed in the case;

   (d) deciding the order in which issues are to be resolved;

   (e) encouraging the parties to use an alternative dispute resolution procedure if the court considers that appropriate;

   (f) fixing timetables or otherwise controlling the progress of the case;

   (g) considering whether the likely benefits of taking a particular step justify the cost of taking it;

   (h) dealing with as many aspects of the case as the court can on the same occasion;

   (i) dealing with the case without the parties needing to attend at court;

   (j) making use of technology; and

   (k) giving directions to ensure that the case proceeds quickly and efficiently.

PART 3
INTERPRETATION AND GENERAL PROVISIONS

Interpretation

6. In these Rules—

   'the Act' means the Mental Capacity Act 2005;

   'applicant' means a person who makes, or who seeks permission to make, an application to the court;

   'application form' means the document that is to be used to begin proceedings in accordance with Part 9 of these Rules or any other provision of these Rules or the practice directions which requires the use of an application form;

   'application notice' means the document that is to be used to make an application in accordance with Part 10 of these Rules or any other provision of these Rules or the practice directions which requires the use of an application notice;

   'attorney' means the person appointed as such by an enduring power of attorney created, or purporting to have been created, in accordance with the regulations mentioned in paragraph 2 of Schedule 4 to the Act;

   'business day' means a day other than—

   (a) a Saturday, Sunday, Christmas Day or Good Friday; or

   (b) a bank holiday in England and Wales, under the Banking and Financial Dealings Act 1971;[5]

   'child' means a person under 18;

   'court' means the Court of Protection;

---

[5] 1971 c. 80.

'deputy' means a deputy appointed under the Act;

'donee' means the donee of a lasting power of attorney;

'donor' means the donor of a lasting power of attorney, except where this expression is used in rule 68 or 201(5) (where it means the donor of an enduring power of attorney);

'enduring power of attorney' means an instrument created in accordance with such of the regulations mentioned in paragraph 2 of Schedule 4 to the Act as applied when it was executed;

'filing' in relation to a document means delivering it, by post or otherwise, to the court office;

'judge' means a judge nominated to be a judge of the court under the Act;

'lasting power of attorney' has the meaning given in section 9 of the Act;

'legal representative' means a barrister or a solicitor, solicitor's employee or other authorised litigator (as defined in the Courts and Legal Services Act 1990)[6] who has been instructed to act for a party in relation to any application;

'LSC funded client' means an individual who receives services funded by the Legal Services Commission as part of the Community Legal Service within the meaning of Part I of the Access to Justice Act 1999;[7]

'order' includes a declaration made by the court;

'P' means any person (other than a protected party) who lacks or, so far as consistent with the context, is alleged to lack capacity to make a decision or decisions in relation to any matter that is the subject of an application to the court and references to a person who lacks capacity are to be construed in accordance with the Act;

'party' is to be construed in accordance with rule 73;

'permission form' means the form that is to be used to make an application for permission to begin proceedings in accordance with Part 8 of these Rules;

'personal welfare' is to be construed in accordance with section 17 of the Act;

'President' and 'Vice-President' refer to those judges appointed as such under section 46(3)(a) and (b) of the Act;

'property and affairs' is to be construed in accordance with section 18 of the Act;

'protected party' means a party or an intended party (other than P or a child) who lacks capacity to conduct the proceedings;

'respondent' means a person who is named as a respondent in the application form or notice, as the case may be;

'Senior Judge' means the judge who has been nominated to be Senior Judge under section 46(4) of the Act, and references in these Rules to a circuit judge include the Senior Judge;

'Visitor' means a person appointed as such by the Lord Chancellor under section 61 of the Act.

Court officers

7.—

(1) Where these Rules permit or require the court to perform an act of a purely formal or administrative character, that act may be performed by a court officer.

(2) A requirement that a court officer carry out any act at the request of any person is subject to the payment of any fee required by a fees order for the carrying out of that act.

---

[6] 1990 c. 41.

[7] 1999 c. 22.

Computation of time

8.—

(1) This rule shows how to calculate any period of time which is specified—
- (a) by these Rules;
- (b) by a practice direction; or
- (c) in an order or direction of the court.

(2) A period of time expressed as a number of days must be computed as clear days.

(3) In this rule 'clear days' means that in computing the number of days—
- (a) the day on which the period begins; and
- (b) if the end of the period is defined by reference to an event, the day on which that event occurs, are not included.

(4) Where the specified period is 7 days or less, and would include a day which is not a business day, that day does not count.

(5) When the specified period for doing any act at the court office ends on a day on which the office is closed, that act will be done in time if done on the next day on which the court office is open.

Application of the Civil Procedure Rules

9. In any case not expressly provided for by these Rules or the practice directions made under them, the Civil Procedure Rules 1998[8] (including any practice directions made under them) may be applied with any necessary modifications, insofar as is necessary to further the overriding objective.

PART 4
COURT DOCUMENTS

Documents used in court proceedings

10.—

(1) The court will seal or otherwise authenticate with the stamp of the court the following documents on issue—
- (a) a permission form;
- (b) an application form;
- (c) an application notice;
- (d) an order; and
- (e) any other document which a rule or practice direction requires to be sealed or stamped.

(2) Where these Rules or any practice direction require a document to be signed, that requirement is satisfied if the signature is printed by computer or other mechanical means.

(3) A practice direction may make provision for documents to be filed or sent to the court by—
- (a) facsimile; or
- (b) other means.

---

[8] S.I. 1998/3132, as amended.

Documents required to be verified by a statement of truth

11.—

(1) The following documents must be verified by a statement of truth—
  (a) a permission form, an application form or an application notice, where the applicant seeks to rely upon matters set out in the document as evidence;
  (b) a witness statement;
  (c) a certificate of—
     (i) service or non-service; or
     (ii) notification or non-notification;
  (d) a deputy's declaration; and
  (e) any other document required by a rule or practice direction to be so verified.
(2) Subject to paragraph (3), a statement of truth is a statement that—
  (a) the party putting forward the document;
  (b) in the case of a witness statement, the maker of the witness statement; or
  (c) in the case of a certificate referred to in paragraph (1)(c), the person who signs the certificate,
  believes that the facts stated in the document being verified are true.
(3) If a party is conducting proceedings with a litigation friend, the statement of truth in—
  (a) a permission form;
  (b) an application form; or
  (c) an application notice,
  is a statement that the litigation friend believes the facts stated in the document being verified are true.
(4) The statement of truth must be signed—
  (a) in the case of a permission form, an application form or an application notice—
     (i) by the party or litigation friend; or
     (ii) by the legal representative on behalf of the party or litigation friend; and
  (b) in the case of a witness statement, by the maker of the statement.
(5) A statement of truth which is not contained in the document which it verifies must clearly identify that document.
(6) A statement of truth in a permission form, an application form or an application notice may be made by—
  (a) a person who is not a party; or
  (b) two or more parties jointly,
  where this is permitted by a relevant practice direction.

Failure to verify a document

12. If a permission form, application form or application notice is not verified by a statement of truth, the applicant may not rely upon the document as evidence of any of the matters set out in it unless the court permits.

Failure to verify a witness statement

13. If a witness statement is not verified by a statement of truth, it shall not be admissible in evidence unless the court permits.

False statements

14.—

(1) Proceedings for contempt of court may be brought against a person if he makes, or causes to be made, a false statement in a document verified by a statement of truth without an honest belief in its truth.

(2) Proceedings under this rule may be brought only—

(a) by the Attorney General; or

(b) with the permission of the court.

Personal details

15.—

(1) Where a party does not wish to reveal—

(a) his home address or telephone number;

(b) P's home address or telephone number;

(c) the name of the person with whom P is living (if that person is not the applicant); or

(d) the address or telephone number of his place of business, or the place of business of any of the persons mentioned in sub-paragraphs (b) or (c),

he must provide those particulars to the court.

(2) Where paragraph (1) applies, the particulars given will not be revealed to any person unless the court so directs.

(3) Where a party changes his home address during the course of the proceedings, he must give notice of the change to the court.

(4) Where a party does not reveal his home address, he must nonetheless provide an address for service which must be within the jurisdiction of the court.

Supply of documents to a party from court records

16. Unless the court orders otherwise, a party to proceedings may inspect or obtain from the records of the court a copy of—

(a) any document filed by a party to the proceedings; or

(b) any communication in the proceedings between the court and—

(i) a party to the proceedings; or

(ii) another person.

Supply of documents to a non-party from court records

17.—

(1) Subject to rules 20 and 92(2), a person who is not a party to proceedings may inspect or obtain from the court records a copy of any judgment or order given or made in public.

(2) The court may, on an application made to it, authorise a person who is not a party to proceedings to—

(a) inspect any other documents in the court records; or

(b) obtain a copy of any such documents, or extracts from such documents.

(3) A person making an application for an authorisation under paragraph (2) must do so in accordance with Part 10.

(4) Before giving an authorisation under paragraph (2), the court will consider whether any document is to be provided on an edited basis.

Subsequent use of court documents

18.—

(1) Where a document has been filed or disclosed, a party to whom it was provided may use the document only for the purpose of the proceedings in which it was filed or disclosed, except where—

    (a) the document has been read to or by the court or referred to at a public hearing; or

    (b) the court otherwise permits.

(2) Paragraph (1)(a) is subject to any order of the court made under rule 92(2).

Editing information in court documents

19.—

(1) A party may apply to the court for an order that a specified part of a document is to be edited prior to the document's service or disclosure.

(2) An order under paragraph (1) may be made at any time.

(3) Where the court makes an order under this rule any subsequent use of that document in the proceedings shall be of the document as edited, unless the court directs otherwise.

(4) An application under this rule must be made in accordance with Part 10.

Public Guardian to be supplied with court documents relevant to supervision of deputies

20.—

(1) This rule applies in any case where the court makes an order—

    (a) appointing a person to act as a deputy; or

    (b) varying an order under which a deputy has been appointed.

(2) Subject to paragraphs (3) and (6), the Public Guardian is entitled to be supplied with a copy of qualifying documents if he reasonably considers that it is necessary for him to have regard to them in connection with the discharge of his functions under section 58 of the Act in relation to the supervision of deputies.

(3) The court may direct that the right to be supplied with documents under paragraph (2) does not apply in relation to such one or more documents, or descriptions of documents, as the court may specify.

(4) A direction under paragraph (3) or (6) may be given—

    (a) either on the court's own initiative or on an application made to it; and

    (b) either—

        (i) at the same time as the court makes the order which appoints the deputy, or which varies it; or

        (ii) subsequently.

(5) 'Qualifying documents' means documents which—

    (a) are filed in court in connection with the proceedings in which the court makes the order referred to in paragraph (1); and

    (b) are relevant to—

        (i) the decision to appoint the deputy;

        (ii) any powers conferred on him;

        (iii) any duties imposed on him; or

        (iv) any other terms applying to those powers and duties which are contained in the order.

(6) The court may direct that any document is to be provided to the Public Guardian on an edited basis.

Provision of court order to Public Guardian

21. Any order of the court requiring the Public Guardian to do something, or not to do something, will be served by the court on the Public Guardian as soon as practicable and in any event not later than 7 days after the order was made.

Amendment of application

22.—

(1) The court may allow or direct an applicant, at any stage of the proceedings, to amend his application form or notice.

(2) The amendment may be effected by making in writing the necessary alterations to the application form or notice, but if the amendments are so numerous or of such a nature or length that written alteration would make it difficult or inconvenient to read, a fresh document amended as allowed or directed may be issued.

Clerical mistakes or slips

23. The court may at any time correct any clerical mistakes in an order or direction or any error arising in an order or direction from any accidental slip or omission.

Endorsement of amendment

24. Where an application form or notice, order or direction has been amended under this Part, a note shall be placed on it showing the date on which it was amended and the alteration shall be sealed.

PART 5
GENERAL CASE MANAGEMENT POWERS

The court's general powers of case management

25.—

(1) The list of powers in this rule is in addition to any powers given to the court by any other rule or practice direction or by any other enactment or any powers it may otherwise have.

(2) The court may—

(a) extend or shorten the time for compliance with any rule, practice direction, or court order or direction (even if an application for extension is made after the time for compliance has expired);

(b) adjourn or bring forward a hearing;

(c) require P, a party, a party's legal representative or litigation friend, to attend court;

(d) hold a hearing and receive evidence by telephone or any other method of direct oral communication;

(e) stay the whole or part of any proceedings or judgment either generally or until a specified date or event;

(f) consolidate proceedings;

(g) hear two or more applications on the same occasion;

(h) direct a separate hearing of any issue;

(i) decide the order in which issues are to be heard;

    (j)   exclude an issue from consideration;

    (k) dismiss or give judgment on an application after a decision is made on a preliminary basis;

    (l)   direct any party to file and serve an estimate of costs; and

    (m) take any step or give any direction for the purpose of managing the case and furthering the overriding objective.

(3) A judge to whom a matter is allocated may, if he considers that the matter is one which ought properly to be dealt with by another judge, transfer the matter to such a judge.

(4) Where the court gives directions it may take into account whether or not a party has complied with any rule or practice direction.

(5) The court may make any order it considers appropriate even if a party has not sought that order.

(6) A power of the court under these Rules to make an order includes a power to vary or revoke the order;

(7) Rules 25.12 to 25.15 of the Civil Procedure Rules 1998 (which make provision about security for costs) apply in proceedings to which these Rules apply as if the references in those Rules to 'defendant' and 'claimant' were to 'respondent' and 'applicant' respectively.

Court's power to dispense with requirement of any rule

26. In addition to its general powers and the powers listed in rule 25, the court may dispense with the requirement of any rule.

Exercise of powers on the court's own initiative

27.—

(1) Except where these Rules or some other enactment make different provision, the court may exercise its powers on its own initiative.

(2) The court may make an order on its own initiative without hearing the parties or giving them the opportunity to make representations.

(3) Where the court proposes to make an order on its own initiative it may give the parties and any person it thinks fit an opportunity to make representations and, where it does so, it will specify the time by which, and the manner in which, the representations must be made.

(4) Where the court proposes—

    (a) to make an order on its own initiative; and

    (b) to hold a hearing to decide whether to make the order,

it will give the parties and may give any other person it thinks likely to be affected by the order at least 3 days' notice of the hearing.

General power of the court to rectify matters where there has been an error of procedure

28. Where there has been an error of procedure, such as a failure to comply with a rule or practice direction—

    (a) the error does not invalidate any step taken in the proceedings unless the court so orders; and

    (b) the court may waive the error or require it to be remedied or may make such other order as appears to the court to be just.

PART 6
SERVICE OF DOCUMENTS

Service generally

Scope

29.—

(1) Subject to paragraph (2), the rules in this Part apply to—

    (a) the service of documents; and

    (b) to the requirement under rule 70 for a person to be notified of the issue of an application form, and references to 'serve', 'service', 'notice' and 'notify', and kindred expressions shall be construed accordingly.

(2) The rules in this Part do not apply where—

    (a) any other enactment, a rule in another Part or a practice direction makes different provision; or

    (b) the court directs otherwise.

Who is to serve

30.—

(1) The general rule is that the following documents will be served by the court—

    (a) an order or judgment of the court;

    (b) an acknowledgment of service or notification; and

    (c) except where the application is for an order for committal, a notice of hearing.

(2) Any other document is to be served by the party seeking to rely upon it, except where—

    (a) a rule or practice direction provides otherwise; or

    (b) the court directs otherwise.

(3) Where the court is to serve a document—

    (a) it is for the court to decide which of the methods of service specified in rule 31 is to be used; and

    (b) if the document is being served on behalf of a party, that party must provide sufficient copies.

Methods of service

31.—

(1) A document may be served by any of the methods specified in this rule.

(2) Where it is not known whether a solicitor is acting on behalf of a person, the document may be served by—

    (a) delivering it to the person personally;

    (b) delivering it at his home address or last known home address; or

    (c) sending it to that address, or last known address, by first class post (or by an alternative method of service which provides for delivery on the next working day).

(3) Where a solicitor–

    (a) is authorised to accept service on behalf of a person; and

    (b) has informed the person serving the document in writing that he is so authorised,

the document must be served on the solicitor, unless personal service is required by an enactment, rule, practice direction or court order.

(4) Where it appears to the court that there is a good reason to authorise service by a method other than those specified in paragraphs (2) or (3), the court may direct that service is effected by that method.

(5) A direction that service is effected by an alternative method must specify—

    (a) the method of service; and

    (b) the date when the document will be deemed to be served.

(6) A practice direction may set out how documents are to be served by document exchange, electronic communication or other means.

Service of documents on children and protected parties

32.—

(1) The following table shows the person on whom a document must be served if it is a document which would otherwise be served on—

    (a) a child; or

    (b) a protected party.

Type of document	Nature of party	Person to be served
Application form	Child	• A person who has parental responsibility for the child within the meaning of the Children Act 1989[9]; or • if there is no such person, a person with whom the child resides or in whose care the child is.
Application form	Protected party	• The person who is authorised to conduct the proceedings in the protected party's name or on his behalf; or • a person who is a duly appointed attorney, donee or deputy of the protected party; or • if there is no such person, a person with whom the protected party lives or in whose care the latter is.
Application for an order appointing a litigation friend, where a child or protected party has no litigation friend	Child or protected party	• See rule 145 (appointment of litigation friend by court order—supplementary).
Any other document	Child or protected party	• The litigation friend or other duly authorised person who is conducting the proceedings on behalf of the child or protected party.

(2) The court may make an order for service on a child or a protected party by permitting the document to be served on some person other than the person specified in the table set out in paragraph (1) above (which may include service on the child or the protected party).

(3) An application for an order under paragraph (2) may be made without notice.

---

[9] 1989, C. 41.

(4) The court may order that, although a document has been served on someone other than the person specified in the table, the document is to be treated as if it had been properly served.

(5) This rule does not apply in relation to the service of documents upon a child in any case where the court has made an order under rule 141(4) permitting the child to conduct proceedings without a litigation friend.

Service of documents on P if he becomes a party

33.—

(1) If P becomes a party to the proceedings, all documents to be served on him must be served on his litigation friend or other person duly authorised to conduct proceedings on P's behalf.

(2) The court may make an order for service on P by permitting the document to be served on some person other than the person specified in paragraph (1) above (which may include service on P).

(3) An application for an order under paragraph (2) may be made without notice.

(4) The court may order that, although a document has been served on someone other than a person specified in paragraph (1), the document is to be treated as if it had been properly served.

(5) This rule does not apply in relation to the service of documents upon P in any case where the court has made an order under rule 147(2) (procedure where appointment of a litigation friend comes to an end – for P).

Substituted service

34. Where it appears to the court that it is impracticable for any reason to serve a document in accordance with any of the methods provided under rule 31, the court may make an order for substituted service of the document by taking such steps as the court may direct to bring it to the notice of the person to be served.

Deemed service

35.—

(1) A document which is served in accordance with these Rules or any relevant practice direction shall be deemed to be served on the day shown in the following table—

Method of service	Deemed day of service
First class post (or other service for next-day delivery)	The second day after it was posted.
Document exchange	The second day after it was left at the document exchange.
Delivering the document to a permitted address	The day after it was delivered to that address.
Fax	If it is transmitted on a business day before 4 p.m., on that day; or in any other case, on the business day after the day on which it is transmitted.
Other electronic means	The second day after the day on which it is transmitted.

(2) If a document is served personally—
   (a) after 5 p.m., on a business day; or
   (b) at any time on a Saturday, Sunday or a Bank Holiday,
   it will be treated as being served on the next business day.

Certificate of service

36.—(1) Where a rule, practice direction or court order requires a certificate of service for the document, the certificate must state the details set out in the following table—

Method of service	Details to be certified
First class post (or any other service for nextday delivery)	Date of posting.
Personal service	Date of personal service
Document exchange	Date when the document was left at the document exchange.
Delivery of document to permitted address	Date when the document was delivered to that address.
Fax	Date of transmission.
Other electronic means	Date of transmission and the means used.
Alternative method permitted by the court	As required by the court.

(2) The certificate must be filed within 7 days after service of the document to which it relates.

Certificate of non-service

37.—

(1) Where an applicant or other person is unable to serve any document under these Rules or as directed by the court, he must file a certificate of non-service stating the reasons why service has not been effected.

(2) The certificate of non-service must be filed within 7 days of the latest date on which service should have been effected.

Power of court to dispense with service

38.—

(1) The court may dispense with any requirement to serve a document.

(2) An application for an order to dispense with service may be made without notice.

Service out of the jurisdiction

Application of Family Procedure (Adoption) Rules 2005

39.—

(1) The rules in Section 2 of Part 6 of the Family Procedure (Adoption) Rules 2005(a) ('the 2005 Rules') apply, with the modifications set out in this rule, to the service of documents out of the jurisdiction.

(2) References in the 2005 Rules to the Hague Convention shall be read in these Rules as references to the Convention on the International Protection of Adults signed at the Hague on 13th January 2000 (Cm. 5881).

(3) References in the 2005 Rules to the Senior Master of the Queen's Bench Division shall be read in these Rules as references to the Senior Judge.

PART 7
NOTIFYING P

General requirement to notify P

General

40.—

(1) Subject to paragraphs (2) and (3), the rules in this Part apply where P is to be given notice of any matter or document, or is to be provided with any document, either under the Rules or in accordance with an order or direction of the court.

(2) If P becomes a party, the rules in this Part do not apply and service is to be effected in accordance with Part 6 or as directed by the court.

(3) In any case the court may, either on its own initiative or on application, direct that P must not be notified of any matter or document, or provided with any document, whether in accordance with this Part or at all.

Who is to notify P

41.—

(1) Where P is to be notified under this Part, notification must be effected by—
   (a) the applicant;
      (a) S.I. 2005/2795.
   (b) the appellant (where the matter relates to an appeal);
   (c) an agent duly appointed by the applicant or the appellant; or
   (d) such other person as the court may direct.

(2) The person within paragraph (1) is referred to in this Part as 'the person effecting notification'.

Circumstances in which P must be notified

Application forms

42.—

(1) P must be notified—
   (a) that an application form has been issued by the court;
   (b) that an application form has been withdrawn; and
   (c) of the date on which a hearing is to be held in relation to the matter, where that hearing is for disposing of the application.

(2) Where P is to be notified that an application form has been issued, the person effecting notification must explain to P—
   (a) who the applicant is;
   (b) that the application raises the question of whether P lacks capacity in relation to a matter or matters, and what that means;
   (c) what will happen if the court makes the order or direction that has been applied for; and
   (d) where the application contains a proposal for the appointment of a person to make decisions on P's behalf in relation to the matter to which the application relates, details of who that person is.

(3) Where P is to be notified that an application form has been withdrawn, the person effecting notification must explain to P–
    (a) that the application form has been withdrawn; and
    (b) the consequences of that withdrawal.
(4) The person effecting notification must also inform P that he may seek advice and assistance in relation to any matter of which he is notified.

Appeals

43.—

(1) P must be notified—
    (a) that an appellant's notice has been issued by the court;
    (b) that an appellant's notice has been withdrawn; and
    (c) of the date on which a hearing is to be held in relation to the matter, where that hearing is for disposing of the appellant's notice.
(2) Where P is to be notified that an appellant's notice has been issued, the person effecting notification must explain to P—
    (a) who the appellant is;
    (b) the issues raised by the appeal; and
    (c) what will happen if the court makes the order or direction that has been applied for.
(3) Where P is to be notified that an appellant's notice has been withdrawn, the person effecting notification must explain to P—
    (a) that the appellant's notice has been withdrawn; and
    (b) the consequences of that withdrawal.
(4) The person effecting notification must also inform P that he may seek advice and assistance in relation to any matter of which he is notified.

Final orders

44.—

(1) P must be notified of a final order of the court.
(2) Where P is notified in accordance with this rule, the person effecting notification must explain to P the effect of the order.
(3) The person effecting notification must also inform P that he may seek advice and assistance in relation to any matter of which he is notified.

Other matters

45.—

(1) This rule applies where the court directs that P is to be notified of any other matter.
(2) The person effecting notification must explain to P such matters as may be directed by the court.
(3) The person effecting notification must also inform P that he may seek advice and assistance in relation to any matter of which he is notified.

Manner of notification, and accompanying documents

Manner of notification

46.—

(1) Where P is to be notified under this Part, the person effecting notification must provide P with the information specified in rules 42 to 45 in a way that is appropriate to P's circumstances (for example, using simple language, visual aids or any other appropriate means).

(2) The information referred to in paragraph (1) must be provided to P personally.

(3) P must be provided with the information mentioned in paragraph (1) as soon as practicable and in any event within 21 days of the date on which—

(a) the application form or appellant's notice was issued or withdrawn;

(b) the order was made; or

(c) the person effecting notification received the notice of hearing from the court and in any event no later than 14 days before the date specified in the notice of the hearing,

as the case may be.

Acknowledgment of notification

47. When P is notified that an application form or an appellant's notice has been issued, he must also be provided with a form for acknowledging notification.

Certificate of notification

48. The person effecting notification must, within 7 days beginning with the date on which notification in accordance with this Part was given, file a certificate of notification which certifies—

(a) the date on which P was notified; and

(b) that he was notified in accordance with this Part.

Dispensing with requirement to notify, etc

49.—

(1) The applicant, the appellant or other person directed by the court to effect notification may apply to the court seeking an order —

(a) dispensing with the requirement to comply with the provisions in this Part; or

(b) requiring some other person to comply with the provisions in this Part.

(2) An application under this rule must be made in accordance with Part 10.

PART 8
PERMISSION

General

50. Subject to these Rules and to section 50(1) of, and paragraph 20 of Schedule 3 to, the Act, the applicant must apply for permission to start proceedings under the Act. (Section 50(1) of the Act specifies persons who do not need to apply for permission. Paragraph 20 of Schedule 3 to the Act specifies an application for which permission is not needed.)

Where the court's permission is not required

51. The permission of the court is not required—

(1) where an application is made by–
  (a) the Official Solicitor; or
  (b) the Public Guardian;

(2) where the application concerns —
  (a) P's property and affairs, unless the application is of a kind specified in rule 52;
  (b) a lasting power of attorney which is, or purports to be, created under the Act; or
  (c) an instrument which is, or purports to be, an enduring power of attorney;

(3) where an application is made in accordance with Part 10; or

(4) where a person files an acknowledgment of service or notification in accordance with this Part or Part 9, for any order proposed that is different from that sought by the applicant.

Exceptions to rule 51(2)(a)

52.—

(1) For the purposes of rule 51(2)(a), the permission of the court is required to make any of the applications specified in this rule.

(2) An application for the exercise of the jurisdiction of the court under section 54(2) of the Trustee Act 1925[10], where the application is made by a person other than—
  (a) a person who has made an application for the appointment of a deputy;
  (b) a continuing trustee; or
  (c) any other person who, according to the practice of the Chancery Division, would have been entitled to make the application if it had been made in the High Court.

(3) An application under section 36(9) of the Trustee Act 1925 for leave to appoint a new trustee in place of P, where the application is made by a person other than—
  (a) a co-trustee; or
  (b) another person with the power to appoint a new trustee.

(4) An application seeking the exercise of the court's jurisdiction under section 18(1)(b) (where the application relates to making a gift of P's property), (h) or (i) of the Act, where the application is made by a person other than—
  (a) a person who has made an application for the appointment of a deputy;
  (b) a person who, under any known will of P or under his intestacy, may become entitled to any property of P or any interest in it;
  (c) a person who is an attorney appointed under an enduring power of attorney which has been registered in accordance with the Act or the regulations referred to in Schedule 4 to the Act;
  (d) a person who is a donee of a lasting power of attorney which has been registered in accordance with the Act; or
  (e) a person for whom P might be expected to provide if he had capacity to do so.

(5) An application under section 20 of the Trusts of Land and Appointment of Trustees Act 1996,[11] where the application is made by a person other than a beneficiary under the trust or, if there is more than one, by both or all of them.

---

[10] 1925 c. 19.
[11] 1996 c. 47.

Permission—supplementary

53.—

(1) The provisions of rule 52(2) apply with such modifications as may be necessary to an application under section 18(1)(j) of the Act for an order for the exercise of any power vested in P of appointing trustees or retiring from a trust.

(2) Where part of the application concerns a matter which requires permission, and part of it does not, permission need only be sought for that part of it which requires permission.

Application for permission

54. The applicant must apply for permission by filing a permission form and must file with it—

    (a) any information or documents specified in the relevant practice direction;

    (b) a draft of the application form which he seeks permission to have issued; and

    (c) an assessment of capacity form, where this is required by the relevant practice direction.

What the court will do when an application for permission to start proceedings is filed

55. Within 14 days of a permission form being filed, the court will issue it and—

    (a) grant the application in whole or in part, or subject to conditions, without a hearing and may give directions in connection with the issue of the application form;

    (b) refuse the application without a hearing; or

    (c) fix a date for the hearing of the application.

Persons to be notified of the hearing of an application for permission

56.—

(1) Where the court fixes a date for a hearing under rule 55(c), it will notify the applicant and such other persons as it thinks fit, and provide them with—

    (a) subject to paragraph (2), the documents mentioned in rule 54; and

    (b) a form for acknowledging notification.

(2) The court may direct that any document is to be provided on an edited basis.

Acknowledgment of notification of permission application

57.—

(1) Any person who is notified of an application for permission and who wishes to take part in the permission hearing must file an acknowledgment of notification in accordance with the following provisions of this rule.

(2) The acknowledgment of notification must be filed not more than 21 days after notice of the application was given.

(3) The court will serve the acknowledgment of notification on the applicant and on any other person who has filed such an acknowledgment.

(4) The acknowledgment of notification must—

    (a) state whether the person acknowledging notification consents to the application for permission;

    (b) state whether he opposes the application for permission, and if so, set out the grounds for doing so;

    (c) state whether he proposes that permission should be granted to make an application for a different order, and if so, set out what that order is;

    (d) provide an address for service, which must be within the jurisdiction of the court; and

    (e) be signed by him or his legal representative.

(5) The acknowledgment of notification may include or be accompanied by an application for directions.

(6) Subject to rules 120 and 123 (restrictions on filing an expert's report and court's power to restrict expert evidence), where a person opposes the application for permission or proposes that permission is granted for a different order, the acknowledgment of notification must be accompanied by a witness statement containing any evidence upon which that person intends to rely.

Failure to file acknowledgment of notification

58. Where a person notified of the application for permission has not filed an acknowledgment of notification in accordance with rule 57, he may not take part in a hearing to decide whether permission should be given unless the court permits him to do so.

Service of an order giving or refusing permission

59. The court will serve—

(a) the order granting or refusing permission;

(b) if refusing permission without a hearing, the reasons for its decision in summary form; and

(c) any directions,

on the applicant and on any other person notified of the application who filed an acknowledgment of notification.

Appeal against a permission decision following a hearing

60. Where the court grants or refuses permission following a hearing, any appeal against the permission decision shall be dealt with in accordance with Part 20 (appeals).

PART 9
HOW TO START PROCEEDINGS

Initial steps

General

61.—

(1) Applications to the court to start proceedings shall be made in accordance with this Part and, as applicable, Part 8 and the relevant practice directions.

(2) The appropriate forms must be used in the cases to which they apply, with such variations as the case requires, but not so as to omit any information or guidance which any form gives to the intended recipient.

(3) If permission to make an application is required, the court shall not issue the application form until permission is granted.

When proceedings are started

62.—

(1) The general rule is that proceedings are started when the court issues an application form at the request of the applicant.

(2) An application form is issued on the date entered on the application form by the court.

Contents of the application form

63. The application form must—
    (a) state the matter which the applicant wants the court to decide;
    (b) state the order which the applicant is seeking;
    (c) name—
        (i) the applicant;
        (ii) P;
        (iii) as a respondent, any person (other than P) whom the applicant reasonably believes to have an interest which means that he ought to be heard in relation to the application (as opposed to being notified of it in accordance with rule 70); and
        (iv) any person whom the applicant intends to notify in accordance with rule 70; and
    (d) if the applicant is applying in a representative capacity, state what that capacity is.

Documents to be filed with the application form

64. When an applicant files his application form with the court, he must also file—
    (a) in accordance with the relevant practice direction, any evidence upon which he intends to rely;
    (b) if permission was required to make the application, a copy of the court's order granting permission;
    (c) an assessment of capacity form, where this is required by the relevant practice direction;
    (d) any other documents referred to in the application form; and
    (e) such other information and material as may be set out in a practice direction.

What the court will do when an application form is filed

65. As soon as practicable after an application form is filed the court will issue the application form in any case where permission—
    (a) is not required; or
    (b) has been granted by the court; and
    do anything else that may be set out in a practice direction.

Steps following issue of application form

Applicant to serve the application form on named respondents

66.—

(1) As soon as practicable and in any event within 21 days of the date on which the application form was issued, the applicant must serve a copy of the application form on any person who is named as a respondent in the application form, together with copies of any documents filed in accordance with rule 64 and a form for acknowledging service.

(2) The applicant must file a certificate of service within 7 days beginning with the date on which the documents were served.

Applications relating to lasting powers of attorney

67.—

(1) Where the application concerns the powers of the court under section 22 or 23 of the Act (powers of the court in relation to the validity and operation of lasting powers of attorney) the

applicant must serve a copy of the application form, together with copies of any documents filed in accordance with rule 64 and a form for acknowledging service—

(a) unless the applicant is the donor or donee of the lasting power of attorney ('the power'), on the donor and every donee of the power;

(b) if he is the donor, on every donee of the power; and

(c) if he is a donee, on the donor and any other donee of the power,

but only if the above-mentioned persons have not been served or notified under any other rule.

(2) Where the application is solely in respect of an objection to the registration of a power, the requirements of rules 66 and 70 do not apply to an application made under this rule by—

(a) a donee of the power; or

(b) a person named in a statement made by the donor of the power in accordance with paragraph 2(1)(c)(i) of Schedule 1 to the Act.

(3) The applicant must comply with paragraph (1) as soon as practicable and in any event within 21 days of date on which the application form was issued.

(4) The applicant must file a certificate of service within 7 days beginning with the date on which the documents were served.

(5) Where the applicant knows or has reasonable grounds to believe that the donor of the power lacks capacity to make a decision in relation to any matter that is the subject of the application, he must notify the donor in accordance with Part 7.

Applications relating to enduring powers of attorney

68.—

(1) Where the application concerns the powers of the court under paragraphs 2(9), 4(5)(a) and (b), 7(2), 10(c), 13, or 16(2), (3), (4) and (6) of Schedule 4 to the Act, the applicant must serve a copy of the application form, together with copies of any documents filed in accordance with rule 64 and a form for acknowledging service—

(a) unless the applicant is the donor or attorney under the enduring power of attorney ('the power'), on the donor and every attorney of the power;

(b) if he is the donor, on every attorney under the power; or

(c) if he is an attorney, on the donor and any other attorney under the power,

but only if the above-mentioned persons have not been served or notified under any other rule.

(2) Where the application is solely in respect of an objection to the registration of a power, the requirements of rules 66 and 70 do not apply to an application made under this rule by—

(a) an attorney under the power; or

(b) a person listed in paragraph 6(1) of Schedule 4 to the Act.

(3) The applicant must comply with paragraph (1) as soon as practicable and in any event within 21 days of the date on which the application form was issued.

(4) The applicant must file a certificate of service within 7 days beginning with the date on which the documents were served.

(5) Where the applicant knows or has reasonable grounds to believe that the donor of the power lacks capacity to make a decision in relation to any matter that is the subject of the application, he must notify the donor in accordance with Part 7.

Applicant to notify P of an application

69. P must be notified in accordance with Part 7 that an application form has been issued, unless the requirement to do so has been dispensed with under rule 49.

Applicant to notify other persons of an application

70.—

(1) As soon as practicable and in any event within 21 days of the date on which the application form was issued, the applicant must notify the persons specified in the relevant practice direction—

    (a) that an application form has been issued;

    (b) whether it relates to the exercise of the court's jurisdiction in relation to P's property and affairs, or his personal welfare, or to both; and

    (c) of the order or orders sought.

(2) Notification of the issue of the application form must be accompanied by a form for acknowledging notification.

(3) The applicant must file a certificate of notification within 7 days beginning with the date on which notification was given.

Requirements for certain applications

71. A practice direction may make additional or different provision in relation to specified applications.

Responding to an application

Responding to an application

72.—

(1) A person who is served with or notified of an application form and who wishes to take part in proceedings must file an acknowledgment of service or notification in accordance with this rule.

(2) The acknowledgment of service or notification must be filed not more than 21 days after the application form was served or notification of the application was given.

(3) The court will serve the acknowledgment of service or notification on the applicant and on any other person who has filed such an acknowledgment.

(4) The acknowledgment of service or notification must—

    (a) state whether the person acknowledging service or notification consents to the application;

    (b) state whether he opposes the application and, if so, set out the grounds for doing so;

    (c) state whether he seeks a different order from that set out in the application form and, if so, set out what that order is;

    (d) provide an address for service, which must be within the jurisdiction of the court; and

    (e) be signed by him or his legal representative.

(5) Subject to rules 120 and 123 (restriction on filing an expert's report and court's power to restrict expert evidence), where a person who has been served in accordance with rule 66, 67 or 68 opposes the application or seeks a different order, the acknowledgment of service must be accompanied by a witness statement containing any evidence upon which that person intends to rely.

(6) In addition to complying with the other requirements of this rule, an acknowledgment of notification filed by a person notified of the application in accordance with rule 67(5), 68(5), 69 or 70 must—

    (a) indicate whether the person wishes to be joined as a party to the proceedings; and

    (b) state the person's interest in the proceedings.

(7) Subject to rules 120 and 123 (restriction on filing an expert's report and court's power to restrict expert evidence), where a person has been notified in accordance with rule 67(5), 68(5), 69, 70, the acknowledgment of notification must be accompanied by a witness statement containing any evidence of his interest in the proceedings and, if he opposes the application or seeks a different order, any evidence upon which he intends to rely.

(8) The court will consider whether to join a person mentioned in paragraph (6) as a party to the proceedings and, if it decides to do so, will make an order to that effect.

(9) Where a person who is notified in accordance with rule 67(5), 68(5), 69 or 70 complies with the requirements of this rule, he need not comply with the requirements of rule 75 (application to be joined as a party).

(10) Where a person has filed an acknowledgment of notification in accordance with rule 57 (acknowledgment of notification of permission application) he must still acknowledge service or notification of an issued application form in accordance with this rule.

(11) A practice direction may make provision about responding to applications.

The parties to the proceedings

Parties to the proceedings

73.—

(1) Unless the court otherwise directs, the parties to any proceedings are—
   (a) the applicant; and
   (b) any person who is named as a respondent in the application form and who files an acknowledgment of service in respect of the application form.

(2) The court may order a person to be joined as a party if it considers that it is desirable to do so for the purpose of dealing with the application.

(3) The court may at any time direct that any person who is a party to the proceedings is to be removed as a party.

(4) Unless the court orders otherwise, P shall not be named as a respondent to any proceedings.

(5) A party to the proceedings is bound by any order or direction of the court made in the course of those proceedings.

Persons to be bound as if parties

74.—

(1) The persons mentioned in paragraph (2) shall be bound by any order made or directions given by the court in the same way that a party to the proceedings is so bound.

(2) The persons referred to in paragraph (1) are—
   (a) P; and
   (b) any person who has been served with or notified of an application form in accordance with these Rules.

Application to be joined as a party

75.—

(1) Any person with sufficient interest may apply to the court to be joined as a party to the proceedings.

(2) An application to be joined as a party must be made by filing an application notice in accordance with Part 10 which must—

(a) state the full name and address of the person seeking to be joined as a party to the proceedings;

(b) state his interest in the proceedings;

(c) state whether he consents to the application;

(d) state whether he opposes the application and, if so, set out the grounds for doing so;

(e) state whether he proposes that an order different from that set out in the application form should be made and, if so, set out what that order is;

(f) provide an address for service, which must be within the jurisdiction of the court; and

(g) be signed by him or his legal representative.

(3) Subject to rules 120 and 123 (restriction on filing an expert's report and court's power to restrict expert evidence), an application to be joined must be accompanied by—

(a) a witness statement containing evidence of his interest in the proceedings and, if he proposes that an order different from that set out in the application form should be made, the evidence on which he intends to rely; and

(b) a sufficient number of copies of the application notice to enable service of the application on every other party to the proceedings.

(4) The court will serve the application notice and any accompanying documents on all parties to the proceedings.

(5) The court will consider whether to join a person applying under this rule as a party to the proceedings and, if it decides to do so, will make an order to that effect.

Applications for removal as a party to proceedings

76. A person who wishes to be removed as a party to the proceedings must apply to the court for an order to that effect in accordance with Part 10.

PART 10
APPLICATIONS WITHIN PROCEEDINGS

Types of applications for which the Part 10 procedure may be used

77.—

(1) The Part 10 procedure is the procedure set out in this Part.

(2) The Part 10 procedure may be used if the application is made by any person—

(a) in the course of existing proceedings; or

(b) as provided for in a rule or practice direction.

(3) The court may grant an interim remedy before an application form has been issued only if—

(a) the matter is urgent; or

(b) it is otherwise necessary to do so in the interests of justice.

(4) An application made during the course of existing proceedings includes an application made during appeal proceedings.

Application notice to be filed

78.—

(1) Subject to paragraph (5), the applicant must file an application notice to make an application under this Part.

(2) The applicant must, when he files the application notice, file the evidence upon which he relies (unless such evidence has already been filed).

(3) The court will issue the application notice and, if there is to be a hearing, give notice of the date on which the matter is to be heard by the court.

(4) Notice under paragraph (3) must be given to—

    (a) the applicant;

    (b) anyone who is named as a respondent in the application notice (if not otherwise a party to the proceedings);

    (c) every party to the proceedings; and

    (d) any other person, as the court may direct.

(5) An applicant may make an application under this Part without filing an application notice if—

    (a) this is permitted by any rule or practice direction; or

    (b) the court dispenses with the requirement for an application notice.

(6) If the applicant makes an application without giving notice, the evidence in support of the application must state why notice has not been given.

What an application notice must include

79. An application notice must state—

    (a) what order or direction the applicant is seeking;

    (b) briefly, the grounds on which the applicant is seeking the order or direction; and

    (c) such other information as may be required by any rule or a practice direction.

Service of an application notice

80.—

(1) Subject to paragraphs (4) and (5), the applicant must serve a copy of the application notice on—

    (a) anyone who is named as a respondent in the application notice (if not otherwise a party to the proceedings);

    (b) every party to the proceedings; and

    (c) any other person, as the court may direct,

as soon as practicable and in any event within 21 days of the date on which it was issued.

(2) The application notice must be accompanied by a copy of the evidence filed in support.

(3) The applicant must file a certificate of service within 7 days beginning with the date on which the documents were served.

(4) This rule does not require a copy of evidence to be served on a person upon whom it has already been served, but the applicant must in such a case give to that person notice of the evidence upon which he intends to rely.

(5) An application may be made without serving a copy of the application notice if this is permitted by—

    (a) a rule;

    (b) a practice direction; or

    (c) the court.

Applications without notice

81.—

(1) This rule applies where the court has dealt with an application which was made without notice having been given to any person.

(2) Where the court makes an order, whether granting or dismissing the application, the applicant must, as soon as practicable or within such period as the court may direct, serve the documents mentioned in paragraph (3) on—

    (a) anyone named as a respondent in the application notice (if not otherwise a party to the proceedings);

    (b) every party to the proceedings; and

    (c) any other person, as the court may direct.

(3) The documents referred to in paragraph (2) are—

    (a) a copy of the application notice;

    (b) the court's order; and

    (c) any evidence filed in support of the application.

(Rule 89 provides for reconsideration of orders made without a hearing or without notice to a person.)

Interim Remedies

Orders for interim remedies

82.—

(1) The court may grant the following interim remedies—

    (a) an interim injunction;

    (b) an interim declaration; or

    (c) any other interim order it considers appropriate.

(2) Unless the court orders otherwise, a person on whom an application form is served under Part 9, or who is given notice of such an application, may not apply for an interim remedy before he has filed an acknowledgment of service or notification in accordance with Part 9.

(3) This rule does not limit any other power of the court to grant interim relief.

PART 11
HUMAN RIGHTS

General

83.—

(1) A party who seeks to rely upon any provision of or right arising under the Human Rights Act 1998 ('the 1998 Act')[12] or who seeks a remedy available under that Act must inform the court in the manner set out in the relevant practice direction specifying—

    (a) the Convention right (within the meaning of the 1998 Act) which it is alleged has been infringed and details of the alleged infringement; and

    (b) the remedy sought and whether this includes a declaration of incompatibility under section 4 of the 1998 Act.

(2) The court may not make a declaration of incompatibility unless 21 days' notice, or such other period of notice as the court directs, has been given to the Crown.

---

[12] 1998 c. 42.

(3) Where notice has been given to the Crown, a Minister or other person permitted by the 1998 Act will be joined as a party on filing an application in accordance with rule 75 (application to be joined as a party).

PART 12
DEALING WITH APPLICATIONS

Dealing with the application

84.—

(1) As soon as practicable after any application has been issued the court shall consider how to deal with it.

(2) The court may deal with an application or any part of an application at a hearing or without a hearing.

(3) In considering whether it is necessary to hold a hearing, the court shall, as appropriate, have regard to—

(a) the nature of the proceedings and the orders sought;

(b) whether the application is opposed by a person who appears to the court to have an interest in matters relating to P's best interests;

(c) whether the application involves a substantial dispute of fact;

(d) the complexity of the facts and the law;

(e) any wider public interest in the proceedings;

(f) the circumstances of P and of any party, in particular as to whether their rights would be adequately protected if a hearing were not held;

(g) whether the parties agree that the court should dispose of the application without a hearing; and

(h) any other matter specified in the relevant practice direction.

(4) Where the court considers that a hearing is necessary, it will—

(a) give notice of the hearing date to the parties and to any other person it directs; and

(b) state whether the hearing is for disposing of the matter or for directions.

(5) Where the court decides that it can deal with the matter without a hearing it will do so and serve a copy of its order on the parties and on any other person it directs.

Directions

85.—

(1) The court may—

(a) give directions in writing; or

(b) set a date for a directions hearing; and

(c) do anything else that may be set out in a practice direction.

(2) When giving directions, the court may do any of the following—

(a) require a report under section 49 of the Act and give directions as to any such report;

(b) give directions as to any requirements contained in these Rules or a practice direction for the giving of notification to any person or for that person to do anything in response to a notification;

(c) if the court considers that P should be a party to the proceedings, give directions joining him as a party;

(d) if P is joined as a party to proceedings, give directions as to the appointment of a litigation friend;

(e) if the court considers that any other person or persons should be a party to the proceedings, give directions joining them as a party;

(f) if the court considers that any party to the proceedings should not be a party, give directions for that person's removal as a party;

(g) give directions for the management of the case and set a timetable for the steps to be taken between the giving of directions and the hearing;

(h) subject to rule 86, give directions as to the type of judge who is to hear the case;

(i) give directions as to whether the proceedings or any part of them are to be heard in public, or as to whether any particular person should be permitted to attend the hearing, or as to whether any publication of the proceedings is to be permitted;

(j) give directions as to the disclosure of documents, service of witness statements and any expert evidence;

(k) give directions as to the attendance of witnesses and as to whether, and the extent to which, cross-examination will be permitted at any hearing; and

(l) give such other directions as the court thinks fit.

(3) The court may give directions at any time—

    (a) on its own initiative; or

    (b) on the application of a party.

(4) Subject to paragraphs (5) and (6) and unless these Rules or a practice direction provide otherwise or the court directs otherwise, the time specified by a rule or by the court for a person to do any act may be varied by the written agreement of the parties.

(5) A party must apply to the court if he wishes to vary –

    (a) the date the court has fixed for the final hearing; or

    (b) the period within which the final hearing is to take place.

(6) The time specified by a rule or practice direction or by the court may not be varied by the parties if the variation would make it necessary to vary the date the court has fixed for any hearing or the period within which the final hearing is to take place.

Allocation of proceedings

Court's jurisdiction in certain kinds of case to be exercised by certain judges

86.—

(1) The court will consider whether the application is of a type specified in the relevant practice direction as being one which must be dealt with by—

    (a) the President;

    (b) the Vice-President; or

    (c) one of the other judges nominated by virtue of section 46(2)(a) to (c) of the Act.

(2) The practice direction made under this rule shall specify the categories of case which must be dealt with by a judge mentioned in paragraph (1).

(3) Applications in any matter other than those specified in the relevant practice direction may be dealt with by any judge.

Disputing the jurisdiction of the court

Procedure for disputing the court's jurisdiction

87.—(1) A person who wishes to—

(a) dispute the court's jurisdiction to hear an application; or

(b) argue that the court should not exercise its jurisdiction,

may apply to the court at any time for an order declaring that it has no such jurisdiction or should not exercise any jurisdiction that it may have.

(2) An application under this rule must be—

(a) made by using the form specified in the relevant practice direction; and

(b) supported by evidence.

(3) An order containing a declaration that the court has no jurisdiction or will not exercise its jurisdiction may also make further provision, including—

(a) setting aside the application;

(b) discharging any order made; and

(c) staying the proceedings.

Participation in hearings

Participation in hearings

88.—

(1) The court may hear P on the question of whether or not an order should be made, whether or not he is a party to the proceedings.

(2) The court may proceed with a hearing in the absence of P if it considers that it would be appropriate to do so.

(3) A person other than P who is served with or notified of the application may only take part in a hearing if—

(a) he files an acknowledgment in accordance with the Rules and is made a party to the proceedings; or

(b) the court permits.

Reconsideration of court orders

Orders made without a hearing or without notice to any person

89.—

(1) This rule applies where the court makes an order—

(a) without a hearing; or

(b) without notice to any person who is affected by it.

(2) Where this rule applies—

(a) P;

(b) any party to the proceedings; or

(c) any other person affected by the order,

may apply to the court for reconsideration of the order made.

(3) An application under paragraph (2) must be made—

(a) within 21 days of the order being served or such other period as the court may direct; and

(b) in accordance with Part 10.

(4) The court will—
  (a) reconsider the order without directing a hearing; or
  (b) fix a date for the matter to be heard, and notify all parties to the proceedings and such other persons as the court may direct, of that date.

(5) Where an application is made in accordance with this rule, the court may affirm, set aside or vary any order made.

(6) Reconsideration may be by any judge of the court—
  (a) including the judge who made the decision in respect of which the reconsideration is sought; but
  (b) may not be by a judge who is not a prescribed higher judge within the meaning of section 53(3) of the Act in relation to the first-mentioned judge.

(7) No application may be made seeking a reconsideration of a decision that has been made under paragraph (5).

(8) An appeal against a decision made under paragraph (5) may be made in accordance with Part 20 (appeals).

(9) Any order made without a hearing or without notice to any person, other than one made under paragraph (5), must contain a statement of the right to apply for a reconsideration of the decision in accordance with this rule.

(10) An application made under this rule may include a request that the court reconsider the matter at a hearing.

PART 13
HEARINGS

Private hearings

General rule – hearing to be in private

90.—

(1) The general rule is that a hearing is to be held in private.

(2) A private hearing is a hearing which only the following persons are entitled to attend—
  (a) the parties;
  (b) P (whether or not a party);
  (c) any person acting in the proceedings as a litigation friend;
  (d) any legal representative of a person specified in any of sub-paragraphs (a) to (c); and
  (e) any court officer.

(3) In relation to a private hearing, the court may make an order—
  (a) authorising any person, or class of persons, to attend the hearing or a part of it; or
  (b) excluding any person, or class of persons, from attending the hearing or a part of it.

Court's general power to authorise publication of information about proceedings

91.—

(1) For the purposes of the law relating to contempt of court, information relating to proceedings held in private may be published where the court makes an order under paragraph (2).

(2) The court may make an order authorising—
  (a) the publication of such information relating to the proceedings as it may specify; or

    (b) the publication of the text or a summary of the whole or part of a judgment or order made by the court.

(3) Where the court makes an order under paragraph (2) it may do so on such terms as it thinks fit, and in particular may—

    (a) impose restrictions on the publication of the identity of—

        (i) any party;

        (ii) P (whether or not a party);

        (iii) any witness; or

        (iv) any other person;

    (b) prohibit the publication of any information that may lead to any such person being identified;

    (c) prohibit the further publication of any information relating to the proceedings from such date as the court may specify; or

    (d) impose such other restrictions on the publication of information relating to the proceedings as the court may specify.

Power to order a public hearing

Court's power to order that a hearing be held in public

92.—

(1) The court may make an order—

    (a) for a hearing to be held in public;

    (b) for a part of a hearing to be held in public; or

    (c) excluding any person, or class of persons, from attending a public hearing or a part of it.

(2) Where the court makes an order under paragraph (1), it may in the same order or by a subsequent order—

    (a) impose restrictions on the publication of the identity of—

        (i) any party;

        (ii) P (whether or not a party);

        (iii) any witness; or

        (iv) any other person;

    (b) prohibit the publication of any information that may lead to any such person being identified;

    (c) prohibit the further publication of any information relating to the proceedings from such date as the court may specify; or

    (d) impose such other restrictions on the publication of information relating to the proceedings as the court may specify.

Supplementary

Supplementary provisions relating to public or private hearings

93.—

(1) An order under rule 90, 91 or 92 may be made—

    (a) only where it appears to the court that there is good reason for making the order;

    (b) at any time; and

    (c) either on the court's own initiative or on an application made by any person in accordance with Part 10.

(2) A practice direction may make further provision in connection with—

    (a) private hearings;

    (b) public hearings; or

    (c) the publication of information about any proceedings.

PART 14
ADMISSIONS, EVIDENCE AND DEPOSITIONS

Admissions

Making an admission

94.—

(1) Without prejudice to the ability to make an admission in any other way, a party may admit the truth of the whole or part of another party's case by giving notice in writing.

(2) The court may allow a party to amend or withdraw an admission.

Evidence

Power of court to control evidence

95. The court may—

(a) control the evidence by giving directions as to—

    (i) the issues on which it requires evidence;

    (ii) the nature of the evidence which it requires to decide those issues; and

    (iii) the way in which the evidence is to be placed before the court;

(b) use its power under this rule to exclude evidence that would otherwise be admissible;

(c) allow or limit cross-examination; and

(d) admit such evidence, whether written or oral, as it thinks fit.

Evidence of witnesses—general rule

96.—

(1) The general rule is that any fact which needs to be proved by evidence of a witness is to be proved—

    (a) where there is a final hearing, by their oral evidence; or

    (b) at any other hearing, or if there is no hearing, by their evidence in writing.

(2) Where a witness is called to give oral evidence under paragraph (1)(a), his witness statement shall stand as his evidence in chief unless the court directs otherwise.

(3) A witness giving oral evidence at the final hearing may, if the court permits—

    (a) amplify his witness statement; and

    (b) give evidence in relation to new matters which have arisen since the witness statement was made.

(4) The court may so permit only if it considers that there is good reason not to confine the evidence of the witness to the contents of his witness statement.

(5) This rule is subject to—

    (a) any provision to the contrary in these Rules or elsewhere; or

    (b) any order or direction of the court.

Written evidence—general rule

97. A party may not rely upon written evidence unless—

  (a) it has been filed in accordance with these Rules or a practice direction;
  (b) it is expressly permitted by these Rules or a practice direction; or
  (c) the court gives permission.

Evidence by video link or other means

98. The court may allow a witness to give evidence through a video link or by other communication technology.

Service of witness statements for use at final hearing

99.—

  (1) A witness statement is a written statement which contains the evidence which that person would be allowed to give orally.
  (2) The court will give directions about the service of any witness statement that a party intends to rely upon at the final hearing.
  (3) The court may give directions as to the order in which witness statements are to be served. (Rules 11 and 100 require witness statements to be verified by a statement of truth.)

Form of witness statement

100. A witness statement must contain a statement of truth and comply with the requirements set out in the relevant practice direction.

Witness summaries

101.—

  (1) A party who wishes to file a witness statement for use at final hearing, but is unable to do so, may apply, without notice, to be permitted to file a witness summary instead.
  (2) A witness summary is a summary of—
    (a) the evidence, if known, which would otherwise be included in a witness statement; or
    (b) if the evidence is not known, the matters about which the party filing the witness summary proposes to question the witness.
  (3) Unless the court directs otherwise, a witness summary must include the name and address of the intended witness.
  (4) Unless the court directs otherwise, a witness summary must be filed within the period in which a witness statement would have had to be filed.
  (5) Where a party files a witness summary, so far as practicable, rules 96(3)(a) (amplifying witness statements) and 99 (service of witness statements for use at a final hearing) shall apply to the summary.

Affidavit evidence

102. Evidence must be given by affidavit instead of or in addition to a witness statement if this is required by the court, a provision contained in any rule, a practice direction or any other enactment.

Form of affidavit

103. An affidavit must comply with the requirements set out in the relevant practice direction.

Affidavit made outside the jurisdiction

104. A person may make an affidavit outside the jurisdiction in accordance with—
    (a) this Part; or
    (b) the law of the place where he makes the affidavit.

Notarial acts and instruments

105. A notarial act or instrument may, without further proof, be received in evidence as duly authenticated in accordance with the requirements of law unless the contrary is proved.

Summoning of witnesses

106.—

(1) The court may allow or direct any party to issue a witness summons requiring the person named in it to attend before the court and give oral evidence or produce any document to the court.

(2) An application by a party for the issue of a witness summons may be made by filing an application notice which includes—
    (a) the name and address of the applicant and of his solicitor, if any;
    (b) the name, address and occupation of the proposed witness;
    (c) particulars of any document which the proposed witness is to be required to produce; and
    (d) the grounds on which the application is made.

(3) The general rule is that a witness summons is binding if it is served at least 7 days before the date on which the witness is required to attend before the court, and the requirements of paragraph (6) have been complied with.

(4) The court may direct that a witness summons shall be binding although it will be served less than 7 days before the date on which the witness is required to attend before the court.

(5) Unless the court directs otherwise, a witness summons is to be served by the person making the application.

(6) At the time of service the witness must be offered or paid—
    (a) a sum reasonably sufficient to cover his expenses in travelling to and from the court; and
    (b) such sum by way of compensation for loss of time as may be specified in the relevant practice direction.

(7) The court may order that the witness is to be paid such general costs as it considers appropriate.

Power of court to direct a party to provide information

107.—

(1) Where a party has access to information which is not reasonably available to the other party, the court may direct that party to prepare and file a document recording the information.

(2) The court will give directions about serving a copy of that document on the other parties.

Depositions

Evidence by deposition

108.—

(1) A party may apply for an order for a person to be examined before the hearing takes place.

(2) A person from whom evidence is to be obtained following an order under this rule is referred to as a 'deponent' and the evidence is referred to as a 'deposition'.

(3) An order under this rule shall be for a deponent to be examined on oath before—

(a) a circuit judge or a district judge, whether or not nominated as a judge of the court;

(b) an examiner of the court; or

(c) such other person as the court appoints.

(4) The order may require the production of any document which the court considers is necessary for the purposes of the examination.

(5) The order will state the date, time and place of the examination.

(6) At the time of service of the order, the deponent must be offered or paid—

(a) a sum reasonably sufficient to cover his expenses in travelling to and from the place of examination; and

(b) such sum by way of compensation for loss of time as may be specified in the relevant practice direction.

(7) Where the court makes an order for a deposition to be taken, it may also order the party who obtained the order to file a witness statement or witness summary in relation to the evidence to be given by the person to be examined.

Conduct of examination

109.—

(1) Subject to any directions contained in the order for examination, the examination must be conducted in the same way as if the witness were giving evidence at a final hearing.

(2) If all the parties are present, the examiner may conduct the examination of a person not named in the order for examination if all the parties and the person to be examined consent.

(3) The examiner must ensure that the evidence given by the witness is recorded in full.

(4) The examiner must send a copy of the deposition—

(a) to the person who obtained the order for the examination of the witness; and

(b) to the court.

(5) The court will give directions as to the service of a copy of the deposition on the other parties.

Fees and expenses of examiners of the court

110.—

(1) An examiner of the court may charge a fee for the examination and he need not send the deposition to the court until the fee is paid, unless the court directs otherwise.

(2) The examiner's fees and expenses must be paid by the party who obtained the order for examination.

(3) If the fees and expenses due to an examiner are not paid within a reasonable time, he may report that fact to the court.

(4) The court may order the party who obtained the order for examination to deposit in the court office a specified sum in respect of the examiner's fees and, where it does so, the examiner will not be asked to act until the sum has been deposited.

(5) An order under this rule does not affect any decision as to the person who is ultimately to bear the costs of the examination.

Examiners of the court

111.—

(1) The Lord Chancellor shall appoint persons to be examiners of the court.

(2) The persons appointed shall be barristers or solicitor-advocates who have been practising for a period of not less than 3 years.

(3) The Lord Chancellor may revoke an appointment at any time.

(4) In addition to appointing persons in accordance with this rule, examiners appointed under rule 34.15 of the Civil Procedure Rules 1998 may act as examiners in the court.

Enforcing attendance of a witness

112.—

(1) If a person served with an order to attend before an examiner—

    (a) fails to attend; or

    (b) refuses to be sworn for the purpose of the examination or to answer any lawful question or produce any document at the examination,

a certificate of his failure or refusal, signed by the examiner, must be filed by the party requiring the deposition.

(2) On the certificate being filed, the party requiring the deposition may apply to the court for an order requiring that person to attend or to be sworn or to answer any question or produce any document, as the case may be.

(3) An application for an order under this rule may be made without notice.

(4) The court may order the person against whom an order is sought or made under this rule to pay any costs resulting from his failure or refusal.

Use of deposition at a hearing

113.—

(1) A deposition ordered under rule 108, 115 or 116 may be put in evidence at a hearing unless the court orders otherwise.

(2) A party intending to put a deposition in evidence at a hearing must file notice of his intention to do so on the court and serve the notice on every other party.

(3) Unless the court directs otherwise, he must file the notice at least 14 days before the day fixed for the hearing.

(4) The court may require a deponent to attend the hearing and give evidence orally.

Taking evidence outside the jurisdiction

Interpretation

114. In this Section—

    (a) 'Regulation State' has the same meaning as 'Member State' in the Taking of Evidence Regulation, that is all Member States except Denmark; and

    (b) 'the Taking of Evidence Regulation' means Council Regulation (EC) No. 1206/2001 of 28 May 2001 on co-operation between the courts of Member States in the taking of evidence in civil and commercial matters.

Where a person to be examined is in another Regulation State

115.—

(1) This rule applies where a party wishes to take a deposition from a person who is—

    (a) outside the jurisdiction; and

    (b) in a Regulation State.

(2) The court may order the issue of the request to a designated court ('the requested court') in the Regulation State in which the proposed deponent is.

(3) If the court makes an order for the issue of a request, the party who sought the order must file—

    (a) a draft Form A as set out in the annex to the Taking of Evidence Regulation (request for the taking of evidence);

    (b) except where paragraph (4) applies, a translation of the form;

    (c) an undertaking to be responsible for the costs sought by the requested court in relation to—

        (i) fees paid to experts and interpreters; and

        (ii) where requested by that party, the use of special procedure or communications technology; and

    (d) an undertaking to be responsible for the court's expenses.

(4) There is no need to file a translation if—

    (a) English is one of the official languages of the Regulation State where the examination is to take place; or

    (b) the Regulation State has indicated, in accordance with the Taking of Evidence Regulation, that English is a language which it will accept.

(5) Where article 17 of the Taking of Evidence Regulation (direct taking of evidence by the requested court) allows evidence to be taken directly in another Regulation State, the court may make an order for the submission of a request in accordance with that article.

(6) If the court makes an order for the submission of a request under paragraph (5), the party who sought the order must file—

    (a) draft Form I as set out in the annex to the Taking of Evidence Regulation (request for direct taking of evidence);

    (b) except where paragraph (4) applies, a translation of the form; and

    (c) an undertaking to be responsible for the requested court's expenses.

Where a person to be examined is out of the jurisdiction – letter of request

116.—

(1) This rule applies where a party wishes to take a deposition from a person who is—

    (a) out of the jurisdiction; and

    (b) not in a Regulation State within the meaning of rule 114.

(2) The court may order the issue of a letter of request to the judicial authorities of the country in which the proposed deponent is.

(3) A letter of request is a request to a judicial authority to take the evidence of that person, or arrange for it to be taken.

(4) If the government of a country permits a person appointed by the court to examine a person in that country, the court may make an order appointing a special examiner for that purpose.

(5) A person may be examined under this rule on oath or affirmation in accordance with any procedure permitted in the country in which the examination is to take place.

(6) If the court makes an order for the issue of a letter of request, the party who sought the order must file—

    (a) the following documents and, except where paragraph (7) applies, a translation of them—

        (i) a draft letter of request;

        (ii) a statement of the issues relevant to the proceedings; and

        (iii) a list of questions or the subject matter of questions to be put to the person to be examined; and

    (b) an undertaking to be responsible for the Secretary of State's expenses.

(7) There is no need to file a translation if—

    (a) English is one of the official languages of the country where the examination is to take place; or

    (b) a practice direction has specified that country is a country where no translation is necessary.

Section 49 reports

Reports under section 49 of the Act

117.—

(1) This rule applies where the court requires a report to be made to it under section 49 of the Act.

(2) It is the duty of the person who is required to make the report to help the court on the matters within his expertise.

(3) Unless the court directs otherwise, the person making the report must—

    (a) contact or seek to interview such persons as he thinks appropriate or as the court directs;

    (b) to the extent that it is practicable and appropriate to do so, ascertain what P's wishes and feelings are, and the beliefs and values that would be likely to influence P if he had the capacity to make a decision in relation to the matter to which the application relates;

    (c) describe P's circumstances; and

    (d) address such other matters as are required in a practice direction or as the court may direct.

(4) The court will send a copy of the report to the parties and to such persons as the court may direct.

(5) Subject to paragraphs (6) and (7), the person who is required to make the report may examine and take copies of any document in the court records.

(6) The court may direct that the right to inspect documents under this rule does not apply in relation to such documents, or descriptions of documents, as the court may specify.

(7) The court may direct that any information is to be provided to the maker of the report on an edited basis.

Written questions to person making a report under section 49

118.—

(1) Where a report is made under section 49 the court may, on the application of any party, permit written questions relevant to the issues before the court to be put to the person by whom the report was made.

(2) The questions sought to be put to the maker of the report shall be submitted to the court, and the court may put them to the maker of the report with such amendments (if any) as it thinks fit and the maker of the report shall give his replies in writing to the questions so put.

(3) The court will send a copy of the replies given by the maker of the report under this rule to the parties and to such other persons as the court may direct.

PART 15
EXPERTS

References to expert

119. A reference to an expert in this Part—

    (a) is to an expert who has been instructed to give or prepare evidence for the purpose of court proceedings; but

    (b) does not include any person instructed to make a report under section 49 of the Act.

Restriction on filing an expert's report

120.—

(1) No person may file expert evidence unless the court or a practice direction permits, or if it is filed with the permission form or application form and is evidence—

    (a) that P is a person who lacks capacity to make a decision or decisions in relation to the matter or matters to which the application relates;

    (b) as to P's best interests; or

    (c) that is required by any rule or practice direction to be filed with the permission form or application form.

(2) An applicant may only rely upon any expert evidence so filed in support of the permission form or application form to the extent and for the purposes that the court allows.

(Rule 64(a) requires the applicant to file any evidence upon which he wishes to rely with the application form and rule 54 requires certain documents to be filed with the application for permission form.)

Duty to restrict expert evidence

121. Expert evidence shall be restricted to that which is reasonably required to resolve the proceedings.

Experts – overriding duty to the court

122. It is the duty of the expert to help the court on the matters within his expertise.

Court's power to restrict expert evidence

123.—

(1) Subject to rule 120, no party may file or adduce expert evidence unless the court or a practice direction permits.

(2) When a party applies for a direction under this rule he must—

    (a) identify the field in respect of which he wishes to rely upon expert evidence;

    (b) where practicable, identify the expert in that field upon whose evidence he wishes to rely;

(c) provide any other material information about the expert; and

(d) provide a draft letter of instruction to the expert.

(3) Where a direction is given under this rule, the court shall specify the field or fields in respect of which the expert evidence is to be provided.

(4) The court may specify the person who is to provide the evidence referred to in paragraph (3).

(5) Where a direction is given under this rule for a party to call an expert or put in evidence an expert's report, the court shall give directions for the service of the report on the parties and on such other persons as the court may direct.

(6) The court may limit the amount of the expert's fees and expenses that the party who wishes to rely upon the expert may recover from any other party.

General requirement for expert evidence to be given in a written report

124. Expert evidence is to be given in a written report unless the court directs otherwise.

Written questions to experts

125.—

(1) A party may put written questions to—

    (a) an expert instructed by another party; or

    (b) a single joint expert appointed under rule 130,

about a report prepared by such person.

(2) Written questions under paragraph (1)—

    (a) may be put once only;

    (b) must be put within 28 days beginning with the date on which the expert's report was served; and

    (c) must be for the purpose only of clarification of the report.

(3) Paragraph (2) does not apply in any case where—

    (a) the court permits it to be done on a further occasion;

    (b) the other party or parties agree; or

    (c) any practice direction provides otherwise.

(4) An expert's answers to questions put in accordance with paragraph (1) shall be treated as part of the expert's report.

(5) Paragraph (6) applies where—

    (a) a party has put a written question to an expert instructed by another party in accordance with this rule; and

    (b) the expert does not answer that question.

(6) The court may make one or both of the following orders in relation to the party who instructed the expert—

    (a) that the party may not rely upon the evidence of that expert; or

    (b) that the party may not recover the fees and expenses of that expert, or part of them, from any other party.

(7) Unless the court otherwise directs, and subject to any final costs order that may be made, the instructing party is responsible for the payment of the expert's fees and expenses, including the expert's costs of answering questions put by any other party.

Contents of expert's report

126.—

(1) The court may give directions as to the matters to be covered in an expert's report.

(2) An expert's report must comply with the requirements set out in the relevant practice direction.

(3) At the end of an expert's report there must be a statement that—

   (a) the expert understands his duty to the court; and

   (b) he has complied with that duty.

(4) The expert's report must state the substance of all material instructions, whether written or oral, on the basis of which the report was written.

(5) The instructions to the expert shall not be privileged against disclosure.

Use by one party of expert's report disclosed by another

127. Where a party has disclosed an expert's report, any party may use that expert's report as evidence at any hearing in the proceedings.

Discussions between experts

128.—

(1) The court may, at any stage, direct a discussion between experts for the purpose of requiring the experts to—

   (a) identify and discuss the expert issues in the proceedings; and

   (b) where possible, reach an agreed opinion on those issues.

(2) The court may specify the issues which the experts must discuss.

(3) The court may direct that following a discussion between the experts they must prepare a statement for the court showing—

   (a) those issues on which they agree; and

   (b) those issues on which they disagree and a summary of their reasons for disagreeing.

(4) Unless the court otherwise directs, the content of the discussions between experts may be referred to at any hearing or at any stage in the proceedings.

Expert's right to ask court for directions

129.—

(1) An expert may file a written request for directions to assist him in carrying out his function as an expert.

(2) An expert must, unless the court directs otherwise, provide a copy of any proposed request for directions under paragraph (1)—

   (a) to the party instructing him, at least 7 days before he files the request; and

   (b) to all other parties, at least 4 days before he files it.

(3) The court, when it gives directions, may also direct that a party be served with a copy of the directions.

Court's power to direct that evidence is to be given by a single joint expert

130.—

(1) Where two or more parties wish to submit expert evidence on a particular issue, the court may direct that the evidence on that issue is to be given by one expert only.

(2) The parties wishing to submit the expert evidence are called 'the instructing parties'.

(3) Where the instructing parties cannot agree who should be the expert, the court may—

   (a) select the expert from a list prepared or identified by the instructing parties; or

   (b) direct the manner by which the expert is to be selected.

Instructions to a single joint expert

131.—

(1) Where the court gives a direction under rule 130 for a single joint expert to be used, each party may give instructions to the expert.

(2) Unless the court otherwise directs, when an instructing party gives instructions to the expert he must, at the same time, send a copy of the instructions to the other instructing parties.

(3) The court may give directions about—

(a) the payment of the expert's fees and expenses; and

(b) any inspection, examination or experiments which the expert wishes to carry out.

(4) The court may, before an expert is instructed, limit the amount that can be paid by way of fees and expenses to the expert.

(5) Unless the court otherwise directs, and subject to any final costs order that may be made, the instructing parties are jointly and severally liable for the payment of the expert's fees and expenses.

PART 16
DISCLOSURE

Meaning of disclosure

132. A party discloses a document by stating that the document exists or has existed.

General or specific disclosure

133.—

(1) The court may either on its own initiative or on the application of a party make an order to give general or specific disclosure.

(2) General disclosure requires a party to disclose—

(a) the documents on which he relies; and

(b) the documents which—

(i) adversely affect his own case;

(ii) adversely affect another party's case; or

(iii) support another party's case.

(3) An order for specific disclosure is an order that a party must do one or more of the following things—

(a) disclose documents or classes of documents specified in the order;

(b) carry out a search to the extent stated in the order; or

(c) disclose any document located as a result of that search.

(4) A party's duty to disclose documents is limited to documents which are or have been in his control.

(5) For the purpose of paragraph (4) a party has or has had a document in his control if—

(a) it is or was in his physical possession;

(b) he has or has had possession of it; or

(c) he has or has had a right to inspect or take copies of it.

Procedure for general or specific disclosure

134.—

(1) This rule applies where the court makes an order under rule 133 to give general or specific disclosure.

(2) Each party must make, and serve on every other party, a list of documents to be disclosed.

(3) A copy of each list must be filed within 7 days of the date on which it is served.

(4) The list must identify the documents in a convenient order and manner and as concisely as possible.

(5) The list must indicate—

    (a) the documents in respect of which the party claims a right or duty to withhold inspection (see rule 138); and

    (b) the documents that are no longer in his control, stating what has happened to them.

Ongoing duty of disclosure

135.—

(1) Where the court makes an order to give general or specific disclosure under rule 133, any party to whom the order applies is under a continuing duty to provide such disclosure as is required by the order until the proceedings are concluded.

(2) If a document to which the duty of disclosure imposed by paragraph (1) extends comes to a party's notice at any time during the proceedings, he must immediately notify every other party.

Right to inspect documents

136.—

(1) A party to whom a document has been disclosed has a right to inspect any document disclosed to him except where—

    (a) the document is no longer in the control of the party who disclosed it; or

    (b) the party disclosing the document has a right or duty to withhold inspection of it.

(2) The right to inspect disclosed documents extends to any document mentioned in—

    (a) a document filed or served in the course of the proceedings by any other party; or

    (b) correspondence sent by any other party.

Inspection and copying of documents

137.—

(1) Where a party has a right to inspect a document, he—

    (a) must give the party who disclosed the document written notice of his wish to inspect it; and

    (b) may request a copy of the document.

(2) Not more than 14 days after the date on which the party who disclosed the document received the notice under paragraph (1)(a), he must permit inspection of the document at a convenient place and time.

(3) Where a party has requested a copy of the document, the party who disclosed the document must supply him with a copy not more than 14 days after the date on which he received the request.

(4) For the purposes of paragraph (2), the party who disclosed the document must give reasonable notice of the time and place for inspection.

(5) For the purposes of paragraph (3), the party requesting a copy of the document is responsible for the payment of reasonable copying costs, subject to any final costs order that may be made.

Claim to withhold inspection or disclosure of document

138.—

(1) A party who wishes to claim that he has a right or duty to withhold inspection of a document, or part of a document, must state in writing—

  (a) that he has such a right or duty; and

  (b) the grounds on which he claims that right or duty.

(2) The statement must be made in the list in which the document is disclosed (see rule 134(2)).

(3) A party may, by filing an application notice in accordance with Part 10, apply to the court to decide whether the claim made under paragraph (1) should be upheld.

Consequence of failure to disclose documents or permit inspection

139. A party may not rely upon any document which he fails to disclose or in respect of which he fails to permit inspection unless the court permits.

PART 17
LITIGATION FRIEND

Who may act as a litigation friend

140.—

(1) A person may act as a litigation friend on behalf of a person mentioned in paragraph (2) if he—

  (a) can fairly and competently conduct proceedings on behalf of that person; and

  (b) has no interests adverse to those of that person.

(2) The persons for whom a litigation friend may act are—

  (a) P;

  (b) a child; or

  (c) a protected party.

Requirement for a litigation friend

141.—

(1) Subject to rule 147, P (if a party to proceedings) must have a litigation friend.

(2) A protected party (if a party to the proceedings) must have a litigation friend.

(3) A child (if a party to proceedings) must have a litigation friend to conduct those proceedings on his behalf unless the court makes an order under paragraph (4).

(4) The court may make an order permitting the child to conduct proceedings without a litigation friend.

(5) An application for an order under paragraph (4)—

  (a) may be made by the child;

  (b) if the child already has a litigation friend, must be made on notice to the litigation friend; and

  (c) if the child has no litigation friend, may be made without notice.

(6) Where—
    (a) the court has made an order under paragraph (4); and
    (b) it subsequently appears to the court that it is desirable for a litigation friend to conduct the proceedings on behalf of the child,
the court may appoint a person to be the child's litigation friend.

Litigation friend without a court order

142.—
(1) This rule does not apply—
    (a) in relation to P;
    (b) where the court has appointed a person under rule 143 or 144; or
    (c) where the Official Solicitor is to act as litigation friend.
(2) A deputy with the power to conduct legal proceedings in the name of the protected party or on the protected party's behalf is entitled to be a litigation friend of the protected party in any proceedings to which his power relates.
(3) If no one has been appointed by the court, or in the case of a protected party, there is no deputy with the power to conduct proceedings, a person who wishes to act as a litigation friend must—
    (a) file a certificate of suitability stating that he satisfies the conditions specified in rule 140(1); and
    (b) serve the certificate of suitability on—
        (i) the person on whom an application form is to be served in accordance with rule 32 (service on children and protected parties); and
        (ii) every other person who is a party to the proceedings.
(4) If the person referred to in paragraph (2) wishes to act as a litigation friend for the protected party, he must file and serve a copy of the court order which appointed him on those persons mentioned in paragraph (3)(b).

Litigation friend by court order

143.—(1) The court may make an order appointing—
    (a) the Official Solicitor; or
    (b) some other person,
to act as a litigation friend.
(2) The court may act under paragraph (1)—
    (a) either on its own initiative or on the application of any person; but
    (b) only with the consent of the person to be appointed.
(3) An application for an order under paragraph (1) must be supported by evidence.
(4) The court may not appoint a litigation friend under this rule unless it is satisfied that the person to be appointed satisfies the conditions specified in rule 140(1).
(5) The court may at any stage of the proceedings give directions as to the appointment of a litigation friend.

Court's power to prevent a person from acting as litigation friend or to order change

144.—
(1) The court may either on its own initiative or on the application of any person—
    (a) direct that a person may not act as a litigation friend;

(b) terminate a litigation friend's appointment; or

(c) appoint a new litigation friend in place of an existing one.

(2) An application for an order under paragraph (1) must be supported by evidence.

(3) The court may not appoint a litigation friend under this rule unless it is satisfied that the person to be appointed satisfies the conditions specified in rule 140(1).

Appointment of litigation friend by court order – supplementary

145. The applicant must serve a copy of an application for an order under rule 143 or 144 on—

(a) the person on whom an application form is to be served in accordance with rule 32 (service on children and protected parties);

(b) every other person who is a party to the proceedings;

(c) any person who is the litigation friend, or who is purporting to act as the litigation friend, when the application is made; and

(d) unless he is the applicant, the person who it is proposed should be the litigation friend, as soon as practicable and in any event within 21 days of the date on which it was issued.

Procedure where appointment of litigation friend comes to an end – for a child or protected party

146.—

(1) This rule applies—

(a) when a child reaches 18, provided he is neither—

(i) P; nor 51

(ii) a protected party; and

(b) where a protected party ceases to be a person who lacks capacity to conduct the proceedings himself.

(2) Where paragraph (1)(a) applies, the litigation friend's appointment ends.

(3) Where paragraph (1)(b) applies, the litigation friend's appointment continues until it is brought to an end by a court order

(4) An application for an order under paragraph (3) may be made by—

(a) the former protected party;

(b) his litigation friend; or

(c) any other person who is a party to the proceedings.

(5) The applicant must serve a copy of the application notice seeking an order under this rule on all parties to the proceedings as soon as practicable and in any event within 21 days of the date on which it was issued.

(6) Where paragraph (2) applies the child must serve notice on every other party—

(a) stating that he has reached full age;

(b) stating that the appointment of the litigation friend has ended; and

(c) providing his address for service.

(7) Where paragraph (3) applies, the former protected party must provide his address for service to all other parties to the proceedings.

Procedure where appointment of litigation friend comes to an end—for P

147.—

(1) This rule applies where P ceases to be a person who lacks capacity to conduct the proceedings himself but continues to lack capacity in relation to the matter or matters to which the application relates.

(2) The litigation friend's appointment continues until it is brought to an end by a court order.

(3) An application for an order under paragraph (2) may be made by—

    (a) P;

    (b) his litigation friend; or

    (c) any other person who is a party to the proceedings.

(4) The applicant must serve a copy of the application notice seeking an order under this rule on all other parties to the proceedings as soon as practicable and in any event within 21 days of the date on which it was issued.

(5) Where the court makes an order under this rule, P must provide his address for service to all other parties to the proceedings.

Procedure where P ceases to lack capacity

148.—

(1) This rule applies where P ceases to lack capacity both to conduct the proceedings himself and in relation to the matter or matters to which the application relates.

(2) The litigation friend's appointment continues until it is brought to an end by a court order.

(3) An application may be made by—

    (a) P;

    (b) his litigation friend; or

    (c) any other person who is a party to the proceedings,

for the proceedings to come to an end.

(4) The applicant must serve a copy of the application notice seeking an order under this rule on all parties to the proceedings as soon as practicable and in any event within 21 days of the date on which it was issued.

Practice direction in relation to litigation friends

149. A practice direction may make additional or different provision in relation to litigation friends.

PART 18
CHANGE OF SOLICITOR

Change of solicitor

150.—

(1) This rule applies where a party to proceedings—

    (a) for whom a solicitor is acting wants to change his solicitor or act in person; or

    (b) after having conducted the proceedings in person, appoints a solicitor to act on his behalf (except where the solicitor is appointed only to act as an advocate for a hearing).

(2) The party proposing the change must—

    (a) file a notice of the change with the court; and

    (b) serve the notice of the change on every other party to the proceedings and, if there is one, on the solicitor who will cease to act.

(3) The notice must state the party's address for service.

(4) The notice filed at court must state that it has been served as required by paragraph (2)(b).

(5) Where there is a solicitor who will cease to act, he will continue to be considered the party's solicitor unless and until—

    (a) the notice is filed and served in accordance with paragraphs (2), (3) and (4); or

    (b) the court makes an order under rule 152 and the order is served in accordance with that rule.

LSC funded clients

151.—

(1) Where the certificate of any person ('A') who is an LSC funded client is revoked or discharged—

    (a) the solicitor who acted for A will cease to be the solicitor acting in the case as soon as his retainer is determined under regulation 4 of the Community Legal Services (Costs) Regulations 2000;[13] and

    (b) if A wishes to continue and appoints a solicitor to act on his behalf, rule 150(2), (3) and (4) will apply as if A had previously conducted the application in person.

(2) In this rule, 'certificate' means a certificate issued under the Funding Code (approved under section 9 of the Access to Justice Act 1999).[14]

Order that a solicitor has ceased to act

152.—

(1) A solicitor may apply for an order declaring that he has ceased to be the solicitor acting for a party.

(2) Where an application is made under this rule—

    (a) the solicitor must serve the application notice on the party for whom the solicitor is acting, unless the court directs otherwise; and

    (b) the application must be supported by evidence.

(3) Where the court makes an order that a solicitor has ceased to act, the solicitor must—

    (a) serve a copy of the order on every other party to the proceedings; and

    (b) file a certificate of service.

Removal of solicitor who has ceased to act on application of another party

153.—

(1) Where—

    (a) a solicitor who has acted for a party—

        (i) has died;

        (ii) has become bankrupt;

        (iii) has ceased to practice; or

        (iv) cannot be found; and

    (b) the party has not served a notice of a change of solicitor or notice of intention to act in person as required by rule 150,

any other party may apply for an order declaring that the solicitor has ceased to be the solicitor acting for the other party in the case.

(2) Where an application is made under this rule, the applicant must serve the application on the party to whose solicitor the application relates, unless the court directs otherwise.

---

[13] S.I. 2000/441.

[14] 1999 c. 22.

(3) Where the court makes an order under this rule—
- (a) the court will give directions about serving a copy of the order on every other party to the proceedings; and
- (b) where the order is served by a party, that party must file a certificate of service.

Practice direction relating to change of solicitor

154. A practice direction may make additional or different provision in relation to change of solicitor.

PART 19

COSTS

Interpretation

155.—

(1) In this Part—
- (a) 'additional liability' means the percentage increase, the insurance premium, or the additional amount in respect of provision made by a membership organisation, as the case may be;
- (b) 'authorised court officer' means any officer of the Supreme Court Costs Office, whom the Lord Chancellor has authorised to assess costs;
- (c) 'costs' include fees, charges, disbursements, expenses, reimbursement permitted to a litigant in person, any additional liability incurred under a funding arrangement and any fee or reward charged by a lay representative for acting on behalf of a party in proceedings;
- (d) 'costs judge' means a taxing Master of the Supreme Court;
- (e) 'costs officer' means a costs judge or an authorised court officer;
- (f) 'detailed assessment' means the procedure by which the amount of costs or remuneration is decided by a costs officer in accordance with Part 47 of the Civil Procedure Rules 1998 (which are applied to proceedings under these Rules, with modifications, by rule 160);
- (g) 'fixed costs' are to be construed in accordance with the relevant practice direction;
- (h) 'fund' includes any estate or property held for the benefit of any person or class of persons and any fund to which a trustee or personal representative is entitled in his capacity as such;
- (i) 'funding arrangement' means an arrangement where a person has—
  - (i) entered into a conditional fee agreement or a collective conditional fee agreement which provides for a success fee within the meaning of section 58(2) of the Courts and Legal Services Act 1990;[15]
  - (ii) taken out an insurance policy to which section 29 of the Access to Justice Act 1999 (recovery of insurance premiums by way of costs) applies; or
  - (iii) made an agreement with a membership organisation to meet his legal costs;
- (j) 'insurance premium' means a sum of money paid or payable for insurance against the risk of incurring a costs liability in the proceedings, taken out after the event that is the subject matter of the claim;

---

[15] 1990 c. 41.

(k) 'membership organisation' means a body prescribed for the purposes of section 30 of the Access to Justice Act 1999 (recovery where body undertakes to meet costs liabilities);

(l) 'paying party' means a party liable to pay costs;

(m) 'percentage increase' means the percentage by which the amount of a legal representative's fee can be increased in accordance with a conditional fee agreement which provides for a success fee;

(n) 'receiving party' means a party entitled to be paid costs;

(o) 'summary assessment' means the procedure by which the court, when making an order about costs, orders payment of a sum of money instead of fixed costs or 'detailed assessment'.

(2) The costs to which the rules in this Part apply include—

(a) where the costs may be assessed by the court, costs payable by a client to his solicitor; and

(b) costs which are payable by one party to another party under the terms of a contract, where the court makes an order for an assessment of those costs.

(3) Where advocacy or litigation services are provided to a client under a conditional fee agreement, costs are recoverable under this Part notwithstanding that the client is liable to pay his legal representative's fees and expenses only to the extent that sums are recovered in respect of the proceedings, whether by way of costs or otherwise.

(4) In paragraph (3), the reference to a conditional fee agreement is to an agreement which satisfies all the conditions applicable to it by virtue of section 58 of the Courts and Legal Services Act 1990.[16]

Property and affairs—the general rule

156. Where the proceedings concern P's property and affairs the general rule is that the costs of the proceedings or of that part of the proceedings that concerns P's property and affairs, shall be paid by P or charged to his estate.

Personal welfare—the general rule

157. Where the proceedings concern P's personal welfare the general rule is that there will be no order as to the costs of the proceedings or of that part of the proceedings that concerns P's personal welfare.

Apportioning costs—the general rule

158. Where the proceedings concern both property and affairs and personal welfare the court, insofar as practicable, will apportion the costs as between the respective issues.

Departing from the general rule

159.—

(1) The court may depart from rules 156 to 158 if the circumstances so justify, and in deciding whether departure is justified the court will have regard to all the circumstances, including–

(a) the conduct of the parties;

(b) whether a party has succeeded on part of his case, even if he has not been wholly successful; and

---

[16] Section 58 was substituted by section 27(1) of the Access to Justice Act 1999 (c. 22).

(c) the role of any public body involved in the proceedings.

(2) The conduct of the parties includes–

    (a) conduct before, as well as during, the proceedings;

    (b) whether it was reasonable for a party to raise, pursue or contest a particular issue;

    (c) the manner in which a party has made or responded to an application or a particular issue;and

    (d) whether a party who has succeeded in his application or response to an application, in whole or in part, exaggerated any matter contained in his application or response.

(3) Without prejudice to rules 156 to 158 and the foregoing provisions of this rule, the court may permit a party to recover their fixed costs in accordance with the relevant practice direction.

Rules about costs in the Civil Procedure Rules to apply

160.—

(1) Subject to the provisions of these Rules, Parts 44, 47 and 48 of the Civil Procedure Rules 1998 ('the 1998 Rules') shall apply with the modifications in this rule and such other modifications as may be appropriate, to costs incurred in relation to proceedings under these Rules as they apply to costs incurred in relation to proceedings in the High Court.

(2) The provisions of Part 47 of the 1998 Rules shall apply with the modifications in this rule and such other modifications as may be appropriate, to a detailed assessment of the remuneration of a deputy under these Rules as they apply to a detailed assessment of costs in proceedings to which the 1998 Rules apply.

(3) Where the definitions in Part 43 (referred to in Parts 44, 47 and 48) of the 1998 Rules are different from the definitions in rule 155 of these Rules, the latter shall prevail.

(4) Rules 44.1, 44.3(1) to (5), 44.6, 44.7, 44.9, 44.10, 44.11. 44.12 and 44.12A of the 1998 Rules do not apply.

(5) In rule 44.17 of the 1998 Rules, the references to Parts 45 and 46 do not apply.

(6) In rule 47.3(1)(c) of the 1998 Rules, the words 'unless the costs are being assessed under rule 48.5 (costs where money is payable to a child or a patient)' are removed.

(7) In rule 47.3(2) of the 1998 Rules, the words 'or a district judge' are removed.

(8) Rule 47.4(3) and (4) of the 1998 Rules do not apply.

(9) Rules 47.9(4), 47.10 and 47.11 of the 1998 Rules do not apply where the costs are to be paid by P or charged to his estate.

(10) Rules 48.2, 48.3, 48.6A, and 48.10 of the 1998 Rules do not apply.

(11) Rule 48.1(1) of the 1998 Rules is removed and is replaced by the following: 'This paragraph applies where a person applies for an order for specific disclosure before the commencement of proceedings'.

Detailed assessment of costs

161.—

(1) Where the court orders costs to be assessed by way of detailed assessment, the detailed assessment proceedings shall take place in the High Court.

(2) A fee is payable in respect of the detailed assessment of costs and on an appeal against a decision made in a detailed assessment of costs.

(3) Where a detailed assessment of costs has taken place, the amount payable by P is the amount which the court certifies as payable.

Employment of a solicitor by two or more persons

162. Where two or more persons having the same interest in relation to a matter act in relation to the proceedings by separate legal representatives, they shall not be permitted more than one set of costs of the representation unless and to the extent that the court certifies that the circumstances justify separate representation.

Costs of the Official Solicitor

163. Any costs incurred by the Official Solicitor in relation to proceedings under these Rules or in carrying out any directions given by the court and not provided for by remuneration under rule 167 shall be paid by such persons or out of such funds as the court may direct.

Procedure for assessing costs

164. Where the court orders a party, or P, to pay costs to another party it may either—
    (a) make a summary assessment of the costs; or
    (b) order a detailed assessment of the costs by a costs officer,
    unless any rule, practice direction or other enactment provides otherwise.

Costs following P's death

165. An order or direction that costs incurred during P's lifetime be paid out of or charged on his estate may be made within 6 years after P's death.

Costs orders in favour of or against non-parties

166.—
(1) Where the court is considering whether to make a costs order in favour of or against a person who is not a party to proceedings—
    (a) that person must be added as a party to the proceedings for the purposes of costs only;and
    (b) he must be given a reasonable opportunity to attend a hearing at which the court will consider the matter further.
(2) This rule does not apply where the court is considering whether to make an order against the Legal Services Commission.

Remuneration of a deputy, donee or attorney

167.—
(1) Where the court orders that a deputy, donee or attorney is entitled to remuneration out of P's estate for discharging his functions as such, the court may make such order as it thinks fit, including an order that—
    (a) he be paid a fixed amount;
    (b) he be paid at a specified rate; or
    (c) the amount of the remuneration shall be determined in accordance with the schedule of fees set out in the relevant practice direction.
(2) Any amount permitted by the court under paragraph (1) shall constitute a debt due from P's estate.
(3) The court may order a detailed assessment of the remuneration by a costs officer, in accordance with rule 164(b).

Practice direction as to costs

168. A practice direction may make further provision in respect of costs in proceedings.

PART 20

APPEALS

Scope of this Part

169. This Part applies to an appeal against any decision of the court except where, in relation to those cases that are to be dealt with in accordance with Part 22 (transitory and transitional provisions), Part 22 makes different provision.

Interpretation

170.—(1) In the following provisions of this Part—
  (a) 'appeal judge' means a judge of the court to whom an appeal is made;
  (b) 'first instance judge' means the judge of the court from whose decision an appeal is brought;
  (c) 'appellant' means the person who brings or seeks to bring an appeal;
  (d) 'respondent' means—
      (i) a person other than the appellant who was a party to the proceedings before the first instance judge and who is affected by the appeal; or
      (ii) a person who is permitted or directed by the first instance judge or the appeal judge to be a party to the appeal.
(2) In this Part, where the expression 'permission' is used it means 'permission to appeal' unless otherwise stated.

Dealing with appeals

171.—
(1) The court may deal with an appeal or any part of an appeal at a hearing or without a hearing.
(2) In considering whether it is necessary to hold a hearing, the court shall have regard to the matters set out in rule 84(3). (Rule 89 provides for reconsideration of orders made without a hearing or without notice to a person.)

Permission to appeal

172.—
(1) Subject to paragraph (8), an appeal against a decision of the court may not be made without permission.
(2) Any person bound by an order of the court by virtue of rule 74 (persons to be bound as if parties) may seek permission to appeal under this Part.
(3) Permission is to be granted or refused in accordance with this Part.
(4) An application for permission to appeal may be made to the first instance judge or the appeal judge.
(5) Where an application for permission is refused by the first instance judge, a further application for permission may be made in accordance with paragraphs (6) and (7).

(6) Where the decision sought to be appealed is a decision of a district judge, permission may be granted or refused by—

    (a) the President;

    (b) the Vice-President;

    (c) one of the other judges nominated by virtue of section 46(2)(a) to (c) of the Act; or

    (d) a circuit judge.

(7) Where the decision sought to be appealed is a decision of a circuit judge, permission may only be granted or refused by one of the judges mentioned in paragraph (6)(a) to (c).

(8) Permission is not required to appeal against an order for committal to prison.

Matters to be taken into account when considering an application for permission

173.—

(1) Permission to appeal shall be granted only where—

    (a) the court considers that the appeal would have a real prospect of success; or

    (b) there is some other compelling reason why the appeal should be heard.

(2) An order giving permission may—

    (a) limit the issues to be heard; and

    (b) be made subject to conditions.

Parties to comply with the practice direction

174. All parties to an appeal must comply with any relevant practice direction.

Appellant's notice

175.—

(1) Where the appellant seeks permission from the appeal judge, it must be requested in the appellant's notice.

(2) The appellant must file an appellant's notice at the court within—

    (a) such period as may be directed or specified in the order of the first instance judge; or

    (b) where that judge makes no such direction or order, 21 days after the date of the decision being appealed.

(3) The court will issue the appellant's notice and unless it orders otherwise, the appellant must serve the appellant's notice on each respondent and on such other persons as the court may direct, as soon as practicable and in any event within 21 days of the date on which it was issued.

(4) The appellant must file a certificate of service within 7 days beginning with the date on which he served the appellant's notice.

Respondent's notice

176.—

(1) A respondent who—

    (a) is seeking permission from the appeal judge to appeal; or

    (b) wishes to ask the appeal judge to uphold the order of the first instance judge for reasons different from or additional to those given by the first instance judge, must file a respondent's notice.

(2) Where the respondent seeks permission from the appeal judge, permission must be requested in the respondent's notice.

(3) A respondent's notice must be filed within—
- (a) such period as may be directed by the first instance judge; or
- (b) where the first instance judge makes no such direction, 21 days beginning with the date referred to in paragraph (4).

(4) The date is the soonest of—
- (a) the date on which the respondent is served with the appellant's notice where—
  - (i) permission to appeal was given by the first instance judge; or
  - (ii) permission to appeal is not required;
- (b) the date on which the respondent is served with notification that the appeal judge has given the appellant permission to appeal; or
- (c) the date on which the respondent is served with the notification that the application for permission to appeal and the appeal itself are to be heard together.

(5) The court will issue a respondent's notice and, unless it orders otherwise, the respondent must serve the respondent's notice on the appellant, any other respondent and on such other parties as the court may direct, as soon as practicable and in any event within 21 days of the date on which it was issued.

(6) The respondent must file a certificate of service within 7 days beginning with the date on which the copy of the respondent's notice was served.

Variation of time

177.—
(1) An application to vary the time limit for filing an appellant's or respondent's notice must be made to the appeal judge.

(2) The parties may not agree to extend any date or time limit for or in respect of an appeal set by—
- (a) these Rules;
- (b) the relevant practice direction; or
- (c) an order of the appeal judge or the first instance judge.

Power of appeal judge on appeal

178.—
(1) In relation to an appeal, an appeal judge has all the powers of the first instance judge whose decision is being appealed.

(2) In particular, the appeal judge has the power to—
- (a) affirm, set aside or vary any order made by the first instance judge;
- (b) refer any claim or issue to that judge for determination;
- (c) order a new hearing;
- (d) make a costs order.

(3) The appeal judge may exercise his powers in relation to the whole or part of an order made by the first instance judge.

Determination of appeals

179.—
(1) An appeal will be limited to a review of the decision of the first instance judge unless—
- (a) a practice direction makes different provision for a particular category of appeal; or
- (b) the appeal judge considers that in the circumstances of the appeal it would be in the interests of justice to hold a re-hearing.

(2) Unless he orders otherwise, the appeal judge will not receive—
    (a) oral evidence; or
    (b) evidence that was not before the first instance judge.
(3) The appeal judge will allow an appeal where the decision of the first instance judge was—
    (a) wrong; or
    (b) unjust, because of a serious procedural or other irregularity in the proceedings before the first instance judge.
(4) The appeal judge may draw any inference of fact that he considers justified on the evidence.
(5) At the hearing of the appeal a party may not rely upon a matter not contained in his appellant's or respondent's notice unless the appeal judge gives permission.

Allocation

180. Except in accordance with the relevant practice direction—
(a) an appeal from a first instance decision of a circuit judge shall be heard by a judge of the court nominated by virtue of section 46(2)(a) to (c) of the Act; and
(b) an appeal from a decision of a district judge shall be heard by a circuit judge.

Appeals to the Court of Appeal

Appeals against decision of a puisne judge of the High Court, etc

181.—
(1) Where the decision sought to be appealed is a decision of a judge nominated by virtue of section 46(2)(a) to (c) of the Act, an appeal will lie only to the Court of Appeal.
(2) The judge nominated by virtue of section 46(2)(a) to (c) of the Act may grant permission to appeal to the Court of Appeal in accordance with this Part, where the decision sought to be appealed was a decision made by a judge so nominated as a first instance judge.

Second appeals

182.—
(1) A decision of a judge of the court which was itself made on appeal from a judge of the court may only be appealed further to the Court of Appeal.
(2) Permission is required from the Court of Appeal for such an appeal.
(3) The Court of Appeal will not give permission unless it considers that—
    (a) the appeal would raise an important point of principle or practice; or
    (b) there is some other compelling reason for the Court of Appeal to hear it.
(4) Nothing in this rule or in rule 181 applies to a second appeal from a decision of a nominated officer.

PART 21
ENFORCEMENT

Enforcement methods—general

183.—
(1) The rules in this Part make provision for the enforcement of judgments and orders.
(2) The relevant practice direction may set out methods of enforcing judgments or orders.

(3) An application for an order for enforcement may be made on application by any person in accordance with Part 10.

Application of the Civil Procedure Rules 1998 and RSC Orders

184. The following provisions apply, as far as they are relevant and with such modifications as may be necessary, to the enforcement of orders made in proceedings under these Rules—

(a) Parts 70 (General Rules about Enforcement of Judgments and Orders), 71 (Orders to Obtain Information from Judgment Debtors), 72 (Third Party Debt Orders) and 73 (Charging Orders, Stop Orders and Stop Notices) of the Civil Procedure Rules 1998; and

(b) Orders 45 (Enforcement of Judgments and Orders: General), 46 (Writs of Execution: General) and 47 (Writs of Fieri Facias) of the Rules of the Supreme Court.[17]

Orders for committal

Contempt of court—generally

185. An application relating to the committal of a person for contempt of court shall be made to a judge and the power to punish for contempt may be exercised by an order of committal.

Application for order of committal

186.—

(1) An application for an order of committal must be made by filing an application notice, stating the grounds of the application, and must be supported by an affidavit made in accordance with the relevant practice direction.

(2) Subject to paragraph (3), the application notice, a copy of the affidavit in support thereof and notice of the date of the hearing of the application must be served personally on the person sought to be committed.

(3) Without prejudice to its powers under Part 6, the court may dispense with service under this rule if it thinks it just to do so.

Oral evidence

187. If on the hearing of the application the person sought to be committed expresses a wish to give oral evidence on his own behalf, he shall be entitled to do so.

Hearing for committal order

188.—

(1) Except where the court permits, no grounds shall be relied upon at the hearing except the grounds set out in the application notice.

(2) Notwithstanding rule 90(1) (general rule—hearing to be in private), when determining an application for committal the court will hold the hearing in public unless it directs otherwise.

(3) If the court hearing an application in private decides that a person has committed a contempt of court, it shall state publicly—

(a) the name of that person;

---

[17] Schedule 1 to the Civil Procedure Rules 1998.

(b) in general terms the nature of the contempt in respect of which the order of committal is being made; and

(c) any punishment imposed.

(4) If the person sought to be committed does not attend the hearing, the court may fix a date and time for the person to be brought before the court.

Power to suspend execution of committal order

189.—

(1) A judge who has made an order of committal may direct that the execution of the order of committal shall be suspended for such period or on such terms and conditions as may be specified.

(2) Where an order is suspended under paragraph (1), the applicant for the order of committal must, unless the court otherwise directs, serve on the person against whom it was made a notice informing him of the making and terms of the direction under that paragraph.

Warrant for arrest

190. A warrant for the arrest of a person against whom an order of committal has been made shall not, without further order of the court, be enforced more than 2 years after the date on which the warrant is issued.

Discharge of person committed

191.—

(1) The court may, on the application of any person committed to prison for contempt of court, discharge him.

(2) Where a person has been committed for failing to comply with a judgment or order requiring him to deliver any thing to some other person or to deposit it in court or elsewhere, and a writ of sequestration has also been issued to enforce that judgment or order, then, if the thing is in the custody or power of the person committed, the commissioners appointed by the writ of sequestration may take possession of it as if it were the property of that person and, without prejudice to the generality of paragraph (1), the court may discharge the person committed and may give such directions for dealing with the thing taken by the commissioners as it thinks fit.

Penal notices

192.—

(1) The court may direct that a penal notice is to be attached to any order warning the person on whom the copy of the order is served that disobeying the order would be a contempt of court punishable by imprisonment or a fine.

(2) Unless the court gives a direction under paragraph (1), a penal notice may not be attached to any order.

(3) A penal notice is to be in the following terms: 'You must obey this order. If you do not, you may be sent to prison for contempt of court.'.

Saving for other powers

193. The rules in this Part do not limit the power of the court to make an order requiring a person guilty of contempt to pay a fine or give security for his good behaviour and those rules, so far

as applicable, shall apply in relation to an application for such an order as they apply in relation to an application for an order of committal.

Power of court to commit on its own initiative

194. The preceding provisions of these Rules shall not be taken as affecting the power of the court to make an order for committal on its own initiative against a person guilty of contempt of court.

PART 22
TRANSITORY AND TRANSITIONAL PROVISIONS

Transitory provision: applications by former receivers

195.—

(1) This rule and rule 196—

(a) apply in any case where a person becomes a deputy by virtue of paragraph 1(2) of Schedule 5 to the Act; but

(b) shall cease to have effect at the end of the period specified in the relevant practice direction.

(2) The deputy may make an application to the court in connection with—

(a) any decision in connection with the day-to-day management of P's property and affairs; or

(b) any supplementary decision which is necessary to give full effect to any order made, or directions given, before 1st October 2007 under Part 7 of the Mental Health Act 1983.[18]

(3) Decisions within paragraph (2) include those that may be specified in the relevant practice direction.

(4) An application—

(a) may relate only to a particular decision or decisions to be made on P's behalf;

(b) must specify details of the decision or decisions to be made; and

(c) must be made using the application form set out in the relevant practice direction.

Transitory provision: dealing with applications under rule 195

196.—

(1) The court may, in determining an application under rule 195, treat the application as if it were an application to vary the functions of the deputy which is made in accordance with the relevant practice direction made under rule 71, and dispose of it accordingly.

(2) In any other case, an application under rule 195 may be determined by an order made or directions given by—

(a) the court; or

(b) a person nominated under paragraph (3).

(3) The Senior Judge or the President may nominate an officer or officers of the court for the purpose of determining applications under rule 195.

(4) Where an officer has been nominated under paragraph (3) to determine an application, he may refer to a judge any proceedings or any question arising in any proceedings which ought, in the officer's opinion, to be considered by a judge.

---

[18] 1983, c. 20.

Appeal against a decision of a nominated officer

197.—(1) This rule applies in relation to decisions made under rules 195 and 196 by a nominated officer.

(2) An appeal from a decision to which this rule applies lies to a judge of the court nominated by virtue of section 46(2)(e) of the Act.

(3) No permission is required for an appeal under paragraph (2).

(4) A judge determining an appeal under paragraph (2) has all the powers that an appeal judge on appeal has by virtue of rule 178.

(5) An appeal from a decision made under paragraph (2) ('a second appeal') lies to a judge of the court nominated by virtue of section 46(2)(d) of the Act.

(6) A second appeal may be made from a decision of a nominated officer, and a judge to whom such an appeal is made may, if he considers the matter is one which ought to be heard by a judge of the court nominated by virtue of section 46(2)(a) to (c), transfer the matter to such a judge.

(7) An appeal from a decision made on a second appeal lies to the Court of Appeal.

Application of Rules to proceedings within paragraphs 3 and 12 of Schedule 5 to the Act

198.—

(1) In this rule, 'pending proceedings' means proceedings on an application within paragraph 3 or 12 of Schedule 5 to the Act.

(2) A practice direction shall make provision for the extent to which these Rules shall apply to pending proceedings.

Practice direction

199. A practice direction may make additional or different provision in relation to transitory and transitional matters.

PART 23
MISCELLANEOUS

Order or directions requiring a person to give security for discharge of functions

200.—

(1) This rule applies where the court makes an order or gives a direction—
    (a) conferring functions on any person (whether as deputy or otherwise); and
    (b) requiring him to give security for the discharge of those functions.

(2) The person on whom functions are conferred must give the security before he undertakes to discharge his functions, unless the court permits it to be given subsequently.

(3) Paragraphs (4) to (6) apply where the security is required to be given before any action can be taken.

(4) Subject to paragraph (5), the security must be given in accordance with the requirements of regulation 33(2)(a) of the Public Guardian Regulations (which makes provision about the giving of security by means of a bond that is endorsed by an authorised insurance company or deposittaker).

(5) The court may impose such other requirements in relation to the giving of the security as it considers appropriate (whether in addition to, or instead of, those specified in paragraph (4)).

(6) In specifying the date from which the order or directions referred to in paragraph (1) are to take effect, the court will have regard to the need to postpone that date for such reasonable period as would enable the Public Guardian to be satisfied that—

(a) if paragraph (4) applies, the requirements of regulation 34 of the Public Guardian Regulations have been met in relation to the security; and

(b) any other requirements imposed by the court under paragraph (5) have been met.

(7) 'The Public Guardian Regulations' means the Lasting Powers of Attorney, Enduring Powers of Attorney and Public Guardian Regulations 2007.[19]

Objections to registration of an enduring power of attorney: request for directions

201.—(1) This rule applies in any case where—

(a) the Public Guardian (having received a notice of objection to the registration of an instrument creating an enduring power of attorney) is prevented by paragraph 13(5) of Schedule 4 to the Act from registering the instrument except in accordance with the court's directions; and

(b) on or before the relevant day, no application for the court to give such directions has been made under Part 9 (how to start proceedings).

(2) In paragraph (1)(b) the relevant day is the later of—

(a) the final day of the period specified in paragraph 13(4) of Schedule 4 to the Act; or

(b) the final day of the period of 14 days beginning with the date on which the Public Guardian receives the notice of objection.

(3) The Public Guardian may seek the court's directions about registering the instrument by filing a request in accordance with the relevant practice direction.

(4) As soon as practicable and in any event within 21 days of the date on which the request was made, the court will notify—

(a) the person (or persons) who gave the notice of objection; and

(b) the attorney or, if more than one, each of them.

(5) As soon as practicable and in any event within 21 days of the date on which the request is filed, the Public Guardian must notify the donor of the power that the request has been so filed.

(6) The notice under paragraph (4) must—

(a) state that the Public Guardian has requested the court's directions about registration;

(b) state that the court will give directions in response to the request unless an application under Part 9 is made to it before the end of the period of 21 days commencing with the date on which the notice is issued; and

(c) set out the steps required to make such an application.

(7) 'Notice of objection' means a notice of objection which is made in accordance with paragraph 13(4) of Schedule 4 to the Act.

Disposal of property where P ceases to lack capacity

202.—

(1) This rule applies where P ceases to lack capacity.

---

[19] S.I. 2007/1253.

(2) In this rule, 'relevant property' means any property belonging to P and forming part of his estate, and which—

(a) remains under the control of anyone appointed by order of the court; or

(b) is held under the direction of the court.

(3) The court may at any time make an order for any relevant property to be transferred to P, or at P's direction, provided that it is satisfied that P has the capacity to make decisions in relation to that property.

(4) An application for an order under this rule is to be made in accordance with Part 10.

Sir Mark Potter
25th June 2007 President
Falconer of Thoroton, C
25th June 2007

EXPLANATORY NOTE
(This note is not part of the Rules)

These Rules set out the practice and procedure to be followed in the new Court of Protection. Section 45 of the Mental Capacity Act 2005 establishes a new, superior court of record called the Court of Protection which replaces the office of the Supreme Court known as the Court of Protection. These Rules revoke the rules governing procedure in the former Court of Protection (the Court of Protection Rules 2001 (S.1. 2001/824, as amended by S.1. 2001/2977, S.I. 2002/833, S.I. 2003/1733, S.I. 2004/1291, S.I. 2005/667 and S.I. 2006/653), and the Court of Protection (Enduring Power of Attorney Rules) 2001 (S.I. 2001/825, as amended by S.I. 2002/832, S.I. 2002/1944, S.I. 2005/668 and S.I. 2005/3126).

Part 2 of the Rules sets out the overriding objective that is to be applied whenever the court exercises its powers under the Rules, or interprets any rule or practice direction. Part 3 contains provisions for interpreting the Rules and for the Civil Procedure Rules 1998 to be applied insofar as may be necessary to further the overriding objective. Part 4 makes provision as to court documents, including the requirement for certain documents to be verified by a statement of truth. Part 5 sets out the court's general case management powers, and includes the power to dispense with the requirement of any rule. The Rules provide procedures for serving documents (Part 6), notifying the person who lacks capacity and who is the subject matter of the application of certain documents and events (Part 7), seeking permission to start proceedings (Part 8), starting proceedings (Part 9), making interim applications and applications within proceedings (Part 10), as to how applications will be dealt with (Part 12) and as to hearings (Part 13), including provisions as to publication of information and as to privacy and publicity of proceedings.

The Rules set out procedures to be followed in relation to evidence (Parts 14 and 15), disclosure (Part 16), appointment of litigation friends (Part 17), change of solicitor (Part 18), costs (Part 19), appeals (Part 20), the enforcement of orders (Part 21) and transitory and transitional matters (Part 22). The detail of the transitional and transitory procedures is provided in the practice directions.

Index